Visual Basic® for Applications

UNLEASHED

Paul McFedries

SAMS

201 West

Indianapol

For Karen (purr)

FIRST EDITION

International Standard Book Number: 0-672-31046-5

Library of Congress Catalog Card Number: 96-72008

2000 99 98 97 4 3 2

Interpretation of the printing code: the rightmost double-digit number is the year of the book's printing; the rightmost single-digit, the number of the book's printing. For example, a printing code of 97-1 shows that the first printing of the book occurred in 1997.

Composed in AGaramond and MCPdigital by Macmillan Computer Publishing

Printed in the United States of America

Trademarks

Publisher and President *Richard K. Swadley*

Publishing Manager *Dean Miller*

Director of Editorial Services *Cindy Morrow*

Managing Editor *Mary Inderstrodt*

Director of Marketing *Kelli S. Spencer*

Assistant Marketing Managers *Kristina Perry*
Rachel Wolfe

Acquisitions Editor
Dean Miller

Development Editor
Brian-Kent Proffitt

Software Development Specialists
Patricia J. Brooks
John Warriner

Production Editor
Gayle L. Johnson

Copy Editor
Bart Reed

Indexers
Bruce Clingaman
Erika Millen

Technical Reviewer
John Charlesworth

Formatter
Katie Wise

Technical Edit Coordinator
Lynette Quinn

Editorial Assistants
Carol Ackerman
Andi Richter
Rhonda Tinch-Mize

Cover Designer
Jason Grisham

Book Designer
Gary Adair

Production Team Supervisors
Brad Chinn
Charlotte Clapp

Production
Georgiana Briggs
Shawn Ring
Janet Seib
Mary Ellen Stephenson

Contents

Part II Unleashing Microsoft Office Objects

Acknowledgments

Robert Pirsig, in *Zen and the Art of Motorcycle Maintenance,* wrote that "a person who sees Quality and feels it as he works, is a person who cares." If this book is a quality product (and I immodestly think that it is), it's because the people at Sams editorial cared enough to make it so.

I would therefore like to thank everyone who helped make this book a reality. I'd like to begin by thanking Acquisitions Editor Dean Miller for, well, acquiring me and for pulling the project together. Many thanks go to Development Editor Brian-Kent Proffitt for doing a great job and for showing compassion to a sore-wristed author. As always, I reserve some special thank-yous for Production Editor Gayle Johnson, who, more than anyone I know in publishing, sees Quality and feels it as she works. I'd also like to thank Copy Editor Bart Reed for his uncanny ability to find my dumb mistakes, and Technical Editor John Charlesworth for making sure my instructions and code cut the technical mustard. Finally, a big thank-you goes to Software Development Specialists Patty Brooks and John Warriner for putting together the excellent CD that appears in the back of this book.

About the Author

Paul McFedries is a computer consultant, programmer, and freelance writer. He has worked with computers in one form or another since 1975, he has a degree in mathematics, and he can swap out a hard drive in seconds flat—yet still, inexplicably, he has a life. McFedries is the author or coauthor of more than two dozen computer books that have sold over 900,000 copies worldwide. His titles include *Paul McFedries' Windows 95 Unleashed, Microsoft Office 97 Unleashed,* and *Navigating the Internet,* all from Sams Publishing.

Other hats worn by McFedries on occasion include video editor, animator, bread maker, Webmaster, brewmaster, cruciverbalist, and neologist. He has no cats, and his favorite hobbies are shooting pool, taking naps, riding his motorcycle, and talking about himself in the third person.

Tell Us What You Think!

As a reader, you are the most important critic and commentator of our books. We value your opinion and want to know what we're doing right, what we could do better, what areas you'd like to see us publish in, and any other words of wisdom you're willing to pass our way. You can help us make strong books that meet your needs and give you the computer guidance you require.

Do you have access to CompuServe or the World Wide Web? Then check out our CompuServe forum by typing `GO SAMS` at any prompt. If you prefer the World Wide Web, check out our site at `http://www.mcp.com`.

> **NOTE**
>
> If you have a technical question about this book, call our technical support line at (800) 571-5840, extension 3668.

As the team leader of the group that created this book, I welcome your comments. You can fax, e-mail, or write me directly to let me know what you did or didn't like about this book—as well as what we can do to make our books stronger. Here's the information:

Fax: (317) 581-4669

E-mail: `opsys_mgr@sams.mcp.com`

Mail: Dean Miller
Comments Department
Sams Publishing
201 W. 103rd Street
Indianapolis, IN 46290

Introduction

Invention in the mother of necessity.

—Thorstein Veblen

When Excel 5 was released in 1994, developers and power users were thrilled that it included the first incarnation of Microsoft's long-awaited new macro language: Visual Basic for Applications (VBA). Many people discarded the creaky old Excel 4 macro language without a second thought and waited eagerly for Microsoft to fulfill its promise to make VBA the common macro language for all its applications.

Other Office products were slowly brought into the VBA fold, but it's only with the release of Office 97 that Microsoft has finally achieved its goal. Now all of the Big Four—Word, Excel, Access, and PowerPoint—have a VBA development environment at their core. Not only that, but just about *everything* in the Office 97 package is programmable: Outlook, Office Binder, even the Office Assistant.

But unprecedented programmatic control over Office objects is only the beginning. Microsoft is now licensing VBA as a separate product—called VBA 5.0—that other companies can incorporate into their own applications. A number of developers have leaped willingly onto the VBA 5.0 bandwagon, including such heavyweights as Adobe, Autodesk, Micrografx, and Visio. And as if that weren't enough, Microsoft has also created a version of VBA—called VBScript—that programmers can use as a scripting tool for Web pages.

There is little doubt, then, that VBA plays a huge role in Microsoft's future plans. Anyone interested in truly unleashing the power of the Office applications, other programs, and Web pages will need to learn the VBA language. The good news is that VBA combines both power and ease of use. So even if you've never programmed before, you won't find it hard to create useful procedures that let your applications perform as they never have before.

VBA 5.0: Something New for Everyone

VBA 5.0 is no mere incremental upgrade. Since the previous version was released with Office 95, Microsoft has spent its time revamping the interface and cramming the VBA tool chest with countless new programming gadgets and gewgaws. (In case you're wondering, the "5.0" designation doesn't mean all that much. It just synchronizes the version numbers of VBA and the latest incarnation of Visual Basic.) I'll be showing you how to take advantage of these new features throughout this book, but let's begin with a sneak preview so you'll know what to expect:

VBA is now Office-wide: As I mentioned earlier, VBA is now the common macro language for the entire Microsoft Office suite. This means that you can leverage your existing knowledge of VBA syntax, statements, and functions and put it to immediate use with the objects exposed by Word and PowerPoint. But that's not all. Thanks to the wonders of OLE Automation, other Office tools expose their objects to VBA. This means, for example, that you can compose and send e-mail messages programmatically by manipulating the appropriate objects in Outlook.

A new integrated development environment: Word, Excel, and PowerPoint now share a new integrated development environment (IDE). This is a separate VBA window that gives you a "big-picture" view of the current VBA project. As you can see in Figure I.1, this view includes a Project Editor that lists the application objects (documents) in the current file and a Properties window that lists the available properties for the current object. You can use this IDE to add new modules and forms to the project, write code, and debug your procedures.

FIGURE I.1.
You now work with VBA in a separate IDE.

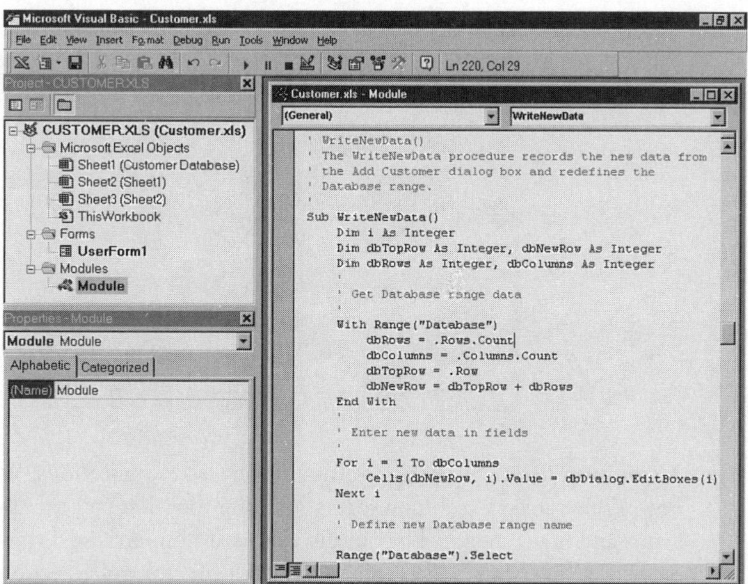

Internet/intranet support: The Internet and intranet features built into Office 97 are fully supported in VBA. This means that your procedures can create and work with hyperlinks, incorporate Internet Explorer's browser objects, send e-mail, and more. Also, you can use VBScript—a subset of the VBA language—to validate Web page form input and establish lines of communication between Web page objects.

Support for ActiveX controls: VBA can work with any of the ActiveX controls (formerly known as OLE controls) that are installed on your system. This lets you set up dynamic forms and dialog boxes with richer content.

Improved code editor: The editor you use to write VBA code has been beefed up with some welcome new features. In addition to existing features such as on-the-fly syntax checking and color-coded keywords, the new editor also includes the *IntelliSense* feature, which provides syntax help on demand. In Figure I.2, for example, you can see that the editor displays a pop-up menu that shows you a list of the properties and methods you can use to complete a line of code. The editor also displays the appropriate arguments when you enter a function or statement.

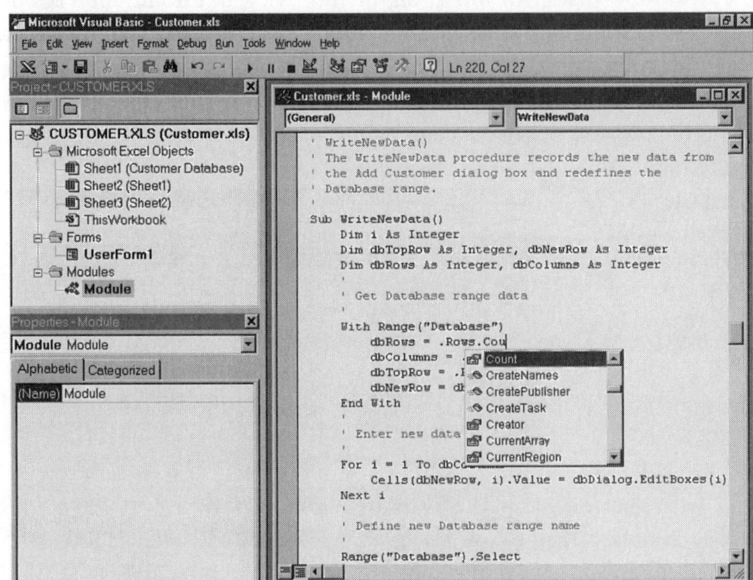

FIGURE I.2.
The new IntelliSense feature provides syntax help on demand.

A common forms-building tool: For interactive applications, Word, Excel, and PowerPoint share a common forms-building tool that you can use to create feedback forms and dialog boxes. The objects you use to build these forms have a number of properties, methods, and events, so you can control any aspect of a form programmatically.

The new and improved Object Browser: Objects are at the heart of VBA, and the vast majority of your VBA procedures will manipulate one or more objects in some way. However, Office exposes well over 500 objects and untold thousands of properties, methods, and events. To help you keep everything straight, the Object Browser has been greatly improved (see Figure I.3). It now groups each object's properties, methods, and events (with separate icons for each type), lets you search for objects and members, provides hypertext links to related objects, and lets you view the associated Help topic for the current item.

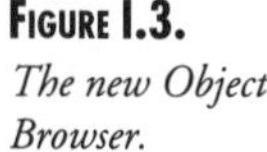

FIGURE I.3.
The new Object Browser.

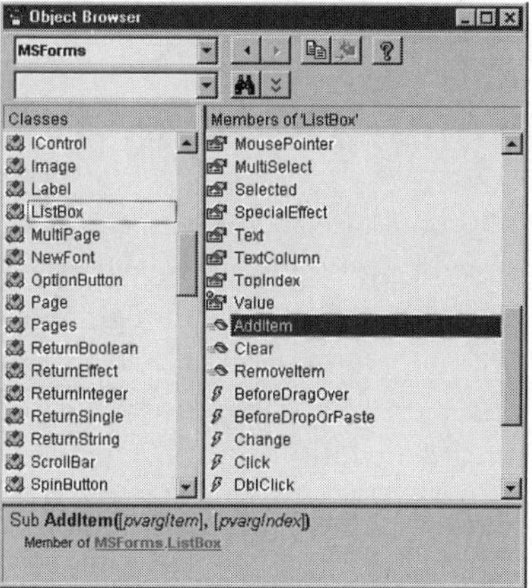

Improvements to Data Access Objects: The Data Access Objects (DAO) model has been enhanced to improve performance, support database replication, and provide better support in multiuser environments. In addition, you can use a new client/server connection mode called ODBCDirect to establish a direct connection to an ODBC database without loading the Jet database engine.

Command bars: Working with menu bars, toolbars, and shortcut menus has been streamlined in VBA 5.0. A new *command bars* object model encapsulates each of these objects into a single structure with common properties and methods.

Class modules: VBA now lets you use *class modules* to set up your own objects. Procedures and functions defined within a class module become the methods and properties of the user-defined object.

Improved security: To prevent users from accessing (and possibly modifying) your code, you can now set up VBA projects with password protection. Because VBA modules and forms are separate from the document objects (for example, Excel no longer has module sheets), securing your project in no way restricts the user from working with the underlying document.

Conditional compilation: Your VBA procedures can now use *conditional compilation* to control which statements get compiled. For example, if you use the Windows API, you'll need to differentiate between 16-bit calls and 32-bit calls. Similarly, you might want to include debugging "flags" in your code and use conditional compilation to turn certain debugging features on when you're testing and off when you distribute the application.

Office 97 Developer Edition: Microsoft has put together a separate version of Office aimed squarely at VBA developers. This "Developer Edition" includes not only Microsoft Office Professional, but also a Setup Wizard for distributing your applications, a Replication Manager for viewing and managing replicated databases on a network, and Visual SourceSafe for managing team development efforts.

What You Should Know Before Reading This Book

My goal in writing this book was to give you complete coverage of the VBA language, as well as numerous examples for putting the language to good use. Note, however, that this book isn't a programming tutorial per se. So although I cover the entire VBA language, many relatively low-level topics are presented quickly so that we can get to meatier topics. Therefore, although you don't need programming experience to read this book, knowledge of some programming basics would be helpful.

I've tried to keep the chapters focused on the topic at hand and unburdened with long-winded theoretical discussions. For the most part, each chapter gets right down to brass tacks without much fuss and bother. To keep the chapters uncluttered, I've made a few assumptions about what you know and don't know:

- I assume you have knowledge of rudimentary computer concepts such as files and folders.
- I assume you're familiar with Windows and that you know how to launch applications and use accessories such as Control Panel.
- I assume you're comfortable with the basic Windows 95 interface. This book doesn't tell you how to work with tools such as menus, dialog boxes, and the Help system.
- I assume you can operate peripherals attached to your computer, such as the keyboard, mouse, printer, and modem.
- I assume you've installed VBA 5.0 (via Office 97 or some other VBA-enabled application) and are ready to dive in at a moment's notice.
- Most of this book's examples involve Office 97. Therefore, I assume you've used the Office programs for a while and are comfortable working with these programs.
- I assume you have a brain and are willing to use it.

How This Book Is Organized

To help you find the information you need, this book is divided into eight parts that group related tasks. The next few sections offer a summary of each part.

Part I: Unleashing the VBA Programming Language

The five chapters in Part I provide intermediate-to-advanced coverage of the fundamentals of VBA programming. Chapter 1 familiarizes you with the layout of the new VBA Editor, and subsequent chapters teach you about variables, operators, expressions, objects, and procedure control.

Part II: Unleashing Microsoft Office Objects

Part II takes an in-depth look at programming all the major Office 97 applications. I'll discuss the objects, properties, methods, and events that are unique to Word, Excel, PowerPoint, and Access.

Part III: Unleashing VBA User Interface Design

The look and feel of your VBA applications is the subject of the three chapters in Part III. We'll begin with some basic methods for interacting with the user, and then I'll show you how to build forms and control them programmatically, how to assign your procedures to menus and toolbars, and how to use VBA to build menus and toolbars using code.

Part IV: Unleashing Application Integration

These days, it's a rare VBA application that operates in splendid isolation. Most applications require at least a little interaction with software other than the underlying VBA program. Integrating multiple applications is the topic of the four chapters in Part IV. You'll learn how to control other programs directly, how to use Dynamic Data Exchange, how to program OLE and ActiveX objects, how to control programs via OLE Automation, and how to work with class modules.

Part V: Unleashing VBA Database Programming

Working with information stored in databases and tables is a crucial topic in this era of client/server setups and intranet-based organizations. From simple Excel list maintenance chores, we'll progress to programming the powerful Data Access Objects model, working with ODBC, dealing with database security, and lots more.

Part VI: Unleashing VBA Internet and Intranet Programming

Part VI shows you how to program VBA's Internet- and intranet-related features. Topics include programming hyperlinks, building a custom Web browser, taking advantage of Outlook's built-in groupware features, building Web pages with the ActiveX Control Pad, and programming Web pages with VBScript.

Part VII: Unleashing Advanced VBA Programming

This part of the book presents a hodgepodge of advanced VBA techniques. You'll learn how to trap errors, how to debug your code, how to use the Windows API, and how to work with low-level file I/O and compiler directives.

Part VIII: Unleashing VBA Applications

Fine words butter no parsnips, as they say, so I've crammed this book full of useful, real-world examples. Most of these examples highlight a specific feature, so they tend to be short. Here in Part VIII, however, I offer up some longer examples that show you how to put together full-fledged VBA applications.

The Appendixes

I've also tacked on a few extra goodies at the end of this book. The appendixes include a complete listing of VBA's statements and functions (Appendixes A and B), the Windows ANSI character set (Appendix C), and an HTML primer (Appendix D).

About the CD

This book comes with a CD-ROM that contains the following:

- All the VBA code used as examples throughout the book
- Miscellaneous files from examples used in the book
- ActiveX controls
- Third-party programs that will help you create VBA applications

Online Resources for This Book

In this age of global communications and speed-of-light conversations, the notion that the relationship between a writer and his readers will go no further than the book you now hold is rather quaint, if not downright antiquated. This is particularly true when the book's subject matter is programming, because learning how to control these unruly electronic beasts through code is a lifelong process. To that end, I've assembled several online resources that you can use to further your VBA education and commune with like-minded souls.

For starters, if you have any comments about this book, or if you want to register a complaint or a compliment (I prefer the latter), please don't hesitate to send an e-mail missive to the following address:

`paul@mcfedries.com`

Better yet, feel free to drop by my Web site, have a look around, and sign the Guest Book:

`http://www.mcfedries.com/`

Note that I have a home page for *Visual Basic for Applications Unleashed* at this site. Here you'll find book excerpts and info, code samples, links to VBA information, programs and utilities written by other readers, and lots more. To go straight there, dial the following address into your Web browser:

```
http://www.mcfedries.com/books/VBAUnleashed/
```

This Book's Special Features

Visual Basic for Applications Unleashed is designed to give you the information you need without making you wade through ponderous explanations and interminable technical background. To make your life easier, this book includes various features and conventions that help you get the most out of the book and VBA itself.

Steps: Throughout this book, each VBA task is summarized in step-by-step procedures.

Things you type: Whenever I suggest that you type something, what you type appears in a `monospace` font.

Commands: I use the following style for application menu commands: File | Open. This means that you pull down the File menu and select the Open command.

Visual Basic keywords: Keywords reserved in the Visual Basic for Applications language appear in `monospace` type.

Function arguments: Throughout this book, I provide you with the proper syntax for VBA's many functions. These syntax constructions contain arguments that fall into two categories: required (arguments that you must include when calling the function) and optional (arguments that you can skip if you don't need them). To help you differentiate between the two, I show required arguments in a ***bold italic monospace*** font, and I show optional arguments in an *italic monospace* font.

The code continuation character (➥): When a line of code is too long to fit on one line of this book, it is broken at a convenient place, and the code continuation character appears at the beginning of the next line.

The VBA 5.0 icon: This icon highlights features that are new to VBA 5.0. VBA 5.0

The CD icon: This icon tells you that the file being discussed is available on the CD that comes with this book.

Toolbar buttons: When a toolbar button is mentioned, a picture of the button appears next to the paragraph in which it is mentioned.

This book also uses the following boxes to draw your attention to important (or merely interesting) information:

NOTE

The Note box presents asides that give you more information about the topic under discussion. These tidbits provide extra insights that give you a better understanding of the task at hand. In many cases, they refer you to other sections of the book for more information.

TIP

The Tip box tells you about VBA methods that are easier, faster, or more efficient than the standard methods.

CAUTION

The Caution box tells you about potential accidents waiting to happen. There are always ways to mess things up when you're working with computers. These boxes help you avoid at least some of the pitfalls.

IN THIS PART

I

PART

Unleashing the VBA Programming Language

Introducing VBA

IN THIS CHAPTER

Well begun is half done.

—Proverb

This chapter gets your VBA education off to a rousing start by introducing you to procedures, functions, and the new Visual Basic Editor. I'll begin by showing you how to use VBA to record simple macros that help automate routine tasks. To get the most out of VBA, however, you need to do some programming. To that end, this chapter gets you started by showing you how to write basic procedures and functions, as well as how to get around in VBA's integrated development environment. This will set the stage for the next few chapters, when we take a closer look at the specifics of the VBA language.

What Is a Macro?

A *macro* is a small program that contains a list of instructions that you want a program to perform. Like DOS batch files (remember those?), macros combine several operations into a single procedure that you can invoke quickly. (Many people also refer to macros as *scripts.*) This list of instructions is composed mostly of *macro statements* that are closely related to program commands. Some of these statements perform specific macro-related tasks, but most just correspond to menu commands and dialog box options. For example, VBA's `ActiveWindow.Close` function works just like File | Close.

How Does VBA Fit In?

VBA is a programming environment designed specifically for application macros. As I mentioned in the Introduction, VBA is now the standard language in the Office suite, and a number of other companies (such as Adobe and Visio) have incorporated VBA into their applications. The ubiquity of VBA has an obvious advantage: A standard language means that you have to learn only one set of statements and techniques for all the programs that support VBA. It also means that applications will get along better than they ever have, because VBA "knows" the functions and commands used by every program.

The power of VBA is clear, but perhaps its biggest advantage is that it's just plain easier to use than most programming languages (including the old macro languages used in Word, Excel, and Access). If you don't want to do any programming, VBA lets you record macros and attach them to buttons either inside a document or on a menu command or toolbar. You also can create dialog boxes by simply drawing the appropriate controls onto a document or onto a separate "user form." Other visual tools let you customize menus and toolbars as well, so you have everything you need to create simple applications without writing a line of code.

Of course, if you want to truly unleash VBA's capabilities, you'll need to augment your interface with programming code. Unlike WordBasic or the Excel 4.0 macro language, VBA 5.0 is a full-blown programming environment that includes most high-level programming constructs as well as access to every feature in the application. Add the powerful debugging tools and the ability to create a Help system, and you have everything you need to create professional-level Office applications.

The Three Types of Procedures

In VBA, a *procedure* is, broadly speaking, a collection of related statements that form a unit. VBA procedures come in three flavors: command macros, user-defined functions, and property procedures. Here's a summary of the differences:

- Command macros (which also are known as *Sub procedures,* for reasons that will become clear later in this chapter) are the most common type of procedure; they usually contain statements that are the equivalent of menu options and other program commands. The distinguishing feature of command macros is that, like regular program commands, they have an effect on their surroundings. (In Word, for example, this would mean the current document, a section of text, and so on.) Whether it's formatting some text, printing a document, or creating custom menus, command macros *change* things. I'll show you how to create command macros in the section titled "Writing Your Own Command Macro."
- User-defined functions (also called *Function procedures*) work just like a program's built-in functions. Their distinguishing characteristic is that they accept arguments and then manipulate those arguments and return a result. A properly designed function has no effect on the current environment. I'll show you how to create these functions in the section titled "Creating User-Defined Functions with VBA."
- Property procedures are new to VBA 5.0 and are used to return or set a property value for an object you've defined. I'll explain objects and properties in detail in Chapter 4, "Working with Objects," but it's enough to know for now that properties describe an object (height, width, color, and so on). If you've defined an object (called a *class module* in VBA lingo), you create property procedures to handle the object's properties. For example, suppose you've defined a "Car" object. If someone using this object wanted to change the car's color to red, you would set up a property procedure that would do the actual painting. I'll talk about class modules and property procedures in more depth in Chapter 26, "VBA Tips and Techniques." VBA 5.0

Recording a VBA Macro

By far the easiest way to create a command macro is to use the Macro Recorder. With this method, you just run through the task you want to automate (including selecting text, running menu commands, and choosing dialog box options), and the Recorder translates everything into the appropriate VBA statements. These are copied to a separate area called a *module,* where you can then replay the entire procedure any time you like. This section shows you how to record a command macro in Word, Excel, or PowerPoint.

NOTE: ACCESS IS UNIQUE

Access implements VBA differently than do Word, Excel, and PowerPoint. Therefore, most of the instructions in this chapter apply only to the latter three applications. I'll show you how to work with Access VBA macros in Chapter 9, "VBA and Access."

To begin, either select Tools | Macro | Record New Macro or click the Record Macro button on the Visual Basic toolbar. You'll see the Record Macro dialog box. Figure 1.1 shows the Excel version.

FIGURE 1.1.
Use the Record Macro dialog box to name and describe your macro.

The application proposes a name for the macro (such as Macro1), but you can use the Macro name text box to change the name to anything you like. However, you must follow a few naming conventions: you can have no more than 255 characters, the first character must be a letter or an underscore (_), and no spaces or periods are allowed.

Word and Excel let you assign shortcuts to the macro:

- In Word, either click Toolbars to assign a toolbar button to the macro or click Keyboard to assign a shortcut key to the macro.
- In Excel, enter a letter in the text box labeled Shortcut key: Ctrl+.

Use the Store macro in drop-down list to specify where the macro will reside:

- In Word, you can store the macro in any open template (which makes the macro available to any document that uses the template) or in any open document (which makes the macro available only to that document).
- In Excel, you can store the macro in the current workbook, in a new workbook, or in the Personal Macro Workbook. If you use the latter, your macros will be available to all your workbooks.

NOTE: THE PERSONAL MACRO WORKBOOK

Excel's Personal Macro Workbook is a hidden workbook that is opened automatically when you start Excel. Its filename is Personal.xls.

- In PowerPoint, you can store the macro in any open presentation.

Finally, enter a description of the macro in the Description text box. When you're ready to go, click OK. The application returns you to the document, displays Recording or REC in the status bar, and displays the Stop Recording Macro toolbar. Now perform the tasks you want to include in the macro.

When you finish the tasks, select Tools | Macro | Stop Recording or click the Stop Macro button.

Viewing the Resulting Module

When you record a macro, the application creates a "VBA project." This is a container that includes both the document you used for the macro and a special object called a *module* that contains the macro code.

To see your macro, select Tools | Macro | Macros (or press Alt-F8) to display the Macro dialog box. In the Macro Name list, highlight the macro you just recorded and then click the Edit button. The application opens the Visual Basic Editor window and then opens the module and displays the macro. As you can see in Figure 1.2, the application (Excel, in this case) translates your actions into VBA code and combines everything into a single macro.

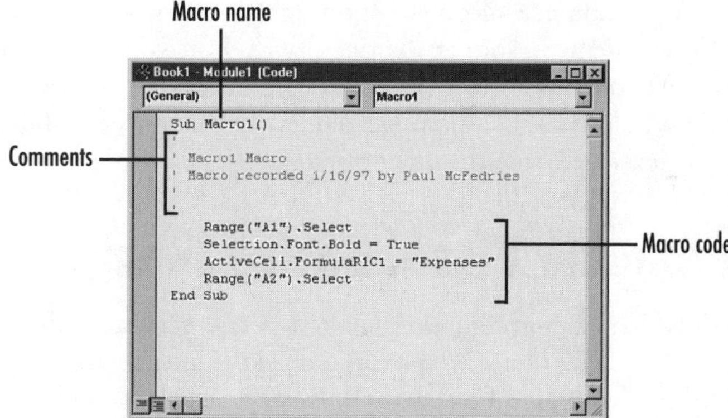

FIGURE 1.2.
A sample recorded macro.

A typical macro has the following features:

`Sub`/`End Sub`: These keywords mark the beginning (`Sub`) and end (`End Sub`) of a macro. The `Sub` keyword is the reason why command macros also are called *Sub procedures.*

Macro Name: After the `Sub` keyword, Excel enters the name of the macro followed by a left and right parenthesis (the parentheses are used for arguments, as you'll see later).

Comments: The first few lines begin with an apostrophe ('), which tells VBA that these lines are *comments.* As the name implies, comments are for show only; they aren't processed when you run the macro. In each recorded macro, the comments display the name of the macro and the description you entered in the Record New Macro dialog box.

Macro code: The main body of the macro (in other words, the lines between `Sub` and `End Sub`) consists of a series of statements. These are the application's interpretations of the actions you performed during the recording. In the example, four actions were performed in Excel:

1. Cell A1 was selected.
2. The cell was formatted as boldface.
3. The string `Expenses` was typed into the cell.
4. The Enter key was pressed (which moved the selection down to cell A2).

Editing a Recorded Macro

As you're learning VBA, you'll often end up with recorded macros that don't turn out quite right the first time. Whether the macro runs a command it shouldn't or is missing a command altogether, you'll often have to patch things up after the fact.

A VBA module is more like a word-processing document than a worksheet, so you make changes the same way you would in a word processor or text editor. If your macro contains statements you want to remove, just delete the offending lines from the module.

If you want to add new recorded actions to the macro, VBA 5.0 doesn't give you any way to record new statements into an existing macro. Instead, you should first record a new macro that includes the actions you want, and then display the macro. From here, you can use the standard Windows cut-and-paste techniques (including drag-and-drop) to move the statements from the new macro into the other macro.

Touring the Visual Basic Editor

The Visual Basic Editor, shown in Figure 1.3, represents an entirely new way of looking at the VBA universe. The idea was to create a separate, integrated VBA development environment modeled on the layout of Microsoft's Visual Basic programming environment. To that end, the Visual Basic Editor is divided into three areas: the Project Explorer, the Properties window, and the work area.

The Project Explorer

The Project Explorer area shows a hierarchical view of the contents of the current VBA project. (If you don't see the Project Explorer, either select View | Project Explorer, press Ctrl-R, or click the Project Explorer button on the toolbar.)

These contents include the open application objects (worksheets, documents, slides, and so on), any modules that have been created either by recording a macro or by creating one from scratch (explained later), and any user forms you've built (see Chapter 11, "Working with Microsoft Forms"). The Project Explorer toolbar contains three icons that let you work with the objects in the tree:

Click the View Code button to open a module window that contains the VBA code associated with the selected object. (You can also view an object's code by double-clicking the object.)

Click the View Object button to switch back to the original application and display the selected object.

Click the Toggle Folders button to alternate the Project Explorer display between a hierarchical view of the objects and a simple list of all the objects.

FIGURE 1.3.
The Visual Basic Editor is a complete programming environment.

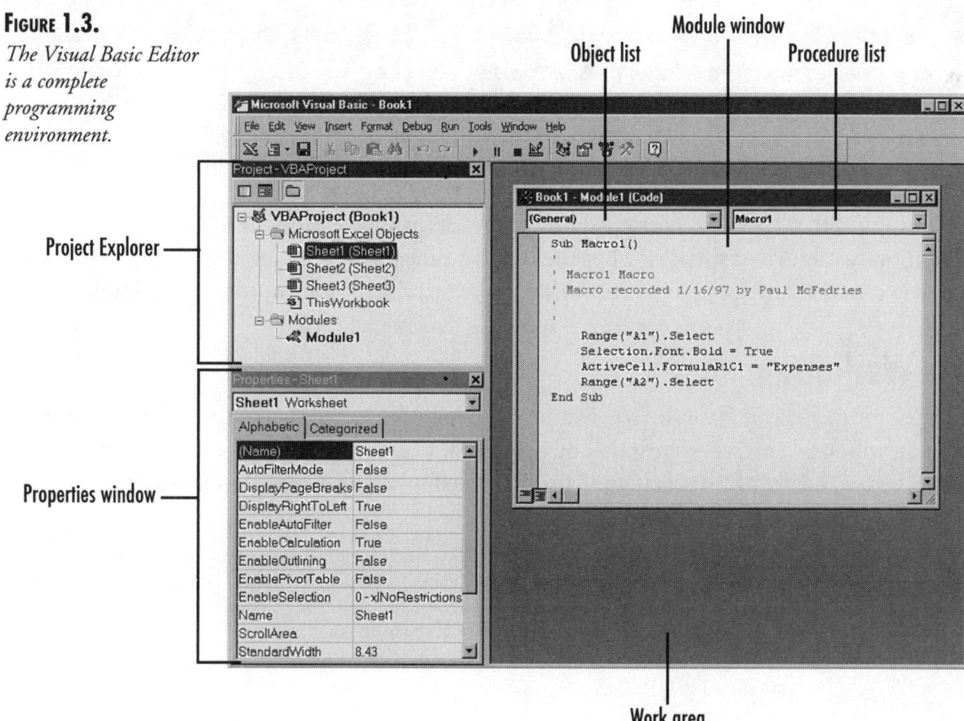

The Properties Window

The Properties window shows the various properties available for whatever object is highlighted in the Project Explorer. If you don't see the Properties window, either select View | Properties Window, press F4, or click the Properties Window button on the toolbar.

As in Visual Basic, the Properties window is divided into two columns. The left column shows you the names of all the properties associated with the object, and the right side shows you the current value of the property. Also note that you can use the tabs in the Properties window to view the properties in either of two ways:

Alphabetic: This tab displays all the properties alphabetically by property name.

Categorized: This tab divides the properties into various categories. (The categories you see depend on the object selected.)

To change the value of a property, click the appropriate box in the right column and then either type in the new value or select it from a drop-down list (the method you use depends on the property).

TIP: DOUBLE-CLICK TO CYCLE THROUGH A PROPERTY LIST

For properties that have a list of possible values, you can cycle through the available items by double-clicking the property. (You can double-click either the property name or the value.)

Bear in mind that these are "design-time" properties you're setting. In other words, these are the property values that will be in effect before you run a macro. As you'll see in Chapter 4, you can also change an object's properties within a program (in other words, at runtime).

The Work Area

The rest of the Visual Basic Editor window is taken up by the work area. This is where the module windows you work with will be displayed. Other VBA objects—such as the custom dialog boxes and user forms that you create yourself—will also appear in this area.

To get a module to appear in the work area, highlight it in the Project Explorer and then use any of the following techniques:

- Click the View Code button on the Project Explorer toolbar.
- Select View | Code.
- Press F7.
- Double-click the module.

Note that each module window has two drop-down lists beneath the title bar:

Object list: This control contains a list of the available objects. Modules don't have objects, so this list contains only `(General)` for a module window.

Procedure list: This is a list of all the procedures and functions in the module. Until you add a procedure, this list shows only `(Declarations)`.

Writing Your Own Command Macro

Although the Macro Recorder makes it easy to create your own macros, there are plenty of macro features that you can't access with mouse or keyboard actions or by selecting menu options. In Excel, for example, VBA has a couple dozen information macro functions that return data about cells, worksheets, workspaces, and more. Also, the VBA control functions let you add true programming constructs such as looping, branching, and decision-making.

To access these macro elements, you need to write your own VBA routines from scratch. This is easier than it sounds, because all you really need to do is enter a series of statements in a module. The next two sections take you through the various steps.

NOTE: A PARADOX

Although the next two sections tell you how to create VBA macros, I realize there's an inherent paradox here: How can you write your own macros when you haven't learned anything about them yet? Making you familiar with VBA's statements and functions is the job of the other four chapters here in Part I. The next couple of sections will get you started, and you can use this knowledge as a base on which to build your VBA skills in subsequent chapters.

Creating a New Module

If you want to enter your macro in an existing module, just display the window as described in the section "Viewing the Resulting Module." If you want to start a new module, first use either of the following techniques to display the Visual Basic Editor (if you're not there already):

- Select Tools | Macro | Visual Basic Editor.
- Click the Visual Basic Editor button on the Visual Basic toolbar. (To display the Visual Basic toolbar, select View | Toolbars | Visual Basic.)

TIP: TOGGLING BETWEEN VBA AND THE APPLICATION

You can also get to the Visual Basic Editor by pressing Alt-F11. In fact, this key combination is a toggle that switches you between the Visual Basic Editor and the original application.

Once you have the Visual Basic Editor displayed, you can open a new module window either by selecting Insert | Module or by dropping down the Insert list on the Standard toolbar (it's the second button from the left) and choosing Module.

Writing a Command Macro

With a module window open and active, follow these steps to write your own command macro:

1. Place the insertion point where you want to start the macro. (Make sure the insertion point isn't inside an existing macro.)
2. If you want to begin your macro with a few comments that describe what the macro does, type an apostrophe (`'`) at the beginning of each comment line.
3. To start the macro, type `Sub` followed by a space and the name of the macro. When you press Enter at the end of this line, VBA automatically adds a pair of parentheses at the end of the macro name. It also tacks on an `End Sub` line to mark the end of the procedure.
4. Between the `Sub` and `End Sub` lines, type the VBA statements you want to include in the macro.

TIP: INDENT STATEMENTS FOR CLARITY

To make your code easier to read, you should indent each line by pressing the Tab key at the beginning of the line. You can also use the following buttons on the Edit toolbar (to display this toolbar, select View | Toolbars | Edit in the Visual Basic Editor):

 Indent

 Outdent (or press Shift-Tab)

Note, however, that VBA preserves the indentation on subsequent lines, so you only have to indent the first line.

When you press Enter to start a new line, VBA analyzes the line you just entered and performs three chores:

- It formats the color of each word in the line. By default, VBA keywords are blue, comments are green, errors are red, and all other text is black. (You can change these colors if you like. To find out how, see the section "Setting Visual Basic Editor Options.")
- VBA keywords are converted to their proper case. For example, if you type `end sub`, VBA converts this to `End Sub` when you press Enter.
- It checks for syntax errors. VBA signifies a syntax error either by displaying a dialog box to let you know what the problem is or by not converting a word to its proper case or color.

TIP: ALWAYS ENTER KEYWORDS IN LOWERCASE

By always entering VBA keywords in lowercase letters, you'll be able to catch typing errors by looking for keywords that VBA doesn't recognize (in other words, the ones that remain in lowercase).

Running a VBA Macro

The Office applications offer several methods for running your VBA macros. Here's a quick rundown:

- Select Tools | Macro | Macros (or press Alt-F8) to display the Macro dialog box, shown in Figure 1.4. If necessary, use the Macros in box to choose the document that contains the macro you want to work with. Use the Macro Name list to highlight the macro, and then click the Run button.

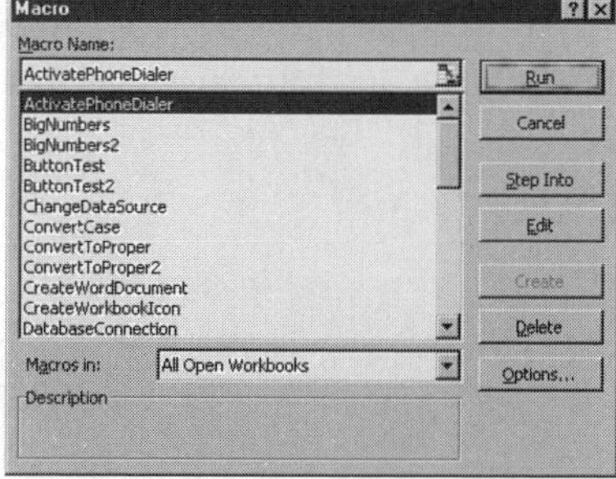

FIGURE 1.4.
The Macro dialog box contains a list of all the macros you've created.

- In a module, place the insertion point anywhere inside the macro, and then either select Run | Run Sub/User Form, press the F5 key, or click the Run Sub/User Form button on the Visual Basic Editor toolbar.
- If you assigned a shortcut key to the macro, press the key combination.
- If you added a new menu command or toolbar button for the macro, select the command or click the button.

Creating User-Defined Functions with VBA

The Office applications come with a large number of built-in functions. Excel, for example, has hundreds of functions—one of the largest function libraries of any spreadsheet package.

However, even with this vast collection, you'll still find that plenty of applications aren't covered. For example, you might need to calculate the area of a circle of a given radius, or the gravitational force between two objects. You could, of course, easily calculate these things on a worksheet, but if you need them frequently, it makes sense to define your own functions that you can use anytime. The next four sections show you how it's done.

Understanding User-Defined Functions

As I mentioned earlier in this chapter, the defining characteristic of user-defined functions is that they return a result. They can perform any number of calculations on numbers, text, logical values, or whatever, but they're not allowed to affect their surroundings. In a worksheet, for example, they can't move the active cell, format a range, or change the workspace settings. In fact, anything you can access using the application menus is off-limits in a user-defined function.

So, what *can* you put in a user-defined function? All of the application's built-in functions are fair game, and you can use any VBA function that isn't the equivalent of a menu command or desktop action.

All user-defined functions have the same basic structure, as shown in Figure 1.5. This is a function named `HypotenuseLength` that calculates the length of a right triangle's hypotenuse given the other two sides.

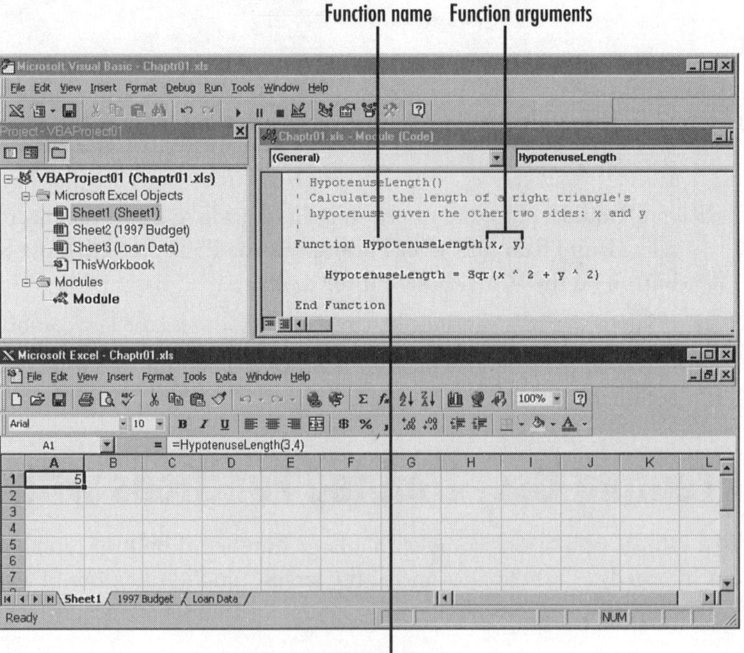

FIGURE 1.5.
A user-defined function that calculates the length of a right triangle's hypotenuse.

NOTE: THE CODE'S ON THE CD

You'll find the code for the `HypotenuseLength` function, as well as all the other procedures in this chapter, on this book's CD. Look for the Chaptr01.xls file. If you don't have Excel, use Chaptr01.bas instead. (These .BAS files are Visual Basic files. However, they contain only text, so you can load them into Notepad or some other text editor. I'll show you how to import from and export to the .BAS format later in this chapter.)

Here's a summary of the various parts of a user-defined function:

The `Function` statement: This keyword identifies the procedure as a user-defined function. The `Function` keyword is the reason that user-defined functions are also known as *Function procedures.*

The function name: This is a unique name for the function. Names must begin with an alphabetic character, they can't include a space or a period, and they can't be longer than 255 characters.

The function arguments: Just as many application functions accept arguments, so do user-defined functions. Arguments (or *parameters,* as they're sometimes called) are typically one or more values that the function uses as the raw materials for its calculations. You always enter arguments between parentheses after the function name, and you separate multiple arguments with commas.

The VBA statements: This is the code that actually performs the calculations. Each expression is a combination of values, operators, variables, and VBA or application functions that produce a result.

The return value: User-defined functions usually return a value. To do this, include a statement where you set the name of the function equal to an expression. For example, in the `HypotenuseLength` function, the following statement defines the return value:

```
HypotenuseLength = Sqr(x ^ 2 + y ^ 2)
```

The `End Function` keywords: These keywords indicate the end of the Function procedure.

All your user-defined functions will have this basic structure, so you need to keep three things in mind when designing these kinds of macros:

- What arguments will the macro take?
- What formulas will you use within the macro?
- What value or values will be returned?

Writing User-Defined Functions

User-defined functions can't contain menu commands or mouse and keyboard actions. This means, of course, that there is no way to record user-defined functions. You have to write them out by hand; the process is very similar to creating a command macro from scratch. Here are the general steps to follow to write a user-defined function:

1. Open the module you want to use for the function.
2. Place the insertion point where you want to start the function.
3. If you like, enter one or more comments that describe what the function does. Be sure to type an apostrophe (`'`) at the beginning of each comment line.
4. Start the procedure by typing `Function` followed by a space and then the name of the macro. If your function uses arguments, enclose them in parentheses after the function name (be sure to separate each argument with a comma). When you press Enter, VBA inserts the `End Function` statement.

> **NOTE: OPTIONAL ARGUMENTS**
>
> The arguments you specify for your user-defined functions won't always be required. For example, you might write a function in which the first argument is required but the second is optional. To tell VBA that a particular argument is optional, include the `Optional` keyword before the argument:
>
> ```
> Function MyFunction(arg1 As String, Optional arg2 As String)
> ```

5. Enter the VBA statements that you want to include in the function. As with Sub procedures, you should indent each line for clarity by pressing the Tab key at the beginning of the line.
6. Be sure to include a line that defines the return value.

Employing User-Defined Functions

You'll probably find that user-defined functions are most useful in Excel. In this case, you can employ these functions only within worksheet formulas or in other VBA statements. You have two choices:

- In the cell, enter the function the same way you would any of Excel's built-in functions. In other words, enter the name of the function and then the necessary arguments enclosed in parentheses. In Figure 1.5, the window at the bottom shows the `HypotenuseLength` function in action. Cell A1 contains the following formula:

  ```
  =HypotenuseLength(3,4)
  ```

- Select Insert | Function, highlight All in the Function category list, and then select the macro from the Function name list. Click OK and enter the arguments. When you're done, click OK.

Working with Procedures

The basic unit of VBA programming is the *procedure*, which is a block of code in a module that you reference as a unit. Earlier in this chapter you learned about the two types of procedures: command macros (also known as Sub procedures) and user-defined functions (or Function procedures).

The Structure of a Procedure

To recap what you learned earlier, a Sub procedure is allowed to modify its environment, but it can't return a value. Here is the basic structure of a Sub procedure:

```
Sub ProcedureName (argument1, argument2, ...)
    [VBA statements]
End Sub
```

For example, Listing 1.1 presents a Sub procedure that enters some values for a loan in various worksheet ranges and then adds a formula to calculate the loan payment. (I'll show you how to work with ranges and other Excel objects in Chapter 7, "Manipulating Excel with VBA.")

Listing 1.1. A sample Sub procedure.

```
Sub EnterLoanData()
    Range("IntRate").Value = .08
    Range("Term").Value = 10
    Range("Principal").Value = 10000
    Range("Payment").Formula = "=PMT(IntRate/12, Term*12, Principal)"
End Sub
```

A Function procedure, on the other hand, can't modify its environment, but it does return a value. Here is its structure:

```
Function ProcedureName (argument1, argument2, ...)
    [VBA statements]
    ProcedureName = returnValue
End Function
```

For example, Listing 1.2 is a Function procedure that sums two ranges, stores the results in variables named `totalSales` and `totalExpenses` (see the next chapter to learn more about variables), and uses these values and the `fixedCosts` argument to calculate the net margin:

Listing 1.2. A sample Function procedure.

```
Function CalcNetMargin(fixedCosts)
    totalSales = Application.Sum(Range("Sales"))
    totalExpenses = Application.Sum(Range("Expenses"))
    CalcNetMargin = (totalSales-totalExpenses-fixedCosts)/totalSales
End Function
```

Calling a Procedure

Once you've written a procedure, you can use it either in a worksheet formula or in another procedure. This is known as *calling* the procedure.

Calling a Procedure Name in the Same Project

If a procedure exists in the current module, or in a different module that's part of the current VBA project, you call it just by entering the procedure name and then including any necessary arguments. For example, as you learned earlier, you can call the `HypotenuseLength` procedure from a worksheet cell by entering a formula such as the following:

```
=HypotenuseLength(3,4)
```

If you like, you can also call a procedure from another procedure. For example, the following VBA statement sets a variable named `TotalPerimeter` equal to the total perimeter of a right triangle that has two sides of length `X` and `Y`:

```
TotalPerimeter = X + Y + HypotenuseLength(X,Y)
```

If the procedure exists in a different module, but it has the same name as a procedure in the current module, you need to preface the call with the name of the module that contains the procedure:

```
ModuleName.ProcedureName
```

For example, the following statement calls the `CalcNetMargin` function from another module:

```
Module.CalcNetMargin(100000)
```

Calling a Procedure in Another Project

If you have a VBA statement that needs to call a procedure in another project, you first need to set up a *reference* to the project. Doing this gives you access to all the project's procedures. The following steps show you what to do:

1. Display the Visual Basic Editor for the project you want to work with.
2. Select Tools | References to display the References dialog box.
3. If the project is from the same application and is open, the name of the project will appear in the Available References list, as shown in Figure 1.6. Highlight the project name and activate its check box. If the project isn't open, click the Browse button, choose the document you want from the Add Reference dialog box that appears, and click Open to return to the References dialog box.

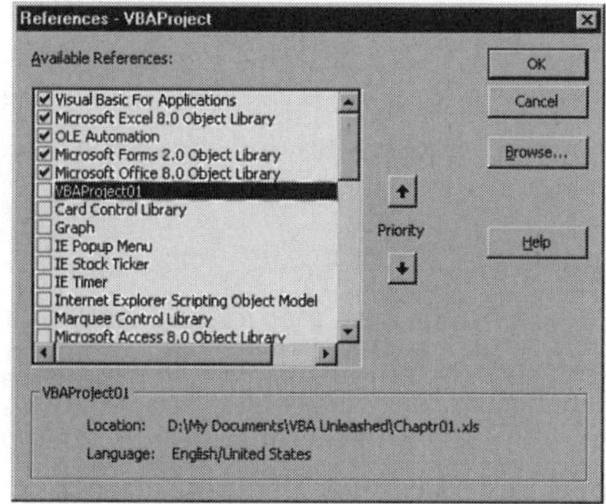

FIGURE 1.6.
Use the References dialog box to set up a reference between a project and another document.

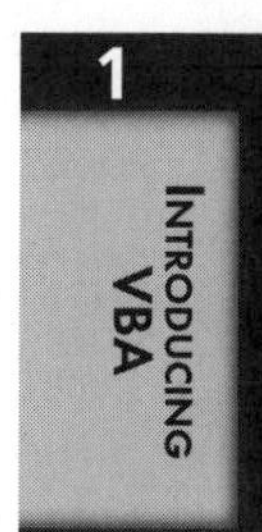

4. Click OK to return to the Visual Basic Editor. You'll see the project added to the Project Explorer.

CAUTION: PROJECT NAMES MUST BE UNIQUE

If the project you select in the References dialog box has the same name as the project in the current document, VBA will display an error message because no two open projects can have the same name. To avoid this, make sure you give each of your VBA projects a unique name. To rename a project, use either of the following methods:

- Click the project name in the Project Explorer and then use the `Name` property in the Properties window to change the name.
- Highlight one of the project's objects in the Project Explorer and then select Tools | *ProjectName* Properties (where *ProjectName* is the name of the project). In the Project Properties dialog box that appears, enter the new name in the Project Name text box and then click OK.

Once you have the reference established, you call the procedure the same way you call the procedures in the current project. If the two projects have procedures with the same names, you need to add the project's name, surrounded by square brackets ([]), to the call:

```
[ProjectName].ProcedureName
```

For example, the following statement calls the `HypotenuseLength` function in the VBAProject01 project:

```
[VBAProject01].HypotenuseLength(3,4)
```

Public Versus Private Procedures

I mentioned in the preceding section that once you've established a reference to a VBA project, you can use that project's procedures and functions directly. Such procedures are called *public* procedures.

There might be times, however, when you don't want to give other projects access to a procedure. For example, you might have a procedure with a name that clashes with an existing name, or you might have an unfinished or untested procedure that you don't want to let loose just yet.

You can make sure that a procedure or function can't be called from another project by preceding the `Sub` or `Function` keyword with the `Private` keyword. This means that the procedure or function can only be used within its own project. For example, the following statement defines the `HypotenuseLength` function as a private function:

```
Private Function HypotenuseLength(x, y)
```

If you prefer to make *all* of a module's procedures and functions unavailable to other projects, add the following line to the top of the module (that is, before your first procedure or function):

```
Option Private Module
```

This is the same as adding `Private` to every `Sub` or `Function` statement.

NOTE: SCOPE

The level of accessibility assigned to a procedure is called its scope.

NOTE: HIDING PROCEDURES FROM THE OBJECT BROWSER

An added bonus that you get with `Option Private Module` is that the module's procedures and functions aren't visible in the Object Browser (the Object Browser shows, among other things, the available procedures in a project; see Chapter 4 for details). If you use just the `Private` keyword, the procedure or function shows up in the Object Browser, which could confuse the users of your application.

VBA 5.0 Another Method for Inserting a Procedure

Now that you know about the difference between public and private procedures, here's an alternative method for inserting a procedure into a module:

1. In the module, position the insertion point where you want the new procedure to appear.

2. Either select Insert | Procedure or drop down the Insert list on the Standard toolbar (the second button from the left) and select Procedure. VBA displays the Insert Procedure dialog box, shown in Figure 1.7.

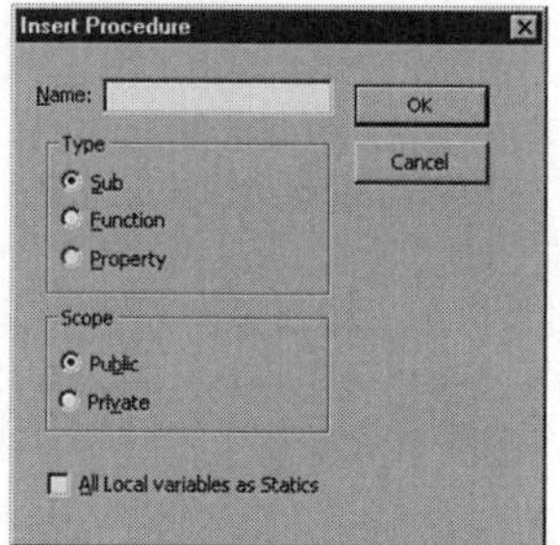

FIGURE 1.7.
Use this dialog box to start a new procedure or function.

3. Use the Name text box to enter a name for the procedure.
4. Use the Type group to choose the kind of procedure you want: Sub, Function, or Property.
5. Use the Scope group to choose the scope you want to use for the procedure: Public or Private.
6. If the All Local variables as Statics check box is activated, VBA adds the `Static` keyword to the procedure definition. This defines the procedure's variables to be *static,* which means they preserve their values between calls to the procedure. I'll talk more about this in the next chapter.
7. Click OK to insert the procedure stub.

Visual Basic Editor Techniques for Easier Coding

If in the past you've used either Visual Basic for Applications or Visual Basic, you'll be pleased to know that the new Visual Basic Editor boasts a number of handy features that make it easier than ever to create and work with procedures. The next few sections discuss four of these features: IntelliSense, comment blocks, Find, and bookmarks.

Taking Advantage of IntelliSense

VBA 5.0

VBA 5.0's new IntelliSense feature is like a mini version of the VBA Help system. It offers you assistance with VBA syntax either on-the-fly or on demand. You should find this an incredibly useful tool because, as you'll see as you work through this book, VBA contains dozens of statements and functions, and VBA-enabled programs offer hundreds of objects to work with. Few people are capable of committing all this to memory, and it's a pain to have to constantly look up the correct syntax. IntelliSense helps by giving you hints and alternatives as you type. To see what I mean, let's look at the five types of IntelliSense help available.

List Properties/Methods

In Chapter 4, you'll learn how to work with the objects that each VBA-enabled application makes available. In particular, you'll learn about *properties* and *methods*, which, put simply, define the characteristics of each object. (In broad terms, properties describe an object's appearance, and methods describe what you can do with an object.)

As you'll see, however, each object can have dozens of properties and methods. To help you code your procedures correctly, IntelliSense can display a list of the available properties and methods as you type your VBA statements. To try this, activate a module in the Visual Basic Editor and type `application` followed by a period (`.`). As shown in Figure 1.8, VBA will display a pop-up menu. The items on this menu are the properties and methods that are available for the Application object. Use the following methods to work with this menu:

- Keep typing to display different items in the list. In Excel, for example, if you type `cap`, VBA highlights `Caption` in the list.
- Double-click an item to insert it in your code.
- Highlight an item (by clicking it or by using the up and down arrow keys) and then press Tab to insert the item and continue working on the same statement.
- Highlight an item and then press Enter to insert the item and start a new line.
- Press Esc to remove the menu without inserting an item.

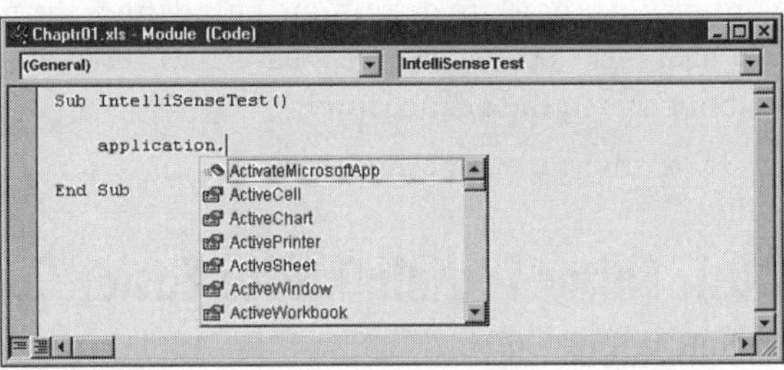

FIGURE 1.8.
IntelliSense displays the available properties and methods as you type.

Note that if you press Esc to remove the pop-up menu, VBA won't display it again for the same object. If you would like to display the menu again, use any of the following techniques:

- Select Edit | List Properties/Methods.
- Press Ctrl-J.
- Right-click the module and select List Properties/Methods.

- Click the List Properties/Methods button on the Edit toolbar.

NOTE: ACTIVATING THE LIST FEATURE

If the Visual Basic Editor doesn't display the pop-up menu automatically, you need to activate this feature. See "Setting Visual Basic Editor Options" later in this chapter.

List Constants

IntelliSense has a List Constants feature that's similar to List Properties/Methods. In this case, you get a pop-up menu that displays a list of the available constants for a property or method. (A *constant* is a fixed value that corresponds to a specific state or result. See Chapter 2, "Understanding Variables," to learn more about them.) For example, type the following in a module:

```
Application.ActiveWindow.WindowState=
```

Figure 1.9 shows the pop-up menu that appears in Excel. This is a list of constants that correspond to the various settings for a window's `WindowState` property. For example, you would use the `xlMaximized` constant to maximize a window. You work with this list using the same techniques that I outlined for List Properties/Methods.

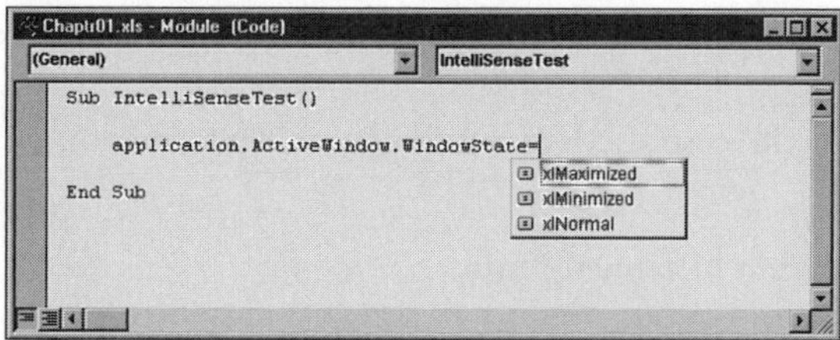

FIGURE 1.9.
The List Constants feature in action.

If you need to display this list by hand, use any of the following methods:

- Select Edit | List Constants.
- Press Ctrl-Shift-J.
- Right-click the module and select List Constants.
- Click the List Constants button on the Edit toolbar.

Parameter Info

You learned earlier that a user-defined function typically takes one or more arguments (or parameters) to use in its internal calculations. Many of the functions and statements built into VBA also use parameters, and some have as many as a dozen separate arguments! The syntax of such statements is obviously very complex, so it's easy to make mistakes. To help you enter a user-defined function or one of VBA's built-in functions or statements, IntelliSense provides the Parameter Info feature. As its name implies, this feature displays information on the parameters you can utilize in a function. To see an example, enter the following text in any Excel module:

```
activecell.formula=pmt(
```

As soon as you type the left parenthesis, a banner pops up that tells you the available arguments for (in this case) VBA's `Pmt` function (see Figure 1.10). Here are the features of this banner:

- The current argument is displayed in boldface. When you enter an argument and then type a comma, VBA displays the next argument in boldface.
- Arguments that are optional are surrounded by square brackets (`[]`).
- The various `As` statements (for example, `As Double`) tell you the *data type* of each argument. I'll explain data types in the next chapter.
- To remove the banner, press Esc.

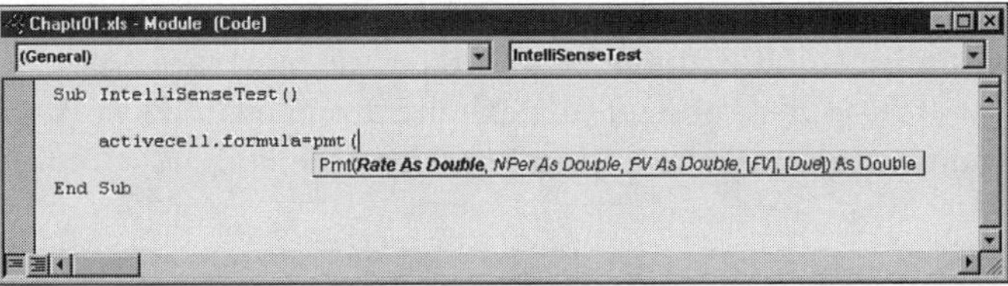

FIGURE 1.10.
The Parameter Info feature shows you the defined arguments for the current function or statement.

As usual, IntelliSense also lets you display this information by hand. Here are the techniques to use:

- Select Edit | Parameter Info.
- Press Ctrl-Shift-I.
- Right-click the module and select Parameter Info.

- Click the Parameter Info button on the Edit toolbar.

Quick Info

IntelliSense also has a Quick Info feature that's similar to Parameter Info, as shown in Figure 1.11. In this case, though, Quick Info provides not only a list of function parameters, but also the syntax of *any* VBA statement, as well as the value of a constant.

Here are the methods you can use to display the Quick Info banner:

- Select Edit | Quick Info.
- Press Ctrl-I.
- Right-click the module and select Quick Info.

- Click the Quick Info button on the Edit toolbar.

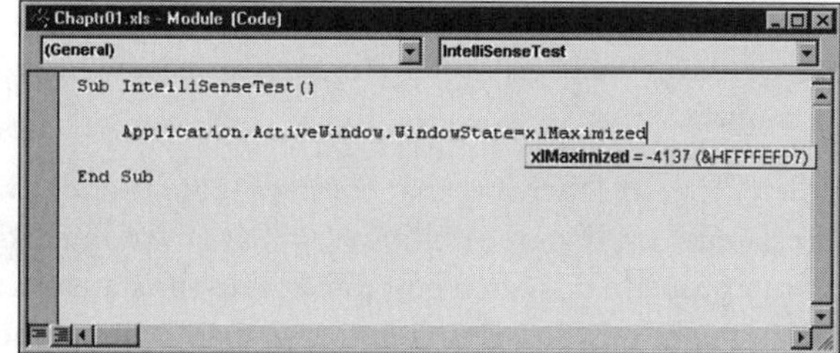

FIGURE 1.11.
Quick Info can help you with constant values as well as statement syntax and function parameters.

Complete Word

The last of the IntelliSense features is Complete Word. You use this feature to get VBA to complete a keyword that you've started typing, and thus save some wear and tear on your typing fingers. To use Complete Word, just type in the first few letters of a keyword and do one of the following:

- Select Edit | Complete Word.
- Press Ctrl-Alt-A.
- Right-click the module and select Complete Word.
- Click the Complete Word button on the Edit toolbar.

If the letters you typed are enough to define a unique keyword, IntelliSense fills in the rest of the word. For example, if you type `appl` and run Complete Word, IntelliSense changes your typing to `Application`. However, if there are multiple keywords that begin with the letters you typed, IntelliSense displays a pop-up menu that you can use to select the word you want.

Working with Comment Blocks

Although comments aren't executed when you run a procedure, they still have an important role to play in VBA programming. In particular, you can use comments to document a procedure:

- You can provide an overall explanation of what the procedure does.
- You can detail any assumptions you've made about how the procedure runs, as well as any background information necessary to operate the procedure.
- You can explain the arguments the procedure uses, if any.
- You can create a "running commentary" throughout the procedure that explains what the procedure is doing and why.

Why go to all this trouble? Well, the VBA language uses a fairly straightforward syntax, but it still suffers (as do most programming languages) from being inherently cryptic. So although *you* might know exactly what your program is trying to accomplish, other people will have a harder time deciphering your code. A copiously commented procedure removes some of this burden and makes it easier for other people to work with it. Not only that, but you'll find that comments are an invaluable tool for getting up to speed when you haven't looked at a procedure for six months.

However, there is yet another way that comments are useful: to prevent VBA from executing troublesome statements. If you're pulling your hair out trying to discover why a particular statement won't run properly, it's often best to just skip the statement altogether and come back to it later. Or you might want to try an alternative statement. Either way, tacking an apostrophe onto the beginning of the statement is all you need to do to "comment out" the pesky line and move on to more productive matters.

Suppose, however, that instead of a single line of troublesome code you have 10 lines, or even 20 or 30. Again, you can bypass these lines by commenting them out, but it's a pain to have to insert apostrophes at the beginning of every line. To relieve you of this hassle, VBA 5.0 has a new Comment Block feature that can toggle any number of statements between "commented" and "uncommented." To use this feature, highlight the statements you want to work with and then do one of the following:

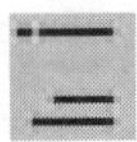

- To comment the statements, click the Comment Block button on the Edit toolbar.

- To uncomment the statements, click the Uncomment Block button on the Edit toolbar.

Finding Code

Once you gain experience with VBA, you'll find that your modules and procedures will get larger and more complex. If you ever find yourself lamenting a long-lost piece of code adrift in some huge megamodule, the folks who designed VBA can sympathize (probably because it has happened to *them* once or twice). In fact, they were even kind enough to build a special Find feature into VBA to help you search for missing code. Find can look for a word or phrase in a procedure, module, or even an entire project. There's even a Replace feature that you can use to replace one or more instances of a word or phrase with another word or phrase.

Using the Find Feature

If you need to find some code in a module that has only a relatively small number of statements, it's usually easiest just to scroll through the module using the mouse or keyboard. But if you're dealing with a few dozen or even a few hundred statements, or with a module that contains dozens of procedures and functions, don't waste your time rummaging through the statements by hand. The Visual Basic Editor's Find feature lets you search for a key word or phrase.

When you're ready to begin, you can select Edit | Find, press Ctrl-F, or click the Find button on the toolbar. The Find dialog box, shown in Figure 1.12, appears.

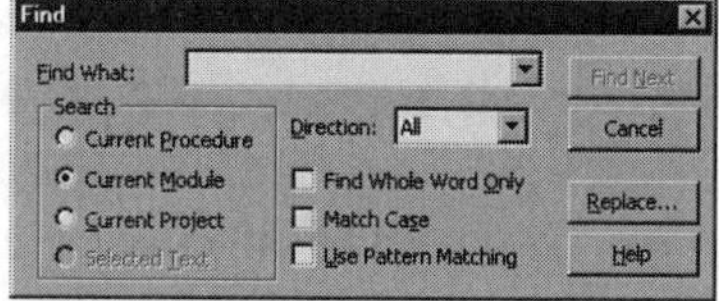

FIGURE 1.12.
Use the Find dialog box to hunt for code in a procedure, module, or project.

Here's a summary of the various controls in this dialog box:

Find What: Use this text box to enter the word or phrase you want to find.

Search: The options in this group define the *search scope*, which tells VBA where to conduct its search. The options are Current Procedure, Current Module, Current Project, and Selected Text.

Direction: If you suspect the code you want is below the current insertion point position, select Down. If you think the code is above the current position, select Up. If you're not sure, select All to run through the entire search scope.

Find Whole Word Only: When this check box is deactivated, VBA will look for text that *contains* the search text. If you only want to find words that match the search text exactly, activate this check box.

Match Case: Activate this check box to make your searches case-sensitive.

Use Pattern Matching: Activate this check box if you want to use VBA's pattern matching feature, which supports the following characters:

Character	*What It Matches*
?	Any single character.
*	Zero or more characters.
#	Any single digit.
`[character-list]`	Any single character in `character-list`, which can be either a series of characters (for example, `[aeiou]`) or a range (for example, `[a-m]`).
`[!character-list]`	Any single character not in `character-list`.

Replace: Clicking this button displays the Replace dialog box. See the next section for details.

Find Next: Click this button to find the next instance of your search text. (In this case, "next" depends on whether you're searching up or down.)

When you start the search, VBA highlights the first instance of your search text if it finds a match. If this is the instance you want, click Cancel. Otherwise, you can continue searching by clicking the Find Next button. If VBA can't find the search text, it lets you know when it has reached the bottom of the search scope (if you're searching down) or the top of the search scope (if you're searching up). Click Yes to search the rest of the scope. If VBA still can't find the search text, it displays a message telling you the bad news.

TIP: SEARCHING IDEAS

Searching for code is a straightforward affair, but VBA gives you lots of options. To make things easier, here are a couple of things to keep in mind when using the Find feature:

- For best results, don't try to match entire statements. A word or two is usually all you really need.
- If you're not sure how to spell a word, just use a piece of it. Access will still find `Application` if you search for app (although it will also find keywords such as `AppActivate` and `DDEAppReturnCode`).

Using the Replace Feature

One of the VBA features you'll probably come to rely on the most is *find and replace.* This means that VBA seeks out a particular bit of code and then replaces it with something else. This might not seem like a big deal for a statement or two, but if you need to change a couple of dozen instances of a variable name, it can be a real time-saver.

Happily, replacing data is very similar to finding it. To get started, you can either click the Replace button in the Find dialog box or select Edit | Replace (you can also press Ctrl-H). You'll see the Replace dialog box, shown in Figure 1.13. Enter the data you want to search for in the Find What text box and then enter the data you want to replace it with in the Replace With text box. The other options are similar to those in the Find dialog box. When you're ready to go, click one of the following buttons:

Find Next: Click this button to find the next matching record without performing a replacement.

Replace: Click this button to replace the currently highlighted data and then move on to the next match.

Replace All: Click this button to replace every instance of the search text with the replacement value. If you click this button, VBA will display a dialog box telling you how many replacements were made (assuming the search text was found). Click OK to dismiss the dialog box.

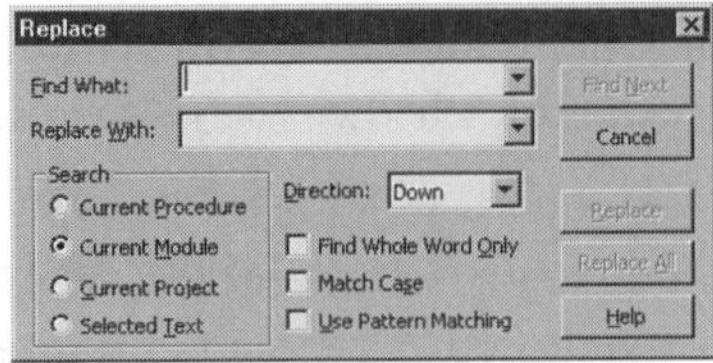

FIGURE 1.13.
Use the Replace dialog box to search for and replace code.

Navigating Modules with Bookmarks

VBA 5.0

If you've used Word for Windows, you probably know that you can define a section of text as a *bookmark*. You can then navigate a document by jumping to specific bookmarks. The Visual Basic Editor now offers a similar feature. In this case, you can set up bookmarks with VBA statements and then navigate a module by jumping from bookmark to bookmark.

Adding Bookmarks

The Visual Basic Editor gives you a number of methods for applying a bookmark to the current statement:

- Select Edit | Bookmarks | Toggle Bookmark.
- Right-click the gray margin to the left of the statement and select Toggle | Bookmark.
- Click the Toggle Bookmark button on the Edit toolbar.

VBA adds a blue, rounded rectangle beside the statement in the module window's margin, as shown in Figure 1.14. This area is called the Margin Indicator Bar, and the bookmark icon is called an *indicator.*

FIGURE 1.14.
You can use bookmarks to navigate a module.

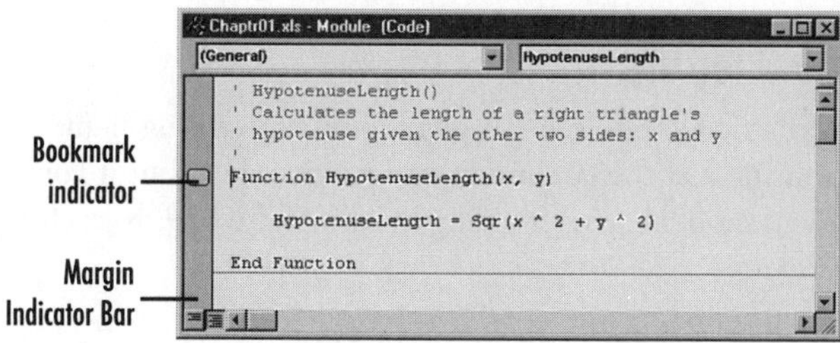

Bookmark Navigation Methods

Once you've set up some bookmarks, here's how you use them to navigate the module:

- To jump to the next bookmark, either select Edit | Bookmarks | Next Bookmark or click the Next Bookmark button on the Edit toolbar.

- To jump to the previous bookmark, either select Edit | Bookmarks | Previous Bookmark or click the Previous Bookmark button on the Edit toolbar.

Deleting Bookmarks

The usefulness of the Bookmarks feature largely depends on not having too many defined at any one time. They're best used for marking a spot where you're doing some work or for jumping between two or three oft-used code areas. If you find that you have too many bookmarks set up, or if you no longer need to bookmark a statement, use the following techniques to remove one or more bookmarks:

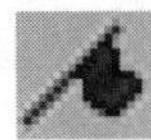

- To remove a single bookmark, highlight the statement and then either select Edit | Bookmarks | Toggle Bookmark or click the Edit toolbar's Toggle Bookmark button. You can also right-click the bookmark indicator and select Toggle | Bookmark.

- To remove *every* bookmark in a module, either select Edit | Bookmarks | Clear All Bookmarks or click the Edit toolbar's Clear All Bookmarks button.

Working with Modules

You've seen so far that modules are where most of the VBA action takes place. As you'll see in subsequent chapters, it's true that you'll also be working in other kinds of code windows, user form windows, and the Properties window, but modules are really the heart of VBA. Given that, it will help to have a few module manipulation techniques under your belt. To that end, the next four sections show you how to rename, export, import, and remove modules.

Renaming a Module

When you insert a new module, VBA gives it an uninspiring name such as Module1. That's fine if you'll be using just the one module in your project, but if you'll be working with multiple modules, you should consider giving meaningful names to each module to help differentiate between them.

To rename a module, make sure the Properties window is displayed, and then select the module in the Project Explorer. As you can see in Figure 1.15, a module has only a single property: `(Name)`. You use this property to rename the module. Make sure the name you use begins with a letter, contains no spaces or punctuation marks (underscores are acceptable, however), and is no longer than 31 characters.

Exporting a Module

The procedures and functions in a module will usually be specific to the application in which the project was created. For example, procedures in an Excel-based module will usually reference Excel-specific objects such as ranges and charts. However, you might have generic procedures and functions that can be used in different contexts. How, then, can you share code between applications?

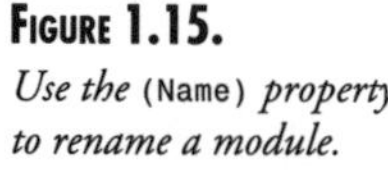

FIGURE 1.15.
Use the `(Name)` *property to rename a module.*

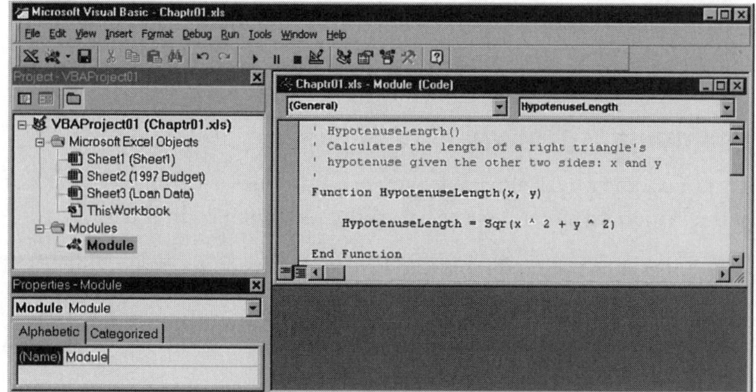

One way to do this would be to use the Clipboard to copy data from one module and paste it in a module in a different application. Another way is to *export* the module to a .BAS file. In the next section, I'll show you how to import .BAS files into your VBA projects.

The .BAS (Basic) file format is the one used by Visual Basic modules (which means you could use your VBA code in a Visual Basic project), but it's really just a simple text file. Here are the steps to follow to export a module:

1. In the Project Explorer, highlight the module you want to export.
2. Select File | Export File or press Ctrl-E. VBA displays the Export File dialog box. (Note that you can also display this dialog box by right-clicking the module and selecting Export File from the context menu.)
3. Select a location and name for the .BAS file.
4. Click Save. VBA creates the new .BAS file.

Importing a Module

If you exported a module to a .BAS file, you can import that file as a module in another application's VBA project. Also, if you've used Visual Basic before, you can leverage your existing code by importing Visual Basic modules into your project. Here are the steps to follow:

Select File | Import, use the Import File dialog box to highlight the appropriate .BAS file, and click Open.

1. If you have multiple projects open, use the Project Explorer to highlight any object in the project you want to use to store the imported file.
2. Select File | Import File or press Ctrl-M to display the Import File dialog box. (You can also display this dialog box by right-clicking the project and selecting Import File.)

3. Highlight the .BAS file that you want to import.
4. Click Open. VBA adds a new module for the .BAS file.

Removing a Module

If you no longer need a module, you should remove it from your project to reduce the clutter in the Project Explorer. Use either of the following techniques:

- Highlight the module in the Project Explorer and select File | Remove *Module,* where *Module* is the name of the module.
- Right-click the module in the Project Explorer and select Remove *Module,* where *Module* is the name of the module.

Either way, a dialog box appears asking if you want to export the module before removing it. If you do, click Yes and use the Export File dialog box to export the module to a .BAS file; otherwise, click No to remove the module.

Setting Visual Basic Editor Options

The VBA designers have set up the Visual Basic Editor so that the features most commonly used by the majority of programmers are activated by default. However, we all work with VBA in our own unique way; what one person uses every day, another needs only once a year. One user's obscure technical feature is another's bread and butter.

To address these differences, the Visual Basic Editor provides a large collection of customization options. The rest of this chapter explores each of these customization features.

To get started, select Tools | Options to display the Options dialog box, shown in Figure 1.16. You use the four tabs to modify the Visual Basic Editor settings and default values. When you finish choosing your options, click OK to return to the Editor.

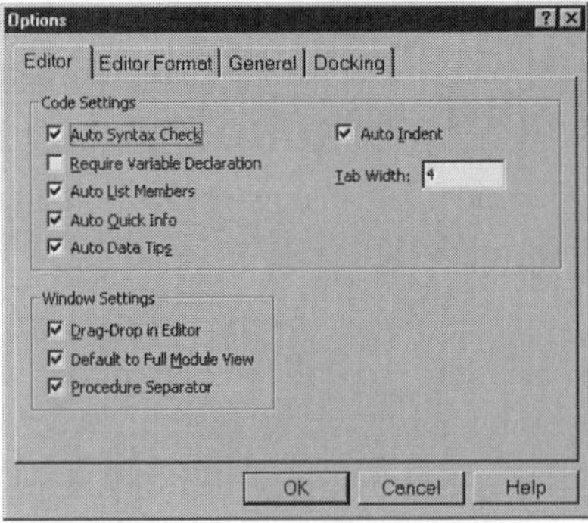

FIGURE 1.16.
You can use the Options dialog box to change dozens of Excel's default settings.

The Editor Tab

The Editor tab contains a few check boxes for controlling the IntelliSense feature and a few other properties of VBA's code windows:

Auto Syntax Check: When this check box is activated, VBA checks the syntax of each line on-the-fly (in other words, after you press Enter or move off the line).

Require Variable Declaration: When this check box is activated, VBA adds the `Option Explicit` statement to the top of each new module. This tells VBA to generate an error if you try to use an undeclared variable. (I'll discuss this in more detail in Chapter 2.)

Auto List Members: This check box toggles the IntelliSense List Properties/Methods feature on and off.

Auto Quick Info: This check box toggles the IntelliSense Quick Info feature on and off.

Auto Data Tips: When this check box is activated, IntelliSense displays a banner showing you the current value of a variable. I'll show you how this works in Chapter 24, "Debugging VBA Procedures."

Auto Indent: If this check box is activated, VBA indents each new line to the same point as the line you just entered. If you deactivate this check box, VBA starts each new line at the left margin.

Tab Width: Use this text box to set the number of spaces VBA moves whenever you press the Tab key in a module.

Drag-Drop in Editor: Activating this check box lets you drag and drop code inside the module window.

Default to Full Module View: When this check box is activated, VBA displays new modules in Full Module view, which means that the module window shows every procedure and function. If you deactivate this check box, VBA uses Procedure view, which shows only one procedure or function at a time. Note that you can switch between these views at any time by clicking the Procedure View and Full Module View buttons in the lower-left corner of the module window, as shown in Figure 1.17.

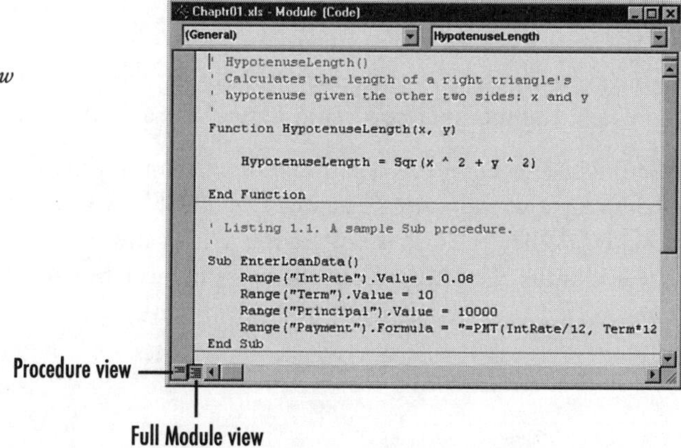

FIGURE 1.17.
Use these buttons to switch module window views.

Procedure Separator: When this check box is activated, VBA displays a line between each procedure.

The Editor Format Tab

As you've seen, VBA displays text such as keywords, comments, and syntax errors in different colors. The Editor Format tab, shown in Figure 1.18, lets you customize these colors as well as the font used in a module. The following procedure shows you how to use this tab to format the appearance of module code:

1. Use the Code Colors list to select the type of code you want to work with.
2. Use the Foreground, Background, and Indicator lists to select the colors to use for the code type you selected in step 1. (The Indicator list controls the color of whatever indicator appears in the Margin Indicator Bar.)
3. Repeat steps 1 and 2 to set the colors for other code types.
4. Use the Font list to select a typeface for the code.
5. Use the Size list to select a type size.
6. Use the Margin Indicator Bar check box to toggle the Margin Indicator Bar on and off.

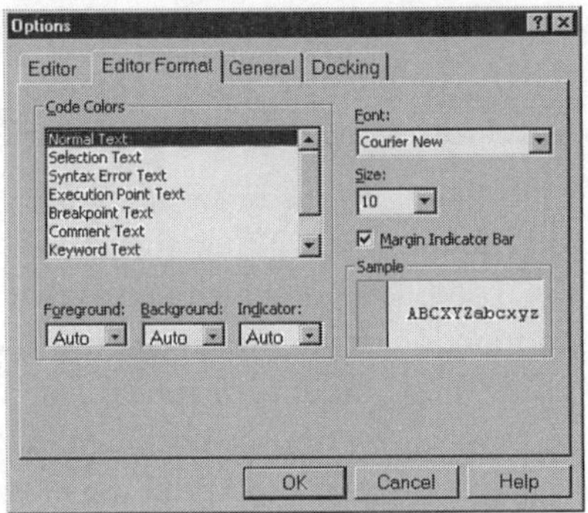

FIGURE 1.18.
Use the Editor Format options to format the text in your VBA modules.

The General Tab

The General tab, shown in Figure 1.19, presents a mixed bag of options that apply to form windows, errors, toolbars, and more. Here's a summary of the available controls:

Form Grid Settings: These controls determine the default settings for the grid that appears in VBA's form windows (see Chapter 11). The Show Grid check box toggles the grid on and off. When the grid is on, use the Width and Height text boxes to determine the grid units. The Align Controls to Grid check box toggles whether or not VBA snaps moved and sized controls to the grid markers.

Show ToolTips: This check box toggles the toolbar ToolTips (the banners that appear when you hover the mouse pointer over a button) on and off.

Collapse Proj. Hides Windows: When this check box is deactivated and you collapse a project (in other words, you click the minus sign (–) beside the project name in the Project Explorer), the Visual Basic Editor leaves the project's open windows on-screen. If you activate this check box, the project's windows are hidden when you collapse it.

Notify Before State Loss: You'll see in Chapter 24 that you can change your code on-the-fly when debugging a procedure. However, some changes require that VBA reset the procedure and start from scratch. When this check box is activated, VBA lets you know when it's going to reset the procedure.

Error Trapping: These options determine when VBA traps errors during program execution. See Chapter 23, "Trapping Program Errors," for a complete discussion of these options.

Compile: These check boxes determine when VBA compiles your project (see Chapter 24 to learn about compiling). If you activate the Compile On Demand check box, VBA compiles the project as the code is needed, which lets the program start faster. Otherwise, the entire project is compiled before it's run. If you activate the Background Compile check box, VBA uses processor idle time to finish compiling the project behind the scenes.

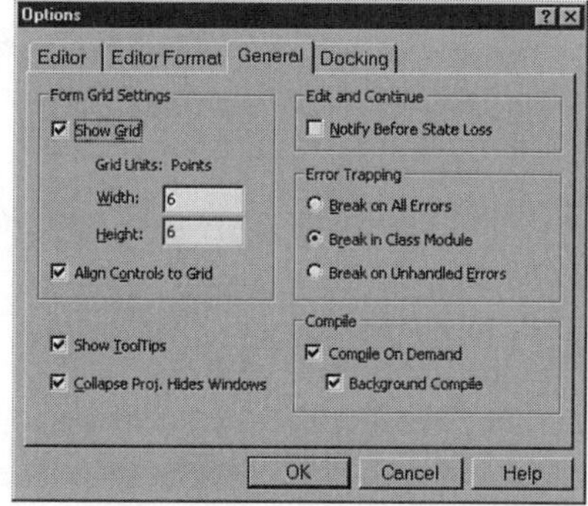

FIGURE 1.19.
The General tab controls the default settings for a number of VBA features.

The Docking Tab

The five check boxes in the Docking tab, shown in Figure 1.20, determine which Visual Basic Editor windows are "dockable." (You'll learn how to work with the Immediate, Locals, and Watch windows in Chapter 24.) A *dockable* window is one that snaps into a preset position when you move it to the edge of the Visual Basic Editor window or to the edge of another window. When a window isn't dockable, it "floats" inside the Visual Basic Editor screen, and you can move it anywhere you like.

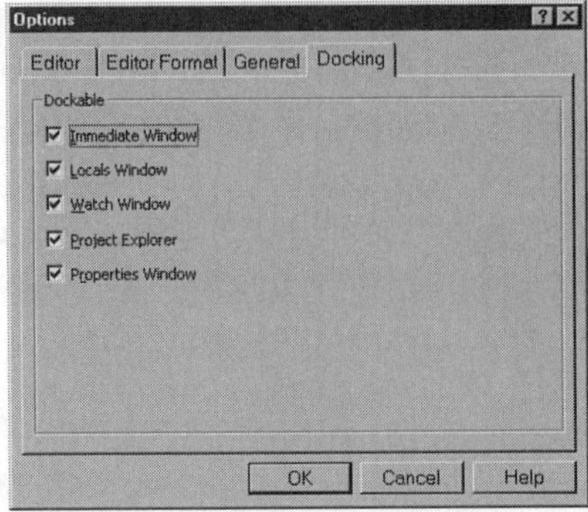

FIGURE 1.20.
Use the Docking tab to determine which windows are dockable.

> **TIP: TOGGLING A WINDOW'S DOCKABLE PROPERTY**
>
> You can also make a window dockable or nondockable by right-clicking the window and then activating or deactivating the Dockable command on the context menu.

Protecting Your Code

VBA 5.0

When you distribute your VBA application, you might not want your users to see your code, either for copyright reasons or because you don't want changes (accidental or otherwise) to be made. VBA 5.0 lets you password-protect your modules to prevent unauthorized access. Here are the steps to follow:

1. In the Visual Basic Editor, select Tools | *ProjectName* Properties, where *ProjectName* is the name of your VBA project.
2. In the Project Properties dialog box that appears, select the Protection tab, shown in Figure 1.21.

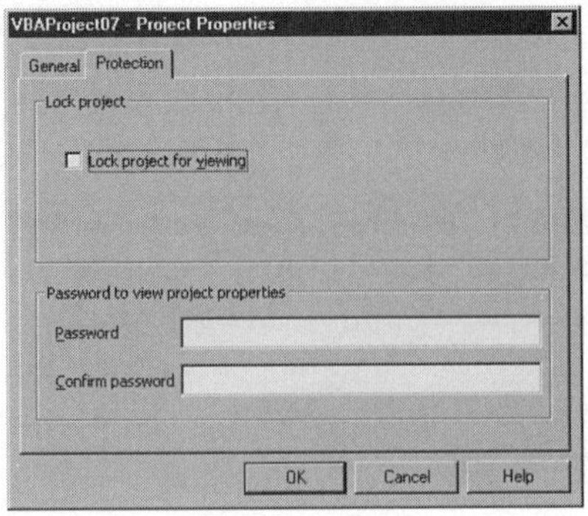

FIGURE 1.21.
Use the Protection tab to prevent users from messing with your code.

3. To prevent any change from being made to the project, activate the check box labeled Lock project for viewing.
4. If you would like to restrict access to the Project Properties dialog box, enter a password in the Password text box and then reenter it in the Confirm password text box.
5. Click OK.

Summary

This chapter introduced you to VBA, Microsoft's powerful macro and development language. I showed you how to record, write, and run a macro, and how to create procedures and user-defined functions. You also learned about VBA 5.0's new Visual Basic Editor, including the IntelliSense feature, comment blocks, find and replace, bookmarks, and a few techniques for working with modules. I closed by looking at the various options available for customizing the Editor. You'll find related information in the following chapters:

- You won't get too far writing VBA code without learning about variables, and you'll do that in Chapter 2, "Understanding Variables."
- Your procedures will also rely heavily on operators and expressions. Turn to Chapter 3, "Building VBA Expressions," to learn more.
- Objects are one of the most important concepts in VBA. You'll find out how they work in Chapter 4, "Working with Objects." Also, see Part II, "Unleashing Microsoft Office Objects," to get the specifics on the objects used in Word, Excel, and other Office applications.
- VBA, like any programming language worth its salt, contains a number of statements that control program flow. I discuss these statements in Chapter 5, "Controlling Your VBA Code."
- I'll show you how to work with the Visual Basic Editor's form window in Chapter 11, "Working with Microsoft Forms."
- To learn how to trap errors while running your programs, head for Chapter 23, "Trapping Program Errors."
- The ability to find and fix coding errors is a crucial programming skill. I discuss the various tools offered by VBA in Chapter 24, "Debugging VBA Procedures."

CHAPTER 2

Understanding Variables

IN THIS CHAPTER

Science is feasible when the variables are few and can be enumerated; when their combinations are distinct and clear.

—*Paul Valéry*

Your VBA procedures often will need to store temporary values for use in later statements and calculations. For example, you might want to store values for total sales and total expenses to use later in a gross margin calculation. Although you probably could get away with using the underlying application to store these values (in, say, a cell in an Excel worksheet), this usually isn't very practical. Instead, VBA (like all programming languages) lets you store temporary values in *variables.* This chapter explains this important topic and shows you how to use variables in your VBA procedures.

Declaring Variables

Declaring a variable tells VBA the name of the variable you're going to use. (It also serves to specify the *data type* of the variable, which I'll explain later in this chapter.) You declare variables by including `Dim` statements (`Dim` is short for *dimension*) at the beginning of each Sub or Function procedure.

NOTE: THE PLACEMENT OF VARIABLE DECLARATIONS

Technically, you can put variable declarations anywhere you like within a procedure, and VBA won't complain. The only real restriction is that the `Dim` statement must precede the first use of the variable in a procedure. Having said all that, however, it's traditional and clearer to lump all your `Dim` statements together at the top of a procedure.

A `Dim` statement has the following syntax:

```
Dim variableName
```

`variableName` is the name of the variable. The name must begin with a letter, it can't be longer than 255 characters, it can't be a VBA keyword, and it can't contain a space or any of the following characters:

```
. ! # $ % & @
```

For example, the following statement declares a variable named `totalSales`:

```
Dim totalSales
```

NOTE: VARIABLE CASE CONSIDERATIONS

To avoid confusing variables with the names of objects, properties, or methods, many programmers begin their variable names with a lowercase letter. This is the style I use in this book.

Also, note that VBA preserves the case of your variable names throughout a procedure. For example, if you declare a variable named `totalSales` and you later enter this variable name as, say, `totalsales`, VBA will convert the name to `totalSales` automatically as part of its syntax checking. This means two things:

- If you want to change the case used in a variable, change the *first* instance of the variable (usually the `Dim` statement).
- Once you've declared a variable, you should enter all subsequent references to the variable entirely in lowercase. Not only is this easier to type, but you'll immediately know if you've misspelled the variable name if you see that VBA doesn't change the case of the variable name once you enter the line.

Most programmers set up a declaration section at the beginning of each procedure and use it to hold all their `Dim` statements. Then, once the variables have been declared, you can use them throughout the procedure. Listing 2.1 shows a `Function` procedure that declares two variables—`totalSales` and `totalExpenses`—and then uses Excel's `Sum` function to store a range sum in each variable. Finally, the `GrossMargin` calculation uses each variable to return the function result.

NOTE: THIS CHAPTER'S CODE LISTINGS

You'll find the code for the `GrossMargin` function, as well as all the other procedures in this chapter, on this book's CD. Look for the Chaptr02.xls file. If you don't have Excel, use Chaptr02.bas instead.

Listing 2.1. A function that uses variables to store the intermediate values of a calculation.

```
Function GrossMargin()

    ' Declarations
    Dim totalSales
    Dim totalExpenses

    ' Code
    totalSales = Application.Sum(Range("Sales"))
    totalExpenses = Application.Sum(Range("Expenses"))
    GrossMargin = (totalSales - totalExpenses) / totalSales
End Function
```

In the `GrossMargin` function, notice that you store a value in a variable with a simple assignment statement of the following form:

```
variableName = value
```

TIP: DECLARE MULTIPLE VARIABLES ON ONE LINE

To conserve space, you can declare multiple variables on a single line. In the `GrossMargin` function, for example, you could declare `totalSales` and `totalExpenses` using the following statement:

```
Dim totalSales, totalExpenses
```

Understanding Variable Scope

In Chapter 1, "Introducing VBA," you learned about the *scope* of a procedure and how this affected whether or not the procedure was accessible or even visible from another project. Variables, too, have a scope that operates in much the same way. In other words, a variable's scope determines which procedures can access and work with the variable. Why is this important? Well, there are two main reasons why you need to be concerned with scope:

- You might want to use the same variable name in multiple procedures. If these variables are otherwise unrelated, you'll want to make sure that there is no confusion about which variable you're working with. In other words, you'll want to restrict the scope of each variable to the procedure in which it is declared.
- You might need to use the same variable in multiple procedures. For example, your procedure might use a variable to store the results of a calculation, and other procedures might need to use that result. In this case, you'll want to set up the scope of the variable so that it's accessible to multiple procedures.

VBA lets you establish three types of scope for your variables:

- Procedure-level scope
- Module-level scope
- Public scope

The next three sections describe each type in detail.

Procedure-Level Scope

When a variable has procedure-level scope, the only statements that can access the variable are those in the *same* procedure in which the variable was declared. The good news is that procedure-level scope is the default for all variables, so you don't have to do any more work. In other words, when you declare a variable in a procedure, VBA sets up the variable with procedure-level scope automatically. Listing 2.2 shows an example.

Listing 2.2. Procedure-level scope demonstration.

```
Sub Procedure1()
    Dim message
    '
    ' All statements in Procedure1 can access the
    ' "message" variable because they're in the scope:
    '
    message = "I'm in the scope!"
    MsgBox message
End Sub
Sub Procedure2()
    '
    ' The statements in Procedure2 can't access the
    ' "message" variable because they aren't in the scope:
    '
    MsgBox message
End Sub
```


Here we have two procedures: `Procedure1` and `Procedure2`. `Procedure1` declares a variable named `message`, sets its value to a text string, and uses VBA's `MsgBox` statement to display the string in the dialog box shown in Figure 2.1. (See Chapter 10, "Interacting with the User," to get the details on the `MsgBox` statement.)

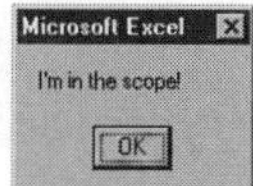

FIGURE 2.1.
`Procedure1` *displays this dialog box.*

`Procedure2` also uses `MsgBox` to display the `message` variable. However, as you can see in Figure 2.2, the dialog box that appears is blank. Why? Because the scope of the `message` variable extends only to `Procedure1`; `Procedure2` can't "see" the `message` variable, so it has nothing to display. In fact, once `Procedure1` finishes executing, VBA removes the `message` variable from memory entirely. This means that the `message` variable referred to in `Procedure2` is a completely different variable.

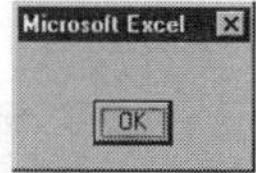

FIGURE 2.2.
`Procedure2` *displays this dialog box.*

NOTE: IMPLICIT DECLARATION

Perhaps you noticed that `Procedure2` used the `message` variable *without* declaring it. This is acceptable in VBA and is known as an *implicit declaration*. However, this is a dangerous programming practice and should be avoided in all your procedures. I'll discuss this in more depth later in this chapter (see "Avoiding Variable Errors").

Module-Level Scope

What if you *do* want to use the same variable in multiple procedures? Let's look at an example to see how such a scenario would be useful. In Listing 2.3, the `CalculateMargins` procedure is designed to calculate margin values and store them in a worksheet.

Listing 2.3. A procedure that calls two functions to calculate margin values. The two functions use the same variables.

```
Sub CalculateMargins()
    Range("GrossMarg").Value = GrossMarginCalc
    Range("NetMarg").Value = NetMarginCalc(Range("FixedCosts").Value)
End Sub
Function GrossMarginCalc()
    Dim totSales
    Dim totExpenses

    totSales = Application.Sum(Range("Sales"))
    totExpenses = Application.Sum(Range("Expenses"))

    GrossMarginCalc = (totSales - totExpenses) / totSales
End Function
Function NetMarginCalc(fixedCosts)
    Dim totSales
    Dim totExpenses

    totSales = Application.Sum(Range("Sales"))
    totExpenses = Application.Sum(Range("Expenses"))

    NetMarginCalc = (totSales - totExpenses - fixedCosts) / totSales
End Function
```

Let's see how this works. For starters, consider the following statement:

```
Range("GrossMarg").Value = GrossMarginCalc
```

This statement calls the `GrossMarginCalc` function and stores the result in a range named `GrossMarg`. (In Chaptr02.xls, this is cell B16 in the 1997 Budget worksheet.) The second statement is similar:

```
Range("NetMarg").Value = NetMarginCalc(Range("FixedCosts").Value)
```

In this case, the `NetMarginCalc` function is called, and the value of the range named `FixedCosts` (cell B15 in the 1997 Budget worksheet) is passed as a parameter. The result is stored in the range named `NetMarg` (cell B17).

However, when you examine the `GrossMarginCalc` and `NetMarginCalc` functions, you see that they use the same variables (`totSales` and `totExpenses`) and that the values assigned to these variables are calculated using the same statements. This is obviously an inefficient way to go about things.

What can we do about it? Well, it would be nice if we could just calculate the `totSales` and `totExpenses` values in one procedure and then use those values again in the other procedure. The easiest way to go about this is to declare `totSales` and `totExpenses` as *module-level* variables. This means that these variables are available to *every* procedure in the module.

To set up a variable with module-level scope, you simply place the appropriate `Dim` statement at the top of the module, outside of (and before) any procedures or functions. Listing 2.4 shows two variables—`totSales2` and `totExpenses2`—declared at the module level and revised functions (`GrossMarginCalc2` and `NetMarginCalc2`) that take advantage of this.

Listing 2.4. When you declare variables at the top of a module, they acquire module-level scope and are therefore available to every procedure in the module.

```
' Module-level declarations
Dim totSales2
Dim totExpenses2
Sub CalculateMargins2()
    Range("GrossMarg").Value = GrossMarginCalc2
    Range("NetMarg").Value = NetMarginCalc2(Range("FixedCosts").Value)
End Sub
Function GrossMarginCalc2()
    totSales2 = Application.Sum(Range("Sales"))
    totExpenses2 = Application.Sum(Range("Expenses"))

    GrossMarginCalc2 = (totSales2 - totExpenses2) / totSales2
End Function
Function NetMarginCalc2(fixedCosts)
    NetMarginCalc2 = (totSales2 - totExpenses2 - fixedCosts) / totSales2
End Function
```

Notice, in particular, that the `totSales2` and `totExpenses2` variables are calculated only once, in the `GrossMarginCalc2` function. The `NetMarginCalc2` function can use these results directly.

Public Scope

Module-level scope is handy, but what if your project has multiple modules and you need to use the same variable in procedures that exist in *different* modules? Or, what if the procedures exist in different projects? You can still provide access to variables in both of these situations, but you have to define the variables with *public* scope by using the `Public` keyword instead of `Dim`:

```
Public variableName
```

This statement makes a variable named *`variableName`* available to every procedure in every module in every open project.

NOTE: RESTRICTING PUBLIC VARIABLES

The rules for a public-scope variable change if the module in which the `Public` declaration is made uses the `Option Private Module` statement. (I discussed this statement in the last chapter.) In this case, the variable is accessible only by the modules and procedures within the project in which the module resides.

Passing Variables as Arguments

You've seen how module-level scoping and public scoping give multiple modules access to a variable. However, there might be times when you don't need such broad coverage. If a module has a large number of procedures, it can be dangerous to declare a module-level variable, because one of the procedures might alter the variable's value in unexpected ways. For example, you might forget that a particular variable has been declared at the module level and redeclare the same variable at the procedure level.

If you need to use a variable in only a couple of procedures, it's probably more efficient to pass the variable from one procedure to another as a parameter. VBA gives you two ways to pass variables: by reference and by value.

Passing Variables by Reference

When you pass a variable by reference, you're sending *the variable itself* to the other procedure. This means that any changes made to the value of the variable in the second procedure will be picked up by the first procedure. Listing 2.5 shows an example that makes this concrete.

Listing 2.5. Passing a variable by reference.

```
Sub Procedure3()
    Dim message
    message = "Pass it on!"
    Procedure4 message
    MsgBox message
End Sub
Sub Procedure4(message)
    MsgBox message
    message = "Thanks for the variable!"
End Sub
```

`Procedure3` declares the `message` variable, assigns it a string value, calls `Procedure4`, and sends `message` as a parameter. Note that passing variables by reference is the VBA default, so you don't need to do anything special with the argument. `Procedure4` then uses `MsgBox` to display the `message` value in the dialog box shown in Figure 2.3.

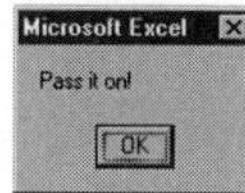

FIGURE 2.3.
`Procedure4` *displays this dialog box.*

Now `Procedure4` sets `message` to a different string and exits. Back in `Procedure3`, another `MsgBox` statement executes and displays the dialog box shown in Figure 2.4. As you can see, this dialog box displays the revised value of the `message` variable. So, in other words, both procedures were working with the same variable all along, which is the whole point of passing variables by reference.

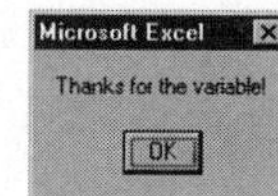

FIGURE 2.4.
`Procedure3` *displays this dialog box showing the* `message` *text that was changed in* `Procedure4`.

Passing Variables by Value

If you would prefer that another procedure *not* have the opportunity to alter the value of a variable, you need to pass the variable *by value.* This means that you don't send the variable itself to the other procedure, just the *value* of the variable.

To specify that a procedure receives a variable by value, you include the `ByVal` keyword in the procedure's argument list, as shown in Listing 2.6.

Listing 2.6. Passing a variable by value.

```
Sub Procedure5()
    Dim message
    message = "Pass it on!"
    Procedure6 message
    MsgBox message
End Sub
Sub Procedure6(ByVal message)
    MsgBox message
    message = "Thanks for the variable!"
End Sub
```

As before, a variable named `message` is declared, set to a string value, and sent to another procedure (`Procedure6`, in this case). Notice how `Procedure6` is defined with the following statement:

```
Sub Procedure6(ByVal message)
```

The `ByVal` keyword ensures that only the value of `message` is received. `Procedure6` then uses `MsgBox` to display this value, as shown in Figure 2.5.

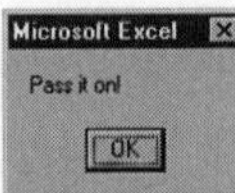

FIGURE 2.5.
`Procedure6` *displays this dialog box.*

Again, `Procedure6` sets `message` to a different string and exits. Back in `Procedure5`, another `MsgBox` statement executes and displays the dialog box shown in Figure 2.6. Notice, though, that `Procedure5` does *not* display the new `message` value. Because the variable was passed by value, anything that `Procedure6` does to the variable is completely ignored by `Procedure5`.

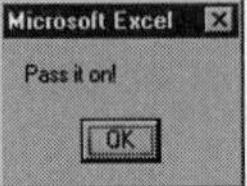

FIGURE 2.6.
`Procedure5` *ignores any changes made to* `message` *in* `Procedure6`.

Working with Static Variables

I mentioned earlier that when a procedure has completed its chores, VBA wipes all trace of the procedure's variables (or, to be more exact, its procedure-level variables) from memory. In other words, if you call the same procedure a second time, all of its local variables (which is another name for procedure-level variables) start from scratch.

If you need to preserve a variable's value between procedure calls, you need to declare the variable as *static*. A static variable retains its value as long as your program is running. To declare a static variable, use the `Static` keyword in place of `Dim` when declaring the variable:

```
Static variableName
```

Note that you can only use a `Static` declaration for procedure-level variables. Listing 2.7 shows the `Static` keyword in action.

Listing 2.7. A static variable example.

```
Sub StaticTest()
    StaticProcedure
    StaticProcedure
End Sub
Sub StaticProcedure()
    Static staticVar
    Dim regularVar

    staticVar = staticVar + 5
    regularVar = regularVar + 5
    MsgBox "staticVar = " & staticVar & " and regularVar = " & regularVar
End Sub
```

The `StaticTest` procedure simply calls `StaticProcedure` twice. `StaticProcedure` declares two variables: `staticVar` is declared with `Static`, and `regularVar` is declared with `Dim`. The next two statements adjust the value of each variable. For example, consider the following statement:

```
staticVar = staticVar + 5
```

This statement says, "Take the current value of `staticVar` and add 5 to it." (I'll talk more about this and other VBA expressions in the next chapter.) A similar statement does the same thing for the `regularVar` variable. Then a `MsgBox` statement displays the results. When you run the `StaticTest` procedure, it calls `StaticProcedure` for the first time and displays the dialog box shown in Figure 2.7. As you can see, both `staticVar` and `regularVar` have the value 5. (When a variable is first declared, VBA assigns it the value 0.)

FIGURE 2.7.
The first time through, `StaticTest` *displays this dialog box.*

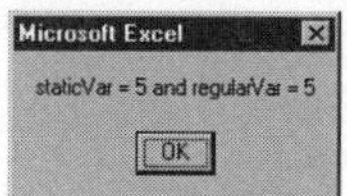

When you click OK, `StaticTest` calls `StaticProcedure` again. This time around, you see the dialog box shown in Figure 2.8. Notice that the value of `regularVar` remains at 5, but `staticVar` is now up to 10. This shows how a static variable retains its value between procedure calls.

FIGURE 2.8.
This dialog box is displayed on the second pass.

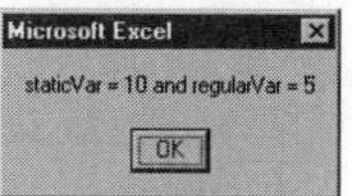

Avoiding Variable Errors

One of the most common errors in VBA procedures is to declare a variable and then later misspell the name. For example, suppose I had entered the following statement in the `GrossMargin` procedure from Listing 2.1:

```
totlExpenses = Application.Sum(Range("Expenses"))
```

Here, `totlExpenses` is a misspelling of the variable named `totalExpenses`. VBA supports *implicit declarations,* which means that if it sees a name it doesn't recognize, it assumes that the name belongs to a new variable. In this case, VBA would assume that `totlExpenses` is a new variable, proceed normally, and calculate the wrong answer for the function.

To avoid this problem, you can tell VBA to generate an error whenever it comes across a name that hasn't been declared explicitly with a `Dim`, `Public`, or `Static` statement. There are two ways to do this:

- For an individual module, enter the following statement at the top of the module:

```
Option Explicit
```

- To force VBA to automatically add this statement to all your modules, select Tools | Options, select the Module General tab in the Options dialog box that appears, and activate the Require Variable Declaration check box in the Editor tab.

NOTE: CHANGE EXISTING MODULES BY HAND

Activating the Require Variable Declaration check box forces VBA to add the `Option Explicit` statement at the beginning of each new module. However, it *doesn't* add this statement to any existing modules; you need to do that by hand.

Variable Data Types

The *data type* of a variable determines the kind of data the variable can hold. Table 2.1 lists all the VBA data types, the kind of values they take, the amount of memory (in bytes) used by each type, and the type-declaration character (explained later).

Table 2.1. The VBA data types.

Data Type	*Storage Size*	*Type-Declaration Character*	*Description*
`Boolean`	2 bytes		Takes one of two logical values: `True` or `False`.
`Byte`	1 byte		Used for small, positive integer values (from 0 to 255).
`Currency`	8 bytes	`@`	Used for monetary or fixed-decimal calculations where accuracy is important. The value range is from –922,337,203,685,477.5808 to 922,337,203,685,477.5807.
`Date`	8 bytes		Used for holding date data. The range is from January 1, 0100 to December 31, 9999. When setting a value to a `Date` variable, enclose the date in pound signs (for example, `newDate = #1/15/97#`).

Data Type	*Storage Size*	*Type-Declaration Character*	*Description*
`Double`	8 bytes	#	Double-precision floating point. Negative numbers range from –1.79769313486232E308 to –4.94065645841247E–324. Positive numbers range from 4.94065645841247E–324 to 1.79769313486232E308.
`Integer`	2 bytes	%	Used for integer values in the range –32,768 to 32,767.
`Long`	4 bytes	&	Large integer values. The range is from –2,147,483,648 to 2,147,483,647.
`Object`	4 bytes		Refers to objects only.
`Single`	4 bytes	!	Single-precision floating point. Negative numbers range from –3.402823E38 to –1.401298E–45. Positive numbers range from 1.401298E–45 to 3.402823E38.
`String`	1 byte per	$	Holds string values. The character strings can be up to 64K.
`Variant` (number)	16 bytes		Can take any kind of data.
`Variant` (string)	22 bytes plus 1 byte per character		Can take any kind of data.

You specify a data type by including the `As` keyword in a `Dim` statement. Here is the general syntax:

```
Dim variableName As DataType
```

`variableName` is the name of the variable, and *`DataType`* is one of the data types from Table 2.1. For example, the following statement declares a variable named `textString` to be of type `String`:

```
Dim textString As String
```

Note, too, that you can also use `As` to assign a data type to variables declared with the `Public` or `Static` keywords. Here are a few notes to keep in mind when using data types:

- If you don't include a data type when declaring a variable, VBA assigns the `Variant` data type. This allows you to store any kind of data in the variable. However, you should read the following Caution sidebar to see why this isn't a good idea.
- If you declare a variable to be one data type and then try to store a value of a different data type in the variable, VBA will often display an error. To help avoid this, many programmers like to use the *type-declaration characters* (listed in Table 2.1). By appending one of these characters to the end of a variable name, you automatically declare the variable to be of the type represented by the character. For example, `$` is the type-declaration character for a string, so the variable `textString$` is automatically a `String` data type variable. Having the `$` (or whatever) at the end of the variable name also reminds you of the data type, so you'll be less likely to store the wrong type of data.
- To specify the data type of a procedure argument, use the `As` keyword in the argument list. For example, the following `Function` statement declares variables `x` and `y` to be `Single`:

  ```
  Function HypotenuseLength(x As Single, y As Single)
  ```
- To specify the data type of the return value for a `Function` procedure, use the `As` keyword at the end of the `Function` statement:

  ```
  Function HypotenuseLength(x, y) As Single
  ```

CAUTION: AVOID `VARIANT` VARIABLES

Since VBA assigns the `Variant` data type by default, you might be tempted to save keystrokes by not bothering to declare a data type at all and just using `Variant` variables. Although this approach will work, it suffers from a number of disadvantages. For one thing, `Variant` variables take up much more memory compared to other data types (see Table 2.1). For another, `Variant` variables are inherently slower, because VBA must convert the variable into a real data type, depending on the value you store. Good programming practice states that not only should you declare all your variables, but you should also assign a data type to all your variables.

Changing the Default Data Type

I mentioned in the preceding section that VBA assigns the `Variant` type to a variable if you don't specify a data type. However, VBA supports a number of `Def`*`Type`* statements that let you redefine the default data type. These statements all use the following syntax:

```
DefType letter1[-letter2]
```

Here, *Type* is a three- or four-letter code that specifies the data type, and *letter1* and *letter2* define a range of letters. Note that this is a module-level statement, so you must place it at the top of a module, before any procedures or functions.

The idea is that any variable (or function argument or function result) that begins with one of these letters will be assigned the specified data type by default. For example, the `DefInt` keyword is used to set the default data type to `Integer`. If you want VBA to assign, say, the `Integer` data type to any variables that begin with the letters X through Z, you would add the following statement at the module level:

```
DefInt X-Z
```

Table 2.2 lists the various `DefType` keywords and the data types they represent.

Table 2.2. VBA's DefType keywords.

DefType	*Data Type*
DefBool	Boolean
DefByte	Byte
DefInt	Integer
DefLng	Long
DefCur	Currency
DefSng	Single
DefDbl	Double
DefDate	Date
DefStr	String
DefObj	Object
DefVar	Variant

Creating User-Defined Data Types

VBA's built-in data types cover a lot of ground and should be sufficient to meet most of your needs. However, VBA also lets you set up *user-defined data types*. These are handy for storing similar types of data in a single structure. For example, suppose your program is working with car makes and models. In this case, you might need to work with values for the manufacturer, the model, the year the car was made, and the purchase price. One way to go about this would be to set up variables for each item of data, like so:

```
Dim carMake As String
Dim carModel As String
Dim yearMade As Integer
Dim carPrice As Currency
```

This approach works, but what if you need to work with the data from multiple cars at once? You could set up new variables for each car, but that seems too inefficient. A better way is to define a "CarInfo" data type that holds all the required information. Here's how you would do so:

```
Type CarInfo
    make As String
    model As String
    made As Integer
    price As Currency
End Type
```

The Type keyword tells VBA that you're creating a user-defined data type. In this example, the new data type is named CarInfo. The statements between Type and End Type define the various elements within the new data type. Note that you need to place this definition at the module level; VBA doesn't let you define new data types within a procedure.

Now you just use the data type as you would any other. For example, the following statement declares a new variable named myCar to be of type CarInfo:

```
Dim myCar As CarInfo
```

From here, you refer to the various elements within the data type by separating the variable name and the element name with a period (.), like so:

```
myCar.make = "Porsche"
myCar.model = "Targa"
myCar.made = 1997
myCar.price = 100,000
```

Using Array Variables

In VBA, an *array* is a group of variables of the same data type. Why would you need to use an array? Well, suppose you wanted to store 20 employee names in variables to use in a procedure. One way to do this would be to create 20 variables named, say, employee1, employee2, and so on. However, it's much more efficient to create a single employee array variable that can hold up to 20 names. Here's how you would do that:

```
Dim employee(19) As String
```

As you can see, this declaration is very similar to one you would use for a regular variable. The difference is the 19 enclosed in parentheses. The parentheses tell VBA that you're declaring an array, and the number tells VBA how many elements you'll need in the array. Why 19 instead of 20? Well, each element in the array is assigned a *subscript,* where the first element's subscript is 0, the second is 1, and so on up to, in this case, 19. Therefore, the total number of elements in this array is 20.

You use the subscripts to refer to any element simply by enclosing its index number in the parentheses, like so:

```
employee(0) = "Ponsonby"
```

By default, the subscripts of VBA arrays start at 0 (this is called the *lower bound* of the array) and run up to the number you specify in the `Dim` statement (this is called the *upper bound* of the array). If you would prefer your array index numbers to start at 1, include the following statement at the top of the module (in other words, before declaring your first array and before your first procedure):

```
Option Base 1
```

Another way to specify a specific lower bound is to add the `To` keyword to your array declaration. Here's the syntax:

```
Dim arrayName(LowerBound To UpperBound) As DataType
```

`arrayName` is the name of the array variable. *`LowerBound`* is a long integer specifying the lower bound of the array, and *`UpperBound`* is a long integer specifying the upper bound of the array. Finally, *`DataType`* is one of the data types from Table 2.1. For example, here's a declaration that creates an array variable with subscripts running from 50 to 100:

```
Dim myArray(50 To 100) As Currency
```

Dynamic Arrays

What do you do if you're not sure how many subscripts you'll need in an array? You could guess at the correct number, but that will almost always leave you with one of the following problems:

- If you guess too low and try to access a subscript higher than the array's upper bound, VBA will generate an error message.
- If you guess too high, VBA will still allocate memory to the unused portions of the array, so you'll waste precious system resources.

To avoid both of these problems, you can declare a *dynamic* array by leaving the parentheses blank in the `Dim` statement:

```
Dim myArray() As Double
```

Then, when you know the number of elements you need, you can use a `ReDim` statement to allocate the correct number of subscripts (notice that you don't specify a data type in the `ReDim` statement):

```
ReDim myArray(52)
```

The following is a partial listing of a procedure named `PerformCalculations`. The procedure declares `calcValues` as a dynamic array and `totalValues` as an integer. Later in the procedure, `totalValues` is set to the result of a function procedure named `GetTotalValues`. The `ReDim` statement then uses `totalValues` to allocate the appropriate number of subscripts to the `calcValues` array.

```
Sub PerformCalculations()
    Dim calcValues() As Double, totalValues as Integer
.
.
.
    totalValues = GetTotalValues()
    ReDim calcValues(totalValues)
.
.
.
End Sub
```

NOTE: PRESERVING ARRAY VALUES

The `ReDim` statement reinitializes the array so that any values stored in the array are lost. If you want to preserve an array's existing values, use `ReDim` with the `Preserve` option:

```
ReDim Preserve myArray(52)
```

NOTE: DETERMINING ARRAY BOUNDS

If your program needs to know the lower bound and the upper bound of an array, VBA provides a couple of functions that can do the job:

`LBound(`*`arrayName`*`)`	Returns the lower bound of the array given by *`arrayName`*.
`UBound(`*`arrayName`*`)`	Returns the upper bound of the array given by *`arrayName`*.

Multidimensional Arrays

If you enter a single number between the parentheses in an array's `Dim` statement, VBA creates a *one-dimensional* array. But you also can create arrays with two or more dimensions (60 is the maximum). For example, suppose you wanted to store both a first name and a last name in your `employee` array. To store two sets of data with each element, you would declare a two-dimensional array, like so:

```
Dim employees(19,1) As String
```

The subscripts for the second number work like the subscripts you've seen already. In other words, they begin at 0 and run up to the number you specify. So this `Dim` statement sets up a "table" (or a *matrix,* as it's usually called) with 20 "rows" (one for each employee) and two "columns" (one for the first name and one for the last name). Here are two statements that initialize the data for the first employee:

```
employees(0,0) = "Biff"
employees(0,1) = "Ponsonby"
```

Working with Constants

Constants are values that don't change. They can be numbers, strings, or other values, but, unlike variables, they keep their value throughout your code. VBA recognizes two types of constants: built-in and user-defined.

Using Built-In Constants

Many properties and methods have their own predefined constants. For Excel objects, these constants begin with the letters `xl`. For Word objects, the constants begin with `wd`. For VBA objects, the constants begin with `vb`. (You'll find all constants referenced in the Object Browser.)

For example, Excel's Window object has a `WindowState` property that recognizes three built-in constants: `xlNormal` (to set a window in its normal state), `xlMaximized` (to maximize a window), and `xlMinimized` (to minimize a window). To maximize the active window, for example, you would use the following statement:

```
ActiveWindow.WindowState = xlMaximized
```

Creating User-Defined Constants

To create your own constants, use the `Const` statement:

```
Public ¦ Private Const CONSTANTNAME [As type] = expression
```

`Public`	Use this keyword at the module level to make the constant available to all modules.
`Private`	Use this keyword at the module level to make this constant available only to the module in which it is defined. (This is the default setting.)
`CONSTANTNAME`	The name of the constant. Most programmers use all-uppercase names for constants.
`As` *`type`*	Use this optional expression to assign a data type to the constant.
`expression`	The value (or a formula that returns a value) that you want to use for the constant.

For example, the following statement creates a constant named `DISCOUNT` and assigns it the value `0.4`:

```
Const DISCOUNT = 0.4
```

Summary

This chapter gave you the nitty-gritty on VBA's variables. You learned how to declare variables, work with variable scope, pass variables as arguments, and work with static variables. I also showed you how to use `Option Explicit` to avoid variable errors. From there, I showed you the various data types supported by VBA, as well as how to change the default data type and create user-defined data types. I finished by showing you how to work with arrays and constants. Here's a list of chapters where you'll find related information:

- You often use operators and expressions to assign values to variables. I discuss this in detail in Chapter 3, "Building VBA Expressions."
- Objects have a separate variable type. I talk about this, as well as about assigning objects to variables, in Chapter 4, "Working with Objects."
- See Chapter 10, "Interacting with the User," to learn more about the details of the `MsgBox` statement.

CHAPTER

Building VBA Expressions

IN THIS CHAPTER

One types the correct incantation on a keyboard, and a display screen comes to life, showing things that never were nor could be...however, if one character, one pause, of the incantation is not strictly in proper form, the magic doesn't work.

—*Frederick Brooks*

The VBA variables you learned about in the preceding chapter don't amount to a hill of beans unless you do something with them. In other words, a procedure is merely a lifeless collection of `Dim` statements until you define some kind of relationship among the variables and your program objects (we'll talk about the latter in the next chapter).

To establish these relationships, you need to create *expressions* that perform calculations and produce results. This chapter takes you through some expression basics and shows you a number of techniques for building powerful expressions using not only variables, but also VBA's built-in functions.

Understanding Expression Structure

You can think of an expression as being like a compact version of a user-defined function. In other words, in the same way that a function takes one or more arguments, combines them in various ways, and returns a value, so too does an expression take one or more inputs (called *operands*), combine them with special symbols (called *operators*), and produce a result. The main difference, though, is that an expression must do all its dirty work in a single VBA statement.

For example, consider the following statement:

```
might = "right"
```

Here, the left side of the equation is a variable named `might`. The right side of the equation is the simplest of all expressions: a text string. So, in other words, a string value is being stored in a variable.

Here's a slightly more complex example:

```
energy = mass * (speedOfLight ^ 2)
```

Again, the left side of the equation is a variable (named `energy`) and the right side of the equation is an expression. For the latter, a variable named `speedOfLight` is squared, and then this result is multiplied by another variable named `mass`. In this example, we see the two main components of any expression:

Operands: These are the "input values" used by the expression. They can be variables, object properties, function results, or literals. (A *literal* is a specific value, such as a number or text string. In the first expression example, `"right"` is a string literal.)

Operators: These are symbols that combine the operands to produce a result. In the example just shown, the * symbol represents multiplication, and the ^ symbol represents exponentiation.

This combination of operands and operators produces a result that conforms to one of the variable data types outlined in the last chapter: `Date`, `String`, `Boolean`, `Object`, `Variant`, or one of the numeric data types (`Byte`, `Integer`, `Long`, `Single`, `Double`, or `Currency`). When building your expressions, the main point to keep in mind is that you must maintain *data type consistency* throughout the expression. This means you must watch for three things:

- The operands must use compatible data types. Although it's okay to combine, say, an `Integer` operand with a `Long` operand (since they're both numeric data types), it wouldn't make sense to use, say, a `Double` operand and a `String` operand.
- The operators you use must match the data types of the operands. For example, you wouldn't want to multiply two strings together.
- If you're storing the expression result in a variable, make sure the variable's data type is consistent with the type of result produced by the expression. For example, don't use a `Currency` variable to store the result of a string expression.

VBA divides expressions into four groups: numeric, string, date, and logical. I'll discuss each type of expression later in this chapter, but let's first run through all the available VBA operators.

VBA Operators

You've already seen the first of VBA's operators: the *assignment operator*, which is just the humble equals sign (=). You use the assignment operator to assign the result of an expression to a variable or to an object property.

Bear in mind that VBA always derives the result of the right side of the equation (that is, the expression) before it modifies the value of the left side of the equation. This seems like obvious behavior, but it's the source of a handy trick that you'll use quite often. In other words, you can use the current value of whatever is on the left side of the equation *as part of the expression* on the right side. For example, consider the following code fragment:

```
currYear = 1997
currYear = currYear + 1
```

The first statement assigns the literal value 1997 to the `currYear` variable. The second statement also changes the value stored in `currYear`, but it uses the expression `currYear + 1` to do it. This looks weird until you remember that VBA always evaluates the expression first. In other words, it takes the current value of `currYear`, which is 1997, and adds 1 to it. The result is 1998, and *that* is what's stored in `currYear` when all is said and done.

NOTE: THE ASSIGNMENT OPERATOR IS NOT "EQUALS"

Because of this evaluate-the-expression-and-*then*-store-the-result behavior, VBA assignment statements shouldn't be read as *variable equals expression*. Instead, it makes more sense to

continues

continued

think of them as *variable is set to expression* or *variable assumes the value given by expression*. This helps to reinforce the important concept that the expression result is being stored in the variable.

VBA has a number of different operators that you use to combine functions, variables, and values in a VBA expression. These operators work much like the operators—such as addition (+) and multiplication (*)—that you use to build formulas in Excel worksheets and Word tables. VBA operators fall into five general categories: arithmetic, concatenation, comparison, logical, and miscellaneous.

Arithmetic Operators

VBA's arithmetic operators are similar to those you use to build Excel formulas. Table 3.1 lists each of the arithmetic operators you can use in your VBA statements. See "Working with Numeric Expressions" later in this chapter for a detailed look at each arithmetic operator.

Table 3.1. The VBA arithmetic operators.

Operator	*Name*	*Example*	*Result*
+	Addition	`10+5`	`15`
–	Subtraction	`10-5`	`5`
–	Negation	`-10`	`-10`
*	Multiplication	`10*5`	`50`
/	Division	`10/5`	`2`
\	Integer division	`11\5`	`2`
^	Exponentiation	`10^5`	`100000`
`Mod`	Modulus	`10 Mod 5`	`0`

The Concatenation Operator

You use the concatenation operator (&) to combine text strings within an expression. One way to use the concatenation operator is to combine string literals. For example, the expression `"soft" & "ware"` returns the string `software`. Note that the quotation marks and ampersand aren't shown in the result. You can also use & to combine any kind of operand, as long as the operands use the `String` data type. For more information on the concatenation operator, check out the section "Working with String Expressions."

Comparison Operators

You use the comparison operators in an expression that compares two or more numbers, text strings, variables, or function results. If the statement is true, the result of the formula is given the logical value `True` (which is equivalent to any nonzero value). If the statement is false, the formula returns the logical value `False` (which is equivalent to 0). Table 3.2 summarizes VBA's comparison operators.

Table 3.2. The VBA comparison operators.

Operator	*Name*	*Example*	*Result*
=	Equal to	`10=5`	`False`
>	Greater than	`10>5`	`True`
<	Less than	`10<5`	`False`
>=	Greater than or equal to	`"a">="b"`	`False`
<=	Less than or equal to	`"a"<="b"`	`True`
<>	Not equal to	`"a"<>"b"`	`True`
`Like`	Like	`"Smith" Like "Sm?th"`	`True`

NOTE: THE `IS` OPERATOR

VBA has an eighth comparison operator: `Is`. You use `Is` to compare two objects, so I'll leave it until we discuss objects in Chapter 4, "Working with Objects."

Using Comparison Operators with String Values

You'll normally use the comparison operators (except `Like`) with numeric values, and the implementation is quite straightforward in this context. (In other words, you don't have to worry about things like data types. VBA is quite happy to compare, say, an `Integer` value and a `Single` value.)

String comparisons are a bit more complex, however. Letters and symbols are stored internally as unique binary numbers, where the value of each letter is determined by the *code page* defined in Windows. The code page is an internal table that Windows uses to map keyboard keys to the characters you see on-screen. You can change the current Windows code page using the Regional Settings icon in Control Panel. The standard Windows code page is English (United States). I've provided the internal values for each symbol used in this code page in Appendix C, "The Windows ANSI Character Set."

In a standard string comparison, VBA compares letters based on their internal values. (This is called a *binary* comparison.) For example, if you examine the character set in Appendix C, you'll see that the character code for the letter *a* is 97 and the code for *b* is 98. Therefore, the expression `"a"<"b"` returns `True`.

Note, however, that Windows assigns a different code to uppercase letters. For example, the default code for *A* is 65, so the comparison `"a"="A"` will return `False`. If you would prefer that your string comparisons be case-insensitive, you can tell VBA to use a *text comparison* instead. To do that, add the following line at the module level (in other words, before any procedures or functions):

```
Option Compare Text
```

Another thing to keep in mind is that most string comparisons involve multiple-letter operands. In these situations, VBA compares each string letter-by-letter. For example, consider the expression `"Smith"<"Smyth"`. The first two letters in each string are the same, but the third letters are different. The *i* in *Smith* is less than the *y* in *Smyth,* so this comparison would return `True`. (Notice that, once a point of difference is found, VBA ignores the rest of the letters in each string.)

Note, too, that a space is a legitimate character for comparison purposes. Its character code is 32, so it comes before all other letters and symbols (see Appendix C). In particular, if you compare two strings of different lengths, VBA will *pad* the shorter string with spaces so that it's the same length as the longer string. Therefore, the comparison `"Marg">"Margaret"` is equivalent to `"Marg    ">"Margaret"`, which returns `False` (because the fifth "letter" of `"Marg    "` is a space, while the fifth letter of `"Margaret"` is *a.*

Using the `Like` Operator

If you need to allow for multiple spellings in a comparison, or if you're not sure how to spell a word you want to use, the *wildcard characters* can help. There are three wildcards: the question mark (?) substitutes for a single character, the asterisk (*) substitutes for a group of characters, and the pound sign (#) substitutes for a single digit. You use them in combination with the `Like` operator, as shown in Table 3.3. In these examples, I'm assuming `strVar` is a `String` variable (the `Like` operator works only with strings).

Table 3.3. Some sample comparisons using the `Like` operator.

Example	*Returns* `True` *if...*
`strVar Like "Re?d"`	`strVar` is `Reid`, `Read`, `Reed`, and so on.
`strVar Like "M?"`	`strVar` is `MA`, `MD`, `ME`, and so on.
`strVar Like "R*"`	`strVar` begins with `R`.
`strVar Like "*office*"`	`strVar` contains the word `office`.
`strVar Like "Fiscal_199#"`	`strVar` is `Fiscal_1997`, `Fiscal_1998`, and so on.

For even more flexibility, the `Like` operator also supports a list of potential letter substitutes. In this case, you replace the wildcard character with a list of the symbols you want to match enclosed in square brackets. For example, suppose you're only interested in matching the names *Reid* and *Reed*. In this case, instead of using `"Re?d"` as your criteria, you would replace the question mark with `[ie]`, like so:

```
strVar Like "Re[ie]d"
```

You can also use character ranges, such as `[a-m]`. (Make sure you enter these ranges from lowest letter to highest letter. If you use, say, `[m-a]`, VBA will generate an error.)

Finally, if you would like to compare strings based on their *not* having a list of characters in a particular position, include an exclamation mark inside the square brackets. For example, the following expression returns `True` if `strVar` isn't *Read* or *Rend*.

```
strVar Like "Re[!an]d"
```

Logical Operators

You use the logical operators to combine or modify `True/False` expressions. Table 3.4 summarizes VBA's logical operators. I'll provide more detail about each operator later in this chapter (see "Working with Logical Expressions").

Table 3.4. The VBA logical operators.

Operator	*General Form*	*What It Returns*
`And`	*`Expr1`* `And` *`Expr2`*	`True` if both *`Expr1`* and *`Expr2`* are `True`; `False` otherwise.
`Eqv`	*`Expr1`* `Eqv` *`Expr2`*	`True` if both *`Expr1`* and *`Expr2`* are `True` or if both *`Expr1`* and *`Expr2`* are `False`; `False` otherwise.
`Imp`	*`Expr1`* `Imp` *`Expr2`*	`False` if *`Expr1`* is `True` and *`Expr2`* is `False`; `True` otherwise.
`Or`	*`Expr1`* `Or` *`Expr2`*	`True` if at least one of *`Expr1`* and *`Expr2`* is `True`; `False` otherwise.
`Xor`	*`Expr1`* `Xor` *`Expr2`*	`False` if both *`Expr1`* and *`Expr2`* are `True` or if both *`Expr1`* and *`Expr2`* are `False`; `True` otherwise.
`Not`	`Not` *`Expr`*	`True` if *`Expr`* is `False`; `False` if *`Expr`* is `True`.

Understanding Operator Precedence

You'll often use simple expressions that contain just two values and a single operator. In practice, however, many expressions you use will have a number of values and operators. In these more complex expressions, the order in which the calculations are performed becomes crucial. For example, consider the expression 3+5^2. If you calculate from left to right, the answer you get is 64 (3+5 equals 8, and 8^2 equals 64). However, if you perform the exponentiation first and then the addition, the result is 28 (5^2 equals 25, and 3+25, equals 28). As this example shows, a single expression can produce multiple answers, depending on the order in which you perform the calculations.

To control this problem, VBA evaluates an expression according to a predefined *order of precedence.* This order of precedence lets VBA calculate an expression unambiguously by determining which part of the expression it calculates first, which part second, and so on.

The Order of Precedence

The order of precedence that VBA uses is determined by the various expression operators I outlined in the preceding section. Table 3.5 summarizes the complete order of precedence used by VBA.

Table 3.5. The VBA order of precedence.

Operator	*Operation*	*Order of Precedence*
^	Exponentiation	First
–	Negation	Second
* and /	Multiplication and division	Third
\	Integer division	Fourth
`Mod`	Modulus	Fifth
+ and –	Addition and subtraction	Sixth
&	Concatenation	Seventh
= < > <= >= <> `Like Is`	Comparison	Eighth
`And Eqv Imp Or Xor Not`	Logical	Ninth

From this table, you can see that VBA performs exponentiation before addition. Therefore, the correct answer for the expression =3+5^2 (just discussed) is 28.

Also notice that some operators in Table 3.4 have the same order of precedence (for example, multiplication and division). This means that it doesn't matter in which order these operators are evaluated. For example, consider the expression =5*10/2. If you perform the multiplication first, the answer you get is 25 (5*10 equals 50, and 50/2 equals 25). If you perform the division first, you also get an answer of 25 (10/2 equals 5, and 5*5 equals 25). By convention, VBA evaluates operators with the same order of precedence from left to right.

Controlling the Order of Precedence

Sometimes you want to override the order of precedence. For example, suppose you want to create an expression that calculates the pre-tax cost of an item. If you bought something for $10.65, including 7 percent sales tax, and you wanted to find the cost of the item less the tax, you would use the expression =10.65/1.07, which gives you the correct answer of $9.95. In general, the expression to use is given by the following formula:

$$\text{Pre-tax cost} = \frac{\text{Total Cost}}{1 + \text{Tax Rate}}$$

Listing 3.1 shows a function that attempts to implement this formula.

Listing 3.1. A first attempt at calculating the pre-tax cost.

```
Function PreTaxCost(totalCost As Currency, taxRate As Single) As Currency
    PreTaxCost = totalCost / 1 + taxRate
End Function
```


NOTE: THIS CHAPTER'S CODE LISTINGS

You'll find the code listings for this chapter on the CD that comes with this book. Look for the file Chaptr03.xls. Non-Excel users can use Chaptr03.bas instead.

Figure 3.1 shows an Excel worksheet that uses this function. The value in cell B4 is passed to the `totalCost` argument, and the value in cell B1 is passed to the `taxRate` argument.

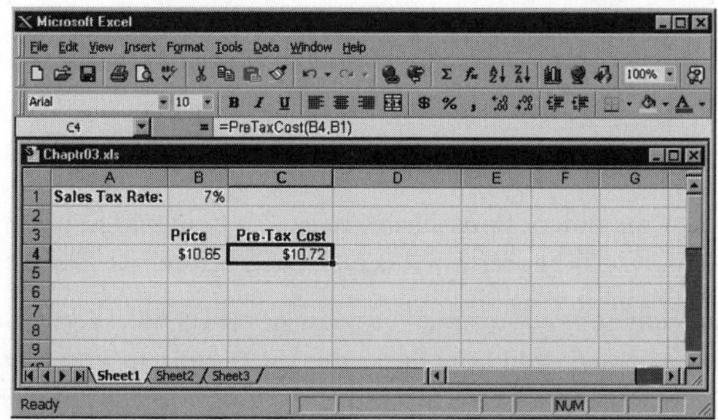

FIGURE 3.1.
A function that attempts to calculate the pre-tax cost of an item.

As you can see, the result is incorrect. What happened? Well, according to the rules of precedence, VBA performs division before addition, so the `totalCost` value first is divided by 1 and then is added to the `taxRate` value, which isn't the correct order.

To get the correct answer, you have to override the order of precedence so that the addition `1 + taxRate` is performed first. You do this by surrounding that part of the expression with parentheses, as in Listing 3.2. Using this revised function, you get the correct answer, as shown in Figure 3.2.

Listing 3.2. The correct way to calculate the pre-tax cost.

```
Function PreTaxCost2(totalCost As Currency, taxRate As Single) As Currency
    PreTaxCost2 = totalCost / (1 + taxRate)
End Function
```

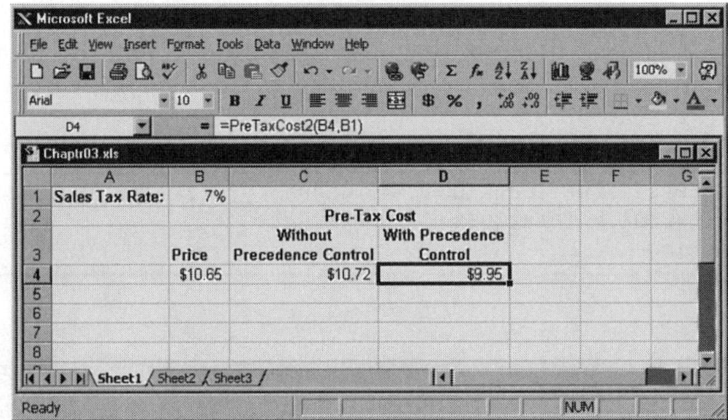

FIGURE 3.2.
The revised function calculates the pre-tax cost correctly.

In general, you can use parentheses to control the order that VBA uses to calculate expressions. Terms inside parentheses are always calculated first; terms outside parentheses are calculated sequentially (according to the order of precedence). To gain even more control over your expressions, you can place parentheses inside one another; this is called *nesting* parentheses, and VBA always evaluates the innermost set of parentheses first. Here are a few sample expressions:

Expression	*First Step*	*Second Step*	*Third Step*	*Result*
3^(15/5)*2–5	3^3*2–5	27*2–5	54–5	49
3^((15/5)*2–5)	3^(3*2–5)	3^(6–5)	3^1	3
3^(15/(5*2–5))	3^(15/(10–5))	3^(15/5)	3^3	27

Notice that the order of precedence rules also hold within parentheses. For example, in the expression (5*2–5), the term 5*2 is calculated before 5 is subtracted.

Using parentheses to determine the order of calculations gives you full control over VBA expressions. This way, you can make sure that the answer given by a expression is the one *you* want.

CAUTION: MAKE SURE PARENTHESES MATCH

One of the most common mistakes when using parentheses in expressions is to forget to close a parenthetic term with a right parenthesis. If you do this, VBA displays an `Expected: )` message. To make sure you've closed each parenthetic term, count all the left parentheses and count all the right parentheses. If these totals don't match, you know you've left out a parenthesis.

Working with Numeric Expressions

Numeric expressions are what we normally think of when we use the generic term "expression." Whether it's calculating gross margin, figuring out commissions, or determining the monthly payment on a loan, many expressions perform some kind of number crunching. This section examines numeric expressions in more depth. I'll discuss the arithmetic operators and numeric data type conversion, and run through some of VBA's built-in math and financial functions.

A Closer Look at the Arithmetic Operators

Table 3.1 outlined VBA's eight arithmetic operators. This section takes a closer look at each operator and talks about the implications that the various numeric data types bring to the table in expressions that use these operators.

The Addition Operator (+)

You use the addition operator to sum two operands. These operands must be either numeric literals, variables declared as one of the numeric data types, functions that return a numeric value, or any expression that evaluates to a number. (Having said all that, you *can* use `Date` values with addition and subtraction. See "Working with Date Expressions" later in this chapter.)

The data type of the result of a numeric expression depends on the data types of the operands. The general VBA rule is that the result takes on the highest precision of any operand in the expression. For example, if you add an `Integer` value and a `Long` value, the result will be a `Long` value.

NOTE: THE ORDER OF PRECISION FOR NUMERIC DATA TYPES

Here is the order of precision (from lowest to highest) based on the definitions of VBA's numeric data types: `Byte`, `Integer`, `Long`, `Single`, `Double`, `Currency`. (See Table 2.1 in the preceding chapter to get the exact precision for each data type.)

However, there are a few exceptions to this rule:

- If you add a `Single` value and a `Long` value, the result is a `Double` value.
- If the result is a `Byte` value that overflows its precision, VBA converts the result to an `Integer` variant.
- If the result is an `Integer` value that overflows its precision, VBA converts the result to a `Long` variant.
- If the result is a `Long` or `Single` value that overflows its precision, VBA converts the result to a `Double` variant.

The Subtraction and Negation Operators (-)

In its basic guise, you use the – operator to subtract one number from another. The rules and requirements for subtraction are the same as those I outlined earlier for addition. In other words, the operands must use one of the numeric data types, and VBA preserves the highest precision of the operands (with the same exceptions).

However, don't confuse subtraction with negation. Both use the same operator, but you wield negation when you want to turn a number into its negative equivalent. For example, the expression `-numVar` takes the negative of whatever value is currently stored in the variable `numVar`. In this sense, negation is like multiplying a value by –1: if the value is positive, the result is negative; if the value is negative, the result is positive.

The Multiplication Operator (*)

The asterisk (*) is the multiplication operator, and you use it to multiply two numbers together. Again, the operands you use must be numeric data types, and the resulting value takes on the data type of the highest-precision operand. The exceptions to this rule are the same as those outlined earlier for addition.

NOTE: THE ORDER OF PRECISION FOR MULTIPLICATION

VBA uses a slightly different order of precision when performing multiplication: `Byte`, `Integer`, `Long`, `Single`, `Currency`, `Double`.

The Division Operator (/)

The forward slash (/) is the division operator, and you use it to divide one number (the *dividend*) by another (the *divisor*). The result (the *quotient*) is usually a `Double` value, with the following exceptions:

- If both the dividend and the divisor are `Byte`, `Integer`, or `Single` values, the quotient is `Single`. If the quotient overflows the legal range for a `Single`, VBA generates an error.
- If both the dividend and the divisor are `Byte`, `Integer`, or `Single` variants, the quotient is a `Single` variant. If the quotient overflows the legal range for a `Single`, VBA converts the result to a `Double` variant.

CAUTION: AVOID DIVIDING BY ZERO

When using division in your procedures, you need to guard against using a divisor that has the value 0, because this will generate an error. In Chapter 5, "Controlling Your VBA Code," I'll show you how to use VBA's `If...Then...Else` statement to check for a 0 divisor before performing a division.

The Integer Division Operator (\)

The backslash (\) is VBA's integer division operator. Unlike regular division (which is also known as *floating-point division*), integer division is concerned only with integer values. In other words, the divisor and dividend are rounded to `Byte`, `Integer`, or `Long` values (as appropriate), the division is performed using these rounded numbers, and only the integer portion of the quotient is returned as the result (which will be `Byte`, `Integer`, or `Long`).

For example, consider the expression `10 \ 2.4`. VBA first rounds 2.4 down to 2 and then divides this value into 10 to give a result of 2. Alternatively, consider the expression `10 \ 2.6`. In this case, VBA rounds 2.6 up to 3 and then divides the new value into 10. The decimal portion of the quotient is discarded, leaving you with a result of 3.

NOTE: INTEGER DIVISION ROUNDING

Bear in mind that VBA rounds .5 values to the nearest even integer during integer division. This means that if your divisor is, say, 2.5, VBA will perform the integer division using 2, but if it's 3.5, VBA will use 4.

The Exponentiation Operator (^)

The caret (^) is VBA's exponentiation operator, which you use to raise one number to the power of a second number. Specifically, the expression `x ^ y` raises the number given by `x` to the power of the number given by `y`. Again, both operands must be legitimate VBA numeric values. However, you can raise a negative number to a power only if the power is an integer. For example, `-5 ^ 3` is a legitimate expression, but `-5 ^ 2.5` is not.

TIP: TAKING *N*TH ROOTS

You can use the exponentiation operator to take the nth root of a number by using the following formula:

```
nth root = number ^ (1/n)
```

For example, the expression `numVar ^ (1/3)` takes the cube root of `numVar`.

The Mod Operator

The `Mod` operator works like Excel's `MOD()` worksheet function. In other words, it divides one number by another and returns the remainder. Here's the general form to use:

```
result = dividend Mod divisor
```

dividend	The number being divided.
divisor	The number being divided into *dividend*.
result	The remainder of the division.

For example, `16 Mod 5` returns 1, because 5 goes into 16 three times with a remainder of 1.

Numeric Data Type Conversion Functions

What do you do if the data you want to use isn't stored in the correct data type? Or, what if you want to coerce the result of an expression into a particular data type? For these situations, VBA provides a half dozen *data conversion functions.* These functions take a string or numeric expression and convert it into a specific numeric data type. Table 3.6 outlines the available functions.

Table 3.6. VBA's numeric data conversion functions.

Function	*What It Returns*
`CByte(`***`expression`***`)`	An ***`expression`*** converted to a `Byte` value.
`CCur(`***`expression`***`)`	An ***`expression`*** converted to a `Currency` value.
`CDbl(`***`expression`***`)`	An ***`expression`*** converted to a `Double` value.
`CInt(`***`expression`***`)`	An ***`expression`*** converted to an `Integer` value.
`CLng(`***`expression`***`)`	An ***`expression`*** converted to a `Long` value.
`CSng(`***`expression`***`)`	An ***`expression`*** converted to a `Single` value.

NOTE: MORE CONVERSION FUNCTIONS

Besides the preceding numeric data conversion functions, VBA also has a few other conversion functions that apply to different data types:

`CBool(expression)`	An ***expression*** converted to a Boolean value.
`CDate(expression)`	An ***expression*** converted to a Date value.
`CVar(expression)`	An ***expression*** converted to a Variant value.
`CStr(expression)`	An ***expression*** converted to a String value.

Here are some notes to bear in mind when using these functions:

- VBA will generate an error if the ***expression*** used in a data conversion function is outside the normal range for the data type (for example, using a number greater than 255 in the `CByte` function).
- VBA has a `Val` function that returns a numeric value that represents all the numbers in a string (or, more accurately, all the numbers in a string that occur before the first nonnumeric character). For example, `Val("123 Mercer Street")` will return 123. You might be tempted to use this function to convert numeric strings to numbers, but you're better off using the data conversion functions. For example, `CCur("1234.95")` not only converts the string `"1234.95"` to a `Currency` value, but it also makes sure that the appropriate thousands separator and currency options are used (depending on the value selected in Windows' Regional Settings).
- If the decimal part of ***expression*** is exactly .5, the `CInt` and `CLng` functions will round ***expression*** to the nearest even number. For example, 0.5 rounds to 0, and 1.5 rounds to 2.

VBA's Math Functions

The operands you use in your numeric expressions will usually be numeric literals or variables declared as one of VBA's numeric data types. However, VBA also boasts quite a few built-in math functions that your expressions can use as operands. These functions are outlined in Table 3.7.

Table 3.7. VBA's math functions.

Function	*What It Returns*
`Abs(number)`	The absolute value of ***number***.
`Atn(number)`	The arctangent of ***number***.
`Cos(number)`	The cosine of ***number***.

continues

Table 3.7. continued

Function	*What It Returns*
`Exp(`***`number`***`)`	*e* (the base of the natural logarithm) raised to the power of ***`number`***.
`Fix(`***`number`***`)`	The integer portion of ***`number`***. If ***`number`*** is negative, `Fix` returns the first negative integer greater than or equal to ***`number`***.
`Hex(`***`number`***`)`	The hexadecimal value, as a `Variant`, of ***`number`***.
`Hex$(`***`number`***`)`	The hexadecimal value, as a `String`, of ***`number`***.
`Int(`***`number`***`)`	The integer portion of ***`number`***. If ***`number`*** is negative, `Int` returns the first negative integer less than or equal to ***`number`***.
`Log(`***`number`***`)`	The natural logarithm of ***`number`***.
`Oct(`***`number`***`)`	The octal value, as a `Variant`, of ***`number`***.
`Oct$(`***`number`***`)`	The octal value, as a `String`, of ***`number`***.
`Rnd(`*`number`*`)`	A random number between 0 and 1, as a `Single`. You use the optional *`number`* as a "seed" value, as follows: ***number*** — **What It Generates** Less than 0 — The same number every time (varies with ***`number`***). Equal to 0 — The most recently generated number. Greater than 0 — The next random number in the sequence.
`Sgn(`***`number`***`)`	The sign of ***`number`***. Returns 1 if ***`number`*** is greater than 0, –1 if ***`number`*** is less than 0, and 0 if ***`number`*** is 0.
`Sin(`***`number`***`)`	The sine of ***`number`***.
`Sqr(`***`number`***`)`	The square root of ***`number`***.
`Tan(`***`number`***`)`	The tangent of ***`number`***.

NOTE: GENERATING RANDOM NUMBERS

The random numbers generated by `Rnd` are only pseudo-random. In other words, if you use the same seed value, you get the same sequence of numbers. If you need truly random numbers, run the `Randomize` statement just before using `Rnd`. This initializes the random number generator with the current system time.

TIP: GENERATING RANDOM NUMBERS IN A RANGE

Instead of random numbers between 0 and 1, you might need to generate numbers within a larger range. Here's the general formula to use to get Rnd to generate a random number between a lower bound and an upper bound:

```
Int((upper - lower) * Rnd + lower)
```

For example, here's some code that generates a random eight-digit number (which would be suitable for use as part of a temporary filename; see the RandomFilename function in Chaptr03.xls):

```
Randomize
filename = Int((99999999 - 10000000) * Rnd + 10000000)
```

VBA's Financial Functions

VBA 5.0

VBA has quite a few financial functions that are new to version 5.0. These functions offer you powerful tools for building applications that manage both business and personal finances. You can use these functions to calculate such things as the monthly payment for a loan, the future value of an annuity, or the yearly depreciation of an asset.

Although VBA has a baker's dozen financial functions that use many different arguments, the following list covers the arguments you'll use most frequently:

rate The fixed rate of interest over the term of the loan or investment.

nper The number of payments or deposit periods over the term of the loan or investment.

pmt The periodic payment or deposit.

pv The present value of the loan (the principal) or the initial deposit in an investment.

fv The future value of the loan or investment.

type The type of payment or deposit. Use 0 (the default) for end-of-period payments or deposits and 1 for beginning-of-period payments or deposits.

For most financial functions, the following rules apply:

- The underlying unit of both the interest rate and the period must be the same. For example, if the ***rate*** is the annual interest rate, you must express ***nper*** in years. Similarly, if you have a monthly interest rate, you must express ***nper*** in months.

- You enter money you receive as a positive quantity, and you enter money you pay as a negative quantity. For example, you always enter the loan principal as a positive number, because it's money you receive from the bank.
- The ***nper*** argument should always be a positive integer quantity.

Table 3.8 lists all of VBA's financial functions.

Table 3.8. The built-in financial functions in VBA 5.0.

Function	*What It Returns*
`DDB(`***`cost,salvage,life,period`***`,`*`factor`*`)`	The depreciation of an asset over a specified period using the double-declining balance method.
`FV(`***`rate,nper,pmt`***`,`*`pv,type`*`)`	The future value of an investment or loan.
`IPmt(`***`rate,per,nper,pv`***`,`*`fv,type`*`)`	The interest payment for a specified period of a loan.
`IRR(`***`values`***`,`*`guess`*`)`	The internal rate of return for a series of cash flows.
`MIRR(`***`values,finance_rate,reinvest_rate`***`)`	The modified internal rate of return for a series of periodic cash flows.
`NPer(`***`rate,pmt,pv`***`,`*`fv,type`*`)`	The number of periods for an investment or loan.
`NPV(`***`rate,value1`***`,`*`value2...`*`)`	The net present value of an investment based on a series of cash flows and a discount rate.
`Pmt(`***`rate,nper,pv`***`,`*`fv,type`*`)`	The periodic payment for a loan or investment.
`PPmt(`***`rate,per,nper,pv`***`,`*`fv,type`*`)`	The principal payment for a specified period of a loan.
`PV(`***`rate,nper,pmt`***`,`*`fv,type`*`)`	The present value of an investment.
`Rate(`***`nper,pmt,pv`***`,`*`fv,type,guess`*`)`	The periodic interest rate for a loan or investment.
`SLN(`***`cost,salvage,life`***`)`	The straight-line depreciation of an asset over one period.
`SYD(`***`cost,salvage,life,period`***`)`	Sum-of-years' digits depreciation of an asset over a specified period.

Working with String Expressions

A *string expression* is an expression that returns a value that has a `String` data type. String expressions can use as operands string literals (one or more characters enclosed in double quotation marks), variables declared as `String`, or any of VBA's built-in functions that return a `String` value. Table 3.9 summarizes all the VBA functions that deal with strings.

Table 3.9. VBA's string functions.

Function	*What It Returns*
`Asc(`**`string`**`)`	The ANSI character code of the first letter in **`string`**.
`Chr(`**`charcode`**`)`	The character, as a `Variant`, that corresponds to the ANSI code given by **`charcode`**.
`Chr$(`**`charcode`**`)`	The character, as a `String`, that corresponds to the ANSI code given by **`charcode`**.
`CStr(`**`expression`**`)`	Converts **`expression`** to a `String` value.
`InStr(`*`start`*`,`**`string1`**`,`**`string2`**`)`	The character position of the first occurrence of **`string2`** in **`string1`**, starting at *`start`*.
`InStrB(`*`start`*`,`**`string1`**`,`**`string2`**`)`	The byte position of the first occurrence of **`string2`** in **`string1`**, starting at *`start`*.
`LCase(`**`string`**`)`	**`string`** converted to lowercase, as a `Variant`.
`LCase$(`**`string`**`)`	**`string`** converted to lowercase, as a `String`.
`Left(`**`string`**`,`**`length`**`)`	The leftmost **`length`** characters from **`string`**, as a `Variant`.
`Left$(`**`string`**`,`**`length`**`)`	The leftmost **`length`** characters from **`string`**, as a `String`.
`LeftB(`**`string`**`)`	The leftmost **`length`** bytes from **`string`**, as a `Variant`.
`LeftB$(`**`string`**`)`	The leftmost **`length`** bytes from **`string`**, as a `String`.
`Len(`**`string`**`)`	The number of characters in **`string`**.
`LenB(`**`string`**`)`	The number of bytes in **`string`**.
`LTrim(`**`string`**`)`	A string, as a `Variant`, without the leading spaces in **`string`**.
`LTrim$(`**`string`**`)`	A string, as a `String`, without the leading spaces in **`string`**.

continues

Table 3.9. continued

Function	*What It Returns*
`Mid(string,start,length)`	`length` characters, as a `Variant`, from **`string`** beginning at **`start`**.
`Mid$(string,start,length)`	`length` characters, as a `String`, from **`string`** beginning at **`start`**.
`MidB(string,start,length)`	`length` bytes, as a `Variant`, from **`string`** beginning at **`start`**.
`MidB$(string,start,length)`	`length` bytes, as a `String`, from **`string`** beginning at **`start`**.
`Right(string)`	The rightmost **`length`** characters from **`string`**, as a `Variant`.
`Right$(string)`	The rightmost **`length`** characters from **`string`**, as a `String`.
`RightB(string)`	The rightmost **`length`** bytes from **`string`**, as a `Variant`.
`RightB$(string)`	The rightmost **`length`** bytes from **`string`**, as a `String`.
`RTrim(string)`	A string, as a `Variant`, without the trailing spaces in **`string`**.
`RTrim$(string)`	A string, as a `String`, without the trailing spaces in **`string`**.
`Trim(string)`	A string, as a `Variant`, without the leading and trailing spaces in **`string`**.
`Trim$(string)`	A string, as a `String`, without the leading and trailing spaces in **`string`**.
`Space(number)`	A string, as a `Variant`, with **`number`** spaces.
`Space$(number)`	A string, as a `String`, with **`number`** spaces.
`Str(number)`	The string representation, as a `Variant`, of **`number`**.
`Str$(number)`	The string representation, as a `String`, of **`number`**.
`StrComp(string2,string2,compare)`	A value indicating the result of comparing **`string1`** and **`string2`**.
`String(number,character)`	**`character`**, as a `Variant`, repeated **`number`** times.
`String$(number,character)`	**`character`**, as a `String`, repeated **`number`** times.

Function	What It Returns
`UCase(`***string***`)`	***string*** converted to uppercase, as a `Variant`.
`UCase$(`***string***`)`	***string*** converted to uppercase, as a `String`.
`Val(`***string***`)`	All the numbers contained in ***string***, up to the first nonnumeric character.

Listing 3.3 shows a procedure that uses some of these string functions.

Listing 3.3. A procedure that uses a few string functions.

```
Function ExtractLastName(fullName As String) As String
    Dim spacePos As Integer
    spacePos = InStr(fullName, " ")
    ExtractLastName = Mid$(fullName, _
                           spacePos +1, _
                           Len(fullName) - spacePos)
End Function
Sub TestIt()
    MsgBox ExtractLastName("Millicent Peeved")
End Function
```

The purpose of this procedure is to take a name (first and last, separated by a space, as shown in the `TestIt` procedure) and extract the last name. The full name is brought into the function as the `fullName` argument. After declaring an `Integer` variable named `spacePos`, the procedure uses the `InStr` function to check `fullName` and find out the position of the space that separates the first and last names. The result is stored in `spacePos`:

```
spacePos = InStr(fullName, " ")
```

The real meat of the function is provided by the `Mid$` string function, which uses the following syntax to extract a substring from a larger string:

`Mid$(`***string,start,***_length_`)`

string The string from which you want to extract the characters. In the `ExtractLastName` function, this parameter is the `fullName` variable.

start The starting point of the string you want to extract. In `ExtractLastName`, this parameter is the position of the space, plus 1 (in other words, `spacePos + 1`).

length The length of the string you want to extract. In the `ExtractLastName` function, this is the length of the full string—`Len(fullName)`—minus the position of the space.

Working with Logical Expressions

A logical expression is an expression that returns a `Boolean` result. A `Boolean` value is almost always either `True` or `False`, but VBA also recognizes some `Boolean` equivalents:

- A `False` result can be used in an expression as though it were 0. Similarly, you can use 0 in a logical expression as though it were `False`.
- A `True` result can be used in an expression as though it were –1. However, *any* nonzero value can be used in a logical expression as though it were `True`.

In Chapter 5, I'll show you various VBA statements that let your procedures make decisions and loop through sections of code. In most cases, the mechanism that controls these statements will be a logical expression. For example, if *x* is a logical expression, you can tell VBA to run one set of statements if *x* returns `True` and a different set of statements if *x* returns `False`.

You'll see that these are powerful constructs, and they'll prove invaluable in all your VBA projects. To help you prepare, let's take a closer look at VBA's logical operators.

The And Operator

You use the `And` operator when you want to test two `Boolean` operands to see if they're both `True`. For example, consider the following generic expression (where *`Expr1`* and *`Expr2`* are `Boolean` values):

```
Expr1 And Expr2
```

- If both *`Expr1`* and *`Expr2`* are `True`, this expression returns `True`.
- If either or both *`Expr1`* and *`Expr2`* are `False`, the expression returns `False`.

The Or Operator

You use the `Or` operator when you want to test two `Boolean` operands to see if one of them is `True`:

```
Expr1 Or Expr2
```

- If either or both *`Expr1`* and *`Expr2`* are `True`, this expression returns `True`.
- If both *`Expr1`* and *`Expr2`* are `False`, the expression returns `False`.

The Xor Operator

`Xor` is the exclusive `Or` operator. It's useful when you need to know if two operands have the opposite value:

```
Expr1 Xor Expr2
```

- If one of the values is `True` and the other is `False`, the expression returns `True`.
- If *`Expr1`* and *`Expr2`* are both `True` or are both `False`, the expression returns `False`.

The Eqv Operator

`Eqv` is the equivalence operator; it tells you whether or not two `Boolean` operands have the same value:

```
Expr1 Eqv Expr2
```

- If *`Expr1`* and *`Expr2`* are both `True` or are both `False`, this expression returns `True`.
- If one of the values is `True` and the other is `False`, the expression returns `False`.

The Imp Operator

`Imp` is the VBA implication operator. What is being implied here? The relationship between two `Boolean` operands:

```
Expr1 Imp Expr2
```

- If *`Expr2`* is `True`, this expression returns `True`.
- If both *`Expr1`* and *`Expr2`* are `False`, this expression returns `True`.
- If *`Expr2`* is `False` and *`Expr1`* is `True`, this expression returns `False`.

The Not Operator

The `Not` operator is the logical equivalent of the negation operator. In this case, `Not` returns the opposite value of an operand. For example, if *`Expr`* is `True`, `Not` *`Expr`* returns `False`.

Working with Date Expressions

A date expression is an expression that returns a `Date` value. For operands in date expressions, you can use either a variable declared as `Date` or a date literal. For the latter, you enclose the date in pound signs, like so:

```
dateVar = #8/23/97#
```

When working with dates, it helps to remember that VBA works with dates internally as *serial numbers*. Specifically, VBA uses December 31, 1899 as an arbitrary starting point and then represents subsequent dates as the number of days that have passed since then. So, for example, the date serial number for January 1, 1900 is 1, January 2, 1900 is 2 and so on. Table 3.10 displays some sample date serial numbers.

Table 3.10. Examples of date serial numbers.

Serial Number	*Date*
366	December 31, 1900
16,229	June 6, 1944
35,430	December 31, 1996

Similarly, VBA also uses serial numbers to represent times internally. In this case, though, VBA expresses time as a fraction of the 24-hour day to get a number between 0 and 1. The starting point, midnight, is given the value 0, noon is 0.5, and so on. Table 3.11 displays some sample time serial numbers.

Table 3.11. Examples of time serial numbers.

Serial Number	*Time*
0.25	6:00:00 AM
0.375	9:00:00 AM
0.70833	5:00:00 PM
.99999	11:59:59 PM

You can combine the two types of serial numbers. For example, 35,430.5 represents 12 noon on December 31, 1996.

The advantage of using serial numbers in this way is that it makes calculations involving dates and times very easy. Since a date or time is really just a number, any mathematical operation you can perform on a number can also be performed on a date. This is invaluable for procedures that track delivery times, monitor accounts receivable or accounts payable aging, calculate invoice discount dates, and so on.

VBA also comes equipped with quite a few date and time functions. Table 3.12 summarizes them all.

Table 3.12. VBA's date and time functions.

Function	*What It Returns*
`CDate(`***`expression`***`)`	Converts ***`expression`*** into a `Date` value.
`Date`	The current system date, as a `Variant`.
`Date$()`	The current system date, as a `String`.
`DateSerial(`***`year`***`,`***`month`***`,`***`day`***`)`	A `Date` value for the specified ***`year`***, ***`month`***, and ***`day`***.
`DateValue(`***`date`***`)`	A `Date` value for the ***`date`*** string.

Function	What It Returns
`Day(`***`date`***`)`	The day of the month given by ***`date`***.
`Hour(`***`time`***`)`	The hour component of ***`time`***.
`Minute(`***`time`***`)`	The minute component of ***`time`***.
`Month(`***`date`***`)`	The month component of ***`date`***.
`Now`	The current system date and time.
`Second(`***`time`***`)`	The second component of ***`time`***.
`Time`	The current system time, as a `Variant`.
`Time$`	The current system time, as a `String`.
`Timer`	The number of seconds since midnight.
`TimeSerial(`***`hour,minute,second`***`)`	A `Date` value for the specified ***`hour`***, ***`minute`***, and ***`second`***.
`TimeValue(`***`time`***`)`	A `Date` value for the ***`time`*** string.
`Weekday(`***`date`***`)`	The day of the week, as a number, given by ***`date`***.
`Year(`***`date`***`)`	The year component of ***`date`***.

Listing 3.4 shows a couple of procedures that take advantage of a few of these date functions.

Listing 3.4. A Function procedure that uses various date functions to calculate a person's age.

```
Function CalculateAge(birthDate As Date) As Byte
    Dim birthdayNotPassed As Boolean
    birthdayNotPassed = CDate(Month(birthDate) & "/" & _
                              Day(birthDate) & "/" & _
                              Year(Now)) > Now
    CalculateAge = Year(Now) - Year(birthDate) + birthdayNotPassed
End Function
' Use this procedure to test CalculateAge.
'
Sub TestIt2()
    MsgBox CalculateAge(#8/23/59#)
End Sub
```

NOTE: THE CODE CONTINUATION CHARACTER

Note the use of the underscore (_) in this listing. This is VBA's *code continuation character*—it's useful for breaking up long statements into multiple lines for easier reading. One caveat, though: Make sure you add a space before the underscore, or VBA will generate an error.

The purpose of the `CalculateAge` function is to figure out a person's age given the date of birth (as passed to `CalculateAge` through the `Date` variable named `birthDate`). You might think the following formula would do the job:

```
Year(Now) - Year(birthDate)
```

This works, but only if the person's birthday has already passed this year. If the person hasn't had his or her birthday yet, this formula reports the person's age as being one year greater than it really is.

To solve this problem, you need to take into account whether or not the person's birthday has occurred. To do this, `CalculateAge` first declares a `Boolean` variable `birthdayNotPassed` and then uses the following expression to test whether or not the person has celebrated his or her birthday this year:

```
CDate(Month(birthDate) & "/" & Day(birthDate) & "/" & Year(Now)) > Now
```

This expression uses the `Month`, `Day`, and `Year` functions to construct the date of the person's birthday this year and uses the `CDate` function to convert this string into a date. The expression then checks to see if this date is greater than today's date (as given by the `Now` function). If it is, the person hasn't celebrated his or her birthday, so `birthdayNotPassed` is set to `True`; otherwise, `birthdayNotPassed` is set to `False`.

The key is that to VBA a `True` value is equivalent to –1, and a `False` value is equivalent to 0. Therefore, to calculate the person's correct age, you need only add the value of `birthdayNotPassed` to the expression `Year(Now) - Year(birthDate)`.

Formatting Numeric and Date Expressions

As you work through this book, I'll show you various methods for displaying data to the user. One of the best ways to improve the readability of your program output is to display the results of your expressions in a format that is logical, consistent, and straightforward. Formatting currency amounts with leading dollar signs, percentages with trailing percent signs, and large numbers with commas are a few of the ways you can improve your expression style.

This section shows you how to format numbers, dates, and times using VBA's built-in formatting options. You'll also learn how to create your own formats to gain maximum control over the appearance of your data.

The `Format` Function

The vehicle you'll be using to format your expressions is, appropriately enough, the `Format` function:

```
Format$(expression,format,firstdayofweek,firstweekofyear)
```

expression	The expression you want to format.
format	Either the name of a predefined format (see the next section) or a user-defined format expression (see "User-Defined Numeric Formats" and "User-Defined Date and Time Formats").
firstdayofweek	A constant that identifies the first day of the week: `vbSunday`, `vbMonday`, and so on. You can also use `vbUseSystem` to set this value to the system default.
firstweekofyear	A constant that identifies the first week of the year. Use `vbUseSystem` to set this value to the system default, or use one of the following values:

`vbFirstJan1`	The year begins with the week that contains January 1.
`vbFirstFourDays`	The year begins with the first week that contains at least four days in the year.
`vbFirstFullWeek`	The year begins with the first week that contains seven days in the year.

VBA's Predefined Formats

VBA comes with a small collection of predefined formats for numbers, dates, and times. If you've ever formatted data in an Excel worksheet, you should be familiar with most of these formats.

Predefined Numeric Formats

By default, VBA displays numbers in a plain style that includes no thousands separators or symbols. If you want your numbers to appear differently, you can choose from among VBA's nine built-in numeric formats, which are described in Table 3.13.

Table 3.13. VBA's built-in numeric formats.

Format	*Description*
General Number	The default numeric format.
Currency	Displays the number using the thousands separator, the dollar sign ($), and with two digits to the right of the decimal. Also, negative numbers are displayed surrounded

continues

Table 3.13. continued

Format	Description
	by parentheses. Note, however, that the exact output of this format depends on the regional currency setting selected in Control Panel.
Fixed	Displays the number with at least one digit to the left of the decimal and at least two digits to the right of the decimal.
Standard	Displays the number with the thousands separator, at least one digit to the left of the decimal, and at least two digits to the right of the decimal.
Percent	Displays the number multiplied by 100, two digits to the right of the decimal, and a percent sign (%) to the right of the number. For example, .506 is displayed as 50.60%.
Scientific	Uses standard scientific notation: The most significant number is shown to the left of the decimal, and 2 to 30 decimal places are shown to the right of the decimal, followed by "E" and the exponent. For example, 123000 is displayed as 1.23E+05.
Yes/No	Displays `No` if the number is 0 and `Yes` for all other values.
True/False	Displays `False` if the number is 0 and `True` for all other values.
On/Off	Displays `Off` if the number is 0 and `On` for all other values.

To use one of these predefined formats, enclose the name in quotation marks as part of the `Format` function:

```
profit = Format(sales - expenses, "currency")
```

Predefined Date and Time Formats

The default date and time formatting used by VBA is based on the current settings selected in the Date and Time tabs of Control Panel's Regional Settings properties sheet. In general, though, if the date serial number doesn't include a fractional part, VBA displays only the date (usually in mm/dd/yy format). Similarly, if the serial number doesn't include an integer part, VBA displays only the time (usually in hh:mm AM/PM format). Table 3.14 shows a complete list of VBA's predefined date and time formats.

Table 3.14. VBA's built-in date and time formats.

Format	*Description*
General Date	The default date/time format.
Long Date	Displays the date according to the long date format defined for the system (for example, Saturday August 23, 1997).
Medium Date	Displays the date according to the medium date format defined for the system (for example, 23-Aug-97).
Short Date	Displays the date according to the short date format defined for the system (for example, 8/23/97).
Long Time	Displays the time according to the long time format defined for the system (for example, 10:30:45 PM).
Medium Time	Displays the time using only hours and minutes and with AM/PM (for example, 10:30 PM).
Short Time	Displays the time using only hours and minutes according to the 24-hour clock (for example, 22:30).

Again, you use one of these formats by including it in quotation marks in the `Format` function:

```
MsgBox "The current time is " & Format(Now, "medium time")
```

User-Defined Numeric Formats

VBA's predefined numeric formats give you some control over how your numbers are displayed, but they have their limitations. For example, unless you alter Windows' Regional Settings, no built-in format lets you display a different currency symbol (the British pound sign, £, for example) or display temperatures using, say, the degree symbol. To overcome these limitations, you need to create your own custom numeric formats. The formatting syntax and symbols are explained in detail later in this section.

Every VBA numeric format has the following syntax:

```
positive format;negative format;zero format;null format
```

The four parts, separated by semicolons, determine how various numbers are presented. The first part defines how a positive number is displayed, the second part defines how a negative number is displayed, the third part defines how zero is displayed, and the fourth part defines how null values are displayed. If you leave out one or more of these parts, numbers are controlled as shown here:

Number of Parts Used	*Format Syntax*
Three	*positive format;negative format;zero format*
Two	*positive and zero format;negative format*
One	*positive, negative, and zero format*

Table 3.15 lists the special symbols you use to define each of these parts.

Table 3.15. VBA's numeric formatting symbols.

Symbol	*Description*
#	Holds a place for a digit. Displays nothing if no number is entered.
0	Holds a place for a digit. Displays zero if no number is entered.
. (period)	Sets the location of the decimal point.
, (comma)	Sets the location of the thousands separator. Marks only the location of the first thousand.
%	Multiplies the number by 100 (for display only) and adds the percent (%) character.
E+ e+ E– e–	Displays the number in scientific format. E– and e– place a minus sign in the exponent; E+ and e+ place a plus sign in the exponent.
$ ( ) – + <space>	Displays the character.
\ (backslash)	Inserts the character that follows the backslash.
"*text*"	Inserts the text that appears within the quotation marks.

Let's check out a few examples. Suppose your procedure is working with 10-digit phone numbers. To display these numbers with parentheses around the area code, use the **`(000) 000-0000`** format, as shown in the following procedure fragment:

```
phoneNum = 2135556543
MsgBox "The phone number is " & Format(phoneNum, "(000) 000-0000")
```

Figure 3.3 shows the resulting dialog box.

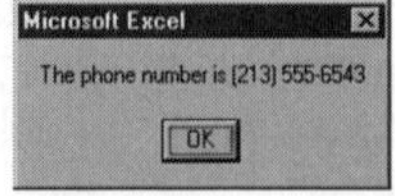

FIGURE 3.3.
The dialog box produced by the code fragment.

For nine-digit Social Security numbers, try the **000-00-0000** format:

```
ssn = 123456789
MsgBox "The social security number is " & Format(ssn, "000-00-0000")
```

If you're working with temperatures, you might want to display each value using the degree symbol, which is ANSI 176. Here's how you would do it:

```
temp = 98.6
MsgBox "The temperature is " & Format(temp, "#,##0.0" & Chr(176) & "F")
```

Figure 3.4 shows how VBA displays the temperature using this format.

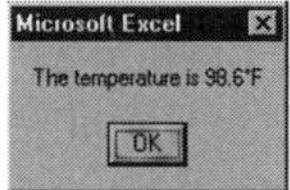

FIGURE 3.4.
You can include symbols (such as the degree symbol shown here) in your formats.

NOTE: THE CHR FUNCTION

You can use VBA's `Chr` function to output any displayable ANSI character. The syntax is `Chr(`***code***`)`, where ***code*** is the ANSI code of the character you want to display. Appendix C lists all the ANSI codes, but here are a few that you might find particularly useful in your numeric formats:

Character Code	ANSI Character
163	£
162	¢
165	¥
169	©
174	®
176	°

User-Defined Date and Time Formats

Although the built-in date and time formats are fine for most applications, you might need to create your own custom formats. For instance, you might want to display the day of the week (for example, "Friday"). Custom date and time formats generally are simpler to create than custom numeric formats since there are fewer formatting symbols. Table 3.16 lists the date and time formatting symbols.

Table 3.16. VBA's date and time formatting symbols.

Symbol	*Description*
	Date Formats
c	Displays the date as ddddd and the time as ttttt.
d	Day number without a leading zero (1 to 31).
dd	Day number with a leading zero (01 to 31).
ddd	Three-letter day abbreviation (Mon, for example).
dddd	Full day name (Monday, for example).
ddddd	Displays the complete date using the system's short date format.
dddddd	Displays the complete date using the system's long date format.
m	Month number without a leading zero (1 to 12).
mm	Month number with a leading zero (01 to 12).
mmm	Three-letter month abbreviation (Aug, for example).
mmmm	Full month name (August, for example).
q	Quarter of the year (1 to 4).
w	Day of the week as a number (1 to 7 for Sunday through Saturday).
ww	Week of the year (1 to 54).
y	Day of the year (1 to 366).
yy	Two-digit year (00 to 99).
yyyy	Full year (1900 to 2078).
	Time Formats
ttttt	Displays the complete time using the system's default time format.
h	Hour without a leading zero (0 to 24).
hh	Hour with a leading zero (00 to 24).
m	Minute without a leading zero (0 to 59).
mm	Minute with a leading zero (00 to 59).
n	Minute without a leading zero (0 to 59).
nn	Minute with a leading zero (00 to 59).
s	Second without a leading zero (0 to 59).

Symbol	Description
ss	Second with a leading zero (00 to 59).
AM/PM, am/pm	Displays the time using a 12-hour clock.
/ : . -	Symbols used to separate parts of dates or times.

NOTE: MINUTE FORMATTING

You might have noticed in Table 3.16 that VBA uses the same symbol (m) for both months and minutes. In general, VBA interprets "m" as a month symbol *unless* it immediately follows an "h" (the hour symbol). To avoid ambiguity in your formats, you might want to use "n" as the minutes symbol.

Here's a code fragment that uses some of the formatting symbols (see Figure 3.5 for the results):

```
thisMoment = Now
MsgBox "It's now " & Format(thisMoment, "h:n AM/PM") & " on " _
    Format(thisMoment, "dddd, mmmm d")
```

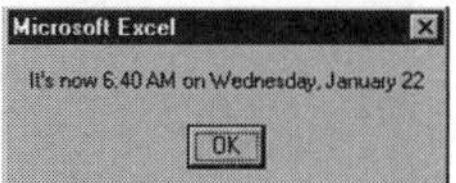

FIGURE 3.5.
The results of the date and time formatting.

Summary

This chapter showed you how to build expressions in VBA. This is a crucial topic, because much of your VBA coding will involve creating expressions of one kind or another. With that in mind, I designed this chapter to give you a solid grounding in expression fundamentals. After first learning about basic expression structure, you were given a quick tour of the various VBA operators and the all-important topic of operator precedence. From there, you went through more detailed lessons on the four main expression types: numeric, string, logical, and date. For related information, see the following chapters:

- Objects will play a big part in your expressions. For example, you'll use expressions to set the values of object properties. I explain all of this and more in Chapter 4, "Working with Objects."
- You can put your newfound knowledge of logical expressions to good use in Chapter 5, "Controlling Your VBA Code."

- VBA boasts an impressive function collection, and you'll be learning about many more of these functions as you progress through this book. However, you also have access to the huge collection of built-in functions exposed by the underlying application (for example, Excel's worksheet functions). The chapters in Part II, "Unleashing Microsoft Office Objects," show you how to access application functions from your VBA procedures.
- You'll find a complete list of VBA functions in Appendix B, "VBA Functions."

CHAPTER

Working with Objects

IN THIS CHAPTER

Nature is a collective idea, and, though its essence exists in each individual of the species, it can never in its perfection inhabit a single object.

—Henry Fuseli

Many of your VBA procedures will perform calculations using simple combinations of numbers, operators, and the host application's built-in functions. You'll probably find, however, that most of your code manipulates the application environment in some way, whether it's formatting document text, entering data in a worksheet range, or setting application options. Each of these items—the document, the range, the application—is called an *object* in VBA. Objects are perhaps the most crucial concept in VBA programming, and I'll explain them in detail in this chapter.

What Is an Object?

The dictionary definition of an object is "anything perceptible by one or more of the senses, especially something that can be seen and felt." Now, of course, you can't feel anything in an Office application, but you can see all kinds of things. To VBA, an object is anything in an application that you can see *and* manipulate in some way. For example, an Excel range is something you can see, and you can manipulate it by entering data, changing colors, setting fonts, and so on. A range, therefore, is an object.

What isn't an object? The Office programs are so customizable that most things you can see qualify as objects, but not everything does. For example, the Maximize and Minimize buttons in document windows aren't objects. Yes, you can operate them, but you can't change them. Instead, the window itself is the object, and you manipulate it so that it is maximized or minimized.

You can manipulate objects in VBA in any of the following three ways:

- You can make changes to the object's *properties.*
- You can make the object perform a task by activating a *method* associated with the object.
- You can define a procedure that runs whenever a particular *event* happens to the object.

To help you understand properties, methods, events, and objects, I'll put things in real-world terms. Specifically, let's look at your computer as though it were an object. For starters, you can think of your computer in one of two ways: as a single object or as a *collection* of objects (such as the monitor, the keyboard, the system unit, and so on).

If you wanted to describe your computer as a whole, you would mention things like the name of the manufacturer, the price, the color, and so on. Each of these items is a *property* of the computer. You can also use your computer to perform tasks, such as writing letters, crunching numbers, and playing games. These are the *methods* associated with your computer. There are also a number of things that happen to the computer that cause it to respond in predefined ways. For example, when the On button is pressed, the computer runs through its Power On Self-Test, initializes its components, and so on. The actions to which the computer responds automatically are its *events.*

The sum total of all these properties, methods, and events gives you an overall description of your computer. In a more general sense, you can think of a generic "computer" object, which also (in an abstract way) has the same properties, uses the same methods, and responds to the same events. This more abstract form is called a *class.* A specific computer object is called an *instance* of the computer class.

But your computer is also a collection of objects, each with its own properties, methods, and events. The CD-ROM drive, for example, has various properties, including its speed and data rate. Its methods would be actions such as ejecting a disk and adjusting the sound level. A CD-ROM event might be the insertion of a disc that contains an AUTORUN.INF file that causes the disc's program to run automatically.

In the end, you have a complete description of the computer: what it looks like (its properties), how you interact with it (its methods), and to what actions it responds (its events).

The Object Hierarchy

As we've seen, your computer's objects are arranged in a hierarchy, with the most general object (the computer as a whole) at the top. Lower levels progress through more specific objects (such as the system unit, the motherboard, and the processor).

Each Office application's objects are also arranged in a hierarchy. The most general object—the `Application` object—refers to the program itself. In Excel, for example, the `Application` object contains no less than 15 objects, some of which are outlined in Table 4.1. Notice that, in most cases, each object is part of a *collection* of similar objects.

Table 4.1. Some Excel objects beneath the `Application` object.

Object	*Collection*	*Description*
AddIn	`AddIns`	An Excel add-in file. The `AddIns` collection refers to all the add-ins available to Excel (in other words, all the add-ins that are listed in the Add-Ins dialog box).
Dialog	`Dialogs`	A built-in Excel dialog box. The `Dialogs` object is a collection of all the Excel built-in dialog boxes.

continues

Table 4.1. continued

Object	*Collection*	*Description*
Name	`Names`	A defined range name. The `Names` object is the collection of all the defined names in all open workbooks.
Window	`Windows`	An open window. The `Windows` object is the collection of all the open windows.
Workbook	`Workbooks`	An open workbook. The `Workbooks` object is the collection of all the open workbooks.
WorksheetFunction	None	A container for Excel's built-in worksheet functions.

Most of the objects in Table 4.1 have objects beneath them in the hierarchy. A Workbook object, for example, contains Worksheet objects and possibly Chart objects. Similarly, a Worksheet object contains many objects of its own, such as Range objects and possibly an Outline object.

To specify an object in the hierarchy, you usually start with the uppermost object and add the lower objects, separated by periods. For example, here's one way you could specify the range B2:B5 on the worksheet named "Sheet1" in the workbook named "Book1":

```
Application.Workbooks("Book1").Worksheets("Sheet1").Range("B2:B5")
```

As you'll see, there are ways to shorten such long-winded "hierarchical paths."

Working with Object Properties

Every object has a defining set of characteristics. These characteristics are called the object's *properties*, and they control the appearance and position of the object. For example, each Window object has a `WindowState` property you can use to display a window as maximized, minimized, or normal. Similarly, a Word Document object has a `Name` property to hold the filename, a `Saved` property that tells you whether or not the document has changed since the last save, a `Type` property to hold the document type (regular or template), and many more.

When you refer to a property, you use the following syntax:

```
Object.Property
```

For example, the following expression refers to the `ActiveWindow` property of the `Application` object:

```
Application.ActiveWindow
```

One of the most confusing aspects of objects and properties is that some properties do double duty as objects. Figure 4.1 uses an Excel example to illustrate this. The `Application` object has an `ActiveWindow` property that tells you the name of the active window. However, `ActiveWindow` is also a Window object. Similarly, the Window object has an `ActiveCell` property that specifies the active cell, but `ActiveCell` is also a Range object. Finally, a Range object has a `Font` property, but a font is also an object with its own properties (`Italic`, `Name`, `Size`, and so on).

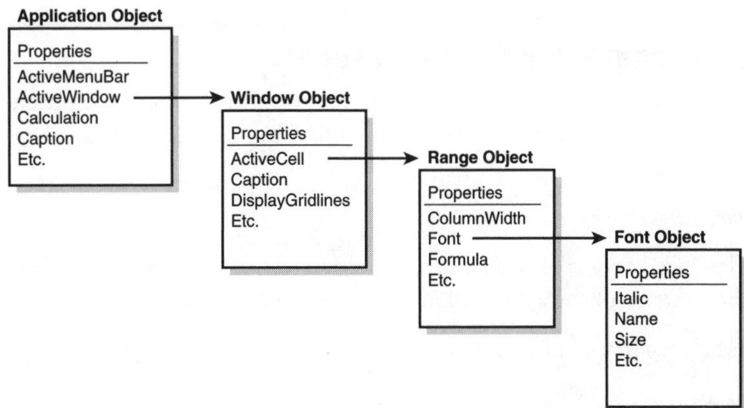

FIGURE 4.1.
Some Excel properties also can be objects.

In other words, lower-level objects in the object hierarchy are really just properties of their parent objects. This idea will often help you to reduce the length of a hierarchical path (and thus reduce the abuse your typing fingers must bear). For example, consider the following object path:

```
Application.ActiveWindow.ActiveCell.Font.Italic
```

Here, an object such as `ActiveCell` implicitly refers to the `ActiveWindow` and `Application` objects, so you can knock the path down to size as follows:

```
ActiveCell.Font.Italic
```


Setting the Value of a Property

To set a property to a certain value, you use the following syntax:

```
Object.Property=value
```

Here, *`value`* is an expression that returns the value to which you want to set the property. As such, it can be any of VBA's recognized data types, including the following:

- A numeric value. For example, the following statement sets the size of the font in the active cell to 14:

  ```
  ActiveCell.Font.Size = 14
  ```

- A string value. The following example sets the font name in the active cell to Times New Roman:

  ```
  ActiveCell.Font.Name = "Times New Roman"
  ```

- A logical value (in other words, `True` or `False`). The following statement turns on the `Italic` property in the active cell:

  ```
  ActiveCell.Font.Italic = True
  ```

Returning the Value of a Property

Sometimes you need to know the current setting of a property before changing the property or performing some other action. You can find out the current value of a property by using the following syntax:

```
variable=Object.Property
```

Here, *`variable`* is a variable or another property. For example, the following statement stores the contents of the active cell in a variable named `cellContents`:

```
cellContents = ActiveCell.Value
```

Working with Object Methods

An object's properties describe what the object is, whereas its *methods* describe what the object *does.* For example, in Word you can spell check a Document object using the `CheckSpelling` method. Similarly, you can sort a Table object by using the `Sort` method.

How you refer to a method depends on whether or not the method uses any arguments. If it doesn't, the syntax is similar to that of properties:

```
Object.Method
```

For example, the following statement saves the active document:

```
ActiveDocument.Save
```

If the method requires arguments, you use the following syntax:

```
Object.Method (argument1, argument2, ...)
```

NOTE: WHEN TO USE METHOD PARENTHESES

Technically, the parentheses around the argument list are necessary only if you'll be storing the result of the method in a variable or object property.

For example, Word's Document object has a `Close` method that you can use to close a document programmatically. Here's the syntax:

```
Object.Close(SaveChanges, OriginalFormat, RouteDocument)
```

Object	The Document object.
SaveChanges	A constant that specifies whether or not the file is saved before closing.
OriginalFormat	A constant that specifies whether or not the file is saved in its original format.
RouteDocument	A `True` or `False` value that specifies whether or not the document is routed to the next recipient.

NOTE: FORMATTING REQUIRED ARGUMENTS

For many VBA methods, not all the arguments are required. For the `Close` method, for example, only the ***SaveChanges*** argument is required. Throughout this book, I differentiate between required and optional arguments by displaying the required arguments in bold type.

For example, the following statement prompts the user to save changes, saves the changes (if applicable) in the original file format, and routes the document to the next recipient:

```
ActiveDocument.Close wdPromptToSaveChanges, wdOriginalFormat, True
```

To make your methods clearer to read, you can use VBA's predefined *named arguments*. For example, the syntax of the `Close` method has three named arguments: `SaveChanges`, `OriginalFormat`, and `RouteDocument`. Here's how you would use them in the preceding example:

```
ActiveDocument.Close SaveChanges:=wdPromptToSaveChanges, _
OrignalFormat:=wdOriginalFormat, _
RouteDocument:=True
```

Notice how the named arguments are assigned values by using the `:=` operator.

TIP: USE NAMED ARGUMENTS IN ANY ORDER

Another advantage of using named arguments is that you can enter the arguments in any order you like, and you can ignore any arguments you don't need (except necessary arguments, of course).

Handling Object Events

In simplest terms, an *event* is something that happens to an object. For example, the opening of an Excel workbook would be an event for that workbook. Don't confuse a method with an event, however. Yes, Excel has an `Open` method that you can use to open a workbook, but this method only *initiates* the procedure; the actual process of the file being opened is the event. Note, too, that events can happen either programmatically (by including the appropriate method in your code) or by user intervention (by selecting, say, File | Open).

In VBA, the event itself isn't as important as how your procedures *respond* to the event. In other words, you can write special procedures called *event handlers* that will run every time a particular event occurs. In a workbook, for example, you can specify event handlers not just for opening the file, but also for other events such as activating the workbook window, saving the file, inserting a new worksheet, closing the file, and so on.

For example, Figure 4.2 shows a module window for a workbook. (Specifically, it's the module window for the project's `ThisWorkbook` object.) Notice that the module window has two drop-down lists just below the title bar:

Object list: This list tells you what kind of object you're working with. If you select (General) in this list, you can use the module window to enter standard VBA procedures and functions. If you select an object from this list, however, you can enter event handlers for the object.

Procedure list: This list tells you which procedure is active in the module. If you select (General) in the Object list, the Procedure list contains all the standard VBA procedures and functions in the module. If you select an object in the Object list, however, the Procedure list changes to show all the events recognized by the object.

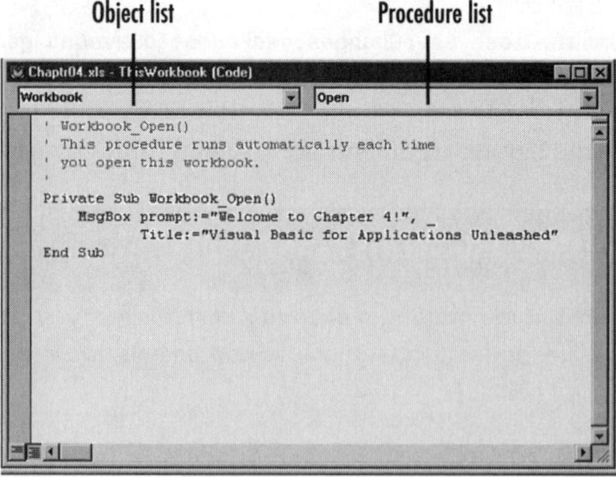

FIGURE 4.2.
An example of an event procedure. Here, this procedure runs each time the workbook is opened.

In Figure 4.2, I've selected Workbook in the Object list, so the Procedure list contains all the events recognized by the Workbook object. For the `Open` event, I've inserted a `MsgBox` statement into the `Workbook_Open` event handler. This statement will display a message each time the workbook is opened. (I'll show you how to use `MsgBox` in Chapter 10, "Interacting with the User.")

Working with Object Collections

A *collection* is a set of similar objects. For example, Excel's `Workbooks` collection is the set of all the open Workbook objects. Similarly, the `Worksheets` collection is the set of all Worksheet objects in a workbook. Collections are objects, too, so they have their own properties and methods, and you can use the properties and methods to manipulate one or more objects in the collection.

The members of a collection are called the *elements* of the collection. You can refer to individual elements using either the object's name or by using an *index*. For example, the following statement closes a workbook named Budget.xls:

```
Workbooks("Budget.xls").Close
```

On the other hand, the following statement uses an index to make a copy of the first picture object in the active worksheet:

```
ActiveSheet.Pictures(1).Copy
```

If you don't specify an element, VBA assumes you want to work with the entire collection.

NOTE: USE COLLECTIONS TO REFER TO OBJECTS

It's important here to reiterate that you can't refer to many application objects by themselves. Instead, you must refer to the object as an element in a collection. For example, when referring to the Budget.xls workbook, you can't just use Budget.xls. You have to use `Workbooks("Budget.xls")` so that VBA knows you're talking about a currently open workbook.

The Object Browser

The Object Browser is a handy tool that shows you the objects available for your procedures as well as the properties, methods, and events for each object. (Technically, it shows you the various *classes* of objects available.) You can also use it to quickly move between procedures and to paste code templates into a module.

To display the Object Browser, activate the Visual Basic Editor and then either select View | Object Browser or click the Object Browser button on the Visual Basic toolbar (you can also press F2). You'll see the Object Browser dialog box, shown in Figure 4.3.

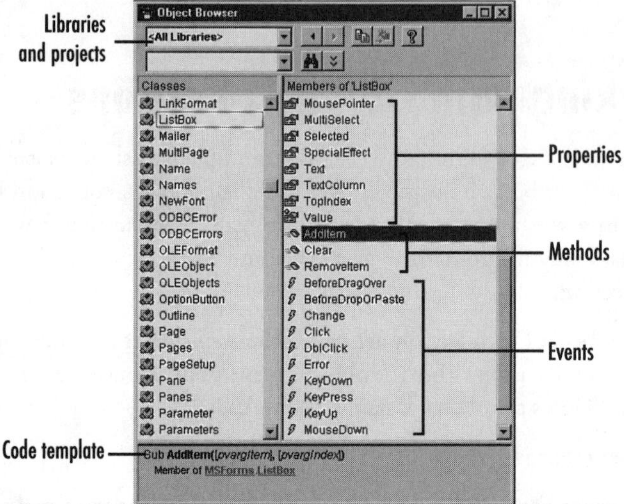

FIGURE 4.3.
VBA's Object Browser.

Object Browser Features

Here's a rundown of the Object Browser's features:

Libraries and projects: This drop-down list contains all the libraries and projects referenced by any module in the current document. A *library* is a file that contains information about the objects in an application. You'll usually see several libraries in this list—for example, the library for the current application, which lists the application objects you can use in your code; the VBA library, which lists the functions and language constructs specific to VBA; and the MSForms library, which contains objects related to building user forms (see Chapter 11, "Working with Microsoft Forms").

Search text: You can use this text box to enter a search string.

Classes: When you select a library, the Classes list shows the available object classes in the library. If you select a VBA project instead, the Classes list shows objects in the project.

Members: When you highlight a class in the Classes list, the Members list shows the methods, properties, and events available for that class. (Each member type has a different icon; see Figure 4.3.) When you highlight a module, Members shows the procedures contained in the module. To move to one of these procedures, double-click it.

Code template: The bottom of the Object Browser window displays code templates that you can paste into your modules. These templates list the method, property, event, or function name followed by the appropriate named arguments, if there are any. You can paste this template into a procedure and then edit the template. (Note, too, that the code template area also includes hyperlinks to related topics. Click one of these links to display the topic.)

Working with the Object Browser

The point of the Object Browser is to give you an easy way to see the available objects in a given library, as well as view the various properties, methods, and events associated with each object. But the Object Browser is more than just an information resource, because you can also use it to learn more about VBA as well as take some of the drudgery out of coding. Here's a quick list of a few techniques you can use with the Object Browser:

Control the Members list: The Members list has two views: grouped (all the properties, methods, and events together) and alphabetical. To toggle between these views, right-click the Object Browser and choose the Group Members command.

Search the objects: As I mentioned earlier, you can enter search text to look for specific items. Once you enter your text, use the following Object Browser buttons:

Click this button to begin the search. VBA expands the Object Browser dialog box to show the search results (see Figure 4.4). Click an item to display it in the Members list.

Click this button to hide the list of found search items.

Click this button to display the list of found search items.

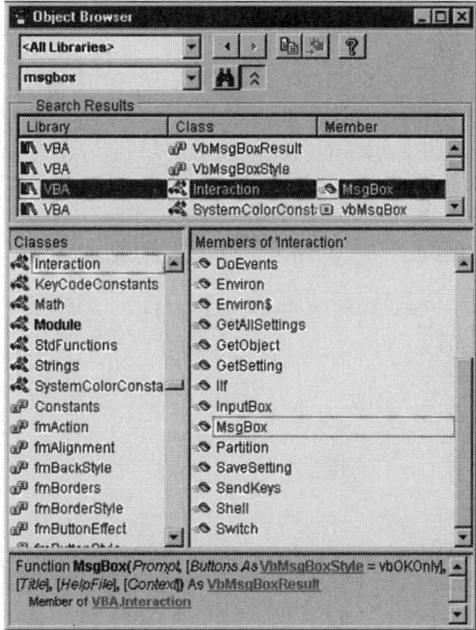

FIGURE 4.4.
When you search, the Object Browser displays an extra panel that shows the matching items.

TIP: WHOLE-WORD SEARCHES

If you would prefer that VBA match only whole words in your searches, right-click the Object Browser and activate the Find Whole Word Only command.

Browse the objects: You can use the following buttons to move back and forth through the members you've highlighted in the current Object Browser session:

Click this button to move backward through the members you've looked at.

Click this button to move forward through the members you've looked at.

Copy an item: For members with long names, you can use the Object Browser's Copy feature to copy the member name to the Clipboard for easy pasting into your procedures. To use this feature, highlight the member and then either right-click the Object Browser and click Copy, or click the Copy button.

Get help for an item: If you would like to know more about the highlighted member or class, you can invoke the Help system topic for that item. To do this, either right-click the Object Browser and click Help, or click the Help button.

Referencing Additional Object Libraries

The default list of libraries that you see in the Object Browser is by no means a complete list. Depending on the applications and controls installed on your system, dozens of object libraries might be available. You saw in Chapter 1, "Introducing VBA," that you need to set up a reference to another VBA project in order to use procedures from that project. It's the same with object libraries: to use their objects, you must first set up a reference to the appropriate library file. (And, yes, the library will then appear in the Object Browser's list of libraries and projects.) Here are the steps to follow:

1. Either select Tools | References or right-click the Object Browser and choose References from the context menu. VBA displays the References dialog box.
2. In the Available References list, activate the check box for each object library you want to use.
3. Click OK to return to the Visual Basic Editor.

Assigning an Object to a Variable

As you learned in Chapter 2, "Understanding Variables," you can declare a variable as an `Object` data type by using the following form of the `Dim` statement:

```
Dim variableName As Object
```

Once you've set up your object variable, you can assign an object to it by using the `Set` statement. `Set` has the following syntax:

```
Set variableName = ObjectName
```

variableName	The name of the variable.
ObjectName	The object you want to assign to the variable.

For example, the following statements declare a variable named `budgetSheet` to be an `Object` and then assigns it to the `1997 Budget` worksheet in the Budget.xls workbook:

```
Dim budgetSheet As Object
Set budgetSheet = Workbooks("Budget.xls").Worksheets("1997 Budget")
```

TIP: DECLARE SPECIFIC OBJECT TYPES

For faster performance, use specific object types instead of the generic `Object` type in your `Dim` statements. For example, the following statement declares the `budgetSheet` variable to be of type `Worksheet`:

```
Dim budgetSheet As Worksheet
```

NOTE: RECLAIMING OBJECT MEMORY

Object variables take up memory. For optimum code performance, you can reclaim the memory used by unneeded object variables by setting the variable equal to `Nothing`:

```
Set budgetSheet = Nothing
```


The `Is` Operator

When we looked at comparison operators in the last chapter, the operands we used were simple numbers and strings. Indeed, most of the comparison operators don't make sense in the context of objects (for example, it's absurd to think of one object as being "greater than" another). However, VBA does have a comparison operator specifically for objects—the `Is` operator:

```
result = Object1 Is Object2
```

Here, ***Object1*** and ***Object2*** are objects or `Object` variables. If they are the same, *`result`* takes the value `True`; otherwise, *`result`* is `False`.

Working with Multiple Properties or Methods

Because most objects have many different properties and methods, you'll often need to perform multiple actions on a single object. You can do this easily with multiple statements that set the appropriate properties or run the necessary methods. However, this can be a pain if you have a long object name.

For example, take a look at the `FormatRange` procedure, shown in Listing 4.1. This procedure formats a range in the `Sheet1` worksheet with six statements. The `Range` object name—`Worksheets("Sheet1").Range("B2:B5")`—is quite long and is repeated in all six statements.

Listing 4.1. A procedure that formats a range.

```
Sub FormatRange()
    Worksheets("Sheet1").Range("B2:B5").Style = "Currency"
    Worksheets("Sheet1").Range("B2:B5").WrapText = True
    Worksheets("Sheet1").Range("B2:B5").Font.Size = 16
    Worksheets("Sheet1").Range("B2:B5").Font.Bold = True
    Worksheets("Sheet1").Range("B2:B5").Font.Color = RGB(255, 0, 0) ' Red
    Worksheets("Sheet1").Range("B2:B5").Font.Name = "Times New Roman"
End Sub
```

NOTE: THIS CHAPTER'S CODE LISTINGS

You'll find the code for Listing 4.1, as well as all the other procedures in this chapter, on this book's CD. Look for either Chaptr04.xls or Chaptr04.bas.

NOTE: THE RGB FUNCTION

When you want to specify colors in VBA, use the `RGB` function:

`RGB(`***`red, green, blue`***`)`

red	An integer value between 0 and 255 that represents the red component of the color.
green	An integer value between 0 and 255 that represents the green component of the color.
blue	An integer value between 0 and 255 that represents the blue component of the color.

To shorten this procedure, VBA provides the `With` statement. Here's the syntax:

```
With object
    [statements]
End With
```

object	The name of the object.
statements	The statements you want to execute on ***object***.

The idea is that you strip out the common object and place it on the `With` line. Then all the statements between `With` and `End With` need only reference a specific method or property of that object. In the `FormatRange` procedure, the common object in all six statements is `Worksheets("Sheet1").Range("B2:B5")`. Listing 4.2 shows the `FormatRange2` procedure, which uses the `With` statement to strip out this common object and make the previous macro more efficient.

Listing 4.2. A more efficient version of `FormatRange()`.

```
Sub FormatRange2()
    With Worksheets("Sheet1").Range("B2:B5")
         .Style = "Currency"
         .WrapText = True
         .Font.Size = 16
         .Font.Bold = True
         .Font.Color = RGB(255, 0, 0) 'Red
         .Font.Name = "Times New Roman"
    End With
End Sub
```

NOTE: NESTING WITH STATEMENTS

You can make the `FormatRange2` procedure even more efficient when you realize that the `Font` object also is repeated several times. In this case, you can nest another `With` statement inside the original one. The new `With` statement would look like this:

```
With .Font
     .Size = 16
     .Bold = True
     .Color = RGB(255, 0, 0)
     .Name = "Times New Roman"
End With
```

The Application Object

You'll be seeing plenty of objects when we turn our attention to Microsoft Office 97 in Part II, "Unleashing Microsoft Office Objects." For now, though, let's take a look at an object that is common to all programs: the `Application` object. The `Application` object refers to the application as a whole; therefore, it acts as a container for all of the program's objects. However, the `Application` object does have a few useful properties and methods of its own, and many of these members are applicable to all the Office applications.

Properties of the Application Object

The `Application` object has dozens of properties that affect a number of aspects of the program's environment. For starters, any control in the application's Options dialog box (select Tools | Options) has an equivalent `Application` object property. For example, the `StatusBar` property takes a `True` or `False` value that toggles the status bar on or off.

Here's a rundown of a few other `Application` object properties you'll use most often in your VBA code:

`Application.ActivePrinter`: Returns or sets the name of the application's current printer driver.

`ActiveWindow`: Returns a Window object that represents the window that currently has the focus.

`Application.Caption`: Returns or sets the name that appears in the title bar of the main application window. In Excel, for example, to change the title bar caption from "Microsoft Excel" to "ACME Coyote Supplies," you would use the following statement:

```
Application.Caption = "ACME Coyote Supplies"
```

`Application.Dialogs`: Returns the collection of all the application's built-in dialog boxes. See Chapter 10 to learn how to display these dialog boxes from your VBA procedures.

`Application.DisplayAlerts`: Determines whether or not the application displays alert dialog boxes. For example, if your code deletes an Excel worksheet, Excel normally displays an alert box asking you to confirm the deletion. To suppress this alert box and force Excel to accept the default action (which is, in this case, deleting the sheet), set the `DisplayAlerts` property to `False`.

NOTE: ALERTS ARE RESTORED AUTOMATICALLY

The application restores the `DisplayAlerts` property to its default state (`True`) when your procedure finishes. If you would prefer to turn the alerts back on before then, set the `DisplayAlerts` property to `True`.

`Application.Height`: Returns or sets the height, in points, of the application window.

`Application.Left`: Returns or sets the distance, in points, of the left edge of the application window from the left edge of the screen.

`Application.Path`: Returns the path of the `Application` object. In other words, it tells you the drive and folder where the application's executable file resides (such as C:\Program Files\Microsoft Office\Office). Note that the returned path doesn't include a trailing backslash (\).

`Application.ScreenUpdating`: Returns or sets the application's screen updating. When `ScreenUpdating` is set to `True` (the default), the user sees the results of all your code actions: cut-and-paste operations, drawing objects added or deleted, formatting, and so on. Applications look more professional (and are noticeably faster) if the user just sees the end result of all these actions. To do this, turn off screen updating (by setting the `ScreenUpdating` property to `False`), perform the actions, and turn screen updating back on.

`Application.Top`: Returns or sets the distance, in points, of the top of the application window from the top of the screen.

`Application.UsableHeight`: The maximum height, in points, that a window can occupy within the application's window. In other words, this is the height of the application window less the vertical space taken up by the title bar, menu bar, toolbars, status bar, and so on.

`Application.UsableWidth`: The maximum width, in points, that a window can occupy within the application's window. This is the width of the application window less the horizontal space taken up by items such as the vertical scroll bar.

`Application.Version`: Returns the version number of the application.

`Application.Visible`: A `Boolean` value that either hides the application (`False`) or displays the application (`True`).

`Application.Width`: Returns or sets the width, in points, of the application window.

`Application.Windows`: The collection of all the application's open Window objects.

`Application.WindowState`: Returns or sets the state of the main application window. This property is controlled via three built-in constants that vary between applications:

Window State	*Excel*	*Word*	*PowerPoint*
Maximized	`xlMaximized`	`wdWindowStateMaximize`	`ppWindowMximized`
Minimized	`xlMinimized`	`wdWindowStateMinimize`	`ppWindowMinimized`
Normal	`xlNormal`	`wdWindowStateNormal`	`ppWindowNormal`

Methods of the `Application` Object

The `Application` object features a few dozen methods that perform actions on the program's environment. Here's a summary of the most common methods:

`Application.CheckSpelling`: When used with the Word or Excel `Application` object, the `CheckSpelling` method checks the spelling of a single word using the following syntax (note that Word's method has a few extra arguments):

`Application.CheckSpelling(`***`word`***`,`*`customDictionary`*`,`*`ignoreUppercase`*`)`

`word`	The word you want to check.
`customDictionary`	The filename of a custom dictionary that the application can search if ***`word`*** wasn't found in the main dictionary.
`ignoreUppercase`	Set to `True` to tell the application to ignore words entirely in uppercase.

For example, the code shown in Listing 4.3 gets a word from the user, checks the spelling, and tells the user whether or not the word is spelled correctly. (You also can use this property with a Document, Worksheet, or Range object, as described in Chapter 6, "Word for Windows VBA Programming," and Chapter 7, "Manipulating Excel with VBA." Also, see Chapter 10 to learn more about the `InputBox` function.)

Listing 4.3. A procedure that checks the spelling of an entered word.

```
Sub SpellCheckTest()
    Dim word2Check As String, result As Boolean
    word2Check = InputBox("Enter a word:")
    result = Application.CheckSpelling(word2Check)
    If result = True Then
        MsgBox "'" & word2Check & "' is spelled correctly!"
    Else
        MsgBox "Oops! '" & word2Check & "' is spelled incorrectly."
    End If
End Sub
```

`Application.EnableCancelKey`: This property controls what the application does when the user presses Esc (or Ctrl-Break), which, under normal circumstances, interrupts the running procedure. If you don't want the user to interrupt a critical section of code, you can disable the Esc key (and Ctrl-Break) by setting the `EnableCancelKey` property to `xlDisabled`. (Note that I'm using the Excel constants here; see the Object Browser for the appropriate constants in other applications.) To restore interrupts to their default state, set the `EnableCancelKey` property to `xlInterrupt`. You can also set `EnableCancelKey` to `xlErrorHandler` to run an error handler routine established by the `On Error Go To` statement. For details on the `On Error Go To` statement, see Chapter 23, "Trapping Program Errors."

CAUTION: LEAVE ESC ENABLED DURING TESTING

Wield the `EnableCancelKey` property with care. If you disable the Esc key and your code ends up in an infinite loop, there's no way to shut down the procedure short of shutting down Excel itself. Therefore, while you're testing and building your application, you should always make sure the `EnableCancelKey` property is set to `True`.

`Application.Help`: Displays the application's Help system.

`Application.Quit`: Quits the application. If there are any open documents with unsaved changes, the application will ask if you want to save the changes. To prevent this, either save the documents before running the `Quit` method (I'll tell you how to do this in the appropriate chapters in Part II), or set the `DisplayAlerts` property to `False`. (In the latter case, note that the application will *not* save changes to the workbooks. Also, Word's version of `Quit` accepts an argument that specifies whether or not to save changes.)

`Application.Repeat`: Repeats the user's last action. This is equivalent to selecting Edit | Repeat.

The Window Object

Another object that's common to almost all applications is the Window object, which represents an open window in an application. Note that this isn't the same as an open document. Rather, the Window object is just a container for a document, so the associated properties and methods have no effect on the document data. You can use VBA to change the window state (maximized or minimized), size and move windows, navigate open windows, and much more. In the next section I'll show you how to specify a Window object in your code; we'll also look at some Window object properties and methods.

Specifying a Window Object

If you need to perform some action on a window or change a window's properties, you need to tell the application which window you want to use. VBA gives you two ways to do this:

Use the `Windows` object: The `Windows` object is the collection of all the open windows in the application. To specify a window, either use its index number (as given by the numbers beside the windows on the application's Windows menu) or enclose the window caption (in other words, the text that appears in the window's title bar) in quotation marks. For example, if the `Budget.xls` window is listed first in the Window menu, the following two statements would be equivalent:

```
Windows(1)
Windows("Budget.xls")
```

Use the `ActiveWindow` object: The `ActiveWindow` object represents the window that currently has the focus.

Opening a New Window

If you need to create a new window, use the Window object's `NewWindow` method:

`Window``.NewWindow`

`Window` The Window object from which you want to create the new window.

Note that this argument is optional in some applications. In Word, for example, if you omit ***`Window`***, the active window is used.

Window Object Properties

Here's a rundown of some common properties associated with Window objects:

`Window``.Caption`: Returns or sets the text that appears in the title bar of the specified *`Window`*.

`Window``.Height`: Returns or sets the height, in points, of the specified *`Window`*.

`Window``.Left`: Returns or sets the distance, in points, of the left edge of the specified *`Window`* from the left edge of the application window.

`Window``.Top`: Returns or sets the distance, in points, of the top of the specified *`Window`* from the top of the application window.

`Window``.UsableHeight`: The maximum height, in points, that data can occupy within the specified *`Window`*.

`Window``.UsableWidth`: The maximum width, in points, that data can occupy within the specified *`Window`*.

`Window.Visible`: A `Boolean` value that either hides the specified *`Window`* (`False`) or displays the *`Window`* (`True`).

`Window.Width`: Returns or sets the width, in points, of the specified *`Window`*.

`Window.WindowNumber`: Returns the window number of the specified *`Window`*. For example, a window named `Chaptr04.xls:2` has window number 2.

`Window.WindowState`: Returns or sets the state of the specified *`Window`*. See the earlier discussion of the `Application.WindowState` property for a list of the constants that control this property.

Window Object Methods

Window objects have a few methods that you can use to control your windows programmatically. Here are a few methods that you'll use most often:

`Window.Activate`: Activates the specified open *`Window`*. For example, the following statement activates the `Finances.xls` window:

```
Windows("Finances.xls").Activate
```

`Window.Close`: Closes the specified *`Window`*.

`Window.LargeScroll`: Scrolls through the specified *`Window`* by screens, using the following syntax:

```
Window.LargeScroll(Down, Up, ToRight, ToLeft)
```

`Window`	The Window object you want to scroll through.
`Down`	The number of screens to scroll down.
`Up`	The number of screens to scroll up.
`ToRight`	The number of screens to scroll to the right.
`ToLeft`	The number of screens to scroll to the left.

`Window.SmallScroll`: Scrolls through the specified *`Window`* by lines, using the following syntax:

```
Window.SmallScroll(Down, Up, ToRight, ToLeft)
```

The arguments are the same as those in the `LargeScroll` method.

Summary

This chapter discussed the all-important topic of objects and how to work with them in your VBA procedures. After some introductory information on objects and the object hierarchy, you learned about the three types of members of any object class: properties, methods, and events. I also showed you how to use the Object Browser, how to assign objects to variables, how to wield the `Is` operator, and how to work with multiple properties and methods. I closed this chapter with a look at the properties and methods of the `Application` and Window objects. Here's a list of chapters where you'll find related information:

- The `With...End With` statement is an example of a VBA control structure. I'll discuss a few more of these control structures in Chapter 5, "Controlling Your VBA Code."
- Part II, "Unleashing Microsoft Office Objects," is a veritable "object fest" as I examine the object hierarchies in the Office applications.
- Tables, queries, and other database-related items have their own object hierarchy called Data Access Objects. You'll learn how to work with this model in Chapter 18, "Programming Data Access Objects."
- You can create your own "objects" by setting up class modules. To find out how it's done, see Chapter 26, "VBA Tips and Techniques."

CHAPTER 5

Controlling Your VBA Code

IN THIS CHAPTER

In a minute there is time
For decisions and revisions which a minute will reverse.

—*T. S. Eliot*

One of the advantages of writing your own VBA procedures instead of simply recording them is that you end up with much more control over what your code does and how it performs its tasks. In particular, you can create procedures that make *decisions* based on certain conditions and that can perform *loops*—the running of several statements repeatedly. The statements that handle this kind of processing—*control structures*—are the subject of this chapter.

Code That Makes Decisions

A smart procedure performs tests on its environment and then decides what to do next based on the results of each test. For example, suppose you've written a Function procedure that uses one of its arguments as a divisor in a formula. You should test the argument before using it in the formula to make sure that it isn't 0 (to avoid producing a `Division by zero` error). If it is, you could then display a message that alerts the user to the illegal argument.

Similarly, a well-designed application will interact with the user and ask for feedback in the form of extra information or a confirmation of a requested action. The program can then take this feedback and redirect itself accordingly.

Using `If...Then` to Make True/False Decisions

The most basic form of decision is the simple true/false decision (which could also be seen as a yes/no or an on/off decision). In this case, your program looks at a certain condition, determines whether it is currently true or false, and acts accordingly. As you might expect from the discussion of expressions in Chapter 3, "Building VBA Expressions," logical expressions (which, you'll recall, always return a `True` or `False` result) play a big part here.

In VBA, simple true/false decisions are handled by the `If...Then` statement. You can use either the *single-line* syntax:

```
If condition Then statement
```

or the *block* syntax:

```
If condition Then
    [statements]
End If
```

`condition`	You can use a logical expression that returns `True` or `False`, or you can use any expression that returns a numeric value. In the latter case, a return value of zero is functionally equivalent to `False`, and any nonzero value is equivalent to `True`.
`statement(s)`	The VBA statement or statements to run if *`condition`* returns `True`. If *`condition`* returns `False`, VBA skips over the statements.

Whether you use the single-line or block syntax depends on the statements you want to run if the *`condition`* returns a `True` result. If you have only one statement, you can use either syntax. If you have multiple statements, you must use the block syntax.

Listing 5.1 shows a revised version of the `GrossMargin` procedure from Chapter 2, "Understanding Variables." This version—called `GrossMargin2`—uses `If...Then` to check the `totalSales` variable. The procedure calculates the gross margin only if `totalSales` isn't zero.

Listing 5.1. An `If...Then` example.

```
Function GrossMargin2()
    Dim totalSales
    Dim totalExpenses
    totalSales = Application.Sum(Range("Sales"))
    totalExpenses = Application.Sum(Range("Expenses"))
    If totalSales <> 0 Then
        GrossMargin2 = (totalSales - totalExpenses) / totalSales
    End If
End Function
```

NOTE: THIS CHAPTER'S CODE LISTINGS

You'll find the `GrossMargin2` procedure (as well as all the procedures listed in this chapter) on the CD that is included with this book. Use either the file Chaptr05.xls or the file Chaptr05.bas.

TIP: YOU DON'T NEED TO TEST FOR ZERO

You can make the `If...Then` statement in the `GrossMargin2` procedure slightly more efficient by taking advantage of the fact that in the condition, zero is equivalent to `False` and any other number is equivalent to `True`. This means you don't have to explicitly test the `totalSales` variable to see whether it's zero. Instead, you can use the following statements:

```
If totalSales Then
    GrossMargin = (totalSales-totalExpenses)/totalSales
End If
```

continues

continued

On the other hand, many programmers feel that including the explicit test for a nonzero value (`totalSales <> 0`) makes the procedure easier to read and more intuitive. Since in this case the efficiency gained is only minor, you're probably better off leaving in the full expression.

Using If...Then...Else to Handle a False Result

Using the `If...Then` statement to make decisions adds a powerful new weapon to your VBA arsenal. However, this technique suffers from an important drawback: A `False` result only bypasses one or more statements; it doesn't execute any of its own. This is fine in many cases, but there will be times when you need to run one group of statements if the condition returns `True` and a different group if the result is `False`. To handle this, you need to use an `If...Then...Else` statement:

```
If condition Then
   [TrueStatements]
Else
   [FalseStatements]
End If
```

`condition`	The logical expression that returns `True` or `False`.
`TrueStatements`	The statements to run if *`condition`* returns `True`.
`FalseStatements`	The statements to run if *`condition`* returns `False`.

If the *`condition`* returns `True`, VBA runs the group of statements between `If...Then` and `Else`. If it returns `False`, VBA runs the group of statements between `Else` and `End If`.

Let's look at an example. Suppose you want to calculate the future value of a series of regular deposits, but you want to differentiate between monthly deposits and quarterly deposits. Listing 5.2 shows a Function procedure called `FutureValue` that does the job.

Listing 5.2. A procedure that uses `If...Then...Else`.

```
Function FutureValue(Rate, Nper, Pmt, Frequency)
    If Frequency = "Monthly" Then
        FutureValue = FV(Rate / 12, Nper * 12, Pmt / 12)
    Else
        FutureValue = FV(Rate / 4, Nper * 4, Pmt / 4)
    End If
End Function
```

The first three arguments—Rate, Nper, and Pmt—are, respectively, the annual interest rate, the number of years in the term of the investment, and the total deposit available annually. The fourth argument—Frequency—is either Monthly or Quarterly. The idea is to adjust the first three arguments based on the Frequency. To do that, the If...Then...Else statement runs a test on the Frequency argument:

```
If Frequency = "Monthly" Then
```

If the logical expression Frequency = "Monthly" returns True, the procedure divides the interest rate by 12, multiplies the term by 12, and divides the annual deposit by 12. Otherwise, a quarterly calculation is assumed, and the procedure divides the interest rate by 4, multiplies the term by 4, and divides the annual deposit by 4. In both cases, VBA's FV function (see Chapter 3) is used to return the future value. (In Chaptr05.xls on the CD, the Sheet1 worksheet shows an example of this function at work.)

TIP: INDENT STATEMENTS FOR EASIER READABILITY

If...Then...Else statements are much easier to read when you indent the expressions between If...Then, Else, and End If, as I've done in Listing 5.2. This lets you easily identify which group of statements will be run if there is a True result and which group will be run if the result is False. Pressing the Tab key once at the beginning of the first line in the block does the job.

Making Multiple Decisions

The problem with If...Then...Else is that normally you can make only a single decision. The statement calculates a single logical result and performs one of two actions. However, plenty of situations require multiple decisions before you can decide which action to take.

For example, the FutureValue procedure discussed in the preceding section probably should test the Frequency argument to make sure it's either Monthly or Quarterly and not something else. The next few sections show you three solutions to this problem.

Using the And and Or Operators

One solution to our multiple-decision problem is to combine multiple logical expressions in a single If...Then statement. From Chapter 3, you'll recall that you can combine logical expressions by using VBA's And and Or operators. In our example, we want to calculate the future value only if the Frequency argument is either Monthly *or* Quarterly. The following If...Then statement uses the And operator to test this:

```
If Frequency <> "Monthly" And Frequency <> "Quarterly" Then
```

If Frequency doesn't equal either of these values, the entire condition returns `True`, and the procedure can return a message to the user, as shown in Listing 5.3.

Listing 5.3. A procedure that uses the And operator to perform multiple logical tests.

```
Function FutureValue2(Rate, Nper, Pmt, Frequency)
    If Frequency <> "Monthly" And Frequency <> "Quarterly" Then
        MsgBox "The Frequency argument must be either " & _
               """Monthly"" or ""Quarterly""!"
        Exit Function
    End If
    If Frequency = "Monthly" Then
        FutureValue2 = FV(Rate / 12, Nper * 12, Pmt / 12)
    Else
        FutureValue2 = FV(Rate / 4, Nper * 4, Pmt / 4)
    End If
End Function
```

Note that this procedure isn't particularly efficient, because you end up testing the `Frequency` argument in two places. However, that just means that this example isn't the best use of the `And` and `Or` operators. The overall principle of using these operators to perform multiple logical tests is a useful one, however, and you should keep it in mind when constructing your decision-making code.

NOTE: EXITING A PROCEDURE PREMATURELY

In Listing 5.3, note the use of the `Exit Function` statement. You use this statement whenever you want a function to bail out before it reaches the `End Function` statement. Similarly, if you want to exit a Sub procedure before reaching `End Sub`, use the `Exit Sub` statement.

Using Multiple If...Then...Else Statements

There is a third syntax for the `If...Then...Else` statement that lets you string together as many logical tests as you need:

```
If condition1 Then
   [condition1 TrueStatements]
ElseIf condition2
   [condition2 TrueStatements]
<etc.>
Else
   [FalseStatements]
End If
```

condition1	A logical expression.
condition1 TrueStatements	The statements to run if *condition1* returns True.
condition2	A different logical expression.
condition1 TrueStatements	The statements to run if *condition2* returns True.
FalseStatements	The statements to run if both *condition1* and *condition2* return False.

VBA first tests *condition1*. If this returns True, VBA runs the group of statements between If...Then and ElseIf...Then. If it returns False, VBA then tests *condition2*. If this test is True, VBA runs the group of statements between ElseIf...Then and Else. Otherwise, VBA runs the statements between Else and End If.

Listing 5.4 shows FutureValue3, a revised version of FutureValue that makes allowances for an improper Frequency argument.

Listing 5.4. A procedure that uses multiple If...Then...Else statements.

```
Function FutureValue3(Rate, Nper, Pmt, Frequency)
    If Frequency = "Monthly" Then
        FutureValue3 = FV(Rate / 12, Nper * 12, Pmt / 12)
    ElseIf Frequency = "Quarterly" Then
        FutureValue3 = FV(Rate / 4, Nper * 4, Pmt / 4)
    Else
        MsgBox "The Frequency argument must be either " & _
               """Monthly"" or ""Quarterly""!"
    End If
End Function
```

As before, the If...Then statement checks to see if Frequency equals Monthly and, if it does, calculates the future value accordingly. If it doesn't, the ElseIf...Then statement checks to see if Frequency equals Quarterly and calculates the future value if the expression returns True. If it returns False, the user entered the Frequency argument incorrectly, so a warning message is displayed.

Using the Select Case Statement

Performing multiple tests with If...ElseIf is a handy technique—it's a VBA tool you'll reach for quite often. However, it quickly becomes unwieldy as the number of tests you need to make gets larger. It's okay for two or three tests, but any more than that makes the logic harder to follow.

For these situations, VBA's Select Case statement is a better choice. The idea is that you provide a logical expression at the beginning and then list a series of possible results. For each possible result—called a *case*—you provide one or more VBA statements to execute should the case prove to be true. Here's the syntax:

```
Select Case TestExpression
   Case FirstCaseList
      [FirstStatements]
    Case SecondCaseList
       [SecondStatements]
    <etc.>
    Case Else
       [ElseStatements]
End Select
```

`TestExpression` This expression is evaluated at the beginning of the structure. It must return a value (logical, numeric, string, and so on).

`CaseList` A list of one or more possible results for `TestExpression`. These results are values or expressions separated by commas. VBA examines each element in the list to see whether one matches the `TestExpression`. The expressions can take any one of the following forms:

`Expression`

`Expression To Expression`

`Is LogicalOperator Expression`

The `To` keyword defines a range of values (for example, `1 To 10`). The `Is` keyword defines an open-ended range of values (for example, `Is >= 100`).

`Statements` These are the statements VBA runs if any part of the associated `CaseList` matches the `TestExpression`. VBA runs the optional `ElseStatements` if no `CaseList` contains a match for the `TestExpression`.

NOTE: HANDLING MULTIPLE MATCHES

If more than one `CaseList` contains an element that matches the `TestExpression`, VBA runs only the statements associated with the `CaseList` that appears *first* in the `Select Case` structure.

Listing 5.5 shows how you would use `Select Case` to handle the `Frequency` argument problem.

Listing 5.5. A procedure that uses `Select Case` to test multiple values.

```
Function FutureValue4(Rate, Nper, Pmt, Frequency)
    Select Case Frequency
        Case "Monthly"
            FutureValue4 = FV(Rate / 12, Nper * 12, Pmt / 12)
        Case "Quarterly"
            FutureValue4 = FV(Rate / 4, Nper * 4, Pmt / 4)
        Case Else
            MsgBox "The Frequency argument must be either " & _
```

```
                    """Monthly"" or ""Quarterly""!"
    End Select
End Function
```

A Select Case Example: Converting Test Scores to Letter Grades

To help you get a better feel for the `Select Case` statement, let's take a look at another example that better showcases the unique talents of this powerful structure. Suppose you want to write a procedure that converts a raw test score into a letter grade according to the following table:

Raw Score	*Letter Grade*
80 and over	A
Between 70 and 79	B
Between 60 and 69	C
Between 50 and 59	D
Less than 50	F

Listing 5.6 shows the `LetterGrade` procedure, which uses a `Select Case` statement to make the conversion.

Listing 5.6. A procedure that uses `Select Case` to convert a raw test score into a letter grade.

```
Function LetterGrade(rawScore As Integer) As String
    Select Case rawScore
        Case Is < 0
            LetterGrade = "ERROR! Score less than 0!"
        Case Is < 50
            LetterGrade = "F"
        Case Is < 60
            LetterGrade = "D"
        Case Is < 70
            LetterGrade = "C"
        Case Is < 80
            LetterGrade = "B"
        Case Is <= 100
            LetterGrade = "A"
        Case Else
            LetterGrade = "ERROR! Score greater than 100!"
    End Select
End Function
```

The `rawScore` argument is an integer value between 0 and 100. The `Select Case` structure first checks to see if `rawScore` is negative and, if so, the function returns an error message. The next `Case` statement checks to see if the score is less than 50, and the function returns the letter grade "F" if it is. The next `Case` statement looks for a score that is less than 60. If we get this far, we already know (thanks to the preceding `Case` statement) that the score is at least 50. Therefore, this case is really checking to see if the score is between 50 and 60 (including 50, but not including 60). If so, the letter grade "D" is returned. The rest of the `Case` statements proceed in the same manner. The `Case Else` checks for a score greater than 100 and returns another error message if it is.

Another Example: Taming the RGB Function

I mentioned briefly in the last chapter that you can use the `RGB(`***`red,green,blue`***`)` VBA function anytime you need to specify a color for a property. Each of the three named arguments (***`red`***, ***`green`***, and ***`blue`***) are integers between 0 and 255 that determine how much of each component color is mixed into the final color. In the ***`red`*** component, for example, 0 means no red is present, and 255 means that pure red is present. If all three values are the same, you get a shade of gray.

Here are some sample values for each component that produce common colors:

Red	*Green*	*Blue*	*Result*
0	0	0	Black
0	0	255	Blue
0	255	0	Green
0	255	255	Cyan
255	0	0	Red
255	0	255	Magenta
255	255	0	Yellow
255	255	255	White

However, rather than memorize these combinations, let's put VBA and `Select Case` to work to make choosing colors easier. Listing 5.7 shows the `VBAColor` function, which lets you set 16 of the most common colors using names (for example, "red" or "blue") rather than cryptic number combinations.

Listing 5.7. A function that accepts a color name as a string and returns the corresponding RGB value.

```
Function VBAColor(colorName As String) As Long

    Select Case LCase$(Trim$(colorName))
        Case "black"
            VBAColor = RGB(0, 0, 0)
        Case "white"
            VBAColor = RGB(255, 255, 255)
        Case "gray"
            VBAColor = RGB(192, 192, 192)
        Case "dark gray"
            VBAColor = RGB(128, 128, 128)
```

```
        Case "red"
            VBAColor = RGB(255, 0, 0)
        Case "dark red"
            VBAColor = RGB(128, 0, 0)
        Case "green"
            VBAColor = RGB(0, 255, 0)
        Case "dark green"
            VBAColor = RGB(0, 128, 0)
        Case "blue"
            VBAColor = RGB(0, 0, 255)
        Case "dark blue"
            VBAColor = RGB(0, 0, 128)
        Case "yellow"
            VBAColor = RGB(255, 255, 0)
        Case "dark yellow"
            VBAColor = RGB(128, 128, 0)
        Case "magenta"
            VBAColor = RGB(255, 0, 255)
        Case "dark magenta"
            VBAColor = RGB(128, 0, 128)
        Case "cyan"
            VBAColor = RGB(0, 255, 255)
        Case "dark cyan"
            VBAColor = RGB(0, 128, 128)
    End Select
End Function
Sub ColorTester()
    ActiveCell.Font.Color = VBAColor("red")
End Sub
```

VBAColor takes a single argument, colorName, which is the name of the color you want to work with. Notice how the Select Case statement massages the argument to prevent errors:

```
Select Case LCase$(Trim$(colorName))
```

The Trim$ function removes any extraneous spaces at the beginning and end of the argument, and the LCase$ function converts colorName to lowercase. This ensures that the function is case-insensitive, which means that whether you send black, BLACK, or Black, the function will still work.

The rest of the function uses Case statements to check for the various color names and return the appropriate RGB value. You can use the ColorTester procedure to give VBAColor a whirl. This procedure just formats the font color of the currently selected worksheet cell.

NOTE: VBA'S COLOR CONSTANTS

VBA also defines eight color constants that you can use when you just need the basic colors: vbBlack, vbBlue, vbCyan, vbGreen, vbMagenta, vbRed, vbWhite, and vbYellow.

Functions That Make Decisions

Much of what we're talking about in this chapter involves ways to make your procedures cleaner and more efficient. These are laudable goals for a whole host of reasons, but the following are the main ones:

- Your code will execute faster.
- You'll have less code to type.
- Your code will be easier to read and maintain.

This section looks at three powerful VBA functions that can increase the efficiency of your procedures.

The `IIf` Function

You've seen how the decision-making prowess of the `If...Then...Else` structure lets you create "intelligent" procedures that can respond appropriately to different situations. However, sometimes `If...Then...Else` just isn't efficient. For example, suppose you want to test the computer on which your code is running to see if it has a flawed Pentium chip. (Some older Pentium processors contain a bug in their floating-point unit that causes incorrect calculations in some rare circumstances.) Here's a code fragment that includes an `If...Then...Else` structure that performs this test:

```
Dim flawedPentium As Boolean
If (4195835 - (4195835/3145727) * 3145727) <> 0 Then
    flawedPentium = True
Else
    flawedPentium = False
End If
```

VBA 5.0

As it stands, there is nothing wrong with this code. However, it seems like a lot of work to go through just to assign a value to a variable. For these types of situations, VBA 5.0 has a new `IIf` function that's more efficient. `IIf`, which stands for "inline `If`," performs a simple `If` test on a single line:

```
IIf (condition, TrueResult, FalseResult)
```

`condition`	A logical expression that returns `True` or `False`.
`TrueResult`	The value returned by the function if ***`condition`*** is `True`.
`FalseResult`	The value returned by the function if ***`condition`*** is `False`.

Listing 5.8 shows a function procedure that checks for a faulty Pentium machine by using `IIf` to replace the `If...Then...Else` statement shown earlier.

Listing 5.8. A function that uses IIf to test for a faulty Pentium chip.

```
Function FlawedPentium() As Boolean
    FlawedPentium = IIf((4195835 - (4195835/3145727) * 3145727), True, False)
End Function
```

If the calculation returns a nonzero value, the chip is flawed; therefore, `IIf` returns `True`. Otherwise, the chip is okay, so `IIf` returns `False`.

The Choose Function

In the preceding section, I showed you how the `IIf` function is an efficient replacement for `If...Then...Else` when all you need to do is assign a value to a variable based on the results of the test. Suppose now you have a similar situation with the `Select Case` structure. In other words, you want to test a number of possible values and assign the result to a variable.

For example, you saw in Chapter 3 that VBA's `Weekday` function returns the current day of the week as a number. What if you want to convert that number into the name of the day (convert 1 into Sunday, for example)? Here's a procedure fragment that will do it:

```
Dim weekdayName As String
Select Case Weekday(Now)
    Case 1
        weekdayName = "Sunday"
    Case 2
        weekdayName = "Monday"
    Case 3
        weekdayName = "Tuesday"
    Case 4
        weekdayName = "Wednesday"
    Case 5
        weekdayName = "Thursday"
    Case 6
        weekdayName = "Friday"
    Case 7
        weekdayName = "Saturday"
End Select
```

VBA 5.0

Again, this seems like *way* too much effort for a simple variable assignment. And, in fact, it *is* too much work now that VBA 5.0's new `Choose` function is available. `Choose` encapsulates the essence of the preceding `Select Case` structure—the test value and the various possible results—into a single statement. Here's the syntax:

```
Choose(index, value1, value2,...)
```

index	A numeric expression that determines which of the values in the list is returned. If ***index*** is 1, ***value1*** is returned. If ***index*** is 2, *value2* is returned (and so on).
value1, *value2...*	A list of values from which `Choose` selects the return value. The values can be any valid VBA expression.

Listing 5.9 shows a function called `WeekdayName` that returns the day name by using `Choose` to replace the `Select Case` structure shown earlier.

Listing 5.9. A function that uses the `Choose` function to select from a list of values.

```
Function WeekdayName(weekdayNum As Integer) As String
    WeekdayName = Choose(weekdayNum, "Sunday", "Monday", _
        "Tuesday", "Wednesday", "Thursday", "Friday", "Saturday")
End Function
```

The `Switch` Function

`Choose` is a welcome addition to the VBA function library, but its use it limited because of two constraints:

- You can use `Choose` only when the ***index*** argument is a number or a numeric expression.
- `Choose` can't handle logical expressions.

To illustrate why the last point is important, consider the `Select Case` structure used earlier in this chapter to convert a test score into a letter grade:

```
Select Case rawScore
    Case Is < 0
        LetterGrade = "ERROR! Score less than 0!"
    Case Is < 50
        LetterGrade = "F"
    Case Is < 60
        LetterGrade = "D"
    Case Is < 70
        LetterGrade = "C"
    Case Is < 80
        LetterGrade = "B"
    Case Is <= 100
        LetterGrade = "A"
    Case Else
        LetterGrade = "ERROR! Score greater than 100!"
End Select
```

At first blush, this structure seems to satisfy the same inefficiency criteria that I mentioned earlier for `If...Then...Else` and `Select Case`. In other words, each `Case` runs only a single statement, and that statement serves only to assign a value to a variable. The difference, though, is that the `Case` statements use logical expressions, so we can't use `Choose` to make this code more efficient.

VBA 5.0 However, we *can* use VBA 5.0's new `Switch` function to do the job:

```
Switch(expr1, value1, expr2, value2,...)
```

expr1, *expr2...*	These are logical expressions that determine which of the values in the list is returned. If ***expr1*** is `True`, ***value1*** is returned. If *expr2* is `True`, *value2* is returned (and so on).
value1, *value2...*	A list of values from which `Switch` selects the return value. The values can be any valid VBA expression.

`Switch` trudges through the logical expressions from left to right. When it comes across the first `True` expression, it returns the value that appears immediately after the expression. Listing 5.10 puts `Switch` to work to create a more efficient version of the `LetterGrade` function.

Listing 5.10. A procedure that uses the `Switch` function to convert a test score into a letter grade.

```
Function LetterGrade2(rawScore As Integer) As String
    LetterGrade2 = Switch( _
        rawScore < 0, "ERROR! Score less than 0!", _
        rawScore < 50, "F", _
        rawScore < 60, "D", _
        rawScore < 70, "C", _
        rawScore < 80, "B", _
        rawScore <= 100, "A", _
        rawScore > 100, "ERROR! Score greater than 100!")
End Function
```

Code That Loops

You've seen in this chapter and in previous chapters that it makes sense to divide up your VBA chores and place them in separate procedures or functions. That way, you only need to write the code once and then call it any time you need it. This is known in the trade as *modular programming*, and it saves time and effort by helping you avoid reinventing too many wheels.

There are also wheels to avoid reinventing *within* your procedures and functions. For example, consider the following code fragment:

```
MsgBox "The time is now " & Time
Application.Wait Now + TimeValue("00:00:05")
MsgBox "The time is now " & Time
Application.Wait Now + TimeValue("00:00:05")
MsgBox "The time is now " & Time
Application.Wait Now + TimeValue("00:00:05")
```

NOTE: THE WAIT METHOD

This code fragment uses the Excel `Application` object's `Wait` method to produce a delay. The argument `Now + TimeValue("00:00:05")` pauses the procedure for about five seconds before continuing.

This code does nothing more than display the time, delay for five seconds, and repeat this two more times. Besides being decidedly useless, this code just reeks of inefficiency. It's clear that a far better approach would be to take just the first two statements and somehow get VBA to repeat them as many times as necessary.

The good news is that not only is it possible to do this, but VBA also gives you a number of different methods to perform this so-called *looping*. I'll spend the rest of this chapter investigating each of these methods.

Using Do...Loop Structures

What do you do when you need to loop but you don't know in advance how many times to repeat the loop? This could happen if, for example, you want to loop only until a certain condition is met, such as encountering a blank cell in an Excel worksheet. The solution is to use a `Do...Loop`.

The `Do...Loop` has four different syntaxes:

`Do While` *`condition`* [*`statements`*] `Loop`	Checks *`condition`* before entering the loop. Executes the *`statements`* only while *`condition`* is `True`.
`Do` [*`statements`*] `Loop While` *`condition`*	Checks *`condition`* after running through the loop once. Executes the *`statements`* only while *`condition`* is `True`. Use this form when you want the loop to be processed at least once.
`Do Until` *`condition`* [*`statements`*] `Loop`	Checks *`condition`* before entering the loop. Executes the *`statements`* only while *`condition`* is `False`.
`Do` [*`statements`*] `Loop Until` *`condition`*	Checks *`condition`* after running through the loop once. Executes the *`statements`* only while *`condition`* is `False`. Again, use this form when you want the loop to be processed at least once.

Listing 5.11 shows a procedure called `BigNumbers` that runs down a worksheet column and changes the font color to magenta whenever a cell contains a number greater than or equal to 1,000.

Listing 5.11. A procedure that uses a `Do...Loop` to process cells until it encounters a blank cell.

```
Sub BigNumbers()
    Dim rowNum As Integer, colNum As Integer, currCell As Range
    rowNum = ActiveCell.Row                              'Initialize row #
    colNum = ActiveCell.Column                           'Initialize column #
```

```
    Set currCell = ActiveSheet.Cells(rowNum, colNum)     'Get first cell
    Do While currCell.Value <> ""                        'Do while not empty
        If IsNumeric(currCell.Value) Then                'If it's a number,
            If currCell.Value >= 1000 Then               'and it's a big one,
                currCell.Font.Color = VBAColor("magenta")'color font magenta
            End If
        End If
        rowNum = rowNum + 1                              'Increment row #
        Set currCell = ActiveSheet.Cells(rowNum, colNum) 'Get next cell
    Loop
End Sub
```

The idea is to loop until the procedure encounters a blank cell. This is controlled by the following `Do While` statement:

```
Do While currCell.Value <> ""
```

`currCell` is an object variable that is `Set` using the `Cells` method (which I describe in Chapter 7, "Manipulating Excel with VBA"). Next, the first `If...Then` uses the `IsNumeric` function to check if the cell contains a number, and the second `If...Then` checks if the number is greater than or equal to 1000. If both conditions are `True`, the font color is set to magenta using the `VBAColor` function described earlier in this chapter.

Using For...Next Loops

The most common type of loop is the `For...Next` loop. Use this loop when you know exactly how many times you want to repeat a group of statements. The structure of a `For...Next` loop looks like this:

```
For counter = start To end [Step increment]
    [statements]
Next [counter]
```

counter	A numeric variable used as a *loop counter*. The loop counter is a number that counts how many times the procedure has gone through the loop.
start	The initial value of *counter*. This is usually 1, but you can enter any value.
end	The final value of *counter*.
increment	This optional value defines an increment for the loop counter. If you leave this out, the default value is 1. Use a negative value to decrement *counter*.
statements	The statements to execute each time through the loop.

The basic idea is simple. When Excel encounters the `For...Next` statement, it follows this five-step process:

1. Set *counter* equal to *start*.
2. Test *counter*. If it's greater than *end*, exit the loop (that is, process the first statement after the `Next` statement). Otherwise, continue. If *increment* is negative, VBA checks to see whether *counter* is less than *end*.
3. Execute each statement between the `For` and `Next` statements.
4. Add *increment* to *counter*. Add 1 to *counter* if *increment* isn't specified.
5. Repeat steps 2 through 4 until done.

Listing 5.12 shows a simple Sub procedure—`LoopTest`—that uses a `For...Next` statement. Each time through the loop, the procedure uses the `Application` object's `StatusBar` property to display the value of `counter` (the loop counter) in the status bar. (See Chapter 10, "Interacting with the User," to learn more about the `StatusBar` property.) When you run this procedure, `counter` gets incremented by 1 each time through the loop, and the new value gets displayed in the status bar.

Listing 5.12. A simple `For...Next` Loop.

```
Sub LoopTest()
    Dim counter
    For counter = 1 To 10
        'Display the message
        Application.StatusBar = "Counter value: " & counter
        ' Wait for 1 second
        Application.Wait Now + TimeValue("00:00:01")
    Next counter
    Application.StatusBar = False
End Sub
```

NOTE: MIMICKING THE `WAIT` METHOD

The `LoopTest` procedure works fine in Excel, but it will fail in the other Office applications because they don't implement the `Wait` method. If you need to get your code to delay for a short while, here's a simple procedure that does the trick:

```
Sub VBAWait(delay As Integer)
    Dim startTime As Long
    startTime = Timer
    Do While Timer - startTime < delay
        DoEvents
    Loop
End Sub
```

Note the use of the `DoEvents` function inside the `Do While...Loop` structure. This function yields execution to the operating system so that events such as keystrokes and application messages are processed while the procedure delays.

If you'd prefer that the user not be able to enter keystrokes in your application, remove the `DoEvents` statement. Since Windows 95 and Windows NT are preemptive multitasking systems, the user will still be able to activate other applications, but he'll get an hourglass icon in your VBA application.

The following are some notes on `For...Next` loops:

- If you use a positive number for *`increment`* (or if you omit *`increment`*), *`end`* must be greater than or equal to *`start`*. If you use a negative number for *`increment`*, *`end`* must be less than or equal to *`start`*.
- If *`start`* equals *`end`*, the loop will execute once.
- As with `If...Then...Else` structures, indent the statements inside a `For...Next` loop for increased readability.
- To keep the number of variables defined in a procedure to a minimum, always try to use the same name for all your `For...Next` loop counters. The letters *i* through *n* traditionally are used for counters in programming. For greater clarity, you might want to use names such as `counter`.
- For the fastest loops, don't use the counter name after the `Next` statement. If you'd like to keep the counter name for clarity (which I recommend), precede the name with an apostrophe (`'`) to comment out the name:

```
For counter = 1 To 10
    [statements]
Next 'counter
```

- If you need to break out of a For...Next loop before the defined number of repetitions is completed, use the `Exit For` statement, described in the section "Using Exit For or Exit Do to Exit a Loop."

Using For Each...Next Loops

A useful variation of the `For...Next` loop is the `For Each...Next` loop, which operates on a collection of objects. You don't need a loop counter, because VBA just loops through the individual elements in the collection and performs on each element whatever operations are inside the loop. Here's the structure of the basic `For Each...Next` loop:

```
For Each element In group
    [statements]
Next [element]
```

element	A variable used to hold the name of each element in the collection.
group	The name of the collection.
statements	The statements to be executed for each element in the collection.

As an example, let's create a command procedure that converts a range of text into proper case (that is, the first letter of each word is capitalized). This function can come in handy if you import mainframe text into your worksheets, because mainframe reports usually appear entirely in uppercase. This process involves three steps:

1. Loop through the selected range with `For Each...Next`.
2. Convert each cell's text to proper case. Use Excel's `PROPER()` function to handle this:

   `PROPER(`*`text`*`)`

text	The text to convert to proper case.

3. Enter the converted text into the selected cell. This is the job of the Range object's `Formula` method:

   `object``.Formula = `*`Expression`*

object	The Range object in which you want to enter *Expression*.
Expression	The data you want to enter into *object*.

Listing 5.13 shows the resulting procedure, `ConvertToProper`. Note that this procedure uses the `Selection` object to represent the currently selected range.

Listing 5.13. A Sub procedure that uses `For Each...Next` to loop through a selection and convert each cell to proper text.

```
Sub ConvertToProper()
    Dim cellObject As Object
    For Each cellObject In Selection
        cellObject.Formula = Application.Proper(cellObject)
    Next
End Sub
```

Using `Exit For` or `Exit Do` to Exit a Loop

Most loops run their natural course, and then the procedure moves on. There might be times, however, when you want to exit a loop prematurely. For example, you might come across a certain type of cell, or an error might occur, or the user might enter an unexpected value. To exit a `For...Next` loop or a `For Each...Next` loop, use the `Exit For` statement. To exit a `Do...Loop`, use the `Exit Do` statement.

Listing 5.14 shows a revised version of the `BigNumbers` procedure, which exits the `Do...Loop` if it comes across a cell that isn't a number.

Listing 5.14. In this version of the `BigNumbers` procedure, the `Do...Loop` is terminated with the `Exit Do` statement if the current cell isn't a number.

```
Sub BigNumbers2()
    Dim rowNum As Integer, colNum As Integer, currCell As Range
    rowNum = ActiveCell.Row                            'Initialize row #
    colNum = ActiveCell.Column                         'Initialize column #
    Set currCell = ActiveSheet.Cells(rowNum, colNum)   'Get first cell
    Do While currCell.Value <> ""                      'Do while not empty
        If IsNumeric(currCell.Value) Then              'If it's a number,
            If currCell.Value >= 1000 Then             'and it's a big one,
                currCell.Font.Color = RGB(255, 0, 255) 'color font magenta
            End If
        Else                                           'If it's not,
            Exit Do                                    'exit the loop
        End If
        rowNum = rowNum + 1                            'Increment row #
        Set currCell = ActiveSheet.Cells(rowNum, colNum) 'Get next cell
    Loop
End Sub
```

Summary

This chapter showed you a number of methods for gaining maximum control over your VBA code. We began with a look at various VBA structures that allow your procedures to make decisions and act accordingly. In particular, I showed you how to work with `If...Then...Else` for true/false decisions; for multiple decisions I told you about the `And` and `Or` operators, the `If...ElseIf...Else` structure, and `Select Case`. I also included material on three decision-making functions: `IIf`, `Choose`, and `Switch`. You then learned about looping, including the structures `Do...Loop`, `For...Next`, and `For Each...Next`.

Here's a list of chapters where you'll find related information:

- This chapter used quite a few Excel objects as examples. To get the full scoop on these and other Excel objects, see Chapter 7, "Manipulating Excel with VBA."
- Controlling code often depends on interaction with the user. For example, you might use `If...Then...Else` to test the value of a check box, or `Select Case` to process a group of option buttons. See Chapter 10, "Interacting with the User," and Chapter 11, "Working with Microsoft Forms," to find out more about these topics.
- A big part of procedure control involves anticipating potential user errors. You'll learn more about this topic in Chapter 23, "Trapping Program Errors."

IN THIS PART

II PART

Unleashing Microsoft Office Objects

CHAPTER 6

Word for Windows VBA Programming

IN THIS CHAPTER

"When I use a word," Humpty Dumpty said in rather a scornful tone, "it means just what I choose it to mean—neither more nor less."

—Lewis Carroll

With the advent of Office 97, Word for Windows programmers finally get to ditch the hoary WordBasic macro language in favor of the relative comforts and power of VBA. Now developers building Word-based applications and power users writing Word macros can take advantage of a modern language that exposes a vast array of objects—from documents to paragraphs to sentences. Not only that, but the simplistic macro development window that was the bane of all Word programmers has given way to the Visual Basic Editor and its large collection of useful tools. Similarly, the clunky Dialog Box Editor has now been relegated to the dustbin of Word programming history and replaced by the user forms of VBA 5.0 (see Chapter 11, "Working with Microsoft Forms").

All of this is great news for people who program Word and who have grown tired of the all-too-glaring limitations of WordBasic. This chapter will serve as your introduction to the Word-specific capabilities of VBA. In case you've used WordBasic in the past, I'll begin with a look at the transition to VBA so you can get up to speed quickly. The rest of this chapter examines some specific Word objects and their properties, methods, and events.

The Transition from WordBasic to VBA

The first thing you need to know about the transition from the WordBasic way of doing things to the VBA way is that you don't have to bother with it if you really don't want to. In other words, if you would prefer to keep programming Word via WordBasic, you can go right ahead, because VBA has a built-in mechanism that lets you continue using WordBasic commands and syntax in your macros. This mechanism is a new object called `WordBasic` that includes methods that correspond to all the WordBasic statements and functions.

For example, consider the following snippet of WordBasic code:

```
StartOfDocument
Insert "Introduction"
Style "Heading 1"
InsertPara
```

These statements move the insertion point to the top of the document, insert the word "Introduction" and format it with the Heading 1 style, and insert a new paragraph. Here's how the equivalent statements look in VBA:

```
With WordBasic
    .StartOfDocument
    .Insert "Introduction"
    .Style "Heading 1"
    .InsertPara
End With
```

As you can see, all you have to do is append "WordBasic." to a WordBasic statement to transform it into a method of the `WordBasic` object.

In fact, this is precisely how Word handles existing WordBasic macros. If you open a template that contains WordBasic procedures and functions, you'll see a few messages in Word's status bar telling you that the program is "converting" these macros. All this means is that Word is tacking on "WordBasic." to each statement.

Of course, if you truly want to unleash Word for Windows programming, you'll need to leave WordBasic behind and start using native VBA statements and functions. The biggest advantage of doing this (and the biggest hurdle WordBasic programmers face) is that you gain access to all of Word's objects. WordBasic really is just a list of a few hundred commands that all exist on the same "level" without any kind of hierarchy. In VBA, on the other hand, statements must take into account the hierarchical nature of the Word object model, from the `Application` object at the top down through lower-level objects such as Document and Paragraph.

This means you need to let go of the traditional way of programming in WordBasic, which involves moving the insertion point to a specific spot and then, say, inserting text or a paragraph, or selecting a section of text and then applying formatting to that selection. With Word's object model, you can usually refer to objects without moving the insertion point or selecting anything. For example, here's a VBA code fragment that performs the same tasks as the WordBasic fragment just shown:

```
With ActiveDocument.Paragraphs(1).Range
    .InsertBefore "Introduction"
    .Style = "Heading 1"
    .InsertParagraphAfter
End With
```

With these ideas in mind, we can now turn to the real meat of this chapter: the Word for Windows object model. The sheer size of the hierarchy (Word has nearly 200 separate objects) prevents me from covering every object, property, and method. However, you'll spend the majority of your Word programming time dealing with a few key objects, and it's to these that I turn my attention in the rest of this chapter.

Reading and Setting Word's Program Options Via VBA

All of the Office 97 applications boast a long list of customization options, and Word's is one of the longest. Many of these features are available via the Options dialog box (which you can display by selecting Tools | Options). The Options dialog box is loaded with check boxes, option buttons, and other controls that let you customize almost every aspect of the Word environment. Almost all of these controls are available to your VBA procedures through the properties of various Word objects (especially the `View` and `Options` objects). The next few sections take you through the equivalent properties for the options in the View, General, and Edit tabs. For the options in the Spelling & Grammar tab, see "Checking Spelling and Grammar with VBA" later in this chapter.

NOTE: PROPERTIES ARE READABLE AND WRITEABLE

Keep in mind that you can use most properties to either read the current state of a property or change the value of a property. For example, you can store the current setting of the `Application.DisplayStatusBar` property in a variable named `currStatusBar` with the following statement:

```
currStatusBar = Application.DisplayStatusBar
```

To set the property, use a statement such as the following:

```
Application.DisplayStatusBar = False
```

The View Tab

The View tab options, shown in Figure 6.1, control several display settings for the Word screen, documents, objects, and windows. Table 6.1 lists the available options in the View tab and their equivalent object properties.

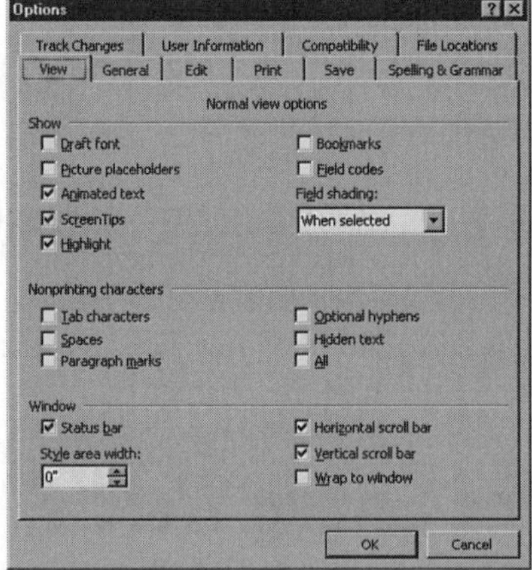

FIGURE 6.1.
The View tab in the Options dialog box.

NOTE: SETTING OPTION VALUES

Most of Word's options are set using either check boxes or option buttons. You work with check box options by assigning the property a `Boolean` value: `True` turns the property on, and `False` turns the property off. For option buttons, Word has predefined constants that correspond to each button.

Table 6.1. Object property equivalents for the View tab controls.

Option	*Property*	*Description*
Draft font	`Window.View.Draft`	Toggles the display of text in `Window` between the regular font and the draft font. For example, the following statement turns the draft font display on: `View.Draft = True`
Picture placeholders	`Window.View.ShowPicture` `➥PlaceHolders`	Toggles picture placeholders (blank boxes that represent embedded pictures) on and off for the specified `Window`.
Animated text	`Window.View.ShowAnimation`	Toggles animated text on and off for the specified `Window`.
Screen tips	`Window.DisplayScreenTips`	Toggles the display of screen tips on and off for the specified `Window`. (Screen tips are pop-up boxes that appear when you hover the mouse pointer over a comment or hyperlink.) To set this property for all windows, use the `Application` object instead of a Window object.
Highlight	`Window.View.Highlight`	Toggles the display of highlight formatting on and off for the specified `Window`.
Bookmarks	`Window.View.ShowBookmarks`	Toggles the display of bookmarks on and off for the specified `Window`.
Field codes	`Window.View.ShowFieldCodes`	Toggles the display of field codes on and off for the specified `Window`.
Field shading	`Window.View.FieldShading`	Reads or sets the behavior of the shading used with document fields in the specified `Window`. The three items in the drop-down list correspond to the following constants:

continues

Table 6.1. continued

Option	Property	Description
		Item / **Constant** Never — `wdFieldShadingNever` Always — `wdFieldShading➥Always` When selected — `wdFieldShadingWhen➥Selected`
Tab characters	`Window.View.ShowTabs`	Toggles the display of tab characters on and off for the specified `Window`.
Spaces	`Window.View.ShowSpaces`	Toggles on and off the display of dots to represent spaces between words for the specified `Window`.
Paragraph marks	`Window.View.ShowParagraphs`	Toggles the display of paragraph marks (¶) on and off for the specified `Window`.
Optional hyphens	`Window.View.ShowHypens`	Toggles on and off the display of optional hyphens that indicate where you want a word divided at the end of a line for the specified `Window`.
Hidden text	`Window.View.ShowHiddenText`	Toggles on and off the display of hidden text with a dotted underline for the specified `Window`.
All	`Window.View.ShowAll`	Toggles the display of all nonprinting characters on and off for the specified `Window`.
Status bar	`Application.DisplayStatusBar`	Toggles the status bar on and off for the specified `Window`.
Style area width	`Window.StyleAreaWidth`	A numeric value that determines the width (in points) of the style area for the specified `Window`. For example, the following statement sets the style area to the points equivalent of 0.2 inches for the active window:

Option	Property	Description
		`ActiveWindow.StyleAreaWidth ➥ = InchesToPoints(0.2)`
Horizontal scroll bar	*Window*.DisplayHorizontal ➥ScrollBar	Toggles the horizontal scroll bar on and off for the specified *Window*.
Vertical scroll bar	*Window*.DisplayVertical ➥ScrollBar	Toggles the vertical scroll bar on and off for the specified *Window*.
Wrap to window	*Window*.View.DisplayVertical ➥ScrollBar	Determines whether or not Word wraps the text at the right edge of the window.

NOTE: MEASUREMENT CONVERSION FUNCTIONS

Word VBA comes with a few functions for converting measurements from one unit to another. Many Word object properties accept values in points, so you can use the following functions to convert other measurements into points:

```
CentimetersToPoints
InchesToPoints
LinesToPoints
MillimetersToPoints
PicasToPoints
```

When reading properties that return values in points, use the following functions to convert these values into different units:

```
PointsToCentimeters
PointsToInches
PointsToLines
PointsToMillimeters
PointsToPicas
```

Toggling these features on an off by hand isn't hard. However, if you have a particular option you activate and deactivate regularly, consider setting up a procedure to do the toggling. For example, Listing 6.1 shows a short procedure that toggles the display of nonprinting characters on and off for the active window.

Listing 6.1. A procedure that toggles the display of nonprinting characters on and off.

```
Sub ToggleNonprinting()
    With ActiveWindow.View
        .ShowAll = Not .ShowAll
    End With
End Sub
```

> **NOTE: CODE LISTINGS FOR THIS CHAPTER**
>
> 
>
> The `ToggleNonprinting` procedure and the other code listings in this chapter can be found in Chaptr06.doc, which is on the CD that comes with this book. If you don't have Word and you would like to view these listings anyway, you'll also find them in the file Chaptr06.bas.

The General Tab

The controls on the General tab, shown in Figure 6.2, affect miscellaneous Word options. Table 6.2 lists the available options in the General tab and their equivalent object properties.

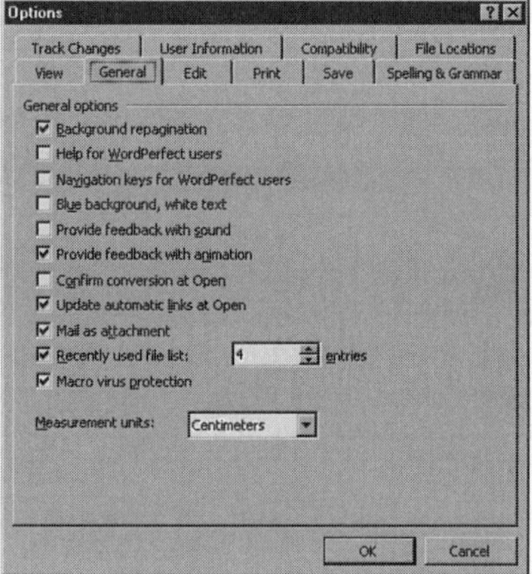

FIGURE 6.2.
The General tab in the Options dialog box.

Table 6.2. Object property equivalents for the General tab options.

Option	*Property*	*Description*
Background repagination	`Options.Pagination`	Toggles background repagination on and off.
Help for WordPerfect users	`Options.WPHelp`	Toggles WordPerfect Help on and off.
Navigation keys for WordPerfect users	`Options.DocNavKeys`	Toggles the WordPerfect navigation keys on and off.
Blue background, white text	`Options.BlueScreen`	Toggles Word between a white screen with black letters (the default) and a blue screen with white letters.

Option	*Property*	*Description*
Provide feedback with sound	`Options.EnableSound`	Toggles whether or not Word plays sounds for events such as opening and closing files.
Provide feedback with animation	`Options.AnimateScreen` `➥Movements`	Toggles mouse animations and other animated movements on and off.
Confirm conversion at Open	`Options.Confirm` `➥Conversions`	Toggles whether or not Word lets you choose the file converter used when you open a non-Word file.
Update automatic links at Open	`Options.UpdateLinks` `➥AtOpen`	Toggles on and off the automatic updating of document links.
Mail as attachment	`Options.SendMailAttach`	Determines whether Word sends documents as e-mail attachments or as text.
Recently used file list	`Application.Display` `➥RecentFiles`	Toggles on and off the File menu's list of the files recently opened. To control the number of entries in the list, use `RecentFiles.Maximum`.
Macro virus protection	`Options.VirusProtection`	Toggles Word's macro virus protection on and off.
Measurement units	`Options.MeasurementUnit`	Returns or sets the current measurement unit. The four items in the drop-down list correspond to the following constants: ***Item*** — ***Constant*** Inches — `wdInches` Centimeters — `wdCentimeters` Points — `wdPoints` Picas — `wdPicas`

The Edit Tab

The options in the Edit tab, shown in Figure 6.3, control various keyboard- and mouse-based editing settings. Table 6.3 lists the available options in the Edit tab and their equivalent object properties.

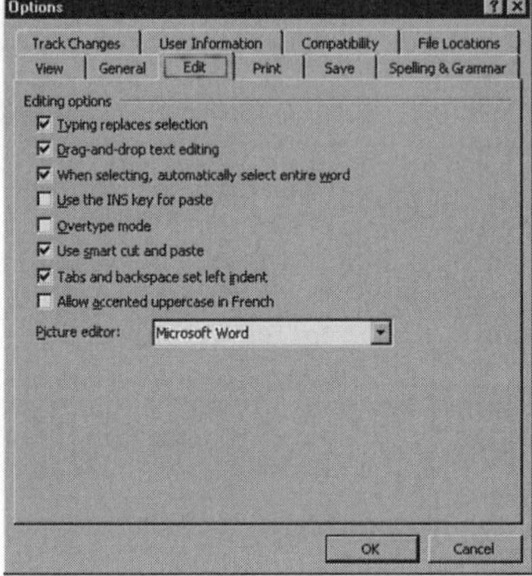

FIGURE 6.3.
The Edit tab in the Options dialog box.

Table 6.3. Object property equivalents for the Edit tab options.

Option	*Property*	*Description*
Typing replaces selection	`Options.ReplaceSelection`	Toggles whether or not a keypress replaces the currently selected text.
Drag and drop text editing	`Options.AllowDragAndDrop`	Toggles drag-and-drop editing on and off.
When selecting, automatically select entire word	`Options.AutoWordSelection`	Toggles whether or not dragging the mouse pointer across text selects entire words at a time.
Use the INS key for paste	`Options.INSKeyForPaste`	Toggles on and off the ability to use the Insert key to paste Clipboard text.
Overtype mode	`Options.Overtype`	Toggles overtype mode on and off.

Option	Property	Description
Use smart cut and paste	`Options.SmartCutPaste`	Toggles whether or not Word deletes extra spaces after cutting text and adds extra spaces when pasting text.
Tabs and backspace set left indent	`Options.TabIndentKey`	Toggles on and off the use of Tab as an indent key and Backspace as an outdent key.
Allow accented uppercase in French	`Options.AllowAccented ➥Uppercase`	Toggles whether or not Word allows text formatted as French to use accent characters on uppercase letters.
Picture editor	`Options.PictureEditor`	Returns or sets the default picture editor.

Word's Application Object

In Chapter 4, "Working with Objects," you learned about some `Application` object properties and methods that are common to all VBA-enabled applications. However, Word also has quite a few unique properties and methods. I'll talk about some of them in this section.

Properties of the Application Object

Here's a rundown of a few `Application` object properties that might prove useful in your VBA applications:

`ActivePrinter`: Returns or sets the name of the active printer. (Note that to set the active printer, you must specify the name of an existing Windows printer.) The following statement sets the active printer:

```
ActivePrinter = "HP LaserJet 5P/5MP PostScript local on LPT1:"
```

`Application.CapsLock`: Returns `True` if the Caps Lock key is activated.

`Application.NumLock`: Returns `True` if the Num Lock key is activated.

`Application.StartupPath`: Returns or sets the path of Word's startup folder.

`Application.UserInitials`: Returns or sets the initials of the user. Word uses these initials when constructing comment marks.

Methods of the Application Object

The Word Application object comes with quite a few methods. Here are a few of the more useful ones:

Application.ChangeFileOpenDirectory: This method specifies the folder that will appear by default in the Open dialog box the next time the user selects File | Open. Here's the syntax:

```
Application.ChangeFileOpenDirectory(Path)
```

Path	The path of the folder that will appear in the Open dialog box.

In the following example, the Dir function is first used to test whether or not a folder exists. If it does, the ChangeFileOpenDirectory method sets the folder to be the File | Open default.

```
If Dir("C:\My Documents\") <> "" Then
    Application.ChangeFileOpenDirectory "C:\My Documents\"
End If
```

Application.OnTime: Runs a procedure at a specified time, using the following syntax:

```
Application.OnTime(When, Name, Tolerance)
```

When	The time (and date, if necessary) you want the procedure to run. Enter a date/time serial number.
Name	The name (entered as text) of the procedure to run when the time given by ***When*** arrives.
Tolerance	If Word isn't ready to run the procedure at ***When***, it will keep trying for the number of seconds specified by *Tolerance*. If you omit *Tolerance*, VBA waits until Word is ready.

The easiest way to enter a time serial number for ***When*** is to use the TimeValue function:

```
TimeValue(Time)
```

Time	A string representing the time you want to use (such as "5:00PM" or "17:00").

For example, the following formula runs a procedure called MakeBackup at 5:00 PM:

```
Application.OnTime _
    When:=TimeValue("5:00PM"), _
    Name:="MakeBackup"
```

TIP: RUNNING A PROCEDURE AFTER A SPECIFIED INTERVAL

If you want the `OnTime` method to run after a specified time interval (for example, an hour from now), use `Now + TimeValue(`***`Time`***`)` for ***`When`*** (where ***`Time`*** is the interval you want to use). For example, the following statement schedules a procedure to run in 30 minutes:

```
Application.OnTime _
    When:=Now + TimeValue("00:30"), _
    Name:="MakeBackup"
```

`Application.Move`: Moves the Word application window according to the following syntax:

`Application.Move(`***`Left, Top`***`)`

`Left`	The horizontal screen position, in points, of the left edge of the application window.
`Top`	The vertical screen position, in points, of the top edge of the application window.

Note that this method causes an error if the window is maximized or minimized. Listing 6.2 shows a procedure that checks to see if the application window is maximized or minimized and, if it's not, moves the window into the top-left corner of the screen.

Listing 6.2. A procedure that moves the Word window into the top-left corner of the screen.

```
Sub TopLeftCorner()
    With Application
        If .WindowState <> wdWindowStateMaximize _
            And .WindowState <> wdWindowStateMinimize _
            Then .Move 0, 0
    End With
End Sub
```

`Application.Resize`: Changes the size of the Word application window. Here's the syntax:

`Application.Resize(`***`Width, Height`***`)`

`Width`	The new width of the application window, in points.
`Height`	The new height of the application window, in points.

As with the `Move` method, this method raises an error if the application window is maximized or minimized.

`Application.Quit`: Quits Word. If there are any open documents with unsaved changes, Word will ask if you want to save the changes. To prevent this, either save the documents before running the `Quit` method (I'll tell you how to save documents in the next section) or set the `DisplayAlerts` property to `False`. (In the latter case, note that Word will *not* save changes to the documents.)

Working with Document Objects

In Microsoft Word, the Document object appears directly below the `Application` object in the object hierarchy. You can use VBA to create new documents, open or delete existing documents, save and close open documents, and more. The next section takes you through various techniques for specifying documents in your VBA code; then we'll look at some Document object properties, methods, and events.

Specifying a Document Object

If you need to do something with a document, or if you need to work with an object contained in a specific document (such as a section of text), you need to tell Word which document you want to use. VBA gives you three ways to do this:

Use the `Documents` object: The `Documents` object is the collection of all open document files. To specify a particular document, either use its index number (where 1 represents the first document opened) or enclose the document name in quotation marks. For example, if Memo.doc was the first document opened, the following two statements would be equivalent:

```
Documents("Memo.doc")
Documents(1)
```

Use the `ActiveDocument` object: The `ActiveDocument` object represents the document that currently has the focus.

Use the `ThisDocument` object: The `ThisDocument` object represents the document where the VBA code is executing. If your code deals only with objects residing in the same document as the code itself, you can use the `ActiveDocument` object. However, if your code deals with other documents, use `ThisDocument` whenever you need to make sure that the code affects only the document containing the procedure.

Opening a Document

To open a document file, use the `Open` method of the `Documents` collection. The `Open` method has 10 arguments you can use to fine-tune your document openings, but only one of these is mandatory. Here's the simplified syntax showing the one required argument (for the rest of the arguments, look up the `Open` method in the VBA Help system):

```
Documents.Open(FileName)
```

`FileName`	The full name of the document file, including the drive and folder that contain the file.

For example, to open a document named Letter.doc in the current drive and folder, you would use the following statement:

```
Documents.Open "Letter.doc"
```

Creating a New Document

If you need to create a new document, use the `Documents` collection's `Add` method:

```
Documents.Add(Template, NewTemplate)
```

`Template`	This optional argument specifies the template file to use as the basis for the new document. Enter a string that spells out the path and name of the .DOT file. If you omit this argument, Word creates the new document based on the Normal template.
`NewTemplate`	If you set this argument to `True`, Word creates a new template file.

Document Object Properties

Most Document object properties return collections of other objects. For example, the `Words` property is a collection of all the words in a document, and the `Bookmarks` property is a collection of all the bookmarks in the document. Here's a list of a few other common properties associated with Document objects:

`Document``.GrammarChecked`: Returns `True` if the entire document has been grammar-checked; returns `False` otherwise.

`Document``.Name`: Returns the filename of the document.

`Document``.Path`: Returns the path of the document file.

> **NOTE: A NEW, UNSAVED DOCUMENT'S PATH PROPERTY**
>
> A new, unsaved document's `Path` property returns an empty string (`""`).

`Document``.Saved`: Determines whether changes have been made to a document since it was last saved.

`Document``.SpellingChecked`: Returns `True` if the entire document has been spell-checked; returns `False` otherwise.

Document Object Methods

Document objects have dozens of methods that let you do everything from saving a document to closing a document. Here are the methods you'll use most often:

Document.Activate: Activates the specified open *Document*. For example, the following statement activates the Tirade.doc document:

```
Documents("Tirade.doc").Activate
```

Document.CheckGrammar: Checks the grammar in the specified *Document*.

Document.CheckSpelling: Checks the spelling in the specified *Document*. This method contains a number of optional arguments that let you set various spell-check options (see "Checking Spelling and Grammar with VBA" later in this chapter).

Document.Close: Closes the specified *Document*. This method uses the following syntax:

```
Document.Close(SaveChanges, OriginalFormat, RouteDocument)
```

Document	The Document object you want to close.
SaveChanges	If the document has been modified, this argument determines whether Word saves those changes: wdSaveChanges — Saves changes before closing. wdDoNotSaveChanges — Doesn't save changes. wdPromptToSaveChanges — Asks the user if he wants to save changes.
OriginalFormat	Specifies the format to use when saving the document: wdOriginalFormat — Saves the document using its original format. wdWordDocument — Saves the document in Word format. wdPromptUser — Asks the user if he wants to save the document in its original format.
RouteDocument	If set to True, this argument tells Word to route the document to the next recipient.

Document.Goto: Returns a Range object (see "The Range Object" later in this chapter) that represents the start of a specified position in the *Document*. Here's the syntax:

```
Document.GoTo(What, Which, Count, Name)
```

Document	The Document object with which you want to work.

What — The type of item to go to. Word uses 17 different constants for this argument. Here's a list of the most common ones you'll use:

`wdGoToBookmark`
`wdGoToComment`
`wdGoToEndnote`
`wdGoToField`
`wdGoToFootnote`
`wdGoToGraphic`
`wdGoToLine`
`wdGoToObject`
`wdGoToPage`
`wdGoToSection`
`wdGoToTable`

Which — A constant that determines how Word goes to the new range:

`wdGoToAbsolute`	Uses the absolute position of the item.
`wdGoToFirst`	Goes to the first instance of the item.
`wdGoToLast`	Goes to the last instance of the item.
`wdGoToNext`	Goes to the next instance of the item.
`wdGoToPrevious`	Goes to the previous instance of the item.
`wdGoToRelative`	Use the relative position of the item.

Count — A positive value that represents the number of the item. For example, the line number of *What* is `wdGoToLine`.

Name — The name of the item, if *What* is `wdGoToBookmark`, `wdGoToComment`, `wdGoToField`, or `wdGoToObject`.

For example, the following statement goes to the second line in the active document:

```
ActiveDocument.Goto _
    What:=wdGoToLine, _
    Which:=wdGoToAbsolute, _
    Count:=2
```

On the other hand, the following statement goes to the second line from the current position in the active document:

```
ActiveDocument.Goto _
    What:=wdGoToLine, _
    Which:=wdGoToRelative, _
    Count:=2
```

`Document.PrintOut`: Prints the specified `Document` using the following syntax:

```
Document.PrintOut(Range, From, To, Copies, Pages, ActivePrinter, PrintToFile)
```

Document	The Document object you want to print.
Range	Specifies the range of text to print, as follows:

`wdPrintAllDocument`	Prints the entire document.
`wdPrintCurrentPage`	Prints only the current page.
`wdPrintFromTo`	Prints a range of pages from a starting page number (see the `From` argument) to an ending page (see the `To` argument).
`wdPrintRangeOfPages`	Prints a range of pages (see the `Pages` argument).
`wdPrintPrintSelection`	Prints only the currently selected text.

From	If *Range* is `wdPrintFromTo`, this argument specifies the page number from which to start printing.
To	If *Range* is `wdPrintFromTo`, this argument specifies the page number of the last page to print.
Copies	The number of copies to print. The default value is 1.
Pages	If *Range* is `wdPrintRangeOfPages`, this argument specifies the page range (for example, `4-8,10`).
ActivePrinter	Specifies the printer to use.
PrintToFile	If `True`, Word prints the document to a file and prompts the user for a filename.

`Document.PrintPreview`: Displays the specified `Document` in the Print Preview window.

`Document.Save`: Saves the specified `Document`. If the document is new, use the `SaveAs` method instead.

`Document.SaveAs`: Saves the specified `Document` to a different file. Here's the simplified syntax for the `SaveAs` method (to see all 11 arguments in their full syntax, look up the `SaveAs` method in the VBA Help system):

```
Document.SaveAs(FileName)
```

Document	The Document object you want to save to a different file.
FileName	The full name of the new document file, including the drive and folder where you want the file to reside.

Listing 6.3 shows a procedure named `MakeBackup` that uses the `SaveAs` method, as well as a few other methods and properties of the Document object.

Listing 6.3. A procedure that creates a backup copy of the active document on a floppy disk.

```
Sub MakeBackup()
    Dim backupFile As String
    Dim currFile As String
    With ActiveDocument
        '
        ' Don't bother if the document is unchanged or new
        '
        If .Saved Or .Path = "" Then Exit Sub
        '
        ' Mark current position in document
        '
        .Bookmarks.Add Name:="LastPosition"
        '
        ' Turn off screen updating
        '
        Application.ScreenUpdating = False
        '
        ' Save the file
        '
        .Save
        '
        ' Store the current file path, construct the path for the
        ' backup file, and then save it to Drive A
        '
        currFile = .FullName
        backupFile = "A:\" + .Name
        .SaveAs FileName:=backupFile
    End With
    '
    ' Close the backup copy (which is now active)
    ActiveDocument.Close
    '
    ' Reopen the current file
    '
    Documents.Open FileName:=currFile
    '
    ' Return to pre-backup position
    '
    ActiveDocument.GoTo What:=wdGoToBookmark, Name:="LastPosition"
End Sub
```

After declaring a couple of variables, this procedures checks to see if the backup operation is necessary. In other words, if the document has no unsaved changes (the `Saved` property returns `True`) or if it's a new, unsaved document (the `Path` property returns `""`), bail out of the procedure.

Otherwise, a new Bookmark object is created to save the current position in the document, screen updating is turned off, and the file is saved.

We're now ready to perform the backup. First, the `currFile` variable is used to store the full path name of the document, and the path name of the backup file is built with the following statement:

```
backupFile = "A:\" + .Name
```

This will be used to save the file to drive A. Note that this statement is easily customized to save the file to a different hard disk or even a network drive. (For the latter, use a UNC network path name in place of `A:\`.)

The actual backup takes place via the `SaveAs` method, which saves the document to the path given by `backupFile`. From there, the procedure closes the backup file, reopens the original file, and uses the `GoTo` method to return to the original position within the document.

NOTE: SCHEDULING REGULAR BACKUPS

Rather than running `MakeBackup` by hand, you might consider using the `OnTime` method to schedule backups at specific times or at regular intervals.

NOTE: TRAPPING ERRORS

The `MakeBackup` procedure should probably check to see if there is a disk in drive A for running the `SaveAs` method. I'll show you how to account for this type of error in Chapter 23, "Trapping Program Errors."

Document Object Events

Document objects respond to three different events: `Close`, `Open`, and `New`. The following is a quick rundown of each event.

NOTE: ENTERING EVENT HANDLER CODE

Remember that you don't create event handlers in a regular VBA module. Instead, you follow these steps:

1. In the Visual Basic Editor's Project Explorer, highlight the Document object you want to work with. For the document containing the VBA code, highlight `ThisDocument`.
2. Select View | Code, press F7, or click the View Code button in the Project Explorer.

3. In the code window that appears, use the Object drop-down list (the one on the left) to select the Document object.
4. Use the Procedure drop-down list (the one on the right) to select the event you want to work with. VBA adds the event handler's procedure stub to the code window.
5. Enter your event handler code within the procedure stub.

`Close`: This event fires when the user selects File | Close, or when your code runs the Document object's `Close` method. Note that the statements you define inside the event handler will run before the workbook is closed, and before the user is asked to save changes. Here's the procedure stub of the event handler:

```
Private Sub Document_Close()
    <Event handler code goes here>
End Sub
```

`New`: This event applies only to templates, and it fires when the user creates a new document based on the template, or when your code runs the Document object's `Add` method and specifies this template. Here's the procedure stub used by the event handler:

```
Private Sub Document_New()
    <Event handler code goes here>
End Sub
```

`Open`: This event fires when the user selects File | Open, or when your code runs the Document object's `Open` method. Here's the procedure stub of the event handler:

```
Private Sub Document_Open()
    <Event handler code goes here>
End Sub
```

Objects That Represent Text in Word

Although you can add lines, graphics, and other objects to a document, text is what Word is all about. So it won't come as any surprise to you that Word has a truckload of objects that give you numerous ways to work with text. The next few sections take you through a few of these objects.

The Range Object

If you've used VBA with Excel, you probably know that Excel has no separate object to represent a cell. Instead, a cell is considered to be just an instance of the generic Range class.

Along similar lines, Word has no separate objects for its most fundamental text units: the character and the word. Like Excel, Word considers these items to be instances of a generic class, which is also called the Range object. A Range object is defined as a contiguous section of text in a document, so it can be anything from a single character to an entire document.

There are two basic methods for returning a Range object: the Document object's `Range` method and the `Range` property.

The Range Method

The Document object has a `Range` method that lets you specify starting and ending points for a range. Here's the syntax:

```
Document.Range(Start,End)
```

Document	The Document object.
Start	The starting character position. Note that the first character in a document is at position 0.
End	The ending character position.

For example, the following statements use the `myRange` object variable to store the first 100 characters in the active document:

```
Dim myRange As Range
myRange = ActiveDocument.Range(0, 99)
```

The Range Property

Many Word objects have a `Range` property that returns a Range object, including the Paragraph and `Selection` objects (discussed later). This is important, because these objects lack certain properties and methods that are handy for manipulating text. For example, the Paragraph object doesn't have a `Font` property. The Range object does, however, so you format a paragraph's font programmatically by referring to its `Range` property, like so:

```
ActiveDocument.Paragraphs(1).Range.Font.Italic = True
```

This statement formats the first paragraph in the active document with italic text. (I'll discuss the `Paragraphs` collection in a moment.)

Range Object Properties

The Range object's properties include many of the standard text formatting commands. Here's a brief review of just a few of these properties:

`Range``.Bold`: Returns `True` if the specified *`Range`* is formatted entirely as bold; returns `False` if no part of the range is bold; returns `wdUndefined` if only part of the range is formatted as bold. You can also set this property using `True` (for bolding), `False` (to remove bolding), or `wdToggle` (to toggle the current setting between `True` and `False`).

`Range``.Case`: Returns or sets the case of the specified *`Range`*. This property uses various Word constants, including `wdLowerCase`, `wdTitleSentence`, `wdTitleWord`, `wdToggleCase`, and `wdUpperCase`.

Range.Characters: Returns a Characters collection that represents all of the characters in the *Range* (see the section titled "The Characters Object").

Range.End: The position of the last character in the *Range*.

Range.Font: Returns or sets a Font object that specifies the character formatting used in the *Range*.

Range.Italic: Returns True if the specified *Range* is formatted entirely as italic; returns False if no part of the range is italic; returns wdUndefined if only part of the range is formatted as italic. You can also set this property using True (for italics), False (to remove italics), or wdToggle (to toggle the current setting between True and False).

Range.Paragraphs: Returns a Paragraphs collection that represents all the Paragraph objects in the *Range* (see the section titled "The Paragraph Object").

Range.Sentences: Returns a Sentences collection that represents all the Sentence objects in the *Range* (see the section titled "The Sentences Object").

Range.Start: The position of the first character in the *Range*.

Range.Text: Returns or sets the text in the *Range*.

Range.Words: Returns a Words collection that represents all of the words in the *Range* (see the section titled "The Words Object").

Range Object Methods

Since it's the fundamental text object, it's not surprising that the Range object boasts a large number of methods that you can use to manipulate text. Here are a few of the ones you'll use most often:

Range.CheckGrammar: Checks the grammar in the specified *Range*.

Range.CheckSpelling: Checks the spelling in the specified *Range*. This method contains a number of optional arguments that let you set various spell-check options (see "Checking Spelling and Grammar with VBA" later in this chapter).

Range.Collapse: If the *Range* is currently selected, use this method to remove the selection and position the cursor according to the following syntax:

Range.Collapse(*Direction*)

Range	The Range object.
Direction	Specifies where you want the cursor to end up. Use wdCollapseStart to position the cursor at the beginning of the **Range** (this is the default). Use wdCollapseEnd to position the cursor at the end of the **Range**.

NOTE: THE SELECTION OBJECT

The `Selection` object represents the currently selected text. To select text programmatically, use the Range object's `Select` method (discussed at the end of this section).

`Range.Copy`: Copies the `Range` to the Clipboard.

`Range.Cut`: Cuts the `Range` from the document and places it on the Clipboard.

`Range.Delete`: If used without arguments, this method deletes the entire `Range`. However, you can fine-tune your deletions by using the following syntax:

`Range.Delete(Unit,Count)`

Range	The Range object containing the text you want to delete.
Unit	A constant that specifies whether you're deleting characters (use `wdCharacter`) or entire words (use `wdWord`). If you omit this argument, VBA assumes you're deleting characters.
Count	The number of units to delete. Use a positive number to delete forward; use a negative number to delete backward.

`Range.InsertAfter`: Inserts text after the specified `Range`:

`Range.InsertAfter(Text)`

Range	The Range object after which you want to insert the text.
Text	The text to insert.

`Range.InsertBefore`: Inserts text before the specified `Range`:

`Range.InsertBefore(Text)`

Range	The Range object before which you want to insert the text.
Text	The text to insert.

`Range.Paste`: Pastes the contents of the Clipboard at the current `Range` position. To avoid overwriting the currently selected Range, use the `Collapse` method before pasting.

`Range.Select`: Selects the specified `Range`.

The Characters Object

The `Characters` object is a collection that represents all the characters in whatever object is specified. For example, `ActiveDocument.Paragraphs(1).Characters` is the collection of all the characters in the Range object given by `ActiveDocument.Paragraphs(1)` (the first paragraph in the active document). Other objects that have the `Characters` property are Document and `Selection`.

Since `Characters` is a collection, you refer to individual characters by including an index number (`Characters(50)`, for example). The following statement formats the first character in the active document to point size 20:

```
ActiveDocument.Words(1).Font.Size = 20
```

To count the number of characters in the specified object, use the `Count` property:

```
totalChars = Documents("Chapter1.doc").Characters.Count
```

This example sets the variable `totalChars` equal to the number of characters in the Chapter1.doc file.

Listing 6.4 shows another example that uses the `Characters` object. In this case, the function procedure named `CountCharacters` takes on an `Object` argument named `countObject` and a `String` argument named `letter`. The procedure determines the number of instances of `letter` that occur within `countObject`.

Listing 6.4. A function that counts the number of instances of a specified character in an object.

```
Function CountCharacters(countObject As Object, letter As String) As Long
    Dim i As Long, char As Range
    i = 0
    For Each char In countObject.Characters
        If char = letter Then i = i + 1
    Next char
    CountCharacters = i
End Function
Sub TestCountCharacters()
    MsgBox CountCharacters(ActiveDocument, "e")
End Sub
```

The Words Object

The `Words` object is a collection that represents all the words in whatever object is specified. For example, `ActiveDocument.Words` is the collection of all the words in the active document. Other objects that have the `Words` property are Paragraph, Range, and `Selection` (all described in a moment).

You refer to individual words by using an index number with the `Words` collection. As I mentioned earlier, however, this doesn't return a "Word" object; there is no such thing in Microsoft Word's VBA universe. Instead, individual words are classified as Range objects (see "The Range Object" earlier in this chapter).

The following statement formats the first word in the active document as bold:

```
ActiveDocument.Words(1).Font.Bold = True
```

To count the number of words in the specified object, use the `Count` property:

```
totalWords = Documents("Article.doc").Words.Count
```

The Sentences Object

The next rung on Word's text object ladder is the `Sentences` object. This is a collection of all the sentences in whatever object you specify, be it a Document, Range, or `Selection`.

As with `Words`, you refer to specific members of the `Sentences` collection using an index number, and the resulting object is a `Range`. For example, the following statement stores the active document's first sentence in the `firstSentence` variable:

```
firstSentence = ActiveDocument.Sentences(1)
```

Again, the `Count` property can be used to return the total number of sentences in an object. In the following procedure fragment, the `Count` property is used to determine the last sentence in a document:

```
With Documents("Remarks.doc")
    totalSentences = .Sentences.Count
    lastSentence = .Sentences(.totalSentences)
End With
```

The Paragraph Object

From characters, words, and sentences, we make the next logical text leap: paragraphs. A Paragraph object is a member of the `Paragraphs` collection, which represents all the paragraphs in the specified Document, Range, or `Selection`. As with the other text objects, you use an index number with the `Paragraphs` object to specify an individual paragraph.

Paragraph Properties

Word's various paragraph formatting options are well-represented in the large set of properties available for the Paragraph object. Here are a few useful ones:

`Paragraph.KeepTogether`: Returns or sets whether the specified `Paragraph` object remains together on the same page when Word repaginates the document.

`Paragraph.KeepWithNext`: Returns or sets whether the specified `Paragraph` remains on the same page with the following paragraph when Word repaginates the document.

`Paragraph.LeftIndent`: Returns or sets the left indent (in points) of the specified `Paragraph`.

`Paragraph.LineSpacing`: Returns or sets the line spacing setting (in points) for the specified `Paragraph`.

Paragraph.RightIndent: Returns or sets the right indent (in points) for the specified *Paragraph*.

Paragraph.SpaceAfter: Returns or sets the spacing (in points) after the specified *Paragraph*.

Paragraph.SpaceBefore: Returns or sets the spacing (in points) before the specified *Paragraph*.

Paragraph.Style: Returns or sets the style of the specified *Paragraph*. Word has a huge number of constants that represent its predefined styles. For example, to set the Heading 1 style, you would use the wdStyleHeading1 constant. To see the other constants, search for wdBuiltInStyle in the Object Browser.

The following procedure fragment applies several properties to the active paragraph (recall that the InchesToPoints function converts values expressed in inches to the equivalent value expressed in points):

```
With Selection.Range
    .LeftIndent=InchesToPoints(1)
    .LineSpacing=12
    .SpaceAfter=6
    .Style=wdStyleNormal
End With
```

Paragraph Methods

To finish our look at the Paragraph object, here are a few methods you can wield in your code:

Paragraph.Indent: Indents the specified *Paragraph* to the next tab stop.

Paragraph.Next: Moves forward in the document from the specified *Paragraph* to return a Paragraph object:

Paragraph.Next(*Count*)

Paragraph	The Paragraph object from which you want to move.
Count	The number of paragraphs to move forward.

Paragraph.Outdent: Outdents the *Paragraph* to the previous tab stop.

Paragraph.Previous: Moves backward in the document from the specified *Paragraph* to return a Paragraph object:

Paragraph.Previous(*Count*)

Paragraph	The Paragraph object from which you want to move.
Count	The number of paragraphs to move backward.

Paragraph.Space1: Sets the specified *Paragraph* to single-spaced.

Paragraph.Space15: Sets the specified *Paragraph* to 1.5-line spacing.

Paragraph.Space2: Sets the specified *Paragraph* to double-spaced.

Checking Spelling and Grammar with VBA

Since words are at the heart of Word, it makes sense that there are a number of properties and methods for checking spelling and grammar via your VBA procedures. The rest of this chapter looks at the various features Word VBA makes available for spelling and grammar checks.

Spell-Checking a Document or Range

To check the spelling in a Document object or a Range object, VBA offers the `CheckSpelling` method, which initiates the spell check procedure:

```
Object.CheckSpelling(CustomDictionary, IgnoreUppercase, AlwaysSuggest,
➥CustomDictionaryX)
```

`Object`	The Document or Range object you want to check.
`CustomDictionary`	The filename of a custom dictionary that the application can search if a word wasn't found in the main dictionary.
`IgnoreUppercase`	Set this argument to `True` to tell Word to ignore words entirely in uppercase.
`AlwaysSuggest`	Set this argument to `True` to tell Word to always suggest alternative spellings for misspelled words.
`CustomDictionaryX`	The name or names of one or more extra custom dictionaries. Here, *`X`* can be any value between 2 and 10.

Spell-Checking a Word

If you only want to spell-check a specific word or phrase, use the following alternative syntax for the `CheckSpelling` method:

```
Application.CheckSpelling(Word, CustomDictionary, IgnoreUppercase, MainDictionary,
➥CustomDictionaryX)
```

`Word`	The word or phrase you want to check.
`CustomDictionary`	The filename of a custom dictionary that the application can search if ***`Word`*** wasn't found in the main dictionary.
`IgnoreUppercase`	Set this argument to `True` to tell Word to ignore words entirely in uppercase.
`MainDictionary`	The name of the main dictionary Word should use to check ***`Word`***.
`CustomDictionaryX`	The name or names of one or more extra custom dictionaries. Here, *`X`* can be any value between 2 and 10.

Checking Grammar

To start a grammar check on a Document or Range object, use the `CheckGrammar` method:

```
Object.CheckGrammar
```

`Object`	The Document or Range object you want to check.

If you would prefer to check the grammar of a string, use the alternative syntax

```
Application.CheckGrammar(String)
```

`String`	The text you want to check.

Word's Spelling and Grammar Options

Earlier in this chapter I took you through a number of the controls in Word's Options dialog box and showed you the VBA property equivalents for each control. The Options dialog box also has a Spelling & Grammar tab, as shown in Figure 6.4, which controls various settings for spelling and grammar checks. Table 6.4 details the VBA equivalents for each option.

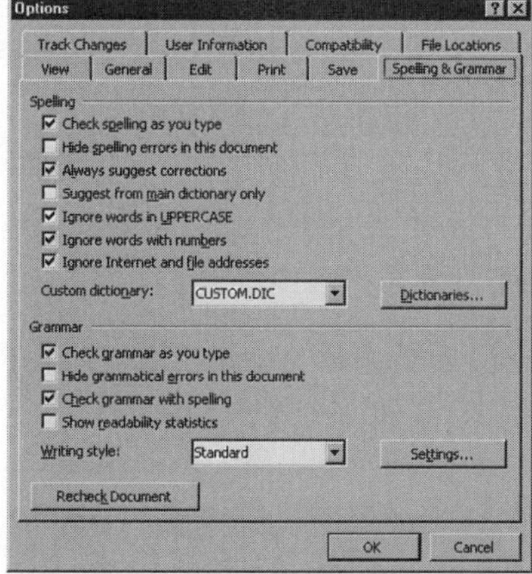

FIGURE 6.4.
The Spelling & Grammar tab.

Table 6.4. Object property equivalents for the Spelling & Grammar tab options.

Option	*Property*	*Description*
Check spelling as you type	`Options.CheckSpelling ➥AsYouType`	Toggles on-the-fly spell checking on and off.
Hide spelling errors in this document	`Document.ShowSpellingErrors`	Toggles underlined spelling errors on and off for the specified `Document`.

continues

Table 6.4. continued

Option	*Property*	*Description*
Always suggest corrections	`Options.SuggestSpelling` `➥Corrections`	Toggles whether or not Word displays alternative spellings automatically.
Suggest from main dictionary only	`Options.SuggestFromMain` `➥DictionaryOnly`	Toggles whether or not Word only takes alternative spellings from the main dictionary.
Ignore words in UPPERCASE	`Options.IgnoreUppercase`	Toggles whether or not Word ignores words entirely in uppercase.
Ignore words with numbers	`Options.IgnoreMixedDigits`	Toggles whether or not Word ignores words that contain numeric characters.
Ignore Internet and file addresses	`Options.IgnoreInternetAnd` `➥FileAddresses`	Toggles whether or not Word ignores Internet addresses (such as URLs) or file paths.
Custom dictionary	`CustomDictionaries.` `➥ActiveCustomDictionary`	A Dictionary object that specifies the custom dictionary to use during the spell check. Use the syntax `customDictionaries.` `➥Item(`***`FileName`***`)`, where ***`FileName`*** is the filename of the custom dictionary.
Check grammar as you type	`Options.CheckGrammar` `➥AsYouType`	Toggles on-the-fly grammar checking on and off.
Hide grammatical errors in this document	*`Document`*`.ShowGrammatical` `➥Errors`	Toggles underlined grammatical errors on and off for the specified *`Document`*.
Show readability statistics	`Options.ShowReadability` `➥Statistics`	Toggles whether or not Word displays the Readability Statistics dialog box after the grammar check is complete.
Writing style	*`Language`*`.DefaultWriting` `➥Style`	A text string that specifies the writing style to use for the specified *`Language`* object, such as `Languages(wdEnglishUS)`.

Summary

This chapter took you on a tour of the new VBA implementation in Word for Windows 97. After discussing the transition from WordBasic to VBA, I showed you various object properties that correspond to the controls available in the View, General, and Edit tabs of the Options dialog box. You then learned more about Word's `Application` object, including a few useful properties and methods. From there, I went through a number of Word-specific objects, including the Document, Range, `Characters`, `Words`, `Sentences`, and Paragraph objects. I closed with a look at spell- and grammar-checking from VBA.

Here are a couple of chapters where you'll find related information:

- For a general discussion of VBA objects, see Chapter 4, "Working with Objects."
- To learn how to integrate Word with other Office applications, see Chapter 15, "Controlling Applications Via OLE Automation."

CHAPTER 7

Manipulating Excel with VBA

IN THIS CHAPTER

Technology is a way of organizing the universe so that man doesn't have to experience it.

—Max Frisch

If you're using VBA in Excel, most of your procedures will eventually do *something* to the Excel environment. They might open a workbook, rename a worksheet, select a cell or range, enter a formula, or even set some of Excel's options. Therefore, knowing how VBA interacts with Excel is crucial if you ever hope to write useful routines. This chapter looks closely at that interaction. I'll show you how to set Excel's options via VBA and how to work with all the most common Excel objects, including the Workbook, Worksheet, and Range objects.

Excel's Macro Options

Before we get to the object fun and games, let's take a quick look at the various options that Excel provides for recording macros. At this point in your VBA career, you might be wondering why you would even bother with recorded macros. After all, the five chapters in Part I, "Introducing VBA," served to expand your VBA horizons so that the larger world of application programming could be glimpsed. Isn't the macro recorder just for novices?

You'd be surprised. The developer's never-ending quest for efficiency applies not just to his programs, but also to his programming. For example, if you needed to put together a few lines of code that manipulate some Excel objects, but you weren't sure of the correct syntax, it might take you a few minutes to look up the objects either in this chapter or in the Excel Help system. However, there's a good chance you can run through those same actions in the macro recorder in just a few seconds. You can then paste the resulting code into your procedure and edit accordingly. With the macro recorder's existence now fully justified, let's examine the available options.

Assigning a Shortcut Key

To assign a shortcut key to an existing macro (or change a macro's current shortcut key), from Excel, select Tools | Macro | Macros (or press Alt-F8). In the Macro Name dialog box, highlight the macro and click Options to display the Macro Options dialog box, shown in Figure 7.1. Use the Shortcut key: Ctrl+ text box to enter the letter you want to use with Ctrl for the key combination. For example, if you enter `e`, you can run the macro by pressing Ctrl-E. Note that Excel shortcut keys are case-sensitive. In other words, if you enter `E` in the Ctrl+ text box, you would have to press Ctrl-Shift-E to run the macro.

FIGURE 7.1.
Use the Macro Options dialog box to assign a shortcut key to a macro.

> **CAUTION: AVOID SHORTCUT KEY CONFLICTS**
>
> Make sure you don't specify a shortcut key that conflicts with Excel's built-in shortcuts (such as Ctrl-B for Bold or Ctrl-C for Copy). If you use a key that clashes with an Excel shortcut, Excel will override its own shortcut and run your macro instead (provided, that is, that the workbook containing the macro is open).
>
> There are only eight letters not assigned to Excel commands that you can use with your macros: e, j, k, l, m, q, t, and y. You can get extra shortcut keys by using uppercase letters. For example, Excel differentiates between Ctrl-b and Ctrl-B (or, more explicitly, Ctrl-Shift-b). Note, however, that Excel uses four built-in Ctrl-Shift shortcuts: A, F, O, and P.
>
> You also can use the `OnKey` method to trigger a macro when the user presses a specific key combination. See the section "Excel's `Application` Object" for details.

While you're in the Macro Options dialog box, you can also use the Description text box to add some descriptive text about the macro. (This text appears in the Description area of the Macro dialog box when you highlight the macro.)

Recording with Relative References

By default, Excel uses absolute references during recording. For example, if you select cell A4, the macro recorder translates this action into the following VBA statement:

```
Range("A4").Select
```

On the other hand, you might prefer that all your cell references be relative to a specific cell. That way, you can apply the code to a different range just by selecting a different cell before running the macro.

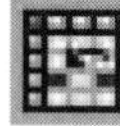

To do this, you need to tell Excel to use relative references during recording. First, select the cell that you want to use as the starting point. Then begin your recording in the usual manner (in other words, select Tools | Macros | Record New Macro, fill in the Record Macro dialog box, and click OK). When the Stop Recording toolbar appears, click the Relative Reference button, and then perform the macro actions normally.

For macros that use relative references, VBA translates cell-related actions as an "offset" from cell A1. For example, suppose you began the macro with cell A1 selected and then you clicked cell A4 during the recording. VBA would translate this into the following VBA statement:

```
ActiveCell.Offset(3,0).Range("A1").Select
```

VBA uses the `Offset` method to refer to a range that's a specified number of rows and columns from the current cell. I'll tell you more about this method later in this chapter (see "Working with Range Objects").

New VBA Features in Excel 97

VBA 5.0

Excel (along with Project) was in the first wave of Microsoft applications to become VBA-enabled. Subsequent Excel versions have tweaked the VBA object model and added new statements and functions to reflect both the new features in Excel and the continuing evolution of the VBA language. Excel 97 is no exception; I'll highlight some of the major changes in this section.

Excel 97's VBA object model has a few significant changes from the Excel 95 model. These changes include not only revisions both major and minor to existing objects, but also some completely new objects. Here's a rundown of the changes to the most important objects:

`CommandBars`: This is a new object in Excel 97 (it's common to every Office application). It's a collection that contains all the menu bars, toolbars, and shortcut menus defined in Excel. It replaces the old `MenuBars` and `Toolbars` objects (although, for backward compatibility, the properties and methods associated with these objects still work in Excel 97).

`UserForms`: This is a new object in the VBA hierarchy. It represents the user forms (dialog boxes) that you create using the Visual Basic Editor (see Chapter 11, "Working with Microsoft Forms"). It replaces the `DialogSheets` object used in previous versions of Excel.

`Hyperlinks`: In keeping with the Web-based focus of Office 97, the object models of Excel 97 and all the Office applications include the `Hyperlinks` object, which represents (in Excel's case) all the hyperlinks used in a worksheet or range. I'll discuss hyperlinks in Chapter 20, "Internet and Intranet Programming Topics."

`Shapes`: This new collection represents all the drawing objects you can create in Excel: lines, ovals, rectangles, and so on. It replaces the individual drawing objects used in previous versions.

`Comment`: This object represents Excel 97's new Comments feature, which replaces the old cell notes feature.

`FormatCondition`: You use this new object to control the conditional range formatting feature, which is new to Excel 97.

Range: This object includes a number of new properties and methods, including the `AddComment` method (for adding a comment to a cell), the `Comment` property (for accessing an existing comment), the `FormatConditions` property (to read or set the conditional formatting in a range), and the `Merge` method (for merging cells).

`RecentFiles`: You can use this new object to access Excel's list of recently used files.

Validation: This new object supports the new range validation feature in Excel 97.

`WorksheetFunction`: You use this new object to access Excel's worksheet functions. (In previous versions, these functions were contained directly in the `Application` object.) See "Accessing Worksheet Functions" later in this chapter.

Using VBA to Read and Set Excel's Program Options

Excel's Options dialog box (which you can display by selecting Tools | Options) is crammed with controls that let you customize almost every aspect of Excel. Almost all the controls in this dialog box can be accessed through the properties of various Excel objects. The next few sections take you through the equivalent properties for the options in the View, Calculation, Edit, and General tabs.

NOTE: PROPERTIES ARE READABLE AND WRITEABLE

Keep in mind that you can use most properties to either read the current state of a property or change the value of a property. For example, you can store the current setting of the `Application.DisplayFormulaBar` property in a variable named `currFormulaBar` with the following statement:

```
currFormulaBar = Application.DisplayFormulaBar
```

To set the property, use a statement such as the following:

```
Application.DisplayFormulaBar = False
```

The View Tab

The View tab options, shown in Figure 7.2, control several display settings for the Excel screen, workbooks, objects, and windows. Table 7.1 lists the available options in the View tab and their equivalent object properties.

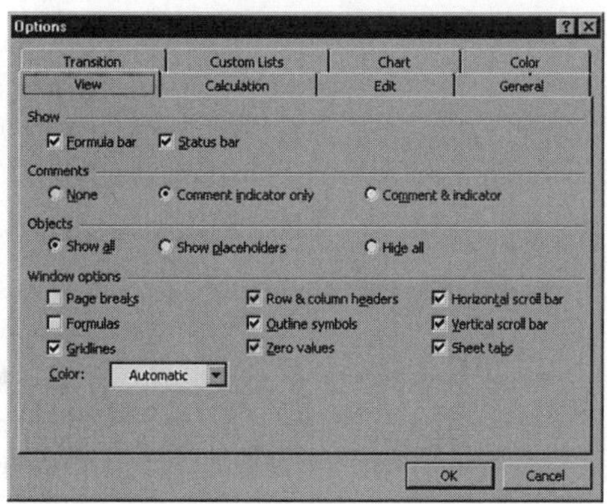

FIGURE 7.2.
The View tab in the Options dialog box.

NOTE: SETTING OPTION VALUES

Most of Excel's options are set using either check boxes or option buttons. You work with check box options by assigning the property a `Boolean` value: `True` turns the property on, and `False` turns the property off. For option buttons, Excel has predefined constants that correspond to each button.

Table 7.1. Object property equivalents for the View tab controls.

Option	*Property*	*Description*
Formula bar	`Application.DisplayFormulaBar`	Toggles the formula bar on and off. For example, the following statement hides the formula bar: `Application.DisplayFormulaBar = False`
Status bar	`Application.DisplayStatusBar`	Toggles the status bar on and off.
Comments	`Application.DisplayCommentIndicator`	Determines how Excel displays comments and comment indicators. Excel uses the following constants for each option button in the `Comments` group: **Option Button** — **Constant** None — `xlNoIndicator` Comment indicator only — `xlCommentIndicatorOnly` Comment & indicator — `xlCommentAndIndicator`
Objects	*`Workbook`*`.DisplayDrawingObjects`	Returns or sets how graphics are displayed in the specified *`Workbook`*. Excel uses the following constants for each option button in the `Objects` group: **Option Button** — **Constant** Show all — `xlDisplayShapes` Show placeholders — `xlPlaceholders` Hide all — `xlHide` For example, the following statement displays the active workbook's graphics as placeholders: `ActiveWorkbook.DisplayDrawingObjects = xlPlaceholders`
Page breaks	*`Worksheet`*`.Display.PageBreaks`	Toggles automatic page breaks on and off for the specified *`Worksheet`*.
Formulas	*`Window`*`.DisplayFormulas`	Toggles formulas on and off for the specified *`Window`*.
Gridlines	*`Window`*`.DisplayGridlines`	Toggles gridlines on and off for the specified *`Window`*. To change the color of the gridlines, use the Window object's `GridlineColorIndex` property.

Option	Property	Description
Row & column headers	`Window.DisplayHeadings`	Toggles row and column headers on and off for the specified `Window`.
Outline symbols	`Window.DisplayOutline`	Toggles outline symbols on and off for the specified `Window`.
Zero values	`Window.DisplayZeros`	Toggles zero values on and off for the specified `Window`.
Horizontal scroll bar	`Window.DisplayHorizontalScrollBar`	Toggles the horizontal scroll bar on and off for the specified `Window`.
Vertical scroll bar	`Window.DisplayVerticalScrollBar`	Toggles the vertical scroll bar on and off for the specified `Window`.
Sheet tabs	`Window.DisplayWorkbookTabs`	Toggles the worksheet tabs on and off for the specified `Window`.

If you find yourself consistently toggling one of these features on or off by hand, you know it's a hassle to constantly fire up the Options dialog box. To make your life easier, it's no problem to set up a procedure to do the toggling for you. For example, I often toggle gridlines on and off, so I created the `ToggleGridlines` procedure, shown in Listing 7.1.

Listing 7.1. A procedure that toggles the active window's gridlines on and off.

```
Sub ToggleGridlines()
    With ActiveWindow
        .DisplayGridlines = Not .DisplayGridlines
    End With
End Sub
```

NOTE: THIS CHAPTER'S CODE LISTINGS

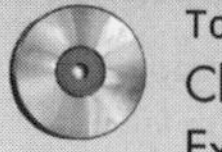

`ToggleGridlines` and all the listings in this chapter can be found in the workbook Chaptr07.xls, which is on the CD that comes with this book. If you don't have Excel and you would like to view these listings anyway (although I can't imagine why!), you'll also find them in the file Chaptr07.bas.

The Calculation Tab

The Calculation tab options contain several settings used to control worksheet calculations, as shown in Figure 7.3. Table 7.2 lists the available options in the Calculation tab and their equivalent object properties.

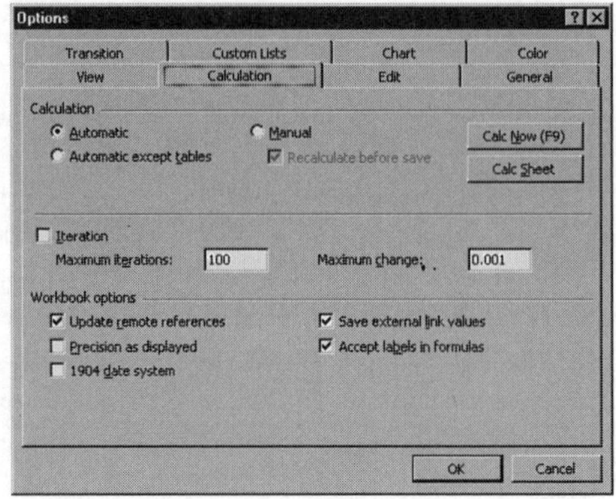

FIGURE 7.3.
The Calculation tab's options.

Table 7.2. Object property equivalents for the Calculation tab options.

Option	*Property*	*Description*
Automatic	`Application.Calculation = xlCalculationAutomatic`	Sets Excel's calculation mode to automatic.
Automatic except tables	`Application.Calculation = xlCalculationSemiautomatic`	Sets Excel's calculation mode to automatic, except for tables.
Manual	`Application.Calculation = xlCalculationManual`	Sets Excel's calculation mode to manual.
Recalculate before save	`Application.CalculateBeforeSave`	If the `Calculation` property is set to `xlManual`, this property returns or sets whether or not Excel recalculates before a workbook is saved.
Iteration	`Application.Iteration`	Returns or sets whether or not Excel uses iteration to resolve circular references.
Maximum iterations	`Application.MaxIterations`	Returns or sets the maximum number of iterations.
Maximum change	`Application.MaxChange`	Returns or sets the maximum amount of change used in each iteration.
Update remote references	*`Workbook`*`.UpdateRemoteReferences`	Returns or sets whether or not Excel updates remote references for the specified *`Workbook`*.
Precision as displayed	*`Workbook`*`.PrecisionAsDisplayed`	Returns or sets whether or not calculations in the specified *`Workbook`* use only the precision of the numbers as they are displayed.
1904 date system	*`Workbook`*`.Date1904`	Returns or sets whether or not the specified *`Workbook`* uses the 1904 date system.
Save external link values	*`Workbook`*`.SaveLinkValues`	Returns or sets whether or not Excel will save link values for the specified *`Workbook`*.
Accept labels in formulas	*`Workbook`*`.AcceptLabelsInFormulas`	Returns or sets whether or not Excel will accept labels in formulas for the specified *`Workbook`*.

The Edit Tab

The options in the Edit tab, shown in Figure 7.4, control various cell and range editing settings. Table 7.3 lists the available options in the Edit tab and their equivalent object properties.

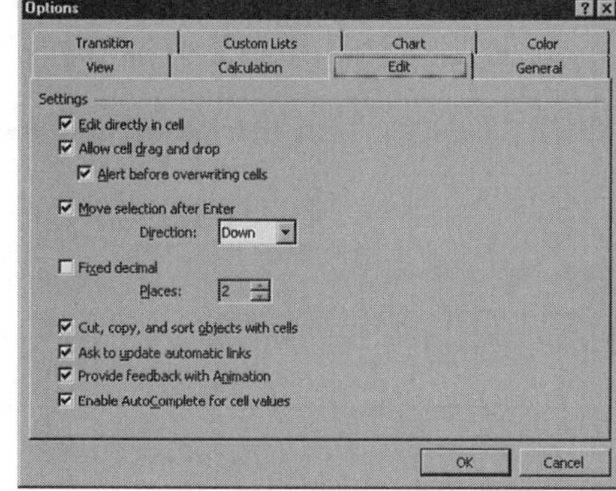

FIGURE 7.4.
The Edit tab in the Options dialog box.

Table 7.3. Object property equivalents for the Edit tab options.

Option	*Property*	*Description*
Edit directly in cell	`Application.EditDirectlyInCell`	Returns or sets whether or not Excel allows editing directly in cells.
Allow cell drag and drop	`Application.CellDragAndDrop`	Toggles cell drag-and-drop editing on and off.
Alert before overwriting cells	`Application.AlertBeforeOverwriting`	If the `CellDragAndDrop` property is set to `True`, this property returns or sets whether or not Excel displays a warning before overwriting non-empty cells during a drag-and-drop operation.
Move selection after Enter	`Application.MoveAfterReturn`	Returns or sets whether or not Excel moves the active cell after the user presses Enter.
Direction	`Application.MoveAfterReturnDirection`	If the `MoveAfterReturn` property is set to `True`, this property returns or sets the direction in which the active cell is moved. You have four choices: `xlToLeft`, `xlToRight`, `xlUp`, and `xlDown`.
Fixed decimal	`Application.FixedDecimal`	Returns or sets whether or not Excel formats entered numbers with the number of decimal places specified by the `FixedDecimalPlaces` property.
Places	`Application.FixedDecimalPlaces`	If the `FixedDecimal` property is set to `True`, this property returns or sets the number of decimal places. For example, to enter all numbers with two decimal places, you would

continues

Table 7.3. continued

Option	*Property*	*Description*
		use the following two statements: `Application.FixedDecimal = True` and `Application.FixedDecimalPlaces = 2`
Cut, copy, and sort objects with cells	`Application.CopyObjectsWithCells`	Returns or sets whether or not graphic objects move with cells that are cut, copied, or sorted.
Ask to update automatic links	`Application.AskToUpdateLinks`	Returns or sets whether or not Excel asks to update links when you open workbooks that contain links.
Provide feedback with Animation	`Application.EnableAnimations`	Toggles animated inserting and deleting on and off.
Enable AutoComplete for cell values	`Application.EnableAutoComplete`	Toggles AutoComplete on and off.

The General Tab

The controls on the General tab, shown in Figure 7.5, affect miscellaneous workspace options. Table 7.4 lists the available options in the General tab and their equivalent object properties.

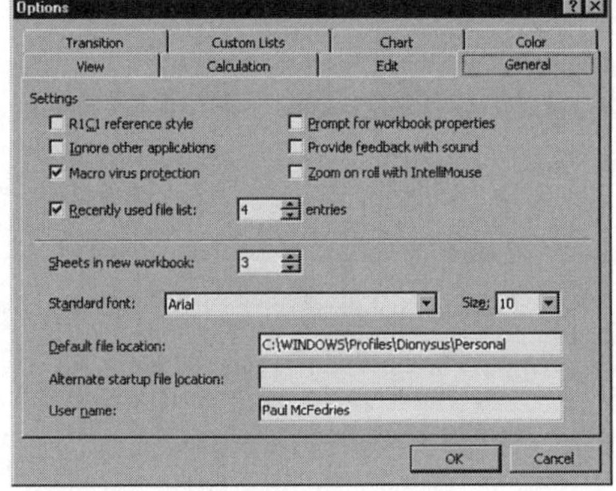

FIGURE 7.5.
The General tab in the Options dialog box.

Table 7.4. Object property equivalents for the General tab options.

Option	*Property*	*Description*
R1C1 reference style	`Application.ReferenceStyle`	Returns or sets the reference style used by Excel. Set this property to `xlA1` to use A1-style references or `xlR1C1` to use R1C1-style references.
Ignore other applications	`Application.IgnoreRemoteRequests`	Returns or sets whether or not Excel ignores Dynamic Data Exchange (DDE) requests from other applications.

Option	Property	Description
Macro virus protection	No VBA equivalent.	
Recently used file list	`Application.DisplayRecentFiles`	Toggles on and off the File menu's list of the last four files you used.
entries	`Application.RecentFiles.Maximum`	Returns or sets the number of files Excel displays in the recently used file list.
Prompt for workbook properties	`Application.PromptForSummaryInfo`	Returns or sets whether or not Excel displays the Properties dialog box whenever you save a new workbook.
Provide feedback with sound	`Application.EnableSound`	Returns or sets whether or not Excel plays sounds for events such as opening and closing files.
Zoom on roll with IntelliMouse	`Application.RollZoom`	Returns or sets whether or not spinning the IntelliMouse wheel zooms in and out of the worksheet. When this property is `False`, rotating the wheel scrolls through the worksheet.
Sheets in new workbook	`Application.SheetsInNewWorkBook`	Returns or sets the default number of sheets in new workbooks. You can use any number between 1 and 255.
Standard font	`Application.StandardFont`	Returns or sets the standard Excel font. When setting this property, use a string that corresponds to a typeface available on the system.

Size	`Application.StandardFontSize`	Returns or sets the default font size. For example, the following two statements set the default font to 12-point Arial:
		`Application.StandardFont = "Arial"`
		`Application.StandardFontSize = 12`

Default file location	`Application.DefaultFilePath`	Returns or sets the initial folder that appears when you first display the Open or Save As dialog boxes.
Alternate startup file location	`Application.AltStartupPath`	Returns or sets a startup directory in addition to \Office\ XLStart.
User name	`Application.UserName`	Returns or sets the user name you want displayed in the Properties dialog box and in scenarios, views, and file sharing.

Excel's Application Object

In Chapter 4, "Working with Objects," I went through a few `Application` object properties and methods that are common to all VBA applications. As you can imagine, though, each application has its own unique set of properties and methods for the `Application` object. Excel is no exception; you saw quite a few in the preceding section. This section shows you a few more.

Accessing Worksheet Functions

VBA 5.0

VBA has dozens of functions of its own, but its collection is downright meager compared to the hundreds of worksheet functions available with Excel. If you need to access one of these worksheet functions, VBA makes them available via a property of the `Application` object called `WorksheetFunctions`. Each function works exactly as it does on a worksheet—the only difference being that you have to append `Application.` to the name of the function.

NOTE: YOUR OLD VBA PROCEDURES WILL STILL WORK

I mentioned earlier that `WorksheetFunctions` is a new element in the VBA 5.0 object model. Previous versions accessed Excel's worksheet functions via the `Application` object directly. However, there's no immediate need to go back and rewrite your old procedures, because VBA 5.0 still supports the old model. There's no telling how long this support will remain in VBA, however, so you should probably put this change on your "to do" list. (This is a perfect example of how the Visual Basic Editor's Replace feature comes in handy. See Chapter 1, "Introducing VBA," for details.)

For example, to run the `SUM()` worksheet function on the range named Sales and store the result in a variable named `totalSales`, you would use the following statement:

```
totalSales = Application.WorksheetFunctions.Sum(Range("Sales"))
```

CAUTION: USE VBA'S FUNCTIONS TO AVOID ERRORS

The `WorksheetFunctions` object includes only those worksheet functions that don't duplicate an existing VBA function. For example, VBA has a `UCase$` function that's equivalent to Excel's `UPPER()` worksheet function (both convert a string into uppercase). In this case, you must use VBA's `UCase$` function in your code. If you try to use `Application.WorksheetFunctions.Upper`, you'll receive the error message `Object doesn't support this property or method.`

NOTE: A LIST OF VBA FUNCTIONS

For a complete list of VBA functions, see Appendix B, "VBA Functions."

Other Properties of the `Application` Object

Besides the properties you saw earlier that control many of Excel's workspace options, the `Application` object has dozens of other properties that affect a number of aspects of the Excel environment. Here's a rundown of some `Application` object properties you'll use most often in your VBA code:

`Application.CanPlaySounds`: This read-only property returns `True` if the system can play sound notes. (See Chapter 10, "Interacting with the User," for a complete description of the `CanPlaySounds` and `CanRecordSounds` properties.)

`Application.CanRecordSounds`: This read-only property returns `True` if the system can record sound notes.

`Application.CutCopyMode`: Returns or sets Excel's Cut or Copy mode status. If your code copies a Range object and then pastes it (as described later in this chapter), Excel stays in Copy mode after the paste. This means that it displays a moving border around the range and displays `Select destination and press ENTER or choose Paste` in the status bar. If you would prefer not to confuse the user with these Copy mode indicators, you can take Excel out of Copy mode (or Cut mode, if you cut the range) by running the following statement:

```
Application.CutCopyMode = False
```

`Application.MemoryFree`: Returns the amount of system memory that is still available to Excel.

`Application.MemoryTotal`: Returns the total amount of system memory (used and free) that is available to Excel.

`Application.MemoryUsed`: Returns the amount of system memory that is being used by Excel.

`Application.MouseAvailable`: Returns `True` if a mouse is present on the system.

`Application.OperatingSystem`: Returns the name and version number of the current operating system. This is a useful way of determining whether or not your procedure should run a feature specific to Windows 95 or to the Macintosh version of Excel.

Methods of Excel's `Application` Object

The `Application` object features a few dozen methods that perform actions on the Excel environment. Here's a summary of the most common methods:

`Calculate`: Calculates all the open workbooks. Note that you don't need to specify the `Application` object. You can just enter `Calculate` by itself.

`Application.DoubleClick`: Equivalent to double-clicking the current cell. If in-cell editing is activated, running this method opens the cell for editing; otherwise, running this method opens the cell's comment (if it has one) for editing.

`Application.Quit`: Quits Excel. If there are any open workbooks with unsaved changes, Excel will ask if you want to save the changes. To prevent this, either save the workbooks before running the `Quit` method (I'll tell you how to save workbooks in the section "Manipulating Workbook Objects"), or set the `DisplayAlerts` property to `False`. (In the latter case, note that Excel will *not* save changes to the workbooks.)

> **NOTE: QUIT IGNORES AUTO_CLOSE PROCEDURES**
>
> Older versions of Excel used `Auto_Close` procedures, which ran automatically whenever the user closed a workbook. If you still use these procedures, note that `Quit` will shut down Excel *without* running any `Auto_Close` procedures. Note, too, that VBA 5.0 supports `BeforeClose` events instead of `Auto_Close` procedures, and that VBA does fire the `BeforeClose` event before quitting Excel via the `Quit` method.

`Application.SaveWorkspace`: Saves the current workspace. Here's the syntax:

```
Application.SaveWorkspace(Filename)
```

`Filename` The name of the workspace file.

`Application.Volatile`: When inserted inside a user-defined function, the `Volatile` method tells Excel to recalculate the function every time the worksheet is recalculated. If you don't include the `Volatile` method, Excel only recalculates the function whenever its input cells change. (Here, the input cells are those cells passed directly to the function as arguments. This doesn't apply to any other cells used indirectly in the calculation.) Use the following statement (again, inside a user-defined function) to change a function's behavior from volatile to nonvolatile:

```
Application.Volatile False
```

`Application.Wait`: Pauses a running macro until a specified time is reached. Here's the syntax:

```
Application.Wait(Time)
```

`Time` The time you want the macro the resume running.

For example, if you wanted your procedure to delay for about five seconds, you would use the following statement:

```
Application.Wait Now + TimeValue("00:00:05")
```

Some Event-Like Methods

Excel's `Application` objects come with a few predefined events, but it takes a bit of work before you can use them. Specifically, you must create a new *class module* and use it to declare an `Application` object. I'll save all this until I discuss class modules in Chapter 26, "VBA Tips and Techniques." In the meantime, the `Application` object comes with several methods that are "event-like." In other words, they respond to outside influences such as the press of a key. This section looks at four of these methods: `OnKey`, `OnTime`, `OnRepeat`, and `OnUndo`.

Running a Procedure When the User Presses a Key

As discussed in the section "Excel's Macro Options," Excel lets you assign a Ctrl-*key* shortcut to a procedure. However, this method has two major drawbacks:

- Excel uses some Ctrl-*key* combinations internally, so your choices are limited.
- It doesn't help if you would like your procedures to respond to "meaningful" keys such as Delete and Esc.

To remedy these problems, use the `Application` object's `OnKey` method to run a procedure when the user presses a specific key or key combination:

```
Application.OnKey(Key, Procedure)
```

Key	The key or key combination that runs the procedure. For letters, numbers, or punctuation marks, enclose the character in quotes (for example, `"a"`). For other keys, see Table 7.5.
`Procedure`	The name (entered as text) of the procedure to run when the user presses a key. If you enter the null string (`""`) for *`Procedure`*, a key is disabled. If you omit *`Procedure`*, Excel resets the key to its normal state.

Table 7.5. Key strings to use with the OnKey method.

Key	*What to Use*
Backspace	`"{BACKSPACE}"` or `"{BS}"`
Break	`"{BREAK}"`
Caps Lock	`"{CAPSLOCK}"`
Delete	`"{DELETE}"` or `"{DEL}"`
Down arrow	`"{DOWN}"`
End	`"{END}"`
Enter (keypad)	`"{ENTER}"`
Enter	`"~"` (tilde)
Esc	`"{ESCAPE}"` or `"{ESC}"`
Help	`"{HELP}"`
Home	`"{HOME}"`
Insert	`"{INSERT}"`
Left arrow	`"{LEFT}"`
Num Lock	`"{NUMLOCK}"`
Page Down	`"{PGDN}"`

continues

Table 7.5. continued

Key	*What to Use*
Page Up	`"{PGUP}"`
Right arrow	`"{RIGHT}"`
Scroll Lock	`"{SCROLLLOCK}"`
Tab	`"{TAB}"`
Up arrow	`"{UP}"`
F1 through F12	`"{F1}"` through `"{F12}"`

You also can combine these keys with the Shift, Ctrl, and Alt keys. You just precede these codes with one or more of the codes listed in Table 7.6.

Table 7.6. Symbols that represent Alt, Ctrl, and Shift in OnKey.

Key	*What to Use*
Alt	`%` (percent)
Ctrl	`^` (caret)
Shift	`+` (plus)

For example, pressing Delete normally wipes out only a cell's contents. If you would like a quick way of deleting everything in a cell (contents, formats, comments, and so on), you could, for example, set up Ctrl-Delete to do the job. Listing 7.2 shows three procedures that accomplish this:

`SetKey`: This procedure sets up the Ctrl-Delete key combination to run the `DeleteAll` procedure. Notice how the *`Procedure`* argument includes the name of the workbook; therefore, this key combination will operate in any workbook.

`DeleteAll`: This procedure runs the `Clear` method on the current selection.

`ResetKey`: This procedure resets Ctrl-Delete to its default behavior.

Listing 7.2. Procedures that set and reset a key combination using the OnKey method.

```
Sub SetKey()
    Application.OnKey _
        Key:="^{Del}", _
        Procedure:="Chaptr07.xls!DeleteAll"
End Sub
Sub DeleteAll()
    Selection.Clear
End Sub
```

```
Sub ResetKey()
    Application.OnKey _
        Key:="^{Del}"
End Sub
```

Running a Procedure at a Specific Time

If you need to run a procedure at a specific time, use the `OnTime` method:

`Application.OnTime(`***`EarliestTime`***`, `***`Procedure`***`, `*`LatestTime`*`, `*`Schedule`*`)`

EarliestTime	The time (and date, if necessary) you want the procedure to run. Enter a date/time serial number.
Procedure	The name (entered as text) of the procedure to run when the ***EarliestTime*** arrives.
LatestTime	If Excel isn't ready to run the procedure at ***EarliestTime*** (in other words, if it's not in Ready, Cut, Copy, or Find mode), it will keep trying until *LatestTime* arrives. If you omit *LatestTime*, VBA waits until Excel is ready. Enter a date/time serial number.
Schedule	A logical value that determines whether or not the procedure runs at ***EarliestTime***. If *Schedule* is `True` or omitted, the procedure runs. Use `False` to cancel a previous `OnTime` setting.

The easiest way to enter the time serial numbers for ***EarliestTime*** and *LatestTime* is to use the `TimeValue` function:

`TimeValue(`***`Time`***`)`

Time	A string representing the time you want to use (such as "5:00PM" or "17:00").

For example, the following formula runs a procedure called `Backup` at 5:00 PM:

```
Application.OnTime _
    EarliestTime:=TimeValue("5:00PM"), _
    Procedure:="Backup"
```

TIP: RUNNING A PROCEDURE AFTER A SPECIFIED INTERVAL

If you want the `OnTime` method to run after a specified time interval (for example, an hour from now), use `Now + TimeValue(`***`Time`***`)` for ***EarliestTime*** (where ***Time*** is the interval you want to use). For example, the following statement schedules a procedure to run in 30 minutes:

```
Application.OnTime _
    EarliestTime:=Now + TimeValue("00:30"), _
    Procedure:="Backup"
```

Running a Procedure When the User Selects Repeat or Undo

Excel has a couple of event-like methods that run procedures when the user selects Edit | Repeat and Edit | Undo.

The `OnRepeat` method customizes the name of the Edit | Repeat menu item and specifies the procedure that runs when the user selects Edit | Repeat. Set this property at the end of a procedure so that the user can easily repeat the procedure just by selecting Edit | Repeat. Here's the syntax:

`Application.OnRepeat(`***`Text`***`, `***`Procedure`***`)`

Text	The name of the Edit | Repeat menu item. This command normally uses R as its accelerator key, so make sure that the ***Text*** argument has an ampersand (`&`) before the `R` (for example, `&Repeat Formatting`).
Procedure	The procedure to run when the user selects Edit | Repeat (this will usually be the name of the procedure that contains the `OnRepeat` statement).

The `OnUndo` method is similar to `OnRepeat`, except that it sets the name of the Edit | Undo menu item and specifies the procedure that runs when the user selects Edit | Undo:

`Application.OnUndo(`***`Text`***`, `***`Procedure`***`)`

Text	The name of the Edit | Undo menu item. Note that the Undo command uses the letter U as its accelerator key.
Procedure	The procedure to run when the user selects Edit | Undo.

Listing 7.3 shows an example that uses both `OnRepeat` and `OnUndo`. The `currCell` variable stores the address of the active cell. Notice that it's declared at the module level to make it available to all the procedures in the module (see Chapter 2, "Understanding Variables"). The `BoldAndItalic` procedure makes the font of the active cell bold and italic and then sets the `OnRepeat` property (to run `BoldAndItalic` again) and the `OnUndo` property (to run the procedure named `UndoBoldAndItalic`).

Listing 7.3. Procedures that set the `OnRepeat` and `OnUndo` properties.

```
Dim currCell As String  ' The module-level variable
Sub BoldAndItalic()
    With ActiveCell
        .Font.Bold = True
        .Font.Italic = True
        currCell = .Address
    End With
    Application.OnRepeat _
        Text:="&Repeat Bold and Italic", _
        Procedure:="BoldAndItalic"
```

```
    Application.OnUndo _
        Text:="&Undo Bold and Italic", _
        Procedure:="UndoBoldAndItalic"
End Sub
Sub UndoBoldAndItalic()
    With Range(currCell).Font
        .Bold = False
        .Italic = False
    End With
End Sub
```


Manipulating Workbook Objects

Workbook objects appear directly below the `Application` object in Excel's object hierarchy. You can use VBA to create new workbooks, open or delete existing workbooks, save and close open workbooks, and much more. The next section takes you through various techniques for specifying workbooks in your VBA code; then we'll look at some Workbook object properties, methods, and events.

Specifying a Workbook Object

If you need to perform some action on a workbook, or if you need to work with an object contained in a specific workbook (such as a worksheet), you need to tell Excel which workbook you want to use. VBA gives you no less than three ways to do this:

Use the `Workbooks` object: The `Workbooks` object is the collection of all the open workbook files. To specify a workbook, either use its index number (where 1 represents the first workbook opened) or enclose the workbook name in quotation marks. For example, if the Budget.xls workbook was the first workbook opened, the following two statements would be equivalent:

```
Workbooks(1)
Workbooks("Budget.xls")
```

Use the `ActiveWorkbook` object: The `ActiveWorkbook` object represents the workbook that currently has the focus.

Use the `ThisWorkbook` object: The `ThisWorkbook` object represents the workbook where the VBA code is executing. If your code only deals with objects residing in the same workbook as the code itself, you can use the `ActiveWorkbook` object. However, if your code deals with other workbooks, use `ThisWorkbook` whenever you need to make sure that the code affects only the workbook containing the procedure.

Opening a Workbook

To open a workbook file, use the `Open` method of the `Workbooks` collection. The `Open` method has a dozen arguments you can use to fine-tune your workbook openings, but only one of these is mandatory. Here's the simplified syntax showing the one required argument (for the rest of the arguments, look up the Open method in the VBA Help system):

```
Workbooks.Open(FileName)
```

FileName	The full name of the workbook file, including the drive and folder that contain the file.

For example, to open a workbook named Data.xls in the current drive and folder, you would use the following statement:

```
Workbooks.Open "Data.xls"
```

> **NOTE: WORKING WITH DRIVES AND FOLDERS**
>
> You can use VBA to change the default drive and folder:
>
> To change the drive, use the ChDrive function. For example, the statement ChDrive "D" changes the current drive to D.
>
> To change the current folder (directory), use the ChDir function. For example, the statement ChDir "\My Documents\Worksheets" changes the default folder to \My Documents\Worksheets on the current drive. If you need to know the name of the current directory, use the CurDir function.

Creating a New Workbook

If you need to create a new workbook, use the Workbooks collection's Add method:

```
Workbooks.Add(Template)
```

Template is an optional argument that determines how the workbook is created. If *Template* is a string specifying an Excel file, VBA uses the file as a template for the new workbook. You also can specify one of the following constants:

xlWBATWorksheet	Creates a workbook with a single worksheet.
xlWBATChart	Creates a workbook with a single chart sheet.
xlWBATExcel4MacroSheet	Creates a workbook with a single Excel 4 macro sheet.
xlWBATExcel4IntlMacroSheet	Creates a workbook with a single Excel 4 international macro sheet.

Here's a sample statement that uses the Add method to open a new workbook based on Excel's Invoice.xlt template file:

```
Workbooks.Add "C:\Program Files\Microsoft Office" & _
    "\Templates\Spreadsheet Solutions\Invoice.xlt"
```

Workbook Object Properties

Here's a rundown of some common properties associated with Workbook objects:

Workbook.FullName: Returns the full pathname of the *Workbook*. The full pathname includes the workbook's path (the drive and folder in which the file resides) and the filename.

Workbook.Name: Returns the filename of the *Workbook*.

Workbook.Path: Returns the path of the *Workbook* file.

NOTE: THE PATH FOR A NEW WORKBOOK

A new, unsaved workbook's Path property returns an empty string ("").

Workbook.ProtectStructure: Returns True if the structure of the *Workbook* is protected; returns False otherwise. (To learn how to use code to protect a workbook, see the next section, which discusses the Workbook object's Protect method.)

Workbook.ProtectWindows: Returns True if the window size and position of the *Workbook* are protected; returns False otherwise. (Again, see the description of the Protect method to learn how to protect windows programmatically.)

Workbook.Saved: Determines whether or not changes have been made to the *Workbook* since it was last saved. If changes have been made, Saved returns False.

TIP: CLOSING WITHOUT SAVING CHANGES

The Saved property is read/write. Therefore, besides reading the current value of Saved, you also can set Saved to either True or False. For example, to allow the user to close a workbook (by selecting File | Close) without saving changes and without Excel asking if she wants to save changes, set the workbook's Saved property to True. (See also the Workbook object's Close method, discussed in the next section.)

Workbook Object Methods

Workbook objects have dozens of methods that let you do everything from saving a workbook to closing a workbook. Here are a few methods that you'll use most often:

Workbook.Activate: Activates the specified open *Workbook*. For example, the following statement activates the Finances.xls workbook:

```
Workbooks("Finances.xls").Activate
```

`Workbook.Close`: Closes the specified `Workbook`. This method uses the following syntax:

```
Workbook.Close(SaveChanges, FileName, RouteWorkbook)
```

`Workbook`	The Workbook object you want to close.
`SaveChanges`	If the workbook has been modified, this argument determines whether or not Excel saves those changes:

`SaveChanges`	*Action*
`True`	Saves changes before closing.
`False`	Doesn't save changes.
Omitted	Asks the user if she wants to save changes.

`FileName`	Save the workbook under this filename.
`RouteWorkbook`	Routes the workbook according to the following values:

`RouteWorkbook`	*Action*
`True`	Sends the workbook to the next recipient.
`False`	Doesn't send the workbook.
Omitted	Asks the user if she wants to send the workbook.

`Workbook.PrintOut`: Prints the specified `Workbook` using the following syntax:

```
Workbook.PrintOut(From, To, Copies, Preview, ActivePrinter, PrintToFile,
➥Collate)
```

`Workbook`	The Workbook object you want to print.
`From`	The page number from which to start printing.
`To`	The page number of the last page to print.
`Copies`	The number of copies to print. The default value is 1.
`Preview`	If `True`, Excel displays the Print Preview window before printing. The default value is `False`.
`ActivePrinter`	Specifies the printer to use.
`PrintToFile`	If `True`, Excel prints the workbook to a file and prompts the user for a filename.
`Collate`	If `True`, and `Copies` is greater than 1, Excel collates the copies.

`Workbook.PrintPreview`: Displays the specified `Workbook` in the Print Preview window.

`Workbook.Protect`: Protects the specified `Workbook`. The `Protect` method uses the syntax shown here:

```
Workbook.Protect(Password, Structure, Windows)
```

Workbook	The Workbook object you want to protect.
Password	A text string that specifies the (case-sensitive) password to use with the protection.
Structure	If `True`, Excel protects the workbook's structure.
Windows	If `True`, Excel protects the workbook's windows.

`Workbook``.Save`: Saves the specified *`Workbook`*. If the workbook is new, use the `SaveAs` method instead.

`Workbook``.SaveAs`: Saves the specified *`Workbook`* to a different file. Here's the simplified syntax for the `SaveAs` method (to see all nine arguments in the full syntax, look up the `SaveAs` method in the VBA Help system):

```
Workbook.SaveAs(FileName)
```

Workbook	The Workbook object you want to save to a different file.
FileName	The full name of the new workbook file, including the drive and folder where you want the file to reside.

`Workbook``.Unprotect`: Unprotects the specified *`Workbook`*. Here's the syntax:

```
Workbook.Unprotect(Password)
```

Workbook	The Workbook object you want to unprotect.
Password	The protection password.

7 MANIPULATING EXCEL WITH VBA

Workbook Object Events

VBA 5.0

Workbook objects respond to a number of events, including opening, closing, activating, deactivating, printing, and saving. Here's a quick look at a few of these events:

`Activate`: This event fires when the workbook gains the focus within Excel:

- When the user selects the workbook from the Window menu.
- When your code runs the workbook's `Activate` method.
- When the user opens the workbook, or when your code runs the workbook's `Open` method.

Note that this event doesn't fire if the workbook has the focus in Excel and the user switches to Excel from a different application. Here's the event handler procedure stub that appears when you select the `Activate` event in a workbook's code module:

```
Private Sub Workbook_Activate()
    <Event handler code goes here>
End Sub
```

NOTE: ENTERING EVENT HANDLER CODE

It's worth repeating that you don't create these event handlers in a regular VBA module. Instead, you follow these steps:

1. In the Visual Basic Editor's Project Explorer, highlight the object you want to work with. For the workbook containing the VBA code, highlight `ThisWorkbook`.

2. Select View | Code, press F7, or click the View Code button in the Project Explorer.
3. In the code window that appears, use the Object drop-down list (the one on the left) to select the Workbook object.
4. Use the Procedures drop-down list (the one on the right) to select the event you want to work with. VBA adds the event handler's procedure stub to the code window.
5. Enter your event handler code within the procedure stub.

`BeforeClose`: This event fires when the user selects File | Close or when your code runs the workbook's `Close` method. Note that the statements you define inside the event handler will run before the workbook is closed and before the user is asked to save changes. Here's the procedure stub of the event handler:

```
Private Sub Workbook_BeforeClose(Cancel As Boolean)
    <Event handler code goes here>
End Sub
```

`Cancel` is a `Boolean` value that determines whether or not the workbook is closed. If you set *`Cancel`* to `True` during this procedure, Excel won't close the workbook.

`BeforePrint`: This event fires when the user selects File | Print or when your code runs the workbook's `PrintOut` method. The statements you define inside the event handler will run before the workbook is printed and before the Print dialog box appears. Here's the event handler's procedure stub:

```
Private Sub Workbook_BeforePrint(Cancel As Boolean)
    <Event handler code goes here>
End Sub
```

`Cancel` is a `Boolean` value that determines whether or not the workbook is printed. If you set *`Cancel`* to `True` during this procedure, Excel won't print the workbook.

`BeforeSave`: Fires when the user selects either File | Save or File | Save As, or when your code runs the workbook's `Save` or `SaveAs` methods. The statements you define inside the event handler will run before the workbook is saved. Here's the procedure stub:

```
Private Sub Workbook_BeforeSave(ByVal SaveAsUI As Boolean Cancel As Boolean)
    <Event handler code goes here>
End Sub
```

`SaveAsUI`	A `Boolean` value that determines whether or not Excel displays the Save As dialog box during a "Save As" operation.

`Cancel`	A `Boolean` value that determines whether or not the workbook is saved. If you set `Cancel` to `True` during this procedure, Excel won't save the workbook.

`Deactivate`: This event fires when the workbook loses the focus within Excel (for example, if the user creates a new workbook or activates another open workbook). This event doesn't fire if the user switches to a different application. Note as well that Excel first switches to the other workbook and *then* runs the event handler. Here's the event handler procedure stub:

```
Private Sub Workbook_Deactivate()
    <Event handler code goes here>
End Sub
```

`NewSheet`: Fires when the user creates a new sheet in the workbook (for example, by selecting Insert | Worksheet) or when your code runs the `Add` method of the `Worksheets` object (see "Dealing with Worksheet Objects" later in this chapter). This event also fires when the user or your code creates a chart in a new sheet. Note that the statements you define inside the event handler will run *after* the new sheet is inserted. Here's the procedure stub used by the event handler:

```
Private Sub Workbook_NewSheet(ByVal Sh As Object)
    <Event handler code goes here>
End Sub
```

`Sh` is an `Object` value that represents the new sheet. `Sh` can be either a Workbook object or a Chart object.

`Open`: This event fires when the user selects File | Open or when your code runs the workbook's `Open` method. Here's the procedure stub of the event handler:

```
Private Sub Workbook_Open()
    <Event handler code goes here>
End Sub
```

Dealing with Worksheet Objects

Worksheet objects contain a number of properties, methods, and events you can exploit in your code. These include options for activating and hiding worksheets, adding new worksheets to a workbook, and moving, copying, and deleting worksheets. The next few sections discuss these and other worksheet operations.

Specifying a Worksheet Object

If you need to deal with a worksheet in some way, or if your code needs to specify an object contained in a specific worksheet (such as a range of cells), you need to tell Excel which worksheet you want to use. To do this, use the `Worksheets` object. `Worksheets` is the collection of all the worksheets in a particular workbook. To specify a worksheet, either use its index number (where 1 represents the first worksheet tab, 2 the second worksheet tab, and so on) or enclose the worksheet name in quotation marks. For example, if Sheet1 is the first worksheet, the following two statements would be equivalent:

```
Workbooks(1)
Worksheets("Sheet1")
```

If you need to work with multiple worksheets (say, to set up a 3-D range), use VBA's `Array` function with the `Workbooks` collection. For example, the following statement specifies the Sheet1 and Sheet2 worksheets:

```
Worksheets(Array("Sheet1","Sheet2"))
```

Creating a New Worksheet

The `Worksheets` collection has an `Add` method you can use to insert new sheets into the workbook. Here's the syntax for this method:

```
Worksheets.Add(Before, After, Count, Type)
```

`Before`	The sheet before which the new sheet is added. If you omit both *`Before`* and *`After`*, the new worksheet is added before the active sheet.
`After`	The sheet after which the new sheet is added. Note that you can't specify both the *`Before`* and *`After`* arguments.
`Count`	The number of new worksheets to add. VBA adds one worksheet if you omit *`Count`*.
`Type`	The type of worksheet. You have three choices: `xlWorksheet` (the default), `xlExcel4MacroSheet`, or `xlExcel4IntlMacroSheet`.

In the following statement, a new worksheet is added to the active workbook before the Sales sheet:

```
Worksheets.Add Before:=Worksheets("Sales")
```

Properties of the Worksheet Object

Let's take a tour through some of the most useful properties associated with Worksheet objects:

`Worksheet``.Name`: Returns or sets the name of the specified *`Worksheet`*. For example, the following statement renames the Sheet1 worksheet to 1994 Budget:

```
Worksheets("Sheet1").Name = "1994 Budget"
```

`Worksheet``.Outline`: Returns an `Outline` object that represents the outline for the specified *`Worksheet`*.

NOTE: WORKING WITH THE OUTLINE OBJECT

Once you have the `Outline` object, use the `ShowLevels` method to select an outline level. For example, the following statement displays the second outline level for the Net Worth worksheet:

```
Worksheets("Net Worth").Outline.ShowLevels 2
```

Here are some other outline-related properties and methods you can use:

> `Range.AutoOutline`: Automatically creates an outline for the specified *`Range`* object.
>
> `Window.DisplayOutline`: Set this property to `True` to display the outline for the specified *`Window`* object.
>
> `Range.ClearOutline`: Clears the outline for the specified *`Range`* object.

`Worksheet.ProtectContents`: Returns `True` if the specified *`Worksheet`* is protected. To set this property (and the next few protection-related properties), run the Worksheet object's `Protect` method, described in the next section.

`Worksheet.ProtectDrawingObjects`: Returns `True` if the drawing objects on the specified *`Worksheet`* are protected.

`Worksheet.ProtectionMode`: Returns `True` if user-interface-only protection is activated for the specified *`Worksheet`*.

`Worksheet.ProtectScenarios`: Returns `True` if the scenarios in the specified *`Worksheet`* are protected.

`Worksheet.StandardHeight`: Returns the standard height of all the rows in the specified *`Worksheet`*.

`Worksheet.StandardWidth`: Returns the standard width of all the columns in the specified *`Worksheet`*.

`UsedRange`: Returns a Range object that represents the used range in the specified *`Worksheet`*.

`Worksheet.Visible`: Controls whether or not the user can see the specified *`Worksheet`*. Setting this property to `False` is equivalent to selecting Format | Sheet | Hide. For example, to hide a worksheet named Expenses, you would use the following statement:

```
Worksheets("Expenses").Visible = False
```

To unhide the sheet, set its `Visible` property to `True`.

Methods of the Worksheet Object

Here's a list of some common Worksheet object methods:

`Worksheet.Activate`: Makes the specified *Worksheet* active (so that it becomes the `ActiveSheet` property of the workbook). For example, the following statement activates the Sales worksheet in the Finance.xls workbook:

```
Workbooks("Finance.xls").Worksheets("Sales").Activate
```

`Worksheet.Calculate`: Calculates the specified *Worksheet*. For example, the following statement recalculates the Budget 1997 worksheet:

```
Worksheets("Budget 1997").Calculate
```

`Worksheet.CheckSpelling`: Displays the Spelling dialog box to check the spelling on the specified *Worksheet*. Here is the syntax of this version of the `CheckSpelling` method:

```
Worksheet.CheckSpelling(CustomDictionary, IgnoreUppercase, AlwaysSuggest)
```

Worksheet	The worksheet you want to check.
CustomDictionary	The filename of a custom dictionary that Excel can search if a word can't be found in the main dictionary.
IgnoreUppercase	Set to `True` to tell Excel to ignore words entirely in uppercase.
AlwaysSuggest	Set to `True` to tell Excel to display a list of suggestions for each misspelled word.

`Worksheet.Copy`: Copies the specified *Worksheet* using the following syntax:

```
Worksheet.Copy(Before, After)
```

Worksheet	The worksheet you want to copy.
Before	The sheet before which the sheet will be copied. If you omit both *Before* and *After*, VBA creates a new workbook for the copied sheet.
After	The sheet after which the new sheet is added. You can't specify both the *Before* and *After* arguments.

In the following statement, the Budget 1997 worksheet is copied to a new workbook:

```
Worksheets("Budget 1997").Copy
```

`Worksheet.Delete`: Deletes the specified *Worksheet*. For example, the following statement deletes the active worksheet:

```
ActiveSheet.Delete
```

`Worksheets.FillAcrossSheets`: Enters data or formatting in a range that applies to the specified *`Worksheets`*. This method uses the following syntax:

```
Worksheets.FillAcrossSheets(Range, Type)
```

`Worksheets`	The `Worksheets` object you want to work with.
`Range`	The Range object in which you want to fill the data or formatting. Note that the specified range must be within one of the sheets specified in ***`Worksheets`***.
`Type`	An optional argument that specifies what you want to fill:

Type	*Action*
`xlFillWithAll`	Fills the sheets with both the contents and the formatting contained in ***`Range`***. This is the default value.
`xlFillWithContents`	Fills the sheets with just the contents of ***`Range`***.
`xlFillWithFormats`	Fills the sheets with just the formatting of ***`Range`***.

For example, the following statement fills the contents of range A1:D5 of worksheet Sheet1 across worksheets named Sheet1, Sheet2, and Sheet3:

```
Worksheets(Array("Sheet1", "Sheet2", "Sheet3")).FillAcrossSheets _
    Range:=Worksheets("Sheet1").Range("A1:D5"), _
    Type:=xlFillWithContents
```

`Worksheet.Move`: Moves the specified *`Worksheet`* using the following syntax:

```
Worksheet.Move(Before, After)
```

`Worksheet`	The worksheet you want to move.
`Before`	The sheet before which the sheet will be moved. If you omit both *`Before`* and *`After`*, VBA creates a new workbook for the moved sheet.
`After`	The sheet after which the new sheet is added. You can't specify both the *`Before`* and *`After`* arguments.

In the following statement, the Budget 1997 worksheet is moved before the Budget 1996 worksheet:

```
Worksheets("Budget 1997").Move Before:=Worksheets("1996 Budget")
```

Worksheet.Protect: Sets up protection for the specified *Worksheet*. Here's the syntax to use:

```
Worksheet.Protect(Password, DrawingObjects, Contents, Scenarios,
➥UserInterfaceOnly)
```

Worksheet	The worksheet you want to protect.
Password	A text string that specifies the (case-sensitive) password to use with the protection.
DrawingObjects	Set to True to protect the worksheet's drawing objects.
Contents	Set to True to protect the worksheet's cell contents.
Scenarios	Set to True to protect the worksheet's scenarios.
UserInterfaceOnly	Set to True to protect the worksheet's user interface, but not its macros.

For example, the following statement protects the Payroll worksheet's contents and scenarios and sets up a password for the protection:

```
Worksheets("Payroll").Protect _
    Password:="cheapskate", _
    Contents:=True, _
    Scenarios:=True
```

Worksheet.Select: Selects the specified *Worksheet*.

Worksheet.SetBackgroundPicture: Adds a bitmap image to the background of the specified *Worksheet*. Here is the syntax:

```
Worksheet.SetBackgroundPicture(FileName)
```

Worksheet	The worksheet you want to use.
FileName	The filename of the bitmap image you want to use.

For example, the following statement sets the background image of Sheet1 to C:\Windows\Clouds.bmp:

```
Worksheets("Sheet1").SetBackgroundPicture "C:\Windows\Clouds.bmp"
```

Worksheet.Unprotect: Unprotects the specified *Worksheet*. Here's the syntax:

```
Worksheet.Unprotect(Password)
```

Worksheet	The Worksheet object you want to unprotect.
Password	The protection password.

Worksheet Object Events

VBA 5.0

Worksheet objects respond to several events, including activating and deactivating the worksheet, calculating the worksheet, and making a change to the worksheet. Here's a rundown of a few of these events:

`Activate`: This event fires when the worksheet gains the focus within Excel (such as when the user clicks the worksheet's tab or when your code runs the worksheet's `Activate` method. Note that this event doesn't fire in the following situations:

- When the user switches from one workbook to another.
- When the user switches to Excel from a different application.

Here's the syntax of this procedure:

```
Private Sub Worksheet_Activate()
    <Event handler code goes here>
End Sub
```

`Calculate`: This event fires when the specified worksheet recalculates, which in turn depends on whether or not any user-defined function has been set up as a volatile function. (See the discussion of the `Application` object's `Volatile` method earlier in this chapter.) If no function is volatile, the `Calculate` event fires as follows:

- When the user reenters a cell containing a formula—that is, when the user highlights the cell, presses F2 to activate in-cell editing, and presses Enter.
- When the value of any input cell changes. An input cell is a cell that is referenced in a formula or is used as an argument in a function.
- When your code runs the worksheet's `Calculate` method.

If a user-defined function has been set up as volatile, the `Calculate` event fires not only in the preceding situations, but also when the following occurs:

- When the user presses F9 or, in the Calculation tab of the Options dialog box, clicks the Calc Now button or the Calc Sheet button.
- When the value of a cell that is used indirectly in a calculation changes.

Here's the procedure stub of the event handler:

```
Private Sub Worksheet_Calculate()
    <Event handler code goes here>
End Sub
```

For example, Listing 7.4 shows the event handler defined for the 1997 Budget worksheet in Chaptr07.xls. The procedure watches a value named `GrossMargin` (cell B16 in the 1997 Budget worksheet). If, after a recalculation, this value dips below 20 percent, the procedure displays a warning message.

Listing 7.4. A `Calculate` event handler that monitors the GrossMargin cell.

```
Sub CheckMargin()
    With Range("GrossMargin")
        If .Value < 0.2 Then
            .Select
            MsgBox "Gross Margin is below 20%!"
        End If
    End With
End Sub
```

`Change`: This event fires when the user changes the value of any cell in the worksheet, or when your code changes the `Value` property of a cell (see "Working with Range Objects" later in this chapter). Here's the event handler procedure stub:

```
Private Sub Worksheet_Change(ByVal Target As Excel.Range)
    <Event handler code goes here>
End Sub
```

`Target` is a Range object that represents the cell in which the new value was entered.

Listing 7.5 shows a sample event handler for the 1997 Budget worksheet. In this case, the code checks to see if the user entered a numeric value in Column B. If not, a message is displayed, and the *`Target`* cell is selected again.

Listing 7.5. A Change event handler that ensures the user enters only numeric values in Column B.

```
Private Sub Worksheet_Change(ByVal Target As Excel.Range)
    With Target
        '
        ' Make sure we're in Column B
        '
        If .Column = 2 Then
            '
            ' The value must be a number
            '
            If Not IsNumeric(.Value) Then
                MsgBox "Please enter a number in cell " & _
                     .Address & "!"
                .Select
            End If
        End If
    End With
End Sub
```

`Deactivate`: This event fires when the worksheet loses the focus within Excel (for example, if the user clicks the tab of another worksheet or if your code runs the `Activate` method for another worksheet). Note that Excel first switches to the other worksheet and *then* runs the event handler. Here's the event handler procedure stub:

```
Private Sub Worksheet_Deactivate()
    <Event handler code goes here>
End Sub
```

Working with Range Objects

Mastering cell and range references is perhaps the most fundamental skill to learn when working with spreadsheets. After all, most worksheet chores involve cells, ranges, and range names. However, this skill takes on added importance when you're dealing with VBA procedures. When you're editing a worksheet directly, you can easily select cells and ranges with the mouse or the keyboard, or you can paste range names into formulas. In a procedure, though, you always have to describe—or even calculate—the range you want to work with.

What you describe is the most common of all VBA objects: the Range object. A Range object can be a single cell, a row or column, a selection of cells, or a 3-D range. The following sections look at various techniques that return a Range object, as well as a number of Range object properties and methods.

Returning a Range Object

Much of your VBA code will concern itself with Range objects of one kind or another. Therefore, you need to be well-versed in the various techniques that are available for returning range objects, be they single cells, rectangular ranges, or entire rows and columns. This section takes you through each of these techniques.

Using the Range Method

The `Range` method is the most straightforward way to identify a cell or range. It has two syntaxes. The first requires only a single argument:

```
Worksheet.Range(Name)
```

`Worksheet`	The Worksheet object to which the `Range` method applies. If you omit *`Worksheet`*, VBA assumes the method applies to the `ActiveSheet` object.
`Name`	A range reference or name entered as text.

For example, the following statements enter a date in cell B2 and then create a data series in the range B2:E10 of the active worksheet (I'll discuss the `Formula` and `DataSeries` methods in more detail later):

```
Range("B2").Value = #01/01/95#
Range("B2:B13").DataSeries Type:=xlDate, Date:=xlMonth
```

The `Range` method also works with named ranges. For example, the following statement clears the contents of a range named `Criteria` in the Data worksheet:

```
Worksheets("Data").Range("Criteria").ClearContents
```

The second syntax for the `Range` method requires two arguments:

```
Worksheet.Range(Cell1, Cell2)
```

`Worksheet`	The Worksheet object to which the `Range` method applies. If you omit *`Worksheet`*, VBA assumes that the method applies to the `ActiveSheet` object.
`Cell1, Cell2`	The cells that define the upper-left corner (***`Cell1`***) and lower-right corner (***`Cell2`***) of the range. Each can be a cell address as text, a Range object consisting of a single cell, or an entire column or row.

The advantage of this syntax is that it separates the range corners into individual arguments. This lets you modify each corner under procedural control. For example, you could set up variables named `upperLeft` and `lowerRight` and then return Range objects of different sizes:

```
Range(upperLeft,lowerRight)
```

Using the `Cells` Method

The `Cells` method returns a single cell as a Range object. Here's the syntax:

Object.Cells(***RowIndex***, ***ColumnIndex***)

Object	A Worksheet or Range object. If you omit *Object*, the method applies to the `ActiveSheet` object.
RowIndex	The row number of the cell. If *Workbook* is a worksheet, a ***RowIndex*** of `1` refers to row 1 on the sheet. If *Object* is a range, ***RowIndex*** `1` refers to the first row of the range.
ColumnIndex	The column of the cell. You can enter a letter as text or a number. If *Object* is a worksheet, a ***ColumnIndex*** of `"A"` or `1` refers to column A on the sheet. If `Object` is a range, ***ColumnIndex*** `"A"` or `1` refers to the first column of the range.

For example, the following procedure fragment loops five times and enters the values `Field1` through `Field5` in cells A1 through E1:

```
For colNumber = 1 To 5
    Cells(1, colNumber).Value = "Field" & colNumber
Next colNumber
```

TIP: A SHORTER CELL REFERENCE

You also can refer to a cell by enclosing an A1-style reference in square brackets (`[]`). For example, the following statement checks the spelling of the text in cell C4 of the active worksheet:

```
ActiveSheet.[C4].CheckSpelling
```

NOTE: THE CELLS COLLECTION

The `Cells` method has a second syntax that doesn't require arguments: *Object*`.Cells`. When *Object* is a worksheet, this method returns a collection of all the cells in the sheet.

Returning a Row

If you need to work with entire rows or columns, VBA has several methods and properties you can use. In each case, the object returned is a Range.

The most common way to refer to a row in VBA is to use the `Rows` method. This method uses the following syntax:

```
Object.Rows(Index)
```

`Object`	The Worksheet or Range object to which the method applies. If you omit *`Object`*, VBA uses the `ActiveSheet` object.
`Index`	The row number. If *`Object`* is a worksheet, an *`Index`* of `1` refers to row 1 on the sheet. If *`Object`* is a range, an *`Index`* of `1` refers to the first row of the range. If you omit *`Index`*, the method returns a collection of all the rows in *`Object`*.

For example, Listing 7.6 shows a procedure named `InsertRangeRow`. This procedure inserts a new row before the last row of whatever range is passed as an argument (`rangeObject`). This would be a useful subroutine in programs that need to maintain ranges (such as an Excel list).

Listing 7.6. A procedure that uses the Rows method to insert a row before the last row of a range.

```
Sub InsertRangeRow(rangeObject As Range)
    Dim totalRows As Integer, lastRow As Integer
    With rangeObject
        totalRows = .Rows.Count          ' Total rows in the range
        lastRow = .Rows(totalRows).Row   ' Last row number
        .Rows(lastRow).Insert            ' Insert before last row
    End With
End Sub
Sub InsertTest()
    InsertRangeRow ThisWorkbook.Worksheets("Sheet1").Range("Test")
End Sub
```

After declaring the variables, the first statement uses the `Rows` method without the *`Index`* argument to return a collection of all the rows in `rangeObject` and uses the `Count` property to get the total number of `rangeObject` rows:

```
totalRows = rangeObject.Rows.Count
```

The second statement uses the `totalRows` variable as an argument in the `Rows` method to return the last row of `rangeObject`, and then the `Row` property returns the row number:

```
lastRow = rangeObject.Rows(totalRows).Row
```

Finally, the last statement uses the `Insert` method to insert a row before `lastRow`. (`Insert` has three different syntaxes. See the Help system for details.)

To use `InsertRangeRow`, you need to pass a Range object to the procedure. For example, the `InsertRange` procedure shown at the end of Listing 7.6 inserts a row into a range named Test.

NOTE: ANOTHER WAY TO RETURN A ROW

You also can use the `EntireRow` property to return a row. The syntax *`Range`*`.EntireRow` returns the entire row or rows that contain the *`Range`* object. This is most often used to mimic the Shift-Spacebar shortcut key that selects the entire row that includes the active cell. To do this, you use the following statement:

```
ActiveCell.EntireRow.Select
```

Returning a Column

To return a column, use the `Columns` method. The syntax for this method is almost identical to the `Rows` method:

```
Object.Columns(Index)
```

`Object`	The Worksheet or Range object to which the method applies. If you omit *`Object`*, VBA uses the `ActiveSheet` object.
`Index`	The column number. If *`Object`* is a worksheet, an *`Index`* of `"A"` or `1` refers to column A on the sheet. If *`Object`* is a range, *`Index`* `"A"` or `1` refers to the first column of the range. If you omit *`Index`*, the method returns a collection of all the columns in *`Object`*.

For example, the following statement sets the width of column B on the active worksheet to 20:

```
Columns("B").ColumnWidth = 20
```

NOTE: ANOTHER WAY TO RETURN A COLUMN

The syntax *`Range`*`.EntireColumn` returns the entire column or columns that contain the specified *`Range`* object.

Using the `Offset` Method

When defining your Range objects, you often won't know the specific range address to use. For example, you might need to refer to the cell that's two rows down and one column to the right of the active cell. You could find out the address of the active cell and then calculate the address of the other cell, but VBA gives you an easier (and more flexible) way: the `Offset` method. `Offset` returns a Range object that is offset from a specified range by a certain number of rows and columns. Here is its syntax:

```
Range.Offset(RowOffset, ColumnOffset)
```

Range	The original Range object.
RowOffset	The number of rows to offset ***Range***. You can use a positive number (to move down), a negative number (to move up), or 0 (to use the same rows). If you omit *RowOffset*, VBA uses 0.
ColumnOffset	The number of columns to offset ***Range***. Again, you can use a positive number (to move right), a negative number (to move left), or 0 (to use the same columns). If you omit *ColumnOffset*, VBA uses 0.

For example, the following statement formats the range B2:D6 as bold:

```
Range("A1:C5").Offset(1,1).Font.Bold = True
```

Listing 7.7 shows a procedure called `ConcatenateStrings` that concatenates two text strings. This is handy, for instance, if you have a list with separate first and last name fields and you want to combine them.

Listing 7.7. A procedure that uses the `Offset` method to concatenate two text strings.

```
Sub ConcatenateStrings()
    Dim string1$, string2$
    ' Store the contents of the cell 2 to the left of the active cell
    string1$ = ActiveCell.Offset(0, -2)
    ' Store the contents of the cell 1 to the left of the active cell
    string2$ = ActiveCell.Offset(0, -1)
    ' Enter combined strings (separated by a space) into active cell
    ActiveCell.Value = string1$ & " " & string2$
End Sub
```

The procedure begins by declaring `string1$` and `string2$`. (The `$` type declaration characters automatically declare these variables as string types; see Chapter 2 for details.) The next statement stores in `string1$` the contents of the cell two columns to the left of the active cell by using the `Offset` method as follows:

```
string1$ = ActiveCell.Offset(0, -2)
```

Similarly, the next statement stores in `string2$` the contents of the cell one column to the left of the active cell. Finally, the last statement combines `string1$` and `string2$` (with a space in between) and stores the new string in the active cell.

Selecting a Cell or Range

If you've used the Excel 4.0 macro language, you know that most of its range operations require you to first select the range and then do something to it. For example, changing the font to Times New Roman in the range B1 to B10 of the active sheet requires two commands:

```
=SELECT(!$B$1:$B$10)
=FORMAT.FONT("Times New Roman")
```

VBA, however, lets you access objects directly without having to select them first. This means that your VBA procedures rarely have to select a range. The preceding example can be performed with a single (and faster) VBA statement:

```
Range("B1:B10").Font.Name = "Times New Roman"
```

However, there are times when you do need to select a range. For example, you might need to display a selected range to the user. To select a range, use the `Select` method:

```
Range.Select
```

Range	The Range object you want to select.

For example, the following statement selects the range A1:E10 in the Sales worksheet:

```
Worksheets("Sales").Range("A1:E10").Select
```

TIP: RETURNING THE SELECTED RANGE

To return a Range object that represents the currently selected range, use the `Selection` property. For example, the following statement applies the Times New Roman font to the currently selected range:

```
Selection.Font.Name = "Times New Roman"
```

Defining a Range Name

In VBA, range names are Name objects. To define them, you use the `Add` method for the `Names` collection (which is usually the collection of defined names in a workbook). Here is an abbreviated syntax for the `Names` collection's `Add` method (this method has 11 arguments; see the VBA Reference in the Help system):

```
Names.Add(Text, RefersTo)
```

Text	The text you want to use as the range name.
RefersTo	The item to which you want the name to refer. You can enter a constant, a formula as text (such as `"=Sales-Expenses"`), or a worksheet reference (such as `"Sales!A1:C6"`).

For example, the following statement adds the range name `SalesRange` to the `Names` collection of the active workbook:

```
ActiveWorkbook.Names.Add _
    Text:="SalesRange", _
    RefersTo:="=Sales!$A$1$C$6"
```

More Range Object Properties

Some of the examples you've seen in the last few sections have used various Range object properties. Here's a review of a few more properties you're likely to use most often in your VBA code:

`Range``.Address`: Returns the address, as text, of the specified *`Range`*.

`Range``.Column`: Returns the number of the first column in the specified *`Range`*.

`Range``.Count`: Returns the number of cells in the specified *`Range`*.

`Range``.CurrentArray`: Returns a Range object that represents the entire array in which the specified *`Range`* resides.

7
MANIPULATING EXCEL WITH VBA

CAUTION: TEST FOR AN ARRAY

If the specified range isn't part of an array, the `CurrentArray` property generates a `No cell found` error message. To prevent this error, use the `HasArray` property to test whether or not the range is part of an array. If the range is part of an array, `HasArray` returns `True`.

`Range``.CurrentRegion`: Returns a Range object that represents the entire region in which the specified *`Range`* resides. A range's "region" is the area surrounding the range that is bounded by at least one empty row above and below, and at least one empty column to the left and right.

`Range``.Formula`: Returns or sets a formula for the specified *`Range`*.

`Range``.FormulaArray`: Returns or sets an array formula for the specified *`Range`*.

`Range``.NumberFormat`: Returns or sets the numeric format in the specified *`Range`*. Enter the format you want to use as a string, as shown in the following statement:

```
Worksheets("Analysis").Range("Sales").NumberFormat = _
    "$#,##0.00_);[Red]($#,##0.00)"
```

`Range``.Row`: Returns the number of the first row in the specified *`Range`*.

`Range``.Value`: Returns or sets the value in the specified *`Range`*.

More Range Object Methods

Here's a look at a few more methods that should come in handy in your VBA procedures:

`Range``.Cut`: Cuts the specified *`Range`* to the Clipboard or to a new destination. The `Cut` method uses the following syntax:

`Range.Cut(Destination)`

Range	The Range object to cut.
Destination	The cell or range where you want the cut range to be pasted.

For example, the following statement cuts the range A1:B3 and moves it to the range B4:C6:

```
Range("A1:B3").Cut Destination:=Range("B4")
```

Range.`Copy`: Copies the specified *Range* to the Clipboard or to a new destination. Copying a range is similar to cutting a range. Here's the syntax for the `Copy` method:

`Range.Copy(Destination)`

Range	The range to copy.
Destination	The cell or range where you want the copied range to be pasted.

Range.`Clear`: Removes everything from the specified *Range* (contents, formats, and comments).

Range.`ClearComments`: Removes the cell comments for the specified *Range*.

Range.`ClearContents`: Removes the contents of the specified *Range*.

Range.`ClearFormats`: Removes the formatting for the specified *Range*.

Range.`DataSeries`: Creates a data series in the specified *Range*. The `DataSeries` method uses the following syntax:

`Range.DataSeries(Rowcol, Type, Date, Step, Stop, Trend)`

Range	The range to use for the data series.
Rowcol	Use `xlRows` to enter the data in rows, or `xlColumns` to enter the data in columns. If you omit *Rowcol,* Excel uses the size and shape of ***Range***.
Type	The type of series. Enter `xlLinear` (the default), `xlGrowth`, `xlChronological`, or `xlAutoFill`.
Date	The type of date series, if you used `xlChronological` for the *Type* argument. Your choices are `xlDay` (the default), `xlWeekday`, `xlMonth`, or `xlYear`.
Step	The step value for the series (the default value is 1).
Stop	The stop value for the series. If you omit *Stop,* Excel fills the range.
Trend	Use `True` to create a linear or growth trend series. Use `False` (the default) to create a standard series.

`Range.FillDown`: Uses the contents and formatting from the top row of the specified *Range* to fill down into the rest of the range.

`Range.FillLeft`: Uses the contents and formatting from the rightmost column of the specified *Range* to fill left into the rest of the range.

`Range.FillRight`: Uses the contents and formatting from the leftmost column of the specified *Range* to fill right into the rest of the range.

`Range.FillUp`: Uses the contents and formatting from the bottom row of the specified *Range* to fill up into the rest of the range.

`Range.Insert`: Inserts cells into the specified *Range* using the following syntax:

`Range.object``.Insert(`*`Shift`*`)`

Range	The range into which you want to insert the cells.
Shift	The direction you want to shift the existing cells. Use either `xlShiftToRight` or `xlShiftDown`. If you omit this argument, Excel determines the direction based on the shape of ***Range***.

`Range.Resize`: Resizes the specified *Range*. Here's the syntax for this method:

`Range``.Resize(`*`RowSize, ColSize`*`)`

Range	The range to resize.
RowSize	The number of rows in the new range.
ColSize	The number of columns in the new range.

For example, suppose you use the `InsertRangeRow` procedure from Listing 7.6 to insert a row into a named range. In most cases, you'll want to redefine the range name so that it includes the extra row you added. Listing 7.8 shows a procedure that calls `InsertRangeRow` and then uses the `Resize` method to adjust the named range.

Listing 7.8. A procedure that uses `Resize` to adjust a named range.

```
Sub InsertAndRedefineName()
    With ThisWorkbook.Worksheets("Sheet1")
        InsertRangeRow .Range("Test")
        With .Range("Test")
            Names.Add _
                Name:="Test", _
                RefersTo:=.Resize(.Rows.Count + 1)
        End With
        .Range("Test").Select
End Sub
```

In the `Names.Add` method, the new range is given by the expression `.Resize(.Rows.Count + 1)`. Here, the `Resize` method returns a range that has one more row than the Test range.

Working with Add-In Applications

If you've used any of Excel's add-in applications, you know they're handy because they add extra functions and commands and look as though they were built right into the program. For your own applications, you can convert your workbooks to add-ins and gain the following advantages:

- The workbook won't be visible, so your application can work behind the scenes.
- Your Function procedures appear in the Function Wizard dialog box in the User Defined category.
- Your Sub procedures do *not* appear in the Macro dialog box. This means users must access your add-in procedures entirely by shortcut keys, menu commands, toolbar buttons, or other indirect means.
- Add-ins execute faster than normal files.

TIP: HOW TO RUN ADD-IN SUB PROCEDURES

Even though your application's Sub procedures don't appear in the Macro dialog box, you can still run them when the dialog box is displayed. Just type a procedure name in the Macro Name text box and click Run.

It's important to keep in mind that add-in applications are *demand-loaded.* This means that, when you install your application, it gets read into memory in two stages:

1. The application's functions are added to the Function Wizard, its shortcut keys are enabled, its menus and menu commands are added to the appropriate menu bar, and its toolbars are displayed.
2. The rest of the application is loaded into memory when the user either chooses one of the add-in functions, presses an add-in shortcut key, selects an add-in menu item, or clicks an add-in toolbar button.

The exception to this is when the add-in file contains an `Open` event handler procedure. In this case, the entire add-in is loaded at the start.

Creating an Add-In Application

When you've fully debugged and tested your code and are ready to distribute the application to your users, it's time to convert the workbook into Excel's .XLA (add-in) format. Before doing that, however, you need to set a couple of workbook properties. Begin by selecting File |

Properties to display the properties sheet for the workbook, as shown in Figure 7.6. You need to fill in at least the Title and Comments boxes in the Summary tab. This information appears in the Add-Ins dialog box (select Tools | Add-Ins; see Figure 7.7):

- The Title text will be the add-in name that appears in the Add-Ins Available list.
- The Comment text appears in the box at the bottom of the dialog box when you highlight your add-in.

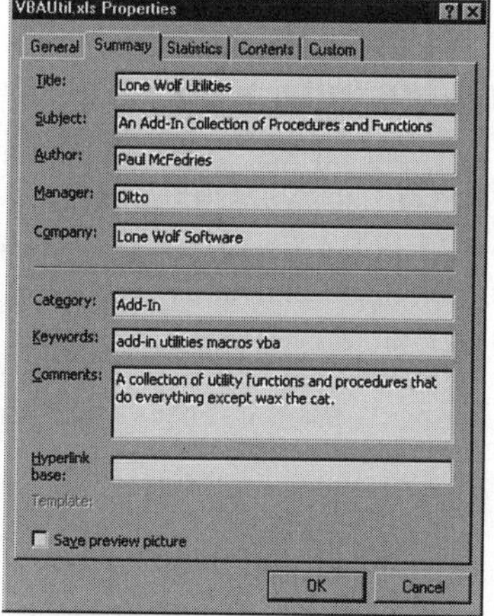

FIGURE 7.6.
Use the Summary tab of the workbook's properties sheet to describe the file before converting it to an add-in.

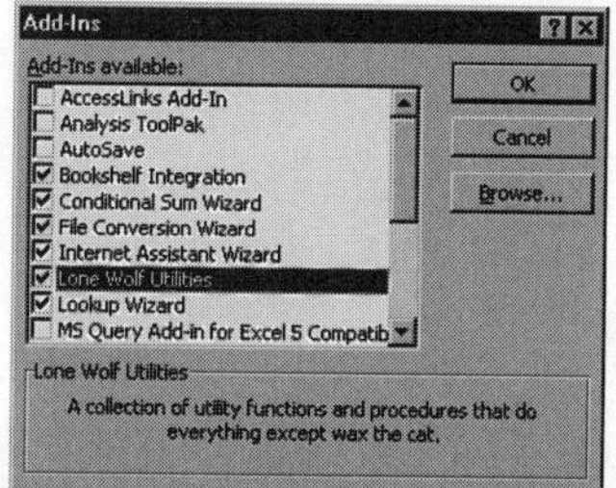

FIGURE 7.7.
The information you enter in the workbook's properties sheet appears in the Add-Ins dialog box.

> **NOTE: PROTECT YOUR ADD-IN**
>
> At this point, it might also be a good idea to set up protection for your add-in project. This will prevent your users from accessing the procedures and functions directly in the Visual Basic Editor. I showed you how to protect a project back in Chapter 1.

When that's done, follow these steps to convert the workbook into the add-in format:

1. Select File | Save As to display the Save As dialog box.
2. Specify a different drive and folder (if required) for the file. You can also change the filename if you like. Note, however, that the next step will change the file's extension to .XLA, so you shouldn't bother editing the file's extension.
3. Use the Save as type drop-down list to select Microsoft Excel Add-In.
4. Click Save.

Controlling Add-Ins with VBA

VBA provides you with several methods and properties that let you control add-in applications at the procedural level. From a VBA point of view, an AddIn object is an individual add-in application, and AddIns is the collection of all the add-in applications available to Excel. The `AddIns` collection is identical to the list of add-ins you see when you display the Add-Ins dialog box (by selecting Tools | Add-Ins).

To refer to an AddIn object, use the `AddIns` method:

```
Addins(Index)
```

`Index`	This argument can be any one of the following: A number representing the add-in you want to use, where 1 signifies the first add-in that appears in the Add-Ins dialog box, 2 is the second add-in that appears, and so on. The name, as text, of the add-in you want to use. For the add-ins that come with Excel, the name of the add-in is the name that appears in the Add-Ins dialog box. For your own add-ins, the name is either the filename (minus the extension) or the text you entered into the Title text box of the workbook's properties sheet. An array of numbers or names.

For example, the following statement refers to the Solver add-in application:

```
AddIns("Solver Add-In")
```

Before you can work with your own add-ins, you need to add them to the `AddIns` collection. VBA provides the `Add` method to do just that:

```
AddIns.Add(FileName, CopyFile)
```

`FileName`	A string containing the full pathname of the add-in file.
`CopyFile`	An optional logical argument to use when the add-in file is stored on a floppy disk, CD-ROM, or network drive. If

`CopyFile` is `True`, Excel copies the add-in file to your hard disk. If it's `False`, Excel leaves the file where it is. If you omit `CopyFile`, Excel displays a dialog box that asks what you want to do. The `CopyFile` argument is ignored if `FileName` references a file on your hard disk.

The `Add` method's only purpose is to tell Excel that the add-in is available. To actually use the file (in other words, to make its commands and functions available to the user), you need to install it by setting its `Installed` property to `True`. (This is the equivalent of activating the add-in's check box in the Add-Ins dialog box.) This does two things:

- It performs the first part of the demand-loading sequence (in other words, the add-in's functions, shortcut keys, menus, and toolbars become available).
- The add-in's `AddinInstall` event handler (if it has one) is executed. This event handler is useful for tasks such as initializing the add-in and telling the user that the add-in is loaded.

Also note that AddIn objects share many of the same properties found in Workbook objects. These properties include `Author`, `Comments`, `FullName`, `Name`, `Path`, `Subject`, and `Title`.

When you no longer need to work with an add-in, you can remove it by setting its `Installed` property to `False`.

Summary

This chapter showed you how to use VBA to manipulate Excel. We examined various properties and methods for common objects, including the `Application`, Workbook, Worksheet, and Range objects. I also showed you how to convert your workbooks into add-in files. Here are some chapters to check out for related information:

- I discuss VBA project protection in Chapter 1, "Introducing VBA."
- For a general discussion of VBA objects, see Chapter 4, "Working with Objects."
- I show you how to use VBA to work with Excel lists in Chapter 17, "Using VBA to Work with Excel Lists."
- See Chapter 27, "A Check Book Application," for an example of an Excel VBA application.

CHAPTER

Programming PowerPoint Presentations

IN THIS CHAPTER

Example moves the world more than doctrine.

—Henry Miller

Previous versions of Office didn't make it easy to incorporate PowerPoint presentations into your VBA applications, because there was no way to program PowerPoint directly. Instead, you had to work with a different VBA-enabled application (such as Excel), use OLE automation to expose PowerPoint's objects, and manipulate those objects via the Automation interface. It worked, but it was a slow and unintuitive way to program.

VBA 5.0 That's all changed with Office 97. Although you can still manipulate PowerPoint via OLE Automation (see Chapter 15, "Controlling Applications Via OLE Automation"), PowerPoint 97 is now fully programmable thanks to its built-in VBA engine. It comes with all the VBA tools we've talked about so far—the macro recorder, the Visual Basic Editor, support for Microsoft Forms, and so on—so all your newfound VBA knowledge can be put to good use programming presentations.

This chapter shows you how to leverage that knowledge in the PowerPoint environment by examining a few PowerPoint objects and their associated properties, methods, and events.

PowerPoint's Application Object

Chapter 4, "Working with Objects," ran through some `Application` object properties and methods that are common to all VBA-enabled applications. You've also seen in the last two chapters how Word and Excel have a few unique `Application` object members. PowerPoint's `Application` object has just a few unique properties and no unique methods. Here's a list of some of PowerPoint's unique properties:

`ActivePresentation`: Returns a Presentation object that represents the presentation file that currently has the focus within PowerPoint. See "PowerPoint's Presentation Object" later in this chapter to learn about the properties and methods of the Presentation object.

`ActivePrinter`: Returns or sets the name of the active printer. (Note that to set the active printer, you must specify the name of an existing Windows printer.) The following statement sets the active printer:

```
ActivePrinter = "HP LaserJet 5P/5MP PostScript local on LPT1:"
```

`Presentations`: Returns the `Presentations` object, which is the collection of all open presentations.

`SlideShowWindows`: Returns the `SlideShowWindows` object, which is the collection of all open slide show windows.

PowerPoint's Presentation Object

In PowerPoint, the Presentation object represents a presentation file (.PPT) that is open in the PowerPoint application window. You can use VBA to create new presentations, open or delete existing presentations, save and close presentations, and more. The next section takes you through various techniques for specifying presentations in your VBA code; then we'll look at some Presentation object properties and methods.

Specifying a Presentation Object

If you need to do something with a presentation, or if you need to work with an object contained in a specific presentation (such as a slide), you need to tell PowerPoint which presentation you want to use. VBA gives you three ways to do this:

Use the `Presentations` object: The `Presentations` object is the collection of all open presentation files. To specify a particular presentation, either use its index number (where 1 represents the first presentation opened) or enclose the presentation filename in quotation marks. For example, if `Proposal.ppt` was the first presentation opened, the following two statements would be equivalent:

```
Presentations("Proposal.ppt")
Presentations(1)
```

Use the `ActivePresentation` object: The `ActivePresentation` object represents the presentation that currently has the focus.

Use the `Presentation` property: Open slide show windows have a `Presentation` property that returns the name of the underlying presentation. For example, the following statement uses the `currPres` variable to store the name of the presentation in the first slide show window:

```
currPres = SlideShowWindows(1).Presentation
```

Opening a Presentation

To open a presentation file, use the `Open` method of the `Presentations` collection. The `Open` method has several arguments you can use to fine-tune your presentation openings, but only one of these is mandatory. Here's the simplified syntax showing the one required argument (for the rest of the arguments, look up the `Open` method in the VBA Help system):

```
Presentations.Open(FileName)
```

Here, ***`FileName`*** is the full name of the presentation file, including the drive and folder that contain the file. For example, to open a presentation named Proposal.ppt in the C:\My Documents\folder, you would use the following statement:

```
Presentations.Open "C:\My Documents\Proposal.ppt"
```

Creating a New Presentation

If you need to create a new presentation, use the `Presentations` collection's `Add` method:

```
Presentations.Add(WithWindow)
```

`WithWindow` is a Boolean value that determines whether or not the presentation is created in a visible window. Use `True` for a visible window (this is the default); use `False` to hide the window.

Presentation Object Properties

Here's a list of a few common properties associated with Presentation objects:

`Presentation``.FullName`: Returns the full pathname of the specified *`Presentation`*. The full pathname includes the presentation's path (the drive and folder in which the file resides) and the filename.

`Presentation``.HandoutMaster`: Returns a Master object that represents the handout master for the specified *`Presentation`*.

`Presentation``.HasTitleMaster`: Returns `True` if the specified *`Presentation`* has a title master.

`Presentation``.Name`: Returns the filename of the *`Presentation`*.

`Presentation``.NotesMaster`: Returns a Master object that represents the notes master for the specified *`Presentation`*.

`Presentation``.Path`: Returns the path of the *`Presentation`* file.

> **NOTE: THE PATH OF A NEW PRESENTATION**
>
> A new, unsaved presentation's `Path` property returns an empty string (`""`).

`Presentation``.Saved`: Determines whether changes have been made to the specified *`Presentation`* since it was last saved.

`Presentation``.SlideMaster`: Returns a Master object that represents the slide master for the specified *`Presentation`*.

`Presentation``.Slides`: Returns a `Slides` object that represents the collection of Slide objects contained in the specified *`Presentation`*.

`Presentation``.SlideShowSettings`: Returns a `SlideShowSettings` object that represents the slide show setup options for the specified *`Presentation`*.

`Presentation``.TemplateName`: Returns the name of the design template underlying the specified *`Presentation`*.

`Presentation``.TitleMaster`: Returns a Master object that represents the title master for the specified *`Presentation`*.

Presentation Object Methods

A Presentation object has methods that let you save the presentation, close it, print it, and more. Here are the methods you'll use most often:

`Presentation.AddTitleMaster`: Adds a title master to the specified *Presentation*. Note that VBA will generate an error if the presentation already has a title master, so your code should use the `HasTitleMaster` property to check for an existing title master before running this method, as shown in the following procedure fragment:

```
With ActivePresentation
    If Not .HasTitleMaster Then .AddTitleMaster
End With
```

`Presentation.ApplyTemplate`: Applies a design template to the specified *Presentation*. This method uses the following syntax:

***Presentation*.ApplyTemplate(*FileName*)**

Presentation	The Presentation object to which you want to apply the template.
FileName	The full name of the template (.POT) file.

For example, the following statement applies the `Dads Tie` template to the active presentation:

```
ActivePresentation.ApplyTemplate _
    "C:\Microsoft Office\Templates\Presentation Designs\Dads Tie.pot"
```

`Presentation.Close`: Closes the specified *Presentation*. If the file has unsaved changes, PowerPoint will ask the user if he wants to save those changes.

`Presentation.NewWindow`: Opens a new window for the specified *Presentation*.

`Presentation.PrintOut`: Prints the specified *Presentation* using the following syntax:

***Presentation*.PrintOut(*From*, *To*, *Copies*, *PrintToFile*, *Collate*)**

Presentation	The Presentation object you want to print.
From	The page number from which to start printing.
To	The page number of the last page to print.
Copies	The number of copies to print. The default value is 1.
PrintToFile	The name of a file to which you want the presentation printed.
Collate	If this argument is `True` and *Copies* is greater than 1, VBA collates the copies.

`Presentation.Save`: Saves the specified *Presentation*. If the presentation is new, use the `SaveAs` method instead.

`Presentation.SaveAs`: Saves the specified `Presentation` to a different file. Here's the syntax for the `SaveAs` method:

```
Presentation.SaveAs(FileName, FileFormat, EmbedTrueTypeFonts)
```

Presentation	The Presentation object you want to save to a different file.
FileName	The full name of the new presentation file, including the drive and folder where you want the file to reside.
FileFormat	The PowerPoint format to use for the new file. Use one of the following constants:

FileFormat	*Format*
`ppSaveAsAddIn`	Add-in (.PPA)
`ppSaveAsPowerPoint3`	PowerPoint 3.0 (.PPT)
`ppSaveAsPowerPoint4`	PowerPoint 4.0 (.PPT)
`ppSaveAsPowerPoint7`	PowerPoint 95 (.PPT)
`ppSaveAsPresentation`	PowerPoint Show (.PPS)
`ppSaveAsRTF`	Rich Text Format (.RTF)
`ppSaveAsTemplate`	Template (.POT)

EmbedTrueTypeFonts	If `True`, PowerPoint embeds the presentation's TrueType fonts in the new file.

The Juggling Application

Throughout this chapter, I'll put the PowerPoint objects, methods, and properties that we talk about to good use in an application that builds an entire presentation from scratch. This presentation will consist of a series of slides that provide instructions on how to juggle.

The code for the application consists of six procedures:

`Main`: This procedure ties the entire application together by calling each of the other procedures in the module.

`CreateJugglingPresentation`: This procedure creates a new Presentation object and saves it.

`CreateJugglingSlides`: This procedure adds the slides to the presentation and then formats them.

`SetUpFirstPage`: This procedure adds and formats text for the presentation title page.

`SetUpJugglingPages`: This procedure adds and formats a title, picture, and instruction text for each of the four pages that explain how to juggle.

`RunJugglingSlideShow`: This procedure asks the user if he or she wants to run the slide show and then runs it if Yes is chosen.

To get started, Listing 8.1 shows the `Main` procedure.

Listing 8.1. This procedure ties everything together by calling each of the code listings individually.

```
' Global variable
Dim pres As Presentation

Sub Main()
    '
    ' Create the presentation file
    '
    CreateJugglingPresentation
    '
    ' Add the slides
    '
    AddJugglingSlides
    '
    ' Set up the title page
    '
    SetUpStartPage
    '
    ' Set up the Juggling pages
    '
    SetUpJugglingPages
    '
    ' Save it and then run it
    '
    pres.Save
    RunJugglingSlideShow
End Sub
```


First, the `pres` variable is declared as a `Presentation` object. Notice that this variable is defined at the module level so that it can be used in all the procedures in the module. Then `Main` begins by calling the `CreateJugglingPresentation` procedure, shown in Listing 8.2. From there, the other procedures (discussed later in this chapter) are called and the presentation is saved.

Listing 8.2. This procedure creates a new presentation and then saves it.

```
Sub CreateJugglingPresentation()
    Dim p As Presentation
    '
    ' If the old one is still open, close it without saving
    '
    For Each p In Presentations
        If p.Name = "Juggling" Then
            p.Saved = True
            p.Close
        End If
    Next p
    '
    ' Create a new Presentation object and store it in pres
    '
    Set pres = Presentations.Add
    pres.SaveAs FileName:="Juggling.ppt"
End Sub
```

A `For Each...Next` loop runs through each open presentation and checks the `Name` property. If it equals Juggling.ppt, we know the file is already open. If it's open (say, from running the application previously), the procedure closes it without saving it. The `pres` variable is `Set`, and then the presentation is saved using the `SaveAs` method.

NOTE: THE JUGGLING APPLICATION CODE

The presentation and code used in this chapter's sample application can be found on the CD that comes with this book. Look for the Chaptr08.ppt file (or Chaptr08.bas, if you don't have PowerPoint but still want to examine the code).

Working with PowerPoint Slide Objects

PowerPoint presentations consist of a series of slides. In PowerPoint VBA, a slide is a Slide object that contains a number of properties and methods that you can wield in your code. These include options for setting the slide's layout, specifying the transition effect, and copying and deleting slides. The next few sections discuss these and other slide techniques.

Specifying a Slide

To work with a slide, you need to specify a Slide object. For a single slide, the easiest way to do this is to use the `Slides` object. `Slides` is the collection of all the slides in a particular presentation. To specify a slide, either use the slide's index number (where 1 represents the first slide in the presentation, 2 the second slide, and so on), or enclose the slide name in quotation marks. For example, if Slide1 is the first slide, the following two statements would be equivalent:

```
ActivePresentation.Slides("Slide1")
ActivePresentation.Slides(1)
```

Alternatively, you can specify a slide by using its *slide ID* number. PowerPoint assigns to each slide you create a unique ID. As you'll see later when we look at slide properties, this value is stored in the `SlideID` property of each Slide object. To refer to a slide by this ID number, use the `FindBySlideID` method of the `Slides` object:

```
Presentation.Slides.FindBySlideID(SlideID)
```

`Presentation`	The Presentation object that contains the slide.
`SlideID`	The slide's ID number.

I'll show you an example of this method in the next section when I discuss how to create a new slide. If you need to work with multiple slides (say, to apply a particular layout to all the slides), use the `Range` method of the `Slides` object:

```
Presentation.Slides.Range(Index)
```

Presentation	The Presentation object that contains the slides.
Index	An array that specifies the slides.

For the ***Index*** argument, use VBA's `Array` function with multiple instances of any of the following: slide index numbers, slide names, or slide ID numbers. For example, the following statement specifies the slides named Slide1 and Slide2:

```
ActivePresentation.Slides.Range(Array("Slide1","Slide2"))
```

TIP: WORKING WITH ALL SLIDES

To work with every slide in the presentation, use the `Range` method without an argument, as in this example:

```
ActivePresentation.Slides.Range
```

You can also use the Presentation object's `SlideMaster` property to work with the slide master. This will change the default settings for every slide in the presentation.

Creating a New Slide

Once you've created a presentation, you need to populate it with slides. To insert a new Slide object into a presentation, use the `Add` method of the `Slides` collection:

```
Presentation.Slides.Add(Index, Layout)
```

Presentation	The Presentation object in which you want to add the slide.
Index	The index number of the new slide within the `Slides` object. Use `1` to make this the first slide; use `Slides.Count + 1` to make this the last slide.
Layout	A constant that specifies the layout of the new slide. PowerPoint defines over two dozen constants, including `ppLayoutText` (for a text-only slide), `ppLayoutChart` (for a chart slide), and `ppLayoutBlank` (for a blank slide). Look up the `Add` method in the VBA Help system to see the full list of constants.

The following statements add an organization chart slide to the end of the active presentation:

```
With ActivePresentation.Slides
    .Add Index:=.Count + 1, Layout:=ppLayoutOrgchart
End With
```

Here's another example of the `Add` method that saves the new slide's ID number:

```
With ActivePresentation.Slides
    newSlideID = .Add(1, ppLayoutText).SlideID
End With
```

Inserting Slides from a File

Instead of creating slides from scratch, you might prefer to pilfer one or more slides from an existing presentation. The `InsertFromFile` method lets you do this. It uses the following syntax:

```
Presentation.Slides.InsertFromFile(FileName, Index, SlideStart, SlideEnd)
```

Presentation	The Presentation object in which you want to add the slides.
FileName	The name of the file (including the drive and folder) that contains the slides you want to insert.
Index	The index number of an existing slide in ***Presentation***. The slides from ***FileName*** will be inserted after this slide.
SlideStart	The index number of the first slide in ***FileName*** that you want to insert.
SlideEnd	The index number of the last slide in ***FileName*** that you want to insert.

For example, the following procedure fragment inserts the first five slides from `Budget.ppt` at the end of the active presentation:

```
With ActivePresentation.Slides
    .InsertFromFile _
        FileName:="C:\Presentations\Budget.ppt", _
        Index:=.Count, _
        SlideStart:=1, _
        SlideEnd:=5
End With
```

Slide Properties

To let you change the look and feel of your slides, PowerPoint VBA offers a number of Slide object properties. These properties control the slide's layout, background, color scheme, name, and more. This section runs through a few of the more useful Slide object properties:

NOTE: A RANGE OF SLIDES ACTS LIKE A SINGLE SLIDE

If you specify multiple slides using the `Range` method described earlier, PowerPoint returns a SlideRange object that references the slides. This object has the same properties and methods as a Slide object, so you can work with multiple slides the same way that you work with a single slide.

`Slide.Background`: Returns or sets the background of the specified `Slide`. Note that this property actually returns a ShapeRange object. (See "Dealing with Shape Objects" later in this chapter.)

You normally use this property with the slide master to set the background for all the slides in the presentation. For example, the following statements store the slide master background in a variable and then use the Shape object's `Fill` property to change the background pattern for all the slides in the active presentation:

```
Set slideBack = ActivePresentation.SlideMaster.Background
slideBack.Fill.PresetGradient _
    Style:=msoGradientHorizontal, _
    Variant:=1, _
    PresetGradientType:=msoGradientFire
```

If you just want to change the background for a single slide, you must first set the slide's `FollowMasterBackground` property to `False`, like so:

```
With ActivePresentation.Slides(1)
    .FollowMasterBackground = False
    .Background.Fill.PresetGradient _
        Style:=msoGradientHorizontal, _
        Variant:=1, _
        PresetGradientType:=msoGradientFire
End With
```

`Slide.DisplayMasterShapes`: Returns or sets whether or not the specified `Slide` displays the Shape objects defined on the slide master. If `True`, objects on the slide master (such as text, graphics, and OLE objects) will also appear on the slide.

`Slide.FollowMasterBackground`: As mentioned earlier, this property returns or sets whether or not the specified `Slide` uses the same `Background` property as the slide master. Set this property to `False` to set a unique background for an individual slide.

`Slide.Layout`: Returns or sets the layout for the specified `Slide`. Again, see the VBA Help system for the full list of layout constants.

`Slide.Master`: Returns the slide master for the specified `Slide`. The following two statements are equivalent:

```
ActivePresentation.SlideMaster
ActivePresentation.Slides(1).Master
```

`Slide.Name`: Returns or sets the name of the specified `Slide`.

`Slide.NotesPage`: Returns a SlideRange object that represents the notes page for the specified `Slide`.

`Slide.Shapes`: Returns a `Shapes` collection that represents all the Shape objects on the specified `Slide`.

`Slide.SlideID`: Returns the ID number of the specified `Slide`.

`Slide.SlideIndex`: Returns the index number of the specified `Slide` within the `Slides` collection.

Slide.SlideShowTransition: Returns a SlideShowTransition object that represents the transition special effects used for the specified *Slide* during a slide show.

The Juggling Application: Creating the Slides

Listing 8.3 shows the AddJugglingSlides procedure, which adds four slides to the Juggling presentation (represented, remember, by the pres variable) and then uses the SlideMaster object to set the default background for the slides.

Listing 8.3. A procedure that adds the slides to the Juggling presentation and formats them.

```
Sub AddJugglingSlides()
    Dim i As Integer

    With pres
        With .Slides
         '
         ' Add the opening slide
         '
         .Add(Index:=1, Layout:=ppLayoutTitle).Name = "Opener"
         '
         ' Now add the slides for each step
         '
         For i = 1 To 4
             .Add(Index:=i + 1, Layout:=ppLayoutTitle).Name = "Juggling" & i
         Next i
    End With
    '
    ' Set the background for all the slides
    '
    .SlideMaster.Background.Fill.PresetGradient _
        Style:=msoGradientHorizontal, _
        Variant:=1, _
        PresetGradientType:=msoGradientNightfall
    End With
End Sub
```

Slide Methods

PowerPoint VBA defines a half dozen Slide object methods that let you copy slides, delete slides, export slides, and more. Here's the complete list:

Slide.Copy: This method copies the specified *Slide* to the Clipboard. If you then want to paste the slide into another presentation, use the Paste method of the Slides object:

Presentation.Slides.Paste(***Index***)

Presentation	The Presentation object into which you want to paste the slide.

Index	The index number of the slide before which the slide will be pasted.

For example, the following statements copy the first slide from the 1996 Budget presentation and paste it before the first slide in the 1997 Budget presentation.

```
Presentations("1996 Budget").Slides(1).Copy
Presentations("1997 Budget").Slides.Paste 1
```

Slide.Cut: This method cuts the specified *Slide* from the presentation and places it on the Clipboard. Again, use the Slides.Paste method to paste the slide into another presentation.

Slide.Delete: This method deletes the specified *Slide*.

Slide.Duplicate: Use this method to make a copy of the specified *Slide* in the same presentation. The new slide is added to the presentation immediately after the specified *Slide*. Note, too, that this method returns a SlideRange object that refers to the new slide.

Slide.Export: This method exports the specified *Slide* to a file in a graphics format of your choice. Here's the syntax:

```
Slide.Export(FileName, FilterName, ScaleWidth, ScaleHeight)
```

Slide	The Slide object you want to export.
FileName	The name of the exported file, possibly including the drive and folder. (If you omit the drive and folder, the slide is exported to the current folder.) Note that you don't need to add a file extension. PowerPoint will add whatever extension is appropriate according to the ***FilterName*** you use.
FilterName	The graphics format to use for the exported file. Use the registered extension for the graphics format (such as JPG for a JPEG file).
ScaleWidth	A number that determines the factor by which the slide is scaled horizontally during the export. For example, a value of 2 doubles the width of the slide in the exported file.
ScaleHeight	A number that determines the factor by which the slide is scaled vertically during the export.

The following statement exports the first slide in the active presentation to a file named Summary.jpg in the C:\Graphics folder.

```
ActivePresentation.Slides(1).Export _
    FileName:="C:\Graphics\Summary", _
    FilterName:="JPG"
```

Slide.Select: This method selects the specified *Slide*. Note that the presentation window must be displayed in a view that supports this method. For example, this method will fail in Slide view, but it works in Outline or Slide Sorter view. Here's some code that uses the `ViewType` property to change the view of the active window to Slide Sorter and then selects a slide:

```
ActiveWindow.ViewType = ppViewSlideSorter
ActivePresentation.Slides(3).Select
```

Dealing with Shape Objects

PowerPoint slides are really just a collection of objects: titles, text boxes, pictures, OLE objects, labels, lines, curves, and so on. In PowerPoint VBA, each of these items is a Shape object. Therefore, in order to get full slide control in your VBA procedures, you must know how to add, edit, format, and otherwise manipulate these objects. That's the goal of this section.

Specifying a Shape

You have to specify a Shape object before you can work with it. The techniques you use for this are similar to those I outlined earlier for Slide objects.

For a single shape, use the `Shapes` object, which is the collection of all Shape objects on a particular slide. To specify a shape, either use the shape's index number (where 1 represents the first shape added to the slide, 2 is the second shape, and so on), or enclose the shape name in quotation marks. For example, if `Rectangle 1` is the first shape, the following two statements would be equivalent:

```
ActivePresentation.Shapes("Rectangle 1")
ActivePresentation.Shapes(1)
```

If you need to work with multiple shapes, use the `Range` method of the `Shapes` object:

`Slide``.Shapes.Range(`***`Index`***`)`

`Slide`	The Slide object that contains the shapes.
`Index`	An array that specifies the shapes.

As with multiple slides, use VBA's `Array` function for the ***`Index`*** argument, like so:

```
Presentations(1).Slides(1).Shapes.Range(Array("Oval 1","TextBox 2"))
```

> **TIP: WORKING WITH ALL SHAPES**
>
> To work with every shape in the slide, use the `Range` method without an argument:
>
> ```
> Presentations(1).Slides(1).Shapes.Range
> ```

Adding Shapes to a Slide

The `Slides` object has 14 different methods you can use to insert shapes into a slide. Many of these methods use similar arguments, so before listing the methods, let's take a quick tour of the common arguments:

`BeginX`	For connectors and lines, the distance (in points) from the shape's starting point to the left edge of the slide window.
`BeginY`	For connectors and lines, the distance (in points) from the shape's starting point to the top edge of the slide window.
`EndX`	For connectors and lines, the distance (in points) from the shape's ending point to the left edge of the slide window.
`EndY`	For connectors and lines, the distance (in points) from the shape's ending point to the top edge of the slide window.
`FileName`	The path and name of the file used to create the shape (such as a picture or an OLE object).
`Height`	The height of the shape (in points).
`Left`	The distance (in points) of the left edge of the shape from the left edge of the slide window.
`Orientation`	The orientation of text within a label or text box. For horizontal text, use the constant `msoTextOrientationHorizontal`; for vertical text, use the constant `msoTextOrientationVerticalFarEast`.
`SafeArrayOfPoints`	For curves, open polylines, and closed polygons, this is an array of coordinate pairs that specify the vertices and control points for the object.
`Top`	The distance (in points) of the top edge of the shape from the top edge of the slide window.
`Width`	The width of the shape (in points).

Here's a list of the `Shapes` object methods and arguments that you can use to create shapes:

`Slide``.Shapes.AddCallout`: Adds a callout to the specified *`Slide`* using the following syntax:

`Slide``.Shapes.AddCallout(`***`Type`***`, `***`Left`***`, `***`Top`***`, `***`Width`***`, `***`Height`***`)`

`Type` A constant that specifies the type of callout to add:

8 PROGRAMMING POWERPOINT PRESENTATIONS

Type	Callout
`msoCalloutOne`	A single-segment callout that can only be oriented horizontally or vertically.
`msoCalloutTwo`	A single-segment callout that can be oriented in any direction.
`msoCalloutThree`	A double-segment callout.
`msoCalloutFour`	A triple-segment callout.

`Slide.Shapes.AddComment`: Adds a comment to the specified *Slide* using the following syntax:

```
Slide.Shapes.AddComment(Left, Top, Width, Height)
```

`Slide.Shapes.AddConnector`: Adds a connector to the specified *Slide* using the following syntax:

```
Slide.Shapes.AddConnector(Type, BeginX, BeginY, EndX, EndY)
```

Type A constant that specifies the connector type:

Type	Connector
`msoConnectorCurve`	A curved connector.
`msoConnectorElbow`	A connector with an elbow.
`msoConnectorStraight`	A straight connector.

NOTE: CONNECTING A CONNECTOR

The `AddConnector` method returns a Shape object that represents the new connector. You use this object's `ConnectorFormat` property to set up the beginning and ending points of the connector. In other words, you use the `ConnectorFormat.BeginConnect` and `ConnectorFormat.EndConnect` methods to specify the shapes attached to the connector.

`Slide.Shapes.AddCurve`: Adds a curved line to the specified *Slide* using the following syntax:

```
Slide.Shapes.AddCurve(SafeArrayOfPoints)
```

`Slide.Shapes.AddLabel`: Adds a label to the specified *Slide* using the following syntax:

```
Slide.Shapes.AddLabel(Orientation, Left, Top, Width, Height)
```

NOTE: LABEL TEXT

I'll show you how to add text to a label and text box when we look at Shape object properties (see "Some Shape Properties").

`Slide.Shapes.AddLine`: Adds a straight line to the specified `Slide` using the following syntax:

```
Slide.Shapes.AddLine(BeginX, BeginY, EndX, EndY)
```

`Slide.Shapes.AddMediaObject`: Adds a multimedia file to the specified `Slide` using the following syntax:

```
Slide.Shapes.AddMediaObject(FileName, Left, Top, Width, Height)
```

`Slide.Shapes.AddOLEObject`: Adds an OLE object to the specified `Slide` using the following syntax:

```
Slide.Shapes.AddOLEObject(Left, Top, Width, Height, ClassName, FileName,
➥DisplayAsIcon, IconFileName, IconIndex, IconLabel, Link)
```

Here's a summary of the extra arguments used in this method:

`ClassName`	The class name or programmatic ID for the OLE object.
`FileName`	The file to use to create the OLE object.
`DisplayAsIcon`	Set to `True` to display the object as an icon. The default value is `False`.
`IconFileName`	If `DisplayAsIcon` is `True`, this is the file that contains the icon.
`IconIndex`	If `DisplayAsIcon` is `True`, this is the index of the icon within `IconFileName`.
`IconLabel`	If `DisplayAsIcon` is `True`, this is the label that appears beneath the icon.
`Link`	If you specify a `FileName`, set this argument to `True` to set up a link to the original file. The default value is `False`.

`Slide.Shapes.AddPicture`: Adds a graphic to the specified `Slide` using the following syntax:

```
Slide.Shapes.AddPicture(FileName, LinkToFile, SaveWithDocument, Left, Top,
➥Width, Height)
```

Here's a summary of the extra arguments used in this method:

`LinkToFile`	Set this argument to `True` to set up a link to the original file. If this argument is `False`, an independent copy of the picture is stored in the slide.
`SaveWithDocument`	Set this argument to `True` to save the picture with the presentation. Note that this argument must be `True` if **`LinkToFile`** is `False`.

`Slide.Shapes.AddPolyline`: Adds an open polyline or a closed polygon to the specified *Slide* using the following syntax:

```
Slide.Shapes.AddPolyline(SafeArrayOfPoints)
```

`Slide.Shapes.AddShape`: Adds an AutoShape to the specified *Slide* using the following syntax:

```
Slide.Shapes.AddShape(Type, Left, Top, Width, Height)
```

Here, the ***Type*** argument is a constant that specifies the AutoShape you want to add. PowerPoint VBA defines dozens of these constants. To see the full list, look up the `AutoShapeType` property in the VBA Help system.

`Slide.Shapes.AddTextbox`: Adds a text box to the specified *Slide* using the following syntax:

```
Slide.Shapes.AddTextbox(Left, Top, Width, Height)
```

`Slide.Shapes.AddTextEffect`: Adds a WordArt text effect to the specified *Slide* using the following syntax:

```
Slide.Shapes.AddTextEffect(PresetTextEffect, Text, FontName, FontSize,
➥FontBold, FontItalic, Left, Top)
```

Here's a summary of the extra arguments used in this method:

PresetTextEffect	A constant that specifies one of WordArt's preset text effects. Look up this method in the VBA Help system to see the few dozen constants that are available.
Text	The WordArt text.
FontName	The font applied to ***Text***.
FontSize	The font size applied to ***Text***.
FontBold	Set to `True` to apply bolding to ***Text***.
FontItalic	Set to `True` to apply italics to ***Text***.

`Slide.Shapes.AddTitle`: Adds a title to the specified *Slide*. This method takes no arguments. However, be aware that the `AddTitle` method will raise an error if the slide already has a title. To check in advance, use the `HasTitle` property, as shown in the following example:

```
With ActivePresentation.Slides(1).Shapes
     If Not .HasTitle Then
        .AddTitle.TextFrame.TextRange.Text = "New Title"
    End If
End With
```

Some Shape Properties

PowerPoint VBA comes equipped with over three dozen Shape object properties that control characteristics such as the dimensions and position of a shape, whether or not a shape displays a shadow, and the shape name. Let's take a quick look at a few of these properties:

`Shape.AnimationSettings`: This property returns an `AnimationSettings` object that represents the animation effects applied to the specified `Shape`. `AnimationSettings` contains various properties that apply special effects to the shape. Here's a sampler (see the VBA Help system for the complete list as well as the numerous constants that work with these properties):

- `AdvanceMode`: A constant that determines how the animation advances. There are two choices: automatically (in other words, after a preset amount of time; use `ppAdvanceOnTime`), or when the user clicks the slide (use `ppAdvanceOnClick`). For the former, you can specify the amount of time by using the `AdvanceTime` property.
- `AfterEffect`: A constant that determines how the shape appears after the animation is complete.
- `Animate`: A `Boolean` value that turns the shape's animation on (`True`) or off (`False`).
- `AnimateTextInReverse`: When this `Boolean` value is `True`, PowerPoint builds the text animation in reverse order. For example, if the shape is a series of bullet points and this property is `True`, the animation displays the bullet points from last to first.
- `EntryEffect`: A constant that determines the special effect applied initially to the shape's animation. For example, you can make the shape fade in by using the `ppEffectFade` constant.
- `TextLevelEffect`: A constant that determines the paragraph level that gets animated.
- `TextUnitEffect`: A constant that determines how PowerPoint animates text: by paragraph, by word, or by letter.

`Shape.AutoShapeType`: For an AutoShape object, this property returns or sets the shape type for the specified `Shape`.

`Shape.Fill`: This property returns a FillFormat object that represents the fill formatting for the specified `Shape`. The FillFormat object defines numerous methods you can wield to apply a fill to a shape:

- `OneColorGradient`: Sets the fill to a one-color gradient.
- `Patterned`: Sets the fill to a pattern.
- `PresetGradient`: A constant that sets the fill to one of PowerPoint's preset gradients.
- `PresetTextured`: A constant that sets the fill to one of PowerPoint's preset textures.
- `Solid`: Sets the fill to a solid color. After running this method, use the `Fill.ForeColor` property to set the fill color.

NOTE: WORKING WITH COLORS

PowerPoint's color properties (such as `ForeColor`) return a ColorFormat object. This object represents either the color of a one-color object, or the background or foreground color of an object with a pattern or gradient. To set a color, use the ColorFormat object's RGB property and VBA's `RGB` function to set a red-green-blue value, as in this example:

```
Shapes(1).Fill.Solid.ForeColor.RGB = RGB(255,0,0)
```

- `TwoColorGradient`: Sets the fill to a two-color gradient.
- `UserPicture`: Sets the fill to a graphics file that you specify.
- `UserTexture`: Sets the fill to a specified graphics image that gets tiled to cover the entire shape.

`*Shape*.HasTextFrame`: A `Boolean` value that tells you if the specified `*Shape*` has a text frame (`True`) or not (`False`). See the `TextFrame` property, discussed in a moment.

`*Shape*.Height`: Returns or sets the height, in points, for the specified `*Shape*`.

`*Shape*.Left`: Returns or sets the distance, in points, between the left edge of the bounding box of the specified `*Shape*` and the left edge of the presentation window.

`*Shape*.Name`: This property returns or sets the name for the specified `*Shape*`.

`*Shape*.Shadow`: This property returns a ShadowFormat object that represents the shadow for the specified `*Shape*`. The ShadowFormat object contains various properties that control the look of the shadow. For example, `Shadow.ForeColor` controls the shadow color, and `Shadow.Visible` is a `Boolean` value that turns the shadow on (`True`) or off (`False`).

`*Shape*.TextEffectFormat`: For a WordArt object, this property returns a TextEffectFormat object that represents the text effects of the specified `*Shape*`.

`*Shape*.TextFrame`: This property returns a `TextFrame` object for the specified `*Shape*`. A text frame is an area within a shape that can hold text. The frame's text, as a whole, is represented by the `TextRange` object, and the actual text is given by the `Text` property of the `TextRange` object. This rather convoluted state of affairs means that you need to use the following property to a refer to a shape's text:

```
Shape.TextFrame.TextRange.Text
```

For example, the following statements add to the active presentation a new slide that contains only a title, and then they set the title text to `1997 Budget Proposal`:

```
With ActivePresentation.Slides
    With .Add(1, ppLayoutTitleOnly).Shapes(1)
        .TextFrame.TextRange.Text = "1997 Budget Proposal"
    End With
End With
```

Also note that the `TextFrame` object has a number of other properties that control the text margins, orientation, word wrap, and more.

`Shape.Top`: Returns or sets the distance, in points, between the top edge of the bounding box of the specified `Shape` and the top edge of the presentation window.

`Shape.Type`: This property returns or (in some cases) sets the shape type for the specified `Shape`.

`Shape.Visible`: A `Boolean` value that makes the specified `Shape` either visible (`True`) or invisible (`False`).

`Shape.Width`: Returns or sets the width, in points, for the specified `Shape`.

The Juggling Application: Creating the Title Page

To put some of these properties through their paces, Listing 8.4 shows the Juggling application's `SetUpStartPage` procedure.

Listing 8.4. A procedure that sets up the text and animation settings for the first page of the Juggling presentation.

```
Sub SetUpStartPage()
    Dim shapeTitle As Shape
    Dim shapeSubTitle As Shape

    With pres.Slides("Opener")
        Set shapeTitle = .Shapes(1)      ' The title
        Set shapeSubTitle = .Shapes(2)   ' The subtitle
        '
        ' Add the title text
        '
        With shapeTitle.TextFrame.TextRange
            .Text = "Juggling"
            With .Font
                .Name = "Arial"
                .Size = 44
                .Bold = True
                .Color.RGB = RGB(255, 255, 255)
            End With
        End With
        '
        ' Set the title animation
        '
        With shapeTitle.AnimationSettings
            .Animate = True
            .AdvanceMode = ppAdvanceOnTime
            .AdvanceTime = 0
            .TextUnitEffect = ppAnimateByCharacter
            .EntryEffect = ppEffectFlyFromLeft
        End With
```

continues

Listing 8.4. continued

```
        '
        ' Add the subtitle text
        '
        With shapeSubTitle.TextFrame.TextRange
            .Text = "A Step-By-Step Course"
            With .Font
                .Name = "Arial"
                .Size = 36
                .Bold = True
                .Color.RGB = RGB(255, 255, 255)
            End With
        End With
        '
        ' Set the subtitle animation
        '
        With shapeSubTitle.AnimationSettings
            .Animate = True
            .AdvanceMode = ppAdvanceOnTime
            .AdvanceTime = 0
            .TextUnitEffect = ppAnimateByWord
            .EntryEffect = ppEffectFlyFromBottom
        End With
    End With
End Sub
```

The first slide is named `Opener`, and this is the object used through most of the procedure. The `shapeTitle` variable is `Set` to the slide's title—`Shapes(1)`—and the `shapeSubTitle` variable is `Set` to the subtitle text box—`Shapes(2)`.

From there, the title's `TextFrame` property is used to add and format the title text. Then its `AnimationSettings` property is used to animate the text. A similar sequence of code adds text, formatting, and animation to the subtitle.

Some Shape Methods

The Shape object comes with a number of methods that let you perform actions such as copying, deleting, and flipping slides. Here's a list of some of the more useful methods:

`Shape``.Apply`: This method applies to the specified *`Shape`* the formatting that was captured from another shape using the `PickUp` method (described in a moment).

`Shape``.Copy`: This method copies the specified *`Shape`* to the Clipboard. If you then want to paste the shape into another slide, use the `Paste` method of the `Shapes` object:

`Slide``.Shapes.Paste`

`Slide`	The Slide object into which you want to paste the shape.

`Shape``.Cut`: This method cuts the specified *`Shape`* from the slide and places it on the Clipboard. Use the `Shapes.Paste` method to paste the shape into another slide.

`Shape``.Delete`: This method deletes the specified *`Shape`*.

`Shape.Duplicate`: This method makes a copy of the specified `Shape` in the same slide. The new shape is added to the `Shapes` object immediately after the specified `Shape`. Note, too, that this method returns a Shape object that refers to the new shape.

`Shape.Flip`: This method flips the specified `Shape` around its horizontal or vertical axis. Here's the syntax:

```
Shape.Flip(FlipCmd)
```

Shape	The Shape object you want to flip.
FlipCmd	A constant that determines how the shape is flipped. Use either `msoFlipHorizontal` or `msoFlipVertical`.

`Shape.IncrementLeft`: Moves the specified `Shape` horizontally using the following syntax:

```
Shape.IncrementLeft(Increment)
```

Shape	The Shape object you want to move.
Increment	The distance, in points, that you want the shape moved. Use a positive number to move the shape to the right; use a negative number to move the shape to the left.

`Shape.IncrementRotation`: Rotates the specified `Shape` around its z-axis using the following syntax:

```
Shape.IncrementRotation(Increment)
```

Shape	The Shape object you want to move.
Increment	The number of degrees you want the shape rotated. Use a positive number to rotate the shape clockwise; use a negative number to rotate the shape counterclockwise.

`Shape.IncrementTop`: Moves the specified `Shape` vertically using the following syntax:

```
Shape.IncrementTop(Increment)
```

Shape	The Shape object you want to move.
Increment	The distance, in points, that you want the shape moved. Use a positive number to move the shape down; use a negative number to move the shape up.

`Shape.PickUp`: Copies the formatting of the specified `Shape`. Use the `Apply` method (discussed earlier) to apply the copied formatting to a different object.

`Shape.Select`: This method selects the specified `Shape` using the following syntax:

```
Shape.Select(Replace)
```

Shape	The Shape object you want to select.
Replace	A `Boolean` value that either adds the shape to the current selection (`False`) or replaces the current selection (`True`). `True` is the default.

The Juggling Application: Creating the Instructions

To continue the Juggling application, the `SetUpJugglingPages` procedure, shown in Listing 8.5, is run. This procedure serves to set up the title, picture, and instruction text for each of the four instruction slides.

Listing 8.5. A procedure that sets up the titles, pictures, and text instructions for each of the Juggling slides.

```
Sub SetUpJugglingPages()
    Dim thisPres As Presentation
    Dim slideTitle As Shape
    Dim slidePicture As Shape
    Dim slideText As Shape
    Dim i As Integer

    For i = 1 To 4
        With pres.Slides("Juggling" & i)
            '
            ' Get pictures from Chaptr08.ppt
            '
            Set thisPres = Presentations("Chaptr08.ppt")
            thisPres.Slides(1).Shapes(i + 1).Copy
            .Shapes.Paste
            '
            ' Adjust the layout and then set the Shape variables
            '
            .Layout = ppLayoutObjectOverText
            Set slideTitle = .Shapes(1)
            Set slideText = .Shapes(2)
            Set slidePicture = .Shapes(3)
            '
            ' Add the title text
            '
            With slideTitle.TextFrame.TextRange
                Select Case i
                    Case 1
                        .Text = "Step 1: The Home Position"
                    Case 2
                        .Text = "Step 2: The First Throw"
                    Case 3
                        .Text = "Step 3: The Second Throw"
                    Case 4
                        .Text = "Step 4: The Third Throw"
                End Select
                With .Font
                    .Name = "Arial"
                    .Size = 44
                    .Bold = True
                    .Color.RGB = RGB(255, 255, 255)
                End With
            End With
            '
            ' Set the picture animation and shadow
            '
            With slidePicture
                With .AnimationSettings
```

```
                .Animate = True
                .AdvanceMode = ppAdvanceOnTime
                .AdvanceTime = 0
                .EntryEffect = ppEffectFade
            End With
            With .Shadow
                .ForeColor.RGB = RGB(0, 0, 0)
                .OffsetX = 10
                .OffsetY = 10
                .Visible = True
            End With
        End With
        '
        ' Add the instruction text
        '
        With slideText.TextFrame.TextRange
            Select Case i
            Case 1
            .Text = "Place two balls in your dominant hand, " & _
                "one in front of the other." & Chr(13) & _
                "Hold the third ball in your other hand." & Chr(13) & _
                "Let your arms dangle naturally and bring your " & _
                "forearms parallel to the ground (as though you " & _
                "were holding a tray.)" & Chr(13) & _
                "Relax your shoulders, arms, and hands."
            Case 2
            .Text = "Of the two balls in your dominant hand, " & _
                "toss the front one towards your other hand " & _
                "in a smooth arc." & Chr(13) & _
                "Make sure the ball doesn't spin too much." & Chr(13) & _
                "Make sure the ball goes no higher than about eye level."
            Case 3
            .Text = "Once the first ball reaches the top of its arc, " & _
                "toss the ball in your other hand." & Chr(13) & _
                "Throw the ball towards your dominant hand, making " & _
                "sure that it flies UNDER the first ball." & Chr(13) & _
                "Again, try not to spin the ball and make sure it goes " & _
                "no higher than eye level."
            Case 4
            .Text = "Now for the tricky part (!). Soon after you release " & _
                "the second ball, the first ball will approach your " & _
                "hand. Go ahead and catch the first ball." & Chr(13) & _
                "When the second ball reaches its apex, throw the " & _
                "third ball (the remaining ball in your dominant hand) " & _
                "under it." & Chr(13) & _
                "At this point, it just becomes a game of catch-and-" & _
                "throw-under, catch-and-throw-under. Have fun!"
            End Select
            With .Font
                .Name = "Times New Roman"
                .Size = 24
                .Bold = False
                .Color.RGB = RGB(255, 255, 255)
            End With
        End With
    End With
Next i

End Sub
```

A `For...Next` loop runs through each of the four instructional slides. (Recall that earlier the `CreateJugglingSlides` procedure gave these slides the names Juggle1 through Juggle4.) Here's a summary of the various chores that are run within this loop:

- The first task is to load the pictures that illustrate each step. These pictures can be found on the slide in Chaptr08.ppt. To get them into the Juggling presentation, the code uses the `Copy` method to copy each one from Chaptr08.ppt to the Clipboard, and then it uses the `Paste` method to add the picture to the Juggling slide. When that's done, the slide's `Layout` property is set to `ppLayoutObjectOverText`, and the three variables that represent the three shapes on each slide are `Set`.
- Next, the title text is added. Here, a `Select Case` structure is used to add a different title to each slide, and then the text is formatted.
- The picture is animated, and a shadow is added.
- The last chunk of code uses another `Select Case` to add the appropriate instructions for each slide, and then the instruction text is formatted.

Operating a Slide Show

With your presentation created and saved, slides added and set up, and shapes inserted and formatted, your file is just about ready to roll. All that remains is to add a few slide show settings and transition effects. This section shows you how to do that, as well as how to run your slide show when it's complete.

Slide Show Transitions

Each Slide object has a `SlideShowTransition` property that determines how the slide advances during a slide show. This property is actually a SlideShowTransition object, and you set up the transition effect by modifying this object's properties. Here's a list of the key properties:

`*Slide*.SlideShowTransition.AdvanceOnClick`: For the specified `*Slide*`, this property returns or sets whether or not the slide advances when it's clicked. Set this property to `True` to advance the slide by clicking it.

`*Slide*.SlideShowTransition.AdvanceOnTime`: For the specified `*Slide*`, this property returns or sets whether or not the slide advances after a period of time has elapsed (as set by the `AdvanceTime` property). Set this property to `True` to advance the slide after a period of time.

`*Slide*.SlideShowTransition.AdvanceTime`: This property returns or sets the amount of time, in seconds, after which the specified `*Slide*` will advance, assuming that the `AdvanceOnTime` property is set to `True`.

NOTE: ENABLING ADVANCE ON TIME

To allow a slide to advance based on time, you also need to set the `SlideShowSettings` object's `AdvanceMode` property to `ppSlideShowUseSlideTimings`. This object is a property of the Presentation object, and I'll discuss it in detail in the next section.

`Slide.SlideShowTransition.EntryEffect`: A constant that determines the special effect used in the transition for the specified `Slide`. Look up this property in the VBA Help system to see the dozens of available constants.

`Slide.SlideShowTransition.Hidden`: This property returns or sets whether or not the specified `Slide` is hidden during the slide show. Use `True` to hide the slide or `False` to make the slide visible.

`Slide.SlideShowTransition.Speed`: This property returns or sets the speed of the transition for the specified `Slide`. Use one of the following constants:

- `ppTransitionSpeedFast`
- `ppTransitionSpeedMedium`
- `ppTransitionSpeedSlow`
- `ppTransitionSpeedMixed`

Slide Show Settings

The Presentation object has a `SlideShowSettings` property that controls various global settings for the slide show. This property is actually a `SlideShowSettings` object, and the settings are the properties of this object. Here's a rundown of the settings you'll utilize most often:

`Presentation.SlideShowSettings.AdvanceMode`: Returns or sets how the slides advance for the specified `Presentation`. Use `ppSlideShowManualAdvance` to advance slides manually (by clicking) or `ppSlideShowUseSlideTimings` to advance slides based on the `AdvanceTime` property for each slide. You can also use the `ppSlideShowRehearseNewTimings` constant to run the slide show in Rehearsal mode (which lets you set the timings by advancing the slides manually).

`Presentation.SlideShowSettings.EndingSlide`: Returns or sets the index number of the last slide that is displayed in the slide show for the specified `Presentation`.

`Presentation.SlideShowSettings.LoopUntilStopped`: Returns or sets whether or not the slide show for the specified `Presentation` plays continuously. Set this property to `True` to play the slide show in a continuous loop until the user presses Esc; set this property to `False` to play the slide show just once.

Presentation.SlideShowSettings.PointerColor: Returns or sets the color of the mouse pointer during the slide show for the specified *Presentation*. For example, the following statements set the color of the slide show pointer to red:

```
With ActivePresentation.SlideShowSettings
    .PointerColor.RGB = RGB(255, 0, 0)
End With
```

Presentation.SlideShowSettings.ShowType: Returns or sets the slide show type for the specified *Presentation*. Use ppShowTypeSpeaker (for the standard, full-screen slide show), ppShowTypeWindow (to run the slide show in a window), or ppShowTypeKiosk (to run the slide show in kiosk mode: full screen with a continuous loop).

Presentation.SlideShowSettings.ShowWithAnimation: Returns or sets whether or not the slide show for the specified *Presentation* uses the animation settings applied to each slide's shapes. Set this property to True to enable animation; use False to disable animation.

Presentation.SlideShowSettings.ShowWithNarration: Returns or sets whether or not the slide show for the specified *Presentation* uses narration. Set this property to True to enable narration; use False to disable narration.

Presentation.SlideShowSettings.StartingSlide: Returns or sets the index number of the first slide that is displayed in the slide show for the specified *Presentation*.

Running the Slide Show

At long last you're ready to display the presentation's slide show for all to see. To do so, simply invoke the Run method of the SlideShowSettings object:

Presentation.SlideShowSettings.Run

For example, Listing 8.6 shows the last of the Juggling application's procedures. In this case, the procedure presents a dialog box that asks the user if he or she wants to run the slide show. If Yes is clicked, some transition effects are applied to the instruction slides, and then the Run method is invoked.

Listing 8.6. This procedure asks the user if he or she wants to run the presentation's slide show.

```
Sub RunJugglingSlideShow
    If MsgBox("Start the slide show?", vbYesNo, "Juggling") = vbYes Then
        With pres
            .Slides("Juggling1").SlideShowTransition.EntryEffect =
            ➥ppEffectBlindsHorizontal
            .Slides("Juggling2").SlideShowTransition.EntryEffect =
            ➥pEffectCheckerboardAcross
            .Slides("Juggling3").SlideShowTransition.EntryEffect =
            ➥ppEffectBoxIn
```

```
            .Slides("Juggling4").SlideShowTransition.EntryEffect =
            ➥ppEffectStripsLeftDown
            .SlideShowSettings.Run
        End With
    End If
End Sub
```

Summary

This chapter showed you the ins and outs of PowerPoint VBA. You began with a look at a few properties of PowerPoint's `Application` object. From there, I went through a number of PowerPoint-specific objects, including the Presentation, Slide, and Shape objects. I closed by showing you how to work with slide shows in your VBA code. Throughout this chapter, I illustrated the concepts with a sample application that creates a PowerPoint presentation from scratch.

Here's a list of chapters where you'll find related information:

- For a general discussion of VBA objects, see Chapter 4, "Working with Objects."
- I show you how to work with `For Each...Next`, `For...Next`, and `Select Case` in Chapter 5, "Controlling Your VBA Code."
- You can also assign sound effects to slide animations and slide show transitions. I show you how it's done in Chapter 10, "Interacting with the User."
- To learn how to integrate PowerPoint with other Office applications, see Chapter 15, "Controlling Applications Via OLE Automation."

CHAPTER

VBA and Access

IN THIS CHAPTER

Data is what distinguishes the dilettante from the artist.

—George V. Higgins

Although Word, Excel, and PowerPoint all have long lists of objects that are unique to their hierarchies, they have quite a few objects in common. In addition, their implementation of VBA is more or less the same. Specifically, all three applications have macro recorders, and they each have the Visual Basic Editor to set up projects, create forms, and sling code.

Access, however, is a different kettle of VBA fish. This might not be too surprising to hear, because Access is unlike any of the other Office applications. For one thing, you don't deal with "documents" in Access. Instead, you have a database "container" that is filled with numerous other objects, such as tables, forms, and reports. For another, how you work with table data programmatically is a little less obvious than with the other applications. In Excel, for example, you can refer to cell B4 and there's no ambiguity about it. In Access, though, it doesn't mean anything to refer to, say, "record 5," because Access has no record numbers. The record that appears fifth in a datasheet depends on how the table is sorted or filtered, or whether you're dealing with a dynaset from a Select query.

Even though VBA is implemented uniquely in Access, you'll find enough similarities that the terrain shouldn't feel too unfamiliar. For example, all the core VBA language constructs that you've seen so far—from variables to operators to control structures such as `If...Then...Else`—are exactly the same in Access VBA. Similarly, the user form concepts that you'll learn about in Chapter 11, "Working with Microsoft Forms," are directly applicable to Access form objects.

What's different about using VBA in Access can be summed up in three points:

- Access objects: Access has its own collection of objects, each with a unique set of properties, methods, and events.
- How you work with Access VBA: Access doesn't use the Visual Basic Editor (VBE). Instead, the functionality of the VBE is built right into Access itself. The database container is equivalent to the VBE Project Editor, the Forms tab is the equivalent of VBE's user forms interface (complete with property sheets), and the Modules tab is the equivalent of VBE's module interface.
- Data Access Objects: This is a separate collection of objects that is independent of Access. (The "access" in Data Access Objects comes from the verb "to access." Don't confuse it with the product Access.) These objects give developers a standard methodology for working with databases, tables, queries, and other data objects.

Thanks to these and other unique features, it's best to treat Access VBA a little differently. In this chapter, I talk about some of the new VBA features in Access 97, I run through some of the objects in the Access hierarchy, and I show you how to set up event handlers for data entry and other chores. I'll hold off on Data Access Objects until we discuss database programming in Part IV, "Unleashing Application Integration."

What's New in Access 97

VBA 5.0

Like the other Office 97 products, Access 97 is no mere upgrade. It's full to bursting with new commands, extra utilities, and performance enhancements. So, of course, the version of VBA that was introduced in Access 95 has also been enhanced to cover these new features and to implement the improvements that are part and parcel of VBA 5.0 (such as the updated Object Browser and the ability to create class modules). Here's a quick look at just a few of the new features in Access 97 VBA:

Module window improvements: The Module window has been enhanced to include the new IntelliSense features in VBA 5.0 (such as Auto List Members and Auto Quick Info). I described these features in Chapter 1, "Introducing VBA."

Protecting your projects: Access 97 now includes a utility that converts a database to a new .MDE file format. This format prevents users from viewing or modifying database modules, forms, and reports, and also speeds the performance of the database. I'll discuss this feature in more depth later in this chapter (see "Protecting Access Projects").

Customizable menus and toolbars: Although Access 95 let you create custom toolbars, Access 97 goes a couple of steps further by also letting you customize menus and shortcut menus. You can also control toolbars and menus programmatically using the new `CommandBars` collection that's part of the Office 97 object model. See Chapter 12, "Creating Custom Menus and Toolbars," for details.

Support for ActiveX controls: You can embed ActiveX controls in your Access forms and control them via VBA.

Support for Internet features: Access 97 has several new Internet features, including Hyperlink columns and the capability to save objects as HTML. All of these features can be controlled programmatically in your VBA procedures (see Chapter 20, "Internet and Intranet Programming Topics").

New objects: The Access 97 object model isn't all that different from the object model used in Access 95. There are a few new objects, however, and they support the following: module windows (the Module object and its corresponding collection, `Modules`), pages in custom tabbed dialog boxes (the Page object and the `Pages` collection), and references to object libraries (the Reference object and the `References` collection).

NOTE: CONVERTING FROM ACCESS BASIC TO VBA

If you're upgrading to Access 97 from an earlier version of Access that used the Access Basic programming language, a number of issues are involved in converting your procedures to VBA. To examine these issues, start the Access Help system and open the book named "Microsoft Access and Visual Basic for Applications Reference." You'll find everything you need to know in the topic titled "Conversion and Compatibility Issues."

The Access Object Hierarchy

The hierarchy of objects in Access begins, as it does with the other Office products, with the `Application` object, which represents Access as a whole. From there, you'll find six objects in the next level:

`Forms`: This is a collection that holds all the open Form objects in the current Access database (see "The Access Form Object" later in this chapter).

`Reports`: This is a collection that holds all the open Report objects in the current Access database (see "The Access Report Object").

`Modules`: This collection represents all the open Module objects in the current Access database. There really isn't much to the Module object from a VBA standpoint—just a few not-very-useful properties. So this chapter will ignore the Module object and just concentrate on using modules to create VBA code.

`References`: This collection represents all the references to object libraries that are activated in Access (in other words, all the object libraries whose check boxes are activated in the References dialog box). When you're using Access to control other applications via OLE Automation (as described in Chapter 15, "Controlling Applications Via OLE Automation"), you can use the `References` collection to manipulate references to object libraries within your VBA procedures. For example, you can use the `AddFromFile` method to add a reference to a specific object library file, and you can use the `Remove` method to delete a reference.

`Screen`: You use this object's properties to refer to the datasheet, form, report, or control that currently has the focus, as follows:

Property	*What It Refers To*
`Screen.ActiveDatasheet`	The currently active datasheet.
`Screen.ActiveForm`	The currently active form.
`Screen.ActiveReport`	The currently active report.
`Screen.ActiveControl`	The form control that currently has the focus.

`DoCmd`: Access defines various *actions* that you can use in a macro procedure. These actions include opening a form (the `OpenForm` action), saving an object (the `Save` action), and printing an object (the `PrintOut` action). The purpose of the `DoCmd` object is to give you access to all of the macro actions within your VBA code. Each action is implemented as a method of the `DoCmd` object.

Controlling Access Options

You saw in Chapter 6, "Word for Windows VBA Programming," and Chapter 7, "Manipulating Excel with VBA," that both Word and Excel let you read and set the values of the various controls in their Options dialog boxes. But whereas these programs enlist the help of object properties to deal with program options, Access uses (once again) a different approach. Specifically, it uses two `Application` object methods: `GetOption` and `SetOption`.

You use the `GetOption` method to read the current value of an option:

```
Application.GetOption(OptionName)
```

OptionName	A string that specifies the option you want to work with.

You use the `SetOption` method to change the value of an option:

```
Application.SetOption OptionName, Setting
```

OptionName	A string that specifies the option you want to work with.
Setting	The new value for the option.

The values returned by `GetOption` and the settings you specify with `SetOption` depend on the type of control you're dealing with:

Check box: This control is represented by `Boolean` values: `True` for an activated check box and `False` for a deactivated check box.

Text box: This control is represented by a string value.

Option button: This control is represented by an integer that specifies the position of the activated option button within its group (where the first option button is 0, the second is 1, and so on).

List box: This control is represented by an integer that specifies the position of the selected item within the list (where the first item is 0, the second item is 1, and so on).

After the nice object-oriented approach used by Word and Excel, the brute-force approach of the `SetOption` and `GetOption` methods seems decidedly archaic:

- Using methods here doesn't make sense. The Options dialog box controls are surely properties of the `Application` object, so we should be able to treat them as such.
- Since each option is only represented by a string instead of an object property, you can't use the IntelliSense feature's List Properties/Methods command to find the option you want. Instead, you have to open the Option dialog box to get the control name and then look up the name in the Help system or in Table 9.1.
- The use of integers to specify list box items and option buttons is unintuitive. It would be better to have built-in constants (as do Word and Excel) that represent each option.
- Since the list box and option button items aren't constants, you can't use the List Constants feature supplied by IntelliSense. Again, you have to open the Options dialog box and display the list or group to calculate the appropriate item number.

Well, all gripes aside, we're stuck with this way of doing things, so we might as well get used to it. Table 9.1 runs through each control in the Options dialog box (except the options in the

Module tab, which can't be manipulated using these methods) and provides the corresponding `OptionName` string value.

Table 9.1. Arguments that correspond to the Access options.

Control	*Type*	`OptionName` *Argument*
	The View Tab	
Status Bar	Check box	Show Status Bar
Startup Dialog Box	Check box	Show Startup Dialog Box
Hidden Objects	Check box	Show Hidden Objects
System Objects	Check box	Show System Objects
Names Column	Check box	Show Macro Names Column
Conditions Column	Check box	Show Conditions Column
	The General Tab	
Left Margin	Text box	Left Margin
Right Margin	Text box	Right Margin
Top Margin	Text box	Top Margin
Bottom Margin	Text box	Bottom Margin
Default Database Folder	Text box	Default Database Directory
New Database Sort Order	List box	New Database Sort Order
Provide Feedback With Sound	Check box	Provide Feedback with Sound
	The Hyperlinks/HTML Tab	
Hyperlink Color	List box	Hyperlink Color
Followed Hyperlink Color	List box	Followed Hyperlink Color
Underline Hyperlinks	Check box	Underline Hyperlinks
Show Hyperlink Addresses In Status Bar	Check box	Show Hyperlink Addresses in Status Bar
HTML Template	Text box	HTML Template
Data Source Name	Text box	Data Source Name
User Name	Text box	User Name
Password	Text box	Password
Server URL	Text box	ActiveX Server URL
Session Timeout	Text box	ActiveX Session Timeout

Control	*Type*	`OptionName` *Argument*
	The Edit/Find Tab	
Default Find/Replace Behavior	Option buttons	Default Find/Replace Behavior
Record Changes	Check box	Confirm Record Changes
Document Deletions	Check box	Confirm Document Deletions
Action Queries	Check box	Confirm Action Queries
Local Indexed Fields	Check box	Show Values in Indexed
Local Nonindexed Fields	Check box	Show Values in Non-indexed
ODBC Fields	Check box	Show Values in Remote
Don't display lists where more than this number of records read	Text box	Show Values Limit
	The Keyboard Tab	
Move After Enter	Option buttons	Move After Enter
Arrow Key Behavior	Option buttons	Arrow Key Behavior
Behavior Entering Field	Option buttons	Behavior Entering Field
Cursor Stops At First/Last Field	Check box	Cursor Stops at First/Last Field
	The Datasheet Tab	
Default Colors: Font	List box	Default Font Color
Default Colors: Background	List box	Default Background Color
Default Colors: Gridlines	List box	Default Gridlines Color
Default Font: Font	List box	Default Font Name
Default Font: Weight	List box	Default Font Weight
Default Font: Size	List box	Default Font Size
Default Font: Italic	Check box	Default Font Italic
Default Font: Underline	Check box	Default Font Underline
Horizontal	Check box	Default Gridlines Horizontal
Vertical	Check box	Default Gridlines Vertical
Default Column Width	Text box	Default Column Width
Default Cell Effect	Option buttons	Default Cell Effect
Show Animations	Check box	Show Animations

continues

Table 9.1. continued

Control	*Type*	`OptionName` *Argument*
	The Tables/Queries Tab	
Text	Text box	Default Text Field Size
Number	List box	Default Number Field Size
Default Field Type	List box	Default Field Type
AutoIndex On Import/Create	Text box	AutoIndex on Import/Create
Show Table Names	Check box	Show Table Names
Output All Fields	Check box	Output All Fields
Enable AutoJoin	Check box	Enable AutoJoin
Run Permissions	Option buttons	Run Permissions
	The Forms/Reports Tab	
Selection Behavior	Option buttons	Selection Behavior
Form Template	Text box	Form Template
Report Template	Text box	Report Template
Always Use Event Procedures	Check box	Always Use Event Procedures
	The Advanced Tab	
Default Record Locking	Option buttons	Default Record Locking
Default Open Mode	Option buttons	Default Open Mode for Databases
Ignore DDE Requests	Check box	Ignore DDE Requests
Enable DDE Refresh	Check box	Enable DDE Refresh
OLE/DDE Timeout (Sec)	Text box	OLE/DDE Timeout (Sec)
Number Of Update Retries	Text box	Number of Update Retries
ODBC Refresh Interval (Sec)	Text box	ODBC Refresh Interval (Sec)
Refresh Interval (Sec)	Text box	Refresh Interval (Sec)
Update Retry Interval (Msec)	Text box	Update Retry Interval (Msec)
Command-Line Arguments	Text box	Command-Line Arguments
Conditional Compilation Arguments	Text box	Conditional Compilation Arguments
Project Name	Text box	Project Name
Error Trapping	Option buttons	Error Trapping

For example, the following code fragment works with several options in the Tables/Queries tab. It first checks the size of the default text field, and, if it's less than 50, it sets the size to 50. It then changes the default field type to Number (item 2 in the Default Field Type list box) and the default number field size to Integer (item 1 in the Number list box).

```
With Application
    If .GetOption("Default Text Field Size") < 50 Then
        .SetOption "Default Text Field Size", 50
    End If
    .SetOption "Default Field Type", 2
    .SetOption "Default Number Field Size", 1
End With
```

More About the Access `Application` Object

You've already seen a few `Application` object properties (the second-level objects mentioned earlier) and a couple of methods (`GetOption` and `SetOption`). However, the Access `Application` object is rich with properties and methods; I discuss a few of them in the next couple of sections.

Some `Application` Object Properties

Most of the `Application` object's properties either have already been mentioned (such as the `Forms` and `Reports` collections discussed earlier) or will be discussed in future chapters (for example, see Chapter 12 to learn about the `CommandBars` and `MenuBar` properties, and Chapter 18, "Programming Data Access Objects," for a description of the `DBEngine` property). However, that still leaves us with a few useful properties, and I've listed them here:

`Application.CodeContextObject`: Returns the object in which the VBA code is running. You'll see later in this chapter (in the section titled "Creating Access Event Handlers") that you can assign procedures to handle events such as the user clicking a form control. Use this property whenever you need to know in which database object the event handler is defined. For example, the following statement returns the name of the database object that is executing the statement:

```
MsgBox Application.CodeContextObject.Name
```

`Application.CurrentObjectName`: Returns the name of the object that either has the focus or in which the code is running. Note that this property returns the name of a database object (table, query, form, report, macro, or module) either if the object is open and has the focus or if the object is highlighted in the database window.

`Application.CurrentObjectType`: Returns the object type for whichever object currently has the focus or in which the code is running. The value returned by this property is a constant that corresponds to each type of database object: `acTable`, `acQuery`, `acForm`, `acReport`, `acMacro`, and `acModule`.

> **NOTE: GETTING MORE OBJECT INFORMATION**
>
> You can use the `CurrentObjectName` and `CurrentObjectType` properties in conjunction with the `SysCmd` function to return data about an object (such as whether the object has unsaved changes). See "Using the Handy `SysCmd` Function" later in this chapter.

`Application.IsCompiled`: This property returns `True` if the current VBA project has been compiled, and `False` otherwise.

`Application.UserControl`: This property returns `True` if the current Access VBA application was launched by the user. If the application was started by another process through OLE Automation (see Chapter 15), this property returns `False`.

`Application.Visible`: This property returns or sets whether the application window is minimized (`False`) or not minimized (`True`).

Some `Application` Object Methods

This section examines a few methods of the `Application` object that you might find useful:

`Application.CloseCurrentDatabase`: This method closes the currently open Access database. You'll rarely use this method within Access since, in most cases, the current database is also the database in which your code will be running. Instead, this method is most useful when you're controlling Access from another application via OLE Automation.

`Application.CodeDB`: This method returns a Database object that represents the database in which the code is running. Database objects are part of the Data Access Objects hierarchy and will be explained in detail in Chapter 18.

`Application.CurrentDB`: This method returns a Database object that represents the database that is currently open in the Access window.

`Application.NewCurrentDatabase`: This method creates a new database using the following syntax:

```
Application.NewCurrentDatabase dbName
```

Here, ***dbName*** is the filename of the new database file, including the path. Again, you'll probably only use this method when controlling Access via OLE Automation.

`Application.OpenCurrentDatabase`: This method opens a database using the following syntax:

```
Application.OpenCurrentDatabase dbName, Exclusive
```

dbName	The filename (including the path) of the database you want to open.
Exclusive	A `Boolean` value that determines whether the database is opened in exclusive mode (`True`) or in nonexclusive mode (`False`; this is the default).

For example, the following statements open the `Northwind.mdb` database:

```
dbStr = "C:\Microsoft Office\Access\Northwind.mdb"
Application.OpenCurrentDatabase dbStr
```

`Application.Quit`: This method quits Access. Here's the syntax:

```
Application.Quit Option
```

`Option` A constant that determines whether Access saves changes:

Option	*Description*
`acSaveYes`	Saves all objects.
`acPrompt`	Prompts the user to save objects before quitting.
`acExit`	Quits without saving any changes.

The Access Form Object

A Form object represents an open form in the current Access database. It's a member of the `Forms` collection, which you use to refer to a specific form, like so:

```
Forms!FormName
```

Here, *`FormName`* is the name of the form you want to work with. Note that if the form name contains spaces, you must enclose the name in square brackets:

```
Forms![Form Name]
```

For example, `Forms![Customer Orders]` refers to the form named Customer Orders.

NOTE: OTHER WAYS TO SPECIFY A FORM

For good measure, Access gives you two other ways to specify a form: `Forms("FormName")`, where *`FormName`* is the name of the form (with or without spaces), and `Forms(Index)`, where *`Index`* is the form's index within the `Forms` collection (the first form opened has index 0, the second has index 1, and so on).

Access also gives you two ways to refer to forms without knowing their names:

- To refer to the active form, use `Screen.ActiveForm`.
- To refer to the form in which the VBA code is running, use `Me`. For example, the following statement sets the caption (title bar text) for the form in which the code is executed:

```
Me.Caption = "Data Entry Form"
```

Opening a Form

When you need to open a form (and, by doing so, add it to the `Forms` collection), use the `DoCmd` object's `OpenForm` method:

```
DoCmd.OpenForm FormName, View, FilterName, WhereCondition, DataMode, WindowMode,
➥OpenArgs
```

FormName The name of the form in the current database that you want to open.

View Determines how the form is opened. Use one of the following constants:

`acNormal`	Opens the form in Form view (the default).
`acDesign`	Opens the form in Design view.
`acFormDS`	Opens the form in Datasheet view.

FilterName The name of a query from the current database.

WhereCondition A valid SQL `WHERE` clause (without the word `WHERE`) that defines the records to display (for example, "`Country='Germany'`").

DataMode Determines the data entry mode in which the form is opened, according to the following constants:

`acAdd`	Opens the form in Add mode (the user can insert new records, but can't edit existing records).
`acEdit`	Opens the form in Edit mode (the user can add new records and edit existing records). This is the default.
`acReadOnly`	Opens the form in Read-only mode (the user can't add or edit records).

WindowMode Determines the window mode in which the form is opened. Again, you specify a constant value:

`acNormal`	Opens the form in Normal view (depends on the form's properties). This is the default.
`acHidden`	Opens the form hidden.
`acIcon`	Opens the form as a minimized icon.
`acDialog`	Opens the form as a modal dialog box.

OpenArgs A string expression that defines one or more arguments. These arguments can be used by your VBA code to modify how the form opens (probably in the form's `Open` event handler).

For example, the following statement opens the Orders form in Add mode and shows only records where the OrderDate field contains dates later than January 1, 1997:

```
DoCmd.OpenForm _
    FormName:="Orders", _
    WhereCondition:="OrderDate > #1/1/97#", _
    DataMode:=acAdd
```

Creating a Form

You can create a form from scratch by running the `Application` object's `CreateForm` method:

```
CreateForm(Database, FormTemplate)
```

Database	The database that contains the form upon which you want to base the new form. If you omit this argument, Access uses the current database.
FormTemplate	The name of the form in *Database* that you want to use as a template for the new form. If you leave out this argument, Access uses the form that's defined in the Form Template text box of the Forms/Reports tab of the Options dialog box.

Note that this method returns a Form object. For example, the following statements declare a variable as a `Form` type and then run `CreateForm` to build a new form based on the existing Suppliers form:

```
Dim newForm As Form
newForm = CreateForm(, "Suppliers")
```

TIP: IMPORT FORMS FOR TEMPLATES

If you specify the *Database* argument in `CreateForm`, the file must be currently open as a library database. To avoid this, use the `DoCmd` object's `TransferDatabase` method to import the form you need into the current database.

Closing a Form

To close a form, use the `DoCmd` object's `Close` method:

```
DoCmd.Close ObjectType, ObjectName, Save
```

ObjectType	The type of object you're closing. Use `acForm` to close a form (the others are `acTable`, `acQuery`, `acReport`, `acMacro`, and `acModule`). If you omit this argument, the active object is closed.
ObjectName	The name of the form you want to close.
Save	A constant that determines how VBA closes a form that has unsaved design changes: `acPrompt` (prompts the user to save changes; this is the default), `acSaveYes` (saves the changes automatically), or `acSaveNo` (doesn't save the changes).

Form Object Properties

The Form object has more than 100 properties that determine the form's look and feel. Most of these properties are straightforward. (For example, to set the form's height and width, you use the `Height` and `Width` properties.) Here's a list of a few of the most useful form properties:

Form.`ActiveControl`: The control that has the focus in the specified *Form*. Remember that you need to use this property in conjunction with the screen object, like so:

```
currControl = Screen.ActiveControl
```

Form.`AllowAdditions`: A `Boolean` value that determines whether the user can add new records in the specified *Form*. If this property is `True`, the user can add records. Similar properties include `AllowDeletions` and `AllowEdits`. Set all these properties to `False` to make the records read-only.

Form.`Caption`: Returns or sets the text that appears in the title bar of the specified *Form*.

Form.`CloseButton`: A `Boolean` value that determines whether or not the specified *Form* displays the Close button.

Form.`ControlBox`: A `Boolean` value that determines whether or not the specified *Form* displays the Control menu box.

Form.`CurrentView`: A value that determines how the specified *Form* is displayed:

Value	*View*
0	Design
1	Form
2	Datasheet

Form.`DataEntry`: If set to `True`, this property tells Access to display only a new record for data entry when you open the specified *Form*. Note that the `AllowAdditions` property must also be set to `True`.

Form.`Dirty`: Returns `True` if the current record in the specified *Form* has changed since it was last saved.

Form.`Filter`: This property filters the records in the specified *Form* to show only a subset of the underlying table. You use a valid SQL `WHERE` clause (without the `WHERE`). You turn the filter on or off by setting the `FilterOn` property to `True` or `False`, respectively. For example, the following statements set the `Filter` property to show only those records in the Customers table in which the Country field is Canada:

```
Forms!Customers.Filter = "Country = 'Canada'"
Forms!Customers.FilterOn
```

Form.`MinMaxButtons`: A value that determines whether or not the specified *Form* displays the Maximize and Minimize buttons:

Value	*Buttons Displayed*
0	None
1	Minimize only
2	Maximize only
3	Minimum and Maximum

`Form.Modal`: Set this property to `True` to open the specified *`Form`* as modal. This means that the user must close the form before he or she can select any other object.

`Form.Name`: This property returns or sets the name of the specified *`Form`*.

`Form.NavigationButtons`: Set this property to `True` to display the usual navigation buttons and record number box at the bottom of the specified *`Form`*.

`Form.NewRecord`: This property returns `True` if the current record in the specified *`Form`* is a new record.

`Form.OrderBy`: Sets the sort order for the records in the specified *`Form`*. For example, to base the active form's sort order on the LastName field with a descending sort, you would use the following statement:

```
ActiveForm.OrderBy = "LastName DESC"
```

`Form.RecordSource`: This all-important property determines the underlying recordset for the specified *`Form`*. You can specify either a table name or a valid SQL `SELECT` expression. For example, the following statement sets the record source for the code's form to just the FirstName and LastName fields from the Employees table:

```
Me.RecordSource = "SELECT FirstName, LastName FROM Employees;"
```

`Form.Visible`: Set this property to `False` to hide the specified *`Form`*.

Form Object Methods

To help you perform actions on your forms, Access offers a few Form object methods, including the following:

`Form.Recalc`: Recalculates all calculated controls in the specified *`Form`*.

`Form.Refresh`: Updates the records in the specified *`Form`* to the latest values in the underlying record source. Use this method in a multiuser environment where a number of people might be working on the same record source.

`Form.Requery`: Reruns the query upon which the records in the specified *`Form`* are based.

`Form.SetFocus`: Moves the focus to the specified *`Form`*.

`Form.Undo`: Discards all changes made to the current record in the specified *`Form`* since it was last saved.

The Access Report Object

A Report object represents an open report in the current Access database. To refer to a specific report, use the `Reports` collection (the collection of all open Report objects), as shown here:

```
Reports!ReportName
```

ReportName is the name of the report you want to work with. As with forms, if the report name contains spaces, enclose the name in square brackets:

```
Reports![Report Name]
```

For example, `Reports![1997 Catalog]` refers to the report named 1997 Catalog.

> **NOTE: ANOTHER METHOD FOR SPECIFYING REPORTS**
>
> Access gives you two other ways to specify a report: `Reports("ReportName")`, where *ReportName* is the name of the report (with or without spaces), and `Reports(Index)`, where *Index* is the report's index within the `Reports` collection (the first report opened has index 0, the second has index 1, and so on).

Access also gives you two ways to refer to reports without knowing their names:

- To refer to the active report, use `Screen.ActiveReport`.
- To refer to the report in which the VBA code is running, use `Me`. For example, the following statement sets the caption (title bar text) for the report in which the code is executed:

```
Me.Caption = "1997 Catalog"
```

Opening a Report

To open a report (and add it to the `Reports` collection), use the `DoCmd` object's `OpenReport` method:

```
DoCmd.OpenReport ReportName, View, FilterName, WhereCondition
```

ReportName	The name of the report in the current database that you want to open.
View	Determines how the report is opened. Use one of the following constants:

`acViewNormal`	Opens the report in Report view (the default).
`acViewDesign`	Opens the report in Design view.
`acViewPreview`	Opens the report in the Print Preview window.

FilterName — The name of a query from the current database.

WhereCondition — A valid SQL WHERE clause (without the word WHERE) that defines the records to display (for example, "Country='Germany'").

For example, the following statement opens the Products By Category report in Print Preview mode and shows only records where the CategoryName field begins with "C":

```
DoCmd.OpenReport _
    ReportName:="Products By Category", _
    View:=acViewPreview, _
    WhereCondition:="CategoryName Like 'C*'"
```

Creating a Report

You can create a report from scratch by running the Application object's CreateReport method:

```
CreateReport(Database, ReportTemplate)
```

Database — The database that contains the report upon which you want to base the new report. If you omit this argument, Access uses the current database.

ReportTemplate — The name of the report in *Database* that you want to use as a template for the new report. If you leave out this argument, Access uses the report that's defined in the Report Template text box of the Forms/Reports tab of the Options dialog box.

Note that this method returns a Report object. For example, the following statements declare a variable as a Report type and then run CreateReport to build a new report based on the existing Suppliers report:

```
Dim newReport As Report
newReport = CreateReport(, "Suppliers")
```

TIP: IMPORT REPORTS FOR TEMPLATES

If you specify the *Database* argument in CreateReport, the file must be currently open as a library database. To avoid this, use the DoCmd object's TransferDatabase method to import the report you need into the current database.

Closing a Report

To close a report, use the DoCmd object's Close method:

```
DoCmd.Close ObjectType, ObjectName, Save
```

ObjectType — The type of object you're closing. Use acReport to close a report. If you omit this argument, the active object it closed.

`ObjectName` The name of the report you want to close.

`Save` A constant that determines how VBA closes a report that has unsaved design changes: `acPrompt` (prompts the user to save changes; this is the default), `acSaveYes` (saves the changes automatically), or `acSaveNo` (doesn't save the changes).

Report Grouping and Sorting

The Report object has dozens of properties that determine the appearance of the report. Most of these properties are the same as those used with the Form object, so I won't repeat them here. Instead, I focus on the `GroupLevel` property, which you can use to control report grouping and sorting.

The `GroupLevel` Object

A report's `GroupLevel` property is both an array and an object. As an array, each element refers to a group level, where `GroupLevel(0)` is the first field or expression upon which the report is grouped or sorted, `GroupLevel(1)` is the second field or expression, and so on.

As an object, `GroupLevel` has various properties that control how the report is grouped and sorted.

Creating Group Levels

Before you can use the properties of a `GroupLevel` object, you need to create the group level (if one doesn't exist already). You do that by running the `CreateGroupLevel` function:

```
CreateGroupLevel(Report, Expression, Header, Footer)
```

`Report` The name of the Report object in which to create the new group level.

`Expression` The field name or expression to use when grouping or sorting the report.

`Header` A `Boolean` value that determines whether the group level has a group header (`True`) or not (`False`).

`Footer` A `Boolean` value that determines whether the group level has a group footer (`True`) or not (`False`).

If you set both the ***`Header`*** and ***`Footer`*** arguments to `False`, Access sorts the report using ***`Expression`***. Otherwise, if either of the ***`Header`*** and ***`Footer`*** arguments is `True` (or if they're both `True`), Access groups the report using ***`Expression`***. Note, too, that the `CreateGroupLevel` function returns an integer that represents the level of the new grouping or sort.

For example, the following statements open a report in Design view, create a new group level that groups the Customers report by Country (with a group footer), and sorts the records within each group by City:

```
DoCmd.OpenReport _
    ReportName:="Customers", _
    View:=acViewDesign
CreateGroupLevel "Customers", "Country", False, True
CreateGroupLevel "Customers", "City", False, False
```

Figure 9.1 shows what the Sorting and Grouping dialog box looks like after you run this code.

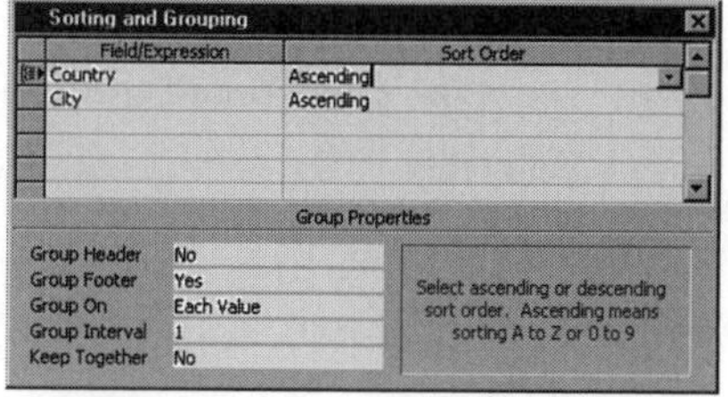

FIGURE 9.1.
Access VBA's sorting and grouping statements are equivalent to setting options in the Sorting and Grouping dialog box.

Properties of the `GroupLevel` Object

Once you've established a group level for a report, you can use the `GroupLevel` object's properties that manipulate the grouping or sorting. Here's a rundown of these properties:

`Report.GroupLevel(n).GroupInterval`: This property specifies a value for group level *n* upon which Access groups the records in the specified `Report`. (This is equivalent to entering a value in the Group Interval field in the Sorting and Grouping dialog box.) For example, in the code shown in the preceding section, the first group level groups the Customers report by Country. If you would prefer to group the records on the first two letters of the Country field (so that, say, Canada and Cameroon appear in the same group), you would use the following statement:

```
Reports!Customers.GroupLevel(0).GroupInterval = 2
```

The value you use depends on the data type of the underlying field and on the current setting of the `GroupOn` property (see Table 9.2). For example, if the field uses the Date/Time data type and `GroupOn` is set to `Month`, setting the `GroupInterval` property to 6 will group the records in half-year intervals.

`Report.GroupLevel(n).GroupOn`: This property determines how group level *n* groups records in the specified `Report`. (This is equivalent to entering a value in the Group On field in the Sorting and Grouping dialog box.) For example, you can group Date/Time fields or expressions by day, week, month, and so on. In each case, you use an integer value to specify the grouping. Table 9.2 outlines the integer values to use.

Table 9.2. Integer values to use when working with the `GroupOn` property.

Use This	*To Group by This*
	All Data Types
0	Items in the field or expression that have the same value (this is the default)
	The Text Data Type
1	Items in the field or expression that begin with the same first *n* characters (where *n* is a value set using the `GroupInterval` property)
	The Date/Time Data Type
2	Year (that is, dates in the same calendar year)
3	Quarter
4	Month
5	Week
6	Day
7	Hour
8	Minute
	Numeric Data Types
9	Values within an interval you specify using `GroupInterval`

For example, the following statements create a group level in the Invoices report based on the `OrderDate` field and then group records in this field every 90 days:

```
CreateGroupLevel "Invoices", "OrderDate", False, True
With Reports!Invoices.GroupLevel(0)
    .GroupOn = 6
    .GroupInterval = 90
End With
```

`Report``.GroupLevel(`*`n`*`).KeepTogether`: This property determines whether Access keeps the header, footer, and detail sections of group level *n* together on the same page for the specified *`Report`*. (This is equivalent to selecting a value in the Keep Together field in the Sorting and Grouping dialog box.) This property has three possible values:

Value	*What It Keeps Together*
0	Nothing (Keep Together field equivalent: No)
1	The header, footer, and detail sections (Keep Together field equivalent: Whole Field)
2	The group header with the first detail record (Keep Together field equivalent: With First Detail)

Report.GroupLevel(*n*).SortOrder: This property specifies the sort order for group level *n* in the specified *Report*. (This is equivalent to selecting a value in the Sort Order field in the Sorting and Grouping dialog box.) Use False for an ascending sort (this is the default) or True for a descending sort.

The Control Object

A Control object represents a control (such as a text box or command button) on a specified form or report. As with Form and Report objects, Access gives you a number of ways to refer to a control. The most straightforward method is to refer to the control directly, like so:

```
Object!ControlName
```

Here, *Object* is a reference to a Form or Report object, and *ControlName* is the name of the control you want to work with. Again, if the control name contains spaces, enclose the name in square brackets. For example, the following statement sets a variable named myControl to the Customer Name control on the Customers form:

```
Dim myControl As Control
Set myCOntrol = Forms!Customers![Customer Name]
```

Also recall that you can use the Screen object to refer to the control that currently has the focus:

```
currControl = Screen.ActiveControl
```

NOTE: SETTING THE FOCUS

To give a particular control the focus, use the SetFocus method:

Control.SetFocus

Here, *Control* is a reference to the control.

Access also has a Controls object that represents all the controls on a given form. This is handy if you need to enumerate a form's controls or apply a particular property value to each control. The following code fragment runs through each control on the form or report in which the code is running and sets the Enabled property for each control to True:

```
Dim c As Control
For Each c in Me.Controls
    c.Enabled = True
Next c
```

Note, too, that the Controls object also gives you a couple of methods for referencing a control: Controls("*ControlName*"), where *ControlName* is the name of the control (with or without spaces), and Controls(*Index*), where *Index* is the control's index within the Controls collection (the first control has index 0, the second has index 1, and so on).

Access also has separate objects for specific controls—CheckBox, ComboBox, CommandButton, and so on. I'll discuss the properties, methods, and events for specific controls in Chapter 11.

Using the Handy SysCmd Function

The Access `Application` object comes equipped with a number of functions, including the `CreateForm` and `CreateReport` functions you saw earlier, as well as some math functions (such as `DAvg`, `DCount`, `DMax`, and `DMin`, to name a few). One of the most versatile functions is `SysCmd`, which lets you display a message or progress meter in the status bar, return the state of a specified database object, and return information about Access. I'll leave the status bar material until Chapter 10, "Interacting with the User," but this section covers the other two `SysCmd` features.

Returning the Current State of an Object

The `SysCmd` function can provide you with information about a database object. Specifically, it will tell if an object is open, new, or has unsaved changes. Here's the syntax to use:

`SysCmd(`***`Action`***`, `***`ObjectType`***`, `***`ObjectName`***`)`

Action	A constant that tells Access you want to return information about a database object. Use the constant `acSysCmdGetObjectState`.
ObjectType	A constant that specifies the type of object you want to work with: `acTable`, `acQuery`, `acForm`, `acReport`, `acMacro`, or `acModule`.
ObjectName	The name of the database object.

With this syntax, the `SysCmd` function returns one of the following constants:

Return Value	*Object State*
`0`	Not open or nonexistent
`acObjStateOpen`	Open
`acObjStateNew`	New
`acObjStateDirty`	Has unsaved changes

For example, the following procedure fragment checks to see if a form is open before running the `OpenForm` method:

```
If SysCmd(acSysCmdGetObjectState, acForm, "Products") = 0 Then
    DoCmd.OpenForm "Products", acDesign
End If
```

Returning Information About Access

The `SysCmd` function can also return valuable information about Access itself. Here's the syntax to use:

```
SysCmd(Action)
```

`Action` A constant that specifies the information to return:

`acSysCmdRuntime`	Returns `True` if this is a runtime version of Access; returns `False` otherwise.
`acSysCmdAccessVer`	Returns the Access version number.
`acSysCmdIniFile`	Returns the name of the .INI file associated with Access.
`acSysCmdAccessDir`	Returns the path of the folder in which the Access executable file (Msaccess.exe) is located.
`acSysCmdProfile`	Returns the /profile setting the user specified when starting Access from the command line.
`acSysCmdGetWorkgroupFile`	Returns the path to System.mdw, the Access workgroup file.

For example, if you're building an application that will be used on multiple versions of Access, you could use the `acSysCmdAccessVer` constant to check the current version and branch your code accordingly:

```
If SysCmd(acSysCmdAccessVer) = 8 Then
    <Do some Access 97-specific things>
Else
    <Do something else>
End If
```


Creating Access Event Handlers

In Chapter 11, I'll show you how to build user forms in the Visual Basic Editor and attach event handlers to controls. For example, you can add code to a command button to handle a `Click` event and to a spin button to handle a `Change` event.

The controls you add to Access forms operate in exactly the same way. In other words, they all have various predefined events. You can "trap" these events by creating event handler procedures. Here are the steps to follow to set up an event handler:

1. In the Form design window, click the control you want to work with and then select View | Properties. Access displays the properties sheet for the control.
2. Activate the Event tab. As you can see in Figure 9.2, this tab includes an entry for every event recognized by the control.

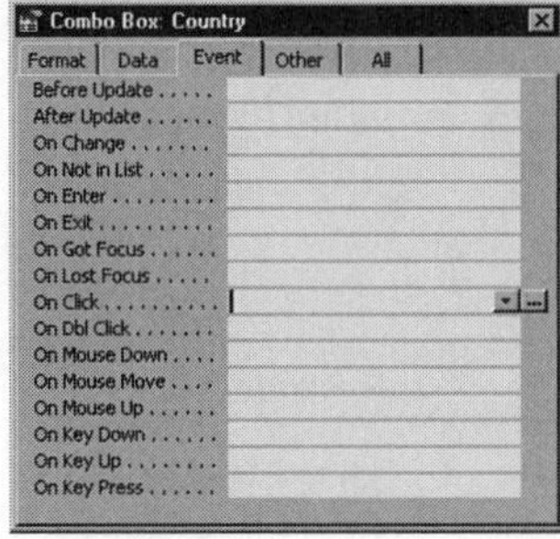

FIGURE 9.2.
The Event tab lists the events associated with the selected control.

3. Click inside the event you want to work with and then click the three-dot button (...) to the right of the event. The Choose Builder dialog box appears, as shown in Figure 9.3.

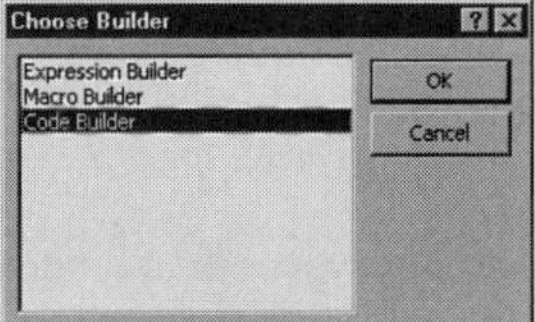

FIGURE 9.3.
Select Code Builder to create a new module for your event handler code.

> **TIP: A FASTER ROUTE**
>
> A quicker way to get to the Choose Builder dialog box is to right-click the control and then choose Build Event.

4. Highlight Code Builder and click OK. Access creates a stub procedure for the event with just `Sub` and `End Sub` statements, as shown in Figure 9.4.

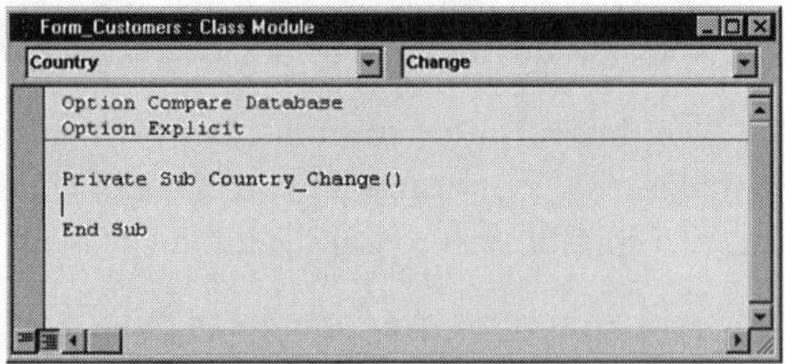

FIGURE 9.4.
Use the stub procedure to fill in the code you want to run whenever the event occurs.

5. Enter your event handler code between the `Sub` and `End Sub` statements.

Working with Access Modules

Event handlers are specific to the form in which they reside. The `Private` keyword that precedes the `Sub` statement ensures that the procedure can only be run within the form. This way, even if another form uses a procedure with the same name (which could easily happen), there will be no ambiguity about which procedure to execute.

What do you do if you want to create a procedure that isn't attached to an event? For example, you might need to design a function procedure or a separate subroutine that can process data from multiple controls.

To handle these situations, Access gives you two choices:

- Insert your procedure as part of the form's module.
- Create a new Module object.

Adding Code to the Form Module

Adding your code to the form module is a good idea if your statements will be referring to the Form object or to any Control object on the form. This lets you use the `Me` keyword to refer to the form, thus saving some keystrokes.

To add a procedure to the form's module, first display the module by selecting View | Code. In the module window that appears, type in your procedure the way you normally would.

To return to the procedure later, open the module, select (General) in the Object drop-down list, and use the procedure list to select your code.

Adding Code to a Module Object

You might have code that you would like to make available to the database as a whole. For example, the Northwind sample database that ships with Access has a module named Startup that contains several functions and procedures related to the startup of the application. The `IsItAReplica` function, for instance, checks to see if the database being opened is a replicated database.

For these more general procedures and functions, create a Module object and use it to insert your procedures. To create a module, activate the Modules tab in the database container and then click New. (Alternatively, you can select Insert | Module from any database tab.) As you can see in Figure 9.5, the window that appears is just the standard module window that you've seen a few times now.

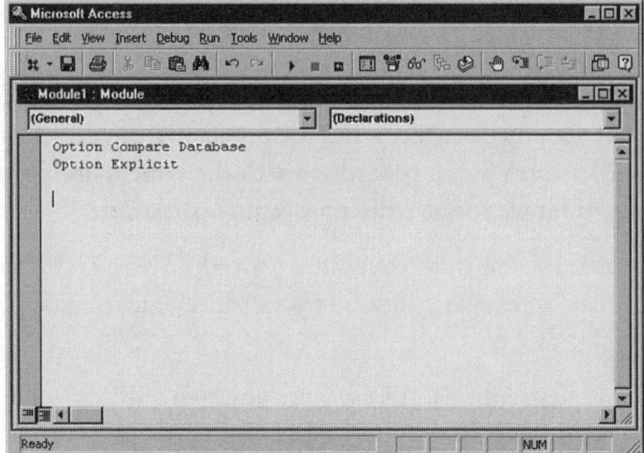

FIGURE 9.5.
A new module window.

Protecting Access Projects

Previous versions of Access didn't offer much in the way of security for the modules included in a database. For example, you could hide a module, but any reasonably savvy user would know how to unhide the module and examine your code.

That's all changed in Access 97 thanks to the new .MDE format. Saving a database in this format leaves the user-level objects—tables, queries, forms, reports, and macros—visible and operational. However, this format makes the following changes to protect your application's code:

- All source code is compiled and then removed from the database. Here, "removed" means that the user can't edit the source code. However, the procedures and functions you set up will still run properly.
- The user can't work with the Module object to alter the application's source code.
- The user can't work with forms or reports in Design view.
- The user can't import or export forms, reports, or modules (but he can still import or export tables, queries, and macros).
- The user can't modify references to object libraries.

CAUTION: KEEP YOUR .MDB FILE

Microsoft has stated that, for security reasons, .MDE files created with Access 97 will *not* work with future versions of Access. You won't even be able to open .MDE files in future versions. For this reason, always keep your original .MDB file. That way, you can load the original into the future version of Access and save it as an .MDE file.

To save an open database as an .MDE file, follow these steps:

1. Select Tools | Database Utilities | Make MDE File. Access displays the Save MDE As dialog box.
2. Choose a location for the .MDE file.
3. For a filename, Access suggest the current name of the database with an .MDE extension. Feel free to modify the primary name if necessary.
4. Click Save. If you have any unsaved changes, Access will prompt you to save the objects.

Summary

This chapter introduced you to Access VBA. I explained how VBA fits into the Access universe, and then you learned about the Access object hierarchy (which included a close look at the Form and Report objects). From there, I showed you how to create event handlers for Access forms, how to work with form modules and Module objects, and how to save database files in the new .MDE format. Here are some chapters to check out for related information:

- To learn about objects, especially object properties and events, see Chapter 4, "Working with Objects."
- To find out more about programming forms and controls, check out Chapter 11, "Working with Microsoft Forms."
- I show you how to work with tables, queries, and other members of the Data Access Objects hierarchy in Chapter 18, "Programming Data Access Objects."
- Advanced database techniques (such as Jet security) are covered in Chapter 19, "Advanced Database Programming."

IN THIS PART

PART

Unleashing VBA User Interface Design

Interacting with the User

IN THIS CHAPTER

Happiness lies outside yourself, is achieved through interacting with others.

—*Valerie Solanas*

A well-designed application not only makes intelligent decisions and streamlines code with loops but also keeps the user involved. It should display messages at appropriate times and ask the user for input. When interacting with the application, the user will feel that he is a part of the process and has some control over what the program does—which means that he won't lose interest in the program and will be less likely to make careless mistakes. This chapter takes you through various methods of giving and receiving user feedback.

Programming Sounds

You'll see later in this chapter that there are a number of ways to present information to the user visually. Also, Chapter 11, "Working with Microsoft Forms," shows you how to create dialog boxes and input forms to gather information from the user. However, these visual cues might get lost in the shuffle if the user has a number of windows and programs open at once. In this case, you might need to supplement visual displays with accompanying sounds that will help focus the user's attention. This section looks at various methods you can employ to work with sounds in your VBA procedures.

Beeping the Speaker

VBA's most rudimentary form of communication is the simple, attention-getting beep. It's VBA's way of saying "Ahem!" or "Excuse me!" and it's handled, appropriately enough, by the `Beep` statement.

For example, Listing 10.1 shows an Excel procedure, called `RecalcAll`, that recalculates all the open workbooks and then sounds three beeps to mark the end of the process.

Listing 10.1. A procedure that recalculates all open workbooks and then sounds three beeps.

```
Sub RecalcAll()

    Dim i As Integer

    Application.Calculate
    For i = 1 To 3
        Beep
        '
        ' Pause for 2 seconds between beeps
        '
        Application.Wait Now + TimeValue("00:00:02")
    Next i

End Sub
```

CAUTION: DON'T OVERDO IT

Avoid overusing the `Beep` statement. You need to get the user's attention, but constant beeping only defeats that purpose; most users get annoyed at any program that barks at them incessantly. Good uses for the `Beep` statement are signaling errors and signaling the end of long operations.

NOTE: EXCEL CODE FOR THIS CHAPTER

This chapter includes code listings for various applications, and you'll find everything on this book's CD. You'll find the Excel listings in Chaptr10.xls (as well as Chaptr10.bas for those without Excel).

Programming PowerPoint Sound Effects

The `Beep` statement is useful, but it's primitive. If you're working with PowerPoint and you have the necessary hardware, you can get your presentations to play much more sophisticated sounds.

PowerPoint has a `SoundEffect` property that lets you assign and play sounds in a presentation. This property is part of the hierarchy of two PowerPoint objects:

`AnimationSettings`: The sound effect is applied to the animation associated with an object (such as a picture) on a slide.

`SlideShowTransition`: The sound effect is applied to a slide's transition.

This property returns or sets a `SoundEffect` object that represents the sound to be played during the animation or transition. To specify a sound, use the `ImportFromFile` method:

`Object``.SoundEffect.ImportFromFile(`***`FileName`***`)`

`Object`	The object to which you want to apply the sound.
`FileName`	The name and path of the sound file.

For example, the following statements import the tada.wav file as the sound effect for the slide named `Start`:

```
Set currSlide = ActivePresentation.Slides("Start")
currSlide.SlideShowTransition.SoundEffect.ImportFromFile _
    FileName:="C:\Windows\Media\tada.wav
```

The `SlideShowTransition` object also has a `LoopSoundUntilNext` property. This property returns or sets whether or not the sound effect for the specified slide loops continuously until the next sound starts. Use `True` to loop the sound, or `False` to play the sound just once.

NOTE: SOUND VIA OLE

Another way to deal with sounds in your application is to embed a sound file or other multimedia file in one of your project's documents. I'll show you how to manipulate OLE objects in Chapter 14, "Programming OLE and ActiveX Objects."

CAUTION: EXCEL SOUND NOTES ARE SILENT

Previous versions of Excel allowed you to add a sound note to a cell and control these notes programmatically. Note, however, that Excel 97 doesn't support sound notes, so you should avoid using any sound note features in your Excel VBA routines.

Displaying Information to the User

Displaying information is one of the best (and easiest) ways to keep your users involved. For example, if an operation will take a long time, make sure the user has some visual clue about the progress of the operation. Similarly, if a user makes an error (for example, he enters the wrong argument in a user-defined function), he should be gently admonished so that he'll be less likely to repeat the error. This section presents several methods of displaying information to the users of your VBA applications.

Changing the Mouse Pointer in Access

When you work in Windows, the mouse pointer often changes shape depending on what you're doing:

- When you're entering text, the pointer changes to an I-beam shape.
- When you're resizing a window, the pointer changes to a two-headed arrow.
- During a lengthy operation, the pointer changes to the dreaded hourglass.
- During most other operations, the pointer assumes its normal arrow shape.

These visual cues provide useful feedback, and you can take advantage of them in Access VBA. The `Screen` object has a `MousePointer` property that lets you control the look of the mouse pointer in your VBA procedures. Here's a list of the acceptable values you can use with this property:

Value	*Mouse Pointer*
0	Default pointer (the pointer that applies to the current Access action)
1	Arrow pointer
3	I-beam pointer
7	Vertical two-headed arrow (the pointer used for resizing a window vertically)
9	Horizontal two-headed arrow (the pointer used for resizing a window horizontally)
11	Hourglass

For example, you could use the following statement to set the pointer to an hourglass to indicate that your application is in the middle of a long operation:

```
Screen.MousePointer = 11
```

Displaying a Message in the Status Bar

Most applications have a status bar at the bottom of the screen that is used for displaying messages and indicating the progress of the current operation. In Office 97, Word, Excel, and Access let you display your own messages in the status bar. The next couple of sections show you how it's done.

Status Bar Messages in Word and Excel

For Word and Excel, you can use the `Application` object's `StatusBar` property to display text messages in the status bar at the bottom of the screen. This gives you an easy way to keep the user informed about what a procedure is doing or how much is left to process.

Listing 10.2 demonstrates the `StatusBar` property with a revised version of the `ConvertToProper` procedure that you saw in Chapter 5, "Controlling Your VBA Code." The goal is to display a status bar message of the form `Converting cell` *`x`* `of` *`y`*, in which *`x`* is the number of cells converted so far and *`y`* is the total number of cells to be converted.

Listing 10.2. A procedure that uses the `StatusBar` property to inform the user of the progress of the operation.

```
Sub ConvertToProper2()

    Dim cellVar As Object
    Dim cellsConverted As Integer, totalCells As Integer
    '
    ' Initialize some variables
    '
```

continues

Listing 10.2. continued

```
    cellsConverted = 0
    totalCells = Selection.Count
    '
    ' Loop through all the selected cells
    '
    For Each cellVar In Selection
        '
        ' Convert to proper case
        '
        cellVar.Value = Application.Proper(cellVar)
        cellsConverted = cellsConverted + 1
        '
        ' Display the message
        '
        Application.StatusBar = "Converting cell " & _
                                cellsConverted & " of " & _
                                totalCells
    Next
    '
    ' Reset the status bar
    '
    Application.StatusBar = False
End Sub
```

The `cellsConverted` variable tracks the number of cells converted, and the `totalsCells` variable stores the total number of cells in the selection (given by `Selection.Count`).

The `For Each...Next` loop does three things:

- It converts one cell at a time to proper case.
- It increments the `cellsConverted` variable.
- It sets the `StatusBar` property to display the progress of the operation. Note the use of the concatenation operator (`&`) to combine text and variable values.

When the loop is done, the procedure sets the `StatusBar` property to `False` to clear the status bar.

Programming the Status Bar in Access

Access uses the status bar to display messages and to display progress meters that let you know the progress of a long operation (such as importing records). You can use the `SysCmd` function to provide the same feedback to the users of your Access applications. Here's the syntax:

`SysCmd(`***`Action`***`, `*`Text`*`, `*`Value`*`)`

`Action` A constant that specifies what Access does to the status bar:

`acSysCmdInitMeter`	Initializes the progress meter.
`acSysCmdUpdateMeter`	Updates the progress meter.

`acSysCmdRemoveMeter`	Removes the progress meter.
`acSysCmdSetStatus`	Displays *`Text`* in the status bar.
`acSysCmdClearStatus`	Clears the status bar.

`Text` The text to be displayed in the status bar. You must specify this argument when ***`Action`*** is `acSysCmdInitMeter` or `acSysCmdSetStatus`.

`Value` Controls the display of the progress meter. You must specify this argument when ***`Action`*** is `acSysCmdInitMeter` or `acSysCmdUpdateMeter`.

If you just want to display text in the status bar, use `acSysCmdSetStatus` for the ***`Action`*** argument and specify the status bar text with the *`Text`* argument. Listing 10.3 shows a procedure that opens a form and then loops depending on the number of controls in the form. While in the loop, the status bar message is updated to indicate the progress of the loop. To slow things down a bit, a `Do While` loop delays for half a second on each pass through the main loop.

Listing 10.3. A procedure that displays text in the status bar.

```
Sub StatusBarText()
    Dim frm As Form
    Dim strStatus As String
    Dim ctrlCount As Integer
    Dim i As Integer
    Dim start As Long
    '
    ' Open the Orders form
    '
    DoCmd.OpenForm "Startup", acDesign
    Set frm = Forms("Startup")
    '
    ' Get the control count
    '
    ctrlCount = frm.Controls.Count
    '
    ' Loop ctrlCount times
    '
    For i = 1 To ctrlCount
        '
        ' Update the status bar text
        '
        strStatus = "Control " & i & " of " & ctrlCount
        SysCmd acSysCmdSetStatus, strStatus
        '
        ' Delay for half a second
        '
        start = Timer
        Do While Timer < (start + 0.5)
            DoEvents
        Loop
    Next i
    '
    ' Clear the status bar
    '
    SysCmd acSysCmdClearStatus
End Sub
```

NOTE: THIS CHAPTER'S ACCESS CODE LISTINGS

The Access code listings for this chapter can be found on the CD in the file named Chaptr10.txt.

Using a progress meter involves three steps:

1. Run `SysCmd` with `acSysCmdInitMeter` to initialize the progress bar. Here, you use the *`Text`* argument to specify text that will appear in front of the progress meter, and you use the *`Value`* argument to set the maximum value of the meter.
2. During the operation whose progress you want to show, run the `SysCmd` function at regular intervals. In this case, the ***`Action`*** argument is `acSysCmdUpdateMeter`, and you use the *`Value`* argument to specify the current value of the meter. For example, if your maximum progress meter value is 100 and you update the meter to 50, the meter will appear half filled in.
3. When the operation is complete, run `SysCmd` once again using `acSysCmdRemoveMeter` as the ***`Action`*** argument to clear the status bar.

Listing 10.4 shows a slightly different example that uses a progress meter instead of text to indicate the loop's progress.

Listing 10.4. A procedure that displays a progress meter in the status bar.

```
Sub StatusBarProgressMeter()
    Dim frm As Form
    Dim ctrlCount As Integer
    Dim i As Integer
    Dim start As Long
    '
    ' Open the Orders form
    '
    DoCmd.OpenForm "Startup", acDesign
    Set frm = Forms!Startup
    '
    ' Get the control count
    '
    ctrlCount = frm.Controls.Count
    '
    ' Initialize the progress meter
    '
    SysCmd acSysCmdInitMeter, "Control Loop:", ctrlCount
    '
    ' Loop ctrlCount times
    '
    For i = 1 To ctrlCount
        '
        ' Update the progress meter
        '
        SysCmd acSysCmdUpdateMeter, i
```

```
        '
        ' Delay for half a second
        '
        start = Timer
        Do While Timer < (start + 0.5)
            DoEvents
        Loop
    Next i
    '
    ' Clear the status bar
    '
    SysCmd acSysCmdRemoveMeter
End Sub
```

Displaying a Message Using MsgBox

The problem with using the `StatusBar` property to display messages is that it's often a bit too subtle. Unless the user knows to look in the status bar, he or she might miss your messages altogether. When the user really needs to see a message, you can use the `MsgBox` function:

`MsgBox(`***`Prompt`***`, `*`Buttons`*`, `*`Title`*`, `*`HelpFile`*`, `*`Context`*`)`

`Prompt` The message you want to display in the dialog box. (You can enter a string up to 1,024 characters long.)

`Buttons` A number or constant that specifies, among other things, the command buttons that appear in the dialog box. (See the next section.) The default value is `0`.

`Title` The text that appears in the dialog box title bar. If you omit the title, VBA uses the name of the underlying application (for example, `Microsoft Excel`).

`HelpFile` The text that specifies the Help file that contains the custom help topic. If you enter *`HelpFile`*, you also have to include *`Context`*. If you include *`HelpFile`*, a Help button appears in the dialog box.

`Context` A number that identifies the help topic in *`HelpFile`*.

For example, the following statement displays the message dialog box shown in Figure 10.1:

```
MsgBox "You must enter a number between one and 100!",,"Warning"
```

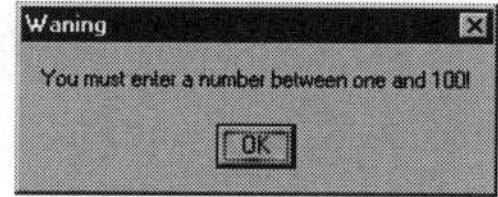

FIGURE 10.1.
A simple message dialog box produced by the `MsgBox` *function.*

> **NOTE: PARENTHESES REMINDER**
>
> The `MsgBox` function, like all VBA functions, needs parentheses around its arguments only when you use the function's return value. See the section later in this chapter called "Getting Return Values from the Message Dialog Box" to learn about the return values produced by the `MsgBox` function.

> **TIP: BREAK PROMPT TEXT INTO MULTIPLE LINES**
>
> For long prompts, VBA wraps the text inside the dialog box. If you would prefer to create your own line breaks, use VBA's `Chr` function and the carriage-return character (ASCII 13) between each line:
>
> ```
> MsgBox "First line" & Chr(13) & "Second line"
> ```

Setting the Style of the Message

The default message dialog box displays only an OK button. You can include other buttons and icons in the dialog box by using different values for the *`Buttons`* parameter. Table 10.1 lists the available options.

Table 10.1. The `MsgBox` *`Buttons`* parameter options.

Constant	*Value*	*Description*
		Buttons
`vbOKOnly`	0	Displays only an OK button. (This is the default.)
`vbOKCancel`	1	Displays the OK and Cancel buttons.
`vbAbortRetryIgnore`	2	Displays the Abort, Retry, and Ignore buttons.
`vbYesNoCancel`	3	Displays the Yes, No, and Cancel buttons.
`vbYesNo`	4	Displays the Yes and No buttons.
`vbRetryCancel`	5	Displays the Retry and Cancel buttons.
		Icons
`vbCritical`	16	Displays the Critical Message icon.
`vbQuestion`	32	Displays the Warning Query icon.
`vbExclamation`	48	Displays the Warning Message icon.
`vbInformation`	64	Displays the Information Message icon.

Constant	Value	Description
		Default Button
`vbDefaultButton1`	0	The first button is the default (that is, the button selected when the user presses Enter).
`vbDefaultButton2`	256	The second button is the default.
`vbDefaultButton3`	512	The third button is the default.
		Modality
`vbApplicationModal`	0	The user must respond to the message box before continuing work in the current application.
`vbSystemModal`	4096	All applications are suspended until the user responds to the message box.

You derive the *`Buttons`* argument in one of two ways:

- By adding up the values for each option
- By using the VBA constants separated by plus signs (+)

For example, Listing 10.5 shows a procedure named `ButtonTest`, and Figure 10.2 shows the resulting dialog box. Here, three variables—*`msgPrompt`*, *`msgButtons`*, and *`msgTitle`*—store the values for the `MsgBox` function's ***`Prompt`***, *`Buttons`*, and *`Title`* arguments, respectively. In particular, the following statement derives the *`Buttons`* argument:

```
msgButtons = vbYesNoCancel + vbQuestion + vbDefaultButton2
```

You also could derive the *`Buttons`* argument by adding up the values that these constants represent (3, 32, and 256, respectively), but the procedure becomes less readable that way.

Listing 10.5. A procedure that creates a message dialog box.

```
Sub ButtonTest()

    Dim msgPrompt As String, msgTitle As String
    Dim msgButtons As Integer, msgResult As Integer

    msgPrompt = "Are you sure you want to copy" & Chr(13) & _
                "the selected files to drive A?"
    msgButtons = vbYesNoCancel + vbQuestion + vbDefaultButton2
    msgTitle = "Copy Files"

    msgResult = MsgBox(msgPrompt, msgButtons, msgTitle)

End Sub
```

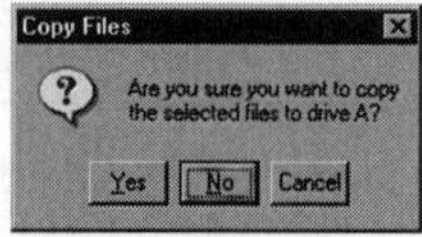

FIGURE 10.2.
The dialog box that's displayed when you run the code in Listing 10.5.

Getting Return Values from the Message Dialog Box

A message dialog box that displays only an OK button is straightforward. The user either clicks OK or presses Enter to remove the dialog from the screen. The multibutton styles are a little different, however; the user has a choice of buttons to select, and your procedure should have a way to find out which button the user chose.

You do this by storing the `MsgBox` function's return value in a variable. Table 10.2 lists the seven possible return values.

Table 10.2. The `MsgBox` function's return values.

Constant	*Value*	*Button Selected*
`vbOK`	1	OK
`vbCancel`	2	Cancel
`vbAbort`	3	Abort
`vbRetry`	4	Retry
`vbIgnore`	5	Ignore
`vbYes`	6	Yes
`vbNo`	7	No

To process the return value, you can use an `If...Then...Else` or `Select Case` structure to test for the appropriate values. For example, the `ButtonTest` procedure shown earlier used a variable called `msgResult` to store the return value of the `MsgBox` function. Listing 10.6 shows a revised version of `ButtonTest` that uses a `Select Case` statement to test for the three possible return values. (Note that the `vbYes` case runs a procedure named `CopyFiles`. The `ButtonTest` procedure assumes that the `CopyFiles` procedure already exists elsewhere in the module.)

Listing 10.6. This example uses `Select Case` to test the return value of the `MsgBox` function.

```
Sub ButtonTest2()

    Dim msgPrompt As String, msgTitle As String
    Dim msgButtons As Integer, msgResult As Integer

    msgPrompt = "Are you sure you want to copy" & Chr(13) & _
                "the selected files to drive A?"
```

```
    msgButtons = vbYesNoCancel + vbQuestion + vbDefaultButton2
    msgTitle = "Copy Files"

    msgResult = MsgBox(msgPrompt, msgButtons, msgTitle)

    Select Case msgResult
        Case vbYes
            CopyFiles
        Case vbNo
            Exit Sub
        Case vbCancel
            Application.Quit
    End Select

End Sub
```

Getting Input from the User

As you've seen, the `MsgBox` function lets your procedures interact with the user and get some feedback. Unfortunately, this method limits you to simple command-button responses. For more varied user input, you need to use more sophisticated techniques.

Prompting the User for Input

The `InputBox` function displays a dialog box with a message that prompts the user to enter data, and it provides a text box for the data itself. Here's the syntax for this function:

`InputBox(`***`Prompt`***`, `*`Title, Default, Xpos, Ypos, HelpFile, Context`*`)`

Prompt	The message you want to display in the dialog box (1,024-character maximum).
Title	The text that appears in the dialog box title bar. The default value is the null string (nothing).
Default	The default value displayed in the text box. If you omit *Default*, the text box is displayed empty.
Xpos	The horizontal position of the dialog box from the left edge of the screen. The value is measured in points (there are 72 points in an inch). If you omit *Xpos*, the dialog box is centered horizontally.
Ypos	The vertical position, in points, from the top of the screen. If you omit *Ypos*, the dialog is centered vertically in the current window.
HelpFile	The text specifying the Help file that contains the custom help topic. If you enter *HelpFile*, you also have to include *Context*. If you include *HelpFile*, a Help button appears in the dialog box.
Context	A number that identifies the help topic in *HelpFile*.

For example, Listing 10.7 shows a procedure called `GetInterestRate` that uses the `InputBox` method to prompt the user for an interest rate value. Figure 10.3 shows the dialog box that appears.

Listing 10.7. A procedure that prompts the user for an interest rate value.

```
Function GetInterestRate()

    Dim done As Boolean
    '
    ' Initialize the loop variable
    '
    done = False

    While Not done
        '
        ' Get the interest rate
        '
        GetInterestRate = InputBox( _
                          Prompt:="Enter an interest rate between 0 and 1:", _
                          Title:="Enter Interest Rate")
        '
        ' First, check to see if the user cancelled
        '
        If GetInterestRate = "" Then
            GetInterestRate = 0
            Exit Function
        Else
            '
            ' Now make sure the entered rate is between 0 and 1
            '
            If GetInterestRate >= 0 And GetInterestRate <= 1 Then
                done = True
            End If
        End If
    Wend

End Function
```

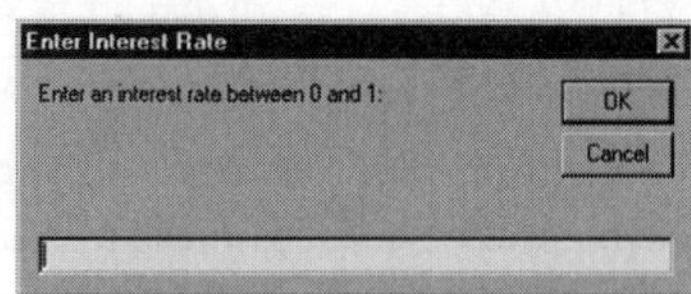

FIGURE 10.3.
A dialog box generated by the `InputBox` *function in Listing 10.7.*

The `InputBox` method returns one of the following values:

- The value entered into the text box if the user clicked OK
- An empty string if the user clicked Cancel

In Listing 10.7, the result of the `InputBox` method is stored in the `GetInterestRate` variable. The procedure first checks to see if `InputBox` returned the empty string (`""`). If so, the `Exit`

`Function` statement bails out of the procedure. Otherwise, an `If...Then` statement checks to make sure the number is between 0 and 1. If it is, the `done` variable is set to `True` so that the `While...Wend` loop will exit; if the number isn't between 0 and 1, the procedure loops and the dialog box is redisplayed.

NOTE: EXCEL'S INPUT BOX METHOD

Excel has its own version of `InputBox` that's an `Application` object method. It has the same syntax as the VBA `InputBox` function, except that it tacks on an extra argument—*Type*:

```
Application.InputBox(Prompt, Title, Default, Xpos, Ypos, HelpFile, Context,
➥Type)
```

Type A number that specifies the data type of the return value, as follows:

Type	*Data Type*
0	Formula
1	Number
2	Text (the default)
4	Boolean (`True` or `False`)
8	Reference (a Range object)
16	Error value
32	An array of values

Accessing an Application's Built-In Dialog Boxes

Many VBA methods are known as *dialog box equivalents* because they let you select the same options that are available in an application's built-in dialog boxes. Using dialog box equivalents works fine if your procedure knows which options to select, but there are times when you might want the user to specify some of the dialog box options.

For example, if your procedure will print a document (using the `PrintOut` method), you might need to know how many copies the user wants or how many pages to print. You could use the `InputBox` method to get this data, but it's usually easier to just display the Print dialog box.

The built-in dialog boxes are Dialog objects, and `Dialogs` is the collection of all the built-in dialog boxes. To reference a particular dialog box, use one of the predefined application constants. Table 10.3 lists a few of the more common ones from Word and Excel.

Table 10.3. Some of Excel's built-in dialog box constants.

Word Constant	*Excel Constant*	*Dialog Box*
`wdDialogFormatFont`	`xlDialogFont`	Font
`wdDialogFileNew`	`xlDialogNew`	New
`wdDialogFileOpen`	`xlDialogOpen`	Open
`wdDialogFilePageSetup`	`xlDialogPageSetup`	Page Setup
`wdDialogEditPasteSpecial`	`xlDialogPasteSpecial`	Paste Special
`wdDialogFilePrint`	`xlDialogPrint`	Print
`wdDialogFilePrintSetup`	`xlDialogPrinterSetup`	Printer Setup
`wdDialogFileSaveAs`	`xlDialogSaveAs`	Save As
`wdDialogInsertObject`	`xlDialogObject`	Object
`wdDialogFormatStyle`	`xlDialogStyle`	Style
`wdDialog`	`xlDialogSort`	Sort

NOTE: DIALOG BOX CONSTANTS

To see a complete list of constants for Word and Excel's built-in dialog boxes, first open the Object Browser. In the list of libraries, select the application (such as Excel or Word), and highlight <globals> in the Classes list. In the Member list, look for the `xxDialog` constants, where *xx* varies between applications: `wdDialog` for Word and `xlDialog` for Excel.

To display any of these dialog boxes, use the Dialog object's `Show` method. For example, the following statement displays Excel's Print dialog box:

```
Application.Dialogs(xlDialogPrint).Show
```

If the user clicks Cancel to exit the dialog box, the `Show` method returns `False`. This means that you can use `Show` inside an `If` statement to determine what the user did:

```
If Not Application.Dialogs(xlDialogPrint).Show Then
    MsgBox "File was not printed"
End If
```

Summary

This chapter introduced you to a few methods for interacting with the users of your VBA applications. We began with a look at sounds, including the simple `Beep` function and PowerPoint's more sophisticated `SoundEffects` object. From there, we progressed to displaying information to the user. I showed you how to change the mouse pointer in Access, display messages in the status bar, and display a message dialog box with the `MsgBox` function. I closed this chapter with two techniques for getting input from the user: the `InputBox` function and the application's built-in dialog boxes.

Here's a list of chapters where you'll find related information on user interaction:

- To get maximum control over your code's user interaction, you'll need to build your own custom dialog boxes and user forms. To find out how, see Chapter 11, "Working with Microsoft Forms."
- To make it easier for users to interact with your procedures, you can assign your procedures to menus and toolbars. I show you how this is done in Chapter 12, "Creating Custom Menus and Toolbars."
- A proper application interface shields the user from program errors. I show you a few techniques for doing this in Chapter 23, "Trapping Program Errors."
- Sophisticated and well-designed applications include a Help system. You'll learn how to create one in Chapter 26, "VBA Tips and Techniques."

CHAPTER 11

Working with Microsoft Forms

IN THIS CHAPTER

The system designer suffers because the better his system does its job, the less its users know of its existence.

—*Gerald M. Weinberg*

VBA procedures are only as useful as they are convenient. There isn't much point in creating a procedure that saves you (or your users) a few keystrokes if you (or they) have to expend a lot of time and energy hunting down a routine. Shortcut keys are true time-savers, but some applications (such as Excel) have only a limited supply to dole out (and our brains can memorize only so many Ctrl-*key* combinations).

Instead, you need to give some thought to the type of user interface you want to create for your VBA application. The interface includes not only the design of the documents, but also three other factors that let the user interact with the model: dialog boxes, menus, and toolbars. Although you certainly can give the user access to the application's built-in dialogs, menus, and toolbars, you'll find that you often need to create your own interface elements from scratch. This chapter starts you off by showing you how to use VBA 5.0's new Microsoft Forms feature to create custom dialog boxes and input forms. Chapter 12, "Creating Custom Menus and Toolbars," shows you how to set up custom menus and toolbars.

Understanding Custom Forms and Dialog Boxes

The `InputBox` function you learn about in Chapter 10, "Interacting with the User," works fine if you need just a single item of information, but what if you need four or five? Or, what if you want the user to choose from a list of items? In some cases, you can use the application's built-in dialog boxes (which I also discussed in Chapter 10), but these might not have the exact controls you need, or they might have controls to which you don't want the user to have access.

The solution is to build your own dialog boxes. You can add as many controls as you need (including list boxes, option buttons, and check boxes), and your procedures will have complete access to all the results. Best of all, the Visual Basic Editor makes constructing even the most sophisticated dialog boxes as easy as dragging the mouse pointer. The next few sections show you how to create dialog boxes and integrate them into your applications.

Forms and Dialog Boxes in VBA 5.0

VBA 5.0 In VBA 5.0, dialog boxes are called *forms* (or *user forms*). This more general term is in keeping with the more general nature of these objects in the latest incarnation of VBA. So, yes, you can use a form as a dialog box to ask the user for confirmation or to set a few options. You can also use forms as data entry screens or query-building mechanisms. In this sense, a VBA form is a close cousin to the form objects that have been available in Access from Day One. In recognition of this, I'll forego the term "dialog box" and instead use the term "form" throughout the rest of this chapter. (The exception to this will be when I'm talking about built-in application dialog boxes.)

NOTE: EXCEL 95'S DIALOG SHEETS

If you've created form objects and worked with Dialog objects in Excel's previous versions of VBA, don't worry—your procedures and objects will still work as they always have. However, VBA 5.0's forms are completely different, so the following discussion will be new to you. You'll find, though, that VBA 5.0 forms are easier to create and much more powerful than the relatively primitive dialog boxes available previously.

Adding a Form to Your Project

Forms are separate objects that you add to your VBA projects. To do this, open the Visual Basic Editor and either select Insert | UserForm or drop down the Insert toolbar button (the second from the left) and select UserForm. As you can see in Figure 11.1, VBA performs the following tasks in response to this command:

- It adds a Forms branch to the project tree in the Project Explorer.
- It creates a new UserForm object and adds it to the Forms branch.
- It displays the form in the work area.
- It displays the Toolbox.

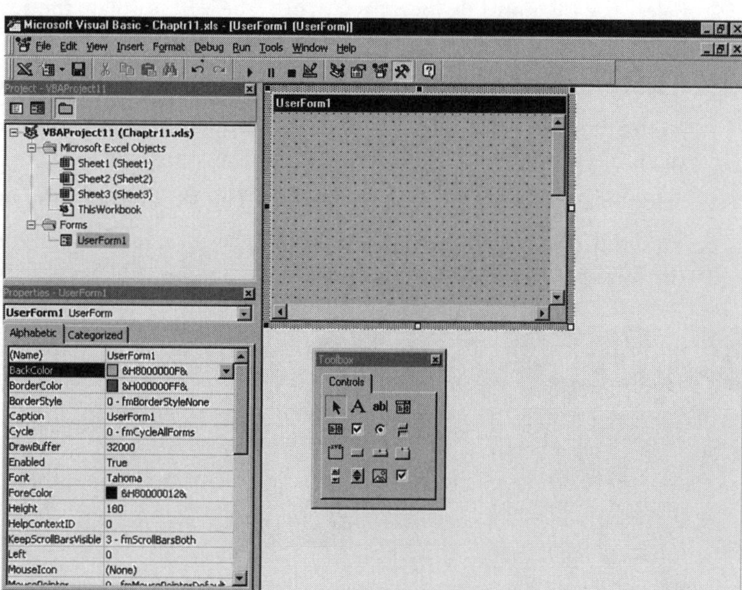

FIGURE 11.1.
Selecting Insert | UserForm adds a new form to the project.

Sharing Forms Between VBA Applications

All VBA applications that use the Visual Basic Editor (VBE) share the Microsoft Forms object library. Therefore, you have a common set of tools for building user forms, which is a giant leap forward from the previous state of affairs, where each application had its own form tools (if it had any at all).

The main advantage here is that you need only learn one set of techniques for building forms and manipulating them programmatically. A secondary (and not insignificant) benefit is that you can share forms between any two VBE-enabled applications. So if you spend time and energy creating a form that is just so in one application, you don't have to rebuild the form from scratch in another environment. VBA gives you two ways to share forms:

- Exporting and importing form files
- Dragging a form object to another project

Importing and Exporting Form Files

The VBE has a couple of commands that let you export a form to a separate file and then import that file into another project (either in the current application or in another VBE-enabled application). Here's how it works:

1. In the Project Explorer, click the form you want to export.
2. Select File | Export File (or press Ctrl-E). The VBE displays the Export File dialog box.
3. Select a location for the file, change the filename if necessary (form files always use the .FRM extension, so you just need to enter the primary name), and click Save.
4. In the Project Explorer (either in the current application or another application), click the project into which you want to import the form file.
5. Select File | Import File (or press Ctrl-M). The VBE displays the Import File dialog box.
6. Find the form file you want to import, highlight it, and click Open. The VBE adds the form to the project.

TIP: EXPORT FORMS AS BACKUPS

The export feature isn't only useful for sharing forms between VBA projects. You can also use it to create a separate form file that can be used as a backup copy in case anything untoward should happen to the form object inside the project (such as the object getting accidentally deleted).

Dragging Form Objects Between Applications

If you don't feel like cluttering your hard drive with form files, or if the export/import procedure feels like too much work, there's an easier method you can use. Just drag the form object from its perch in the Project Explorer and drop it on the other project:

- If the other project is in the same application, you drop the form on the name of another project in the Project Explorer.
- If the other project is in a different VBE-enabled application, you have to arrange the VBE windows in advance so that you can see the Project Explorer in the other application.

TIP: DRAGGING FORMS WITHOUT ARRANGING WINDOWS

If, like me, you prefer to work with the VBE window maximized, there's a way to avoid having to arrange the VBE windows for dragging. Just drag the form from the Project Explorer and let it hover over the taskbar button of the other VBE window. After a second or two, Windows will bring the other VBE window to the front and you can then drop the form onto the appropriate project in the other window.

Changing the Form's Design-Time Properties

One of Microsoft's design goals in VBA 5.0 was to create a common user interface between the Visual Basic Editor and Visual Basic 5.0, the stand-alone programming environment. To that end, forms (and all the control objects you can add to a form) have an extensive list of properties that you can manipulate by entering or selecting values in the Properties window. (Recall that you display the Properties window by selecting View | Properties Window or by pressing F4.)

For a form, there are over 30 properties arranged into seven categories (in the Properties window, activate the Categories tab to see the properties arranged by category), as described in the next few sections.

NOTE: CONTROLLING FORM PROPERTIES PROGRAMMATICALLY

Besides modifying form properties at design time, you can also modify many of the properties at runtime by including the appropriate statements in your VBA procedures. I talk about this in greater detail later in this chapter (see the section "Using a Form in a Procedure").

The Appearance Category

The properties in the Appearance category control the look of the form:

BackColor: Sets the color of the form's background. For all color properties, you can either enter the hexadecimal equivalent of the color you want (surround by & signs), or click the drop-down arrow to display a color menu. In this menu, you can either choose a predefined color from the System tab or a built-in color from the Palette tab.

BorderColor: Sets the color of the form's border. Note that for this property to have any effect, you have to assign a border to the form using the BorderStyle property.

BorderStyle: Choose fmBorderStylSingle to apply a border around the form. Use fmBorderStyleNone for no border.

Caption: Specifies the text that's displayed in the form's title bar.

ForeColor: Sets the default color of text used in the form's controls.

SpecialEffect: Controls how the form appears relative to the form window (for example, raised or sunken).

The Behavior Category

The properties in the Behavior category control two aspects of how the user interacts with the form:

Cycle: Determines what happens when the user presses Tab while the focus is on the last control in the form. If this property is set to fmCycleAllForms and the form has multiple pages, focus is set to the first control on the next page. If this property is set to fmCycleCurrentForm, focus is set to the first control on the current page.

Enabled: Set this property to True to enable the form or False to disable it.

The Font Category

The Font property determines the default font used throughout the form. When you activate this property, click the three-dot (...) button to display the Font dialog box from which you can select the font, style, size, and effects.

The Misc Category

As its name implies, the Misc category contains a collection of properties that don't fit anywhere else:

Name: You use this property to refer to the form in your VBA code.

TIP: USE DESCRIPTIVE NAMES

Although you might be tempted to stick with the default form name supplied by VBA (such as UserForm1), your code will be easier to read if you give the form a more descriptive name. Indeed, this advice applies not only to forms, but to *all* controls.

`DrawBuffer`: This value is the number of pixels that VBA sets aside in memory for rendering the frame. You can enter an integer value between 16,000 and 1,048,576.

`HelpContextID`: Specifies the topic number in a Help file that refers to Help topic for the form. See Chapter 26, "VBA Tips and Techniques," to learn more about defining Help systems for your projects.

`MouseIcon`: Assigns a picture that will appear as the mouse pointer whenever the pointer is inside the form. Note that you must also set the `MousePointer` property to `fmMousePointerCustom`.

`MousePointer`: Determines the appearance of the mouse pointer when the pointer is inside the form.

`Tag`: This property defines a hidden string that is assigned to the form. You can use this string to specify extra information about the form that isn't available with the other properties (such as a version number, the creation date or developer name, or a description of the form's purpose).

`WhatsThisButton`: When this property is set to `True`, VBA displays a "What's This?" Help button (it has a question mark) in the upper-right corner, which signifies that What's This? Help is available for the form.

`WhatsThisHelp`: When this property is set to `True`, VBA displays a pop-up Help window when the user clicks a control after clicking the "What's This?" Help button. The displayed text is defined in a custom Help file (see Chapter 26).

`Zoom`: This property specifies a percentage by which the form is enlarged (for values between 100 and 400) or reduced (for values between 10 and 100).

The Picture Category

In the Picture category, use the `Picture` property to set a background image for the form. (Again, click the three-dot button to select a picture file from a dialog box.) The other properties determine how the picture is displayed:

`PictureAlignment`: Specifies where on the form the picture is displayed.

`PictureSizeMode`: Specifies how the picture is displayed relative to the form. Use `fmPictureSizeModeClip` to crop any part of the picture that's larger than the form; use `fmPictureSizeModeStretch` to stretch the picture so that it fits the entire form; use `fmPictureSizeModeZoom` to enlarge the picture until it hits the vertical or horizontal edge of the form.

`PictureTiling`: For small images, set this property to `True` to fill the background with multiple copies of the image.

The Position Category

The properties in the Position category specify the dimensions of the form (`Height` and `Width`), and the position of the form within the application window. For the latter, you can either use the `StartUpPosition` property to center the form relative to the application window (`CenterOwner`) or to the screen (`CenterScreen`), or you can choose `Manual` and specify the `Left` and `Top` properties. (The latter two properties set the form's position in points from the application window's left and top edges, respectively.)

The Scrolling Category

The properties in the Scrolling category determine whether the form displays scroll bars and, if it does, what format the scroll bars have:

`KeepScrollBarsVisible`: Determines which of the form's scroll bars remain visible even if they aren't needed.

`ScrollBars`: Determines which scroll bars are displayed on the form.

`ScrollHeight`: Specifies the total height of the form's scrollable region. For example, if the form's `Height` property is set to 200 and you set the `ScrollHeight` property to 400, you double the total vertical area available in the form.

`ScrollLeft`: If `ScrollWidth` is greater than the width of the form, use the `ScrollLeft` property to set the initial position of the horizontal scroll bar's scroll box. For example, if the `ScrollWidth` is 200, setting `ScrollLeft` to 100 starts the horizontal scroll bar at the halfway position.

`ScrollTop`: If `ScrollHeight` is greater than the height of the form, use the `ScrollTop` property to set the initial position of the vertical scroll bar's scroll box.

`ScrollWidth`: Specifies the total width of the form's scrollable region.

`VerticalScrollBarSide`: Determines whether the vertical scroll bar appears on the right or left side of the window.

Working with Controls

Now that your form is set up with the design-time properties you need, you can get down to the brass tacks of form design. In other words, you can start adding controls to the form, adjusting those controls to get the layout you want, and setting the design-time properties of each control. I discuss the unique characteristics of each type of control later in this chapter (see the section "Types of Form Controls"). For now, though, I'll run through a few techniques that you can apply to any control.

Inserting Controls on a Form

The new form object is an empty shell that doesn't become a useful member of society until you populate it with controls. As with the form-building tools in Word and Access, the idea is that you use this shell to "draw" the controls you need. Later, you can either link the controls directly to other objects (such as Excel worksheet cells) or create procedures to handle the selections.

The Toolbox contains buttons for all the controls you can add to a form. Here are the basic steps to follow to add any control to the form:

1. Click the button you want to use.
2. Move the mouse pointer into the form and position it where you want the top-left corner of the control to appear.
3. Drag the mouse pointer. VBA displays a gray border indicating the outline of the control.
4. When the control is the size and shape you want, release the mouse button. VBA creates the control and gives it a default name (such as CheckBox*n,* where *n* signifies that this is the *n*th check box you've created on this form).

TIP: ADDING MULTIPLE COPIES OF A CONTROL

If you want to add multiple instances of the same type of control, double-click the appropriate Toolbox button. The button will remain pressed, and you can draw as many instances of the control as you need. When you're done, click an empty part of the Toolbox to reset the control.

NOTE: GRID OPTIONS

When you're dragging most controls, the VBE adjusts the control's border so that it aligns with the form's grid. Don't forget that the VBE has a few useful options for setting up this grid to your liking (I discuss these options in detail in Chapter 1, "Introducing VBA"). To see these options, select Tools | Options and then activate the General tab in the Options dialog box. The Form Grid Settings group lets you turn the grid on and off, adjust the grid size, and set whether or not controls are aligned to the grid.

Selecting Controls

Before you can work with a control, you must select it. For a single control, you select it simply by clicking it. If you prefer to work with multiple controls, the Visual Basic Editor gives you a number of techniques:

- Hold down the Ctrl key and click each control.
- You also can "lasso" multiple controls by dragging the mouse. Move the mouse pointer to an empty part of the form, hold down the left button, and drag. The VBE displays a box with a dashed outline, and any control that falls within this box (in whole or in part) will be selected.
- To select every control, make sure the form is active and then select Edit | Select All. (For faster service, you can also either press Ctrl-A or right-click an empty part of the form and choose Select All from the shortcut menu.)

To exclude a control from the selection, hold down the Ctrl key and click inside the control.

After you've selected multiple controls, you can set properties for all the controls at once. Note, however, that the Properties window will show only those properties that are common to all of the controls. (See "Common Control Properties" later in this chapter.) Not only that, but if you size, move, copy, or delete one of the selected controls (as described in the next few sections), your action will apply to all of the controls.

Each control is surrounded by an invisible rectangular *frame*. When you select a control, the VBE displays a gray outline that represents the control's frame and this outline is studded with white *selection handles* at the frame's corners and midpoints, as shown in Figure 11.2.

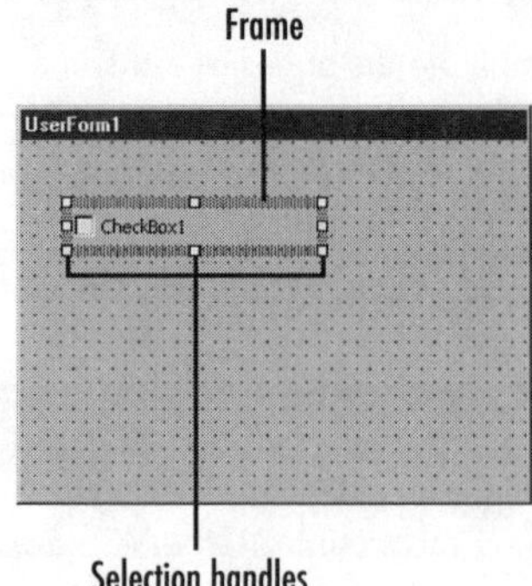

FIGURE 11.2.
A selected control displays a frame and various selection handles.

Sizing Controls

You can resize any control to change its shape or dimensions. The following procedure outlines the steps to work through:

1. Select the object you want to size.

2. Position the mouse pointer over the selection handle you want to move. The pointer changes to a two-headed arrow. To change the size horizontally or vertically, use the appropriate handle on the middle of a side. To change the size in both directions at once, use the appropriate corner handle.
3. Drag the handle to the position you want.
4. Release the mouse button. The VBE redraws the object and adjusts the frame size.

NOTE: SIZING THE FORM

To size the form itself, click an empty part of the form and then drag the selection handles that appear around the form.

To reduce some of the drudgery of control sizing, the VBE also offers a number of automatic sizing techniques. The next few sections give you a quick tour of these techniques.

Sizing to the Grid

If you've turned off the option that causes the VBE to size controls to the grid marks, you can still adjust a control's size to the grid by hand. To do this, select the control and then select Format | Size to Grid. The VBE will then adjust the control's frame to the nearest grid marks.

Sizing to the Caption

If you want to make a control only large enough to display its caption, select the control and then select Format | Size to Fit.

Making Controls the Same Size

If you've added similar controls (such as command buttons), your form will look its best if these controls are the same size. The easy way to do this is with the Make Same Size command, which gives the selected controls either the same width or the same height (or both).

Note that the VBE always uses one of the selected controls as the "base" upon which the other controls are sized. For example, suppose you want to size controls named CommandButton1 and CommandButton2, and that they have widths of 100 and 50 pixels, respectively. If CommandButton1 is the base, the Make Same Size command will adjust the width of CommandButton2 to 100 pixels.

Therefore, before running this command, you must decide which of the controls has the width or height that you want to use as the base. Then, when you're selecting the controls, make sure the base control is the one you select *last.* (Note that the base control is the one with white selection handles. The other controls in the selection will have black handles.)

When that's done, select Format | Make Same Size. (Or you can right-click one of the controls and select Make Same Size from the shortcut menu.) In the cascade menu that appears, choose one of the following commands:

Width: Adjusts the horizontal dimensions of all the selected controls so that they have the same width as the base control.

Height: Adjusts the vertical dimensions of all the selected controls so that they have the same height as the base control.

Both: Adjusts both the horizontal and vertical dimensions of all the selected controls so that they have the same width and height as the base control.

Note, too, that the UserForm toolbar also has a Make Same Size drop-down button from which you can select these commands, as shown in Figure 11.3.

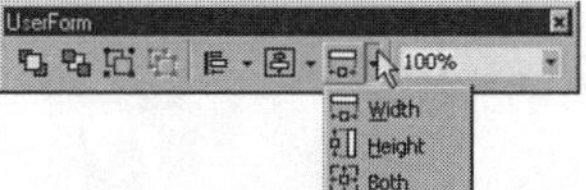

FIGURE 11.3.
The Make Same Size drop-down button.

> **NOTE: THE USERFORM TOOLBAR**
>
> The UserForm toolbar contains many useful one-click shortcuts for working with forms. To display this toolbar, either select View | Toolbars | UserForm or right-click the Standard toolbar and select UserForm from the shortcut menu.

Moving Controls

You can move any control to a different part of the form by following these steps:

1. Select the control you want to move.
2. Position the mouse pointer inside the control. (You can also position the pointer over the control's frame, although you need to make sure the pointer isn't over a selection handle. In this case, the pointer changes to a four-headed arrow.)
3. Drag the control to the position you want. As you drag the object, a dashed outline shows you the new position.
4. Release the mouse button. The VBE redraws the control in the new position.

As with sizing, the VBE also boasts quite a collection of commands that can adjust the position of one or more controls automatically. The next few sections give you the rundown.

Aligning to the Grid

If you've turned off the option that causes the VBE to align moved controls to the grid marks, you can still align to the grid by hand. Select the control and then select Format | Align | to Grid. The VBE will move the control to the nearest grid marks.

Aligning Control Edges

Forms look best when the controls are aligned in apple-pie order. The simplest way to do this is to use the Align command. This command is similar to Make Same Size in that it operates on multiple controls and lets you align, say, their left edges. Again, you must decide which of the controls to use as the alignment base and then select this control last.

When you're ready, select Format | Align (or right-click one of the controls and select Align from the shortcut menu). In the cascade menu that appears, choose one of the following commands:

Lefts: Adjusts the horizontal position of all the selected controls so that they line up on the left edge of the base control.

Centers: Adjusts the horizontal position of all the selected controls so that the center of each control lines up with the center of the base control.

Rights: Adjusts the horizontal position of all the selected controls so that they line up on the right edge of the base control.

Tops: Adjusts the vertical position of all the selected controls so that they line up on the top edge of the base control.

Middles: Adjusts the vertical position of all the selected controls so that the middle of each control lines up with the middle of the base control.

Bottoms: Adjusts the vertical position of all the selected controls so that they line up on the bottom edge of the base control.

The UserForm toolbar also has an Align drop-down button from which you can select these commands, as shown in Figure 11.4.

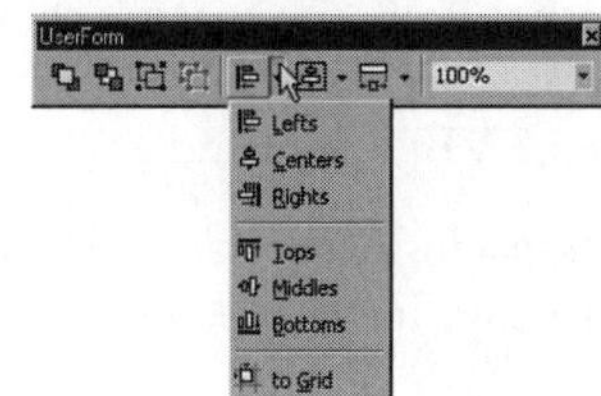

FIGURE 11.4.
The Align drop-down button.

Centering Controls

If you want one or more controls to appear in the center of the form, don't bother adjusting the control positions by hand. Instead, just select the control or controls you want to center, select Format | Center in Form, and select one of the following commands from the cascade menu:

Horizontally: Adjusts the controls left or right so that they appear in the horizontal center of the form.

Vertically: Adjusts the controls up or down so that they appear in the vertical center of the form.

Again, you can also take advantage of the UserForm toolbar. In this case, drop down the Center button, as shown in Figure 11.5.

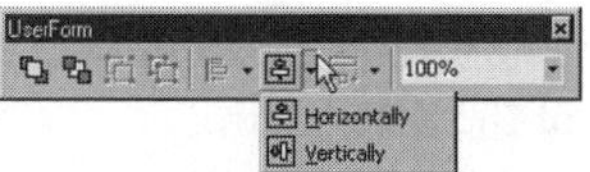

FIGURE 11.5.
The Center drop-down button.

Arranging Command Buttons

Command buttons traditionally are placed either along the bottom of a form or along the right side of the form. If you have multiple command buttons, the VBE will be only too happy to align these controls for you automatically. To try this, select the command buttons you want to move, select Format | Arrange Buttons, and choose one of these cascade menu commands:

Bottom: Moves the controls to the bottom of the form and aligns the bottom edges of each button.

Right: Moves the controls to the right side of the form and aligns the right edges of each button.

Adjusting the Spacing Between Controls

To make your forms easy to read, the controls shouldn't be crammed together edge-to-edge, nor should they be too far apart. Again, you can avoid making subtle spacing adjustments by hand thanks to a few more VBE commands.

To adjust the horizontal spacing between multiple controls, select the controls and then select Format | Horizontal Spacing. In the cascade menu that appears, select one of the following commands:

Make Equal: If you have three or more controls selected, use this command to adjust the horizontal spacing so that it's the same between each control.

Increase: This command increases the horizontal spacing between each control by one grid mark, relative to the base control.

Decrease: This command decreases the horizontal spacing between each control by one grid mark, relative to the base control.

Remove: This command removes the horizontal spacing between each control. The base control remains in place and the other controls are aligned relative to this control.

Adjusting the vertical spacing between multiple controls is similar. Select the controls, select Format | Vertical Spacing, and choose one of these commands from the cascade menu:

Make Equal: If you have three or more controls selected, use this command to adjust the vertical spacing so that it's the same between each control.

Increase: This command increases the vertical spacing between each control by one grid mark, relative to the base control.

Decrease: This command decreases the vertical spacing between each control by one grid mark, relative to the base control.

Remove: This command removes the vertical spacing between each control. The base control remains in place and the other controls are aligned relative to this control.

Copying Controls

If you've formatted a control and then decide that you need a similar control, don't bother building the new control from scratch. Instead, follow the steps outlined next to make as many copies of the existing control as you need:

1. Select the control you want to copy.
2. Hold down the Ctrl key, position the mouse pointer inside the control, and press the left mouse button. The pointer changes to an arrow with a plus sign.
3. Drag the pointer to the position you want. As you drag the mouse, a dashed outline shows you the position of the copied control.
4. Release the mouse button. The VBE copies the control to the new position.

You also can use the Clipboard to copy controls. In this case, you click the control, select Edit | Copy, and select Edit | Paste. The VBE will add a copy of the control to the form that you can then move to the appropriate position.

TIP: FASTER COPYING

You also can right-click the control and select Copy from the control's shortcut menu. To paste the control, right-click an empty part of the form, and then click Paste. Alternatively, use Ctrl-C to copy a selected control and Ctrl-V to paste it.

Deleting Controls

To delete a control, select it and then select Edit | Delete. The VBE deletes the control.

> **TIP: FASTER DELETING**
>
> To delete a control quickly, select it and press the Delete key. Alternatively, you can right-click the control and select Delete from the shortcut menu.

Grouping Controls

The VBE lets you create control *groups.* A group is a collection of controls you can format, size, and move—similar to the way you format, size, and move a single control. To group two or more controls, select them and then use any of the following techniques:

- Select the Format Group command.
- Right-click inside any one of the selected controls and select Group from the shortcut menu.

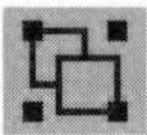

- Click the UserForm toolbar's Group button.

The VBE treats a group as a single control with its own frame. To select an entire group, you just need to select one control from the group.

To ungroup controls, select the group and use one of these methods:

- Select Format | Ungroup.
- Right-click inside any one of the selected controls and select Ungroup from the shortcut menu.

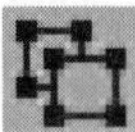

- Click the UserForm toolbar's Ungroup button.

Ordering Overlapped Controls

When you're inserting controls, you'll usually want to avoid overlapping the controls so that the user won't be confused and so the captions won't get mixed together. However, there might be times when you do want controls to overlap. For example, if you've added two or more picture controls, you might be able to produce interesting effects by superimposing one picture on another.

When you have two controls that overlap, the most recently created control covers part of the other control. The newer control is "in front" of the older one. The overlap order of these controls is called the Z-order. (Think of the Z-axis in a graph.) To change the Z-order, select one of the overlapping controls, select Format | Order, and choose one of the following cascade menu commands:

Bring to Front: Moves the control to the top of the Z-order, which places it in front of every other control. You can also run this command by pressing Ctrl-J, right-clicking the control and selecting Bring to Front, or by clicking the Bring to Front button on the UserForm toolbar.

Send to Back: Moves the control to the bottom of the Z-order, which places it behind every other control. You can also run this command by pressing Ctrl-K, right-clicking the control and selecting Send to Back, or by clicking the Send to Back button on the UserForm toolbar.

Bring Forward: Moves the control one position toward the front of the Z-order.

Send Backward: Moves the control one position toward the back of the Z-order.

Setting Control Properties

Form controls are objects with their own set of properties. A check box, for example, is a CheckBox object, and it has properties that control the name of the check box, whether it is initially checked, what its accelerator key is, and more.

You can manipulate control properties during program execution (in other words, at runtime) either before you display the form or while the form is displayed. (For example, you might want to disable a control in response to a user's action.) However, you can also set some control properties in the Visual Basic Editor (in other words, at design time) by using the Properties window. To display a particular control's properties in the Properties window, you have two choices:

- Click the control in the form.
- Select the control from the drop-down list in the Properties window.

Common Control Properties

Later in this chapter I'll run through each of the default controls and explain their unique features. However, a few properties are common to many of the controls. Many of these properties perform the same function as those I outlined for a form earlier in this chapter. These properties include the following: `BackColor`, `ForeColor`, `SpecialEffect`, `Enabled`, `Font`, `HelpContextID`, `MouseIcon`, `MousePointer`, `Tag`, `Picture`, `PicturePosition`, `Height`, `Width`, `Left`, and `Top`. (Note that the latter two are relative to the left and top edges of the form.)

Here's a list of a few other properties that are common to some or all of the default controls:

`Accelerator`: Determines the control's accelerator key. (In other words, the user will be able to select this control by holding down Alt and pressing the specified key.) The letter you enter into this property will appear underlined in the control's caption.

TIP: ACCELERATORS FOR CONTROLS WITHOUT CAPTIONS

Some controls (such as list boxes and text boxes) don't have a `Caption` property. However, you can still assign an accelerator key to these controls by using a Label control. I'll show you how this is done when I discuss labels in the section "Types of Form Controls."

`AutoSize`: If this property is set to `True`, the control resizes automatically to fit its text (as given by the `Caption` property).

`BackStyle`: Determines whether the control's background is opaque (use `fmBackStyleOpaque`) or transparent (use `fmBackStyleTransparent`).

`Control Source`: In the VBE, this property specifies which cell will be used to hold the control's data. You can enter either a cell reference or a range name.

CAUTION: AVOID CONTROL SOURCE FOR SAFER CODE

The value of a cell linked to a control changes whenever the value of the control changes, even when the user clicks Cancel to exit the form. It's usually better (and safer) to assign the value of a control to a variable and then, if appropriate, place the value in the cell under program control.

`Caption`: Sets the control's text.

`ControlTipText`: Sets the "control tip" that pops up when the user lets the mouse pointer linger over the control for a second or two.

`Locked`: Set this property to `True` to prevent the user from editing the current value of the control.

`TabIndex`: Determines where the control appears in the tab order (in other words, the order in which VBA navigates through the controls when the user presses the Tab key). See the next section.

`TabStop`: Determines whether the user can navigate to the control by pressing Tab. If this property is set to `False`, the user won't be able to select the control using the Tab key.

`Visible`: Determines whether the user can see the control (`True`) or not (`False`).

Setting the Tab Order

As you know, you can navigate a form by pressing the Tab key. The order in which the controls are selected is called the *tab order*. VBA sets the tab order according to the order you create the controls on the form. You'll often find that this order isn't what you want to end up with, so the VBE lets you control the tab order yourself. The following procedure shows you how it's done:

1. Select View | Tab Order. (You can also right-click an empty part of the form and select Tab Order from the shortcut menu.) The VBE displays the Tab Order dialog box, shown in Figure 11.6.

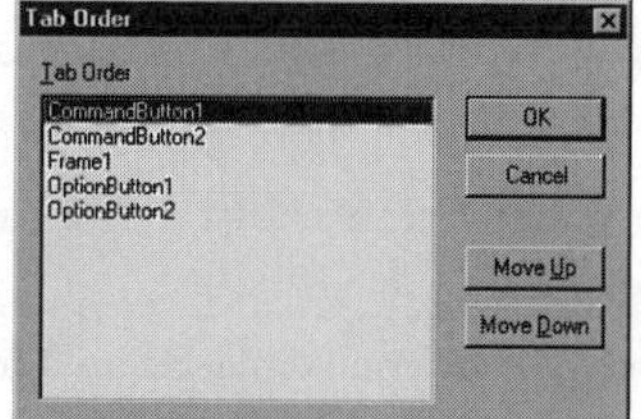

FIGURE 11.6.
Use the Tab Order dialog box to set the order in which the user navigates the form when pressing the Tab key.

2. In the Tab Order list, highlight the control you want to work with.
3. Click Move Up to move the item up in the tab order, or click Move Down to move the control down.
4. Repeat steps 2 and 3 for other controls you want to move.
5. Click OK.

Adding Controls to the Toolbox

At first, the Toolbox just displays the default set of controls. However, Office 97 ships with a number of extra controls—including a collection of ActiveX controls—that you can add to the Toolbox. Also, any other controls installed on your system (such as those installed with Visual Basic, for example) can also be used in your Toolbox.

To add another control to the Toolbox, click the toolbox to activate it, and select Tools | Additional Controls. In the Additional Controls dialog box, shown in Figure 11.7, use the Available Controls list to activate the check boxes beside each control you want to add, and then click OK. The controls will now appear as icons in the Toolbox, and you can use them exactly as you would the default controls.

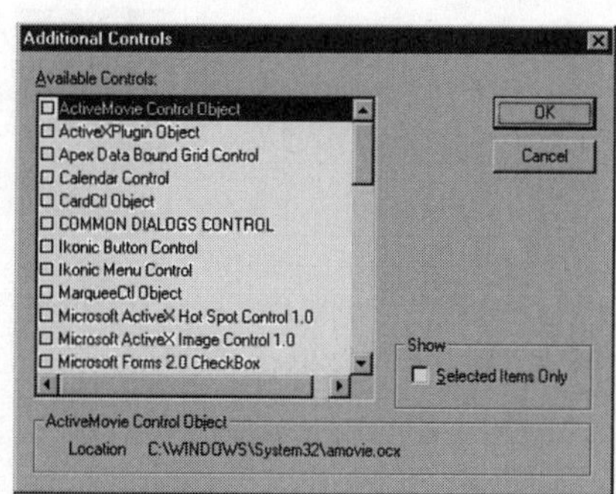

FIGURE 11.7.
The Additional Controls dialog box displays a complete list of the available controls on your system.

Creating User-Defined Controls

One of the secrets of programming productivity is the maxim "Don't reinvent the wheel." You've already seen a few techniques that let you avoid starting certain operations from scratch: the modular programming concept of dividing code into separate, reusable procedures and functions; using loops to repeat chunks of code; and sharing user forms among projects.

This section looks at yet another "wheel reinvention avoidance" technique: creating user-defined controls that you can reuse in other forms or even in other projects. In this case, a "user-defined" control is either of the following:

- A regular control that you've set up with a particular collection of properties (caption, colors, size, and so on).
- A group of controls that you've placed on a form. In this case, the user-defined control includes not only the defined properties of each control, but also the relative position of the controls within the form.

Adding a Page to the Toolbox

Your first task should be to create a new page in the Toolbox. (This is optional because you can add user-defined controls to the main Toolbox page. However, adding these controls to a separate page will avoid confusion down the road.) Here are the steps to follow:

1. Right-click the title (Controls) of the toolbox tab and select New Page from the shortcut menu. VBA adds a new page to the Toolbox, as shown in Figure 11.8.

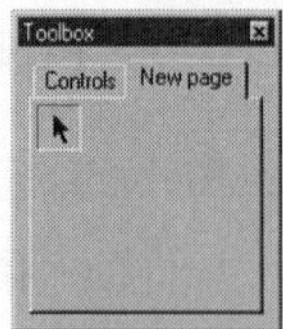

FIGURE 11.8.
The Toolbox with a new page added.

2. Right-click the title (New Page) of the new Toolbox tab, and then click Rename. VBA displays the Rename dialog box, shown in Figure 11.9.

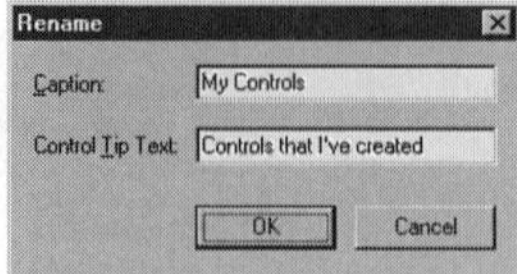

FIGURE 11.9.
Use the Rename dialog box to edit the name of the new Toolbox tab.

3. Edit the Caption and Control Tip Text (this will be the message that appears when you hover the mouse pointer over the tab).

4. Click OK. VBA updates the tab name, as shown in Figure 11.10.

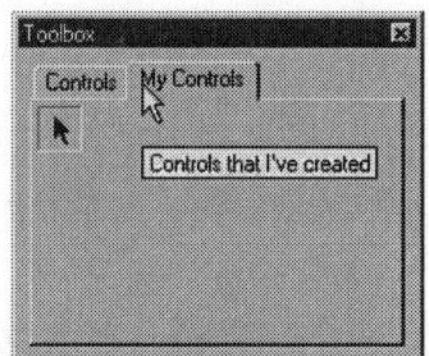

FIGURE 11.10.
The new Toolbox page is now ready for action.

Adding User-Defined Controls to the New Page

Once your new Toolbox page is established, populating it with user-defined controls is easy. First, add a regular control to any form and then format the control's design-time properties to your liking. Now simply drag the control from the form and drop it on your new Toolbox page. The VBE adds an icon for the control. From here, you can reuse the control on the same form or another form by clicking it and then drawing the control in the form. The VBE will add the form and include all of the design-time properties that you defined for the original control.

Creating a user-defined control group is similar. Again, you add the controls to any form and set up their design-time properties. Then select all the controls, drag the selection from the form, and drop it on the new Toolbox page. Once again, the VBE adds a new icon to the Toolbox. You can re-create the entire group by clicking this icon and drawing the control in any form.

Customizing User-Defined Controls

The VBE just uses default icons and a default tooltip for each user-defined control added to the toolbox. This can get confusing once you've added several user-defined controls, so the VBE lets you customize both the icon and the tooltip. Here are the steps to follow:

1. Right-click the user-defined control and select Customize New *Control*, where *Control* is the type of user-defined control you're working with (for example, CheckBox). You'll see a Customize Control dialog box similar to the one shown in Figure 11.11.

FIGURE 11.11.
Use this dialog box to customize the tooltip and icon image for a user-defined control.

2. Use the Tool Tip Text box to define a new tooltip for the control.

3. To change the icon, you have two options:

   Edit Picture: Click this button to display the Edit Image dialog box, shown in Figure 11.12. The basic idea here is that you click a color and then click inside the Picture box to "draw" the image. When you're done, click OK to exit.

   Load Picture: Click this button to display the Load Picture dialog box, from which you can select an existing picture file (such as a .BMP or .ICO bitmap). Highlight the file and then click Open.

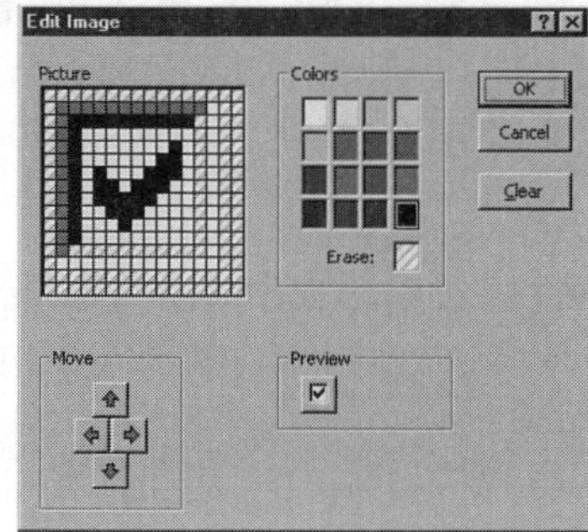

FIGURE 11.12.
Use the Edit Image dialog box to create a custom image for the icon.

4. Click OK to return to the Toolbox.

> **TIP: SHARE USER-DEFINED CONTROLS BETWEEN APPLICATIONS**
>
> Earlier in this chapter, I showed you how to share a form object between applications. You can do the same thing with user-defined controls; there are two methods you can use:
>
> - In the other application, open the VBE, display the Toolbox, and create a new page. Return to the original application, drag the user-defined control, and drop it on the new page in the other Toolbox. (If you can't see the other Toolbox, drag the control to the other application's VBE taskbar button and wait for the VBE window to come to the front.)
> - You can share an entire page of controls. First, right-click the tab of the page you want to share and select Export Page. In the Export Page dialog box, select a location, enter a primary name for the page file (they use the .PAG extension), and click Save. In the other application, right-click any page tab, select Import Page, and open the .PAG file in the Import Page dialog box that appears.

Handling Form Events

VBA 5.0

An *event-driven* language is one in which code can respond to specific events, such as a user's clicking a command button or selecting an item from a list. The procedure can then take appropriate action, whether it's validating the user's input or asking for confirmation of the requested action. Previous versions of VBA had only rudimentary event handlers, and therefore could hardly be described as event-driven. VBA 5.0, however, is fully event-driven thanks to its support of many different kinds of events. For example, a form responds to more than 20 separate events, including activating and deactivating the form, displaying the form, clicking the form, and resizing the form.

For each event associated with an object, VBA has set up stub procedures called *event handlers*. These procedures are really just `Sub` and `End Sub` statements. You process the event by filling in your own VBA code between these statements. Here are the steps to follow:

1. Click the object for which you want to define an event handler.
2. Either select View | Edit Code or double-click the object. (You can also right-click the object and select Edit Code from the shortcut menu.) VBA displays the code module for the object, as shown in Figure 11.13.

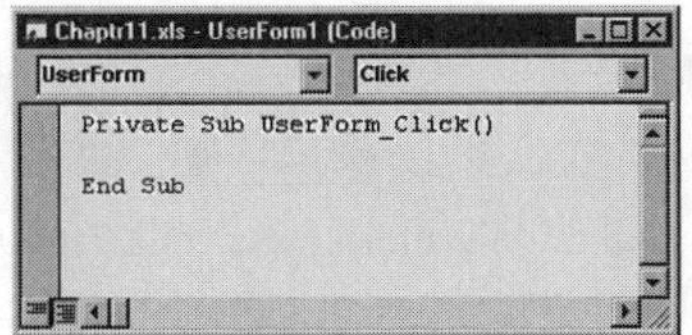

FIGURE 11.13.
For each event, VBA defines a stub procedure. You define the procedure by entering code into this stub.

3. Use the procedure drop-down list (the one on the right) to select the event you want to work with.
4. Enter the rest of the procedure code between the `Sub` and `End Sub` statements.

Types of Form Controls

The default Toolbox offers 14 different controls for your custom forms. The next few sections introduce you to each type of control and show you the various options and properties associated with each object.

Command Buttons

Most forms include command buttons to let the user accept the form data (an OK button), cancel the form (a Cancel button), or carry out some other command at a click of the mouse.

To create a command button, use the CommandButton tool in the Toolbox. A command button is a CommandButton object that includes many of the common control properties mentioned earlier as well as the following design-time properties (among others):

`Cancel`: If this property is set to `True`, the button is selected when the user presses Esc.

`Caption`: Returns or sets the text that appears on the button face.

`Default`: If this property is set to `True`, the button is selected when the user presses Enter. Also, the button is displayed with a thin black border.

Labels

You use labels to add text to the form. To create labels, use the Label button in the Toolbox to draw the label object, and then edit the `Caption` property. Although labels are mostly used to display text, you can also use them to name controls that don't have their own captions—such as text boxes, list boxes, scroll bars, and spinners.

It's even possible to define an accelerator key for the label and have that key select another control. For example, suppose you want to use a label to describe a text box, but you also want to define an accelerator key that the user can press to select the text box. The trick is that you must first create a label and set its `Accelerator` property. You then create the text box immediately after. Since the text box follows the label in the tab order, the label's accelerator key will select the text box.

TIP: ACCELERATORS FOR EXISTING CONTROLS

To assign a label and accelerator key to an existing control, add the label and then adjust the Tab order so that the label comes immediately before the control in the tab order.

Text Boxes

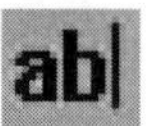

Text boxes are versatile controls that let the user enter text, numbers, cell references, and formulas. To create a text box, use the TextBox button in the Toolbox. Here are a few useful properties of the TextBox object:

`EnterFieldBehavior`: Determines what happens when the user tabs into the text box. If you select 0 (`fmEnterFieldBehaviorSelectAll`), the text within the field is selected. If you select 1 (`fmEnterFieldBehaviorRecallSelect`), only the text that the user selected the last time he was in the field will be selected.

TIP: ENTERING THE TEXT BOX WITHOUT SELECTING

If you want to make sure that the text inside a text box isn't selected when the user tabs into the control, set the `EnterFieldBehavior` property to `fmEnterFieldBehaviorRecallSelect` and then enter the following two lines in the control's `Enter` event (assuming the control is named `TextBox1`):

```
TextBox1.SelStart = 0
TextBox1.SelLength = 0
```

`SelStart` and `SelLength` are runtime properties that determine, respectively, the start and length of the selection. If you would prefer to place the cursor at the end of the text, replace the preceding `SelStart` statement with the following:

```
TextBox1.SelStart = Len(TextBox1.Text)
```

`EnterKeyBehavior`: When set to `True`, this property lets the user start a new line within the text box by pressing Enter. (Note that this is applicable only if you set `MultiLine` to `True`, as described in a moment.) When this property is `False`, pressing Enter moves the user to the next field.

`MaxLength`: This property determines the maximum number of characters that the user can enter.

`MultiLine`: Set this property to `True` to let the user enter multiple lines of text.

`PasswordChar`: If this property is set to `True`, the text box displays the user's entry as asterisks.

`Text`: Returns or sets the text inside the text box.

`WordWrap`: When this property is `True`, the text box wraps to a new line when the user's typing reaches the right edge of the text box.

Frames

You use frames to create groups of two or more controls. There are three situations in which frames come in handy:

To organize a set of controls into a logical grouping: Let's say your form contains controls for setting program options and obtaining user information. You could help the user make sense of the form by creating two frames: one to hold all the controls for the program options, and one to hold the controls for the user information.

To move a set of controls as a unit: When you draw controls inside a frame, these controls are considered to be part of the frame object. Therefore, when you move the frame, the controls move right along with it. This can make it easier to rearrange multiple controls on a form.

To organize option buttons: If you enter multiple option buttons inside a frame (see the next section), VBA treats them as a group and therefore allows the user to activate only one of the options.

To create a frame, click the Frame button in the Toolbox and then drag a box inside the form. Note that you use the Frame object's `Caption` property to change the caption that appears at the top of the box.

Option Buttons

Option buttons are controls that usually appear in groups of two or more; the user can select only one of the options. To create an option button, use the OptionButton tool. You can determine whether an option button starts off activated or deactivated by setting the `Value` property: If it's `True`, the option is activated; if it's `False`, the option is deactivated.

In order for option buttons to work effectively, you need to group them so that the user can select only one of the options at a time. VBA gives you three ways to do this:

- Create a frame and then draw the option buttons inside the frame.
- Use the same `GroupName` property for the options you want to group.
- If you don't draw the option buttons inside a frame or use the `GroupName` property, VBA treats all the option buttons in a form as one group.

> **TIP: INSERTING UNFRAMED OPTION BUTTONS**
>
> If you already have one or more "unframed" option buttons on your form, you can still insert them into a frame. Just select the buttons, cut them to the Clipboard, select the frame, and paste. VBA will add the buttons to the frame.

Check Boxes

Check boxes let you include options that the user can toggle on or off. To create a check box, use the CheckBox button in the Toolbox.

As with option buttons, you can control whether a check box is initially activated (checked). Set its `Value` property to `True` to activate the check box, or to `False` to deactivate it.

Toggle Buttons

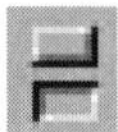

A toggle button is a cross between a check box and a command button: Click it once, and the button stays pressed; click it again, and the button returns to its normal state. You create toggle buttons by using the ToggleButton tool in the Toolbox.

You control whether a toggle button is initially activated (pressed) by setting its `Value` property to `True` to press the button or to `False` to "unpress" the button.

List Boxes

VBA offers two different list objects you can use to present the user with a list of choices: a ListBox and a ComboBox.

The ListBox Object

The ListBox object is a simple list of items from which the user selects an item or items. Use the ListBox button to create a list box. Here are some ListBox object properties to note:

`ColumnCount`: The number of columns in the list box.

`ColumnHeads`: If this property is `True`, the list columns are displayed with headings.

`MultiSelect`: If this property is `True`, the user may select multiple items in the list.

`RowSource`: Determines the items that appear in the list. In Excel, enter a range or a range name.

`Text`: Sets or returns the selected item.

The ComboBox Object

The ComboBox object is a control that combines a text box with a list box. The user clicks the drop-down arrow to display the list box and then selects an item from the list or enters an item in the text box. Use the ComboBox button to create this control.

Because the ComboBox is actually two separate controls, the available properties are an amalgam of those discussed earlier for a text box and a list box. You can also work with the following properties that are unique to a ComboBox object:

`ListRows`: Determines the number of items that appear when the user drops the list down.

`MatchRequired`: If this property is `True`, the user can only enter values from the list. If it's `False`, the user can enter new values.

`Style`: Determines the type of ComboBox. Use 0 (`fmStyleDropDownCombo`) for list that includes a text box; use 2 (`fmStyleDropDownList`) for a list only.

List Box Techniques

How do you specify the contents of a list if the `RowSource` property isn't applicable (that is, if you're not working in Excel or if the data you want in the list isn't part of an Excel range)? In this case, you must build the list at runtime. You can use the `AddItem` method, described later in this section, or you can set the List property. For the latter, you must specify an array of values. For example, the following statements use a form's `Initialize` event to populate a list box with the days of the week:

```
Private Sub UserForm_Initialize()
    ListBox1.List() = Array("Monday", "Tuesday", "Wednesday", "Thursday", "Friday",
    ➥"Saturday", "Sunday")
End Sub
```

List boxes also have a few useful methods for controlling from your VBA code the items that appear in a list box:

`AddItem`: Adds an item to the specified list box. Here's the syntax:

```
object.AddItem(text,index)
```

object	The name of the ListBox object to which you want to add the item.
text	The item's text.
index	The new item's position in the list. If you omit this argument, VBA adds the item to the end of the list.

`Clear`: Removes all the items from the specified list box.

`RemoveItem`: Removes an item from the specified list box using the following syntax:

```
object.RemoveItem(index)
```

object	The ListBox object from which you want to remove the item.
index	The index number of the item you want to remove.

Scroll Bars

Scroll bars are normally used to navigate windows, but by themselves you can use them to enter values between a predefined maximum and minimum. Use the ScrollBar button to create either a vertical or horizontal scroll bar. Here's a rundown of the ScrollBar object properties you'll use most often in your VBA code:

`LargeChange`: Returns or sets the amount that the scroll bar value changes when the user clicks between the scroll box and one of the scroll arrows.

`Max`: Returns or sets the maximum value of the scroll bar.

`Min`: Returns or sets the minimum value of the scroll bar.

`SmallChange`: Returns or sets the amount that the scroll bar value changes when the user clicks one of the scroll arrows.

`Value`: Returns or sets the current value of the scroll bar.

Spin Buttons

A spin button is similar to a scroll bar in that the user can click the button's arrows to increment or decrement a value. To create a spin button, use the SpinButton tool in the Toolbox. The properties for a SpinButton object are the same as those for a ScrollBar (except that there is no `LargeChange` property).

Most spin buttons have a text box control beside them to give the user the choice of entering the number directly or selecting the number by using the spin button arrows. You have to use VBA code to make sure that the values in the text box and the spinner stay in sync. (In other words, if you increment the spinner, the value shown in the text box increments as well, and vice versa.)

To do this, you have to add event handler code for both controls. For example, suppose you have a text box named TextBox1 and a spin button named SpinButton1. Listing 11.1 shows the basic event handler code that will keep the values of these two controls synchronized.

Listing 11.1. Event handler code that keeps a text box and a spin button in synch.

```
Private Sub TextBox1_Change()
    SpinButton1.Value = TextBox1.Value
End Sub

Private Sub SpinButton1_Change()
    TextBox1.Value = SpinButton1.Value
End Sub
```

Tab Strips and MultiPage Controls

I mentioned earlier that you can use frames to group related controls visually and help the user make sense of the form. However, there are two situations in which a frame falls down on the job.

The first situation is when you need the form to show multiple sets of the same (or similar) data. For example, suppose you have a form that shows values for sales and expense categories. You might want the form to be capable of showing separate data for various company divisions. One solution would be to create separate frames for each division and populate each frame with the same controls, but this is clearly inefficient. A second solution would be to use a list or a set of option buttons. This will work, but it might not be obvious to the user how he is supposed to display different sets of data, and these extra controls just serve to clutter the frame. A better solution is to create a tabbed form where each tab represents a different set of data.

The second situation is when you have a lot of controls. In this case, even the judicious use of frames won't be enough to keep your form from becoming difficult to navigate and understand. In situations where you have a large number of controls, you're better off creating a tabbed form that spreads the controls over several tabs.

In both of these situations, the tabbed form solution acts much like the tabbed dialog boxes you work with in Windows, Office, and other modern programs. To create tabs in your forms, VBA offers two controls: TabStrip and MultiPage.

The TabStrip Control

The TabStrip is an ideal way to give the user an intuitive method of displaying multiple sets of data. The basic idea behind the TabStrip control is that as the user navigates from tab to tab, the visible controls remain the same, and only the data displayed inside each control changes. The advantage here is that you need to create only a single set of controls on the form, and you use code to adjust the contents of these controls.

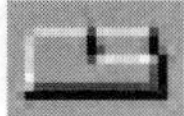

You create a TabStrip by clicking the TabStrip button in the Toolbox and then dragging the mouse until the strip is the size and shape you want. Here are a few points to keep in mind:

- The best way to set up a TabStrip is to add it as the first control on the form and then add the other controls inside the TabStrip.
- If you already have controls defined on the form, draw the TabStrip over the controls and then use the Send to Back command (described earlier) to send the TabStrip to the bottom of the Z-order.
- You can also display a series of buttons instead of tabs. To use this format, select the TabStrip and change the `Style` property to `fmTabStyleButtons` (or 1).

Figure 11.14 shows a form that contains a TabStrip control and an Excel worksheet that shows budget data for three different divisions. The goal here is to use the TabStrip to display budget data for each division as the user selects the tabs.

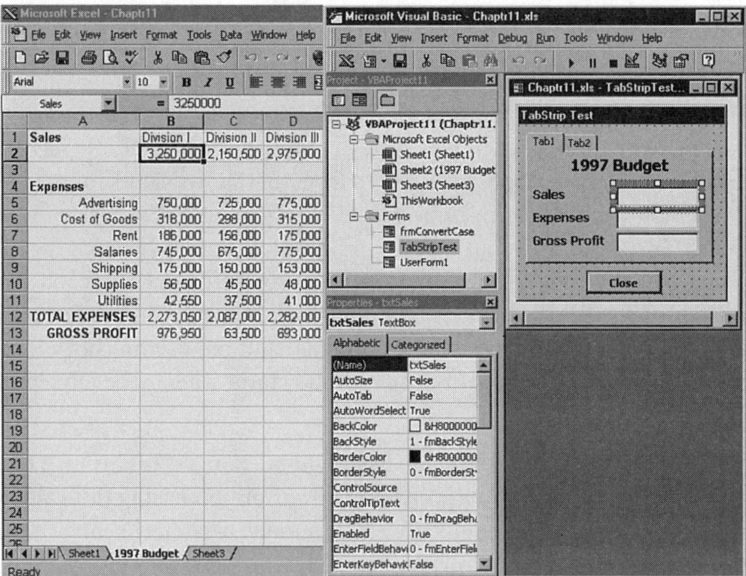

FIGURE 11.14.
Using the form's TabStrip to display budget data from the three divisions in the Excel worksheet.

The first order of business is to use code to change the tab captions, add a third tab, and enter the initial data. Listing 11.2 shows an `Initialize` event procedure that does just that.

Listing 11.2. An `Initialize` event procedure that sets up a TabStrip.

```
Private Sub UserForm_Initialize()
    '
    ' Rename the existing tabs
    '
    With TabStrip1
        .Tabs(0).Caption = "Division I"
```

```
        .Tabs(1).Caption = "Division II"
        '
        ' Add a new tab
        '
        .Tabs.Add "Division III"
    End With
    '
    ' Enter the intial data for Division I
    '
    With Worksheets("1997 Budget")
        txtSales = .[B2]
        txtExpenses = .[B12]
        txtGrossProfit = .[B13]
    End With
End Sub
```

The code first uses the `Tabs` collection to change the captions of the two existing tabs. The `Tabs` collection represents all the tabs in a TabStrip, and you refer to individual tabs using an index number (where the first tab is 0, the second is 1, and so on). Then the `Tabs` collection's `Add` method is used to add a third tab titled Division III to the TabStrip. Finally, the three text boxes within the TabStrip (named `txtSales`, `txtExpenses`, and `txtGrossProfit`) are set to their respective values for Division I in the 1997 Budget worksheet.

Now you must set up a handler for when the user clicks a tab. This fires a `Change` event for the TabStrip, so you use this event handler to adjust the values of the text boxes, as shown in Listing 11.3.

Listing 11.3. A Change event procedure that modifies the controls within a tab strip whenever the user selects a different tab.

```
Private Sub TabStrip1_Change()
        With Worksheets("1997 Budget")
            Select Case TabStrip1.Value
                Case 0
                '
                ' Enter the data for Division I
                '
                txtSales = .[B2]
                txtExpenses = .[B12]
                txtGrossProfit = .[B13]
                Case 1
                '
                ' Enter the data for Division II
                '
                txtSales = .[C2]
                txtExpenses = .[C12]
                txtGrossProfit = .[C13]
                Case 2
                '
                ' Enter the data for Division III
                '
```

continues

Listing 11.3. continued

```
                txtSales = .[D2]
                txtExpenses = .[D12]
                txtGrossProfit = .[D13]
            End Select
        End With
End Sub
```

Here, a `Select Case` checks the `Value` property of the TabStrip (where the first tab has the value 0, the second tab has the value 1, and so on). Figure 11.15 shows the form in action. (See "Displaying the Form" later in this chapter to learn how to run a form.)

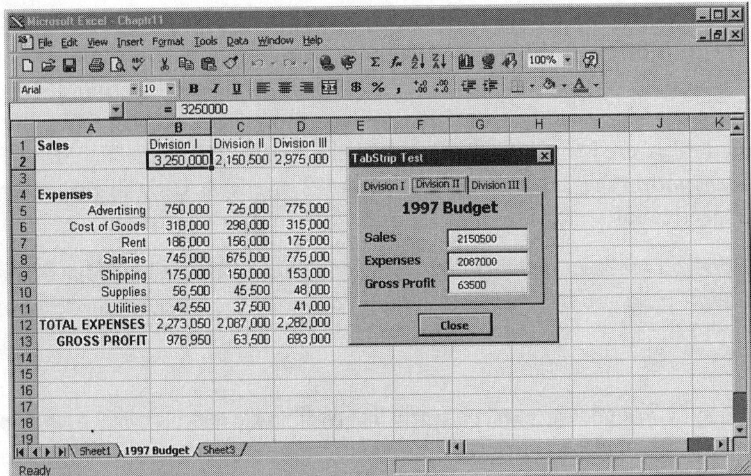

FIGURE 11.15.
Clicking each tab displays the data for the appropriate division.

The MultiPage Control

The MultiPage control is similar to a TabStrip in that it displays a series of tabs along the top of the form. The major difference, however, is that each tab represents a separate form (called a *page*). Therefore, you use a MultiPage control whenever you want to display a different set of controls each time the user clicks a tab.

You add a MultiPage control to your form by clicking the MultiPage button in the Toolbox and then dragging the mouse until the control is the size and shape you want.

It's important to remember that each page in the control is a separate object (a Page object). So each time you select a page, the values that appear in the Properties window apply only to the selected page. For example, the `Caption` property determines the text that appears in the page's tab. Also, you set up a page by selecting it and then drawing controls inside the page. (If you have controls on the form already, you can put them inside a page by cutting them to the Clipboard, selecting the page, and pasting the controls.)

Working with a MultiPage control in code is very similar to working with a TabStrip:

- The `Pages` collection represents all the pages inside a MultiPage control. You refer to individual pages using their index number.
- Use the `Pages.Add` method to add more pages to the control.
- When the user selects a different tab, the MultiPage control's `Change` event fires.

Using a Form in a Procedure

After you've created your form, the next step is to incorporate your handiwork into some VBA code. This involves three separate techniques:

- Displaying the form
- Handling events while the form is displayed
- Processing the form results

Displaying the Form

Each UserForm object has a `Show` method that you use to display the form to the user. For example, to display a form named UserForm1, you would use the following statement:

```
UserForm1.Show
```

Alternatively, you might want to load the form into memory but keep it hidden from the user. For example, you might need to perform some behind-the-scenes manipulation of the form before showing it to the user. You can do this by executing the `Load` statement:

```
Load Form
```

`Form` The name of the form you want to load.

This statement brings the form object into memory and fires the form's Initialize event. From there, you can display the form to the user at any time by running the form's `Show` method, as just discussed.

TIP: DISPLAYING A FORM BY HAND

Before getting to the code stage, you might want to try out your form to make sure it looks okay. To do this, activate the form and then either select Tools | Run Sub/UserForm, press F5, or click the Run Sub/UserForm button on the toolbar.

Handling Events While the Form Is Displayed

Once the user has the form in front of him, your code should watch for and react to events. Although you'll rarely have to account for every possible event, there are a few common ones to keep an eye on.

For starters, here are a few form events that are often handy to trap:

`Click`: Fires when the user clicks an empty part of the form.

`DblClick`: Fires when the user double-clicks an empty part of the form.

`Initialize`: This event fires when the form loads (that is, after you run the `Show` method). Use this event to set up the controls' and the form's properties at runtime.

`KeyDown`: Fires when the user presses and holds down a key or key combination. The event handler is passed two values:

- A `KeyCode` variable that contains the ANSI code of the key (see Appendix C, "The Windows ANSI Character Set")
- A `Shift` variable that tells you which of the following keys was also pressed:

Key	`Shift` *Value*
Shift	`fmShiftMask` or 1
Ctrl	`fmCtrlMask` or 2
Alt	`fmAltMask` or 4)

To check for a combination, use the sum of the values. For example, use 3 to see if both Shift and Ctrl were pressed.

`KeyPress`: Fires when the user presses and releases a key. The event handler is passed a variable named `KeyANSI` that represents the ANSI value of the key that was pressed.

`KeyUp`: This event is similar to `KeyDown`, except that it fires when the user releases the key or key combination that he had previously held down.

`MouseDown`: Fires when the user presses and holds down a mouse button. The event handler is passed four variables:

- `Button` specifies the button that was pressed (`fmButtonLeft` or 1 for the left button, `fmButtonRight` or 2 for the right button, or `fmButtonMiddle` or 4 for the middle button).
- `Shift` specifies whether any combination of Shift, Ctrl, and Alt was also pressed (see the description of the `KeyDown` event).
- `X` specifies the horizontal position, in points, of the mouse pointer from the left edge of the form.
- `Y` specifies the vertical position, in points, of the mouse pointer from the top edge of the form.

`MouseMove`: Similar to `MouseDown`, except that it fires when the user moves the mouse pointer within the form window.

`MouseUp`: Similar to `MouseDown`, except that it fires when the user releases the mouse button.

`Resize`: Fires when the user resizes the form. You might want to use this event to adjust the relative sizes of your controls to account for the new form size.

Control objects support most of the events in this list for a form, and quite a few others. Here's a quick look at a few that you should find useful:

`AfterUpdate`: This event fires after the user has changed the control's data. Note, however, that this event occurs after the `BeforeUpdate` event and before the `Exit` event.

`BeforeUpdate`: Fires before the data in a control is updated with the user's changes. The event procedure passes a `Cancel` variable which, if you set it to `True`, will void the update and return the user to the control. This event is particularly useful if the control is bound to, say, a worksheet cell and you want to validate the entry before allowing changes to the cell.

`Change`: Fires when the `Value` property of a control changes. See Table 11.1 for a list of controls with the `Value` property.

`Enter`: Fires just before the control gets the focus.

`Exit`: Fires just before the control loses the focus. The event procedure passes a `Cancel` variable which, if you set it to `True`, will leave the focus on the control.

Unloading the Form

Once the user has filled out the form, you'll probably want her to click a command button to put whatever values she entered into effect. Alternatively, she could click some sort of Cancel button to dismiss the form without affecting anything.

However, just clicking a command button doesn't get rid of the form—even if you've set up a command button with the `Default` or `Cancel` property set to `True`. Instead, you have to add the following statement to the event handler for the command button:

```
Unload Me
```

The `Unload` command tells VBA to dismiss the form. Note that the `Me` keyword refers to the form in which the event handler resides. For example, the following event handler processes a click on a command button named `cmdCancel`:

```
Private Sub cmdCancel_Click()
    Dim result as Integer
    result = MsgBox("Are you sure you want to Cancel?", vbYesNo + vbQuestion)
    If result = vbYes Then Unload Me
End Sub
```

You should note, however, that simply unloading a form doesn't remove the form object from memory. To ensure proper cleanup (technically, to ensure that the form object class fires its internal `Terminate` event), `Set` the form object to `Nothing`. For example, the following two lines `Show` the `frmConvertCase` form and then `Set` it to `Nothing` to ensure termination:

```
frmConvertCase.Show
Set frmConvertCase = Nothing
```

Processing the Form Results

When the user clicks OK or Cancel (or any other control that includes the `Unload Me` statement in its `Click` event handler), you usually need to examine the form results and process them in some way.

Obviously, how you proceed depends on whether the user has clicked OK or Cancel, because this almost always determines whether the other form selections should be accepted or ignored.

- If OK is clicked, the `Click` event handler for that button can process the results. In other words, it can read the `Value` property for each control (for example, by storing them in variables for later use in the program or by entering the values into the VBE cells).
- If Cancel is clicked, the code can move on without processing the results. (As shown earlier, you can include code to ask the user if he's sure he wants to cancel.)

Table 11.1 lists all the controls that have a `Value` property and provides a description of what kind of data gets returned.

Table 11.1. `Value` properties for some form controls.

Object	*What It Returns*
CheckBox	`True` if the check box is activated; `False` if it's deactivated; `Null` otherwise.
ComboBox	The position of the selected item in the list (where 1 is the first item).
ListBox	The position of the selected item in the list (where 1 is the first item).
MultiPage	An integer that represents the active page (where 0 is the first page).
OptionButton	`True` if the option is activated; `False` if it's deactivated; `Null` otherwise.
ScrollBar	A number between the scroll bar's minimum and maximum values.
SpinButton	A number between the spinner's minimum and maximum values.
TabStrip	An integer that represents the active tab (where 0 is the first tab).
TextBox	The value entered in the box.
ToggleButton	`True` if the button is pressed; `False` otherwise.

For example, Figure 11.16 shows the Convert Case form created in the Visual Basic Editor. The idea behind this form is to convert the selected cells to proper case, uppercase, or lowercase, depending on the option chosen.

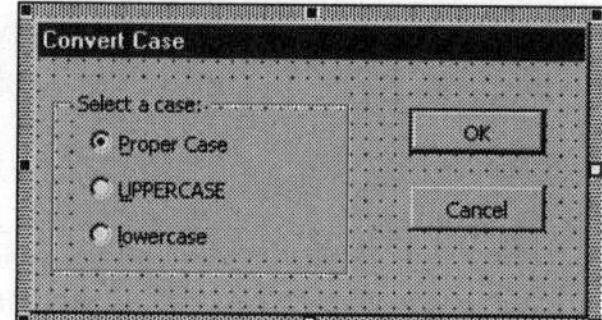

FIGURE 11.16.
A custom form that lets the user change the case of the selected worksheet cells.

To load this form, I created a macro named `ConvertCase` that contains the two statements shown earlier:

```
frmConvertCase.Show
Set frmConvertCase = Nothing
```

Here, `frmConvertCase` is the name of the form shown in Figure 11.16. The three option buttons are named `optProper`, `optUpper`, and `optLower`; the OK button is named `cmdOK`. Listing 11.4 shows the event handler that runs when the user clicks OK.

Listing 11.4. A procedure that processes the Convert Case custom form.

```
Private Sub cmdOK_Click()
    Dim c As Range
    For Each c In Selection
        If optProper.Value = True Then
            c.Value = StrConv(c, vbProperCase)
        ElseIf optUpper.Value = True Then
            c.Value = StrConv(c, vbUpperCase)
        ElseIf optLower.Value = True Then
            c.Value = StrConv(c, vbLowerCase)
        End If
    Next 'c
    Unload Me
End Sub
```

The procedure runs through the selected cells, checking to see which option button was chosen, and then converts the text by using VBA's `StrConv` function:

`StrConv(`***`String, Conversion`***`)`

`String`	The string you want to convert.
`Conversion`	A constant that specifies the case you want:

`Conversion`	*Resulting Case*
`vbProperCase`	Proper Case
`vbUpperCase`	UPPERCASE
`vbLowerCase`	lowercase

Summary

This chapter showed you how to work with VBA 5.0's new Microsoft Forms feature. After a brief introduction to user forms, I showed you how to add a form to your project, how to share forms between applications, and how to set a number of form design-time properties. From there we turned our attention to controls, and you learned numerous techniques for working with the various Toolbox objects, including inserting, selecting, sizing, moving, copying, and deleting controls. After a brief discussion of form event handlers, I took you on a tour of the various control types that are available in the Toolbox. You finished by learning how to handle forms inside your VBA procedures. Here are some places to go for related material:

- Handling form results often means using loops and control structures (such as `If...Then...Else` and `Select Case`). I explain these VBA statements in Chapter 5, "Controlling Your VBA Code."
- The `MsgBox` and `InputBox` functions provide simple form capabilities in a single statement. I show you how to use these functions in Chapter 10, "Interacting with the User." This chapter also shows you how to access the built-in dialog boxes available in VBA applications.
- We complete our look at VBA user-interface design in Chapter 12, "Creating Custom Menus and Toolbars."
- For a good example of how to create dynamic forms and process their results, see Chapter 17, "Using VBA to Work with Excel Lists."

CHAPTER 12

Creating Custom Menus and Toolbars

IN THIS CHAPTER

Make things as simple as possible, but no simpler.

—Albert Einstein

In Chapter 1, "Introducing VBA," I showed you a number of methods for running your VBA macros. However, all these methods assume that you know which task each macro performs. If you're constructing procedures for others to wield, they might not be so familiar with what each macro name represents. Not only that, but you might not want novice users scrolling through a long list of procedures in the Macro dialog box or, even worse, having to access the Visual Basic Editor.

To help you avoid these problems, this chapter presents some techniques for making your macros more accessible. To wit, I'll show you how to give your users the ability to use familiar tools—namely, menus and toolbars—to run your macros. You'll learn not only how to modify menus and toolbars by hand using the built-in application tools, but also how to build custom menus and toolbars using VBA code.

Assigning Macros to Menu Commands

The Windows environment offers the developer many advantages:

- The ability to open multiple windows
- The ability to multitask applications (such as a VBA application and the Visual Basic Editor)
- Graphical goodies such as color-coded syntax and mouse-based form tools
- The ever-useful drag-and-drop feature, which makes it a breeze to move things around and share data among applications

However, one of Windows' biggest advantages is something that developers don't often consider: the consistent user interface. For example, pull-down menus are now such a common feature of the PC landscape that we hardly notice them; we just assume that anybody with even a modicum of Windows experience knows how to work with them. That's a huge plus for your interface design chores, because it means you have a built-in mechanism for delivering access to your procedures—a mechanism, moreover, that requires no support or training on your part. In other words, you can add your macros as commands on the application's existing menu system, and therefore put your application within easy reach. You can even create your own menus so as not to clutter the application's built-in menus. This section shows you how to create custom menus and commands and associate macros with them.

NOTE: THE APPLICATIONS I'M DEALING WITH

The instructions in this section, as well as those in the next section on creating toolbars, apply to the Big Four Office applications: Word, Excel, PowerPoint, and Access.

First, a Game Plan

Before you dive into the menu customization techniques outlined in the next few sections, you need to take a step back and plan what you want to do. For starters, bear in mind that these techniques require access to the user's computer, so they apply only to the following situations:

- You're a corporate developer and your application is designed for a limited number of employees. (After all, you wouldn't want to tweak the menu systems of a thousand machines!)
- You're a consultant putting together a system for a client.
- You want easier access to the macros and procedures you've developed for your own use.

In each case, I'm assuming you can sit down in front of the computer, load the underlying application, and make the appropriate menu customizations.

On the other hand, there will be plenty of situations where you can't access the user's computer directly—for example, if you distribute your application electronically or via some other means where you have no direct contact with the user. Similarly, you might be building an application for use on hundreds or thousands of computers, and it's impractical to customize each system by hand. For these and similar cases, you need to use code to customize your menus. I'll tell you how to do this later in this chapter (see "Menus, Toolbars, and VBA 5.0").

The next thing you have to consider is the layout of your custom menus. You can use three levels of customization:

Menu commands: This level involves tacking a new command or two onto one or more of the application's built-in menus. Use this level when you have just a few procedures.

Cascade menus: This level involves adding one or more cascade menus to the application's built-in menu system. Use this level if you have several related procedures that you want to group together.

Menus: This level involves creating an entirely new menu that appears in the application's menu bar. Use this level when you have many different procedures and you don't want to cram them all into the application's built-in menus.

Creating a New Menu

If you'll be adding a lot of new commands to the application's menu system, you might not want to bog down the existing menus with too many items. To keep things clean, you can create a custom menu just for your procedures. Here are the steps to follow:

1. Either select Tools | Customize (in Access, select View | Toolbars | Customize) or right-click the menu bar and select Customize from the shortcut menu. The application displays the Customize dialog box.
2. Activate the Commands tab, shown in Figure 12.1.

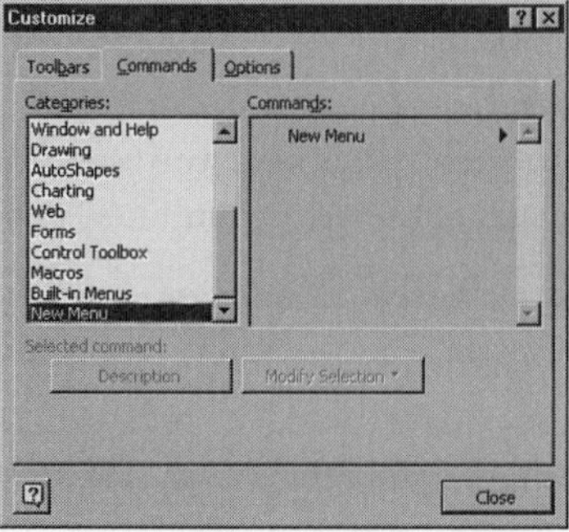

FIGURE 12.1.
Use the Commands tab in the Customize dialog box to create new menus in the application.

3. In the Categories list, highlight New Menu.
4. In the Commands list, drag the New Menu item up to the menu bar. You'll see a vertical bar that marks the spot where the new menu will appear. When the bar is positioned where you want your menu, drop the New Menu item.
5. Either click Modify Selection or right-click the new menu, and then use the Name box in the shortcut menu to name your new menu, as shown in Figure 12.2. Place an ampersand (&) before whichever letter you want to use as an accelerator key. (Make sure the key you choose doesn't conflict with an accelerator key used by any other menu.)

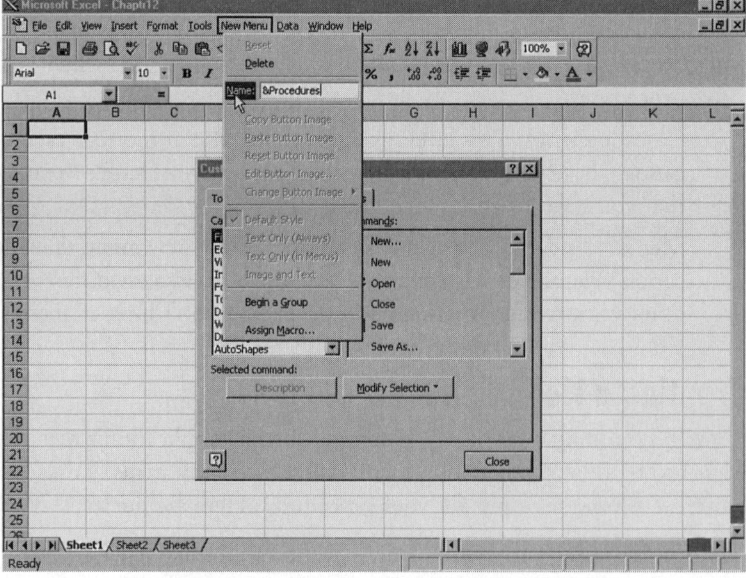

FIGURE 12.2.
Use this shortcut menu to rename the new menu bar item.

6. Press Enter.

Creating a New Cascade Menu

To work with cascade menus, you have two choices:

- Add the cascade menu to the new menu you created in the preceding section.
- Add the cascade menu to one of the application's built-in menus.

Either way, you follow the steps outlined in the preceding section. However, instead of dragging the New Menu item to the menu bar, drag it to an existing menu. When the menu pulls down, drag the mouse pointer down into the menu to the position where you want the cascade menu to appear. When you drop the item, a new cascade menu is created.

To rename the cascade menu item, either right-click the item or highlight the item and click Modify Selection. Then use the Name text box to enter the new name (including an accelerator key).

Adding Menu Commands and Assigning Macros

You're now ready to create the custom menu commands for your macros. Remember that you can create these commands in any of the following locations:

- On a custom menu you've created
- On a custom cascade menu you've created
- On one of the application's built-in menus

Here are the steps you need to work through:

1. Follow the steps outlined earlier to display the Commands tab in the Customize dialog box.
2. In the Categories list, highlight the Macros item.
3. In the Commands list, drag the Custom Menu item to a custom menu, a custom cascade menu, or a built-in menu.
4. When the menu opens, drag the item down into the menu and then drop the item at the position where you want the command to appear.
5. Right-click the new command, or click Modify Selection, and then use the Name box in the shortcut menu to name your new menu. As before, place an ampersand (&) before whichever letter you want to use as an accelerator key. (To ensure that the Modify Selection menu remains on-screen, don't press Enter when you're done.)
6. From the Modify Selection menu, choose Assign Macro. The Assign Macro dialog box appears, as shown in Figure 12.3.

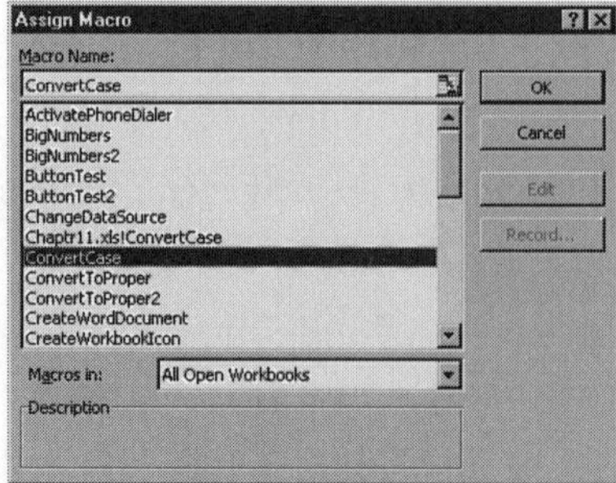

FIGURE 12.3.
Use this dialog box to choose the macro you want to assign to the new menu item.

7. Use the Macro Name list to highlight the macro you want to assign to the new menu command, and then click OK.

> **NOTE: MORE MENU CUSTOMIZATIONS**
>
> Although my focus in this chapter is only on creating menu items to run macros and procedures, you can use the Customize dialog box to remake any of the application's menus in your own image. Just follow the basic instructions in the last couple of sections to create cascade menus and menu commands. Instead of macros, however, you use the other items in the Categories list to create commands for application features that don't have existing commands.

Deleting Menus and Menu Commands

If you don't need a custom menu, cascade menu, or command any longer, you can use a couple of methods to delete these items. First, display the Customize dialog box, and then try either of the following techniques:

- Use the mouse to drag the item off the menu or menu bar and drop it outside the application's menu system.
- Right-click the item and choose Delete from the shortcut menu.

Creating Custom Toolbars for Your Macros

Menu commands are fine, but there's nothing like a toolbar's one-click access for making your macros easy to run. This section shows you how to create custom toolbars, populate them with buttons, and assign macros to these buttons.

Creating a New Toolbar

Theoretically, you *could* add new buttons to the application's built-in toolbars, but you would run the risk of overcrowding them and possibly confusing your users. Instead, you can create a toolbar from scratch and add custom buttons to it. Here are the steps to follow:

1. Either select Tools | Customize (in Access, select View | Toolbars | Customize) or right-click a toolbar and select Customize from the shortcut menu. The application displays the Customize dialog box.
2. Activate the Toolbars tab.
3. Click the New button. The New Toolbar dialog box appears, as shown in Figure 12.4.

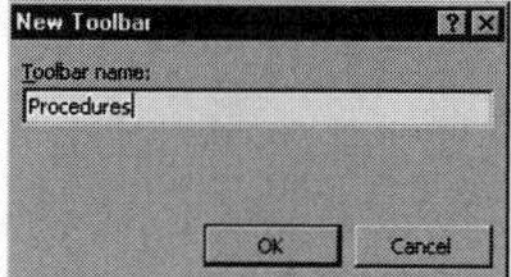

FIGURE 12.4.
Use this dialog box to name your new toolbar.

4. Use the Toolbar name text box to enter the name you want to use for the toolbar, and then click OK. The application displays a new, empty toolbar.

Adding a Toolbar Button and Assigning a Macro

Once you have your new toolbar, you can start adding buttons to it for your macros. Follow these steps:

1. In the Customize dialog box, select the Commands tab.
2. In the Categories list, highlight the Macros item.
3. In the Commands list, drag the Custom Button item and drop it on your new toolbar.
4. Either right-click the button or click Modify Selection and then use the Name box on the shortcut menu to name your new button. This is the text that will appear when the user hovers the mouse pointer over the button for a second or two.
5. To change the button face, click Change Button Image and then choose an image from the menu that appears. Alternatively, you can click Edit Button Image and use the Button Editor to create a custom image.
6. In the Modify Selection list, click Assign Macro to display the Assign Macro dialog box.
7. Use the Macro Name list to highlight the macro you want to assign to the new menu command, and then click OK.

Menus, Toolbars, and VBA 5.0

As I mentioned earlier, there might be times when it's inconvenient, impractical, or downright impossible to make design-time modifications to a user's menus or toolbars. What do you do in these situations if you want to give the user pull-down menu or toolbar access to your application's procedures? Easy: Get your application to build its own menus, cascade menus, commands, and toolbars at runtime. For example, the document that contains your VBA application has an `Open` event that you can use to construct the necessary menu structure each time the user runs the application, as well as a `Close` event to remove the custom items when the application shuts down.

> **TIP: ATTACH TOOLBARS TO EXCEL WORKBOOKS**
>
> If you're building an Excel application, there *is* a way to distribute custom toolbars with your project:
>
> 1. Activate the workbook to which you want to attach the custom toolbar.
> 2. Select Tools | Customize and choose the Toolbars tab in the Customize dialog box.
> 3. Highlight your custom toolbar and then click Attach. Excel displays the Attach Toolbars dialog box.
> 4. Highlight the custom toolbar and then click Copy.
> 5. Click OK.

> **NOTE: WHICH APPLICATION?**
>
> In this chapter, I use the word "application" in two contexts: your VBA application and the underlying application in which your VBA code runs (such as Word or Excel). To avoid confusion, I refer to the underlying application as the *container application*.

VBA 5.0

The secret of controlling menus and toolbars programmatically is a new object in VBA 5.0: `CommandBars`. This Microsoft Office 97 object is a collection that represents all the command bars in the current application, where a "command bar" can be any of the following: a menu bar, a shortcut menu, or a toolbar. This single object replaces the multiple objects used in older versions of Excel (such as `MenuBars` and `Toolbars`), although code that uses these older objects still works in VBA 5.0.

You can use the properties and methods of the `CommandBars` collection to make modifications to the container application's menus and toolbars within procedures. This includes not only simulating the basic design-time techniques of adding menus, commands, and toolbars, but also some techniques that are available only at runtime, such as renaming, disabling, and enabling menus and commands. The rest of this chapter takes you on a brief tour of some of these techniques.

NOTE: REFERENCE THE OFFICE OBJECT LIBRARY

Since `CommandBars` is a Microsoft Office 97 object, you won't be able to use it unless you've established a reference to the Office object library. This is usually set up automatically when you install Office 97. However, if you don't see the `CommandBars` object in the Object Browser, select Tools | References from the Visual Basic Editor and use the References dialog box to activate the reference for the Microsoft Office 8.0 Object Library.

Understanding Command Bars

To work with command bars effectively, you'll likely need to change the way you think about menu bars, shortcut menus, and toolbars. In other words, instead of thinking of these as distinct objects, you need to start thinking of them as variations on the same theme. What theme? Well, for lack of anything better, how about the palette-of-controls-that-you-click-on-to-perform-an-action theme? Think about it. Whether it's a menu bar, a shortcut menu, or a toolbar, you interact with the object in the same way: you click a control (a menu bar item, a menu command, a toolbar button, and so on) and something happens (a menu pulls down, a command is executed, a cascade menu appears, a pop-up box appears, and so on).

This, in a nutshell, is why Microsoft decided to gather menu bars, shortcut menus, and toolbars under the umbrella of the `CommandBars` object. Each of these items is now a CommandBar object, and the only difference between them is that they have a different `Type` property.

In a similar vein, the objects that can appear on a command bar—menu commands, toolbar buttons, pop-up boxes, drop-down menus, and so on—are called *controls*, and they're all variations of the new CommandBarControl object.

Specifying a Command Bar

As with any collection object, you use the `CommandBars` object to specify individual members of the collection (which are CommandBar objects in this case). You can specify either an index number or the name of the command bar. For example, both of the following statements refer to the menu bar that appears when the focus is on an Excel worksheet:

```
CommandBars(1)
CommandBars("Worksheet Menu Bar")
```

Unlike most collections, the index numbers used in the `CommandBars` object aren't all that useful. For example, Excel's `Worksheets` collection contains all the worksheets in a workbook, and the index numbers correspond to the order the sheets appear in the workbook. In the `CommandBars` collection, however, the index numbers for the built-in menus and toolbars have been assigned by the container application's design team, so they have no intrinsic meaning. This means that you'll usually have to refer to individual CommandBar object by their names:

Custom CommandBar objects: Any menu or toolbars that you create at runtime can also be named within the code. Therefore, your procedures will always know the names of these objects.

Built-in toolbars: The names of the container application's built-in toolbars are easy enough to figure out: The name of the toolbar is just the text that appears in the toolbar's title bar (when the toolbar is floating, that is).

Built-in menu bars and shortcut menus: The container application supplies a name for each built-in menu bar and shortcut menu, but there's no easy method for determining the names of these objects.

To help you solve the latter problem, Listing 12.1 presents an Excel procedure that runs through the entire `CommandBars` collection and displays the name, type, and index number for each command bar.

Listing 12.1. A procedure that runs through Excel's `CommandBars` collection and writes the name, type, and index number of each command bar.

```
Sub ListExcelCommandBars()
    Dim i As Integer
    Dim cb As CommandBar
    Dim cbType As String
    i = 0
    For Each cb In CommandBars
        Select Case cb.Type
            Case msoBarTypeNormal     '0
                cbType = "Toolbar"
            Case msoBarTypeMenuBar    '1
                cbType = "Menu Bar"
            Case msoBarTypePopup      '2
                cbType = "Shortcut Menu"
        End Select
        With Worksheets("Sheet1").[a2]
            .Offset(i, 0) = cb.Name
            .Offset(i, 1) = cbType
            .Offset(i, 2) = cb.Index
        End With
        i = i + 1
    Next
    Set cb = Nothing
End Sub
```

NOTE: LISTING WORD'S COMMAND BARS

If you would like to list the command bars in Word, substitute the `With...End With` statement in Listing 12.1 with the following (see either Chaptr12.doc or Chaptr12.bas on the CD):

```
With ActiveDocument.Paragraphs(2).Range
    With .ParagraphFormat.TabStops
        .Add Position:=InchesToPoints(2)
        .Add Position:=InchesToPoints(3.5)
    End With
    .InsertAfter cb.Name & vbTab
    .InsertAfter cbType & vbTab
    .InsertAfter cb.Index
    .InsertParagraphAfter
End With
```


Properties of the CommandBars Object

Before we get to the properties and methods of individual command bars, let's examine a few properties of the `CommandBars` object. These properties control the look and feel of all the command bars, including the animation style used with menus, whether or not buttons display tooltips, and more:

`CommandBars.ActiveMenuBar`: Returns a CommandBar object that represents the active menu bar in the container application.

`CommandBars.Count`: Returns the number of command bars in the `CommandBars` collection.

`CommandBars.DisplayKeysInTooltips`: Returns or sets whether or not the container application includes a control's shortcut key inside the tooltip that is displayed when the user hovers the mouse pointer over the control. Use `True` to include the shortcut key.

`CommandBars.DisplayTooltips`: Returns or sets whether or not the container application displays a tooltip when the user hovers the mouse pointer over a command bar control. Use `True` to display tooltips.

`CommandBars.LargeButtons`: Returns or sets whether or not the container application displays large toolbar buttons. Use `True` to display the large buttons.

`CommandBars.MenuAnimationStyle`: Returns or sets the animation style the container application uses for pulled-down menus. Use one of the following constants:

MenuAnimationStyle	*Resulting Animation*
`msoMenuAnimationUnfold`	Unfold
`msoMenuAnimationSlide`	Slide

continues

`MenuAnimationStyle`	*Resulting Animation*
`msoMenuAnimationNone`	None
`msoMenuAnimationRandom`	Switches randomly between Unfold, Slide, and None

Working with Command Bars

Now that you're familiar with the `CommandBars` object, you can put it to good use creating your own custom command bars and modifying the container application's built-in command bars. This section shows you how to perform these actions.

Creating a New Command Bar

Whether you want to create a new toolbar, shortcut menu, or menu bar, the procedure is exactly the same. In other words, you invoke the `Add` method of the `CommandBars` object and use it to specify the type of command bar you want. Here's the syntax:

```
CommandBars.Add(Name, Position, MenuBar, Temporary)
```

`Name` The name you want to use for the new command bar. Although this argument is optional, it's always a good idea to include it so that you can be sure of the command bar's name. Otherwise, the container application assigns a generic name such as "Custom1."

`Position` Determines where the command bar appears within the container application's window:

`Position`	*Description*
`msoBarTop`	Command bar is docked at the top of the window.
`msoBarBottom`	Command bar is docked at the bottom of the window.
`msoBarLeft`	Command bar is docked on the left side of the window.
`msoBarRight`	Command bar is docked on the right side of the window.
`msoBarFloating`	Command bar is undocked.
`msoBarPopup`	Command bar is a shortcut menu.
`msoBarMenuBar`	(Macintosh only) Command bar replaces the system menu bar.

`MenuBar` A `Boolean` value that determines whether or not the new command bar replaces the active menu bar. Use `True` to replace the menu bar; use `False` to leave the active menu bar in place (this is the default).

Temporary A `Boolean` value that determines when the command bar is deleted. Use `True` to have the command bar deleted when the container application is closed; use `False` to keep the command bar (this is the default).

For example, Listing 12.2 shows a procedure that uses the `Add` method to create a new temporary toolbar named My Toolbar. Before doing so, the procedure runs through the `CommandBars` collection to make sure there is no existing command bar with the same name. (The container application generates an error if you attempt to create a new command bar with the name of an existing command bar.)

Listing 12.2. A procedure that creates a new toolbar after first checking to see if a command bar with the same name already exists.

```
Sub AddToolbar()
    Dim cb As CommandBar
    Dim cbExists As Boolean

    cbExists = False
    For Each cb In CommandBars
        If cb.Name = "My Toolbar" Then
            cbExists = True
            Exit For
        End If
    Next cb
    If cbExists Then
        MsgBox "A command bar named ""My Toolbar"" already exists!"
    Else
        Set cb = CommandBars.Add( _
            Name:="My Toolbar", _
            Position:=msoBarFloating, _
            Temporary:=True)
    End If
    Set cb = Nothing
End Sub
```

Command Bar Properties

Whether you're dealing with one of the container application's built-in command bars or a custom command bar that you've created via code, you can exploit a number of CommandBar object properties in your VBA procedures. Here's a look a few useful ones:

CommandBar`.BuiltIn`: Returns `True` if the specified *CommandBar* is native to the container application; returns `False` for custom command bars.

CommandBar`.Controls`: Returns a `CommandBarControls` object that represents the collection of all the controls contained in the specified *CommandBar*.

CommandBar`.Enabled`: When this property is `True`, the user can work with the specified *CommandBar*. The command bar is disabled when this property is set to `False`.

CommandBar`.Height`: Returns or sets the height, in pixels, for the specified *CommandBar*.

This property only has an effect on a non-empty command bar. Also, note that setting this property results in an error in two situations:

- If the command bar is docked (in other words, the command bar's `Position` property isn't set to `msoBarFloating`; see the `Position` property, discussed later).
- If the command bar is protected against resizing (in other words, the command bar's `Protection` property is set to `msoNoResize`; see the `Protection` property, discussed later).

Here's a procedure fragment that checks a command bar's `Position` and `Protection` properties before changing the height:

```
With CommandBars("My Toolbar")
    If .Position = msoBarFloating And _
       Not .Protection = msoBarNoResize Then
        .Height = 100
    End If
End With
```

CommandBar`.Index`: Returns the index number in the `CommandBars` collection for the specified *CommandBar*.

CommandBar`.Left`: If the command bar is floating, this property returns or sets the distance, in pixels, of the left edge of the specified *CommandBar* from the left edge of the screen (not the container application window). If the command bar is docked, this property returns the distance from the left edge of the docking area.

CommandBar`.Name`: Returns or sets the name of the specified *CommandBar*.

CommandBar`.Position`: Returns or sets the position of the specified *CommandBar*. This property uses the same constants that I outlined earlier for the `Position` argument in the `CommandBars` object's `Add` method.

CommandBar`.Protection`: Returns or sets the protection options for the specified *CommandBar*. You use these options to prevent (or allow) user customization of the object. When setting this property, use any one of the following constants (or you can apply multiple levels of protection by using the sum of two or more constants):

Protection	*Value*	*Resulting Protection*
`msoBarNoProtection`	0	None.
`msoBarNoCustomize`	1	Prevents the user from adding, modifying, or deleting controls.
`msoBarNoResize`	2	Prevents the user from resizing the command bar.
`msoBarNoMove`	4	Prevents the user from moving the command bar.
`msoBarNoChangeVisible`	8	Prevents the user from hiding or unhiding the command bar.
`msoBarNoChangeDock`	16	Prevents the user from docking or undocking the command bar.

`Protection`	*Value*	*Resulting Protection*
`msoBarNoVerticalDock`	32	Prevents the user from docking the command bar on the left or right side of the window.
`msoBarNoHorizontalDock`	64	Prevents the user from docking the command bar on the top or bottom of the window.

`CommandBar.RowIndex`: Returns or sets the row number in the docking area for the specified `CommandBar`. You use this property to determine where in the docking area your command bar will appear. You can use any positive integer or the constants `msoBarRowFirst` (to place the command bar at the beginning of the docking area) or `msoBarRowLast` (to place the command bar at the end of the docking area).

`CommandBar.Top`: If the command bar is floating, this property returns or sets the distance, in pixels, of the top edge of the specified `CommandBar` from the top edge of the screen (*not* the container application window). If the command bar is docked, this property returns the distance from the top edge of the docking area.

`CommandBar.Type`: Returns the object type for the specified `CommandBar`, as follows:

`Type`	*Type of Command Bar*
`msoBarTypeNormal`	Toolbar
`msoBarTypeMenuBar`	Menu bar
`msoBarTypePopup`	Shortcut menu

`CommandBar.Visible`: Returns or sets whether or not the specified `CommandBar` is visible. Use `True` to display the command bar; use `False` to hide the command bar. Note that VBA sets this property to `False` by default when you create a custom command bar.

`CommandBar.Width`: Returns or sets the width, in pixels, of the specified `CommandBar`. This property only has an effect on a non-empty command bar, and, as with `Height`, this property results in an error if the command bar is docked or if the command bar is protected against resizing.

Deleting a Custom Command Bar

Unless you specify otherwise, the command bars you create become a permanent part of the container application. This might be a desirable situation in certain circumstances. For example, if your VBA application contains utilities that are applicable to any document in the container application, it makes sense to give the user full-time access to the procedures.

On the other hand, your procedures might be applicable only while the VBA application is running. In this case, there are a number of reasons why you should delete the command bars when your application shuts down:

- You avoid confusing the user with extra command bars.
- You prevent damage to the user's other files that might be caused by running one of your procedures on a document that wasn't designed for your application.
- You save memory and resources.

I mentioned earlier that you can create your command bars with the `Add` method's *`Temporary`* argument set to `True`. This tells the container application to delete the command bar upon exiting. For immediate deleting, however, use the CommandBar object's `Delete` method:

`CommandBar``.Delete`

Here, ***`CommandBar`*** is the custom CommandBar object you want to delete. Note that you can't delete built-in command bars.

Resetting a Built-In Command Bar

If you make changes to one of the container application's built-in command bars, you can restore the command bar to its default state by using the `Reset` method:

`CommandBar``.Reset`

`CommandBar` is the built-in CommandBar object you want to reset. For example, Listing 12.3 shows the `CleanUpCommandBars` procedure that loops through the `CommandBars` collection and performs one of two tasks: If the command bar is built-in, it's restored to its default state; if the command bar is a custom object, it's deleted.

Listing 12.3. A procedure that runs through the `CommandBars` collection and resets the built-in command bars and deletes the custom command bars.

```
Sub CleanUpCommandBars()
    Dim cb As CommandBar
    For Each cb In CommandBars
        If cb.BuiltIn Then
            cb.Reset
        Else
            cb.Delete
        End If
    Next cb
    Set cb = Nothing
End Sub
```

Working with Command Bar Controls

At this point, your custom command bars aren't particularly useful, because they can't do much of anything. In other words, they don't contain any controls that the user can click or otherwise execute. This section solves that problem by giving you the lowdown on VBA's command bar controls and by showing you how to add and modify custom command bar controls.

The Microsoft Office 97 object model divides command bar controls into three categories:

CommandBarButton: This is an object that the user clicks to execute a command or run a procedure. Menu commands and toolbar buttons are examples of CommandBarButton objects.

CommandBarPopup: This is an object that the user clicks to display a menu of items. Examples of CommandBarPopup objects are menu bar commands and menu commands that display cascade menus.

CommandBarComboBox: This object takes one of three forms: a text box into which the user enters text (for example, the Name text box in the Modify Selection menu shown in Figure 12.2), a drop-down list from which the user selects an item, or a combo box that combines a text box and a drop-down list (for example, the Font and Font Size controls on the Formatting toolbar in Word and Excel).

Specifying a Control

As you learned earlier, each CommandBar object has a `Controls` property that returns the collection of all the controls on the command bar. You use this collection to specify individual controls using their index number, where `Controls(1)` is the first control on the command bar, `Controls(2)` is the second control, and so on. In each case, a CommandBarControl object is returned.

Another way to specify a control is to use the CommandBar object's `FindControl` method:

```
CommandBar.FindControl(Type, Id, Tag, Visible, Recursive)
```

`CommandBar`	The CommandBar object in which you want to search.
`Type`	A constant that specifies the type of CommandBarControl object you want to find. For custom controls, use one of the following constants that correspond to the control types just discussed: `msoControlButton`, `msoControlPopup`, `msoControlEdit`, `msoControlDropdown`, or `msoControlComboBox`. For built-in controls, Office also defines quite a number of other constants. To see these constants, look up the `Type` property of the CommandBarControl object in the Office VBA Help system.
`Id`	This is a unique identifier that the container application supplies for each control. This identifier is returned by the CommandBarControl object's `Id` property.
`Tag`	Specifies the `Tag` property of the control you want to find.
`Visible`	Use `True` to search only for controls that are visible; use `False` to search for hidden controls as well (this is the default).

Recursive — Use `True` to search not only the command bar, but all its cascade menus and pop-up menus; use `False` to search only the command bar (this is the default).

If `FindControl` is successful, it returns a CommandBarControl object for the first control that matches your search criteria. If the search fails, `FindControl` returns the value `Nothing`.

Adding a Control to a Command Bar

When customizing command bars, you have a number of different routes to take:

- You can modify a built-in command bar by adding built-in controls.
- You can modify a built-in command bar by adding custom controls that execute your VBA procedures.
- You can modify a custom command bar by adding built-in controls.
- You can modify a custom command bar by adding custom controls.

Whichever route you take, you insert a control into a command bar by using the `Controls` object's `Add` method:

```
CommandBar.Controls.Add(Type, Id, Parameter, Before, Temporary)
```

CommandBar — The CommandBar object into which you want to insert the control.

Type — A constant that determines the type of custom control to add:

Type	*Control Object*
`msoControlButton`	CommandBarButton
`msoControlPopup`	CommandBarPopup
`msoControlEdit`	CommandBarComboBox
`msoControlDropdown`	CommandBarComboBox
`msoControlComboBox`	CommandBarComboBox

Id — An integer that specifies the built-in control you want to add.

Parameter — You use this argument to send a parameter to a built-in control. (The container application uses this parameter to modify how it runs the command associated with the control.) For custom controls, you can use this argument to send information to the procedure associated with the control.

Before — The index number of the control before which the new control will be added. If you omit this argument, VBA adds the control to the end of the command bar.

Temporary — A `Boolean` value that determines when the control is deleted. Use `True` to have the control deleted when the container application is closed; use `False` to keep the control (this is the default).

For example, the following statement adds a CommandBarButton object to the end of the toolbar named My Toolbar:

```
CommandBars("My Toolbar").Controls.Add Type:=msoControlButton
```

The Command Bar Info Utility

One of the problems you face when working with command bars and controls is that you're often flying blind. For example, you saw earlier that there's no easy way to tell the name of a menu bar or shortcut menu. Similarly, you can't add a built-in control to a command bar unless you know its `Id` property, but VBA gives you no easy way to determine this property.

To help you out, I put together a small utility that solves this dilemma. In Chaptr12.xls on this book's CD, you'll see a form named CommandBarInfo. If you run this form, you'll see the dialog box shown in Figure 12.5. The idea is that you use the Name list to select the name of a command bar and then use the Caption list to choose a control. The labels beneath this list tell you the control's `Id`, `Type`, and `Index` properties.

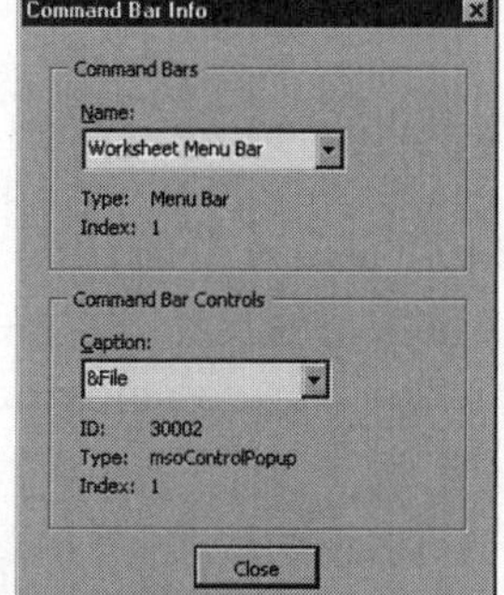

FIGURE 12.5.
Use the Command Bar Info utility to find out the `Id` property of a built-in control.

NOTE: THERE'S ALSO A FORM FILE

If you don't have Excel, you'll also find the Command Bar Info utility in the file Chaptr12.frm on this book's CD.

Control Properties

To make your custom controls do something useful, you have to set a few properties. For example, you'll want to specify the procedure to run when the user clicks the control, and you'll probably want to define a tooltip for a your toolbar-based controls. Here's a quick rundown of these and other control properties:

`Control.BeginGroup`: Returns `True` if the specified *`Control`* is at the beginning of a group of controls on a command bar. If `True`, the underlying application displays a separator bar before the *`Control`*.

`Control.BuiltIn`: Returns `True` if the specified *`Control`* is native to the container application; returns `False` for custom controls.

`Control.Caption`: Returns or sets the caption for the specified *`Control`*. If the control is a menu bar command or a menu command, the `Caption` property determines the command text, so you should include an ampersand (`&`) before the letter you want to use as an accelerator key, like so:

```
Set newMenu = CommandsBars(1).Controls.Add(Type:=msoControlPopup)
newMenu.Caption = "&My Menu"
```

NOTE: BUTTON CAPTION IS DEFAULT TOOLTIP

If the control is a toolbar button, the `Caption` property sets the default text used as the control's tooltip. Note, however, that each control also has a `ToolTipText` property that you can use to manipulate the tooltip text.

`Control.Controls`: If the specified *`Control`* is a CommandBarPopup object, this property returns the collection of all the controls on the pop-up. For example, you can use this property to return all the menu items in a pull-down menu.

`Control.DropDownLines`: If the specified *`Control`* is a CommandBarComboBox object, this property returns or sets the number of items that appear when the user drops down the list.

`Control.DropDownWidth`: If the specified *`Control`* is a CommandBarComboBox object, this property returns or sets the width of the control in pixels.

`Control.Enabled`: When this property is `True`, the user can work with the specified *`Control`*. The control is disabled when this property is set to `False`.

`Control.FaceId`: If the specified *`Control`* is a CommandBarButton object, this property returns or sets the ID number of the icon on the button's face. Note that this number is the same as the control's `Id` property in most cases.

`Control.Id`: As you've seen, this property returns a unique ID for the specified built-in *`Control`*. Note that all custom controls return 1 for the `Id` property.

`Control.Index`: Returns the index number in the `Controls` collection for the specified *`Control`*.

`Control.List(`**`Index`**`)`: If the specified *`Control`* is a CommandBarComboBox object, this property returns or sets the value of the list item given by **`Index`** (where 0 is the first item).

`Control.ListCount`: If the specified *`Control`* is a CommandBarComboBox object, this property returns the number of items in the list.

`Control.ListIndex`: If the specified *`Control`* is a CommandBarComboBox object, this property returns or sets the selected item in the list.

`Control``.OnAction`: Returns or sets the name of the VBA procedure that will execute when the user clicks the specified *`Control`*. Listing 12.4 shows a procedure that adds a new command to the Tools menu.

Listing 12.4. A procedure that modifies the Tools menu by adding a command to execute the `RunCommandBarInfo` procedure.

```
Sub AddToolsMenuCommand()
    Dim cb As CommandBar
    Dim menuTools As CommandBarControl
    Dim ctrl As CommandBarControl
    Dim ctrlExists As Boolean

    ctrlExists = False
    '
    ' Get the Tools menu (ID=30007)
    '
    Set menuTools = Application.CommandBars.FindControl(Id:=30007)
    '
    ' Make sure the command doesn't exist
    '
    For Each ctrl In menuTools.Controls
        If ctrl.Caption = "Command &Bar Info" Then
            ctrlExists = True
            Exit For
        End If
    Next ctrl
    '
    ' If the command doesn't exist, add it
    '
    If Not ctrlExists Then
        Set ctrl = menuTools.Controls.Add(Type:=msoControlButton)
        With ctrl
            .Caption = "Command &Bar Info"
            .OnAction = "RunCommandBarInfo"
        End With
    End If
    Set cb = Nothing
End Sub

' This procedure runs the CommandBarInfo utility.
'
Sub RunCommandBarInfo()
    CommandBarInfo.Show
End Sub
```

The procedure first checks to see if the command already exists. It does this by using the `FindControl` method to find the Tools menu (which the Command Bar Info utility tells us has ID 30007) and then using a `For Each...Next` loop to check the `Caption` of each item on the menu. If the command doesn't exist, the `Add` method tacks it onto the end of the menu, the `Caption` property is set to `Command &Bar Info`, and the `OnAction` property is set to `RunCommandBarInfo`. The latter procedure appears at the end of the listing. It just runs the `Show` method to display the `CommandBarInfo` form.

`Control.ShortcutText`: If the specified *`Control`* is a CommandBarButton object that appears on a menu, this property returns or sets the shortcut key text that appears to the right of the control.

`Control.State`: If the specified *`Control`* is a CommandBarButton object, this property returns or sets the appearance of the button:

`State`	*How the Button Appears*
`msoButtonUp`	Unpressed
`msoButtonDown`	Pressed
`msoButtonMixed`	Mixed

`Control.Style`: If the specified *`Control`* is a CommandBarButton object, this property returns or sets how the container application displays the button:

`Style`	*How the Button Is Displayed*
`msoButtonAutomatic`	Using the container application's default display
`msoButtonIcon`	With an icon only
`msoButtonCaption`	With a caption only
`msoButtonIconandCaption`	With both an icon and a caption

`Control.Text`: If the specified *`Control`* is a CommandBarComboBox object, this property returns or sets the text that appears in the text box part of the control.

`Control.ToolTipText`: Returns or sets the tooltip text for specified *`Control`*.

`Control.Type`: Returns the object type for the specified *`Control`*. To see a complete list of control types, open the code window for the CommandBarInfo form and examine the `ControlType` function.

`Control.Visible`: Returns or sets whether or not the specified *`Control`* is visible. Use `True` to display the control; use `False` to hide the control.

Control Methods

To complete our examination of controls, this section looks at a few methods associated with controls. With these methods you can copy and move a control, execute the action that underlies a control, set the focus on a control, delete a control, and more. Here's the rundown:

`Control.AddItem`: If the specified *`Control`* is a CommandBarComboBox object, this method adds an item to the control's list using the following syntax:

```
Control.AddItem(Text, Index)
```

Control	The control to which you want to add the list item.
Text	A string that specifies the item to be added to the list.
Index	The position of the new item in the list. If you omit this argument, VBA adds the item to the end of the list.

Control.: If the specified *Control* is a CommandBarComboBox object, this method clears the contents of the list. Note that you can't apply this method to a built-in control.

Control.Copy: Makes a copy of the specified *Control* using the following syntax:

Control.Copy(*Bar*, *Before*)

Control	The control you want to copy.
Bar	The CommandBar object to which you want to copy the control. If you omit this argument, VBA makes a copy of this control on the command bar that contains ***Control***.
Before	The index number of the control before which the copied control will be inserted. If you omit this argument, VBA adds the control to the end of the command bar.

Control.CopyFace: If the specified *Control* is a CommandBarButton object, this method copies the icon on the button's face to the Clipboard. You can then use the PasteFace method (which appears later in this list) to apply the copied face to another button.

Control.Delete: Deletes the specified *Control* using the following syntax:

Control.Delete(*Temporary*)

Control	The control you want to delete.
Temporary	A Boolean value that determines the permanence of the deletion. If you use True, VBA deletes the control, but then restores the control the next time the container application is started. If you use False, VBA deletes the control permanently (this is the default).

Control.Execute: Runs the built-in command or VBA procedure associated with the specified *Control*.

Control.Move: Moves the specified *Control* using the following syntax:

Control.Move(*Bar*, *Before*)

Control	The control you want to move.
Bar	The CommandBar object to which you want to move the control. If you omit this argument, VBA moves the control to the end of the command bar that contains ***Control***.
Before	The index number of the control before which the moved control will be inserted. If you omit this argument, VBA adds the control to the end of the command bar.

`Control.PasteFace`: If the specified *Control* is a CommandBarButton object, this method pastes the current contents of the Clipboard onto the button's face. You normally use this method after having first copied another button's face to the Clipboard using the `CopyFace` method (which appears earlier in this list).

`Control.RemoveItem`: If the specified *Control* is a CommandBarComboBox object, this method removes an item from the list using the following syntax:

```
Control.RemoveItem(Index)
```

Control	The control from which you want to remove the item.
Index	The number of the item you want to remove.

`Control.Reset`: Restores the specified *Control* to its default state.

`Control.SetFocus`: Sets the focus on the specified *Control*.

Summary

This chapter rounded out your VBA user interface education by showing you how to set up menus and toolbars to run your procedures. In the first part of this chapter, you learned how to use the built-in tools of the Office applications to create new menus and toolbars and to assign procedures to menu commands and toolbar buttons. From there, I showed you how to wield Office 97's `CommandBars` object model to create custom command bars and controls and to modify the container application's built-in command bars and controls.

Here's a list of chapters where you'll find related information:

- I go through some basic user interface features—such as the `MsgBox` and `InputBox` functions—in Chapter 10, "Interacting with the User."
- The Command Bar Info utility is a custom user form, and the underlying code manipulates various objects in this form. To learn about user forms and their objects, see Chapter 11, "Working with Microsoft Forms."
- I set up a custom menu structure in the database application discussed in Chapter 17, "Using VBA to Work with Excel Lists."
- For another example of a custom menu system, see Chapter 27, "A Check Book Application."

IV PART

IN THIS PART

Unleashing Application Integration

CHAPTER

Working with Other Applications

IN THIS CHAPTER

There is nothing new under the sun, but there are lots of old things we don't know.

—*Ambrose Bierce*

Your VBA code will likely spend most of its time working with its native application's objects and their associated properties and methods. However, there will be times when you need your code to interact with other applications. Happily, VBA offers a number of functions and methods for working with other applications inside your procedures. This chapter shows you how to start and activate other programs, how to send them keystrokes, and how to use Dynamic Data Exchange.

Starting Another Application

I suppose the most obvious way to work with another application is to simply start it up and work with it directly. As is usually the case with most computer tasks, there's a hard way and an easy way to do this. The "hard" way is to open the Start menu and then either wade through all those submenus to launch the program from its icon or select the Run command and enter the program's executable filename in the Run dialog box.

The easy way is to use the `Shell` function to start the program from a VBA procedure:

`Shell(`***`PathName`***`, `*`WindowStyle`*`)`

`PathName` The name of the file that starts the application. Unless the file is in the Windows folder, you should include the drive and folder to make sure that VBA can find the file.

`WindowStyle` A constant or number that specifies how the application window will appear:

`WindowStyle`	*Window Appearance*
`vbHide` (or 0)	Hidden
`vbNormalFocus` (or 1)	Normal size with focus
`vbMinimizedFocus` (or 2)	Minimized with focus (this is the default)
`vbMaximizedFocus` (or 3)	Maximized with focus
`vbNormalNoFocus` (or 4)	Normal without focus
`vbMinimzedNoFocus` (or 6)	Minimized without focus

If successful, `Shell` returns a number (called the *task ID* number). If unsuccessful, `Shell` generates an error. Listing 13.1 shows an example of the `Shell` function.

Listing 13.1. Using the `Shell` function to start an application.

```
Sub StartControlPanelIcon(cplFile As String)

    On Error GoTo BadStart

    Shell "CONTRO L.EXE " & cplFile, 1
    Exit Sub

BadStart:
    MsgBox "Could not start Control Panel!", _
        vbOKOnly + vbExclamation
End Sub

' This procedure calls StartControlPanelIcon with
' "INETCPL.CPL" to open the Data Sources dialog box
'
Sub ChangeDataSource()
    StartControlPanelIcon ("INETCPL.CPL")
End Sub
```

NOTE: THIS CHAPTER'S CODE LISTINGS

To use the code listings from this chapter, look for the file named Chaptr13.xls on the CD. If you don't have Excel, you can still view the code by opening the file named Chaptr13.bas.

The Windows Control Panel is a frequently used accessory that lets you control many aspects of the Windows environment, including printer settings, fonts, and colors. The `StartControlPanelIcon` procedure takes advantage of the fact that you can start any Control Panel icon directly by using the following command-line syntax:

```
CONTROL.EXE cplFile
```

Here, *`cplFile`* is a .CPL (Control Panel Library) file that corresponds to the Control Panel icon you want to start. Table 13.1 lists some of the Control Panel icons and their corresponding .CPL files.

Table 13.1. Control Panel icons and their .CPL files.

Icon	*.CPL File*
Accessibility Options	ACCESS.CPL
Add/Remove Programs	APPWIZ.CPL
Date/Time	TIMEDATE.CPL
Desktop Themes	THEMES.CPL

continues

Table 13.1. continued

Icon	*.CPL File*
Display	DESK.CPL
Fonts	MAIN.CPL FONTS
Internet	INETCPL.CPL
Joystick	JOY.CPL
Keyboard	MAIN.CPL KEYBOARD
Mail and Fax	MLCFG32.CPL
Microsoft Mail Postoffice	WGPOCPL.CPL
Modems	MODEM.CPL
Mouse	MAIN.CPL MOUSE
Multimedia	MMSYS.CPL
Network	NETCPL.CPL
Passwords	PASSWORD.CPL
Printers	MAIN.CPL PRINTERS
Regional Settings	INTL.CPL
System	SYSDM.CPL

The `StartControlPanelIcon` procedure takes a *`cplFile`* argument that specifies the Control Panel icon you want to work with. The procedure sets up an `On Error` handler just in case Control Panel doesn't start properly. (See Chapter 23, "Trapping Program Errors," to learn more about the `On Error` statement.) Then it runs the `Shell` function to load Control Panel and run the module specified by *`cplFile`*.

The `ChangeDataSource` procedure shows an example of how you call `StartControlPanelIcon`. In this case, the Internet Properties dialog box appears so that you can modify the setup of Internet Explorer.

NOTE: CHANGING DIRECTORIES

Use the `ChDir` statement if you need to change to an application's directory before starting the program:

```
ChDir Path
```

The *`Path`* argument is a string that specifies the directory to change to.

CAUTION: SHELL IS ASYNCHRONOUS

Don't enter statements after a `Shell` function if you want the statements to execute only when you've finished with the other application. The `Shell` statement runs an application *asynchronously*, which means that VBA starts the program and then immediately resumes executing the rest of the procedure.

Activating a Running Application

Once you have some other programs up and running, your VBA application might need to switch between them. For example, you might want the user to switch between Excel and Control Panel to change various settings. To switch to any running application, use the `AppActivate` statement:

```
AppActivate(Title, Wait)
```

Title	The name of the application as it appears in the title bar, or its *task ID* number (as returned by the `Shell` function).
Wait	A logical value that determines when VBA switches to the application. If *Wait* is `True`, `AppActivate` waits until you activate the application in which the VBA code is running before switching. If *Wait* is `False` or omitted, `AppActivate` immediately switches to the other application.

Note that, for some applications, the title bar might include both the name of the application and the name of the active document. If ***Title*** doesn't match any application's title bar exactly, VBA tries to find a title bar that begins with ***Title***.

Listing 13.2 shows `AppActivate` in action.

Listing 13.2. Using the AppActivate statement to switch to a running application.

```
' This procedure loads the Phone Dialer accessory
'
Sub LoadPhoneDialer()

    On Error GoTo BadStart
    '
    ' Start Phone Dialer without the focus
    '
    If InStr(1, Application.OperatingSystem, "NT") Then
        '
        ' Use this line with Windows NT:
        '
        Shell "C:\Program Files\Windows NT\dialer.exe", 4
```

continues

Listing 13.2. continued

```
    Else
        '
        ' Use this line with Windows 95:
        '
        Shell "C:\Windows\dialer.exe", 4
    End If
    '
    ' Set up the Ctrl+Shift+P shortcut key
    '
    Application.OnKey _
        Key:="^+P", _
        Procedure:="ActivatePhoneDialer"

    MsgBox "Phone Dialer loaded!" & Chr(13) & _
        "Press Ctrl+Shift+P to activate.", _
        vbInformation

    Exit Sub
BadStart:
    MsgBox "Could not start Phone Dialer!", _
        vbOKOnly + vbExclamation

End Sub

' This procedure copies the current cell and activates
' Phone Dialer when the user presses Ctrl+Shift+P
'
Sub ActivatePhoneDialer()

    Dim result As Integer

    On Error GoTo NotRunning
    '
    ' Copy the contents (a phone number?) of the current cell
    '
    ActiveCell.Copy
    '
    ' Activate Phone Dialer
    '
    AppActivate "Phone Dialer"

    Exit Sub

NotRunning:
    result = MsgBox("Phone Dialer is not loaded! " & _
                    "Do you want to load it now?", _
                    vbYesNo + vbExclamation)

    If result = vbYes Then
        LoadPhoneDialer
    End If

End Sub
```

In this example, the LoadPhoneDialer procedure loads the Phone Dialer accessory that's available in Windows 95 and Windows NT 4.0. (Note that Excel's Application object has an OperatingSystem property that returns a string identifying the running operating system.) The procedure then sets up a shortcut key for activating Phone Dialer.

The Shell function starts Phone Dialer without focus. Then an OnKey method sets up the Ctrl-Shift-P key combination to run the ActivatePhoneDialer procedure. (The OnKey method assigns a procedure to a key combination. When the user presses the keys, the procedure executes; see Chapter 7, "Manipulating Excel with VBA.") Finally, a MsgBox function displays a message to tell the user that Phone Dialer has been loaded.

If Phone Dialer doesn't load, a different MsgBox function alerts the user to the problem.

The ActivatePhoneDialer procedure copies the contents of the active cell (which contains, ideally, a phone number you want to dial) and then activates Phone Dialer using the AppActivate statement. (You can then paste the copied number into Phone Dialer's Number to dial text box.) If an error occurs, the code jumps to the NotRunning label and asks the user if he or she wants to start Phone Dialer.

NOTE: ACTIVATING A MICROSOFT APPLICATION

If the application you want to activate is a Microsoft application, you can use the Excel Application object's ActivateMicrosoftApp(***Index***) method. Here, ***Index*** is a constant that represents the Microsoft application you want to activate: xlMicrosoftAccess, xlMicrosoftFoxPro, xlMicrosoftMail, xlMicrosoftPowerPoint, xlMicrosoftProject, xlMicrosoftSchedulePlus, or xlMicrosoftWord.

If the application isn't running, ActivateMicrosoftApp starts it. For example, the following statement activates Microsoft Word:

```
Application.ActivateMicrosoftApp xlMicrosoftWord
```


Sending Keystrokes to an Application

As you'll see later in this chapter, you can use DDE to run a server application's macro commands. Also, as you'll see in Chapter 15, "Controlling Applications Via OLE Automation," the OLE automation interface makes it easy to program a server application's objects. However, the majority of Windows applications don't have a macro language and don't support OLE automation. What's to be done with these less-sophisticated programs?

Well, one solution is to simply load the application using the Shell function and let the user work with the program directly. This is fine if the user is familiar with the application, but your real goal here is to control programs from within a VBA procedure. The solution is to use the `SendKeys` statement to send keystrokes to the application. You can send any key or key combination (including those that use the Alt, Ctrl, and Shift keys), and the result is exactly the same as if you typed it yourself. Here is the syntax of the `SendKeys` statement:

```
SendKeys String, Wait
```

String	The key or key combination you want to send to the active application. For letters, numbers, or punctuation marks, enclose the character in quotes (for example, `"a"`). For other keys, use the strings outlined in Table 13.2.
Wait	A logical value that determines whether VBA waits for the keys to be processed before continuing the procedure. If *Wait* is `True`, VBA waits for the application to finish processing the keys before moving to the next statement in the procedure. It doesn't wait if the *Wait* argument is `False` or omitted.

Table 13.2. Strings to use for the SendKeys method's *String* argument.

Key	*String to Use*
Backspace	`"{BACKSPACE}"` or `"{BS}"`
Break	`"{BREAK}"`
Caps Lock	`"{CAPSLOCK}"`
Delete	`"{DELETE}"` or `"{DEL}"`
Down arrow	`"{DOWN}"`
End	`"{END}"`
Enter (keypad)	`"{ENTER}"`
Enter	`"~"` (tilde)
Esc	`"{ESCAPE}"` or `"{ESC}"`
Home	`"{HOME}"`
Insert	`"{INSERT}"`
Left arrow	`"{LEFT}"`
Num Lock	`"{NUMLOCK}"`
Page Down	`"{PGDN}"`
Page Up	`"{PGUP}"`
Right arrow	`"{RIGHT}"`
Scroll Lock	`"{SCROLLLOCK}"`
Tab	`"{TAB}"`
Up arrow	`"{UP}"`
F1 through F12	`"{F1}"` through `"{F12}"`

NOTE: SENDING MULTIPLES OF A KEY

For most of the keys listed in Table 13.2, you can send the key multiple times by enclosing a number within the braces. For example, to send the up arrow key three times, use `{UP 3}`.

By combining these keys with the Alt, Ctrl, and Shift keys, you can create any key combination. Just precede a string from Table 13.2 with one or more of the codes listed in Table 13.3.

Table 13.3. Codes for the Alt, Ctrl, and Shift keys.

Key	*Code to Use*
Alt	`%` (percent)
Ctrl	`^` (caret)
Shift	`+` (plus)

All you have to do is start a program with `Shell`, and then you can send whatever keystrokes you need. (You can sometimes get away with activating a running application with `AppActivate` and then sending the keys, but I've found that this doesn't work consistently. You'll need to experiment with the applications you want to use.) For example, you can close any active Windows application by sending the Alt-F4 key combination, as follows:

```
SendKeys "%{F4}"
```

Listing 13.3 shows a more complex example that dials a phone number using the Phone Dialer accessory.

Listing 13.3. Controlling an application using the SendKeys statement.

```
Sub LoadAndDialPhoneDialer()

    Dim msg As String, buttons As Integer, response As Integer
    On Error GoTo BadStart

    msg = "About to dial the following number:" & _
          Chr(13) & Chr(13) & _
          "   " & ActiveCell & _
          Chr(13) & Chr(13) & _
          "Please make sure your modem is turned on."
    buttons = vbOKCancel + vbExclamation
    response = MsgBox(msg, buttons)

    If response = vbCancel Then Exit Sub
    '
    ' Copy the contents (a phone number?) of the current cell
    '
```

continues

Listing 13.3. continued

```
    ActiveCell.Copy
    '
    ' Start Phone Dialer with the focus
    '
    If InStr(1, Application.OperatingSystem, "NT") Then
        '
        ' Use this line with Windows NT:
        '
        Shell "C:\Program Files\Windows NT\dialer.exe", 1
    Else
        '
        ' Use this line with Windows 95:
        '
        Shell "C:\Windows\dialer.exe", 1
    End If
    '
    ' Paste the copied phone number with Ctrl+V and
    ' then press Enter to select the Dial button
    '
    SendKeys "^v~", True
    '
    ' Wait eight seconds to give the modem time to dial
    '
    Application.Wait Now + TimeValue("00:00:08")
    '
    ' Close the dialog boxes and exit Phone Dialer
    '
    SendKeys "~{ESC}%{F4}"
    '
    ' Get rid of Excel's Copy mode indicators
    '
    Application.CutCopyMode = False

    Exit Sub

BadStart:
    MsgBox "Could not start Phone Dialer!", _
        vbOKOnly + vbExclamation
End Sub
```

This procedure uses a modem and the Phone Dialer accessory to dial the phone number contained in the active cell. After displaying a `MsgBox` that tells the user the number that will be dialed and makes sure that his or her modem is on, the procedure copies the active cell and starts Phone Dialer. (A good exercise would be to add code that checks to make sure the cell isn't blank.)

A `SendKeys` statement sends Ctrl-V and then Enter to paste the phone number and click the Dial button. After a few seconds, Phone Dialer displays the Call Status dialog box. Go ahead and pick up the receiver, but don't press Enter to clear the dialog box. The procedure waits eight seconds to give your phone time to dial; then another `SendKeys` statement sends the following keys: Enter (to remove the dialog box), Esc (to cancel the Dialing dialog box), and Alt-F4 (to exit Phone Dialer). Finally, the `CutCopyMode` property is set to `False` to take Excel out of copy mode.

NOTE: SENDKEYS IS CASE-SENSITIVE

Keep in mind that the `SendKeys` statement is case-sensitive. For example, the strings `"^P"` and `"^+p"` both send the key combination Ctrl-Shift-P. If you want to send just Ctrl-P, `"^p"` is the string to use.

TIP: SENDING THE SENDKEYS PUNCTUATION MARKS

Enclose the following characters in braces (`{}`) to send them in a `SendKeys` string: `~ % ^ ( ) + { } [ ]`. For example, you send a percent sign as follows:

```
SendKeys "{%}"
```


Using Dynamic Data Exchange

In Chapter 14, "Programming OLE and ActiveX Objects," and Chapter 15, you'll learn how the advanced technologies of OLE and OLE automation make it easier than ever to work and exchange data with other Windows applications. However, of the thousands of Windows applications that exist, only a few support the OLE standard, and a relative handful (for now) support OLE automation. OLE might one day be the de facto standard for application interoperability, but until that day comes, we'll need a few more tricks in our programming bag to work with other applications.

One of those tricks is the predecessor of OLE: *dynamic data exchange* (*DDE*). DDE is an internal communications protocol that lets some Windows applications exchange data and even execute each others' commands. Because it's implemented unevenly in different applications, DDE is nowhere near as clean (or as straightforward) as OLE, but it's often the only choice we have. The good news is that VBA provides plenty of tools to control the DDE protocol at the procedure level. The next few sections examine each of these tools.

DDE: The Basics

Human conversations can take two forms: static and dynamic. A static conversation—such as the exchange of letters or e-mail—is one in which information is passed back and forth intermittently. A dynamic conversation, on the other hand, is one in which information is exchanged continuously. Face-to-face meetings or telephone calls are examples of dynamic conversations.

A *dynamic* data exchange, then, is one where two applications continuously send data and commands to each other. As in OLE, the two applications involved in this process are called *client* and *server*. The *client* is the application that initializes the conversation and sends requests for data (the client is also sometimes called the *destination*). The *server* is the application that responds to the client's requests by executing its own commands and sending its data (the server is also called the *source*).

DDE conversations unfold in three stages:

1. Initiate a link between the client and the server: This link—it's called a *channel*—is the path along which the two applications will communicate. In our case, VBA will be initiating the conversation, so it will be the client.
2. Work with the server: Once the link is established, the client can exchange data with the server and can control the server by invoking its internal macro commands or by sending keystrokes.
3. Terminate the link: When the client is finished working with the server, your procedure needs to close the channel.

Initiating a Link Between VBA and a Server Application

Just as you need to call someone before you can have a phone conversation, so too must your procedure "call" a server application to initiate a DDE conversation. To establish a channel between VBA and another DDE application, use the `DDEInitiate` method:

```
DDEInitiate(App, Topic)
```

App	The DDE name of the server application with which you want to open a link.
Topic	This is the "topic of conversation" that the two applications will be using. For most applications, you use either `System` (the application as a whole) or the name of a document in the application (in other words, the name as it appears in the title bar).

The DDE name used in the ***App*** argument depends on the application—it's almost always the name of the executable file that starts the application (without the extension). For example, the DDE name for Excel is `Excel`, for Word for Windows it's `Winword`, and for Access it's `MSAccess`. For other applications, you can check your documentation or contact the application's technical support department. However, you might be able to figure it out for yourself. Here are the steps to follow:

1. In Windows Explorer, select View | Options and then activate the File Types tab in the Options dialog box.
2. In the Registered file types list, highlight a file type that corresponds to the application you want to work with, and then click Edit.

3. In the Edit File Type dialog box, use the Actions list to highlight Open, and then click Edit. You'll see a dialog box similar to the one shown in Figure 13.1.

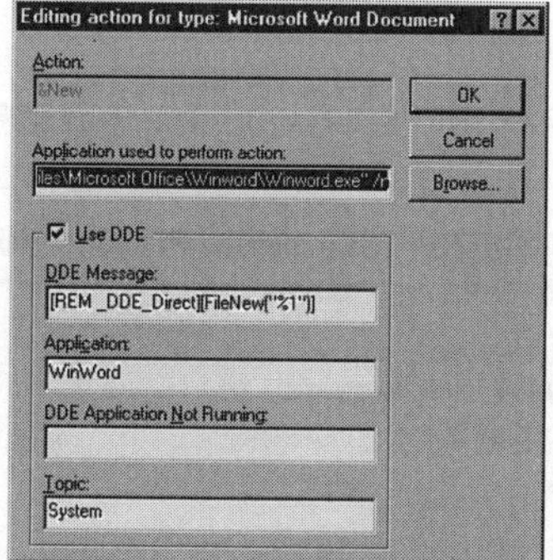

FIGURE 13.1.
If the application supports DDE, editing its Open action will tell you its DDE name and topic.

4. If the application supports DDE, the Use DDE check box will be activated. You'll find the program's DDE name in the Application text box and its application-level topic in the Topic text box.

Make sure you include the full pathname of a document in the `DDEInitiate` method's *`Topic`* argument if you're trying to access a document that isn't already open. Here's an example:

```
DDEInitiate("Winword", "C:\WINWORD\MEMO.DOC")
```

If `DDEInitiate` is successful, it returns an integer identifying the channel. You'll need to refer to this number in all subsequent DDE exchanges between the client and server, so make sure you store the result of the `DDEInitiate` method in a variable.

The server application needs to be open before you can initiate a DDE session. Therefore, one decision you need to make before running the `DDEInitiate` method is whether you want to open the server beforehand with the `Shell` function or whether you want `DDEInitiate` to handle it for you. In most cases, a `Shell` function is the way to go, because the `DDEInitiate` startup method has two annoying quirks:

- VBA displays a dialog box similar to the one shown in Figure 13.2. You need to click Yes to start the application. If you like, you can prevent this message from appearing by setting the `Application.DisplayAlerts` property to `False`.

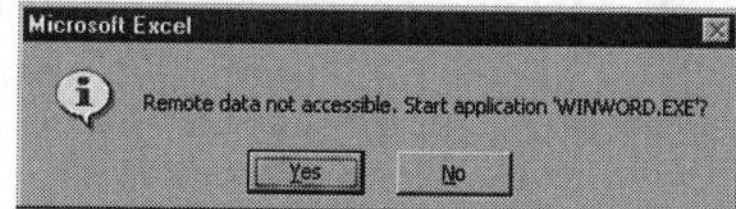

FIGURE 13.2.
The dialog box Excel displays if you let `DDEInitiate` *start a server application that isn't already running.*

- If the application isn't in the current directory or the DOS search path, `DDEInitiate` won't be able to find it. You can solve this problem by first using the `ChDir` statement to change to the application's directory:

  ```
  ChDir "C:\WINWORD"
  ```

Listing 13.4 shows a sample `Function` procedure that uses the `DDEInitiate` method.

Listing 13.4. Using the `DDEInitiate` method to open a DDE channel.

```
Sub TestIt()
   Dim result as integer
    result = OpenHailingFrequencies
    DDETerminate result
End Sub

Function OpenHailingFrequencies() As Integer
    Dim channel As Integer

    On Error GoTo BadConnection
    '
    ' Establish the DDE connection to Program Manager
    '
    channel = DDEInitiate("Progman", "Progman")

    MsgBox "A channel to Program Manager is now open.", vbInformation
    '
    ' Return the channel number
    '
    OpenHailingFrequencies = channel
    Exit Function

BadConnection:
    MsgBox "Could not open a channel to Program Manager!", vbExclamation
    '
    ' Return 0
    '
    OpenHailingFrequencies = 0

End Function
```

The `TestIt` procedure calls the `OpenHailingFrequencies` function, which is designed to open a DDE channel between VBA and Windows' Program Manager (which is still a component of Windows 95 and Windows NT 4.0). In `OpenHailingFrequencies`, a variable named `channel` is declared to store the channel number returned by the `DDEInitiate` method. An `On Error GoTo` handler is established just in case something goes wrong. (This is always a good idea, because DDE connections are notoriously flaky.)

If all goes well, the channel number is stored in the `channel` variable, a `MsgBox` function tells the user the connection has been established, and the channel number is returned. If an error occurs, the code jumps to the `BadConnection` label, displays an error message, and returns 0.

When your procedure is finished with its DDE conversation, you need to terminate the link between the client and server. You do this by running the DDETerminate method:

```
DDETerminate Channel
```

Here, *Channel* is the channel number returned by the DDEInitiate method.

Controlling the Server Application

Once you have an open channel, you can use the DDEExecute method to control the other application. You can send either commands the server application understands (such as commands from its macro language, if it has one) or keystrokes. DDEExecute has the following syntax:

```
DDEExecute(Channel, String)
```

Channel	The channel returned by the DDEInitiate method.
String	A text string representing the commands to run in the application.

The tricky part of the DDEExecute method is the ***String*** argument; its form depends entirely on the application. Excel and Word for Windows let you use their macro commands, provided that you enclose the commands in square brackets ([]). Other applications also let you use their macro commands, but they don't support the square-brackets standard. Other programs have no macro language, but they do have special DDE commands. Finally, some applications have no special commands to use, but they let you control the application by sending keystroke sequences with the DDEExecute method.

NOTE: SENDING DDE KEYSTROKES

To send keystrokes with DDEExecute, use the same key formats I showed you earlier for the SendKeys statement. For example, the DDEExecute(Channel,"^v") statement sends the key combination Ctrl-V to the application linked to VBA by Channel. Note, however, that you can't use DDEExecute to send keys to a dialog box. For that you need to use the SendKeys method.

Listing 13.5 uses a couple of examples of the DDEExecute method.

Listing 13.5. Using DDEExecute to control a server application.

```
Sub CreateWorkbookIcon()

    Dim channel As Integer
    Dim strPath As String, strName As String, strApp As String

    On Error GoTo BadConnection
```

continues

Listing 13.5. continued

```
    '
    ' Get info required for program item
    '
    strPath = ActiveWorkbook.Path & "\" & ActiveWorkbook.Name
    strName = Left(ActiveWorkbook.Name, Len(ActiveWorkbook.Name) - 4)
    strApp = Application.Path & "\Excel.exe"
    '
    ' Establish the DDE connection to Program Manager
    '
    channel = DDEInitiate("Progman", "Progman")
    '
    ' Create the group and item
    '
    DDEExecute channel, "[CreateGroup(""Excel Workbooks"")]"
    DDEExecute channel, "[AddItem(""" & strPath & """,""" & strName & """,""""" &
    ➥strApp & """"")]"
    DDETerminate channel

    Exit Sub

BadConnection:
    MsgBox "Could not open a channel to Program Manager!", vbExclamation

End Sub
```

The `CreateWorkbookIcon` procedure uses a DDE link with Program Manager to create a new folder on the Programs menu and add an icon for the active workbook. The procedure begins by setting up an error handler and gathering the information you need to create a group and icon:

- The `strPath` variable holds the full path and filename for the active workbook.
- The `strName` variable strips off the file's extension so that you can use just the primary name as the icon's title.
- The `strApp` variable combines the application's path with the name of its executable file. Program Manager will use this data to determine the icon to use with the new program item.

With that out of the way, the procedure opens a channel to Program Manager's "Progman" topic. The first `DDEExecute` method runs Program Manager's `CreateGroup` function to create a new group called Excel Workbooks. The second `DDEExecute` method runs Program Manager's `AddItem` function to create the new program item. The `DDETerminate` method then closes the channel.

Exchanging Data with the Server Application

As you've seen, each DDE conversation between the client and server is established on a specified topic. Everything else the two applications "discuss" in the current DDE session is limited to subjects related to the topic. For example, in the preceding section, you saw how the server's built-in functions are a fit subject to include in the conversation.

We'll now turn to another subject you can use in your DDE dialogues: data items. Each server application that supports DDE defines one or more items that can be shared with the client. For example, a typical spreadsheet item is a cell, and a typical word processor item is a bookmark (in other words, a named chunk of text). These items are always composed of simple text and numbers; graphics and other high-level objects can't be transferred in a DDE conversation.

The next two sections show you how to use the `DDERequest` and `DDEPoke` methods to exchange data items between the client and server.

Receiving Data from the Server

If the server has data you would like to transfer into, say, a worksheet cell, you can establish a DDE link between the two applications and then use the `DDERequest` method to retrieve the data:

`DDERequest(`***`Channel`***`, `***`Item`***`)`

`Channel`	The channel returned by the `DDEInitiate` method.
`Item`	A string that specifies the data item you want to retrieve from the server.

Listing 13.6 runs through an example. Note that for this listing (and others in this chapter) you'll likely need to adjust the paths used in order to get these procedures to work on your system.

Listing 13.6. Using `DDERequest` to retrieve data from an application.

```
Sub RequestWordData()

    Dim channel As Integer
    Dim wordData As Variant
    Dim getString As String
    On Error GoTo BailOut
    '
    ' Start Word
    '
    Application.StatusBar = "Starting Word..."
    Shell "C:\Program Files\Microsoft Office\Office\Winword.exe", 6
    '
    ' Initiate channel with System topic
    '
    channel = DDEInitiate("Winword", "System")
    '
    ' Open the document you want to work with
    '
```

continues

Listing 13.6. continued

```
    Application.StatusBar = "Opening Word document..."
    DDEExecute channel, "[FileOpen ""C:\My Documents\Memo.doc""]"
    DDETerminate channel
    '
    ' Initiate new channel with document
    '
    channel = DDEInitiate("Winword", "C:\My Documents\Memo.doc")
    '
    ' Find keyword and add a bookmark
    '
    DDEExecute channel, "[StartOfDocument]"
    DDEExecute channel, "[EditFind .Find = ""ACME""]"
    DDEExecute channel, "[SelectCurSentence]"
    DDEExecute channel, "[EditBookmark .Name = ""Gotcha""]"
    '
    ' Retrieve the bookmark and store it
    '
    wordData = DDERequest(channel, "Gotcha")
    getString = wordData(1)
    Worksheets("Sheet1").[A2].Value = getString
    '
    ' Quit Word and terminate channel
    '
    DDEExecute channel, "[FileExit 1]"
    DDETerminate channel

    Exit Sub

BailOut:
    DDETerminate channel
    MsgBox "DDE operation failed!", vbExclamation

End Sub
```

The idea behind the `RequestWordData` procedure is to find a particular section of text in a word document and then read it into Excel. The procedure begins by setting up an error handler, starting Word, establishing the channel, and opening the document.

The first `DDEExecute` method moves to the start of the document. The second `DDEExecute` looks for the text string `"ACME"` in the document. Then the entire sentence containing "ACME" is selected, and a final `DDEExecute` creates a bookmark named "Gotcha" for the selected sentence.

To retrieve the text, the `DDERequest` method asks Word for the "Gotcha" item and stores it in the `wordData` variable. Note that the `wordData` variable is declared as a `Variant`. This is required because the `DDERequest` method always returns an array. To save the bookmark text, you set the `getString` variable equal to `wordData(1)`. The retrieved data is stored in cell A1 of Sheet1; then Word is closed (note that `FileExit 1` saves changes) and the channel is terminated.

NOTE: THE TOPICS TOPIC

You can use DDERequest to get a list of all the server's open documents. Just initiate a DDE channel on the System topic and then use DDERequest to return the Topics item. Here's an example:

```
openFiles = DDERequest(channel, "Topics")
```

Here, openFiles is a Variant variable. The server will return the list of open files as an array.

Sending Data to the Server

Like all good conversations, the exchange between the client and server is a two-way street. Therefore, just as your procedures can request data from the server, so too can the client send data to the server. This is handled by the DDEPoke method:

DDEPoke(***Channel***, ***Item***, ***Data***)

Channel	The channel returned by the DDEInitiate method.
Item	A string that specifies the data item to which the data will be sent.
Data	The data you want to send to the server application (it must be plain text or numbers).

Listing 13.7 shows an example.

Listing 13.7. Using DDEPoke to send data to an application.

```
Sub SendDataToWord()

    Dim channel As Integer, pokeData As Variant
    On Error GoTo BailOut
    '
    ' Start Word
    '
    Application.StatusBar = "Starting Word..."
    Shell "C:\Program Files\Microsoft Office\Office\Winword.exe", 6
    '
    ' Initiate channel with System topic
    '
    channel = DDEInitiate("Winword", "System")
    '
    ' Open the document we want to work with
    '
    Application.StatusBar = "Opening Word document..."
    DDEExecute channel, "[FileOpen ""C:\My Documents\Memo.doc""]"
    DDETerminate channel
```

continues

Listing 13.7. continued

```
    '
    ' Initiate new channel with document
    '
    channel = DDEInitiate("Winword", "C:\My Documents\Memo.doc")
    '
    'Get the data to be sent
    '
    Application.StatusBar = "Sending data..."
    Set pokeData = Worksheets("Sheet1").[B2]
    '
    'Send it to the "Gotcha" bookmark
    '
    DDEPoke channel, "Gotcha", pokeData
    '
    ' Quit Word and terminate channel
    '
    Application.StatusBar = "Shutting down Word..."
    DDEExecute channel, "[FileExit 1]"
    DDETerminate channel
    Application.StatusBar = False

    Exit Sub

BailOut:
    DDETerminate channel
    MsgBox "DDE operation failed!", vbExclamation
    Application.StatusBar = False
End Sub
```

This procedure performs the opposite function of the procedure we looked at in Listing 13.6. Here, VBA takes text from a cell and sends it to a bookmark in Word. The procedure begins by setting up the error handler, starting Word, and establishing the link. The cell data to send is stored in the `pokeData` variable. Note that the procedure uses `Set` to store a Range object in `pokeData`. Then the `DDEPoke` method sends the cell's data to the "Gotcha" bookmark in the Word document. A `DDEExecute` statement shuts down Word and saves changes to the document, the link is then terminated, and the procedure exits.

Summary

This chapter walked you through a number of techniques for working with other applications. The most straightforward of these techniques is the simple `Shell` function, which starts another application. You can activate any running application by using the `AppActivate` statement, and you can send keystrokes to a running application by using the `SendKeys` method.

You also learned about dynamic data exchange (DDE). This protocol lets DDE-enabled applications "talk" to each other and exchange data items. VBA has several DDE functions that let you initialize a DDE channel, execute the server application's commands, send data back and forth, and terminate the link.

Here's a list of chapters where you'll find related information:

- To learn how to send OLE objects back and forth between applications, see Chapter 14, "Programming OLE and ActiveX Objects."
- I'll show you how to deal with other programs using OLE automation in Chapter 15, "Controlling Applications Via OLE Automation."
- Chapter 20, "Internet and Intranet Programming Topics," shows you how to manipulate Internet Explorer via VBA code running in another application.
- In Chapter 22, "E-Mail and Groupware Programming with Outlook," you'll learn how to control Outlook from your VBA applications.
- For detailed information on VBA's error-trapping techniques, see Chapter 23, "Trapping Program Errors."
- VBA lets you get and set entries in the Windows Registry. I show you how it's done in Chapter 25, "Programming the Windows API."

CHAPTER 14

Programming OLE and ActiveX Objects

IN THIS CHAPTER

You can't have everything. Where would you put it?

—*Steven Wright*

The techniques outlined in the preceding chapter are certainly useful, and you'll turn to them often enough to solve particular programming problems. However, our goal here in Part IV is to unleash "application integration," and merely activating another application or sending it a few keystrokes hardly qualifies. No, to achieve true integration, you need to be able to exchange data and manipulate other programs behind the scenes without the user's necessarily being aware of what your program is up to.

The Dynamic Data Exchange techniques discussed in the last chapter took us a step closer to that goal. By establishing a channel between applications, you can control the other program and exchange data in a relatively quick and reliable manner. Unfortunately, DDE is limited both by the level of interaction you can achieve (macro commands or a few DDE-specific commands) and by the types of data it can exchange (text only).

For richer interaction and more flexible data exchange, you need to turn to OLE—Object Linking and Embedding. OLE is one of Microsoft's most important technologies. It can be described without hyperbole as the foundation of all of Microsoft's future development efforts in operating systems, applications, and the Internet. OLE offers two major advantages to the VBA developer:

- The ability to expose the object model used in other applications and then manipulate those objects in much the same way you manipulate the objects in the client application. Working with an application's objects, properties, and methods—this is known as OLE Automation—gives you far more power than the measly commands provided by DDE.
- The ability to work with richer data types—namely, the OLE objects that are supported by other applications. For example, instead of inserting text from a Word document in an Excel spreadsheet, you can insert an entire Word document as a linked or embedded object.

This chapter introduces you to OLE and then shows you how to work with OLE objects (or ActiveX objects, as they're now called) within your VBA procedures. I'll show you how to manipulate other applications via OLE Automation in Chapter 15, "Controlling Applications Via OLE Automation."

First, Some OLE Fundamentals

Although for the most part this book has shunned long-winded technical explanations in favor of practical know-how, it's important to know some OLE background in order to get the most out of it as a developer. To that end, this section explores some important OLE underpinnings.

Before diving into these theoretical waters, however, you should know about three crucial OLE concepts: *objects, servers,* and *clients:*

Object: In the OLE world, an object is not only data—a slice of text, a graphic, a sound, a chunk of a spreadsheet, or whatever—but also one or more functions for creating, accessing, and using that data.

Server application: The application that you use to create and edit an object. Also known as the *source application.*

Client application: The application that you use to store a linked or embedded object created with a server application. Also known as the *container application.*

With these simple fundamentals in hand, you can now take a closer look at OLE architecture. However, OLE is a large, complicated standard, so I'll only scratch the surface here by restricting your look at OLE's plumbing to just the following four topics:

- Compound documents
- The Component Object Model
- OLE Automation
- ActiveX controls (formerly known as OLE controls)

Compound Documents

A *compound document* is a document that contains, along with its native data, one or more objects that were created using other applications. The key point is that the compound document's native data and its objects can have entirely different data formats. For example, a word processing document can include a spreadsheet range object or a sound clip object. The client application doesn't need to know a thing about these alien data formats. All it has to know is the name of the server application that created the data and how to display the data. All this information (and more) is included free of charge as part of the object, so it's readily available to the client application.

As the name Object Linking and Embedding implies, you create a compound document by either linking objects to the document or embedding objects in the document. The next few sections explain linking and embedding in more depth.

Understanding Linking

Linking is one of the OLE methods you can use to insert an object into a file from a client application and thus create a compound document. In this case, the object includes only the following information:

- The Registry key needed to invoke the object's server application (see "OLE and the Registry" later in this chapter for details).

- A metafile that contains GDI (Windows' Graphics Device Interface) instructions on how to display the object. These instructions simply generate the primitives (lines, circles, arcs, and so on) that create an image of the object. These primitives are the heart of the GDI, and they form the basis of any image you see on-screen. So the client application doesn't have to know a thing about the object itself; it just follows the metafile's instructions blindly, and a perfect replica of the object's image appears.
- A pointer to the server application file (the *source document)* that contains the original data.

Linking offers many advantages, but three are most relevant to our purposes. First, the link lets the client application check the source document for changes. If it finds that the data has been modified, OLE can use the link to update the object automatically. For example, suppose you insert a linked spreadsheet object into a word processing document. If you revise some of the numbers in the spreadsheet sometime down the road, the object inside the document is automatically updated to reflect the new numbers. However, this updating is automatic only under certain conditions:

- If the client application is running and has the compound document open, the update is automatic.
- If the compound document isn't open when the data is changed, the object gets updated automatically the next time you open the compound document.
- Most OLE applications let you disable automatic updating either for individual documents or for the application as a whole. In this case, you need to perform the updates either manually or programmatically. (I'll show you how this is done later in this chapter.)

Second, since the object "knows" where to find both the server application and the source document, you can edit the object from within the client application. In most cases, double-clicking the object invokes the server and loads the appropriate source file. However, as you'll see a bit later, you can also load an object for editing from within a VBA procedure. Either way, you can then edit the original data and exit the server application, and your object is once again updated automatically.

Third, since the source data exists in a separate file, you can easily reuse the data in other compound documents, and you can edit the data directly from within the server application.

Understanding Embedding

One of the problems associated with linking is that if you distribute the compound document, you also have to distribute the source document. Similarly, if you move the source document to a different location on your system, the link breaks. (However, you can edit the link by hand or via code to reflect the new location.)

NOTE: LINK TRACKING

Microsoft promises that future versions of Windows will support *link tracking*. This means that the operating system will monitor links and update them automatically if you move a source file to a new location.

Embedding solves these problems by inserting an object not only with the server's Registry information and the metafile for displaying the object, but also with the object's *data*. This way, everything you need to display and work with the object exists within the object itself. There's no need for a separate source file, so you can distribute the compound document knowing that the recipient will receive the data intact.

In fact, embedding lets you *create* server objects from within the client application. If you're working with Word for Windows, for example, you can insert a new spreadsheet object right from Word. OLE will start Excel so that you can create the new object, but when you exit Excel, the object will exist only within the Word compound document. There will be no separate Excel file. Once again, this process is also available via VBA code.

Note that many applications can operate only as OLE servers. This means that they aren't standalone applications and therefore have no way to create files on their own. They exist only to create OLE objects for compound documents. Microsoft Office ships with several examples of such applications, including WordArt and Microsoft Graph.

Should You Link or Embed?

Perhaps the most confusing aspect of OLE is determining whether you should link your objects or embed them. As you've seen, the only major difference between linking and embedding is that a linked object stores only a pointer to its data, while an embedded object stores its own data internally.

With this in mind, you should link your objects if any of the following situations apply:

- You want to keep your compound documents small. The information stored in a linked object—the pointers to the server and source document, and the metafile—consume only about 1.5 KB, so very little overhead is associated with linking. If you're using WordPad as the client, you can check this out for yourself. Click the object and select Edit | Object Properties, or right-click the object and select Object Properties from the shortcut menu. The properties sheet that appears shows you the size of the object, as shown in Figure 14.1.

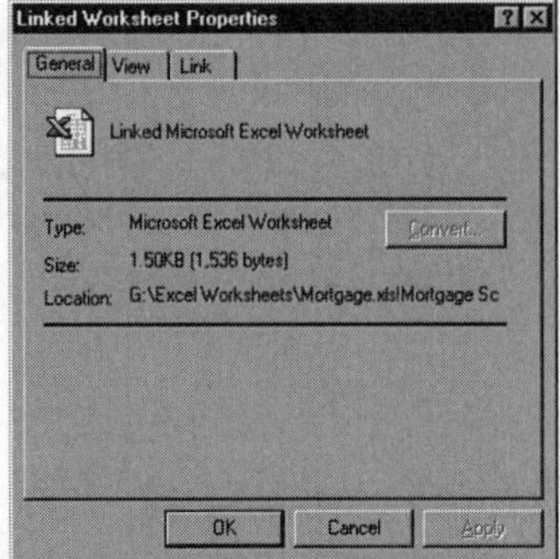

FIGURE 14.1.
The WordPad properties sheet for a linked object. Notice that the linked object takes up only 1.5 KB.

- You're sure the source document won't be moved or deleted. To maintain the link, OLE requires that the source file remain in the same place. If the document gets moved or deleted, the link is broken (although, as I've said, most OLE applications let you reestablish the link by modifying the path to the source document).
- You need to keep the source file as a separate document in case you want to make changes to it later, or in case you need it for other compound documents. You're free to link an object to as many client files as you like. If you think you'll be using the source data in different places, you should link it to maintain a separate file.
- You won't be sending the compound document via e-mail or floppy disk. Again, OLE expects the linked source data to appear in a specific place. If you send the compound document to someone else, he might not have the proper source file to maintain the link.

Similarly, you should embed your objects if any of the following situations apply:

- You don't care how big your compound documents get. Embedding works best in situations in which you have lots of hard disk space and lots of memory. For example, Figure 14.2 shows the WordPad properties sheet for an embedded object. This is the same Excel worksheet that was linked in Figure 14.1, but you can see that the embedded object is much larger.

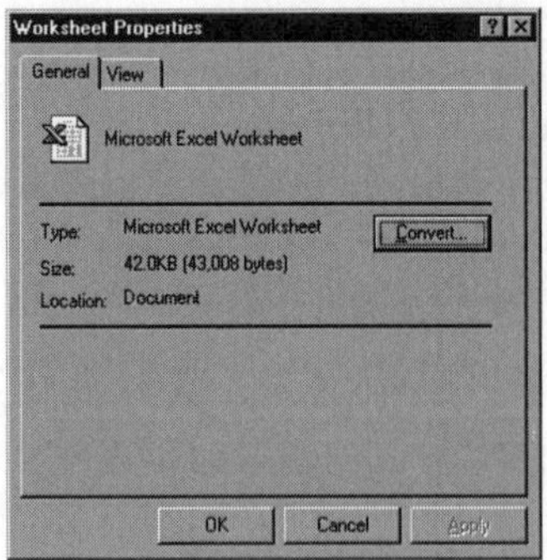

FIGURE 14.2.
The WordPad properties sheet for an embedded object. Because embedded objects store their own data, they're much larger than linked objects.

- You don't need to keep the source file as a separate document. If you need to use the source data only once, embedding it means you can get rid of the source file (or never have to create one in the first place) and reduce the clutter on your hard disk.
- You'll be sending the compound documents, and you want to make sure the object arrives intact. If you send a file containing an embedded object, the other person will see the data complete and unaltered. If he wants to edit the object, however, he'll need to have the server application installed.

NOTE: OLE NEEDS MEMORY

Whether you link or embed, OLE will still put a strain on your system's memory resources. Although Microsoft has made some strides in improving the efficiency of the OLE standard (particularly with the new, slimmed down, ActiveX interface), the memory cost is still high. You'll need a minimum of 12 MB of physical RAM to achieve anything approaching reasonable performance out of OLE.

Visual Editing

In the original incarnation of OLE, double-clicking an object opened a new window for the server application and loaded the source document (if the object was linked) or loaded the object's data (if the object was embedded). This process is called *open editing.*

When OLE 2.0 debuted a couple of years ago, it introduced the idea of *visual editing* (also known as *in-place editing*). When you double-click an embedded object, instead of your seeing the server application in a separate window, certain features of the client application's window are temporarily hidden in favor of the server application's features. (Linked objects still use open editing.) Here's a summary of the changes that occur in the client application:

- The document window's title bar changes to tell you what kind of object you're now working with. (Not all applications do this.)
- The menu bar (with the exception of the File and Window menus) is replaced by the server application's menu bar.
- The toolbars are replaced by the server application's toolbars.

Essentially, the client application "becomes" the server application while still maintaining the object's context in the compound document. Let's look at an example. First, Figure 14.3 shows the normal Microsoft Excel window.

If you now insert a Microsoft Word document into Excel, OLE changes the menu bar and toolbars from Excel's to Word's, as you can see in Figure 14.4. However, the rest of the Excel interface—including the row and column headers, the underlying worksheet cells, and the sheet tabs—remain visible to give context to the embedded object. (To exit visual editing, click outside the object.)

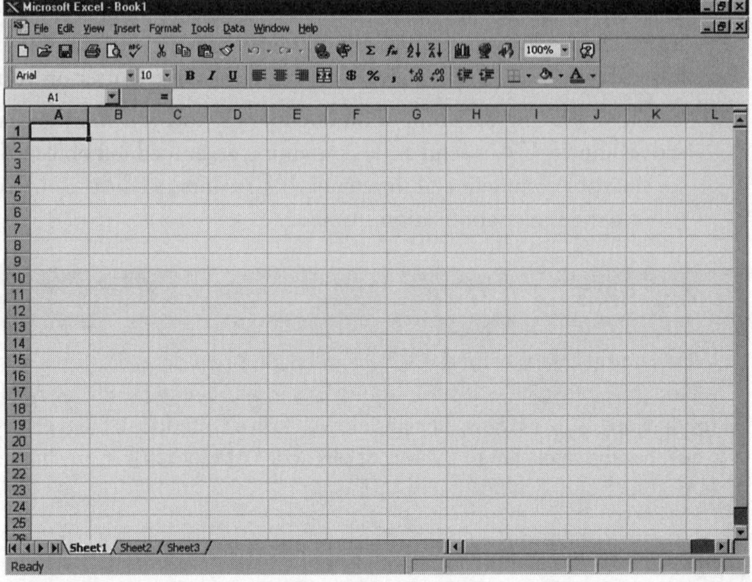

FIGURE 14.3.
The Microsoft Excel window before you insert an object.

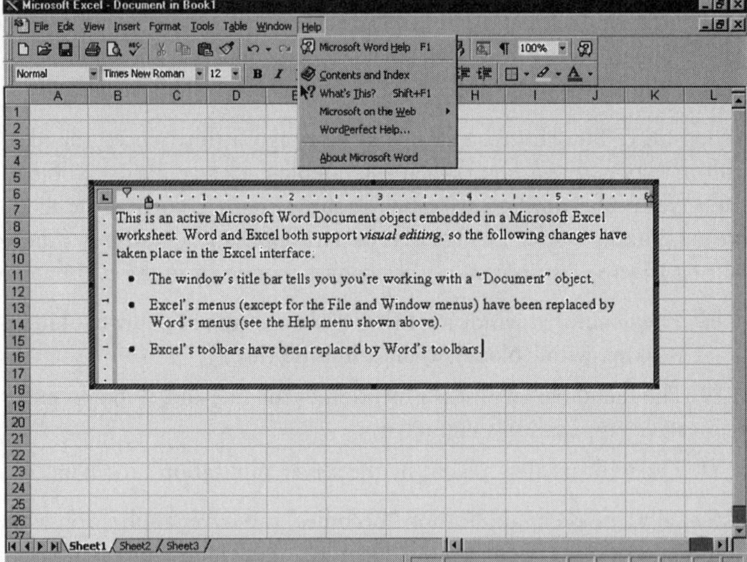

FIGURE 14.4.
During visual editing, the Excel window assumes many features of the Word window.

The Component Object Model

The Component Object Model (COM) is the heart and soul of OLE. It defines not only the standards that server applications use to create objects, but also the mechanisms by which server and client applications interact when dealing with objects.

These features are implemented as *interfaces,* which are collections of related functions. A server application makes an OLE component (that is, an object) available by implementing an interface for the component. When a client application needs to work with a server's OLE components, it just uses the appropriate interface. The client application doesn't have to know anything about the underlying structure of the component. It just works with the interface functions, and the linking or embedding (or whatever) happens in a consistent manner.

This is what's happening when you use VBA code to interact with the container application's objects. You don't have to know anything about how these objects operate internally or what data structures they use; you just have to manipulate the object interface: the properties, methods, and events exposed by each object.

One of the chief features of COM is that the interfaces it supports are extensible. In other words, when a vendor upgrades its components, it doesn't change the existing behavior of the interface; it just adds new functionality. (This is done either by extending an existing interface or by creating new interfaces; client applications can query the server to find out what's new.) This way, client applications know they can work with a server reliably and that an interface function used today will work exactly the same 10 years from now. The *OLE Programmer's Reference* says that, metaphorically, an object's interface acts like a "contract" that guarantees its behavior for prospective client applications.

NOTE: OLE VERSION NUMBERS NO LONGER EXIST

This explains why Microsoft has dropped version numbering from OLE. A new version number for a software product implies that the underlying functionality of the product has changed. However, thanks to its extensibility, that will never happen with OLE, because existing functions will always work the same. So, in a sense, you'll never get a "new" version of OLE, just a better implementation of the existing version.

The starting point for COM is the *class factory.* This is an object in the server application that creates instances of OLE components. When you tell your client application that you want to insert a particular object, the client notifies the appropriate server's class factory that an instance of the object is required. The class factory then creates the object and informs the client application of the appropriate interface to use in order to access the new object.

After the class factory has done its work, the server and client communicate (with COM as the intermediary) through various interfaces. These interfaces control a number of OLE features, including compound documents, visual editing, how data is transferred between server and client, how an object is stored in the client, how the server notifies the client of changes, and many more.

OLE Automation

The beauty of OLE is not only how easy it is to insert objects in a client application (especially via drag-and-drop), but the access you have to the object's original tools. With a simple double-click, you can edit the object with the full power of the server's menus and commands.

However, until recently, the one thing that was missing was the ability to control the server via code. For example, it would be nice to be able to create new objects using VBA procedures. This is especially true if you're developing corporate applications for end-users. Editing or creating an object, whether you use visual editing or open editing, has meant that you must at least be familiar with the server application. And although *you* might be willing to spend time and effort learning a new program, the users of your VBA applications might not be.

This has all changed with the advent of OLE Automation (now usually called just Automation). Applications that support OLE Automation "expose" their objects to VBA (and any other applications and development tools that support the OLE Automation standard). So, just as, say, Excel VBA can recognize and manipulate an Excel worksheet range (a Range object), it can also recognize and manipulate objects from other OLE Automation applications. For example, all the Office object models that you examined in Part II, "Unleashing Microsoft Office Objects," are also available via OLE Automation. This means you could also use Excel VBA to manipulate a Word Document object or a PowerPoint Presentation object. Also, many applications that don't use the Visual Basic Editor development environment are still programmable via OLE Automation. In Office 97, for example, this includes Outlook, Binder, and even Internet Explorer.

ActiveX Controls

If you use any modern, full-featured application, you've probably gasped at the disk real estate that the program gobbles up. Executable files that are 3 or 4 MB in size aren't that unusual these days. These behemoth files are indicative of the biggest disease facing software today: code bloat. Each new iteration of an application crams in more bells, more whistles, and more gee-aren't-our-programmers-clever features. If you can use these new baubles, the toll on your hard disk free space is probably worth it. More likely, however, you might use one or two of the new features, and the rest you couldn't care less about. In the end, most software programs follow the old 80-20 rule: you spend 80 percent of your time using 20 percent of the features.

In response to user complaints, the software industry is finally doing something about this problem. Someday soon you'll be able to install only the features you'll actually use and consign the rest to the obscurity they deserve. The engine behind this change is *component-based software.* These are small software modules that perform specific tasks. For example, a spell-checking component would do nothing but check an application's spelling. By combining such modules, you can create a customized version of a software package that's tailored to your needs.

The current standard for these software components is the ActiveX control (formerly known as the OLE control). These are prebuilt OLE objects that developers can plug into existing applications. These objects expose various properties and methods, so the developer can manipulate how the program appears and how it interacts with the user.

ActiveX controls first appeared on the Internet in Microsoft's Internet Explorer 3.0 browser. When developers insert ActiveX controls into Web pages, Internet Explorer downloads them to the user's computer and executes them. This technique is used mostly to spice up Web pages with dynamic content, such as an animation or an order form that includes running totals. However, you can also use ActiveX controls in your VBA applications by inserting them into your user forms.

OLE and the Registry

Windows 95 and Windows NT make extensive use of the Registry to store all kinds of information about your system. So it will come as no surprise that the Registry plays a big part in OLE as well.

NOTE: VIEWING THE REGISTRY

To view the Registry data, click Windows' Start button and select the Run command. In Windows 95, type `regedit` and click OK; in Windows NT, type `regedt32` and click OK. If you would like to know more about how the Registry works in Windows 95, see my book *Paul McFedries' Windows 95 Unleashed, Premier Edition* (Sams Publishing, 1996).

Programmatic Identifier Keys

Most OLE-related Registry data can be found in the `HKEY_CLASSES_ROOT` key (which is an alias of `HKEY_LOCAL_MACHINE\SOFTWARE\Classes`). `HKEY_CLASSES_ROOT` consists of a long list of extensions, followed by an equally long list of file types, which are known, officially, as *programmatic identifiers*. For example, Figure 14.5 shows the key for the programmatic ID for an Excel worksheet.

The key's default value is the name of the file type that the programmatic ID represents (Microsoft Excel Worksheet in Figure 14.5). Here's a rundown of the OLE-related subkeys that you'll find in the programmatic ID key:

`CLSID`: This is the object's *class ID*, a 16-byte (32 hexadecimal digit) value that's also known as the object's Globally Unique Identifier (GUID). As the latter name implies, `CLSID`s are values that uniquely identify an object. The value of the `CLSID` key points to a subkey of the `HKEY_CLASSES_ROOT\CLSID` key (discussed in a moment).

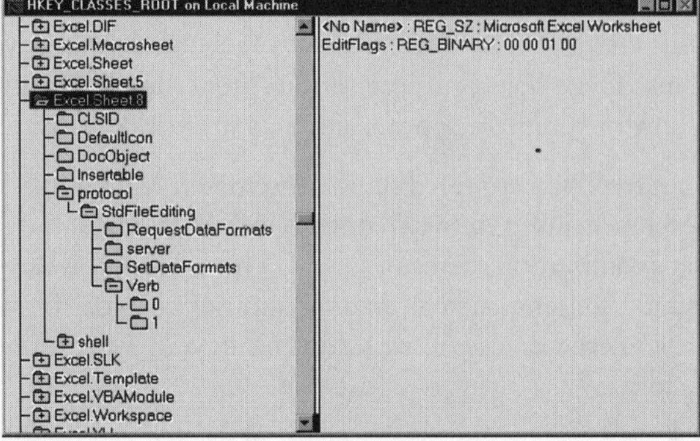

FIGURE 14.5.
The programmatic ID keys contain lots of useful OLE information.

> **NOTE: HOW `CLSID` VALUES ARE GENERATED**
>
> `CLSID`s are either assigned by Microsoft or generated by a program that comes in the Microsoft Software Development Kit. How can a vendor be sure that its object's `CLSID` is unique? Well, if you get the value from Microsoft, Microsoft can check its database to ensure uniqueness. All Microsoft-generated `CLSID` values use the following format (where *xxxxxxxx* is a unique sequence of eight hexadecimal digits):
>
> `{xxxxxxxx-0000-0000-C000-000000000046}`
>
> If you use the program, consider how each value is generated. The first eight digits are random, the next four digits are generated by the current date and time, and the last 20 digits are generated based on the hardware details of the developer's computer. That combination is about as unique as it gets!

`Insertable`: This key is a flag that tells COM that this type of object can be inserted into a client document. When you select Insert | Object in an OLE client application, COM gathers all the objects that have the `Insertable` key and displays them in the Object dialog box.

`DefaultIcon`: If you elect to insert an object as an icon, OLE uses the data in this key to determine which icon to display.

`StdExecute\server`: This subkey gives the client application the pathname of the server application to be used to execute the object.

`StdFileEditing\server`: This subkey gives the client application the pathname of the server application to be used to edit the object.

`Verb`: This subkey lists the actions you can take with a linked or embedded object. Most objects have two verbs: `Edit` (which activates visual editing) and `Open` (which activates open editing). Others—such as `AVIFile` (video files) and `SoundRec` (audio files)—also have a `Play` verb that plays the object. As you'll see, VBA has methods that you can use to invoke these verbs.

CLSID Keys

As I said, the `CLSID` subkey contains a setting that points to a subkey of `HKEY_CLASSES_ROOT\CLSID`. For example, the Excel worksheet object's `CLSID` subkey points to the following key, as shown in Figure 14.6:

```
HKEY_CLASSES_ROOT\CLSID\{00020820-0000-0000-C000-000000000046}
```

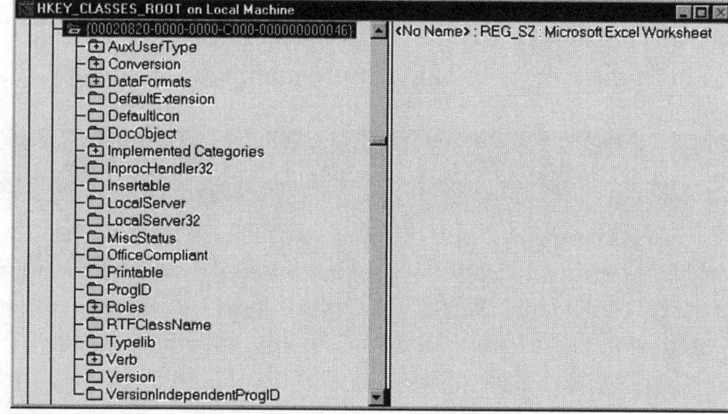

FIGURE 14.6. *Each OLE object has a subkey in the* `HKEY_CLASSES_ROOT\CLSID` *key.*

The default value of this key is the name of the object. The subkeys contain lots of OLE-related data. Here's a summary of a few of these keys:

`AuxUserType`: Alternative (shorter) names for the object type.

`Conversion`: Information used during object conversion. Items in the `Readable` subkey are formats that the server application can convert into the object's format; items in the `Readwritable` subkey are file formats into which the server can convert the object.

`DataFormats`: The data formats supported by the server application. Most of the formats are listed as integer values that correspond to default formats defined by Windows.

`DefaultExtension`: The default extension for this type of object. If you leave off the extension when you enter a filename in the Insert Object dialog box, OLE tacks on the extension specified in this subkey.

`DefaultIcon`: If you elect to insert an object as an icon, OLE uses the data in this key to determine which icon to display. (This is the same as `DefaultIcon` in the programmatic ID subkey, discussed earlier.)

`InProcHandler32`: 32-bit in-process handlers (DLL files) used to help the server and client applications communicate.

`InProcServer32`: 32-bit in-process servers (DLL files) that a client application can call instead of a full-blown server application.

`Insertable`: This key is a flag that tells COM that this type of object can be inserted into a client document. When you select Insert | Object in the client, COM gathers all the objects that have the `Insertable` key and displays them in the Object dialog box. (This is the same as `Insertable` in the programmatic ID subkey, discussed earlier.)

`LocalServer` and `LocalServer32`: The full pathname of the server application. 32-bit applications need only the `LocalServer32` subkey, but the `LocalServer` subkey is also added for backwards compatibility with 16-bit client applications.

`ProgID`: A pointer to the object's programmatic ID.

`Verb`: This subkey lists the actions you can take with a linked or embedded object. (This is the same as `Verb` in the programmatic ID subkey, discussed earlier.)

TIP: MICROSOFT'S OLE/COM OBJECT VIEWER

Instead of making you grope blindly through these Registry settings, Microsoft offers a handy tool designed to present your system's OLE object information in a structured format. This utility is called the OLE/COM Object Viewer, and you can get it from Microsoft's Web site by dialing the following address into your favorite browser:

`http://www.microsoft.com/oledev/olecom/oleview.htm`

Programming Linked and Embedded Objects

Object Linking and Embedding (OLE) can add some slick new tricks to your Office arsenal. However, the price you pay for this advanced technology is added complexity. This is especially true for novice users, who might be uncomfortable with the various choices available in a typical OLE operation. For example, if you've copied data from the server application, the client's Paste Special command gives you a number of choices: You can paste the information as an object or, depending on the data, you can paste it as a picture or as text; you can paste the data linked or unlinked; or you can paste the data as an icon or in full view.

VBA can help, because it gives you control over each of these decisions at the procedural level. You can give your users a single command or toolbar button that creates a specified OLE object and hides the gory details. The rest of this chapter shows you how to create and work with OLE objects using VBA.

Inserting OLE Objects

VBA 5.0

In previous versions of VBA, each linked or embedded OLE object was an instance of the OLEObject class, and the collection of all OLE objects in a document was represented by `OLEObjects`. These objects still exist in Excel VBA, but they've been superseded by more general objects in VBA 5.0.

In particular, a linked or embedded object is now an instance of the Shape class, which represents graphical objects. (This makes sense when you remember that a linked or embedded object is represented visually in the client application as a metafile drawn by the GDI, as explained earlier.) The collection of all OLE objects (and, indeed, all graphical objects) in a document is represented by the `Shapes` class. This section shows you how to use the `Shapes` object to link and embed OLE objects in the container application.

Understanding the AddOLEObject Method

To insert a new OLE object, the `Shapes` collection provides the `AddOLEObject` method. Here's the syntax of this method in all its 12-argument glory:

```
Document.Shapes.AddOLEObject(ClassType, FileName, LinkToFile, DisplayAsIcon,
➥IconFileName, IconIndex, IconLabel, Left, Top, Width, Height, Anchor)
```

Document	The document to which you want to add the OLE object.
ClassType	If you're inserting a new object, use *ClassType* to specify the type of object you want to insert. For example, to insert a new Word for Windows 97 document, you would use `Word.Document.8` for *ClassType* (see the next section for more information).
FileName	If you're inserting an object from an existing server file, use *FileName* to specify the name of the file. If you use this parameter, don't specify a *ClassType*.
LinkToFile	A logical value that determines whether the object created from *FileName* is linked or embedded. If `True`, the object is linked to the original file; if `False` or omitted, the object is embedded.
DisplayAsIcon	A logical value that determines how the object is displayed. If `True`, the object is displayed as an icon; if `False` or omitted, the object is displayed in its normal picture form.
IconFileName	If *DisplayAsIcon* is `True`, use *IconFileName* to specify the name of the file that contains the icon you want to display. If you omit *IconFileName*, the default icon for the OLE class is used.
IconIndex	Some files contain multiple icons, so you can use *IconIndex* to select the icon you want to use (where the first icon is 0, the second is 1, and so on). For this to work, *DisplayIcon* must be `True`, *IconFileName* must point to a valid icon file, and you must specify the *IconLabel* argument.
IconLabel	If *DisplayAsIcon* is `True`, *IconLabel* spells out a text string that appears underneath the icon.
Left	The distance, in points, from the left edge of the object to the left edge of the document window (the default value is 0).

`Top`	The distance, in points, from the top edge of the object to the top edge of the document window (the default value is 0).
`Width`	The width of the object in points.
`Height`	The height of the object in points.
`Anchor`	(Word only) The Range object to which the control is bound. In other words, if you move the range, the OLE object will move along with it.

I'll show you how to use the `AddOLEObject` method and its arguments in the next few sections.

NOTE: EXCEL AND POWERPOINT ARE DIFFERENT

Excel and PowerPoint use a slightly different syntax for the `AddOLEObject` method. In these programs, use `Link` instead of the `LinkToFile` argument.

Looking Up an Object's Class Type

Before you see the `AddOLEObject` method in action, let's take a quick look at how you find out an object's class type (also known as its *programmatic ID*) for the `ClassType` argument.

I mentioned earlier that the Windows Registry contains information about applications installed on your system and, in particular, it contains data related to applications that support OLE. To find out the class types of the OLE objects available on your system, first start the Registry Editor, and then open `HKEY_CLASSES_ROOT`.

Now you have two ways to proceed:

- If the object has a default file extension, find the extension in `HKEY_CLASSES_ROOT` and click it. For a Paint bitmap, for example, you would highlight the `.bmp` key. On the right side of the Registry Editor window, look at the entry in the first line: in Windows 95, this entry has the name `(Default)`; in Windows NT, the name is `<No Name>`, as shown in Figure 14.7. The value of this entry is the class type for this object. (In NT, ignore the `REG_SZ` part.)
- For ActiveX controls and OLE servers, there is no default extension. For these objects, scroll down `HKEY_CLASSES_ROOT` until you get past the list of extensions. The rest of `HKEY_CLASSES_ROOT` (except the `CLSID` branch) is a list of the class types installed on your system. You'll have to trudge through this list until you find a class type that corresponds to the object you want to insert.

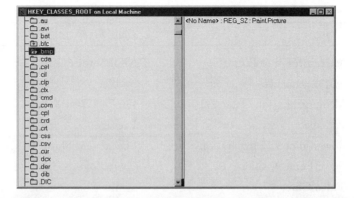

FIGURE 14.7.
In HKEY_CLASSES_ROOT, *highlight the object's file extension to find out its class type.*

> **TIP: AN EASIER WAY TO GET THE CLASS TYPE**
>
> If you're having trouble finding the appropriate class type, or if the object has multiple class types and you're not sure which one to use, you might be able to use the Macro Recorder to do the dirty work for you. Just start the Recorder (see Chapter 1, "Introducing VBA") and then insert the object you want by hand. Stop the recorder, switch to the Visual Basic Editor, and examine the module to see the appropriate `ClassType` argument.

To save you some legwork, Table 14.1 lists some class types for common objects.

Table 14.1. Class types for common objects.

Object	*Class Type*
Bitmap Image	Paint.Picture
Calendar Control	MSCAL.MSCalCtrl.8
Excel 97 Chart	Excel.Chart.8
Excel 97 Worksheet	Excel.Sheet.8
Media Clip	mplayer
Microsoft Clip Gallery	MS_ClipArt_Gallery.2
Microsoft Equation 3.0	Equation.3
Microsoft Graph 97	MSGraph.Chart.8
Microsoft Map	MSMap.8
Microsoft Organization Chart 2.0	OrgPlusWOPX.4
Microsoft Photo Editor Scan	MDPhotoEdScan.3

continues

Table 14.1. continued

Object	*Class Type*
Microsoft Photo Editor	MDPhotoEd.3
MIDI Sequence	midfile
MS Organization Chart 2.0	OrgPlusWOPX.4
Package	Package
PowerPoint 97 Presentation	PowerPoint.Show.8
PowerPoint 97 Slide	PowerPoint.Slide.8
Video Clip	avifile
Wave Sound	SoundRec
Word 97 Document	Word.Document.8
Word 97 Picture	Word.Picture.8
WordPad Document	Wordpad.Document.1

Inserting a New Embedded Object

To insert a new embedded object into a worksheet, you need to run the `AddOLEObject` method with the *`ClassType`* argument. Listing 14.1 provides an example.

Listing 14.1. Using the `AddOLEObject` method to embed a new object in a Word document.

```
Sub InsertOrgChart()

    Dim msgPrompt As String, msgButtons As Integer
    Dim response As Integer, embeddedOrgChart as Object

    msgPrompt = "Are you sure you want to insert a new Organization Chart object?"
    msgButtons = vbOKCancel + vbQuestion
    response = MsgBox(msgPrompt, msgButtons)

    If response = vbOK Then
        Application.StatusBar = "Loading Organization Chart..."
        Set embeddedOrgChart = ActiveDocument.Shapes.AddOLEObject _
            (ClassType:="OrgPlusWOPX.4")
        Application.StatusBar = False
    End If
    Set embeddedOrgChart = Nothing
End Sub
```

The `InsertNewOrgChart` procedure is designed to insert a new Organization Chart object into a worksheet. The procedure begins by constructing the prompt and buttons for a `MsgBox` function, which asks the user if he's sure he wants to insert the object. If OK is clicked, the procedure displays a message in the status bar about loading Organization Chart. Then the `AddOLEObject` method inserts the Organization Chart object into Sheet1 and stores it in the `Object` variable `embeddedOrgChart`.

CAUTION: SET YOUR OBJECT VARIABLES TO NOTHING

Notice at the end of Listing 14.1 that I `Set` the `embeddedOrgChart` variable to `Nothing`. This ensures that the object is terminated and that your procedures don't waste precious system resources.

NOTE: THIS CHAPTER'S CODE LISTINGS

You'll find all the code listings for this chapter on the CD in the file named Chaptr14.doc. If you don't have Word, use Chaptr14.bas instead.

Inserting an Existing File as an Embedded Object

To embed an OLE object from an existing file, you need to run the `AddOLEObject` method with the *`FileName`* argument, and you need to either set the *`LinkToFile`* argument to `False` or omit it altogether. Listing 14.2 shows you how it's done.

Listing 14.2. Using the `AddOLEObject` method to embed an existing file in a Word document.

```
Sub EmbedWorksheet()

    Dim dirOffice as String
    '
    ' Specify the location of the Office files
    '
    dirOffice = "C:\Program Files\Microsoft Office\Office\"
    '
    ' Insert the Excel Samples.xls file
    '
    ActiveDocument.Shapes.AddOLEObject _
        FileName:=dirOffice & "Examples\Samples.xls", _
        DisplayAsIcon:=True, _
        IconFileName:=dirOffice & "Excel.exe", _
        IconIndex:=1, _
        IconLabel:="Excel Sample File - Double-click to open"

End Sub
```

This procedure embeds an Excel worksheet by specifying the filename in the `AddOLEObject` method and by omitting the *`LinkToFile`* argument. For good measure, the procedure also displays the object as an icon by setting the *`DisplayAsIcon`* argument to `True`, specifying both an icon file (the Excel executable) and an icon index, and entering a label to appear beneath the icon.

Inserting an Existing File as a Linked Object

If you would rather insert an existing file as linked instead of embedded, you need to set the `AddOLEObject` method's *`LinkToFile`* argument to `True`, as shown in Listing 14.3.

Listing 14.3. Using the `AddOLEObject` method to insert an existing file as a linked object.

```
Sub InsertPictureAsLinked()

    Dim strPicture As String
    '
    ' Specify the location of the picture, depending
    ' on the operating system
    '
    If InStr(System.OperatingSystem, "NT") <> 0 Then
        strPicture = "C:\Windows\winnt256.bmp"
    Else
        strPicture = "C:\Windows\clouds.bmp"
    End If

    ActiveDocument.Shapes.AddOLEObject _
        FileName:=strPicture, _
        LinkToFile:=True

End Sub
```

This procedure inserts a bitmap file into a Word document as a linked object. The code first checks the current operating system and then assigns a pathname to the `strPicture` variable accordingly. Then the `AddOLEObject` method is run to insert the file. The *`FileName`* argument specifies the bitmap file, and the *`LinkToFile`* argument is set to `True` to establish the link.

Instead of merely inserting the object, you might prefer that the server application load so that the user can edit the object. To do this, add the `Activate` method after inserting the object, like this:

```
Dim objPicture As Object
Set objPicture = ActiveDocument.Shapes.AddOLEObject( _
        FileName:=strPicture, _
        LinkToFile:=True)
objPicture.Activate
```

Alternatively, you can insert an object and activate it in one command:

```
ActiveDocument.Shapes.AddOLEObject( _
        FileName:=strPicture, _
        LinkToFile:=True).Activate
```

OLE Objects and Word's InlineShape Object

OLE objects inserted via the `Shapes` object's `AddOLEObject` method are placed in the "drawing layer" of the client application. This means that the object is rendered as a free-floating shape that the user (or your code) can move around at will. In Word, particularly, the object covers any existing text in the document.

If you would prefer that your OLE objects not cover your Word document text, you can insert the object as an "inline" shape instead. In this case, the object is placed in the "text layer" of the client application, which means the object becomes part of the document text and is moved along with the surrounding text as you edit the document.

To do this, you work with the `InlineShapes` object instead of the `Shapes` object. The syntax of the `InlineShapes` object's `AddOLEObject` method is similar to that of the `Shapes` object, except that it doesn't use the *`Left`*, *`Top`*, *`Width`*, and *`Height`* arguments, and it adds an extra *`Range`* argument:

```
Document.InlineShapes.AddOLEObject(ClassType, FileName, LinkToFile, DisplayAsIcon,
➥IconFileName, IconIndex, IconLabel, Range)
```

`Range` The Range object where the OLE object will be inserted. Note that the object will replace the specified range if the range is currently selected. Otherwise, the object is inserted at the beginning of the range. If you omit this argument, VBA inserts the object at the top of the document.

For example, Listing 14.4 shows a procedure that embeds a GIF file from the Office 97 clip art collection as an inline image. In this case, the image is embedded at the beginning of the second paragraph in the active document.

Listing 14.4. Using the `InlineShapes` object's `AddOLEObject` method to embed a picture file as an embedded inline image.

```
Sub InsertInlineObject()

    Dim dirClipArt As String
    '
    ' Specify the location of the Office clipart
    '
    dirClipArt = "C:\Program Files\Microsoft Office\Clipart\"
    '
    ' Insert the picture as an inline shape
    '
    With ActiveDocument
        .InlineShapes.AddOLEObject _
            FileName:=dirClipArt & "Icons\Globe.gif", _
            Range:=.Paragraphs(2).Range
    End With
End Sub
```

Inserting ActiveX Controls in Word

Word has a separate method for inserting ActiveX controls in a document. The method is called `AddOLEControl`, and it's available with both the `Shapes` object and the `InlineShapes` object:

```
Document.Shapes.AddOLEControl(ClassType, Left, Top, Width, Height, Anchor)
```

```
Document.InlineShapes.AddOLEControl(ClassType, Range)
```

Document	The document to which you want to add the OLE control.
ClassType	The programmatic ID of the control.
Left	The distance, in points, from the left edge of the control to the left edge of the document window.
Top	The distance, in points, from the top edge of the control to the top edge of the document window (the default value is 0).
Width	The width of the control in points.
Height	The height of the control in points.
Anchor	The Range object to which the control is bound.
Range	The Range object where the control will be inserted. The control will replace the specified range if the range is currently selected. Otherwise, the control is inserted at the beginning of the range. If you omit this argument, VBA inserts the control at the top of the document.

For example, the following statement adds an ActiveX check box:

```
ActiveDocument.Shapes.AddOLEControl ClassType:="Forms.CheckBox.1"
```

Working with Linked and Embedded Objects

Once you have a linked or embedded object inserted into a document, you can work with the object using its properties and methods. To access the OLE-specific properties and members of the Shape and (in Word) InlineShape objects, you use the `OLEFormat` property. Among other things, this will let you change the object's size and formatting, update the object data, edit the object, and delete it from the document.

Before examining these techniques, though, you need to know how to refer to OLE objects once you've added them to a document. One way is to use an index value with the `Shapes` collection. For example, `Shapes(1)` refers to the first Shape object added to the document. How do you know you're dealing with an OLE object? Well, in many cases you don't know, so your code will need to test the Shape object's `Type` property to see if it returns either `msoEmbeddedOLEObject` or `msoLinkedOLEObject`. (In Word, you can also use an index with the `InlineShapes` collection to return an InlineShape object, and you can test this object's `Type` property. Note that Word also supports the `msoOLEControlObject` constant that identifies ActiveX controls.)

Alternatively, you can use the object's name as the argument in the `Shapes` collection. For example, `Shapes("Object 1")` refers to an object named `Object 1`.

Notice that neither of these methods produces particularly meaningful object representations. To make your code easier to read, try to assign meaningful names to your OLE objects by adjusting the object's `Name` property (see the next section for details).

Some OLE Object Properties

Like most objects, an OLE object has a number of properties you can take advantage of in your code. As I mentioned earlier, you access these properties via the `OLEFormat` object, which is a property of the Shape class. For example, you would use the following partial statement to refer to the `Name` property of the first shape on the active document:

```
ActiveDocument.Shapes(1).OLEFormat.Name
```

Note, however, that the `OLEFormat` object doesn't give you access to link-related properties. For that you need to use a separate object called `LinkFormat`.

Here's a summary of a few of the more commonly used OLEObject properties:

CAUTION: WATCH THE IMPLEMENTATION

Not all of these properties are implemented in all VBA applications. Check the Object Browser or Help system for the container application you're using before adding any of these properties to your code.

`Object.LinkFormat.AutoUpdate`: Returns or sets whether or not the linked *`Object`* updates automatically when the server data changes. Use `True` for automatic updating; use `False` for manual updating.

`Object.OLEFormat.ClassType`: Returns or sets the class type for the specified *`Object`*.

`Object.OLEFormat.DisplayAsIcon`: Returns or sets the display mode for the specified *`Object`*. Use `True` to display the object as an icon; use `False` to display the object as a picture.

`Object.OLEFormat.IconIndex`: Returns or sets the index of the icon for the specified *`Object`*.

`Object.OLEFormat.IconLabel`: Returns or sets the text that is displayed below the icon for the specified *`Object`*.

`Object.OLEFormat.IconPath`: Returns or sets the path of the icon file for the specified *`Object`*.

`Object.LinkFormat.SourceFullName`: Returns or sets the full pathname (drive, folder, and filename) for the linked *`Object`*.

Object.LinkFormat.SourceName: Returns or sets the filename for the linked *Object*.

Object.LinkFormat.SourcePathName: Returns or sets the pathname (drive and folder) for the linked *Object*.

NOTE: SHAPE PROPERTIES

If you want to change the height, width, and position of the OLE object, or if you want to format the object's appearance (such as adding a shadow), use the properties of the Shape object.

Some OLE Object Methods

OLE objects also come equipped with several methods you can use to manipulate the objects after you've inserted them. Many of these methods (such as Copy, Cut, Delete, and Select) are available via the Shape object and are straightforward. However, a few OLE-specific methods are available via the OLEFormat and LinkFormat objects. I'll close this chapter by looking at two of these methods—Update and Verb.

The Update Method

If you inserted the OLE data as a linked object, the link between the object and the server file is usually automatic. This means that anytime the server file changes, the client object is updated automatically. There are two circumstances in which updating is *not* automatic:

- If you've changed the link to manual. You can do this by selecting Edit | Links, highlighting the source file in the Links dialog box, and selecting the Manual update option. You can also set the AutoUpdate property to False.
- If you closed and then reopened the client document and clicked No when the application asked if you wanted to reestablish the links.

In these situations, you need to update the object using the LinkFormat.Update method (which takes no arguments). Listing 14.5 provides an example.

Listing 14.5. Using the Update method to update linked OLE objects.

```
Sub UpdateAllObjects()

    Dim obj As Object

    Application.StatusBar = _
        "Now updating linked objects..."
    For Each obj In ActiveDocument.Shapes
        If obj.Type = msoLinkedOLEObject Then
```

```
        obj.LinkFormat.Update
    End If
Next obj

Application.StatusBar = False
MsgBox "Link update complete."
Set embeddedOrgChart = Nothing

End Sub
```

This procedure has a `For Each...Next` statement to loop through every Shape object in the current document. If the object is linked (that is, its `Type` property equals `msoLinkedOLEObject`), it gets updated with the `LinkFormat.Update` method.

NOTE: BREAKING A LINK

If you decide that you no longer need an object to be linked to its source file, you can break the link by running the ***`Object`***`.LinkFormat.BreakLink` method, where ***`Object`*** is the object you want to "unlink."

The Verb Method

Each OLE object has one or more *verbs* that specify what actions you can perform on the object. Unlike methods, which tell you what actions can be performed on the object from the point of view of the client application, verbs tell you what actions can be performed on the object from the point of view of the *server* (that is, the application used to create the object). For example, a typical verb is "edit." Running this verb opens the server application so that you can edit the object.

To run a verb, use the `Verb` method:

`Object``.OLEFormat(`***`Verb`***`)`

`Object`	The OLE object you want to work with.
`Verb`	A constant or integer that specifies the verb to run.

Note that Word doesn't support the `Verb` method. Instead, it implements the more sophisticated `DoVerb` method, which I'll discuss in the next section.

Here are some notes to keep in mind when dealing with the *`Verb`* argument:

- All OLE objects have a *primary* verb, which is the same as the action taken when you double-click the object. The constant you use to specify the primary verb depends on the application. In Excel, for example, use the constant `xlPrimary` or the number `1`.

- For most objects, the primary verb lets you edit the object. If you want to edit an object but you're not sure what its primary verb does, use the *open* verb. Again, the constant depends on the application; in Excel, use `xlOpen`.
- If the object supports a secondary verb, you can specify this verb by using `2` for the *`Verb`* argument.
- For embedded objects that support OLE 2.0, the primary verb lets you edit the object in place, and the secondary verb lets you open the object in a separate server window.

NOTE: VIEWING VERBS

To find out which verbs are available for an object, look up the object in the Registry Editor, as described earlier. The object's supported verbs are shown in the Verb subkey.

Table 14.2 lists the available verbs for some common OLE objects.

Table 14.2. Verbs for common OLE objects.

Object	*Primary Verb*	*Other Verb*
Bitmap Image	Edit	Open
Calendar Control	Edit	Properties
Media Clip	Play	Edit
Microsoft Clip Gallery	Replace	None
Microsoft Map	Open	Edit
Microsoft Equation	Edit (in-place)	Open
Microsoft Excel Chart	Edit (in-place)	Open
Microsoft Excel Worksheet	Edit (in-place)	Open
Microsoft Graph	Edit (in-place)	Open
Microsoft Word Document	Edit (in-place)	Open
Microsoft Word Picture	Edit (in-place)	Open
MIDI Sequence	Play	Edit
MS Organization Chart	Edit	None
Package	Activate Contents	Edit
Video Clip	Play	Edit
Wave Sound	Play	Edit
WordPad Document	Edit (in-place)	Open

OLE Verbs in Word VBA

Microsoft Word 97 implements no less than three methods in the `OLEFormat` object that let you invoke the verbs for an OLE object. Here's a summary:

`Object.OLEFormat.Edit`: Invokes the primary verb for the specified `Object`.

`Object.OLEFormat.Open`: Invokes the secondary verb for the specified `Object`.

`Object.OLEFormat.DoVerb`: Invokes one of verbs associated with the specified `Object` using the following syntax:

```
Object.OLEFormat.DoVerb(VerbIndex)
```

`Object`	The OLE object you want to work with.
`VerbIndex`	A constant that specifies the verb to run. If you omit this argument, Word invokes the object's primary verb.

Table 14.3 lists the constants you can use with the `VerbIndex` argument.

Table 14.3. Available constants for the `DoVerb` method's *`VerbIndex`* argument.

Constant	*Verb Description*
`wdOLEVerbPrimary`	Runs the object's primary verb.
`wdOLEVerbShow`	Shows the object for editing or viewing. This constant is normally used when you first insert an object that doesn't normally activate its server application for initial editing.
`wdOLEVerbOpen`	Runs the open verb to open the object in a separate window.
`wdOLEVerbHide`	Hides the object's user interface tools (that is, the server application's menus and toolbars).
`wdOLEVerbUIActivate`	Edits the object in place.
`wdOLEVerbInPlaceActivate`	Edits the object in place but doesn't display the server application's interface tools.
`wdOLEVerbDiscardUndoState`	Tells the object to discard any current undo information.

Summary

This chapter showed you how to work with OLE objects via VBA. It began with an extensive look at the technology behind the OLE standard, including some background on linking, embedding, visual editing, the Component Object Model, OLE Automation, ActiveX controls, and how OLE works with the Windows Registry. From there you got down to more practical matters as I showed you how to insert linked and embedded objects using VBA techniques. I closed with a look at a few OLE object properties and methods.

Here's a list of chapters where you'll find related information:

- For the full scoop on OLE Automation, see Chapter 15, "Controlling Applications Via OLE Automation."
- To learn how to create custom objects, complete with their own properties and methods, see Chapter 16, "Rolling Your Own Objects with Class Modules."
- I show you how to use OLE Automation to control Internet Explorer and Netscape Navigator in Chapter 20, "Internet and Intranet Programming Topics."
- Once you add ActiveX controls to an HTML document, you can use VBScript—a subset of VBA—to program the controls. Surf to Chapter 21, "Web Page Programming: ActiveX and VBScript," to find out the details.
- You learn how to program Outlook via OLE Automation in Chapter 22, "E-Mail and Groupware Programming with Outlook."

CHAPTER 15

Controlling Applications Via OLE Automation

IN THIS CHAPTER

We are continually faced with a series of great opportunities brilliantly disguised as insoluble problems.

—*John W. Gardner*

Linking and embedding OLE objects via VBA code is a great way to share data between applications and to remove some of the object creation burden from your users. However, unless you're simply dropping an existing object into a document, linking and embedding still requires the user to interact with the server application to create or edit the object. This might be exactly what you need, but in many cases you'll prefer that your code do at least some of the interacting. For example, once you've inserted a new Word document object inside an Excel worksheet, you might want to set up the document by adding and formatting some text before handing things over to the user.

As you learned in Chapter 13, "Working with Other Applications," you could accomplish this by using dynamic data exchange. In other words, you could use DDE to establish a communications channel between Excel and Word, use Word's macro (that is, WordBasic) commands to set up and save the document, and then use OLE to bring the document into the worksheet.

The fly in this DDE ointment is that you're required to take a technological leap backward by having to use Word's old WordBasic commands. Similarly, to control Excel via DDE, you have to use the ancient Excel 4.0 macro language. In other words, this solution in no way leverages all the VBA language information that you've absorbed up to this point in the book. Not only that, but since these commands are embedded within strings, you lose all the benefits of working in the Visual Basic Editor, including on-the-fly syntax checking, color-coded keywords, IntelliSense shortcuts, and more.

The solution is to turn to OLE Automation, which, in applications that support this standard, lets you directly manipulate an external application's objects—including setting its properties and running its methods. This chapter introduces you to this powerful concept and shows you how to implement OLE Automation technology into your VBA applications.

NOTE: TO OLE OR NOT TO OLE?

At the time I wrote this, Microsoft seemed to be in the process of quietly eliminating the phrase "object linking and embedding" from its corporate vocabulary. For example, OLE controls are now officially called ActiveX controls. Also, OLE Automation is now often called simply Automation. Since the latter seems to be Microsoft's term of choice, I'll use it throughout the rest of this chapter.

Understanding Automation

As you learned in the last chapter, applications that support Automation implement object libraries that expose the application's native objects to VBA. Such applications are called *Automation servers*, and the applications that manipulate the server's objects are called *Automation controllers*. In Office 97, Word, Excel, PowerPoint, and Access are all Automation servers because, as you saw in Part II, "Unleashing Microsoft Office Objects," they expose extensive object libraries. However, these applications are also Automation controllers because they have the VBA development environment that, as you'll see, lets you write code to control a server's objects.

Note, too, that some applications can function only as Automation servers. Outlook, for example, implements an object library, but it has no development environment from which to access external objects. (I'll show you how to use VBA to work with some of Outlook's objects later in this chapter.) Other examples of Automation servers are the Binder (also covered in this chapter) and Graph programs that come with Office 97, the Internet Explorer and Netscape Navigator Web browsers (see Chapter 20, "Internet and Intranet Programming Topics"), and any ActiveX objects that are installed on your system.

Finally, there are programs that are happy to act as OLE object servers, but they don't support Automation and therefore can't be manipulated by Automation controllers. Examples include Paint, WordPad, and the WordArt, Organization Chart, and Equation Editor components of Office 97.

Referencing Object Libraries

The trick to using Automation isn't really much of a trick at all since you've seen it used already. Namely, before you can work with an Automation server's objects, you must set up a reference to the server's object library in your VBA project. Recall that you do this by first highlighting your project in the Project Explorer and then selecting Tools | References in the Visual Basic Editor to display the References dialog box. In the Available References list, activate the check box for the object library you want to work with. For example, if you want to control Word's objects from within Excel, you would activate the Microsoft Word 8.0 Object Library item, as shown in Figure 15.1. (Alternatively, click Browse to add other object libraries, executable files, or projects to the References dialog box.)

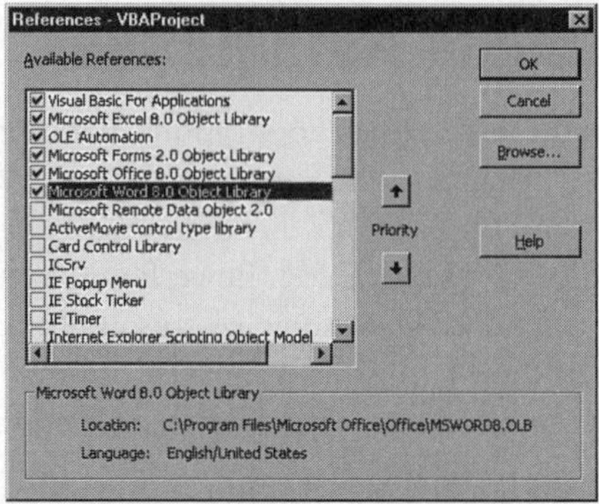

FIGURE 15.1.
Use the References dialog box to activate the object library for the Automation server you want to control.

> **NOTE: THE ORDER OF THE REFERENCES**
>
> The order of the items in the Available References list appears random, but the items are actually ordered in two ways:
>
> - Unchecked items are listed alphabetically.
> - Checked items are listed by priority.
>
> This priority determines how VBA treats objects that have the same name in multiple object libraries. Consider the `Application` object. This object is part of the libraries of both Excel and Word (among others), so when you refer to this object in your code, how does VBA know which one you mean? It uses the reference priority. In Excel VBA, for instance, the Excel object library has a higher priority than the Word object library, so VBA assumes that an unqualified use of the `Application` object is a reference to Excel. You'll see later that you can qualify these object references and thus avoid this ambiguity.

Click OK to return to the Visual Basic Editor and then launch the Object Browser. In the list of libraries and projects, you'll now see an item that corresponds to the object library you just referenced. In Figure 15.2, for example, you see that the entire Word object model is now available to the Excel VBA project.

Note, too, that this reference remains in place when you distribute your project to your users. (This assumes, of course, that the other application—and hence its object library—is installed on the user's computer.) Not only that, but the dirty work of adjusting the path to the object library is handled automatically. Therefore, if the user installed the application in a different folder, the object library reference will be adjusted to point to the correct location (this is all determined by Registry entries).

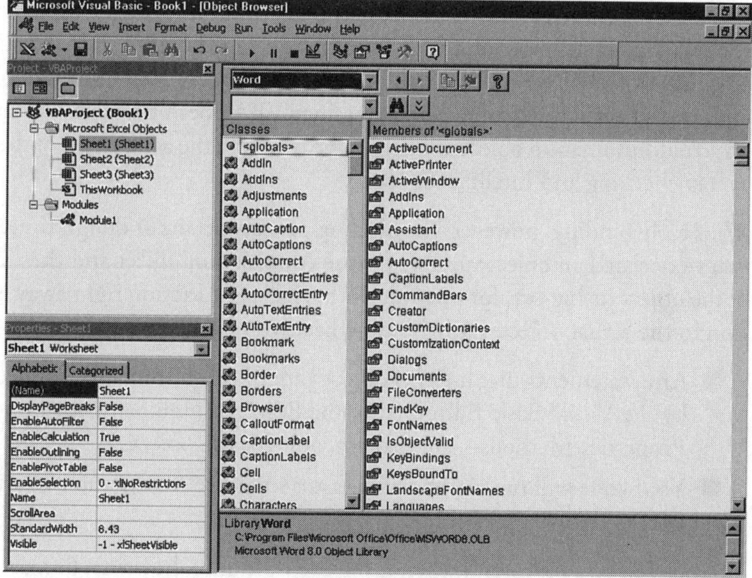

FIGURE 15.2.
Word's object model is now available to the Excel project.

As Figure 15.2 suggests, setting up a reference to an Automation server's object model means that you can now use the exposed objects more or less as you use the objects in the container application. With just a minimum of preparation, your Excel code can refer to, say, a Word Document object just as easily as it can refer to a Workbook object. Not only that, but your procedures can manipulate any exposed object's properties and methods, just as if you were working in the Automation server directly. Therefore, your Excel project could use the `Add` method of Word's `Documents` object to create a new document.

With a minimum of effort on your part, and using all of the VBA syntax and language constructs that you've learned about so far, you can create procedures that manipulate other Automation applications to your heart's content. The only real work that's required is learning the Automation server's object model, but the Object Browser and its instant access to the server's Help system should reduce some of that burden.

Late Binding Versus Early Binding

Binding is the method by which the Component Object Model connects the Automation controller and the Automation server. In essence, binding is the mechanism that associates an object variable in your VBA procedure with an actual Automation object on the server. Before getting down to the Automation nitty-gritty, you need to understand a couple of binding-related concepts that are crucial if you want to develop Automation-based applications quickly and reliably. These concepts are *late binding* and *early binding*.

Late binding means that the binding process occurs at runtime. In other words, VBA doesn't resolve your object variables into Automation objects until you actually run the code. The advantage of this method is that all Automation servers support late binding, so there's no guesswork involved. On the downside, since VBA doesn't associate your object variables with an actual Automation object at design time, you lose the advantages of the Visual Basic Editor's syntax checking and IntelliSense features.

With early binding, however, the binding process occurs at design time. In other words, after you've declared an object variable for the Automation object and then you create an instance of the object (using `Set`, for example), VBA leaps into action right away and sets up an association to the actual object. Early binding has two major advantages:

- Any statements that use this object variable are automatically checked for syntax errors by the Visual Basic Editor. Also, the Editor's IntelliSense features—such as List Properties/Methods—are also available for the object.
- Your code will run significantly faster since the Automation interface requires fewer calls to resolve the object.

You need to be a bit careful when using early binding, however, because it's not supported by all applications. These are mostly older applications, though, and any Automation server that has an object library will support early binding.

I'll show you the specifics of setting up late and early binding in the next section.

Accessing Automation Objects

Although you can reference the container application's objects directly in your VBA code, referencing Automation objects takes a bit more work (although, as you'll see, it's really just a few extra keystrokes). Specifically, you need to use the `Dim` and `Set` statements to let VBA know that you want to work with an Automation object. There are three ways to go about this: the `New` keyword, the `CreateObject` function, and the `GetObject` function.

The New Keyword

The `New` keyword is used within the `Dim` statement when you declare an Automation object. Using `New` tells VBA to create the object implicitly, which means a new instance of the object will be created the first time your code references the object. In other words, you don't have to bother with an explicit `Set` statement to instance the object.

Here's the general syntax of a `Dim` statement that uses the `New` keyword:

```
Dim varName As New Application.ObjectType
```

Here, `varName` is the name of the object variable, and `Application.ObjectType` specifies the Automation object class, where `Application` is the name of the application as it appears in the Object Browser's Project/Library drop-down list, and `ObjectType` is the object class type.

NOTE: NOT ALL OBJECTS CAN BE REFERENCED DIRECTLY

Not all of the objects in an application's hierarchy can be referenced directly via the `Application.ObjectType` class syntax. Although there are no hard-and-fast rules, generally only the first one or two levels in the hierarchy are available. In Word, for example, this means the `Application` object and the Document object. In Excel, it's the `Application` object and the Workbook object. You access all other objects by using the properties of these top-level objects.

NOTE: AVOIDING AMBIGUOUS OBJECT NAMES

Earlier I mentioned that VBA uses the priority order in the References list to resolve ambiguous object names. By specifying the `Application` part of the `Application.ObjectType` class ID, you avoid ambiguity and save VBA the extra work of resolving the object's application.

For example, the following statement references Word's `Application` object:

```
Dim wordApp As New Word.Application
```

Here are some notes to keep in mind when using the `New` keyword:

- This method results in early binding of the specified object.
- Some Automation servers don't support the `New` keyword, so you'll need to test your code.
- Some programmers avoid the `New` keyword because it creates an object before you ever use it, and this seems wasteful (especially if, due to program branching, your code never does make use of the object).

Because of the last two points, use of the `New` keyword has fallen out of favor, and most VBA programmers use the `CreateObject` function instead.

The `CreateObject` Function

Instead of using the `New` keyword to create an object implicitly, you can use VBA's `CreateObject` function to create the object explicitly. Here's the syntax used with this function:

```
CreateObject(Class)
```

`Class`	The *programmatic identifier* that specifies the Automation server application and the type of object to create.

The ***`Class`*** argument is a string that always takes the following form (where *`Application`* and *`ObjectType`* are the same as I described earlier for the `New` keyword):

```
Application.ObjectType
```

Note that you normally use `CreateObject` within a `Set` statement, and that the function serves to create a new instance of the specified Automation object. For example, if `wordApp` is an object variable, you would use the following statement to create a new instance of Word's `Application` object:

```
Set wordApp = CreateObject("Word.Application")
```

It's important to understand the effect your object variable declaration has on your program. You have two ways to proceed:

- VBA will use late binding if you declare the variable as an `Object`, as in this example:

  ```
  Dim wordApp As Object
  Set word = CreateObject("Word.Application")
  ```

- VBA will use early binding if you declare the variable as a specific class type (using the *`Application.ObjectType`* class syntax), as shown here:

  ```
  Dim wordApp As Word.Application
  Set word = CreateObject("Word.Application")
  ```

Note that there's nothing else you need to do to use the Automation object. With your variable declared and an instance of the object created, you can use that object's properties and methods directly. Listing 15.1 shows an example.

Listing 15.1. Using Automation to create a new Word document.

```
Sub CreateWordDocument()
    Dim wordApp As Word.Application
    '
    ' Create the Word Application object
    '
    Application.StatusBar = "Creating Word Application object..."
    Set wordApp = CreateObject("Word.Application")
    '
    ' Work with Application object directly
```

```
    With wordApp
        '
        ' Create a new document and add some text
        '
        Application.StatusBar = "Creating new Word document..."
        .Documents.Add
        .ActiveDocument.Paragraphs(1).Range.InsertBefore "This is an Automation
        ➥test."
        '
        ' Save the document
        '
        Application.StatusBar = "Saving Word document..."
        .ActiveDocument.SaveAs "C:\My Documents\OLETest.doc"
        '
        ' We're done, so quit Word
        '
        Application.StatusBar = "Shutting down Word..."
        .Quit
    End With
    Set wordApp = Nothing
    Application.StatusBar = False
End Sub
```

CAUTION: NO ERROR CHECKING

To keep things simple, the examples in this chapter don't use any kind of error checking. However, production code should check for Automation errors as a matter of routine. To learn about VBA's error-trapping features, see Chapter 23, "Trapping Program Errors."

This procedure creates and saves a new Word for Windows document from within Excel by working with Word's Application object via Automation. The procedure begins by declaring a variable called `wordApp`. Note the use of a specific class type in the `Dim` statement to force early binding. Then the `CreateObject` function is invoked to create a new Word Application object, and the object is stored in the `wordApp` variable. From here, you can wield the `wordApp` variable just as though it were the Word Application object. (Note that all the `Application.StatusBar` statements refer to the *Excel* `Application` object.)

For example, the `wordApp.Documents.Add` statement uses the `Documents` collection's `Add` method to create a new Word document, and the `InsertBefore` method adds some text to the document. Then the `SaveAs` method saves the new file. With the Word-related chores complete, the Application object's `Quit` method is run to shut down Word. Note as well that the `wordApp` variable is cleared (in other words, it's `Set` to `Nothing`) to reclaim the memory used by the object. (This is always a good idea when you're working with Automation objects.)

TIP: MAKING THE AUTOMATION SERVER VISIBLE

The `CreateObject` function loads Word, but you never see Word on-screen. This is the desired behavior in most Automation situations. However, if you *do* want to see what Word is up to, set the Application object's `Visible` property to `True`, like so:

```
wordApp.Visible = True
```

NOTE: THIS CHAPTER'S CODE LISTINGS

To grab the code listings used in this chapter, open the file named Chaptr15.xls on the CD. Those without Excel can still examine the code by opening the Chaptr15.bas file.

The GetObject Function

If you know that the object you want to work with already exists or is already open, the `CreateObject` function isn't the best choice. In Listing 15.1, for example, if Word is already running, the code will start up a second copy of Word, which is a waste of resources.

For these situations, it's better to work directly with the existing object. To do this, use the `GetObject` function:

```
GetObject(PathName, Class)
```

`PathName`	The pathname (drive, folder, and filename) of the file you want to work with (or the file that contains the object you want to work with). If you omit this argument, you have to specify the *`Class`* argument.
`Class`	The *programmatic ID* that specifies the Automation server application and the type of object to work with (that is, the *`Application.ObjectType`* class syntax).

Listing 15.2 shows the `GetObject` function at work.

Listing 15.2. Using Automation to work with a Word document.

```
Sub DocumentWordCount()
    Dim wordDoc As Word.Document
    '
    ' Get the Word Document object
    '
```

```
    Application.StatusBar = "Getting Word Document object..."
    Set wordDoc = GetObject("C:\My Documents\OLETest.doc", "Word.Document")
    '
    ' Get the word count
    '
    Application.StatusBar = "Getting word count..."
    MsgBox wordDoc.Name & " has " & wordDoc.Words.Count & " words."
    '
    ' We're done, so quit Word and release object variable
    '
    Application.StatusBar = "Shutting down Word..."
    wordDoc.Application.Quit
    Set wordDoc = Nothing
    Application.StatusBar = False
End Sub
```

The `GetObject` function assigns the Word Document object named `OLETest.doc` to the `wordDoc` variable. Again, once you've set up this reference, you can use the object's properties and methods directly. For example, the `MsgBox` statement uses `wordDoc.Name` to return the filename and `wordDoc.Words.Count` to determine the number of words in the document.

Note as well that even though you're working with a Document object, you still have access to Word's `Application` object. That's because most objects have an `Application` property that refers to the `Application` object. In Listing 15.2, for example, the following statement uses the `Application` property to quit Word:

```
wordDoc.Application.Quit
```

Handling Automation Errors

If you attempt to reference an `Application` object using `GetObject` and the application isn't running, VBA generates an Automation error. On the other hand, if you use `CreateObject` to reference an `Application` object and the application *is* running, VBA creates a second instance of the application. To avoid both of these problem scenarios, your procedure should include error handling code that does the following:

- If the application is already running, use `GetObject` to reference the `Application` object.
- If the application isn't running, use `CreateObject` to instance the `Application` object.

Listing 15.3 shows a procedure that does just that.

Listing 15.3. Using Automation to run a PowerPoint presentation slide show.

```
Sub RunPresentation()
    On Error GoTo OpenPowerPoint
    Dim ppApp As PowerPoint.Application
    '
    ' Reference the existing PowerPoint Application object
    '
    Set ppApp = GetObject(, "PowerPoint.Application")
    '
    ' Work with PowerPoint's Application object directly
    '
    With ppApp
        '
        ' Display PowerPoint
        '
        .Visible = True
        '
        ' Open and then run the presentation's slide show
        '
        .Presentations.Open "C:\My Documents\Juggling.ppt"
        .Presentations("Juggling.ppt").SlideShowSettings.Run
    End With
    Set ppApp = Nothing
'
' Program branches here if PowerPoint isn't running
'
OpenPowerPoint:
    '
    ' Create a new instance of PowerPoint's Application object
    '
    Set ppApp = CreateObject("PowerPoint.Application")
    '
    ' Continue after the statement that caused the error
    '
    Resume Next
End Sub
```

This procedure is designed to open a PowerPoint presentation and then run its slide show. Although we could reference the Presentation object directly, I'll use PowerPoint's `Application` object so that I can illustrate my point. (Don't forget to set up a reference to the PowerPoint object library.)

The first statement is part of VBA's error handling repertoire, and it says, in effect, "If any errors occur, jump down to the `OpenPowerPoint:` line." Therefore, when the `GetObject` function is executed, everything proceeds normally if PowerPoint is already running. However, if PowerPoint isn't open, an Automation error occurs, and the program branches down the `OpenPowerPoint:` label. Here, the `CreateObject` function is executed to open a new instance of the PowerPoint `Application` object. The `Resume Next` statement tells VBA to resume execution with the statement *after* the one that raised the error.

From here, the procedure displays the PowerPoint window, opens a Presentation object, and runs the presentation's slide show.

> **NOTE: ERROR-HANDLING SPECIFICS**
>
> Listing 15.3 assumes that the generated error is the one caused by invoking `GetObject` on an unopened application. There are many different Automation errors, however, so you should probably check for specific error numbers (particularly if you're using late binding). To get the full scoop on error numbers and all of VBA's error handling features, see Chapter 23.

Summary

This chapter showed you how to use Automation (formerly known as OLE Automation) to manipulate other applications from within your VBA procedures. After some background information, I showed you how to set up references to object libraries and explained the difference between early binding and late binding. You then learned how to access Automation objects using the `New` keyword and the `CreateObject` and `GetObject` functions. I closed with a quick look at how you handle Automation errors.

Here's a list of chapters where you'll find related information:

- To learn how to create custom Automation objects, complete with their own properties and methods, see Chapter 16, "Rolling Your Own Objects with Class Modules."
- I show you how to use OLE Automation to control Internet Explorer and Netscape Navigator in Chapter 20, "Internet and Intranet Programming Topics."
- Once you add ActiveX controls to an HTML document, you can use VBScript and Automation to manipulate the controls. Head for Chapter 21, "Web Page Programming: ActiveX and VBScript," to find out the details.
- You learn how to program Outlook via OLE Automation in Chapter 22, "E-Mail and Groupware Programming with Outlook."

CHAPTER 16

Rolling Your Own Objects with Class Modules

IN THIS CHAPTER

If you wish to be well-served, serve yourself.

—Spanish proverb

You saw in the preceding chapter how Automation makes it easy to manipulate the objects exposed by Automation servers. Indeed, setting up a reference to an `Application` object gives you access to that server's entire object model, including all the associated properties and methods. This is truly the state of the application integration art, because it means you can now establish one VBA application as a "home base" and manipulate other applications remotely via the Automation interface.

VBA 5.0

With VBA 5.0, you can take Automation a step further by creating custom Automation objects, complete with their own properties and methods. You can then use these custom creations as regular objects within your VBA code. The secret of building custom objects is the class module, and it's the subject of this chapter. You'll learn how to create new class modules, how to define properties and methods for the new objects, and how to use these objects in your code. Along the way, I'll provide plenty of examples that you can put to good use.

Partway There: Custom Collections

Before diving into the deep end of user-defined classes, let's start off by just dipping a toe or two into these new waters. Specifically, let's see how VBA 5.0 lets you define custom collections.

A collection, as you know, is a set of similar objects. In Excel, for example, the `Worksheets` collection holds all the Worksheet objects contained in a particular workbook. Similarly, Word's `Paragraphs` collection holds all the Paragraph objects in a specified document. Collections have varying implementations, properties, and methods, but the following items are constant throughout all collections:

- You can cycle through every object in the collection by using a `For Each...Next` loop.
- You can refer to any object in the collection using an index value, such as `Worksheets("Sheet1")` or `Paragraphs(1)`.
- You can determine the number of items in the collection by examining the `Count` property.
- You can insert new items into the collection by running the `Add` method.

This collection object functionality also forms the core of the new custom collections, which are nothing more or less than sets of objects that you define yourself. You'll see later that custom collections are most useful when you're working with your own classes, but it's perfectly acceptable to use them with an application's built-in objects.

One common use for custom collections is to work with a subset of objects from a built-in collection. For example, suppose you've created a user form that contains a number of controls, including text boxes, labels, and command buttons. What do you do if you want to show the form's data, but you don't want the user to modify what's in the text boxes? The best way to do this is to change the `Enabled` property for each text box to `False`. However, there's no such thing as a "TextBoxes" collection that contains only a form's TextBox objects. And you can't just loop through the form's `Controls` collection, because you would end up disabling all the non-TextBox controls as well. The solution is to create a custom collection that includes just the form's TextBox objects. You can then use `For Each...Next` to loop through the custom collection's objects, setting their `Enabled` properties to `False`.

Also note that you're free to reuse your custom collections wherever you need them. In the text boxes example, you could use the same custom collection to clear the text boxes, hide them, or set any property that's available with a TextBox object.

Why not use an array of objects instead? That would work, but custom collections offer three significant advantages:

- Custom collections are easier to work with and maintain than arrays. Not only do collections come with built-in properties and methods for counting, adding, and removing items, but you also can work with individual collection items using either an index number or a more intuitive string value (called a *key*).
- You don't have to worry about allocating memory as you do with dynamic arrays. The collection object handles all memory management chores behind the scenes.
- Collections have lower memory requirements than arrays.

Declaring a Custom Collection

Custom collections are `Collection` objects. You create them by declaring an object variable of data type `Collection`, where you include the `New` keyword in the `Dim` statement:

```
Dim myCollection As New Collection
```

This creates the object, but it won't be instanced until the first time you use the object in your code.

Adding Objects to a Custom Collection

Once you've declared the `Collection` object, you use the `Add` method to populate the collection with the objects of your choice. Note in particular that VBA really doesn't care what kinds of objects you place inside your custom collection. In fact, you can even store objects that have *different* data types!

Here's the syntax of the `Add` method:

```
Collection.Add Item, Key, Before, After
```

Collection	The custom `Collection` object.
Item	The object you want to add to the collection.
Key	A unique string value that identifies the object within the collection. You can use this value instead of a positional index to reference the object.
Before	The object before which the new object is added. You can specify either the positional index or the *Key* value of the object.
After	The object after which the new object is added. Again, you can specify either the positional index or the *Key* value of the object.

For example, Listing 16.1 presents a procedure that loops through all the worksheets in a workbook. Those sheets that contain the word "Budget" in the name are added to the custom collection named `myCollection`. (Note, too, that the worksheet's name is stored as the *Key* value.) The procedure closes with a message that displays the number of worksheets in the collection (as returned by the `Collection` object's `Count` property).

Listing 16.1. A procedure that places all "Budget" worksheets into a custom collection.

```
Sub GatherBudgetSheets()
    Dim myCollection As New Collection
    Dim ws As Worksheet
    For Each ws In ThisWorkbook.Worksheets
        If InStr(ws.Name, "Budget") Then
            myCollection.Add Item:=ws, Key:=ws.Name
        End If
    Next 'ws
    MsgBox "The custom collection contains " & _
        myCollection.Count & " worksheets."
End Sub
```

NOTE: THIS CHAPTER'S CODE LISTINGS

The code listings and class modules used in this chapter can be found on the CD in the file named Chaptr16.xls. If you don't have access to Excel, you can read the code listings in the Chaptr16.bas text file.

Earlier I mentioned that a common use for custom collections is to define a subset of a form's controls. Unfortunately, there's no straightforward way to go about this. If would be nice if you could just loop through the `Controls` collection and check some sort of "Type" property, but there's no such thing in VBA. Here are a couple of ideas:

- Use a consistent naming convention for your controls. For example, most people place `txt` at the beginning of text box names, `chk` at the beginning of check box names, and so on. You could then use code similar to the following to create a custom collection of the form's text box controls:

```
For Each c in Me.Controls
    If Left(c.Name, 3) = "txt" Then myCollection.Add c
Next 'c
```

- Take advantage of the `Tag` property. For each control, you could enter into the `Tag` property a string that specifies the type of control and then use code similar to the following to create the collection:

```
For Each c in Me.Controls
    If c.Tag = "Text Box" Then myCollection.Add c
Next 'c
```

NOTE: CREATE CONTROLS COLLECTIONS DURING INITIALIZATION

These code examples loop through the `Me.Controls` collection. Recall that the `Me` keyword refers to the form in which the code is running. I used this format because the ideal spot for creating your custom control collection is the form's `Initialize` or `Activate` event.

Working with Objects in a Custom Collection

With your custom collection now populated with objects, you can work with the items in the collection. As with any collection object, you'll do this in one of two ways: by looping through the collection or by referring to individual items.

Looping through a custom collection is identical to looping through a built-in collection. In other words, you use a `For Each...Next` loop, as in this example:

```
Dim ws As Worksheet
For Each ws In myCollection
    ws.Protect Contents:=True
Next 'ws
```

To refer to an individual member of a collection, you can either use an index number that represents the object's position in the collection, or you can use the *`Key`* argument that you specified during the `Add` method. For example, if the first item in a custom collection named `myCollection` was added with the key value `Address`, the following statements are equivalent:

```
myCollection(1)
myCollection("Address")
```

> **NOTE: THE ITEM METHOD**
>
> The `Collection` object also has an `Item(`***`Index`***`)` method that returns the object associated with the specified ***`Index`***. This is the default method for the collection, however, so you don't need to include the `Item` keyword. For example, the following two statements are equivalent:
>
> ```
> myCollection(1)
> myCollection.Item(1)
> ```

Removing Objects from a Custom Collection

To delete an item from a custom collection, use the `Remove` method:

`Collection``.Remove `***`Item`***

`Collection`	The custom `Collection` object that contains the object you want to remove.
`Item`	The object you want to remove from the collection. You can specify either the positional index or the key value of the object.

Listing 16.2 shows a procedure that accepts a `Collection` object as an argument. A `Do Loop` runs the `Remove` method on the first item of the collection until there are no objects left (in other words, until `Count` is 0).

Listing 16.2. A procedure that clears all objects from a custom collection.

```
Sub ClearCollection(coll As Collection)
    Do While coll.Count > 0
        coll.Remove Index:=1
    Loop
End Sub
```

Understanding Class Modules

Back in Chapter 2, "Understanding Variables," I told you about VBA's user-defined data types, and you saw that they were useful for storing related data in a single structure. As our entrance into the world of class modules, let's examine the limitations of user-defined data types and see how class modules can overcome these limitations.

First, let's build a sample user-defined data type. Suppose you want to work with invoice data in your VBA procedure. In a simplified model, you would want to track seven pieces of data for each invoice: a unique ID number, the customer's account number, the amount, the date of the invoice, the due date of the invoice, the date the invoice was paid, and whether or not the invoice is overdue. You could track these items by setting up variables for each one:

```
Dim ID As Long
Dim custAcct As String
Dim amount As Currency
Dim invDate As Date
Dim dueDate As Date
Dim pmtDate As Date
Dim overdue As Boolean
```

However, this approach suffers from two major drawbacks:

- If you need to work with multiple invoices simultaneously, you'll have to create separate sets of variables (ID2, ID3, and so on), which is clearly inefficient.
- There's no built-in mechanism for checking or manipulating the data stored in these variables.

As you learned in Chapter 2, you can solve the first problem by creating a user-defined data type that holds all the required information:

```
Type Invoice
    ID As Long
    custAcct As String
    amount As Currency
    invDate As Date
    dueDate As Date
    pmtDate As Date
    overdue As Boolean
End Type
```

From here, you can declare new variables that use this data type. For example, the following statements declare a new variable named `testInvoice` to be of type `Invoice` and assign values to the elements:

```
Dim testInvoice As Invoice
testInvoice.ID = 95512
testInvoice.custAcct = "12-3456"
testInvoice.amount = 1234.56
testInvoice.invDate = Date
testInvoice.dueDate = Date + 30
testInvoice.overdue = False
```

This certainly makes it easier to work with multiple invoices, but we're still just adding static data to each element.

To overcome this problem, you can set up a custom "Invoice" object that has the following characteristics:

- The ID, customer account number, amount, invoice date, invoice due date, invoice payment date, and overdue flag become properties of the object.
- When you create a new object, you can assign values to certain properties automatically.

- When you assign a value to any of the properties, you can set up VBA code to check the value to make sure it's within a certain range or satisfies your company's business rules.
- You can implement object methods (say, to check if the invoice is overdue).

As you'll see, all of this is extremely easy to do thanks to VBA 5.0's new class modules. In the object-oriented world, a *class* acts as a sort of object "template." A cookie cutter provides a good analogy. The cookie cutter isn't a cookie, but, when implemented, it defines the characteristics of the actual cookie. A class is the same way. It's not an object, but implementing it (or *instancing* it, to use the vernacular) creates an object that uses the class characteristics. These characteristics are governed by the *members* of the class, which are its properties and methods.

Until now, the classes you've worked with have been built into the object libraries that come with the container application. You instance one of these classes either by working with a specific object directly or by using `Set` to assign an object variable to a specific object.

However, the purpose of a class module is to let you define your own custom classes, complete with custom properties and methods. Once that's done, you can then work with the class just like you do with the built-in classes: you instance a class object and manipulate its properties and methods. The great thing about class modules is that they are completely reusable. Your VBA project becomes a sort of mini object library, and any other project that references your project—in any application that can act as an Automation controller—can then implement your classes.

The next few sections give you the details on putting together a class module in VBA.

Setting Up a Class Module

For our purposes, a class module is really no different from a regular code module. In other words, it's just a window into which you type your code, and it comes complete with all the usual Visual Basic Editor bells and whistles (color-coded syntax, IntelliSense, and so on). As you'll see, the key to a class module is what you put inside it.

Creating the Class Module

To create a new class module, make sure the VBA project you want to work with is highlighted in the Project Explorer, and then use any of the following techniques:

- Select Insert | Class Module.
- Right-click the project name and select Insert | Class Module from the shortcut menu.
- Drop down the Insert toolbar button (the second from the left) and choose the Class Module command.

Now use the Properties window to adjust the `Name` property to whatever name you want to use for the object. (When naming a class module, it's traditional to preface the name with an uppercase C.) You'll then use this name to create an object based on the class.

For example, if you name the class module `CInvoice`, you can set up an object variable named `newInvoice` to be of type `CInvoice` with the following statement:

```
Dim newInvoice As New CInvoice
```

Although this creates the object and allocates memory for it, note that the object isn't instanced until you refer to it in code (say, by setting one of its properties or running one of its methods.)

If you would prefer that VBA not allocate memory for a custom object until your code actually needs it, you can create and instance the object in one shot with the following statements:

```
Dim newInvoice As CInvoice
Set newInvoice = New CInvoice
```

Defining the Data Members

When you assign a value to an object's property, that value is stored internally in a variable that's accessible only within the object itself. An outsider (that is, a person or program using the object) can manipulate only the exposed property, so the "real" object data is protected from direct manipulation and possible corruption.

Your first chore after you've created a class module is to declare these internal class variables, which are called *data members*. You'll normally declare one variable for each item of data you want to store in the object, and you follow these guidelines:

- Declare each variable using the `Private` keyword to ensure that the variables are available only within the class module.
- It's traditional to preface these variable names with `m_` to indicate that they are data members of the class.

In the invoice example, we'll declare one variable for each of the seven items of information we want to work with:

```
Private m_ID As Long
Private m_CustAcct As String
Private m_Amount As Currency
Private m_InvDate As Date
Private m_DueDate As Date
Private m_PmtDate As Date
Private m_Overdue As Boolean
```

NOTE: THIS CLASS EXAMPLE IS ON THE CD

The class module example that I'll be building over the next few sections is called `CInvoice`, and you'll find it in the Chaptr16.xls file on the CD. I've also made a copy of the class module in the text file named CInvoice.cls.

Implementing Class Properties

Okay, your class module is set up and is now ready for the next step, which is to define the properties for the class. As with the data members, the basic idea is to create a property for each item of information you want to store. This step involves setting up two things for each property: a mechanism for returning the current value of the property, and an optional mechanism for changing the value of the property. (You can omit the latter mechanism if you want to define the property as read-only.)

These "mechanisms" are really just special VBA procedures that are defined with the keywords `Property Get` and `Property Set`. These are explained in detail in the next two sections.

The `Property Get` Procedure

You use a `Property Get` procedure to return the current value of a property. This type of procedure uses the following general format:

```
Public Property Get PropertyName() As DataType
    [Extra statements, if needed, go here]
    PropertyName = m_DataMember
End Property
```

Using the `Public` keyword ensures that this procedure (and, hence, the property) is available to external processes. *`PropertyName`* is the name of the property, *`DataType`* is the data type of the property, and *`m_DataMember`* is the data member variable that holds the current value of the property. You can also add extra statements within the procedure, but this is rarely done with `Property Get` procedures.

For the `CInvoice` object example, here's the `Property Get` procedure we'll use to return the current value of the `ID` property:

```
Public Property Get ID() As Long
    ID = m_ID
End Property
```

With this in place, the user can then return the ID number of an instanced `CInvoice` class by referencing the `ID` property. For example, if `newInvoice` is an instance of the `CInvoice` class, the following statement stores the value of the `ID` property in a variable named `currID`:

```
currID = newInvoice.ID
```

Listing 16.3 is the complete listing of the `Property Get` procedures for all seven properties in the `CInvoice` class.

Listing 16.3. The `Property Get` procedures for the `CInvoice` class.

```
' Returns the current value of the CInvoice.ID property
'
Public Property Get ID() As Long
    ID = m_ID
End Property
'
' Returns the current value of the CInvoice.CustomerAccount property
'
Public Property Get CustomerAccount() As String
    CustomerAccount = m_CustAcct
End Property
'
' Returns the current value of the CInvoice.Amount property
'
Public Property Get Amount() As Currency
    Amount = m_Amount
End Property
'
' Returns the current value of the CInvoice.InvoiceDate property
'
Public Property Get InvoiceDate() As Date
    InvoiceDate = m_InvDate
End Property
'
' Returns the current value of the CInvoice.DueDate property
'
Public Property Get DueDate() As Date
    DueDate = m_DueDate
End Property
'
' Returns the current value of the CInvoice.PaymentDate property
'
Public Property Get PaymentDate() As Date
    PaymentDate = m_PmtDate
End Property
'
' Returns the current value of the CInvoice.Overdue property
'
Public Property Get Overdue() As Boolean
    Overdue = m_Overdue
End Property
```

The `Property Let` Procedure

Unless you want a property to be read-only, you must also define a procedure that lets the user assign a new value to the property. To do this, you set up a `Property Let` procedure within the class module:

```
Public Property Let PropertyName(NewValue As DataType)
    [Extra statements, if needed, go here]
    m_DataMember = NewValue
End Property
```

As before, `PropertyName` is the name of the property. Also, `NewData` is the value the user is attempting to assign to the property, `DataType` is the data type that must be used for the property value, and `m_DataMember` is the data member variable whose value will be adjusted. You can also add extra statements to test the new value to make sure it passes muster before changing the data member.

For the `CInvoice` object example, here's the `Property Let` procedure we'll use to set the current value of the `InvoiceDate` property:

```
Public Property Let InvoiceDate(InvDate As Date)
    If InvDate < Date Then
        InvDate = Date
        MsgBox "Can't set an invoice date in the past!" & _
            Chr(13) & "Today's date will be used, instead."
    End If
    m_InvDate = InvDate
    m_DueDate = m_InvDate + 30
End Property
```

This procedure first checks to see if the new value (the `InvDate` argument) is less than today's date. If it is, `InvDate` is set to today's date, and a message is displayed to warn the user of the change. Then the `m_InvDate` data member is set to `InvDate`, and the `m_DueDate` member is set to the invoice date plus 30 days.

The user can now assign an invoice date of an instanced `CInvoice` class by referencing the `InvoiceDate` property. If `newInvoice` is an instance of the `CInvoice` class, for example, the following statement sets the value of the `InvoiceDate` property to today's date:

```
newInvoice.InvoiceDate = Date
```

Listing 16.4 shows all the `Property Let` procedures for the seven properties in the `CInvoice` class.

Listing 16.4. The `Property Let` procedures for the `CInvoice` class.

```
' Changes the value of the CInvoice.CustomerAccount property
'
Public Property Let CustomerAccount(CustAcct As String)
    m_CustAcct = CustAcct
End Property
'
' Changes the value of the CInvoice.Amount property
'
Public Property Let Amount(Amt As Currency)
    If Amt < 0 Then
        Amt = 0
        MsgBox "Can't enter a negative amount!" & _
            Chr(13) & "$0.00 will be used, instead."
```

```
    End If
    m_Amount = Amt
End Property
'
' Changes the value of the CInvoice.InvoiceDate property
'
Public Property Let InvoiceDate(InvDate As Date)
    If InvDate < Date Then
        InvDate = Date
        MsgBox "Can't set an invoice date in the past!" & _
            Chr(13) & "Today's date will be used, instead."
    End If
    m_InvDate = InvDate
    m_DueDate = m_InvDate + 30
End Property
'
' Changes the value of the CInvoice.PaymentDate property
'
Public Property Let PaymentDate(PmtDate As Date)
    m_PmtDate = PmtDate
    m_Overdue = False
End Property
```

Note in particular that there is no `Property Let` procedure for the `ID`, `DueDate`, and `Overdue` properties. By leaving out these `Property Let` procedures, we set up these properties as read-only.

Setting Up the Class Methods

A typical object comes equipped with one or more methods that act upon the object, and you can establish similar functionality in your custom classes. All you need to do is add one or more Sub or Function procedures defined with the `Public` keyword to make them available to controlling applications.

For example, you could define an `Update` method for the `CInvoice` class. In this method, the procedure should check to see if the invoice due date is prior to today's date and if the invoice hasn't yet been paid. If both conditions are true, the invoice is overdue. Here's a procedure that does this:

```
Public Sub Update()
    If m_DueDate < Date And m_PmtDate = 0 Then
        m_Overdue = True
    End If
End Sub
```

Defining the Class Events

Custom classes support only two events: `Initialize` and `Terminate`.

The Initialize Event

The `Initialize` event fires when the class is first instanced as an object:

- If you declare a class object variable with the `New` keyword, the event fires the first time you use the variable in code (say, when you assign a value to a property). Here's an example:

  ```
  Dim testInvoice As New CInvoice
  testInvoice.ID = 1234 ' Initialize event fires here
  ```

- If you declare a class object variable without the `New` keyword, the `Initialize` event fires when you `Set` the variable equal to a new instance of the class, as in this example:

  ```
  Dim testInvoice As CInvoice
  Set testInvoice = New CInvoice ' Initialize event fires here
  ```

To trap this event, add to the class module a `Private` procedure that uses the following format:

```
Private Sub Class_Initialize()
    [Initialization code goes here]
End Sub
```

For example, the following procedure initializes a `CInvoice` object by setting `m_ID` to a random six-digit number, `m_InvDate` to today's date, and `m_DueDate` to 30 days from now:

```
Private Sub Class_Initialize()
    Randomize
    m_ID = Int((999999 - 100000) * Rnd + 100000)
    m_InvDate = Date
    m_DueDate = m_InvDate + 30
End Sub
```

The Terminate Event

The `Terminate` event fires when all references to class objects are set to `Nothing`. This is useful for running code that performs cleanup chores. To trap this event, add to the class module a `Private` procedure that uses the following format:

```
Private Sub Class_Terminate()
    [Termination code goes here]
End Sub
```

Creating Class Collections

If you need to work with multiple instances of your custom class, you should consider creating a *collection class* that can hold one or more of your class objects. As you might expect, the information you learned earlier about user-defined `Collection` objects will prove useful here.

Setting Up a Class Module for a Collection

To get started, create a new class module and use the plural of the object name as the name of the new class. For the `CInvoice` class example, the collection class is named `CInvoices`. Only one data member is required for a collection class, and that member is a `Private` variable declared as a `Collection` object, like so:

```
Private m_Invoices As New Collection
```

Providing Wrappers for Each Member

As you learned earlier, custom collections come with four members: the `Count` property and the `Add`, `Item`, and `Remove` methods. Since you've declared the `Collection` object as `Private`, external processes won't be able to access this object directly (which is what you want). Therefore, to implement these members in your collection class, you have to create procedures within the class module that mimic the underlying `Collection` object members.

The `Count` property is easy enough. You just set up a `Property Get` procedure that returns the `Count` property of the `Collection` object, like so:

```
Public Property Get Count() As Long
   Count = m_Invoices.Count
End Property
```

A procedure that encapsulates a method or function within it is called a *wrapper*. You normally implement a wrapper either to shield the user from the complexity of the encapsulated method or function, or to insert new functionality.

For example, when adding new `CInvoice` objects to the `CInvoices` collection, I would like to do two things:

- Hide the `Collection` object's `Add` method arguments completely.
- Let the user specify the customer account number and invoice amount at the time the `CInvoice` object is added.

To accomplish these goals, I inserted the following `Add` function into the `CInvoices` class module:

```
Public Function Add(CustAcct As String, Amt As Currency) As CInvoice
    Dim newInvoice As New CInvoice
    With newInvoice
        .CustomerAccount = CustAcct
        .Amount = Amt
        m_Invoices.Add Item:=newInvoice, Key:=CStr(.ID)
    End With
    Set Add = newInvoice
End Function
```

As you can see, this function accepts arguments for the customer account and invoice amount, and it will return a new CInvoice object. The latter is created by declaring an object variable (newInvoice) to be of type CInvoice. Then a With...End With sets the CustomerAccount and Amount properties for this new object and invokes the Add method for the private Collection object:

- The Item argument is the newInvoice object.
- The Key argument is the string equivalent of the ID property of the newInvoice object. How can we do this if we haven't set the ID property yet? Well, recall from earlier in this chapter that the ID property is assigned during the Initialize event for the CInvoice class. In this case, this event fires the first time we refer to the object in code, which is when VBA runs the With newInvoice statement. Therefore, the ID property is already initialized by the time we run the Add method.

Finally, a Set statement returns newInvoice as the function value.

To use this method in code, you would write statements similar to the following:

```
Dim myInvoices As New CInvoices
Dim myInvoice As New CInvoice
Set myInvoice = myInvoices.Add(CustAcct:="12-3456", Amt:=1234.56)
```

Note in particular that the arguments specified in the Add function can be used as named arguments in the CInvoices object's Add method.

Here are two more CInvoices class module procedures that serve as wrappers for the Collection object's Item and Remove methods:

```
' This function is a wrapper for the Item method
'
Public Function Item(Index As Variant) As CInvoice
    Set Item = m_Invoices.Item(InvID)
End Function
'
' This procedure is a wrapper for the Remove method
'
Public Sub Delete(Index As Variant)
    m_Invoices.Remove InvID
End Sub
```

Note the use of Variant arguments in these procedures. You need to use the Variant data type here because the Index argument can be either a number or a string.

It's also important to note that there is no such thing as a default method for a custom class. Earlier you learned that, for a Collection object, the Item method is the default, so the following statements are equivalent:

```
myCollection(1)
myCollection.Item(1)
```

With a collection class, however, the `Item` method is *not* the default. Therefore, you must specify the `Item` method any time you need to return an object from the collection:

```
Dim myInvoices As New CInvoices
Dim myInvoice As New CInvoice
myInvoices.Add CustAcct:="12-3456", Amt:=1234.56
Set myInvoice = myInvoices(1)        ' This statement generates an error
Set myInvoice = myInvoices.Item(1)   ' This statement is correct
```

Implementing Class Properties for Objects

You've seen throughout this book that object properties often double as objects themselves. For example, an Excel Range object has a `Font` property that also corresponds to the Font object. Similarly, a Workbook object has a `Worksheets` property that doubles as the `Worksheets` collection—the set of all worksheets in the workbook.

You can implement objects as properties in your custom classes as well. For example, suppose you wanted to create a custom class called `CCustomer` to store customer data. In a simplified model, you would want to track the customer's account number, name, and address. Therefore, your `CCustomer` class module would start off with the following data members:

```
Private m_CustAcct As String
Private m_CustName As String
Private m_CustAddress As String
```

However, suppose you also wanted to include in this class all the invoices for a particular customer. That sounds like a job for our `CInvoices` class, so you would add the following data member to the `CCustomer` class module:

```
Private m_CustInvoices As CInvoices
```

How do you manipulate this new data member? Returning the current collection of the customer's invoices is a simple matter of creating a `Property Get` procedure. For example, if the collection of customer invoices will be given by the `Invoices` property, you would define the following `Property Get` procedure:

```
Public Property Get Invoices() As CInvoices
    Set Invoices = m_CustInvoices
End Property
```

To assign a collection to this `Invoices` property, you need to use a `Property Set` procedure. This type of procedure is used to assign an object to a property, and it uses the following format:

```
Public Property Set PropertyName(NewObject As DataType)
    [Extra statements, if needed, go here]
    Set m_DataMember = NewObject
End Property
```

As before, *PropertyName* is the name of the property. Also, *NewObject* is the object you want to assign, *DataType* is the object's data type, and *m_DataMember* is the object data member variable. Here's an example:

```
Public Property Set Invoices(InvoicesObject As CInvoices)
    Set m_CustInvoices = InvoicesObject
End Property
```

Listing 16.5 shows an example of how you would implement this in code.

Listing 16.5. Using an object in a custom class.

```
Sub CustomClassObjectTest()
    Dim newCustomer As New CCustomer
    With newCustomer
        .Account = "12-3456"
        .Name = "ACME Coyote Supplies"
        .Address = "123 Wily Way"
        Set .Invoices = New CInvoices
    End With
    With .Invoices
        .Add CustAcct:=newCustomer.Account, Amt:=1234.56
        .Add CustAcct:=newCustomer.Account, Amt:=432.10
    End With
End Sub
```

Using Events with the Excel Application Object

Excel's `Application` object recognizes quite a few events, but you can't use them directly. Instead, you have to tell VBA that you want the `Application` object to trap events. Let's work through the steps you have to follow.

First, start a new class module and name it (I named mine `CEvents`). This class module will contain the event procedures for the `Application` object.

Next, at the top of the class module, declare a new `Application` object variable. Make it `Public` so that it can be referenced by external processes, and use the `WithEvents` keyword to connect the variable to the object's events. Here's an example:

```
Public WithEvents XLEvents As Application
```

For each event you want to trap, create an event handler in the class module. These event handlers use the following format:

```
Private Sub AppVariable_Event(Parameters)
    [Event handler code goes here]
End Sub
```

`AppVariable` is the name of the `Application` object variable that you declared at the top of the module, `Event` is the event you want to trap, and `Parameters` is a list of the parameters required by the event (if any). For example, the following procedure handles the `NewWorkbook` event by tiling all the open windows:

```
Private Sub XLEvents_NewWorkbook(ByVal Wb As Workbook)
    Application.Windows.Arrange xlArrangeStyleTiled
End Sub
```

To use these event handlers in your code, first add a global variable at the module level. This variable must use the object type of the class module you created, as in this example:

```
Dim EventsApp As New CEvents
```

Now you need to instance this object variable by associating it with Excel's `Application` object, as shown here:

```
Set EventApp.XLEvents = Application
```

For convenience, you can place this statement in the `Open` event for your workbook (which is what I've done in Chaptr16.xls).

Summary

This chapter showed you how to create custom objects. I began by showing you how to work with custom collections, including how to declare a `Collection` object and how to add, reference, and remove objects. From there I turned to class modules and showed you how to use them to create user-defined objects. You learned how to set up a class module, how to define properties using `Property Get` and `Property Let` procedures, and how to implement class methods. I also touched on the `Initialize` and `Terminate` events and showed you how to create a class collection. I closed by showing you how to use a class module to work with the events in Excel's `Application` object.

Here are a couple of chapters where you'll find related information:

- In Chapter 17, "Using VBA to Work with Excel Lists," I use a custom collection to work with the text boxes on a user form.
- Chapter 25, "Programming the Windows API," shows you how to use the Windows API functions in your VBA code. These functions are often complex, so I also show you how to use class modules to act as wrappers for these functions.

Part V

Unleashing VBA Database Programming

IN THIS PART

CHAPTER 17

Using VBA to Work with Excel Lists

IN THIS CHAPTER

Information appears to stew out of me naturally, like the precious ottar of roses out of the otter.

—Mark Twain

These days, there's no shortage of dedicated database programs for the Windows market. There's the Access package that comes with Microsoft Office, of course, and there are also Windows versions of FoxPro, Paradox, and dBASE, to name a few. These high-end programs are full relational database management systems designed to handle complex, interrelated tables, queries, and reports.

If your database needs aren't quite so grandiose, however, these programs probably provide more than you need. If all you want is to store a few names and addresses, for example, it's overkill to fire up Access every time you need to edit your data or find a name.

Fortunately, when it comes to simple tables of data, you don't have to bother with all the bells and whistles of the big-time database systems. Excel is more than capable of handling flat-file databases right in a worksheet. You can create simple data-entry forms with a few mouse clicks, and you can sort the data, summarize it, extract records based on criteria, and lots more.

These techniques give you powerful ways to work with both native Excel data and external data in various formats. However, what if you need to set up Excel so that other, less experienced users can work with data? In this case, you need to establish a custom user interface that shields these users from the intricacies of Excel databases and lists. This chapter shows you how to do just that. We'll look at using VBA to work with Excel lists, including entering, editing, filtering, deleting, sorting, and subtotaling data.

What Is a List?

A database can be defined as any collection of related information with an organizational structure that makes it easy to find or extract data from its contents. Examples of real-world databases are a phone book organized by name and a library card catalog organized by book title.

In Excel, a database is called a *list,* and it refers to a worksheet range that has the following properties:

Field: A single type of information, such as a name, address, or phone number. In Excel lists, each column is a field.

Field value: A single item in a field. In an Excel list, the field values are the individual cells.

Field name: A unique name you assign to every list field (worksheet column). These names are always found in the first row of the list.

Record: A collection of associated field values. In Excel lists, each row is a record.

List range: The worksheet range that includes all the records, fields, and field names of a list.

Working with List Data

If the data you want to work with exists on an Excel worksheet, VBA offers a number of list-related properties and methods for both Range objects and Worksheet objects. To demonstrate these VBA techniques, I'll take you through an example: a simple database application that stores information on customers.

The application's workbook is called Customer.xls, and you'll find it on the CD that comes with this book. When you open Customer.xls, you'll see the screen shown in Figure 17.1. The workbook consists of a single Customer Database worksheet on which you enter and work with data. There are two sections: Customer Database is where you enter your data, and Customer Criteria is where you enter your advanced filter criteria.

FIGURE 17.1.
The Customer Database worksheet.

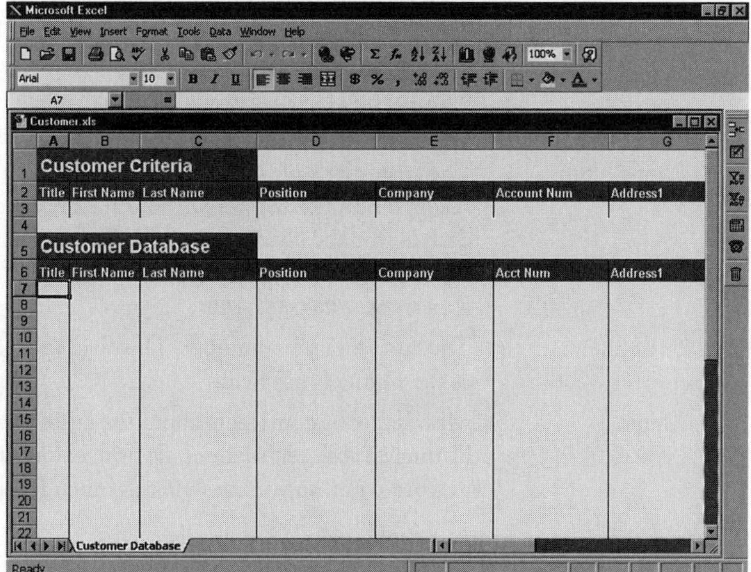

The Customer Database section consists of the following 15 fields:

Field	*Description*
Title	The form of address you use with the customer (for example, Miss, Ms., Mr.).
First Name	The customer's first name.
Last name	The customer's surname.
Position	The customer's job title.

continues

Field	*Description*
Company	The name of the company the customer works for.
Acct Num	The account number of either the customer or the company he works for.
Address1	The first part of the customer's street address.
Address2	The second part of the address.
City	The customer's city.
State	The customer's state.
Country	The customer's country.
ZIP Code	The customer's ZIP code. This field has been formatted to accept both the normal five-digit ZIP codes and the newer nine-digit codes. Note that a dash is added automatically whenever you enter a nine-digit code. For example, if you enter `123456789`, the data appears as `12345-6789`. Canadian postal codes are displayed as they are entered.
Phone Num	The customer's phone number. This field has been formatted to accept a number with or without the area code and to enter the dash automatically. For example, if you enter `1234567`, the number appears as `123-4567`. If you enter `12345678901`, the number appears as `1-234-567-8901`.
Fax Num	The customer's fax number. This field uses the same formatting as the Phone Num field.
Memo	Miscellaneous comments about the customer (for example, birthdays, children's names, favorite color). The field is formatted as word wrap, so you can enter as much information as you need.

The workbook also contains the following VBA objects:

`Customer` module: A collection of VBA procedures. I'll describe each procedure in this chapter.

`frmCustomer` form: A custom user form you can use to add, edit, and delete customer records (see Figure 17.2). This form consists of three tabs that contain text boxes corresponding to each field in the list. The form shown in Figure 17.2 is used for adding customers, but as you'll soon see, it's quite simple to customize the form for use with other procedures.

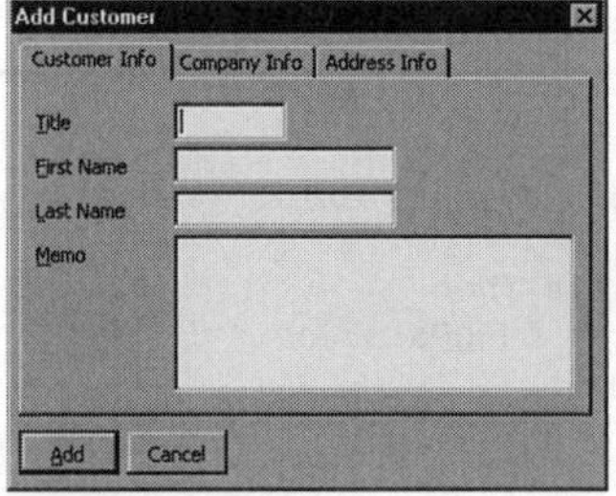

FIGURE 17.2.
The form used in the customer database application.

Setting Up the Application

Before learning how to use the Customer Database application and examining the VBA code that makes it tick, let's take a second to see how the application sets itself up.

In addition to the user form shown in Figure 17.2, the application provides two other user interface features: custom menu commands and a custom toolbar. These features are put in place when you first open the workbook. The code that adds the menu and displays the toolbar is part of the workbook's `Open` event, which is shown in Listing 17.1.

Listing 17.1. The code for the Customer.xls workbook's Open event.

```
Private Sub Workbook_Open()
    Dim menuData As CommandBarPopup
    Dim dbMenu As CommandBarPopup
    Dim ctrl As CommandBarControl
    Dim menuExists As Boolean
    '
    ' Set up Customer Database submenu on the Data menu
    '
    Application.StatusBar = "Setting up the Customer Database submenu..."
    menuExists = False
    '
    ' Get the Data menu (ID=30011)
    '
    Set menuData = Application.CommandBars.FindControl(Id:=30011)
    '
    ' Make sure the submenu doesn't exist
    '
    For Each ctrl In menuData.Controls
        If ctrl.Caption = "C&ustomer Database" Then
            menuExists = True
            Exit For
        End If
```

continues

Listing 17.1. continued

```
    Next 'ctrl
    '
    ' If the submenu doesn't exist, add it
    '
    If Not menuExists Then
        Set dbMenu = menuData.Controls.Add(Type:=msoControlPopup)
        With dbMenu
            '
            ' Set up the submenu
            '
            .Caption = "C&ustomer Database"
            .Tag = "Customer Database Popup"
            .BeginGroup = True
            '
            ' Add the submenu commands
            '
            Set ctrl = .Controls.Add(Type:=msoControlButton)
            ctrl.Caption = "&Add Customer..."
            ctrl.OnAction = "AddCustomer"
            Set ctrl = .Controls.Add(Type:=msoControlButton)
            ctrl.Caption = "&Edit Customer..."
            ctrl.OnAction = "EditCustomer"
            Set ctrl = .Controls.Add(Type:=msoControlButton)
            ctrl.Caption = "&Filter Customers"
            ctrl.OnAction = "FilterCustomers"
            ctrl.BeginGroup = True
            Set ctrl = .Controls.Add(Type:=msoControlButton)
            ctrl.Caption = "&Show All Customers"
            ctrl.OnAction = "ShowAllCustomers"
            Set ctrl = .Controls.Add(Type:=msoControlButton)
            ctrl.Caption = "&Count Customers..."
            ctrl.OnAction = "CountCustomers"
            ctrl.BeginGroup = True
            Set ctrl = .Controls.Add(Type:=msoControlButton)
            ctrl.Caption = "&Phone Customer..."
            ctrl.OnAction = "PhoneCustomer"
            Set ctrl = .Controls.Add(Type:=msoControlButton)
            ctrl.Caption = "&Delete Customer..."
            ctrl.OnAction = "DeleteCustomer"
            ctrl.BeginGroup = True
        End With
    End If
    '
    ' Display the Customer Database toolbar
    '
    With Application.CommandBars("Customer Database")
        .Visible = True
        .Position = msoBarRight
    End With
    '
    ' Select first database cell and reset the status bar
    '
    ActiveSheet.Cells(Range("Database").Row + 1, 1).Select
    Application.StatusBar = False
End Sub
```

The bulk of this procedure is used to create a new submenu named Customer Database on Excel's Data menu. To do this, the code runs through the following tasks:

- The Data menu is found and stored in the `menuData` object variable.
- A `For Each...Next` loop checks each Data menu command to see if the Customer Database command already exists.
- If it doesn't exist, a new Control object is added to the Data menu. This is an `msoControlPopup` item, which means it will appear on the Data menu as a submenu command.
- The commands are then added to this submenu. For each control, the `Caption` property sets the command name, and the `OnAction` property sets the procedure that runs when you select the command.

NOTE: VBA MENU TECHNIQUES

All of these menu techniques were discussed in detail in Chapter 12, "Creating Custom Menus and Toolbars."

The procedure then displays the Customer Database toolbar (which is attached to the workbook) and positions it docked on the right side of the screen. Note that each button on this toolbar corresponds to one of the commands just added to the Customer Database submenu.

The Customer Database submenu and toolbar work only with the Customer.xls workbook. Therefore, these tools need to be disabled when the user activates a different workbook. To handle this, the appropriate objects are disabled in the workbook's `Deactivate` event, as shown in Listing 17.2.

Listing 17.2. The code for the Customer.xls workbook's `Deactivate` event.

```
Private Sub Workbook_Deactivate()
    Dim dbMenu As CommandBarControl
    '
    ' Disable the Customer Database command
    '
    Set dbMenu = Application.CommandBars.FindControl(Tag:="Customer Database
    ➥Popup")
    If Not dbMenu Is Nothing Then dbMenu.Enabled = False
    '
    ' Hide the Customer Database toolbar
    '
    Application.CommandBars("Customer Database").Visible = False
End Sub
```

This procedure returns the Customer Database menu by using the `FindControl` method to search for the menu's `Tag` property (which was set in Listing 17.1). It then sets the menu's `Enabled` property to `False`, and sets the toolbar's `Visible` property to `False`.

When the user returns to the workbook, the menu and toolbar must be restored, and that's what happens in the workbook's `Activate` event handler, shown in Listing 17.3.

Listing 17.3. The code for the Customer.xls workbook's `Activate` event.

```
Private Sub Workbook_Activate()
    Dim dbMenu As CommandBarControl
    '
    ' Enable the Customer Database command
    '
    Set dbMenu = Application.CommandBars.FindControl(Tag:="Customer Database
    ➥Popup")
    If Not dbMenu Is Nothing Then dbMenu.Enabled = True
    '
    ' Display the Customer Database toolbar
    '
    Application.CommandBars("Customer Database").Visible = True
End Sub
```

Finally, when the user closes the workbook, the application should delete the Customer Database menu. (The toolbar is hidden automatically.) Listing 17.4 shows the `BeforeClose` event handler, which does just that.

Listing 17.4. The code for the Customer.xls workbook's `BeforeClose` event.

```
Private Sub Workbook_BeforeClose(Cancel As Boolean)
    Dim dbMenu As CommandBarControl
    '
    ' Delete the Customer Database command
    '
    Set dbMenu = Application.CommandBars.FindControl(Tag:="Customer Database
    ➥Popup")
    If Not dbMenu Is Nothing Then dbMenu.Delete
End Sub
```

Entering Data

You can use two basic methods to enter database records on a worksheet: Enter the data directly, or use the built-in list form that comes with Excel. However, there are a few reasons why neither method is ideal for a database application:

- Entering data directly on the worksheet becomes a problem for a database that's wider than the screen (as is the customer database). Not all the fields appear on-screen at once, which means you can never see the entire record you're adding, and it can be a chore to navigate between fields at either end of the database.
- As you'll see, if you want to control a database using VBA, it simplifies your code immeasurably if the database range has a defined name (such as "Database"). However, if you add new records at the end of the list manually, you have to redefine the database range name.
- The Excel form solves the aforementioned problems, but there's no way to manipulate the form's fields from VBA.

Entering Data Using a Custom Form

To overcome these problems, the Customer Database application comes with the custom form shown in Figure 17.2. Using this form to enter your customers' information gives you the following advantages:

- There is an edit box for every field in the database, so you always see the entire record before you add it.
- Navigating the fields is easy. If you have a mouse, just click on the field you want to work with. From the keyboard, use each field's accelerator key (the underlined letter) to select the field.
- When you click Add, the form stays on-screen so that you can add another customer.
- The Database range name is updated automatically.

The following procedure shows you how to add customers with the custom form:

1. Select Data | Customer Database | Add Customers or click the Add Customer button on the Customer Database toolbar. The Add Customer form appears.

2. Fill in the fields for the customer.
3. Click the Add button. The customer is added to the list and a fresh Add Customer form appears.
4. Repeat steps 2 and 3 to add more customers.
5. When you're done, click Close to return to the worksheet.

Handling Data Entry with VBA

When you select Data | Customer Database | Add Customers or click the Add Customer button on the Customer Database toolbar, the application launches the `AddCustomer` procedure, shown in Listing 17.5.

Listing 17.5. The AddCustomer procedure runs when you select the Add Customer command or click the Add Customer button.

```
Sub AddCustomer()
    frmCustomer.Show
    Set frmCustomer = Nothing
End Sub
```

This simple procedure just runs the form's `Show` method to display the form. When the user is done with the form, it's `Set` to `Nothing` to remove it from memory.

Preparing the Data Entry Form

After the form's `Show` method is run, but before the form appears on-screen, the form's `Activate` event fires. Trapping this event gives you a chance to perform any other setup chores that are necessary to get the form ready for the user. Listing 17.6 shows an event handler that does this.

Listing 17.6. Some global variables and the code for the form's Activate event.

```
Dim textBoxes As New Collection ' Holds the form's text boxes
Dim totalFields As Integer      ' The total number of fields
Dim textboxNames() As String    ' Holds the names of the text boxes
'
' This event fires just before the form appears on-screen
'
Private Sub UserForm_Activate()
    Dim ctrl As Control
    '
    ' Set up the custom textBoxes collection
    '
    For Each ctrl In Me.Controls
        If Left(ctrl.Name, 3) = "txt" Then
            textBoxes.Add Item:=ctrl, key:=ctrl.Name
        End If
    Next 'ctrl
    '
    ' Get the total number of fields in the list
    ' and then redimension the array of text box names
    '
    totalFields = Range("Database").Columns.Count
    ReDim textboxNames(totalFields)
    '
    ' Initialize the array of text box names in the
    ' order they appear in the list
    '
    textboxNames(0) = "txtTitle"
    textboxNames(1) = "txtFirst"
    textboxNames(2) = "txtLast"
    textboxNames(3) = "txtPosition"
```

```
    textboxNames(4) = "txtCompany"
    textboxNames(5) = "txtAccount"
    textboxNames(6) = "txtAddress1"
    textboxNames(7) = "txtAddress2"
    textboxNames(8) = "txtCity"
    textboxNames(9) = "txtState"
    textboxNames(10) = "txtZIP"
    textboxNames(11) = "txtCountry"
    textboxNames(12) = "txtPhone"
    textboxNames(13) = "txtFax"
    textboxNames(14) = "txtMemo"
    '
    ' Set up the form using the caption on the cmdAction
    ' button to differentiate the various modules
    '
    Select Case cmdAction.Caption
        Case "Add"     ' The Add Customer command
            ' Nothing to do!
        Case "OK"      ' The Edit Customer command
            ReadData ActiveCell.Row
        Case "Delete" ' The Delete Customer command
            ReadData ActiveCell.Row
            '
            ' Disable the text boxes
            '
            For Each ctrl In textBoxes
                ctrl.Enabled = False
            Next 'ctrl
            cmdCancel.SetFocus
    End Select
End Sub
```


Here's a quick rundown of all the tasks performed by this event handler:

- First, several module-level variables are declared: `textBoxes` is a custom collection object that will store all the form's text boxes (I explained these objects in the last chapter), `totalFields` is the number of fields in the database, and `textboxNames` is a dynamic array that holds the names assigned to each text box.
- The text boxes are added to the custom `textBoxes` collection. A `For Each...Next` loop runs through all the controls on the form. Every text box name begins with `txt` (for example, `txtTitle` and `txtFirst`), so just these controls are inserted into the collection. Note, too, that the name of each text box is stored as the `Key` value.
- The total number of fields in the database (as given by the `Columns.Count` property of the `Database` range) is stored in the `totalFields` variable, and then the `textboxNames` array is redimensioned accordingly.
- The individual elements in the `textboxNames` array are set to the names used for each text box control. Note in particular that these names are assigned in the order the fields appear in the database. As you'll see, this will save us some work later.

- This form is used with the Add Customer, Edit Customer, and Delete Customer commands. Each of these commands uses a different `Caption` property for the `cmdAction` button (the one on the left). In order, the captions used are Add, OK, and Delete. Since each command requires a slightly different setup, a `Select Case` checks the button's `Caption` property and branches accordingly:

    Add: This is the default setup for the form, so there's nothing to do.

    OK: This case runs the `ReadData` command to load the data for the current customer into the form's text boxes. I'll show you this procedure later in this chapter.

    Delete: Runs `ReadData` and loops through the `textBoxes` collection to disable all the text boxes (we don't want the user to make changes here).

Writing Data to the Database

With the `Activate` event handled, the form is then displayed on-screen. At this point, the user can do one of two things:

- Click Cancel to bail out of the form. In this case, the Cancel button's `Click` event fires. The event handler (which is named `cmdCancel_Click`) runs the `Unload Me` statement to shut down the form.
- Fill in the text boxes and then click Add.

If the user clicks Add, the `cmdAction` button's `Click` event fires, and the event handler shown in Listing 17.7 kicks in.

Listing 17.7. This event handler fires when the user clicks the `cmdAction` button. It uses the button caption to differentiate between the various actions.

```
Private Sub cmdAction_Click()
    Dim dbTopRow As Integer
    Dim dbRows As Integer
    Dim dbNewRow As Integer
    Dim ctrl As Control
    Select Case cmdAction.Caption
        Case "Add"
            With Range("Database")
                '
                ' Insert the new row
                '
                dbTopRow = .Row
                dbRows = .Rows.Count
                dbNewRow = dbTopRow + dbRows
                WriteData dbNewRow
                '
                ' Define new Database range name
                '
                .Select
```

```
            Selection.Resize(RowSize:=dbRows + 1, ColumnSize:=
            ➥totalFields).Select
            Names.Add Name:="Database", RefersTo:=Selection
            '
            ' Select first cell in new record
            '
            Cells(dbNewRow, 1).Select
        End With
        '
        ' Clear the text boxes
        '
        For Each ctrl In textBoxes
            ctrl.Text = ""
        Next 'ctrl
        '
        ' Change Cancel to Close
        '
        cmdCancel.Caption = "Close"
    Case "OK"
        WriteData ActiveCell.Row
        Unload Me
    Case "Delete"
        ActiveCell.EntireRow.Delete
        Unload Me
    End Select
End Sub
```


Once again, a `Select Case` structure examines the `Caption` property of the `cmdAction` button to differentiate between each action. For the `Add` case, the procedure performs the following chores:

- The `With` statement sets several variables that define the boundaries of the `Database` range. In particular, the `dbNewRow` variable points to the first row below the database.
- The `WriteData` procedure is called to place the text box data onto the worksheet (see Listing 17.8).
- The next three statements redefine the `Database` range name. The existing range is selected, and the `Resize` method adds one row. With this new range selected, the `Names.Add` method redefines `Database` to refer to the selection.
- The selection is collapsed by moving to the first cell of the new record.
- A `For Each...Next` loop runs through the `textBoxes` collection, setting each text box value to the null string. This clears the data so that the user can enter another customer.
- The next line changes the name of the `cmdCancel` button to Close. Because you're adding a customer, it's too late to cancel the procedure. Therefore, it's normal programming practice to rename a Cancel button "Close" in this situation.

Listing 17.8 shows the code for the `WriteData` procedure.

Listing 17.8. The `WriteData` procedure writes the form data to the specified row in the database.

```
Sub WriteData(dbRow As Integer)
    Dim i As Integer, fieldValue As Variant
    '
    ' Enter data in fields
    '
    For i = 1 To totalFields
        fieldValue = textBoxes(textboxNames(i - 1)).Text
        Cells(dbRow, i).Value = fieldValue
    Next 'i
    '
    ' Select first cell in record
    '
    Cells(dbRow, 1).Select
End Sub
```

Note, first, that this procedure accepts an integer argument that represents the row in the database where the data will be stored.

A `For...Next` loop is used to add the data. Recall that earlier the individual elements of the `textboxNames` array were set to the names of each text box in the order that the fields appear in the database. Therefore, the expression `textboxNames(i - 1)` will return the name of a text box, and plugging this name into the `textBoxes` collection will return the corresponding TextBox object. (Note that the `For...Next` loop ensures that these names are returned in database order.) Given that object, we use the `Text` property to store the value of the field in the `fieldValue` variable.

The `Cells` method is then used to return the individual cells in the specified database row. As `i` increases, we move from left to right through the database fields, which is why it was important that we set up the `textboxNames` array in database order. Each time through the loop, the cell value is assigned the derived text box value.

Editing Data

If you need to make changes to a record, you can just edit the worksheet cells directly. However, the Customer Database application lets you edit the data using the convenience of the custom form.

Editing Data Using the Custom Form

To see how data editing works, follow these steps to edit a record:

1. Select any cell within the record you want to edit.

2. Select Data | Customer Database | Edit Customer or click the Edit Customer button on the Customer Database toolbar. The Edit Customer form appears, as shown in Figure 17.3.

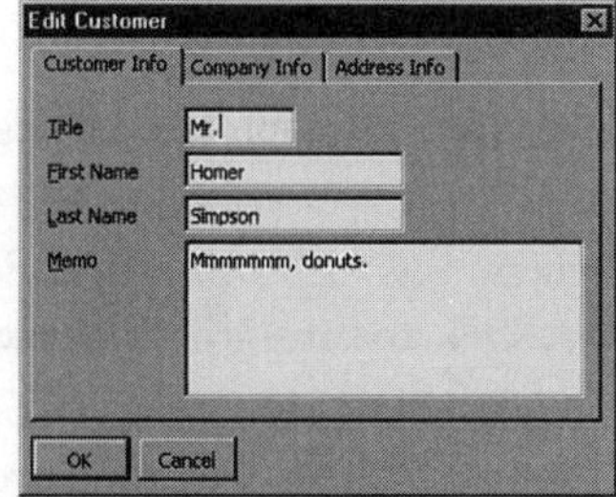

FIGURE 17.3.
The Edit Customer form.

CAUTION: SELECT A DATABASE CELL BEFORE EDITING

Be sure to select a cell within the database when you run the Edit Customer command. If you don't, the application displays a warning message. If you get this message and you've selected a record, you might have to redefine the Database range name to include the entire list.

3. Make your changes to the record.
4. Click OK. The application writes the changes to the worksheet.

Handling Data Editing with VBA Code

When you select the Edit Customer command, the application runs the `EditCustomer` procedure, shown in Listing 17.9.

Listing 17.9. The `EditCustomer` procedure runs when you select the Edit Customer command or click the Edit Customer toolbar button.

```
Sub EditCustomer()
    '
    ' Make sure selection is inside database
    '
    If Not InsideDatabase(ActiveCell.Row) Then
        Exit Sub
    End If
    '
    ' Set up the form and then Show it
    '
    With frmCustomer
        .Caption = "Edit Customer"
        .Controls("cmdAction").Caption = "OK"
        .Show
    End With
    Set frmCustomer = Nothing
End Sub
```

Here's how events unfold when you run the Edit Customer command:

- First, the `InsideDatabase` function (see Listing 17.10) is called to make sure the active cell is within the `Database` range and that the range isn't empty.
- Next, a `With` statement sets the form title to Edit Customer, sets the `cmdAction` button's caption to OK, and runs the `Show` method.
- In the form's `Activate` event (see Listing 17.6), the `Select Case` runs the `ReadData` procedure (see Listing 17.11) to read the current customer's data into the form's text boxes.
- As before, the user can then either cancel or edit the customer data. For the latter, if she then clicks OK, the `cmdAction` button's `Click` event handler (see Listing 17.7) calls `WriteData` to record the changes in the database, and then the form exits.

Listing 17.10 shows the `InsideDatabase` function.

Listing 17.10. The `InsideDatabase` function tests whether or not the active cell is inside the Database range.

```
' InsideDatabase()
' Function that determines whether or not the
' active cell is inside the Database range
'
Function InsideDatabase(currRow As Integer)
    With Range("Database")
        If .Rows.Count = 1 Then
            MsgBox Prompt:="There are no records in the database.", _
                   Title:="Customer Database", _
                   Buttons:=vbExclamation
            InsideDatabase = False
            Exit Function
        End If
        If currRow <= .Row Or currRow >= (.Row + .Rows.Count) Then
            MsgBox Prompt:="You must select a record inside the database.", _
                   Title:="Customer Database", _
                   Buttons:=vbExclamation
            InsideDatabase = False
        Else
            InsideDatabase = True
        End If
    End With
End Function
```

First, the `Rows.Count` property of the `Database` range is checked. If it's 1, the range includes only the column headings, so the database is empty and the user is warned accordingly. Otherwise, the variable `currRow` holds the row number of the active cell. If this number is less than or equal to the first row of the database (as given by the `Row` property) or below the database (in other words, greater than or equal to the sum of `Row` and `Rows.Count`), a `MsgBox` function displays a warning message.

Listing 17.11 shows the `ReadData` procedure.

Listing 17.11. The `ReadData` procedure reads database data from the specified row into the form.

```
Sub ReadData(dbRow As Integer)
    Dim i As Integer, fieldValue As Variant
    '
    ' Enter data into form text boxes
    '
    For i = 1 To totalFields
        fieldValue = Cells(dbRow, i).Value
        textBoxes(textboxArray(i - 1)).Text = fieldValue
    Next 'i
End Sub
```

As you might expect, this procedure is really the opposite of the `WriteData` procedure. The `For...Next` loop grabs each value in the current database row in turn and then stores the value in the corresponding text box.

Filtering Data

You can filter any Excel list to see only certain records. If you have simple criteria, the Data | Filter | AutoFilter command is probably your best bet.

Filtering the Customer Database

For more complex filtering, use the Customer Criteria range to enter your compound or computed criteria. When you're ready to filter the list, you can do it in one step either by selecting Data | Customer Database | Filter Customers or by clicking the Filter Customers button on the Customer Database toolbar.

When you want to exit filter mode and return to the normal view, either select Data | Customer Database | Show All Customers or click the Show All Customers button.

CAUTION: WATCH THE CRITERIA RANGE

The Advanced Filter button uses a range named Criteria to filter the records. By default, this range consists of the Customer Criteria column headings and the first row beneath them (A2:O3). If you use multiline criteria to display records that match one criterion or another, you'll need to redefine the Criteria range appropriately.

Filtering Data with VBA

The Filter Customers command is attached to the `FilterCustomers` procedure, shown in Listing 17.12.

Listing 17.12. The `FilterCustomers` procedure runs when you select the Filter Customers command or click the Filter Customers toolbar button.

```
Sub FilterCustomers()
    Dim criteriaCells As Range
    Dim c As Range
    Dim criteriaEmpty As Boolean
    '
    ' Make sure the Criteria range contains a value
    '
    criteriaEmpty = True
    Set criteriaCells = Range("Criteria").Offset(1).Resize(RowSize:=1)
    For Each c In criteriaCells
        If c.Value <> "" Then criteriaEmpty = False
    Next 'c
    If criteriaEmpty Then
        MsgBox "The Criteria range is empty!" & Chr(13) & _
               "Please enter criteria before filtering the database."
        Exit Sub
    End If
    '
    ' Filter the database according the the Criteria range values
    '
    Range("Database").AdvancedFilter _
        Action:=xlFilterInPlace, _
        CriteriaRange:=Range("Criteria")
End Sub
```

First, a `For Each...Next` loop runs through the second row of the Criteria range to make sure there's a value in at least one of the cells. If there isn't one, a warning message is displayed.

Otherwise, `FilterCustomers` runs the `AdvancedFilter` method on the `Database` range object:

Range`.AdvancedFilter(`***Action***`,` *`CriteriaRange, CopyToRange, Unique`*`)`

Range	The Range object you want to filter.
Action	A constant that specifies where you want the data filtered. You can use either `xlFilterInPlace` or `xlFilterCopy`.
CriteriaRange	A Range object that specifies the criteria range to use for the filter. (In the application, the `CriteriaRange` argument uses the `Criteria` named range. If you use multiple lines for your criteria, you have to redefine the `Criteria` name before running this procedure.)

CopyToRange	If ***Action*** is xlFilterCopy, use *CopyToRange* to specify the destination for the copied rows.
Unique	If you set this argument to True, Excel filters only unique records. If it's set to False (the default), Excel filters all records that meet the criteria.

The Show All Customers command is attached to the ShowAllCustomers procedure, which is shown in Listing 17.13. This procedure just runs the ShowAllData method for the active sheet.

Listing 17.13. The ShowAllCustomers procedure runs when you select the Show All Customers command or click the Show All Customers toolbar.

```
Sub ShowAllCustomers()
    ActiveSheet.ShowAllData
End Sub
```

Autofiltering a Worksheet

If you need to place a worksheet in AutoFilter mode from within VBA, use the Range object's AutoFilter method. If you just want to add the AutoFilter drop-down arrows to each field, run the AutoFilter method without any arguments. For example, the following statement adds AutoFilter drop-down arrows to the Database range:

```
Range("Database").AutoFilter
```

To remove the AutoFilter arrows, run the AutoFilter method again.

As an alternative, you can use the AutoFilter method to filter a list. Here's the syntax:

Range.AutoFilter(***Field***, *Criteria1*, *Operator*, *Criteria2*)

Range	The Range object you want to filter.
Field	An integer that specifies the offset of the field to use for the filter (where the leftmost field is 1).
Criteria1	The criterion for the filter, entered as a string (for example, "CA"). If you omit *Criteria1*, VBA uses All. If *Operator* is xlTop10Items, use *Criteria1* to specify the number of items to return (for example, "20").
Operator	If you specify both *Criteria1* and *Criteria2*, use *Operator* to build compound criteria. In this case, you can use either xlAnd (the default) or xlOr. You also can use xlTop10Items to use the Top 10 AutoFilter.
Criteria2	A second criteria string to use for compound criteria.

For example, the following statement filters the `Database` range to show only those customers where the State field (Field 10) is "CA" or "NY":

```
Range("Database").AutoFilter _
    f=Field:=10, _
    Criteria1:="CA", _
    Operator:=xlOr, _
    Criteria2:="NY"
```

NOTE: CHECKING FOR A FILTERED LIST

Use the Worksheet object's `AutoFilterMode` property to determine whether or not the AutoFilter drop-down arrows are currently displayed on the worksheet. (The `AutoFilterMode` property returns `True` if the sheet is currently in AutoFilter mode.) If you want to know whether or not a worksheet contains filtered data, use the Worksheet object's `FilterMode` property. (The `FilterMode` property returns `True` if the sheet is currently filtered.)

Getting a Count of the Database Records

As your database grows, you might need to know how many records it contains. You can find out by selecting Data | Customer Database | Count Customers or by clicking the Count Customers button on the Customer Database toolbar. The dialog box that appears will tell you the current count.

The Count Customers command and the Count Customers button are attached to the `CountCustomers` procedure, shown in Listing 17.14. The `totalRows` variable holds the count, which is given by the `Rows.Count` property, minus 1 (because you don't want to count the column headings). Then, the variables `alertMsg`, `alertButtons`, and `alertTitle` are assigned values, and the `MsgBox` function displays the count message.

Listing 17.14. The `CountCustomers` procedure runs when you select the Count Customers command or click the Count Customers toolbar button.

```
Sub CountCustomers()
    Dim totalRows As Integer
    Dim alertMsg As String, alertButtons As Integer, alertTitle As String
    '
    ' Customer count is total rows in Database, minus 1
    '
    totalRows = Range("Database").Rows.Count - 1
    alertMsg = "There are currently " & _
        totalRows & _
        " customers in the database."
    alertButtons = vbInformation
    alertTitle = "Customer Database"
    MsgBox alertMsg, alertButtons, alertTitle
End Sub
```

Deleting Records

To save memory and make the database easier to manage, you should delete customer records you no longer need. The next two sections show you the interface and the underlying code.

Deleting a Customer Database Record

Here are the steps to follow for deleting a customer from the Customer Database application:

1. Select any cell within the record of the customer you want to delete.
2. Select Data | Customer Database | Delete Customer or click the Delete Customer button on the Customer Database toolbar. The Delete Customer form appears. 
3. If you're sure you want to delete this customer, click the Delete button. The application deletes the record and returns you to the worksheet.

Handling Record Deletion with VBA

The `DeleteCustomer` procedure, shown in Listing 17.15, handles the customer deletions.

Listing 17.15. The `DeleteCustomer` procedure runs when you select the Delete Customer command or click the Delete Customer toolbar button.

```
Sub DeleteCustomer()
    '
    ' Make sure selection is inside database
    '
    If Not InsideDatabase(ActiveCell.Row) Then
        Exit Sub
    End If
    '
    ' Set up the form and then Show it
    '
    With frmCustomer
        .Caption = "Delete Customer"
        .Controls("cmdAction").Caption = "Delete"
        .Show
    End With
    Set frmCustomer = Nothing
End Sub
```

This procedure is almost identical to the `EditCustomer` procedure discussed earlier, except that the `cmdAction` button's `Caption` property is set to Delete. Once the `Show` method is invoked, the following actions occur:

- In the form's `Activate` event (see Listing 17.6), the `Select Case` runs the `ReadData` procedure (see Listing 17.11) to read the current customer's data into the form's text boxes. However, we don't want the user to edit the data, so a `For Each...Next` loop runs through the `textBoxes` collection and sets each `Enabled` property to `False`. Also, to prevent accidental deletions, the `cmdCancel` button is given the focus.

- The user can then click either Cancel or Delete. For the latter, the `cmdAction` button's `Click` event handler (see Listing 17.7) deletes the records by running the following statement:

```
ActiveCell.EntireRow.Delete
```

Sorting Data

The Customer Database application doesn't include any code for sorting data, but it's easy enough to handle using VBA. The mechanism is the Range object's `Sort` method, which uses the following syntax:

```
Range.Sort(Key1, Order1, Key2, Order2, Key3, Order3, Header, OrderCustom,
➥MatchCase, Orientation)
```

Range	The Range object you want to sort. If ***Range*** is a single cell, Excel sorts the cell's current region.
Key1	The first key field. You can enter either a range name or a Range object.
Order1	The order for *Key1*. Use either `xlAscending` (the default) or `xlDescending`.
Key2	The second key field. You can enter either a range name or a Range object.
Order2	The order for *Key2* (`xlAscending` or `xlDescending`).
Key3	The third key field. You can enter either a range name or a Range object.
Order3	The order for *Key3* (`xlAscending` or `xlDescending`).
Header	Tells Excel whether or not the sort range contains a header in the first row. Use `xlYes` (the default), `xlNo`, or `xlGuess` (to let Excel try to figure out if the range contains a header row).
OrderCustom	An integer value that specifies which of Excel's custom sort orders to use. The default value is 1 (which corresponds to the Normal sort order).
MatchCase	Specifies whether or not the sort is case-sensitive. If `True`, the sort is case-sensitive; if `False` (the default), the sort isn't case-sensitive.
Orientation	Specifies whether Excel sorts by rows (top to bottom) or columns (left to right). Use either `xlTopToBottom` (the default) or `xlLeftToRight`.

For example, the following statement sorts the `Database` range by State and then in descending order by City:

```
Range("Database").Sort _
    Key1:=Worksheets("Customer Database").Range("J6"), _
    Key2:=Worksheets("Customer Database").Range("I6"), _
    Order2:=xlDescending, _
    Header:=xlYes
```

Subtotaling Data

If your list contains numeric data, you can use VBA code to add automatic subtotals to the list. The Range object has a `Subtotal` method that does the job:

***Range*.Subtotal(*GroupBy*, *Function*, *TotalList*, *Replace*, *PageBreaks*, *SummaryBelowData*)**

Range	The Range object you want to subtotal. If ***Range*** is a single cell, Excel applies the subtotals to the cell's current region.
GroupBy	An integer that represents the field to use for the subtotal groupings (where the first field in ***Range*** is 1).
Function	The function to use for these subtotals: `xlAverage`, `xlCount`, `xlCountNums`, `xlMax`, `xlMin`, `xlProduct`, `xlStDev`, `xlStDevP`, `xlSum`, `xlVar`, or `xlVarP`.
TotalList	The fields to which the subtotals are added. Use an array of integers, where each integer represents a field (where the first field in ***Range*** is 1).
Replace	Set this argument to `True` to replace the existing subtotals. The default value is `False`.
PageBreaks	Set this argument to `True` to add page breaks after each grouping. The default value is `False`.
SummaryBelowData	Specifies where Excel places the subtotals in relation to the detail. Use either `xlBelow` (the default) or `xlAbove`.

The following statement sets up subtotals for a range named `Invoices`. The records are grouped by the values in the first field, and the subtotals are added to Fields 5 and 6.

```
Range("Invoices").Subtotal _
    GroupBy:=1, _
    Function:=xlSum, _
    TotalList:=Array(5,6), _
    Replace:=True
```

NOTE: REMOVING SUBTOTALS

To remove subtotals from a range, use the Range object's `RemoveSubtotals` method. For example, the following statement removes the subtotals from the `Invoices` range:

```
Range("Invoices").RemoveSubtotals
```

Summary

This chapter showed you how to program Excel lists. You saw how to use VBA to perform a number of basic list chores, including entering and editing data; filtering, deleting, and sorting records; and subtotaling data.

Here's a list of chapters where you'll find related information:

- I examine the basic Excel objects—including the Workbook, Worksheet, and Range objects—in Chapter 7, "Manipulating Excel with VBA."
- To learn how to build custom user forms, see Chapter 11, "Working with Microsoft Forms."
- I show you how to manipulate menus and toolbars via VBA in Chapter 12, "Creating Custom Menus and Toolbars."
- To learn how to deal with data in Access and ODBC databases, read Chapter 18, "Programming Data Access Objects," and Chapter 19, "Advanced Database Programming."

Programming Data Access Objects

IN THIS CHAPTER

Give us the tools, and we will finish the job.

—*Winston Churchill*

When you investigate the Access object hierarchy (as we did back in Chapter 9, "VBA and Access"), it seems strange at first that there are no references to database, table, or query objects. After all, these are the most fundamental objects in the Access world. How can you possibly work with Access programmatically if you can't work with such objects?

Well, it turns out that you can. The secret is that these objects are defined in a separate object hierarchy altogether: the *Data Access Objects* (DAO) hierarchy. These objects are the link between your Access VBA programs and the databases, tables, queries, and recordsets you want to work with. Note, too, that you can use the DAO model to work with Access databases from other Office applications. For example, you could use DAO to insert external data into an Excel range without having to use Microsoft Query. This chapter takes you through the basics of using DAO to access and work with Access databases.

NOTE: REFERENCE THE DAO LIBRARY

To use DAO from an application other than Access, you must make sure that your VBA project has a reference to the correct library. To do this, switch to the Visual Basic Editor and select Tools | References. In the References dialog box, activate the check box beside Microsoft DAO 3.5 Object Library and then click OK.

About Data Access Objects

As I said, DAO is a separate library of objects and their associated properties and methods. These objects expose the full functionality of the Microsoft Jet database engine—the engine used in Access. In other words, DAO is an Automation server, and you use it the same way you use the objects exposed by any other Automation server. (I discuss Automation in depth in Chapter 15, "Controlling Applications Via OLE Automation.") In particular, make sure that you add a reference to the DAO object library in your VBA project. To do this, select Tools | References, activate the check box beside the Microsoft DAO 3.5 Object Library item, and click OK.

VBA 5.0 In VBA 5.0, the DAO object hierarchy supports two different environments (or *workspaces*):

Microsoft Jet: This is the standard environment, and it's used for working with Microsoft Jet databases (.MDB files), Jet-connected Open Database Connectivity (ODBC) databases, and installable Indexed Sequential Access Method (ISAM) databases.

ODBCDirect: This new workspace is useful for connecting to remote ODBC databases directly without having to load the entire Jet engine. I discuss ODBCDirect in the next chapter.

Figure 18.1 shows the DAO hierarchy that is used with Jet workspaces.

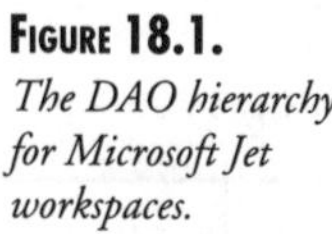

FIGURE 18.1.
The DAO hierarchy for Microsoft Jet workspaces.

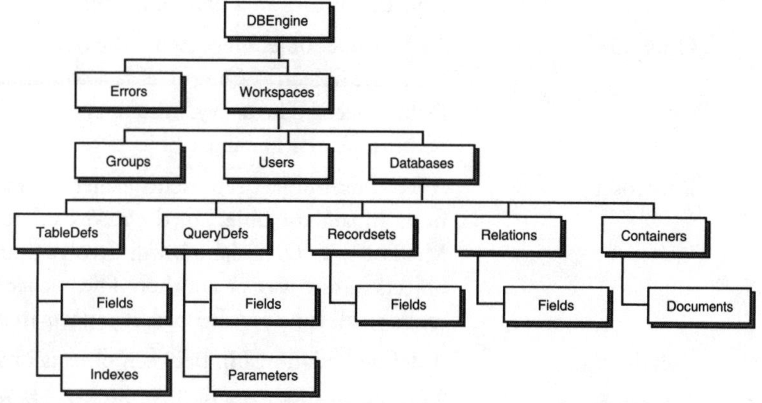

With the exception of the top-level `DBEngine` object, the hierarchy shown in Figure 18.1 lists just the collections in the DAO model. Each of these collections has, of course, a corresponding singular object. Here's a rundown of these DAO objects:

`DBEngine`	This top-level object represents the Microsoft Jet database engine as a whole. Although this object has methods that let you compact a database (the `CompactDatabase` method) and repair a database (the `RepairDatabase` method), you'll use it most often to create a Workspace object in which to open a database.
Workspace	A particular session of the `DBEngine` object (in other words, the time between when a user logs in to the database and when he logs off).
Error	This object represents a data access error that occurs when you're working with any of the DAO members.
Database	A Database object represents an open database in the workspace. (In Access VBA, you can use the `CurrentDB` keyword to reference the current database.) The `Databases` collection refers to all the Database objects open in the workspace.
User	The User object represents a user account defined in a workgroup database.

Group	The Group object represents a group that has been defined in a workgroup database.
TableDef	A TableDef object represents the definition of a table in a Database object. A TableDef is a container for the table's Field and Index objects. The `TableDefs` collection refers to all the table definitions in a Database object.
QueryDef	A QueryDef object represents the definition of a query in a Database object. A QueryDef is a container for the query's Field objects. The `QueryDefs` collection refers to all the query definitions in a Database object.
Recordset	A Recordset object represents either the records in a base table from a Database object or the records that result from a query. Most of your DAO labors will involve manipulating Recordset objects in one way or another. The `Recordsets` collection refers to all the open Recordset objects in a Database object.
Relation	A defined relationship between objects in a database.
Container	This object stores the built-in objects contained in a database. In an Access database, for example, the Container object includes the forms, reports, and modules. Each of these items is a Document object.
Field	A Field object represents a column of data. For a TableDef or QueryDef object, a Field object contains the specifications for a field used in a table or query. For a Recordset object, a Field object represents the value in a particular field for the current record. The `Fields` collection refers to all the fields in a TableDef, QueryDef, or Recordset object.
Index	An Index object specifies an order for the records in a TableDef object. The `Indexes` collection refers to all the Index objects stored in a TableDef object. Note that each Index object has an associated `Fields` collection that contains the fields used for the index.

We'll now turn our attention to using these objects in your VBA procedures.

Accessing Data in an External Database

Accessing the data contained in an external database from a VBA procedure takes four or five steps, depending on the type of database:

1. Declare variables for the objects you'll be using (you'll usually need variables for at least a Database and a Recordset object).

2. Establish a new workspace session.
3. Open the database. If you're using a non-Jet external database (such as a FoxPro, Paradox, dBASE, or SQL Server database), open a Jet database to use for attaching the external database.
4. For a non-Jet external database, attach the database to the open Jet database.
5. Open the Recordset for the table you want to work with.

The next few sections supply the details for these steps.

Creating a Workspace

Before you can open a database, you need to establish a new workspace session. You do this by invoking the `DBEngine` object's `CreateWorkspace` method:

```
DBEngine.CreateWorkspace(Name, User, Password, UseType)
```

Name	A string that provides a unique name for the workspace.
User	The username of the person logging in to this database session.
Password	The password of the person logging in to this session.
UseType	The type of workspace. Use `dbUseJet` for a Microsoft Jet workspace (this is the default) or `dbUseODBC` for an ODBCDirect workspace.

Here's an example:

```
Dim ws As WorkSpace
Set ws = DBEngine.CreateWorkspace( _
    Name:="MySpace", _
    User:="Biff", _
    Password:="ssshhhh", _
    UseType:=dbUseJet)
```

Bear in mind that you often won't have to bother creating an explicit workspace. That's because the Jet engine creates a default workspace each time you open a database. You only need to create a workspace if the following conditions apply (both of which are discussed in the next chapter):

- You want to apply the Jet engine's security features to control access to a database.
- You want to implement transaction processing (that is, the ability to commit or roll back multiple edits).

Connecting to a Jet Database

As you might expect, the Jet database engine has the easiest time connecting to databases in its native Jet format (.MDB files, such as those created with Access). Listing 18.1 shows an example.

Listing 18.1. A procedure that connects to an Access database.

```
Sub DatabaseConnection()
    Dim db As Database
    Dim rs As Recordset
    ' Open the Northwind database
    Set db = OpenDatabase("C:\Program Files\Microsoft Office\Access\Northwind.mdb")
    ' Open the Customers table (recordset)
    Set rs = db.OpenRecordset("Customers", dbOpenTable)
    ' Display confirmation message
    MsgBox "Opened " & db.Name & " Successfully!" & _
           Chr(13) & Chr(13) & _
    "The open Recordset is " & rs.Name
    ' Close the database
    db.Close
End Sub
```

NOTE: THIS CHAPTER'S CODE LISTINGS

Although most of the code in this chapter can be used in any application that can serve as an Automation controller, I used Excel to create the examples. Therefore, you'll find the code in the Excel file named Chaptr18.xls on the CD. However, I've also provided a text file named Chaptr18.bas just in case you don't have Excel.

First, the Database and Recordset object variables are declared (`db` and `rs`, respectively). Then the `OpenDatabase` method is invoked to open the database. `OpenDatabase` is a method of the Workspace object (but notice that I didn't bother to create a new workspace; I just let Jet handle that for me). Here's the syntax of the `OpenDatabase` method:

`Workspace``.OpenDatabase(`***`Name`***`, `***`Options`***`, `*`ReadOnly`*`, `*`Connect`*`)`

`Workspace`	The Workspace object in which you want to open the database. If you omit *`Workspace`*, VBA uses the current workspace. I showed you how to create a new workspace in the preceding section.
`Name`	The full pathname (including the drive and directory) of the database file.
`Options`	For a Jet workspace, set this argument to `True` to open the database with exclusive access. The default value is `False`.
`ReadOnly`	Set this argument to `True` to open the database with read-only access. The default value is `False`.
`Connect`	A string that specifies extra parameters for opening the database (see the next section for details).

NOTE: ADJUST NORTHWIND PATH AS NEEDED

The `OpenDatabase` statements in this chapter's code listings use a path to the Northwind database file as an example. Note that you might have to adjust this path in order for these procedures to work on your machine.

TIP: AN ACCESS SHORTCUT

As I mentioned earlier, if you're working with Access VBA, you can open the current Access database by using the `CurrentDB` property:

```
Set db = CurrentDB
```

Once the database is open, the procedure then opens a Recordset object using the Database object's `OpenRecordset` method:

```
Database.OpenRecordset(Name, Type, Options, LockEdit)
```

Database	The Database object that contains the data you want to use for the recordset.
Name	A string specifying the source for the Recordset. You can use a table name, a query name, or a SQL statement.
Type	The type of recordset you want to create. For an explanation of each type of recordset, see the section "Understanding the Recordset Types."
Options	One or more (integer) constants that specify the characteristics of the new recordset:

`dbAppendOnly`	You can append only new records. (Used only with dynaset types.)
`dbSQLPassThrough`	Lets you pass SQL statements through to an ODBC database.
`dbSeeChanges`	Generates an error if another user changes a record you're editing.
`dbDenyWrite`	Prevents others from editing and adding records.

	`dbDenyRead`	Prevents others from viewing records. (Used only with table types.)
	`dbInconsistent`	You can update all fields in a multiple-table query Recordset. (Used only with dynaset types.)
	`dbConsistent`	You can only make changes to a field in a multiple-table query Recordset that keeps the records consistent with each other. (Used only with dynaset types.)
`LockEdit`	A constant that specifies the locking characteristics of the new recordset:	
	`dbReadOnly`	Prevents users from making changes to the records.
	`dbPessimistic`	In a multiuser environment, the current recordset is locked as soon as you run the `Edit` method.
	`dbOptimistic`	In a multiuser environment, the current recordset isn't locked until you run the `Update` method.
	`dbOptimisticValue`	Implements value-based optimistic concurrency for ODBCDirect workspaces only.
	`dbOptimisticBatch`	Implements batch optimistic updating for ODBCDirect workspaces only.

Finally, a `MsgBox` statement displays the name of the open database (using the Database object's `Name` property) and the name of the open Recordset (using the Recordset object's `Name` property).

Connecting to a Non-Jet Database

If the data you want to work with exists in a non-Jet database, you need to attach the data source to an existing Jet database as a new TableDef object. (It's possible to run the `OpenDatabase` method directly on a non-Jet database, but it's more efficient—and your Recordset operations will perform faster—if you link the database to a Jet database.)

> **NOTE: CREATING A JET DATABASE**
>
> What do you do if you don't have access to a Jet database? The answer is easy: Create your own using the `CreateDatabase` method. For example, the following statement creates a Jet database named MyJetDB.mdb and assigns it to a `Database` object variable:
>
> ```
> Dim db As Database
> Set db = CreateDatabase("MyJetDB.mdb", dbLangGeneral)
> ```
>
> The `dbLangGeneral` argument specifies the collating order used for string comparisons. You'll learn more about this when I provide a detailed discussion of the `CreateDatabase` method in the next chapter.

Listing 18.2 shows the `NonJetConnection` procedure that connects to a FoxPro database.

Listing 18.2. A procedure that connects to a non-Jet database.

```
Sub NonJetConnection()
    Dim db As Database
    Dim tdFox As TableDef
    Dim rs As Recordset
    '
    ' Open the Jet database (check the path!)
    '
    Set db = OpenDatabase("C:\Program Files\Microsoft Office\Access\Northwind.mdb")
    '
    ' Create TableDef and set the connection information.
    ' This code assumes the CUSTOMER.DBF file is in the same
    ' folder as this workbook.
    '
    Set tdFox = db.CreateTableDef("Linked FoxPro Table")
    tdFox.Connect = "FoxPro 2.5;DATABASE=" & ThisWorkbook.Path
    tdFox.SourceTableName = "Customer"
    '
    ' Append the TableDef to create the link
    '
    db.TableDefs.Append tdFox
    '
    ' Open the recordset
    '
    Set rs = db.OpenRecordset("Linked FoxPro Table", dbOpenSnapshot)
    '
    ' Display confirmation message
    '
    MsgBox "Opened " & db.Name & " Successfully!" & _
            Chr(13) & Chr(13) & _
            "The open Recordset is " & rs.Name & _
            Chr(13) & _
            "The source table is   " & tdFox.SourceTableName
    '
    ' Close the database
    '
    db.Close
End Sub
```

A TableDef object variable named `tdFox` is declared to hold the new TableDef. A Jet database is opened, and then the new TableDef object is created using the Database object's `CreateTableDef` method. This method has a number of arguments, but your code will be easier to read if you use the TableDef object's properties to set up the TableDef. In most cases, all you need to include in the `CreateTableDef` method is a name for the new TableDef (`Linked FoxPro Table` in Listing 18.2).

The next two lines set the `Connect` and `SourceTableName` properties. Here's a simplified syntax for the `Connect` property:

`TableDef``.Connect=`*`databasetype`*`;DATABASE=`*`path`*

`TableDef` The TableDef object.

`databasetype` A string indicating the type of database you're attaching. Here are your choices:

dBASE III	FoxPro 2.0	Excel 3.0
dBASE IV	FoxPro 2.5	Excel 4.0
dBASE 5.0	FoxPro 2.6	Excel 5.0
Paradox 3.x	HTML Import	Excel 97
Paradox 4.x	HTML Export	Text
Paradox 5.x		

`path` The drive and directory (folder) containing the table you want to use (such as a FoxPro .DBF file). Note that you'll usually have to specify directory names using MS-DOS eight-character names.

The `SourceTableName` property specifies the table you want to use. In Listing 18.2, setting this property to `Customer` tells DAO that you want to work with the Customer.dbf table.

Once the new TableDef object is ready, you add it to the Database object's `TableDefs` collection by using the `Append` method. When that's done, you can use the TableDef as though it were a Jet table (including opening a new recordset on the table, as I've done in Listing 18.2).

NOTE: CUSTOMER.DBF IS ON THE CD

The CUSTOMER.DBF FoxPro file used in Listing 18.2 is on the CD. To run the code in Listing 18.2 successfully, make sure you place this .DBF file in the same folder as Chaptr18.xls.

Connecting to an ODBC Data Source

For ODBC data sources in client/server environments, the `Connect` property usually requires a few more parameters. When linking to a SQL Server data source, for example, you'll need to specify not only a database but also a user name, a password, and a data source name (DSN). For these kinds of ODBC databases, the *`databasetype`* argument is `ODBC`, and you specify the other parameters using the `UID` (user ID), `PWD` (password), and `DSN` (data source name) keywords. Here's the general form:

```
object.Connect = "ODBC;DATABASE=dbname;UID=userID;PWD=password;DSN=datasource"
```

For example, the following statement connects a linked TableDef object named `tdSQLServer` to a SQL Server data source named Publishers, specifies the database named Pubs as the default database, and also specifies a user ID and password:

```
tdSQLServer.Connect = "ODBC;DATABASE=pubs;UID=bwana;PWD=nottelling;DSN=Publishers"
```

TIP: LETTING THE USER CHOOSE THE DATA SOURCE

If the `Connect` string is only `ODBC;` (for example, `tdWhatever="ODBC;"`), VBA displays the Select Data Source dialog box with a list of all the defined data sources so the user can choose (or even create) the one he or she wants. Note that if the user cancels this dialog box, a trappable runtime error occurs (error number 3059). (See Chapter 23, "Trapping Program Errors," to learn more about trapping errors.)

NOTE: DIRECT ODBC CONNECTIONS

As I mentioned earlier, it's possible to use the `OpenDatabase` method to connect to a non-Jet database directly. This also holds, naturally, for ODBC databases located on servers; you simply use the `OpenDatabase` method's *`Connect`* argument to specify the appropriate connection string (the user ID, password, and so on).

However, you'll find your work with the resulting recordset (and especially your queries) will be noticeably faster if, instead, you link the server data to a Jet database on the client machine. That's because the Jet database engine caches information (such as the field and index data) locally, which greatly improves performance. Note, however, that if you change any fields or indexes on the server, you need to update the cached data by running the TableDef object's `RefreshLink` method.

Having said all that, however, you might find that the new ODBCDirect workspace environment offers your best level of performance since it doesn't require the full Jet engine. I discuss this in greater detail in the next chapter.

Working with Recordsets

As I mentioned earlier, once you've opened a database and created a new recordset, you'll spend most of your time manipulating the recordset in some way. This section gives you more information about recordsets and takes you through a few useful properties and methods.

Understanding the Recordset Types

As you know from the discussion of the `OpenRecordset` method, you can specify one of three different recordset types. Table 18.1 provides a rundown of the available types and what they mean.

Table 18.1. A summary of the DAO recordset types.

`Type` Constant	*Recordset Type*	*Description*
`dbOpenTable`	Table	This type refers to a base table or attached table in an open Database object. Certain actions, such as sorting and indexing, can be performed only on table-type recordsets.
`dbOpenDynamic`	Dynamic	This type creates a recordset with characteristics similar to an ODBC dynamic cursor. (This type is available only for ODBCDirect workspaces.)
`dbOpenDynaset`	Dynaset	This type refers to a dynamic, virtual table that is (usually) the result of a query. Dynasets can include fields from multiple tables. They are dynamic because you can update the records by adding, editing, or deleting.
`dbOpenSnapshot`	Snapshot	This type is similar to a dynaset, except that the records are static: You can't make changes, add records, or delete records. This is the fastest type, and it's the one you should use if you only want to view the data.
`dbOpenForwardOnly`	Forward-only	This type refers to a forward-scrolling snapshot. Use this option for faster performance if you're making just a single pass through the records.

Getting Field Information

Before working with a recordset, you might need to find out some information about the fields in the recordset. For example, you might want to find out the names of all the fields, their sizes, whether a field requires a value, and the type of data each field uses. Each Recordset object is a container for all the Field objects in the Recordset. Therefore, you can get information on each field by running through the `Fields` collection. Listing 18.3 shows a procedure that does this.

Listing 18.3. A procedure that displays information on all the fields in a Recordset.

```
Sub DisplayFieldInfo()
    Dim db As Database
    Dim rs As Recordset
    Dim fld As Field
    Dim i As Integer
    Dim fieldInfo As String
    ' Open the Northwind database
    Set db = OpenDatabase("C:\Program Files\Microsoft Office\Access\Northwind.mdb")
    ' Open the Categories table
    Set rs = db.OpenRecordset("Categories", dbOpenSnapshot)
    ' Enumerate all fields in the Recordset
    For i = 0 To rs.Fields.Count - 1
        fieldInfo = "Recordset: " & rs.Name & Chr(13) & _
            "Field " & _
            i + 1 & " of " & _
            rs.Fields.Count & Chr(13) & Chr(13)
        ' Set the Field variable and then run through the properties
        Set fld = rs.Fields(i)
        fieldInfo = fieldInfo & _
            "Name: " & fld.Name & Chr(13) & _
            "Allow Zero Length: " & fld.AllowZeroLength & Chr(13) & _
            "Attributes: " & fld.Attributes & Chr(13) & _
            "Collating Order: " & fld.CollatingOrder & Chr(13) & _
            "Default Value: " & fld.DefaultValue & Chr(13) & _
            "Ordinal Position: " & fld.OrdinalPosition & Chr(13) & _
            "Required: " & fld.Required & Chr(13) & _
            "Size: " & fld.Size & Chr(13) & _
            "Source Field: " & fld.SourceField & Chr(13) & _
            "Source Table: " & fld.SourceTable & Chr(13) & _
            "Type of Field: " & TypeOfField(fld.Type) & Chr(13) & _
            "Validation Rule: " & fld.ValidationRule & Chr(13) & _
            "Validation Text: " & fld.ValidationText
        MsgBox Prompt:=fieldInfo, Title:="Field Information"
    Next i
    ' Close the database
    db.Close
End Sub
' TypeOfField()
' Function to translate the constant returned by a Field object's
' Type property into a descriptive string.
'
```

continues

Listing 18.3. continued

```
Function TypeOfField(fldConstant As Integer) As String
    Select Case fldConstant
        Case 1  ' dbBoolean
            TypeOfField = "Boolean"
        Case 2  ' dbByte
            TypeOfField = "Byte"
        Case 3  ' dbInteger
            TypeOfField = "Integer"
        Case 4  ' dbLong
            TypeOfField = "Long Integer"
        Case 5  ' dbCurrency
            TypeOfField = "Currency"
        Case 6  ' dbSingle
            TypeOfField = "Single"
        Case 7  ' dbDouble
            TypeOfField = "Double"
        Case 8  ' dbDate
            TypeOfField = "Date"
        Case 10 ' dbText
            TypeOfField = "Text"
        Case 11 'dbLongBinary
            TypeOfField = "OLE Object"
        Case 12 ' dbMemo
            TypeOfField = "Memo"
        Case 15 ' dbGUID
            TypeOfField = "GUID"
    End Select
End Function
```

The `For...Next` loop runs from 0 (the first field number) to one less than the number of fields in the recordset `rs` (the number of fields is given by `rs.Fields.Count`). In each pass through the loop, the `fld` variable is set to `rs.Fields(i)`, and then the properties of this `Field` object are enumerated (such as `Name`, `AllowZeroLength`, `Size`, and `Type`) and stored in the `fieldInfo` string. Note that the procedure doesn't return the `Type` property directly. Instead, the constant is translated into a string by the `TypeOfField` function. (If you want to, you can create similar functions that translate the constants returned by the `Attributes` and `CollatingOrder` fields.)

Recordset Properties

Here's a look at some Recordset object properties you'll use most often:

> `Recordset.AbsolutePosition`: Returns or sets the relative record number in the specified *`Recordset`*. (Note that the relative position of a particular record might change each time you create the recordset, so you can't use this property as a substitute for the xBASE `RECNO()` function.)
>
> `Recordset.BOF`: Returns `True` if the current record position in the specified *`Recordset`* is before the first record.

`Recordset.Bookmark`: Sets or returns a `Variant` value that uniquely identifies the current record in the specified `Recordset`. For example, the following code saves the current position to a `Variant` variable named `currRecord`, moves to the end of the recordset (using the `MoveLast` method, which is discussed later), and returns to the previous position:

```
currRecord = rs.Bookmark
rs.MoveLast
rs.Bookmark = currRecord
```

`Recordset.Bookmarkable`: Returns `True` if the specified `Recordset` supports bookmarks. You should always test your recordset's `Bookmarkable` property before attempting to set a bookmark.

`Recordset.DateCreated`: The date and time the specified `Recordset` was created.

`Recordset.EOF`: Returns `True` if the current record position in the specified `Recordset` is after the last record.

`Recordset.Filter`: Returns or sets the criteria that determines which records are included in the `Recordset`. For example, the following statements set the variable `rsCustomer` to the Customers table and the `Filter` property to include only those records in which the Country field is "Canada," and then they open a new `Recordset` (`rsCanada`) based on the filtered records:

```
Set rsCustomer = OpenRecordset("Customers")
rsCustomer.Filter = "Country = 'Canada'"
Set rsCanada = rsCustomer.OpenRecordset()
```

`Recordset.Index`: Returns or sets the current Index object for the specified table-type `Recordset`. Use the `TableDef` object's `Indexes` collection to find out the available indexes for a table.

`Recordset.LastModified`: Returns a bookmark for the specified `Recordset` that identifies the most recently added or modified record.

`Recordset.LastUpdated`: The date and time of the most recent change made to the specified `Recordset`.

`Recordset.NoMatch`: Returns `True` if the `Seek` method or one of the `Find` methods failed to find the desired record in the specified `Recordset`. Returns `False` otherwise.

`Recordset.RecordCount`: The number of records in the specified `Recordset`.

`Recordset.Sort`: Returns or sets the sort order for the specified dynaset-type or snapshot-type `Recordset`. (Use the `Index` property to sort a table-type recordset.) To set the sort order, set this property equal to a field name, followed by either `Asc` (the default) or `Desc`. Here are a couple of examples (where `rs` is a `Recordset` variable):

```
rs.Sort = "Country"
rs.Sort = "LastName Desc"
```

Recordset Methods

Here are a few methods you can use to manipulate a recordset:

Recordset.AddNew: Adds a new record to the specified table-type or dynaset-type *Recordset*.

Recordset.CancelUpdate: Cancels any pending changes made in the specified *Recordset* by the AddNew or Edit methods. (Changes aren't written to the recordset until you run the Update method, which I'll discuss in a moment.)

Recordset.Close: Closes the specified *Recordset*.

Recordset.Delete: Deletes the current record in the specified table-type or dynaset-type *Recordset*.

Recordset.Edit: Copies the current record in the specified table-type or dynaset-type *Recordset* to the copy buffer for editing. For example, the following code uses the FindFirst method to find the first record where the Country field equals *Czechoslovakia*. The record is opened for editing using the Edit method, the Country field is modified, and the recordset is updated with the Update method. The FindNext method looks for more instances of *Czechoslovakia*. Here is the code:

```
strFind = "Country = 'Czechoslovakia'"
strReplace = "Czech Republic"
rs.FindFirst strFind                        ' Find first occurrence
Do While rs.NoMatch                         ' Loop until no more matches
    rs.Edit                                 ' Open record for editing
    rs.Fields("Country") = strRreplace      ' Modify Country field
    rs.Update                               ' Update the Recordset
    rs.FindNext strFind                     ' Find the next match
Loop
```

Recordset.FindFirst, *Recordset*.FindLast, *Recordset*.FindNext, *Recordset*.FindPrevious: Searches the specified *Recordset* for the first, last, next, or previous records that meet the specified criteria. If no record matches the criteria, the NoMatch property returns True.

Recordset.Move: Moves the current record pointer in the specified *Recordset* by a specified number of records. Here's the syntax:

***Recordset*.Move(*Rows*, *Start*)**

Recordset	The Recordset object.
Rows	A long integer specifying the number of records to move. Use a negative number to move backwards.
Start	A variable name that identifies a bookmark from which to start the move. If you omit *Start*, the move occurs from the current record.

Recordset.MoveFirst, *Recordset*.MoveLast, *Recordset*.MoveNext, *Recordset*.Move Previous: Moves the current record to the first, last, next, or previous record in the specified *Recordset*. Use the BOF property to determine if MovePrevious moves the record pointer before the first record. Use EOF to determine if MoveNext moves the record pointer past the last record.

Recordset.Seek: Searches the indexed table-type *Recordset* for a record that meets the specified criteria. Here's the syntax for the Seek method:

Recordset.Seek(*Comparison*, *Key1*, *Key2...*)

Recordset	The indexed table-type Recordset object.
Comparison	A comparison operator: =, >, >=, <, <=, or <>.
Key1, Key2...	One or more values that correspond to the fields in the current index.

Note that you need to set the current index for the recordset before you use the Seek method. For example, the following code sets a Recordset object's Index property and then uses Seek to find a matching record:

```
Set rs = db.OpenRecordset("Customers")
rs.Index = "Country"
rs.Seek "=", "Czechoslovakia"
```


TIP: USE SEEK WHENEVER POSSIBLE

Index-based Seek searches are much faster than any of the Find methods, so you should always use Seek if an appropriate Index object is available.

Recordset.Update: Writes changes made by AddNew or Edit to a table-type or dynaset-type *Recordset*.

Querying a Recordset

In general, the recordsets you open will contain all the records in the underlying table. If you want to filter the records, however, DAO gives you three choices:

- Specify the Recordset object's Filter property and then run the OpenRecordset method on the filtered records. (The Filter property was described earlier in this chapter.)
- Run the OpenRecordset method and specify a SQL expression instead of a table name.
- Run the OpenRecordset method on a QueryDef object.

Opening a Recordset Using a SQL Expression

Using a SQL SELECT statement to query a recordset affords you more control over the resulting dynaset than does the Filter method, and it also lets you avoid creating a separate QueryDef object. For example, Listing 18.4 shows a procedure that opens a recordset based on the Customers table in the Northwind sample database. The strSELECT variable holds a SELECT statement that filters the data as follows:

- Only the CompanyName, Region, and Country fields are used.
- The records are restricted to those in which the Country field is Canada.
- The recordset is ordered by the CompanyName field.

Listing 18.4. A procedure that opens a Recordset using a SQL SELECT expression.

```
Sub QueryCustomers()
    Dim db As Database
    Dim strSELECT As String
    Dim rs As Recordset
    ' Open the Northwind database
    Set db = OpenDatabase("C:\Program Files\Microsoft Office\Access\Northwind.mdb")
    ' Store the SELECT statement in a string variable
    strSELECT = "SELECT CompanyName,Region,Country " & _
                "FROM Customers " & _
                "WHERE Country = 'Canada' " & _
                "ORDER BY CompanyName"
    ' Open the Recordset
    Set rs = db.OpenRecordset(strSELECT)
    ' Display confirmation message
    MsgBox "The filtered Recordset contains " & _
    rs.RecordCount & " records."
    ' Close the database
    db.Close
End Sub
```

TIP: GET SQL SYNTAX FROM ACCESS

Are you unsure of the correct syntax for SQL SELECT statements? One easy way to avoid errors is to create a temporary Select query in Access. When the resulting dynaset is what you want, select View | SQL View to display the underlying SELECT statement. You can then copy this statement to your VBA code and delete the query.

Opening a Recordset from a QueryDef Object

If the Database object already contains one or more queries in the form of QueryDef objects, you can open a recordset by using the QueryDef object's OpenRecordset method. For example,

Listing 18.5 opens a database, assigns the variable qd to the "Products Above Average Price" QueryDef object, and creates the recordset from the QueryDef.

Listing 18.5. A procedure that creates a recordset from a QueryDef object.

```
Sub QueryDefExample()
    Dim db As Database
    Dim qd As QueryDef
    Dim rs As Recordset
    ' Open the Northwind database
    Set db = OpenDatabase("C:\Program Files\Microsoft Office\Access\Northwind.mdb")
    ' Assign the QueryDef object
    Set qd = db.QueryDefs("Products Above Average Price")
    ' Open the Recordset
    Set rs = qd.OpenRecordset()
    ' Display confirmation message
    MsgBox "The filtered Recordset contains " & _
        rs.RecordCount & " records."
    ' Close the database
    db.Close
End Sub
```


NOTE: CREATING NEW QUERYDEF OBJECTS

You can create new QueryDef objects by using the Database object's CreateQueryDef method. This method takes two arguments: the name of the new QueryDef object and the SQL expression that defines the query. For example, the following statement creates a new QueryDef object called "Canadian Customers" based on the SQL expression used in Listing 18.5:

```
Dim db As Database, qd As QueryDef
Set db = OpenDatabase("Northwind.mdb")
strSELECT = "SELECT CompanyName,Region,Country " & _
            "FROM Customers " & _
            "WHERE Country = 'Canada' " & _
"ORDER BY CompanyName"
Set qd = db.CreateQueryDef("Canadian Customers",strSELECT)
```

Retrieving Data into Excel

To get data from an external database into an Excel worksheet, you have three choices:

- Retrieve an individual field value
- Retrieve one or more entire rows
- Retrieve an entire Recordset

Retrieving an Individual Field Value

For individual field values, move to the record you want to work with and then use the Field object's `Value` property. For example, the following statement returns the value of the current record's Country field in the Recordset named `rs` and stores it in cell A1 of the active worksheet:

```
ActiveSheet.[A1] = rs.Fields("Country").Value
```

Note, however, that the `Value` property is the default for a Field object. Therefore, you can save some typing by referring to just the field itself, like so:

```
ActiveSheet.[A1] = rs.Fields("Country")
```

You can shorten this even further by using the bang (!) notation, as follows:

```
ActiveSheet.[A1] = rs!Country
```

Retrieving One or More Entire Rows

To get full records, use the Recordset object's `GetRows` method. The `GetRows(`***n***`)` method returns ***n*** records in a two-dimensional array, where the first subscript is a number that represents the field (the first field is 0) and the second subscript represents the record number (where the first record is 0). Listing 18.6 shows a procedure that opens a recordset from a QueryDef and enters the first 100 rows into a worksheet named Database Records.

Listing 18.6. A procedure that reads 100 rows from a Recordset into a worksheet.

```
Sub ReadDataIntoExcel()
    Dim db As Database, qd As QueryDef, rs As Recordset
    Dim recArray As Variant
    Dim i As Integer, j As Integer
    ' Open the Jet database, QueryDef, and Recordset
    Set db = OpenDatabase("C:\Program Files\Microsoft Office\Access\Northwind.mdb")
    Set qd = db.QueryDefs("Invoices")
    Set rs = qd.OpenRecordset()
    ' Head for Database Records and clear the sheet
    Worksheets("Database Records").Activate
    With Worksheets("Database Records").[A1]
        .CurrentRegion.Clear
        ' Read the data using GetRows
        recArray = rs.GetRows(100)
        For i = 0 To UBound(recArray, 2)
            For j = 0 To UBound(recArray, 1)
                .Offset(i + 1, j) = recArray(j, i)
            Next j
        Next i
        ' Enter the field names and format the cells
        For j = 0 To rs.fields.Count - 1
            .Offset(0, j) = rs.fields(j).Name
            .Offset(0, j).Font.Bold = True
            .Offset(0, j).EntireColumn.AutoFit
        Next j
```

```
    End With
    ' Close the database
    db.Close
End Sub
```

Retrieving an Entire Recordset

If you need to retrieve an entire recordset into a worksheet, you can do so easily with the Range object's `CopyFromRecordset` method:

Range`.CopyFromRecordset(`***Data***`, `*MaxRows*`, `*MaxColumns*`)`

Range	A Range object that specifies the upper-left corner of the destination range.
Data	The recordset containing the data you want to retrieve.
MaxRows	The maximum number of records to retrieve. If you omit *MaxRows*, Excel copies every record.
MaxColumns	The maximum number of fields to retrieve. If you omit *MaxColumns*, Excel copies every field.

Here are a few notes to bear in mind when working with `CopyFromRecordset`:

- Excel begins the copying from the current record. If you want to retrieve every record, make sure you run the `MoveFirst` method to move to the first record.
- When the `CopyFromRecordset` method is done, the Recordset object's `EOF` property is `True`.
- `CopyFromRecordset` will choke if the Recordset object has a field that contains OLE objects.

Listing 18.7 shows the `RetrieveCategories` procedure that uses the `CopyFromRecordset` method.

Listing 18.7. A procedure that filters out OLE Object fields before retrieving a Recordset.

```
Sub RetrieveCategories()
    Dim db As Database, rs As Recordset, fld As Field
    Dim strSELECT As String, i As Integer
    ' Open the Jet database
    Set db = OpenDatabase("C:\Program Files\Microsoft Office\Access\Northwind.mdb")
    ' Open the full Categories table
    Set rs = db.OpenRecordset("Categories")
    ' The strSELECT variable will hold the SQL SELECT statement
    ' that filters the Recordset to remove OLE Object fields
    strSELECT = "SELECT "
    ' Run through the Recordset fields
    For Each fld In rs.fields
        ' Check for OLE Object fields
```

continues

Listing 18.7. continued

```
        If fld.Type <> dbLongBinary Then
            ' If it's not an OLE Object field, add it to the SELECT statement
            strSELECT = strSELECT & fld.Name & ","
        End If
    Next fld
    ' Remove the trailing comma
    strSELECT = Left(strSELECT, Len(strSELECT) - 1)
    ' Add the FROM clause
    strSELECT = strSELECT & " FROM Categories"
    ' Open the filtered Recordset
    Set rs = db.OpenRecordset(strSELECT)
    ' Retrieve the records
    Worksheets("Database Records").Activate
    With Worksheets("Database Records").[a1]
        .CurrentRegion.Clear
        ' Retrieve the records
        .Offset(1).CopyFromRecordset rs
        ' Enter the field names and format the cells
        For i = 0 To rs.fields.Count - 1
            .Offset(0, i) = rs.fields(i).Name
            .Offset(0, i).Font.Bold = True
            .Offset(0, i).EntireColumn.AutoFit
        Next i
    End With
    ' Close the database
    db.Close
End Sub
```

`RetrieveCategories` connects to a Jet database and opens the Categories table as the `rs` Recordset variable. You want to make sure that you don't try to copy any OLE Object fields, so the procedure constructs a SQL `SELECT` statement that excludes any fields that contain OLE objects. The `strSELECT` variable will hold the `SELECT` statement, so it's initialized to `"SELECT "`. Then a `For...Next` loop runs through each field in `rs` and looks for OLE Object fields where the `Type` property is `dbLongBinary`. If a field isn't an OLE Object type, its name (and a comma separator) is appended to the `SELECT` statement.

Next, the trailing comma is removed, and the `FROM` clause is concatenated to the `SELECT` statement. A new recordset is opened based on `strSELECT`, and then the `CopyFromRecordset` method retrieves the records.

Summary

This chapter showed you how to use the Data Access Objects model to work with external data in both Jet and non-Jet databases. After a quick tour of the DAO hierarchy, I showed you a number of methods for connecting to databases. From there, you learned how to open a recordset and work with some recordset properties and methods. I also showed you how to use QueryDef objects and how to retrieve external data into Excel.

Here are a few related chapters to check out:

- For information on working with Access VBA objects, see Chapter 9, "VBA and Access."
- If you only need to work with simple flat-file data, Excel lists are your best bet. I show you how to manipulate lists in Chapter 17, "Using VBA to Work with Excel Lists."
- I discuss a few more advanced DAO topics in Chapter 19, "Advanced Database Programming."

CHAPTER

Advanced Database Programming

IN THIS CHAPTER

Handle your tools without mittens.

—Benjamin Franklin

You got your database programming education off to a rousing start in the preceding chapter. This chapter continues the learning process by presenting you with a few advanced topics that should prove useful. In particular, you'll learn some techniques for maintaining databases, implementing transaction processing, and opening ODBCDirect workspaces to work with remote server data.

Maintaining a Jet Database

I briefly touched upon a few database maintenance chores in the preceding chapter. I'll begin our look at advanced database programming by covering these techniques in more detail and introducing you to a few more helpful maintenance routines for Jet databases. Although everything I'll show you in this chapter is more easily accomplished by working with Access directly, there are still plenty of situations in which this code will come in handy:

- You don't have Access but want to take advantage of the power of the Jet database engine.
- You have Access but you would prefer to avoid loading it because of memory constraints.
- You're building an application for others to use, and you need to perform database maintenance behind the scenes.
- You want to create a front-end that others can use to maintain their own databases.

Creating a New Database

As I mentioned in the preceding chapter, the Workspace object has a `CreateDatabase` method that you can wield to produce a Jet Database object from scratch. Here's the syntax of this method:

```
Workspace.CreateDatabase(Name, Locale, Option)
```

`Workspace` The Workspace object in which you want to create the database. If you omit *`Workspace`*, Jet uses the default workspace.

`Name` The filename and (optionally) the local path or network path of the new database. Use a string up to 255-characters long. If no extension is specified, Jet appends .MDB automatically.

`Locale` A constant that specifies the collating order used in the database. The collating order is used when performing string comparisons or sorting on text fields. The default value is `dbLangGeneral`,

which applies to English, French, German, Italian, Modern Spanish, and Portuguese. Other languages have their own constants (see the DAO Help file for the complete list).

Option — One or more constants that determine whether or not the database is encrypted and which Jet database version is used:

`dbEncrypt`	The new database will be encrypted. `dbEncrypt` has the value 2.
`dbVersion10`	The new database uses the Jet 1.0 file format.
`dbVersion11`	The new database uses the Jet 1.1 file format.
`dbVersion20`	The new database uses the Jet 2.0 file format.
`dbVersion30`	The new database uses the Jet 3.0 file format (this is the default).

NOTE: SET UP A REFERENCE TO THE JET LIBRARY

As explained in the preceding chapter, don't forget that you won't be able to use DAO in your code until you set up a reference to the Microsoft DAO 3.5 Object Library in your project.

To help demonstrate this method and many of the other techniques described in this section, I've put together an application called Jet Database Maintainer (JDM). You'll find it on the CD in the file named Chaptr19.xls. When you open this file and click the Run Jet Database Maintainer worksheet button, you'll see the form shown in Figure 19.1. (This is `frmDBMaintainer` in the application. Note that you can also display this dialog box by running the macro named Main.)

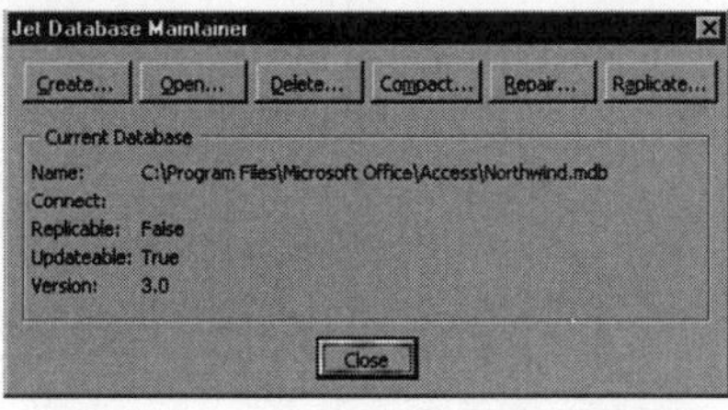

FIGURE 19.1.
The main form of the Jet Database Maintainer application.

To use this application to create a new Jet database, follow these steps:

1. Click the Create button to display the form shown in Figure 19.2 (this is `frmCreateDB` in the application).

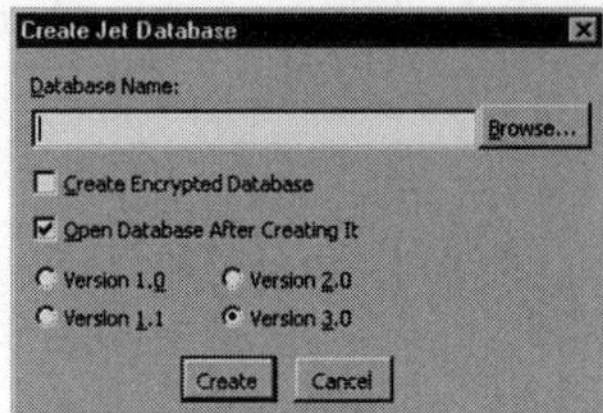

FIGURE 19.2.
Use this custom form to create a new database.

2. Either enter a path and filename in the Database Name text box, or click Browse and use the displayed dialog box to choose a location and enter a filename.
3. Activate the Create Encrypted Database check box to make the new database encrypted.
4. If you want the application to open the database, leave the Open Database After Creating It check box activated.
5. Select the database version you want to use.
6. Click Create.

Listing 19.1 shows the event handler procedures used in the Create Jet Database form. Here's a summary of the actions performed by each procedure:

`cmdBrowse_Click`: When you click the Browse button, this procedure runs Excel's `GetSaveAsFilename` method. This method displays the built-in Save As dialog box and returns the path and filename entered by the user.

`txtDBName_Exit`: This procedure checks the text box value to make sure the filename uses the .MDB extension.

`cmdCreate_Click`: This event handler runs the `CreateDatabase` method to create the new database. Note that the code assumes you want to use the `dbLangGeneral` constant for the *`Locale`* argument. If the Open Database After Creating It check box (named `chkOpenDB`) is activated, the `OpenDatabase` method is invoked on the new file and the resulting Database object is stored in the global `db` variable.

Listing 19.1. Event handler code for the Create Jet Database form.

```
' The Browse button event handler. This
' procedure displays the built-in Save As dialog box and
' grabs the specified file path and name.
'
Private Sub cmdBrowse_Click()
    Dim dbFile As Variant
    Dim td As TableDef
```

```
    '
    ' Get the database filename
    '
    dbFile = Application.GetSaveAsFilename( _
        filefilter:="Jet Databases (*.mdb),*.mdb", _
        Title:="Create Jet Database")
    If dbFile = False Then Exit Sub
    txtDBName = dbFile
End Sub
'
' The Exit event handler for the text box. This procedure
' ensures that the filename uses the .MDB extension.
'
Private Sub txtDBName_Exit(ByVal Cancel As MSForms.ReturnBoolean)
    Dim dbName As String
    Dim dotPosition As Integer

    dbName = txtDBName
    If dbName = "" Or UCase$(Left(dbName, 4)) = ".MDB" Then
        '
        ' Filename is blank or okay, so never mind
        '
        Exit Sub
    Else
        dotPosition = InStr(dbName, ".")
        If dotPosition = 0 Then
            '
            ' If there's no extension, add one
            '
            dbName = dbName + ".mdb"
        Else
            '
            ' If there's a different extension, change it
            '
            dbName = Left$(dbName, dotPosition) + "mdb"
        End If
        txtDBName = dbName
    End If
End Sub
'
' The Create button event handler. This
' procedure creates the new database.
'
Private Sub cmdCreate_Click()
    On Error GoTo ErrorHandler
    '
    ' Make sure a database name was entered
    '
    If txtDBName <> "" Then
        '
        ' Create the database. Multiply the check box
        ' value by -2 to get either 2 (checked) or
        ' 0 (unchecked)
        '
        CreateDatabase _
            Name:=txtDBName, _
            locale:=dbLangGeneral, _
            Option:=dbVersion30 + chkEncrypt * (-2)
```

continues

Listing 19.1. continued

```
        If chkOpenDB = True Then
            Set db = OpenDatabase(txtDBName)
        End If
        Unload Me
    Else
        MsgBox "You must enter a name for the new database!", _
            vbExclamation + vbOKOnly, _
            "Jet Database Maintainer"
        txtDBName.SetFocus
    End If
    Exit Sub
'
' Trap the "Database already exists" error (3204)
'
ErrorHandler:
    If Err = 3204 Then
        If MsgBox("The database name you entered already exists. Do you want to
        ➥replace the existing database?", _
            vbQuestion + vbYesNo, _
            "Jet Database Maintainer") = vbYes Then
            Kill txtDBName
            Resume
        Else
            txtDBName.SetFocus
            Exit Sub
        End If
    End If

End Sub
Private Sub cmdCancel_Click()
    Unload Me
End Sub
```

Compacting a Database

When you delete a table from a Jet database, you can no longer view the table, but it still takes up the same amount of space in the database file. This is analogous to the way Windows (and DOS before it) deletes a file. In other words, the file's data remains intact, but the file system no longer refers to the file.

As you may know, once you delete a file or two from a hard disk, the disk becomes fragmented, and data retrieval becomes less efficient. The same thing happens to a Jet database in which one or more tables have been deleted. To reduce the disk space requirements for such a database and to improve the efficiency of data retrieval, you need to *compact* the database. You can do this programmatically by using the `CompactDatabase` method:

```
DBEngine.CompactDatabase(SrcName, DstName, DstLocale, Options, SrcLocale)
```

`SrcName` The filename and (optionally) the local path or network path of the database you want to compact. Note that this database must be closed.

DstName	The filename and (optionally) the local path or network path of the database to which the file specified by ***SrcName*** will be compacted. ***DstName*** must be different than ***SrcName***.
DstLocale	A constant that specifies the collating order used in the compacted database. This is the same as the *Locale* argument of the `CreateDatabase` method.
Options	One or more constants that determine whether or not the database is encrypted and which Jet database version is used. (See the *Option* argument in the `CreateDatabase` method.)
SrcLocale	A string specifying the source database password, preceded by `;pwd=` (for example, `;pwd=mondocanuck`).

TIP: MAKING BACKUP COPIES

The `CreateDatabase` method could also be used as a makeshift backup function. During an idle period (say, while waiting for user input), you could close the database, run `CompactDatabase` to create a compact copy in a backup location (such as a network drive), and reopen the database.

If you click the Compact button in the Jet Database Maintainer form, you see the Compact Jet Database form, shown in Figure 19.3. Here are the steps to follow to fill in this form:

1. In the Source group, use the Database Name text box to enter the name of the database you want to compact. You can also click the Browse button to select the file from a dialog box. The name is copied to the Database Name text box in the Destination group.
2. If you want to compact to a different database, use the Destination group's Database Name text box to enter the name of the compacted database. You can also click the Browse button to select the file from a dialog box.
3. Activate the Encrypt Destination Database check box to make the compacted database encrypted.
4. If you want the application to open the encrypted database, leave the Open Destination Database After Compacting check box activated.
5. Select the database version of the compacted database.
6. Click Compact.

FIGURE 19.3.
Use this form to compact a Jet database.

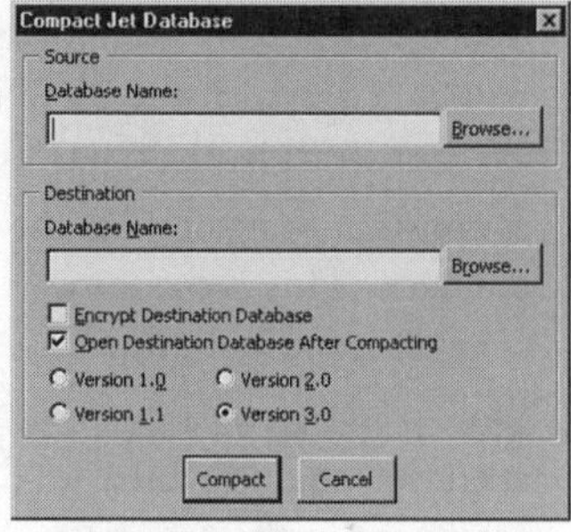

Listing 19.2 shows you the event handler code that underlies the Compact Jet Database form (`frmCompactDB` in the project). Here's a summary of the procedures:

`cmdSrcBrowse_Click`: When you click the Browse button in the Source group, this procedure runs Excel's `GetSaveAsFilename` method. This method displays the built-in Save As dialog box and returns the selected path and filename for the source database.

`cmdDstBrowse_Click`: When you click the Browse button in the Destination group, this procedure returns the selected path and filename for the destination database.

`txtSrcName_Exit`: This procedure checks the text box in the Source group to make sure the filename exists.

`cmdCompact_Click`: This event handler runs the `CompactDatabase` method to compact the new database. Note that the code assumes you want to use the `dbLangGeneral` constant for the *`DstLocale`* argument. If the source and destination are the same, the destination is changed to a temporary filename for the compact process. This file is then renamed to the source after compacting. If the Open Destination Database After Compact check box (named `chkOpenDB`) is activated, the `OpenDatabase` method is invoked on the compacted file and the resulting Database object is stored in the global `db` variable.

Listing 19.2. Event handler code for the Compact Jet Database form.

```
' The Source database Browse button event handler. This
' procedure displays the built-in Save As dialog box and
' grabs the specified file path and name.
'
Private Sub cmdSrcBrowse_Click()
    Dim dbFile As Variant
    '
    ' Get the source database filename
    '
    dbFile = Application.GetSaveAsFilename( _
        filefilter:="Jet Databases (*.mdb),*.mdb", _
        Title:="Source Database")
    If dbFile = False Then Exit Sub
    txtSrcName = dbFile
    txtDstName = dbFile
End Sub
```

```
'
' The Destination database Browse button event handler. This
' procedure displays the built-in Save As dialog box and
' grabs the specified file path and name.
'
Private Sub cmdDstBrowse_Click()
    Dim dbFile As Variant
    '
    ' Get the database file to be compacted
    '
    dbFile = Application.GetSaveAsFilename( _
        filefilter:="Jet Databases (*.mdb),*.mdb", _
        Title:="Destination Database")
    If dbFile = False Then Exit Sub
    txtDstName = dbFile
End Sub
'
' The Exit event handler for the Source Database Name text box.
' This procedure ensures that the source file exists.
'
Private Sub txtSrcName_Exit(ByVal Cancel As MSForms.ReturnBoolean)
    Dim dbName As String
    dbName = txtSrcName.Text
    If dbName = "" Then
        '
        ' Filename is blank, so never mind
        '
        Exit Sub
    ElseIf Dir(dbName) <> "" Then
        '
        ' File exists, so copy name to destination and bail out
        '
        txtDstName = dbName
        Exit Sub
    Else
        MsgBox "Source database does not exist!", _
            vbExclamation, _
            "Jet Database Maintainer"
        txtSrcName.SetFocus
    End If
End Sub
'
' The Compact button event handler. This
' procedure compacts the source database.
'
Private Sub cmdCompact_Click()
    On Error GoTo ErrorHandler
    Dim intOptions As Integer
    Dim compactToSource As Boolean
    compactToSource = False
    '
    ' Make sure the source database name was entered
    '
    If txtSrcName = "" Then
        MsgBox "You must enter a name for the source database!", _
            vbExclamation + vbOKOnly, _
            "Jet Database Maintainer"
```

19 ADVANCED DATABASE PROGRAMMING

continues

Listing 19.2. continued

```
        txtSrcName.SetFocus
    '
    ' Make sure the destination database name was entered
    '
    ElseIf txtDstName = "" Then
        MsgBox "You must enter a name for the destination database!", _
            vbExclamation + vbOKOnly, _
            "Jet Database Maintainer"
        txtDstName.SetFocus
    Else
        '
        ' Close the current database if it's the source or
        ' if the Open Destination Database After Compacting
        ' check box is activated
        '
        If Not db Is Nothing Then
            With db
                If txtSrcName = .Name Or chkOpenDb Then .Close
            End With
        End If
        '
        ' If source and destination are the same,
        ' use a temporary name for the destination
        '
        If txtSrcName = txtDstName Then
            Randomize
            txtDstName = CStr(Int(89999999 * Rnd + 10000000)) & ".mdb"
            compactToSource = True
        End If
        '
        ' Calculate the Options argument
        '
        If opt10 Then
            intOptions = opt10.Tag
        ElseIf opt11 Then
            intOptions = opt11.Tag
        ElseIf opt20 Then
            intOptions = opt20.Tag
        Else
            intOptions = opt30.Tag
        End If
        intOptions = intOptions + chkEncrypt * (-2)
        '
        ' Compact the source database
        '
        DBEngine.CompactDatabase _
            srcname:=txtSrcName, _
            dstname:=txtDstName, _
            dstlocale:=dbLangGeneral, _
            Options:=intOptions
        '
        ' If the source and destination are the same,
        ' delete the source and then rename the temporary
        ' file to the source name
        '
```

```
        If compactToSource = True Then
            Kill txtSrcName
            Name txtDstName As txtSrcName
            txtDstName = txtSrcName
        End If
        '
        ' Open the destination, if applicable
        '
        If chkOpenDB = True Then
            Set db = OpenDatabase(txtDstName)
        End If
        Unload Me

    End If
    Exit Sub
'
' Trap errors
'
ErrorHandler:
    '
    ' Destination database already exists
    '
    If Err = 3204 Then
        If MsgBox("The destination database name you entered already exists. Do
➥you want to replace the existing database?", _
            vbQuestion + vbYesNo, _
            "Jet Database Maintainer") = vbYes Then
            Kill txtDstName
            Resume
        Else
            txtDstName.SetFocus
            Exit Sub
        End If
    '
    ' Can't compact to an earlier version
    '
    ElseIf Err = 3301 Then
        MsgBox "Can't compact to an earlier version!", _
            vbExclamation, _
            "Jet Database Maintainer"
            Exit Sub
    End If
End Sub
Private Sub cmdCancel_Click()
    Unload Me
End Sub
```

Repairing a Database

If an application (or even Windows itself) crashes while a database is open, the database structure might become corrupted. In this case, you'll receive an error message when you attempt to open or compact the file. To fix a corrupted database, Data Access Objects offer the `RepairDatabase` method:

```
DBEngine.RepairDatabase Name
```

Name	The filename and (optionally) the local path or network path of the database you want to repair. This database must be closed before running the `RepairDatabase` method.

In the Jet Database Maintainer application, clicking the Repair button produces the Repair Jet Database dialog box (`frmRepairDB` in the project), shown in Figure 19.4. Enter the name of the database you want to repair (or click Browse to select the file from dialog box) and then click Repair.

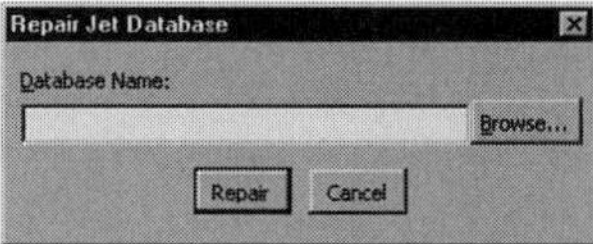

Figure 19.4.
Use this form to repair a Jet database.

Listing 19.3 shows the event handler for the Repair button. This procedure performs the following tasks:

- Closes the currently open database if it's the same as the one to be repaired. (This is unlikely since a corrupted database will usually fail to open in the first place.)
- Runs the `RepairDatabase` method.
- Compacts the repaired database. (This is always a good idea after repairing a database.) Note that the database is compacted to a temporary file which is then restored to the original file.
- The `ErrorHandler` section traps any errors that occur during the repair. In this case, I use the DAO `Errors` object to display the error messages.

Listing 19.3. Event handler code for the Repair button in the Repair Jet Database form.

```
' The Repair button event handler. This procedure
' attempts to repair the specified database.
'
Private Sub cmdRepair_Click()
    On Error GoTo ErrorHandler
    Dim tmpDBName As String
    Dim dbError As Error
    '
    ' Make sure a database name was entered
    '
    If txtDBName <> "" Then
        '
        ' Close the current database if it's the same as the
        ' one to be repaired
        '
        If Not db Is Nothing Then
            With db
                If txtDBName = .Name Then .Close
```

```
            End With
        End If
        '
        ' Attempt to repair the database
        '
        DBEngine.RepairDatabase txtDBName
        '
        ' Compact the repaired database
        '
        Randomize
        tmpDBName = CStr(Int(89999999 * Rnd + 10000000)) & ".mdb"
        DBEngine.CompactDatabase txtDBName, tmpDBName
        Kill txtDBName
        Name tmpDBName As txtDBName
        '
        ' Unload the form and display a message
        '
        Unload Me
        MsgBox "Repair completed successfully!"
    Else
        MsgBox "You must enter a name for the database!", _
            vbExclamation + vbOKOnly, _
            "Jet Database Maintainer"
        txtDBName.SetFocus
    End If
    Exit Sub
'
' Trap any errors that occur during the repair
'
ErrorHandler:
    For Each dbError In DBEngine.Errors
        MsgBox "Repair failed!" & _
            Chr(13) & _
            "Error number: " & dbError.Number & _
            Chr(13) & _
            "Error description: " & dbError.Description
    Next 'dbError
End Sub
```


Replicating a Database

One of Access 97's handiest features is replication. *Replication* lets you create replicas, or "special copies," of a database to distribute to users in different locations so they can work on their copy of the database independent of other users. Replicas allow for data synchronization so that all the replicas can be put together into a single entity, incorporating all the changes that have been introduced in the individual users' copies.

Note, however, that once you convert a regular database into a replicated database, there's no going back—you can't convert it back to a nonreplicable database. Here's a summary of the changes Access makes to a database during replication:

- Several fields are added to each table. Access uses these fields to keep track of, among other things, changes made to the tables.

- Several new system tables are added to the database. These tables keep track of errors and conflicts that occur during synchronization.
- AutoNumber fields are changed so that they generate random numbers.
- The original database is converted into a *Design Master*, and a single replica is created. You use the Design Master to make changes to the structure and design of the database objects. When you synchronize the replicas, these changes are propagated through to each replica. You can't use a replica to alter the structure of database objects.

Replicating Via VBA

When you click the Replicate button in the Jet Database Manager, you see the Replicate Jet Database dialog box, shown in Figure 19.5. First, use the Database Name text box to enter the name of the database you want to replicate (or, as usual, click Browse to choose the database you want). If necessary, enter the name of the replica in the Replica Name text box. (This might not be necessary, because the application automatically adds "Replica of" to the database filename.) When you click Replicate, the database is backed up (to a file with the same name with a .BAK extension), and the replica is created.

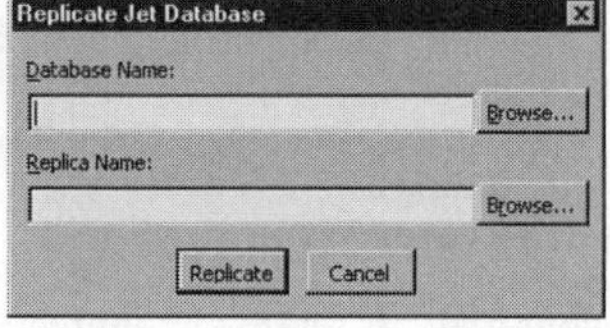

FIGURE 19.5.
Use this form to create a replica of a Jet database.

Replicating a database within a VBA procedure requires the following steps:

1. Make the database replicable.
2. Close the database.
3. Make a backup copy.
4. Create the replica.

Listing 19.4 shows the click event handler for the Replicate button on the Replicate Jet Database form (`frmReplicateDB` in the project), which goes through each of the following steps:

- A series of `If` tests checks the current database and decides if it's the one we want to replicate. If so, the database is closed. The `MakeBackup` function creates a backup copy of the database file using the extension .BAK. The database is then opened in exclusive mode and stored in the `repDB` variable.
- The database is then made replicable by creating a new Property object named `Replicable` for the database. This property is appended to the Database object's `Properties` collection and then set to `T` (for "True").

- The replica is then created using the `MakeReplica` method:

Database`.MakeReplica(`***PathName, Description,*** *`Options`*`)`

Database	The Database object that you want to replicate.
PathName	The filename and (optionally) the local path or network path of the replica.
Description	A description of the replica.
Options	One or more constants that determine the characteristics of the replica. Use `dbRepMakePartial` to create a filtered replica; use `dbRepMakeReadOnly` to make the replica read-only.

Listing 19.4. Event handler code for the Replicate button in the Replicate Jet Database form.

```
' The Replicate button event handler. This procedure
' replicates the specified database.
'
Private Sub cmdReplicate_Click()
    On Error GoTo ErrorHandler
    Dim prop As Property
    Dim dbError As Error
    Dim repDB As Database
    Dim backupFile As String
    '
    ' Make sure the database name was entered
    '
    If txtDBName = "" Then
        MsgBox "You must enter a name for the database!", _
            vbExclamation + vbOKOnly, _
            "Jet Database Maintainer"
        txtDBName.SetFocus
    '
    ' Make sure the replica database name was entered
    '
    ElseIf txtRepName = "" Then
        MsgBox "You must enter a name for the replica database!", _
            vbExclamation + vbOKOnly, _
            "Jet Database Maintainer"
        txtRepName.SetFocus
    Else
        '
        ' We need to open the database in exclusive mode
        ' to make it replicable
        '
        If db Is Nothing Then
            '
            ' No database is open
            '
            backupFile = MakeBackup(txtDBName)
            Set repDB = OpenDatabase(txtDBName, True)
        ElseIf txtDBName <> db.Name Then
```

continues

Listing 19.4. continued

```
            '
            ' The open database is not the one we
            ' want to replicate
            '
            backupFile = MakeBackup(txtDBName)
            Set repDB = OpenDatabase(txtDBName, True)
        Else
            '
            ' The open database is the one we
            ' want to replicate
            '
            CloseDB db.Name
            backupFile = MakeBackup(txtDBName)
            Set repDB = OpenDatabase(txtDBName, True)
        End If
        '
        ' Do the replication
        '
        With repDB
            '
            ' Make the database replicable
            '
            On Error Resume Next
            Set prop = .CreateProperty("Replicable", dbText, "T")
            .Properties.Append prop
            .Properties("Replicable") = "T"
            On Error GoTo ErrorHandler
            Unload Me
            '
            ' Create the replica
            '
            .MakeReplica txtRepName, "Replica of " & txtDBName
            .Close
        End With
        '
        ' Unload the form and display a message
        '
        MsgBox "Replication completed successfully!" & _
            Chr(13) & _
            "Original file backed up as " & backupFile

    Else
        MsgBox "You must enter a name for the database!", _
            vbExclamation + vbOKOnly, _
            "Jet Database Maintainer"
        txtDBName.SetFocus
    End If
    Exit Sub
'
' Trap any errors that occur during the replication
'
ErrorHandler:
    For Each dbError In DBEngine.Errors
        MsgBox "Replication failed!" & _
            Chr(13) & _
```

```
            "Error number: " & dbError.Number & _
            Chr(13) & _
            "Error description: " & dbError.Description
    Next 'dbError
End Sub
```

If you need to create more replicas, simply click the Replicate button as often as you wish. Each time you run this command, the application creates a new replica in the location you specify. (The various replicas you create are known as the *replica set.*)

Synchronizing Replicas

To make sure that each replica contains the most current information, you need to *synchronize* the replicas. During synchronization, Access checks the changes made to each replica and then incorporates these changes into each copy of the file. To synchronize two replicas via VBA, use the `Synchronize` method:

Database`.Synchronize(`***DBPathName,*** *ExchangeType*`)`

Database	The Database object that's a replica.
DBPathName	The filename and (optionally) the local path or network path of the replica with which ***Database*** will be synchronized.
ExchangeType	A constant that determine how the synchronization takes place:

`dbRepExportChanges`	Sends the changes from ***Database*** to ***DBPathname***.
`dbRepImportChanges`	Sends the changes from ***DBPathname*** to ***Database***.
`dbRepImpExpChanges`	Sends the changes both ways.
`dbRepSyncInternet`	Sends the changes via the Internet.

Working with Transaction Processing

In the world of database programming, a *transaction* is a sequence of operations that is treated as a unit. In particular, each of these operations acts a *sine qua non* for the transaction as a whole. In other words, if any one of the operations fails, the entire transaction must not be processed.

For example, consider a transaction that transfers money from a bank savings account into a checking account. This transaction actually consists of two operations: a debit from the savings account and a credit for the same amount to the checking account. Ideally, if either one of these operations fails (not enough money in the savings account, for example), the entire process should be canceled.

To help preserve data integrity, your database applications might need to implement some kind of transaction processing. To do this, the Jet engine provides several methods that let you begin transactions and then either save the changes made during the transaction or else discard these changes. The key here is that once you begin a transaction, the Jet engine no longer writes any changes directly to the database or table with which you're working. Instead, it saves the changes in a special buffer and does the following:

- If you decide to save these changes (this is called *committing* the changes), the Jet engine applies each operation to the underlying object.
- If you decide to discard the changes (this is called *rolling back* the changes), the Jet engine clears the buffer and the underlying object remains untouched.

NOTE: TRANSACTIONS IMPROVE PERFORMANCE

Another benefit of transaction processing is that it's much faster than direct database work. The reason is that, while you're in a transaction, the changes are written to the memory buffer. This process is significantly faster than writing changes to the disk.

In the DAO hierarchy, the Workspace object provides three methods that you can use to set up transaction processing in your VBA applications:

`BeginTrans`: This method starts a new transaction.

`CommitTrans`: This method writes to the database all the changes made since you invoked the `BeginTrans` method.

`Rollback`: This method discards all the changes made since you invoked the `BeginTrans` method.

Listing 19.5 runs through an example. In this procedure, the Northwind sample database is opened, and the Customers table is used as the recordset. The transaction is begun, and a `Do While` loop runs through every record, looking for those in which the `ContactTitle` field is "Owner" and changing this field to "Head Honcho." Then a `MsgBox` asks the user if he or she wants to save these changes. If Yes is clicked, `CommitTrans` saves the changes to disk; otherwise, `Rollback` discards the changes.

Listing 19.5. A procedure that demonstrates transaction processing.

```
Sub TransactionTest()
    Dim nwDB As Database
    Dim rs As Recordset
    Dim newTitle As String
    '
    ' Open the Northwind database (check the path!)
    '
    Set nwDB = OpenDatabase("C:\Program Files\Microsoft Office\Access\
    ➥Northwind.mdb")
```

```
    '
    ' Open the Customers table
    '
    Set rs = nwDB.OpenRecordset("Customers")
    '
    ' Start the transaction
    '
    BeginTrans
    '
    ' Make the changes
    '
    With rs
        Do While Not .EOF
            If !ContactTitle = "Owner" Then
                .Edit
                !ContactTitle = "Head Honcho"
                .Update
            End If
            .MoveNext
        Loop
        '
        ' Ask to save changes
        '
        If MsgBox("Do you want to save all the changes?", vbYesNo) = vbYes Then
            '
            ' Save the changes to disk
            '
            CommitTrans
        Else
            '
            ' Discard the changes
            '
            Rollback
        End If
    End With
    '
    ' Close the database
    '
    nwDB.Close
End Sub
```


Using the ODBCDirect Workspace

As you've seen, the DAO hierarchy gives you direct access to Jet databases via the Jet engine. For other types of databases, you saw in the preceding chapter that you can either attach a table to an existing Jet database or use the Jet engine to work with a table directly. However, these methods suffer from a number of problems, including the following:

- The attached table method requires an existing Jet database.
- The direct method is slow.
- Both methods require the use of the Jet engine to access non-Jet data.

It has always seemed wasteful to have to use the Jet engine as an intermediary for working with Open Database Connectivity (ODBC) data. For one thing, the extra layer used to translate calls from Jet to ODBC slows down database applications. For another, the Jet engine is none too svelte and therefore requires a rather large memory footprint.

VBA 5.0 To solve these problems, VBA 5.0 introduces a new type of workspace called ODBCDirect that lets your applications work with ODBC data directly, thus foregoing the Jet engine entirely. This results in noticeable speed increases and reduced memory requirements for your application. This section shows you how to set up an ODBCDirect workspace as well as how to use the new features of ODBCDirect.

Creating an ODBCDirect Workspace

I mentioned briefly in the preceding chapter that you establish an ODBCDirect workspace by specifying a special constant in the `DBEngine` object's `CreateWorkspace` method. Here's the syntax to use:

```
DBEngine.CreateWorkspace(Name, User, Password, UseType)
```

Name	A string that provides a unique name for the workspace.
User	The user name of the person logging in to this database session.
Password	The password of the person logging in to this session.
UseType	You must specify `dbUseODBC` for an ODBCDirect workspace.

Here's an example:

```
Dim wsODBC As WorkSpace
Set wsODBC = DBEngine.CreateWorkspace( _
    Name:="ODBCWorkSpace", _
    User:="Biff", _
    Password:="ssshhhh", _
    UseType:=dbUseODBC)
```

TIP: SETTING THE DEFAULT WORKSPACE TYPE

You can change the `DBEngine` object's default workspace type by setting the `Type` property equal to either `dbUseJet` or `dbUseODBC`.

NOTE: SETTING THE CURSOR TYPE

ODBCDirect workspaces have a new `DefaultCursorDriver` property that you can use to set the cursor (recordset) type used within the workspace. You can set this property to one of the following constants:

`dbUseDefaultCursor`	Lets the ODBC driver decide which cursor to use. (This is the default constant used by this property.) Server cursors are used if the server supports them (as does SQL Server 6.x); otherwise, a local cursor is used.
`dbUseODBCCursor`	Uses a local cursor. This is ideal for small recordsets.
`dbUseServerCursor`	Uses a server cursor. This is the setting to use for larger recordsets on servers that support cursors.
`dbUseClientBatchCursor`	Uses an optimistic batch cursor.
`dbUseNoCursor`	Uses no cursor, which means the workspace sets up forward-only, read-only recordsets that fetch one record at a time from the server.

Connecting to a Database

With your ODBCDirect workspace ready to roll, you can then establish a connection to the data with which you want to work. You saw in the preceding chapter that the `OpenDatabase` method lets you connect to a data source. You can still use this method in an ODBCDirect workspace, but you can also establish a new Connection object as well. The next two sections explain both techniques.

The OpenDatabase Method for ODBCDirect Workspaces

Let's take a closer look at how the various arguments associated with the `OpenDatabase` method apply to ODBCDirect workspaces. Here's the general syntax once again:

```
ODBCWorkspace.OpenDatabase(Name, Options, ReadOnly, Connect)
```

ODBCWorkspace	The ODBCDirect Workspace object in which you want to open the database.
Name	The name of the data source to which you want to connect. If you'll be using the *Connect* argument to specify the data source instead, you can either set ***Name*** to the empty string (`""`) or to a user-defined name that will become the `Name` property of the returned Database object.
Options	For an ODBCDirect workspace, this argument is a constant that determines whether or not the user is prompted to establish the connection:

`dbDriverNoPrompt`	The user isn't prompted. If the *Connect* string is incomplete or wrong, a runtime error occurs.

`dbDriverPrompt`	The Select Data Source dialog box appears so the user can choose a data source.
`dbDriverComplete`	Only prompts the user with the ODBC Data Sources dialog box if the *`Connect`* string is incomplete or in error.
`dbDriverCompleteRequired`	The same as `dbDriverComplete`, except that the user can't change any information already contained in the *`Connect`* argument.

`ReadOnly` Set this argument to `True` to open the database with read-only access. The default value is `False`.

`Connect` A string that specifies extra parameters for opening the database.

For ODBC data sources, the *`Connect`* argument is used to specify any of the following optional information: the data source name (DSN), the database, a user name, and a password. The *`Connect`* string always begins with `ODBC;`, and you specify the other parameters using the `DSN` (data source name), `UID` (user ID), and `PWD` (password) keywords. Here's the general form:

```
"ODBC; DSN=datasource;DATABASE=dbname;UID=userID;PWD=password;"
```

Listing 19.6 runs through an example that creates an ODBCDirect workspace and then opens an ODBC database.

Listing 19.6. Using OpenDatabase to connect to a SQL Server database in an ODBCDirect workspace.

```
Sub OpenDatabaseTest()
    Dim wsODBC As Workspace
    Dim db As Database
    '
    ' Create the ODBCDirect workspace
    '
    Set wsODBC = DBEngine.CreateWorkspace( _
        Name:="ODBCWorkspace", _
        UserName:="sa", _
        Password:="", _
        usetype:=dbUseODBC)
    '
    ' Connect to the database
    '
    Set db = wsODBC.OpenDatabase( _
        Name:="Publisher Database", _
        Options:=dbDriverNoPrompt, _
        ReadOnly:=False, _
        Connect:="ODBC;DSN=Publishers;DATABASE=pubs;UID=sa;PWD=;")
    '
    ' Display the database name. Notice that the Name property is
    ' the same as the string specified in the OpenDatabase method's
```

```
    ' Name argument.
    '
    MsgBox db.Name
    '
    ' Shut everything down
    '
    db.Close
    wsODBC.CLose
    Set wsODBC = Nothing
    Set db = Nothing
End Sub
```

Creating a Connection Object

Using `OpenDatabase` to return a Database object is a perfectly legitimate way to work with data in an ODBCDirect workspace. However, ODBCDirect gives you a second method—called `OpenConnection`—that connects to a data source by using a Connection object. This might be the preferable way to go, because the Connection object operates much like the familiar Database object, and it's also tuned for remote data connectivity. You can use a Connection object to run asynchronous queries and to create temporary QueryDef objects.

The `OpenConnection` method uses the same syntax as the `OpenDatabase` method:

ODBCWorkspace`.OpenConnection(`***Name, Options,*** *ReadOnly, Connect*`)`

There are two differences you should bear in mind:

- The *Options* argument also supports the `dbRunAsync` constant, which tells ODBCDirect to open the connect asynchronously. Note that you combine this constant with the other *Options* argument constants.
- If you omit the `UID` or `PWD` elements from the *Connect* argument, ODBCDirect uses the user name and password values that you specified when you created the ODBCDirect workspace.

Listing 19.7 presents a sample procedure that illustrates how you would use `OpenConnection` to establish a connection to an ODBC data source.

Listing 19.7. Using `OpenConnection` to connect to a SQL Server database in an ODBCDirect workspace.

```
Sub OpenConnectionTest()
    Dim con As Connection
    '
    ' We don't have to create an explicit ODBCDirect workspace if we
    ' set the DBEngine object's DefaultType property to dbUseODBC
    '
    DefaultType = dbUseODBC
    '
    ' Create the Connection object
    '
```

continues

Listing 19.7. continued

```
    Set con = OpenConnection( _
        Name:="Connection Test", _
        Options:=dbDriverNoPrompt, _
        ReadOnly:=False, _
        Connect:="ODBC;DSN=Publishers;DATABASE=pubs;UID=sa;PWD=;")
    '
    ' Display the connection name
    '
    MsgBox con.Name
    '
    ' Shut everything down
    '
    con.Close
    Set con = Nothing
End Sub
```

NOTE: DATABASES AND CONNECTIONS

When you run the `OpenConnection` method, ODBCDirect also creates a Database object. You can refer to this object by using the `Database` property of the Connection object. Similarly, the Database object has a `Connection` property that refers to its associated Connection object.

Working with ODBCDirect Recordsets

Whether you're using a Database or a Connection object, you still invoke the `OpenRecordset` method whenever you want to work with records from an ODBC data source table. The syntax is identical to what you saw in the preceding chapter:

`Object``.OpenRecordset(`***`Name`***`, `*`Type`*`, `*`Options`*`, `*`LockEdit`*`)`

However, you need to keep the following notes in mind when working within an ODBCDirect workspace:

- In the *`Type`* argument, ODBCDirect workspaces don't support table-type recordsets, so you can't use the `dbOpenTable` constant.
- The default value for *`Type`* is `dbOpenForwardOnly`.
- The default value for *`LockEdit`* is `dbReadOnly`.
- Not all ODBC drivers support all combinations of the *`Type`* and *`LockEdit`* arguments. For example, if you specify `dbOpenSnapShot` as the *`Type`*, SQL Server 6.x only supports `dbReadOnly` for *`LockEdit`*. See the ODBC driver documentation to learn which restrictions you face.
- It's possible to return multiple Recordset objects from a single `OpenRecordset` method (see the next section).

CAUTION: MORE RECORDSET RESTRICTIONS

You should also know that ODBCDirect recordsets don't support indexes and the following methods: `Seek`, `FindFirst`, `FindLast`, `FindNext`, and `FindPrevious`.

Returning Multiple Recordset Objects

One of the more interesting new features you get with ODBCDirect is the ability to return two or more recordsets with a single call to the `OpenRecordset` method. The trick is to specify multiple SQL SELECT statements in the ***Name*** argument, as in this example:

```
Set rs = con.OpenRecordset( _
    "SELECT * FROM authors; " & _
    "SELECT * FROM titles;")
```

Here are some notes about this technique:

- The returned recordsets are read-only, so you can't do any updating.
- For simplicity, you should use local cursors.
- The returned object acts like a forward-only snapshot recordset where each "record" is itself a recordset. You traverse this "meta-recordset" by invoking its `NextRecordset` method. This discards the current recordset and loads the next one (and you can't return to the previous recordset).
- The returned object's `NextRecordset` method returns `True` if it contains a valid recordset, and it returns `False` if there are no recordsets left.

Listing 19.8 shows a procedure that uses this technique. The `OpenRecordset` method uses two SELECT statements to return two recordsets. Then a couple of loops are constructed: one to run through the Recordset objects and another to run through the records in each of the recordsets.

Listing 19.8. A procedure that returns multiple recordsets.

```
Sub MultipleRecordsetTest()
    Dim wsODBC As Workspace
    Dim con As Connection
    Dim rs As Recordset
    Dim i As Integer, j As Integer
    '
    ' Set up the workspace
    '
    Set wsODBC = DBEngine.CreateWorkspace( _
        Name:="ODBCWorkspace", _
        UserName:="sa", _
        Password:="", _
        UseType:=dbUseODBC)
```

continues

Listing 19.8. continued

```
    '
    ' Use local cursors
    '
    wsODBC.DefaultCursorDriver = dbUseODBCCursor
    '
    ' Create the Connection object
    '
    Set con = wsODBC.OpenConnection( _
        Name:="Multiple Recordsets", _
        Options:=dbDriverNoPrompt, _
        ReadOnly:=False, _
        Connect:="ODBC;DSN=Publishers;DATABASE=pubs;")
    '
    ' Use multiple SELECTs to return the recordsets
    '
    Set rs = con.OpenRecordset( _
        "SELECT * FROM authors; " & _
        "SELECT * FROM titles;")
    '
    ' Loop through the returned objects
    '
    i = 1
    With rs
        Do
            j = 0
            '
            ' Loop through the current recordset
            '
            Do While Not .EOF
                j = j + 1
                .MoveNext
            Loop
            MsgBox "Recordset #" & i & " has " & j & " records."
            i = i + 1
        Loop Until (rs.NextRecordset = False)
    End With
    '
    ' Shut everything down
    '
    rs.Close
    con.Close
    wsODBC.Close
    Set wsODBC = Nothing
    Set con = Nothing
    Set rs = Nothing
End Sub
```

Programming Jet Database Security

If you're programming in a multiuser environment, security issues are always paramount. Sure, it's possible that all the databases you work with might be needed by and available to all the users on the network, but it's more likely that you'll want to place some restrictions on database access. Outside of creating a secure Jet database (which must be done directly in Access),

VBA lets you control security programmatically, including creating new users and groups, setting passwords and permissions, deleting users and groups, and more. I discuss all of these techniques in this section.

Creating a Secure Database

Jet database security is controlled by a *workgroup information file,* which is used to manage account names and passwords for individual users and for groups of users. In 32-bit environments, the default workgroup information file is named System.mdw, but for tightest security you need to create custom workgroup information files. However, VBA offers no way to create these files and no way to manipulate these files to secure a database, so you must do this by hand within Access. The next few sections take you through the steps necessary to accomplish this.

Step 1: Create a New Workgroup File

When implementing Jet database security, it's best to start fresh with a new workgroup information file. This ensures that you begin with only the default set of users and groups, and it adds extra security because the default file (System.mdw) is identified by the name and organization you specified when installing Access, and this information is relatively easy for an unauthorized user to determine. Here are the steps to follow to create a new workgroup information file:

1. Click the Start button in the Windows taskbar, select the Run command, enter `wrkgadm.exe` in the Run dialog box, and click OK. This starts the Workgroup Administrator application.
2. Click the Create button to display the Workgroup Owner Information dialog box, shown in Figure 19.6.

FIGURE 19.6.
Use this dialog box to specify the data that will be used to create the new workgroup information file.

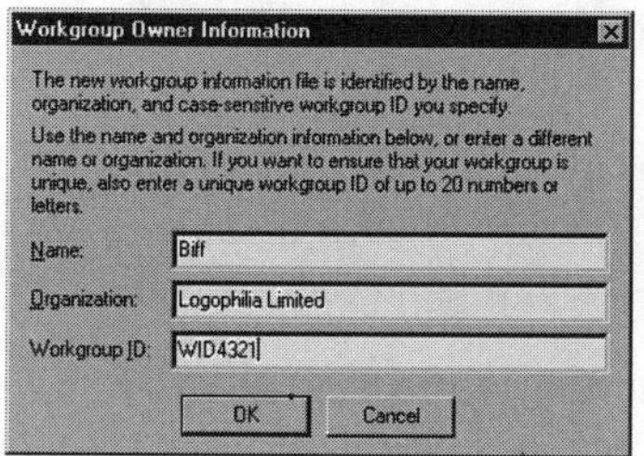

3. Enter a name of up to 39 alphanumeric characters in the Name text box.
4. Enter an organization name of up to 39 alphanumeric characters in the Organization text box.
5. Enter a workgroup ID between 4 and 20 alphanumeric characters long in the Workgroup ID text box. Note that this ID is case-sensitive.

CAUTION: SAVE THE INFORMATION

You should write down the information you enter in this dialog box and store the data in a safe place. This way, you'll always be able to re-create the workgroup information file down the road should anything happen to it.

6. Click OK. The Workgroup Information File dialog box appears.
7. Enter a name and location for the new file and then click OK. The Confirm Workgroup Information dialog box appears.

TIP: SHARE THE WORKGROUP INFORMATION FILE

If you want others on the network to log on to Access using this workgroup information file, be sure to save it to a shared folder.

8. Click OK and, when the Workgroup Administrator lets you know the file has been created, click OK again.
9. Click Exit and then start Access. (If Access was already open when you ran through these steps, you must exit and restart Access so that you can log in to the new workgroup.)

In order for other users to log on to Access using this workgroup information file, they must run the Workgroup Administrator, click Join, select the file using the Workgroup Information File dialog box that appears, and click OK.

Step 2: Assign a Password to the Admin User Name

When you create a new workgroup information file, you're assigned a default user name of Admin. This user is given a default password, which is the null string (""), and is assigned membership in the Admins group. This combination gives you full read/write permissions on every database object and doesn't require you to log in when you launch Access.

The next step in creating a secure database is to activate the Logon dialog box so that users have to log in to the workgroup you established in the preceding section. Here's how it's done:

1. Select Tools | Security | User and Group Accounts. (Note that this command is available even without an open database.) The User and Group Accounts dialog box appears, as shown in Figure 19.7.

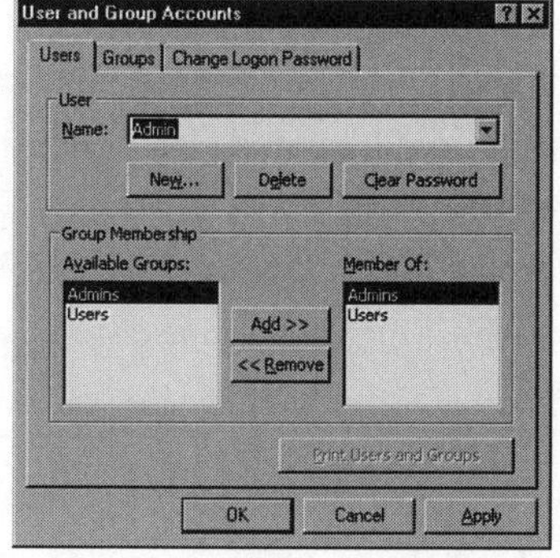

FIGURE 19.7.
Use this dialog box to make adjustments to user and group accounts.

2. Activate the Change Logon Password tab.
3. The default password for the Admin user is empty, so you can ignore the Old Password text box. Enter a new password for the Admin user in both the New Password and Verify text boxes.
4. Click OK.

By assigning a password to the Admin user, Access will now display the Logon dialog box to any user who attempts to log in to the workgroup you created earlier.

Step 3: Create an Administrator Account

Your next chore is to create a new administrator account for the workgroup. This account will be responsible for maintaining the security for each workgroup database, including creating user and group accounts, setting permissions on database objects, and more. Here are the steps to follow:

1. Select Tools | Security | User and Group Accounts to display the User and Group Accounts dialog box.
2. In the Users tab, click New. Access displays the New User/Group dialog box, shown in Figure 19.8.

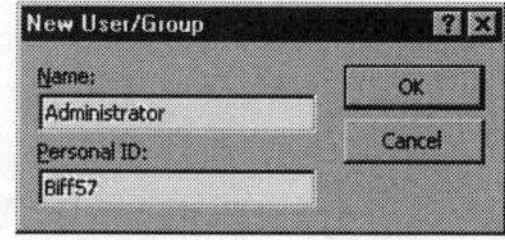

FIGURE 19.8.
Use this dialog box to define a new user account.

3. Enter a user name in the Name text box, a personal ID for the user in the Personal ID text box, and click OK.
4. In the Available Groups list, make sure Admins is highlighted and then click Add >>.
5. Click OK to create the new account.

6. Exit and then restart Access. When the Logon dialog box appears, enter the user name for the new administration account you just created and click OK.
7. Select Tools | Security | User and Group Accounts to display the User and Group Accounts dialog box.
8. Activate the Change Logon Password tab.
9. Enter a new password for the administrator account in both the New Password and Verify text boxes.
10. Click OK.

Step 4: Remove the Admin User from the Admins Group

The next item on your security agenda is to remove the default Admin user from the Admins group. Here's the procedure:

1. Select Tools | Security | User and Group Accounts to display the User and Group Accounts dialog box.
2. In the Users tab, select Admin in the Name drop-down list.
3. In the Member Of list, highlight Admins and then click << Remove.
4. Click OK.

Step 5: Convert to a Secure Database

To complete the procedure for securing a database, you need to run the User-Level Security Wizard, which will convert your database into a secure database. Here's what you do:

1. Open the database you want to secure.
2. Select Tools | Security | User-Level Security Wizard to display the dialog box shown in Figure 19.9.

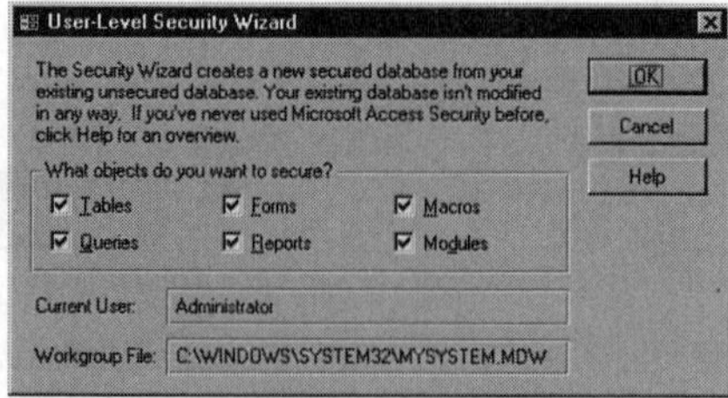

FIGURE 19.9.
The User-Level Security Wizard converts a file into a secured database.

3. Use the check boxes to decide which database objects you want to secure.
4. Click OK. The Wizard displays the Destination Database dialog box.
5. Select a location and name for the secured database and click Save. (Note that the original database isn't changed during this procedure.)

6. When the conversion is complete, the Wizard displays a dialog box to let you know. Click OK.

At this point, your database is secure and only the new administration account has permission to make changes to the database objects. From here, you need to open the secure database and do the following:

- Select Tools | Security | User and Group Accounts and use the dialog box to add new users and groups. (For the latter, activate the Groups tab, click New, and enter a group name and ID.)
- Select Tools | Security | User and Group Permissions and use the dialog box that appears (see Figure 19.10) to set database object permissions for each user and group.

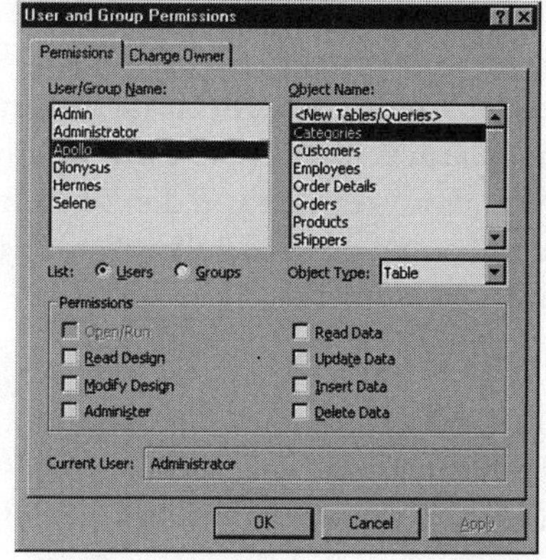

FIGURE 19.10.
Use this dialog box to set permissions for users and groups.

The next few sections show you how to perform these security techniques programmatically in your VBA applications.

Opening a Secure Database

With your secure database ready for action, you can start implementing security measures in your VBA applications. The first thing you need to know is how to open a secured database via DAO. This is controlled by some properties of the `DBEngine` object.

For starters, you use the `SystemDB` property to specify the workgroup information file you want to use. (Note that you must set this property before using `DBEgine` to create a workspace or open a database.) Set this property to a string value that spells out the path and filename of the workgroup information file, like so:

```
DBEgine.SystemDB = "C:\Windows\System32\MySystem.mdw"
```

The next step is to create a workspace and log on using the user name and password of the administration account you set up earlier, or some other account in the Admins group. You have two ways to do this:

- Specify the *UserName* and *Password* arguments in the CreateWorkspace method.
- Use the DBEngine object's DefaultUser and DefaultPassword properties to set the user name and password for the default workspace.

The following procedure fragment shows one way of opening a secure database:

```
Dim db As Database
With DBEngine
    .SystemDB = "C:\Windows\System32\Secure.mdw"
    .DefaultUser = "Administrator"
    .DefaultPassword = "shhhhh"
    Set db = OpenDatabase("C:\Program Files\Microsoft Office\Access\Northwind.mdb")
End With
```

Working with the User Object

In the Data Access Objects hierarchy, the User object represents an individual user account in a secure workspace. You can use VBA to create new users, remove users, and assign database permissions to users. The next few sections show you these and other methods for manipulating User objects. Note, however, that you don't need to have a database opened to use these techniques. User accounts are stored in the workgroup information file, not a database, so you only need to create the appropriate workspace.

Adding a User

As I've said, User objects represent user accounts in a secure workspace (that is, a workgroup information file). Defining a new user involves three steps:

1. Use the Workspace object's CreateUser method to create a new user account:

   ```
   Workspace.CreateUser(Name, PID, Password)
   ```

Workspace	The Workspace object in which you want to create the user account.
Name	The user's name.
PID	The user's personal identifier.
Password	The user's password.

2. Add the new user account to the Users collection by invoking the collection's Append method:

   ```
   Workspace.Users.Append Object
   ```

Workspace	The Workspace object in which you created the user account.
Object	The User object.

3. Assign the user to one or more groups. I'll show you how to do this later when I discuss the Group object.

Listing 19.9 shows a sample procedure that implements steps 1 and 2. The default workspace is set to the secure workgroup information file, the new user is created, and the user is added to the `Users` collection.

Listing 19.9. A procedure that creates a new user account, appends the user to the Users collection, and assigns the user to the Users group.

```
Sub AddNewUser()
    Dim ws As Workspace
    Dim newUser As User
    '
    ' Set up the secure default workspace
    '
    With DBEngine
        .SystemDB = "C:\Windows\System32\Secure.mdw"
        .DefaultUser = "Administrator"
        .DefaultPassword = "shhhhh"
        Set ws = Workspaces(0)
    End With
    '
    ' Create the user
    '
    Set newUser = ws.CreateUser( _
        Name:="Biff", _
        PID:="Biff123", _
        Password:="DoNotTell")
    '
    ' Add the user to the Users collection
    '
    ws.Users.Append newUser
End Sub
```

Once you've added a user, you can use the `Users` collection to refer to the user. You can either use an index value (where 0 is the first user, 1 is the second user, and so on) or the user name. For example, if Admin is the first user, the following statements are equivalent:

```
Users(0)
Users("Admin")
```


Deleting a User

When you no longer need a particular user, the `Users` object has a `Delete` method you can wield to remove the user from the collection:

Workspace*.Users.Delete *Name

Workspace	The Workspace object in which you created the user account.
Name	The name of the user.

Here's an example:

```
With DBEngine
    .SystemDB = "C:\Windows\System32\Secure.mdw"
    .DefaultUser = "Administrator"
    .DefaultPassword = "shhhhh"
    Workspaces(0).Users.Delete "Biff"
End With
```

User Object Properties and Methods

The User object has a few properties and methods that will often come in handy in your VBA procedures. Here's a rundown:

User.`CreateGroup`: This method creates a new Group object for the specified *User*. See "Adding a User to a Group" later in this chapter.

User.`Groups`: This property returns a `Groups` collection that represents the groups in which the specified *User* is a member.

User.`Name`: This property returns or sets the user name for the specified *User*.

User.`NewPassword`: This method changes the password for the specified existing *User*. Here's the syntax:

User*.NewPassword *bstrOld, bstrNew

User	The User object you want to work with.
bstrOld	The current password.
bstrNew	The password you want to assign.

User.`Password`: This property sets the password for the specified new *User*. Note that you can't use this property to return the user's password.

User.`PID`: This property returns or sets the personal identifier for the specified *User*.

Working with the Group Object

In secure database environments, it's usually preferable to work with groups of users rather than individual users. This makes it much easier to manipulate database access, because you can apply permissions to a group, and every user in that group inherits the permissions. Moreover, adding a user to a group automatically sets up that user with the group's permissions. This section shows you how to add new groups, add users to a group, delete groups, and work with group properties and methods.

Adding a Group

To create a new group, use the Workspace object's `CreateGroup` method:

***Workspace*.CreateGroup(*Name*, *PID*)**

Workspace	The secure workspace in which you want to create the group.
Name	The name of the group.
PID	The group identifier.

Once you've created the group, you use the Workspace object's `Groups` collection to invoke the `Append` method and add the group to the collection. For example, Listing 19.10 shows a procedure that creates a new group named Marketing.

Listing 19.10. A procedure that creates a new group.

```
Sub AddGroup()
    Dim ws As Workspace
    Dim grp As Group
    '
    ' Set up the secure default workspace
    '
    With DBEngine
        .SystemDB = "C:\Windows\System32\MySystem.mdw"
        .DefaultUser = "Administrator"
        .DefaultPassword = "dio1459"
        Set ws = Workspaces(0)
    End With
    '
    ' Create the new group and append it
    '
    Set grp = ws.CreateGroup( _
        Name:="Marketing", _
        PID:="mktg1234")
    ws.Groups.Append grp
End Sub
```

Adding a User to a Group

Earlier I ran through the steps necessary to create a new user, but I didn't show you how to assign a user to a group. To do this, you must do two things:

- Invoke the User object's `CreateGroup` method (which has the same syntax as the Workspace object's `CreateGroup` method) to "create" a Group object for an existing group.
- Append that Group object to the User object's `Groups` collection.

Listing 19.11 shows a revised version of the `AddNewUser` procedure that also adds the user to the Marketing group created in the preceding section.

Listing 19.11. A procedure that creates a new user account, appends the user to the Users collection, and assigns the user to the Marketing group.

```
Sub AddNewUser2()
    Dim ws As Workspace
    Dim newUser As User
    Dim grp As Group
    '
    ' Set up the secure default workspace
    '
    With DBEngine
        .SystemDB = "C:\Windows\System32\Secure.mdw"
        .DefaultUser = "Administrator"
        .DefaultPassword = "shhhhh"
        Set ws = Workspaces(0)
    End With
    '
    ' Create the user and set their properties
    '
    Set newUser = ws.CreateUser("Alphonse")
    newUser.PID = "Al123"
    newUser.Password = "WhoKnows"
    '
    ' Add the user to the Users collection
    '
    ws.Users.Append newUser
    '
    ' Create an object for the Users group and then add
    ' this object to the new user's Groups collection
    '
    Set grp = newUser.CreateGroup("Marketing")
    newUser.Groups.Append grp
End Sub
```

Deleting a Group

If a group has worn out its welcome, the `Groups` object has a `Delete` method that removes a group from the collection:

`Workspace``.Groups.Delete `***`Name`***

`Workspace`	The Workspace object in which you created the group.
`Name`	The name of the group.

Here's an example:

```
With DBEngine
    .SystemDB = "C:\Windows\System32\Secure.mdw"
    .DefaultUser = "Administrator"
    .DefaultPassword = "shhhhh"
    Workspaces(0).Groups.Delete "Marketing"
End With
```

Group Object Properties and Methods

You can manipulate Group objects in your VBA procedures by taking advantage of their properties and methods:

`Group.CreateUser`: This method creates a new User object in the specified `Group`:

`Group.CreateUser(Name, PID, Password)`

`Group`	The Group object in which you want to create the user.
`Name`	The user's name.
`PID`	The user's personal identifier.
`Password`	The user's password.

`Group.Name`: This property returns or sets the name of the specified `Group`.

`Group.PID`: This property returns or sets the identifier for the specified `Group`.

`Group.Users`: This property returns a `Users` collection that represents the users that are members of the specified `Group`.

Setting Object Permissions

With your users and groups in place, you can then begin the process of adjusting the permissions for the database objects. The permissions available depend on the object you're dealing with. For a Database object, you can set up a user or group with permissions to create new databases, replicate databases, and so on. Similarly, for a Table object, you can set up permissions for adding, modifying, and deleting records.

Permissions are controlled by the `Permissions` property of either the Container object or the Document object. A Document object represents a particular type of database object (such as a table) and a Container object groups similar types of Document objects together. Container objects are handy for setting permissions on multiple objects, such as, say, all of the tables in a database. In this case, you would simply refer to the "Tables" container. For example, if `db` is a `Database` object variable, here are some containers and the type of documents they hold:

Container	*Documents*
`db.Containers("Databases")`	Saved databases
`db.Containers("Forms")`	Forms
`db.Containers("Modules")`	Modules
`db.Containers("Relationships")`	Relationships
`db.Containers("Reports")`	Reports
`db.Containers("Tables")`	Tables or queries

If you want to work with a particular Document object, use the `Documents` property of the appropriate Container object. For example, to refer to a table named Customers, you would use a statement like the following:

```
db.Containers("Tables").Documents("Customers")
```

Once you know which Container or Document object you want to work with, setting permissions is a two-step procedure:

1. Use the Container or Document object's `UserName` property to specify the user or group for which you want to set permissions.
2. Use the Container or Document object's `Permissions` property to set the type of permissions you want for the user or group.

To set the permissions, you assign one or more constants to the `Permissions` property. The available constants depend on the Container or Document object you're working with, as outlined in Table 19.1.

Table 19.1. Constants used for setting permissions.

Constant	*User/Group Permission*
`dbSecNoAccess`	No access to the object.
`dbSecFullAccess`	Full access to the object.
`dbSecDelete`	Can delete the object.
`dbSecReadSec`	Can read the object's security-related information.
`dbSecWriteSec`	Can modify access permissions.
`dbSecWriteOwner`	Can modify Owner property setting.
`dbSecCreate`	Can create new documents (Container objects only).
`dbSecReadDef`	Can read table or query definition.
`dbSecWriteDef`	Can modify or delete table or query definition.
`dbSecRetrieveData`	Can read data from the table or query object.
`dbSecInsertData`	Can add table records.
`dbSecReplaceData`	Can update table records.
`dbSecDeleteData`	Can delete table records.
`dbSecDBAdmin`	Can replicate a database and change the database password.
`dbSecDBCreate`	Can create new databases.
`dbSecDBExclusive`	Has exclusive access to the database.
`dbSecDBOpen`	Can open the database.

Listing 19.12 shows a sample procedure that sets permissions for a group and for a user.

Listing 19.12. A procedure that sets various permissions.

```
Sub SetPermissions()
    Dim db As Database
    Dim ws As Workspace
    '
    ' Set up the secure default workspace
    '
    With DBEngine
        .SystemDB = "C:\Windows\System32\Secure.mdw"
        .DefaultUser = "Administrator"
        .DefaultPassword = "shhhhh"
        Set ws = Workspaces(0)
    End With
    '
    ' Open a secure version of the Northwind database
    '
    Set db = ws.OpenDatabase("C:\Program Files\Microsoft Office\Access\Secure
    ➥Northwind.mdb")
    '
    ' Set permissions on Customers table for user "Biff"
    '
    With db.Containers("Tables").Documents("Customers")
        .UserName = "Biff"
        .Permissions = dbSecInsertData + _
                       dbSecReplaceData + _
                       dbSecDeleteData
    End With
    '
    ' Set permissions on all Report objects for "Marketing" group
    '
    With db.Containers("Reports")
        .UserName = "Marketing"
        .Permissions = dbSecFullAccess
    End With
    db.Close
End Sub
```

NOTE: CHANGING THE OWNER

If you want to change the owner of a Container or Document object, set the `Owner` property equal to a user name.

Summary

This chapter took you through a few advanced database programming topics. You first learned how to maintain a database via VBA, including how to create, compact, repair, and replicate a database. I then showed you how to implement transaction processing in your applications. From there, I discussed the new ODBCDirect workspaces, showed you a couple of methods for connecting to ODBC databases, and showed you how to work with ODBC recordsets. I closed this chapter with a look at some Jet database security issues, including how to create a secure database and how to use the User and Group objects to control security via VBA.

If you're looking for related material, try the following chapters:

- I show you how to work with the Access object hierarchy in Chapter 9, "VBA and Access."
- For a complete look at user forms, head for Chapter 11, "Working with Microsoft Forms."
- I introduce the Data Access Objects hierarchy in Chapter 18, "Programming Data Access Objects."

IN THIS PART

VI PART

Unleashing VBA Internet and Intranet Programming

CHAPTER 20

Internet and Intranet Programming Topics

IN THIS CHAPTER

> *We're not forming an Internet division. To us, you know, it's like having an electricity division or a software division. The Internet is pervasive in everything that we're doing.*
>
> *—Bill Gates*

The last couple of years have seen a huge increase in the popularity of the World Wide Web. Not only are people surfing like there's no tomorrow, but everyone from individuals to Fortune 500 corporations is rushing to set up shop in cyberspace. For individuals, a Web site is a great way to let other surfers know you're out there. (On my Web site, for example, I have data about my books, updates to the printed material, extra chapters, mailing list archives, and more.) For corporations, the Web is useful for customer contact: tech support, marketing information, product announcements, contests, and even online commerce.

However, Web technology hasn't only spurred massive growth in the Internet's public highways and byways. IT managers all over the world have come to the realization that they can leverage existing technologies such as TCP/IP, Web servers, and Web browsers to create private, internal internets—or *intranets,* as they're usually called. In fact, it's likely that the majority of corporations are sinking more money into developing intranet sites than Internet sites. Why? Well, there are many reasons:

- Once you "get" the idea of an intranet, you can usually think of dozens of ways that it can benefit your business. Corporate reporting, financial data, announcements, archives of frequently used files (such as proprietary graphics files), scheduling, document collaboration—the list is endless.
- Intranets can work with existing content. For example, years ago I worked at a large corporation that maintained a database with thousands of internal employee phone numbers. This database was printed each month, and a copy was distributed to everyone in the company. Needless to say, the printed version was out of date the moment the ink was dry. If we had had an intranet, we could have created an online phone book that was updated dynamically from the database. One of the major goals of Office 97 is to allow existing documents (such as Word and Excel files) to be posted seamlessly (in other words, without conversion to HTML) on intranets.
- An intranet usually doesn't have the same bandwidth limitations that exist with an Internet connection. This means that there are fewer restrictions on the number of files you can post and on the size of those files. It's also possible to provide richer content (such as multimedia files).
- An intranet, since it is by definition not connected to the public Internet, is inherently more secure (although precautions must still be taken if the network has an Internet gateway).

Given these two success stories, the big question nowadays is how to deliver Web-based content quickly and cheaply, yet still maintain a high level of quality. Well, Office 97 certainly has no shortage of end-user tools to do just that. However, there are also a number of resources that the VBA programmer can turn to. We'll examine quite a few of them in this chapter.

Controlling Office 97 Hyperlinks

One of the most interesting innovations in Office 97 is the capability to create hyperlinks in any kind of Office document: Word documents, Excel worksheets, Access databases, PowerPoint presentations, and even Outlook e-mail messages. This lets you create "active" documents that let the reader click special text sections and "surf" to another document, which might be on the World Wide Web, your corporate intranet, or your hard drive.

For example, consider the Word document shown in Figure 20.1. The phrase "amortization schedule" is displayed underlined and in a different color (blue). This formatting indicates that this phrase is a hyperlink. Clicking this link displays the Excel worksheet shown in Figure 20.2.

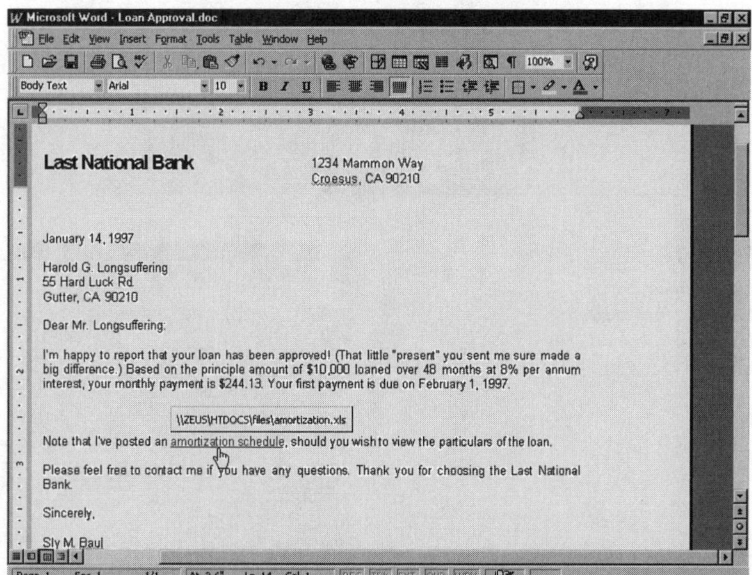

FIGURE 20.1.
A Word document containing a hyperlink.

> **TIP: VIEWING LINK INFORMATION**
>
> As shown in Figure 20.1, you can see where a hyperlink will take you by moving the mouse pointer over the link text. After a second or two, a banner appears that tells you the name of the hyperlink document.

The Office products boast a number of different methods for creating these hyperlinks, but the most common is to enter the appropriate information by hand by selecting Insert | Hyperlink. The application displays the Insert Hyperlink dialog box, shown in Figure 20.3, so that you can define the particulars of the hyperlink, including the network path or URL, and a named location (such as a bookmark) within the file.

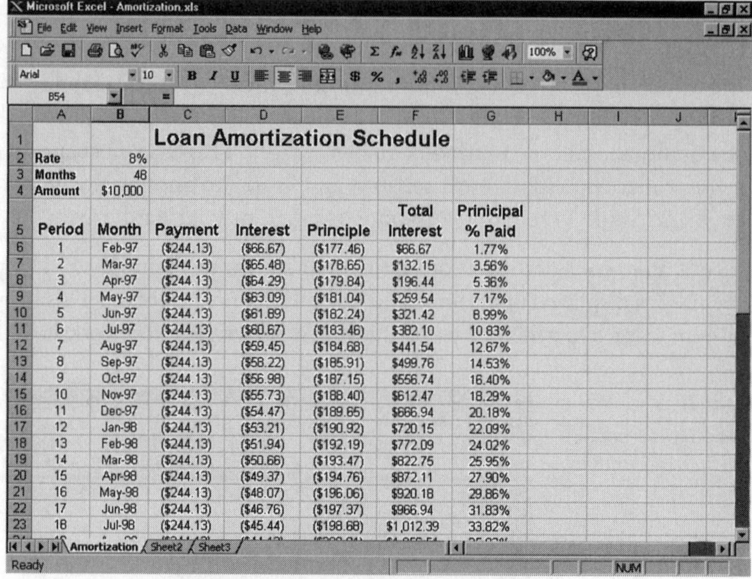

Loan Amortization Schedule

	A	B	C	D	E	F	G
2	Rate	8%					
3	Months	48					
4	Amount	$10,000					
5	Period	Month	Payment	Interest	Principle	Total Interest	Principal % Paid
6	1	Feb-97	($244.13)	($66.67)	($177.46)	$66.67	1.77%
7	2	Mar-97	($244.13)	($65.48)	($178.65)	$132.15	3.56%
8	3	Apr-97	($244.13)	($64.29)	($179.84)	$196.44	5.36%
9	4	May-97	($244.13)	($63.09)	($181.04)	$259.54	7.17%
10	5	Jun-97	($244.13)	($61.89)	($182.24)	$321.42	8.99%
11	6	Jul-97	($244.13)	($60.67)	($183.46)	$382.10	10.83%
12	7	Aug-97	($244.13)	($59.45)	($184.68)	$441.54	12.67%
13	8	Sep-97	($244.13)	($58.22)	($185.91)	$499.76	14.53%
14	9	Oct-97	($244.13)	($56.98)	($187.15)	$556.74	16.40%
15	10	Nov-97	($244.13)	($55.73)	($188.40)	$612.47	18.29%
16	11	Dec-97	($244.13)	($54.47)	($189.65)	$666.94	20.18%
17	12	Jan-98	($244.13)	($53.21)	($190.92)	$720.15	22.09%
18	13	Feb-98	($244.13)	($51.94)	($192.19)	$772.09	24.02%
19	14	Mar-98	($244.13)	($50.66)	($193.47)	$822.75	25.95%
20	15	Apr-98	($244.13)	($49.37)	($194.76)	$872.11	27.90%
21	16	May-98	($244.13)	($48.07)	($196.06)	$920.18	29.86%
22	17	Jun-98	($244.13)	($46.76)	($197.37)	$966.94	31.83%
23	18	Jul-98	($244.13)	($45.44)	($198.68)	$1,012.39	33.82%

FIGURE 20.2.
Clicking the hyperlink displays this Excel worksheet.

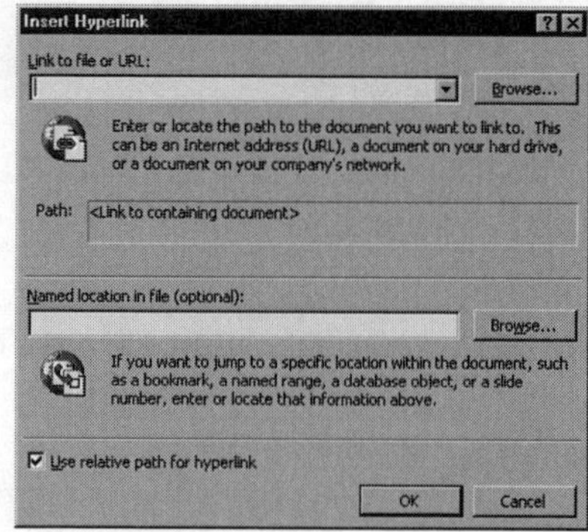

FIGURE 20.3.
Use the Insert Hyperlink dialog box to create your hyperlinks from scratch.

You can duplicate this technique in your VBA code, and I'll show you how to do just that in the next few sections.

Working with the Hyperlink Object

VBA5.0

Each Office 97 application's object model includes the Hyperlink object, which represents a hyperlink in a document. Using VBA, you can insert Hyperlink objects into a document, add hyperlinks to the Favorites folder, and even "surf" the hyperlinks.

`Hyperlinks` is the object that represents the collection of all hyperlinks in an entire document or in part of a document (such as a range). You use `Hyperlinks(`***`Index`***`)` to refer to a specific hyperlink, where ***`Index`*** can be either of the following:

- A number that represents the Hyperlink object, where 1 represents the first hyperlink, 2 the second hyperlink, and so on.
- A string that contains the hyperlink address (a file path, UNC path, or a URL).

Adding New Hyperlink Objects

The `Hyperlinks` collection has an `Add` method that you can use to insert a new Hyperlink object into a document:

Object`.Hyperlinks.Add(`***Anchor, Address,*** *SubAddress*`)`

Object	The object in which you want to insert the hyperlink (such as a Document or Range object in Word, or a Worksheet or Range object in Excel).
Anchor	The object the user will click to follow the hyperlink. This could be a section of text, a Range object, or a graphic.
Address	The address of the link, which can be a file path, a UNC path, or a URL.
SubAddress	A named location within the linked file (such as a bookmark in a Word document or a named range in an Excel workbook).

Listing 20.1 shows a procedure that uses the `Add` method to insert a link to a URL in a Word document.

Listing 20.1. A procedure that adds a Hyperlink object.

```
Sub AddLink()
    Dim r As Range
    Set r = ThisDocument.Paragraphs(1).Range
    r.InsertAfter "Sams' Home Page"
    r.Hyperlinks.Add _
        Anchor:=r, _
        Address:="http://www.mcp.com/sams/"
End Sub
```

NOTE: THIS CHAPTER'S CODE LISTINGS

You'll find the code for Listings 20.1 and the other sample procedures in this chapter on this book's CD in the file named Chaptr20.doc. If you don't have Word, look for Chaptr20.bas instead.

Hyperlink Object Properties

Once you've added a hyperlink or two, you can use the properties of the Hyperlink object to manipulate these links as needed. Here's a quick rundown of some useful properties:

`Hyperlink.Address`: Returns or sets the address associated with the specified *Hyperlink*.

`Hyperlink.Range`: Returns the Range object associated with the specified *Hyperlink*.

`Hyperlink.Shape`: Returns the Shape object associated with the specified *Hyperlink*.

`Hyperlink.SubAddress`: Returns or sets the named location within the target associated with the specified *Hyperlink*.

`Hyperlink.Type`: Returns a `Long` value that specifies the kind of link associated with the specified *Hyperlink*. This property returns one of the following constants: `msoHyperlinkInlineShape`, `msoHyperlinkRange`, or `msoHyperlinkShape`.

Hyperlink Object Methods

The Hyperlink object has only three methods:

`Hyperlink.AddToFavorites`: Adds the specified *Hyperlink* to the current user's Favorites folder.

`Hyperlink.Delete`: Deletes the specified *Hyperlink*.

`Hyperlink.Follow`: Displays the linked document associated with the specified *Hyperlink*. Here's the syntax to use:

```
Hyperlinks.Follow(NewWindow, AddHistory, ExtraInfo, Method, HeaderInfo)
```

Hyperlink	The Hyperlink object.
NewWindow	Set this argument to `True` to display the document in a new window. Use `False` (the default) to display the document in the current window. (Note that this depends on the application used to display the linked document.)
AddHistory	This argument is reserved for future use.
ExtraInfo	Use this argument to specify additional information that HTTP requires to resolve the hyperlink. The most common uses for this argument are to send a Web server the contents of a form, the coordinates of an image map, or a search parameter for an ASP or IDC file.
Method	This argument determines how the data specified with *ExtraInfo* is sent to the server. Use `msoMethodGet` to append the data to the link address; use `mspMethodPost` to post the data either as a `String` or as a `Byte` array (depending on the data type of the data).

HeaderInfo Use this argument to specify header data for the HTTP header.

For example, the Yahoo! Web site has a search engine that lets you query the Yahoo! database of Web pages. Here's the general syntax for a Yahoo search query:

`http://search.yahoo.com/bin/search?p=`*`keyword`*

Here, *keyword* is a keyword you want to use as the criterion for your search. If you wanted to implement this in the `Follow` method, the part after the question mark (`?`) would correspond to the *ExtraInfo* argument, and since this data is appended to the address, the *Method* argument must be `msoMethodGet`.

To demonstrate this, Listing 20.2 contains two procedures: `AddYahoo` creates a link to the Yahoo! search engine, and `SearchYahoo` prompts for a keyword and then runs the `Follow` method.

Listing 20.2. Procedures that add a link for the Yahoo! search engine and run a query on the Yahoo! database.

```
Sub AddYahoo()
    Dim r As Range
    Set r = ThisDocument.Paragraphs(1).Range
    r.InsertAfter Chr(13) & "Yahoo Search"
    r.Hyperlinks.Add _
        Anchor:=r, _
        Address:="http://search.yahoo.com/bin/search"

End Sub
Sub SearchYahoo()
    Dim link As Hyperlink
    Dim keyword As String
    Set link = ThisDocument.Hyperlinks("http://search.yahoo.com/bin/search")
    keyword = InputBox("Enter a search keyword:")
    link.Follow _
        extrainfo:="p=" & keyword, _
        Method:=msoMethodGet
End Sub
```

The `FollowHyperlink` Method

You saw in the preceding section that you can use the `Follow` argument to display a target document associated with an existing Hyperlink object. What do you do, however, if you would rather not clutter a document with hyperlinks? For these situations, the Office 97 applications each have a `FollowHyperlink` method that displays a target document without requiring an existing Hyperlink object. Here are the various syntaxes:

Word:

```
Document.FollowHyperlink(Address, SubAddress, NewWindow, AddHistory, ExtraInfo,
➥Method, HeaderInfo)
```

20 INTERNET AND INTRANET PROGRAMMING

Excel:

```
Workbook.FollowHyperlink(Address, SubAddress, NewWindow, AddHistory, ExtraInfo,
➥Method, HeaderInfo)
```

PowerPoint:

```
Presentation.FollowHyperlink(Address, SubAddress, NewWindow, AddHistory,
➥ExtraInfo, Method, HeaderInfo)
```

Access:

```
Application.FollowHyperlink(Address, SubAddress, NewWindow, AddHistory, ExtraInfo,
➥Method, HeaderInfo)
```

For example, Listing 20.3 shows how you would use this method in Word to perform the same Yahoo! search you saw earlier.

Listing 20.3. Using the `FollowHyperlink` method to display a target document without an existing Hyperlink object.

```
Sub FollowHyperlinkTest()
    Dim keyword As String
    keyword = InputBox("Enter a search keyword:")
    ThisDocument.FollowHyperlink _
        Address:="http://search.yahoo.com/bin/search", _
        ExtraInfo:="p=" & keyword, _
        Method:=msoMethodGet
End Sub
```

Building a Custom Web Browser

These simple hyperlink manipulations are certainly useful, but they hardly qualify as "browsing." However, you might have been intrigued by the possibilities inherent in the `FollowHyperlink` method. Wouldn't it be possible to set up a user form with a text box to accept URLs and then use `FollowHyperlink` to display these URLs? Perhaps you could set up some kind of array or custom collection object to store the visited URLs, and thus implement some sort of "Back" and "Forward" features.

Well, yes, I suppose you *could* do all that, but there's a much easier way to build browsing capabilities into your VBA applications: the WebBrowser control. This is an ActiveX control that encapsulates the basic functionality of Internet Explorer 3.0. By adding this control to a user form, you can create a custom Web browser with the following features:

- The capability to display any URL as well as basic navigation features—such as Back, Forward, Refresh, and Stop—all invoked with simple WebBrowser object methods.
- Support for embedded ActiveX controls and VBScript (or JavaScript) procedures.
- The capability to display multiple data types, including Office 97 documents.
- Support for a number of events (such as `BeforeNavigate`).

Best of all, this is ridiculously easy to implement, because all you really have to do is build an interface and then tie in the WebBrowser object's properties, methods, and events. Why bother with all this when you have Internet Explorer itself sitting on your computer? Well, you might want to shield your users from the complexity of Internet Explorer, you might like the idea of being able to browse the Web or your intranet without having to leave whatever Office application you're using to host the browser form, or you might want the ability to tailor a browser to suit your intranet's needs.

Whatever the reason, this section shows you how easy it is to build a browser from scratch and control it via VBA. In particular, I'll take you through the steps necessary for building a fully functional Web browser in Word.

Referencing the WebBrowser Control

The first thing you need to do is activate your project in the Visual Basic Editor and then establish a reference to the object library that contains the WebBrowser class. (Note that you need to have Internet Explorer 3.0 installed to have access to this library.) To do this, select Tools | References, activate the check box beside the Microsoft Internet Controls library, and click OK. To view the members of the WebBrowser class, open the Object Browser, select the SHDocVw library, and select WebBrowser in the Classes list.

Next, you need to add the WebBrowser control to the Visual Basic Editor toolbox by following these steps:

1. Select Insert | UserForm to create a new form.
2. Select Tools | Additional Controls to display the Additional Controls dialog box.
3. In the Available Controls list, activate the check box beside the Microsoft Web Browser Control item, as shown in Figure 20.4.

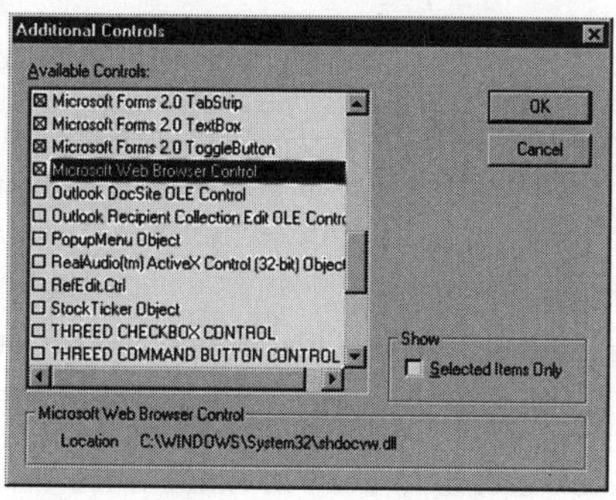

FIGURE 20.4.
Use the Additional Controls dialog box to add the WebBrowser control to the toolbox.

4. Click OK. VBA adds the control to the toolbox.

Displaying Web Pages with the WebBrowser Control

To get started, I'll show you how to use the WebBrowser control to display a specified URL. You use the `Navigate` method to do this. It uses the following syntax:

```
WebBrowser.Navigate(URL, Flags, TargetFramename, PostData, Headers)
```

WebBrowser	A reference to the WebBrowser object you're working with.
URL	The address of the Web page you want to display.
Flags	One or more constants that control various aspects of the navigation:

`navOpenInNewWindow` or 1	Opens the URL in a new window.
`navNoHistory` or 2	Prevents the URL from being added to the history list.
`navNoReadFromCache` or 4	Prevents the browser from reading the page from the disk cache.
`navNoWriteToCache` or 8	Prevents the URL from being added to the disk cache.

TargetFrameName	The name of the frame in which to display the URL.
PostData	Specifies additional POST information that HTTP requires to resolve the hyperlink. The most common uses for this argument are to send a Web server the contents of a form, the coordinates of an image map, or a search parameter for an ASP or IDC file. If you leave this argument blank, this method issues a GET call.
Headers	Specifies header data for the HTTP header.

The WebBrowser object also has a few properties that come in handy when navigating URLs:

WebBrowser`.Busy`: This property returns `True` if the specified *WebBrowser* is in the process of downloading text or graphics. This property returns `False` when the complete document has been downloaded. You can bail out of a download in progress by invoking the WebBrowser object's `Stop` method.

WebBrowser`.LocationName`: This property returns the title of the current document.

WebBrowser`.LocationURL`: This property returns the URL of the current document.

There are also a few events to keep in mind when designing the navigation section of your application:

`BeforeNavigate`: This event fires just before the WebBrowser control navigates to a different URL. Here's the event handler syntax:

```
Private Sub WebBrowser_BeforeNavigate(ByVal URL As String, ByVal Flags As
➥Long, ByVal TargetFrameName As String, PostData As Variant, ByVal
➥Headers As String, Cancel As Boolean)
```

The first five arguments are identical to the ones you saw earlier with the `Navigate` method. You can set the `Cancel` argument to `True` to stop the browser from navigating to the URL.

`DownloadBegin`: This event fires once the download of the page begins. You can use this event to initiate a message or animation that indicates the browser is busy. Here's the syntax for the event handler:

```
Private Sub WebBrowser_ DownloadBegin()
```

`DownloadComplete`: This event fires once the page has been completely downloaded, or when the download is stopped. Use this event to turn off any busy indicators you might have started in the `DownloadBegin` event handler. The event procedure uses the following syntax:

```
Private Sub WebBrowser_ DownloadComplete()
```

`NavigateComplete`: This event fires once the browser has successfully navigated to the URL. Note that the document might still be downloading (especially images) when this event fires. Here's the syntax for the event handler:

```
Private Sub WebBrowser_ NavigateComplete(ByVal URL As String)
```

The `URL` argument is the address of the page that is being downloaded.

`StatusTextChange`: This event fires when the WebBrowser control's status message text changes. These status messages provide information about the current download operation (you see them in the status bar of Internet Explorer). Here's the event handler syntax:

```
Private Sub WebBrowser_ StatusTextChange(ByVal Text As String)
```

The `Text` argument holds the status message. You can add a label control to your form and use the `Caption` property to display these messages.

`TitleChange`: This event fires when the WebBrowser control learns the title of the page you're downloading. Here's the syntax of the event handler:

```
Private Sub WebBrowser_ TitleChange(ByVal Text As String)
```

The `Text` argument holds the Web page title. If you like, you can use the form's `Caption` property to display the title of the Web page.

Application: The World Wide Web Browser

For our World Wide Web browser example, I created a form named `frmWWW`. I began this form with the following controls:

Name	Type	Description
webWWW	WebBrowser	The WebBrowser control.
txtLocation	Text box	Use this text box to enter a URL. It also displays the address of the current URL.
cmdSurf	Command button	You click this button (its caption is Surf!) to display the URL specified in the txtLocation text box.
lblStatus	Label	Displays the WebBrowser control's status messages.
lblProgress	Label	Displays Downloading... while the page is being downloaded; displays Done once the download is complete.

Listing 20.4 shows the code for several event handlers that are used to display a Web page:

UserForm_Initialize: This event fires when you first show the form. It uses the Navigate method to display the initial URL, which is defined at design time in the Text property of the txtLocation text box. This value is also stored in a global variable named topPage so that you can return to this page later.

cmdSurf_Click: This event fires when you click the Surf! button. It checks to make sure the text box isn't empty and, if it's not, it uses Navigate to display the URL specified in the text box.

webWWW_BeforeNavigate: This procedure checks the Busy property and, if it returns True, it invokes the Stop method to shut down the current operation.

webWWW_DownloadBegin: This procedure displays the Downloading... message in the lblProgress label.

webWWW_NavigateComplete: This procedure displays the address of the new Web page in the txtLocation text box.

webWWW_DownloadComplete: This procedure displays the Done message in the lblProgress label.

webWWW_TitleChange: This procedure updates the form's caption so that it displays the title of the current Web page.

webWWW_StatusTextChange: This procedure updates the lblStatus label to display the current status message.

Listing 20.4. Some event handlers that are used to display a Web page.

```
' This event handler fires when you first open the form
'
Private Sub UserForm_Initialize()
    With webWWW
        '
        ' Display and save the initial URL
        '
        If txtLocation <> "" Then
            topPage = txtLocation
            .Navigate txtLocation
        End If
    End With
End Sub
'
' This event handler fires when you enter the text box
'
Private Sub txtLocation_Enter()
    '
    ' Make sure Surf! button is the default
    '
    cmdSurf.Default = True
End Sub
'
' This event handler fires when you click the Surf! button
'
Private Sub cmdSurf_Click()
    '
    ' Surf to the URL specified in the Location text box
    '
    If txtLocation <> "" Then
        webWWW.Navigate txtLocation
    Else
        txtLocation.SetFocus
        Beep
    End If
End Sub
'
' This event handler fires before the browser navigates to a new URL
'
Private Sub webWWW_BeforeNavigate(ByVal URL As String, ByVal Flags As Long, ByVal
➥TargetFrameName As String, PostData As Variant, ByVal Headers As String,
➥Cancel As Boolean)
    With webWWW
        '
        ' Stop the current operation
        '
        If .Busy Then .Stop
    End With
End Sub
'
' This event handler fires at the start of the download
'
Private Sub webWWW_DownloadBegin()
    lblProgress = " Downloading..."
End Sub
```

continues

Listing 20.4. continued

```
'
' This event handler fires after the browser has navigated
' successfully to the URL
'
Private Sub webWWW_NavigateComplete(ByVal URL As String)
    txtLocation = URL
End Sub
'
' This event handler fires once the download is finished
'
Private Sub webWWW_DownloadComplete()
    lblProgress = " Done"
End Sub
'
' This event handler fires when the URL title changes
'
Private Sub webWWW_TitleChange(ByVal Text As String)
    '
    ' Update the form's caption to reflect the new title
    '
    Me.Caption = "The World Wide Web - " & webWWW.LocationName
End Sub
'
' This event handler fires when the status text changes
'
Private Sub webWWW_StatusTextChange(ByVal Text As String)
    lblStatus = Text
End Sub
```

NOTE: EXPORTED FORM FILE

I exported the form used in this example to a file named Browser.frm, which you'll find on the CD. Note that you can import this form into Excel or PowerPoint, and it should run with modifications. (You might only need to adjust the size of the WebBrowser control.)

Navigating with the WebBrowser Control

Displaying a specified Web page isn't the only trick up the WebBrowser control's sleeve. It also has quite a few methods that let you navigate backward and forward through visited Web pages, refresh the current page, stop the current download, and more. Here's a summary of these methods:

`*WebBrowser*.GoBack`: This method tells the specified *`WebBrowser`* to navigate backward to a previously visited page.

`*WebBrowser*.GoForward`: This method tells the specified *`WebBrowser`* to navigate forward to a previously visited page.

`WebBrowser.GoHome`: This method tells the specified `WebBrowser` to display the default Home page. Note that this is the same as the Start page defined by Internet Explorer. The URL of the Start page is stored in the Registry in the following key:

```
\HKEY_CURRENT_USER\Software\Microsoft\Internet Explorer\Main\
```

The address is given by the Start Page value.

`WebBrowser.GoSearch`: This method tells the specified `WebBrowser` to display the default Search page. Again, this is the Search page as defined by Internet Explorer. The URL of the Search page is stored in the Registry in the following key:

```
\HKEY_CURRENT_USER\Software\Microsoft\Internet Explorer\Main\
```

The address is given by the Search Page value.

`WebBrowser.Refresh`: This method tells the specified `WebBrowser` to refresh the current page.

`WebBrowser.Refresh2`: This method also tells the specified `WebBrowser` to refresh, but it uses the following syntax:

```
WebBrowser.Refresh2(Level)
```

WebBrowser	A reference to the WebBrowser object you're working with.
Level	A constant that determines how the page is refreshed:

`REFRESH_NORMAL` or 0	Refreshes the page with a cached copy.
`REFRESH_IFEXPIRED` or 1	Refreshes the page with a cached copy only if the page has expired.
`REFRESH_COMPLETELY` or 3	Performs a full refresh (doesn't use a cached copy).

`WebBrowser.Stop`: This method tells the specified `WebBrowser` to cancel the current download or to shut down dynamic page objects, such as background sounds and animations.

Navigating in the World Wide Web Browser

The World Wide Web browser example contains a number of buttons that implement these methods. Here's a summary of these controls:

Button Name	*Description*
`cmdBack`	Invokes the `GoBack` method.
`cmdForward`	Invokes the `GoForward` method.

continues

Button Name	*Description*
`cmdTop`	Invokes the `Navigate` method to return to the initial page (which, you'll recall, is stored in the `topPage` global variable).
`cmdRefresh`	Invokes the `Refresh` method.
`cmdStop`	Invokes the `Stop` method.
`cmdHome`	Invokes the `GoHome` method.
`cmdSearch`	Invokes the `GoSearch` method.
`cmdExit`	Closes the form.

Listing 20.5 presents the event handler code for these buttons.

Listing 20.5. Event handlers for the navigation buttons in the custom Web browser.

```
' This event handler fires when you click the Back button
'
Private Sub cmdBack_Click()
    '
    ' An error occurs if there is no page to go back to
    '
    On Error Resume Next
    webWWW.GoBack
End Sub
'
' This event handler fires when you click the Forward button
'
Private Sub cmdForward_Click()
    '
    ' An error occurs if there is no page to go forward to
    '
    On Error Resume Next
    webWWW.GoForward
End Sub
'
' This event handler fires when you click the Top button
'
Private Sub cmdTop_Click()
    webWWW.Navigate topPage
End Sub
'
' This event handler fires when you click the Refresh button
'
Private Sub cmdRefresh_Click()
    webWWW.Refresh
End Sub
'
' This event handler fires when you click the Stop button
'
Private Sub cmdStop_Click()
    webWWW.Stop
End Sub
'
' This event handler fires when you click the Home button
'
```

```
Private Sub cmdHome_Click()
    webWWW.GoHome
End Sub
'
' This event handler fires when you click the Search button
'
Private Sub cmdSearch_Click()
    webWWW.GoSearch
End Sub
'
' This event handler fires when you click the Exit button
'
Private Sub cmdExit_Click()
    Unload Me
End Sub
```

Figure 20.5 shows the completed browser.

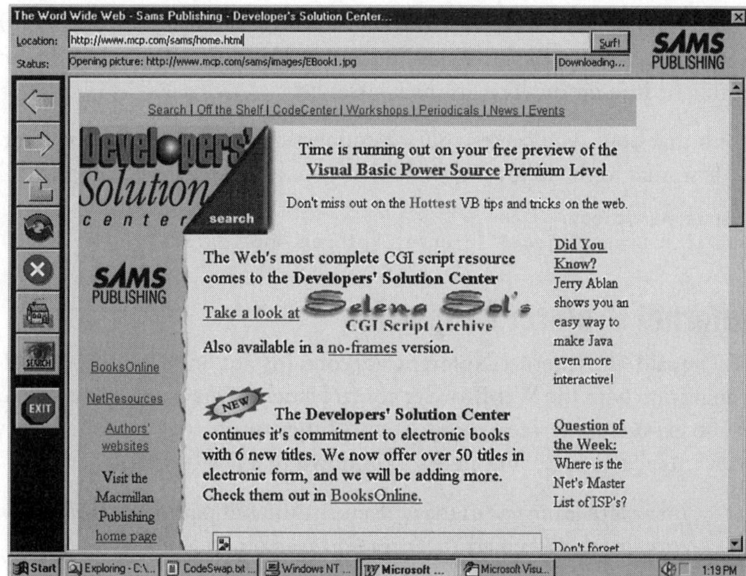

FIGURE 20.5.
A fully functional Web browser created with the WebBrowser ActiveX control.

Controlling Internet Explorer Via Automation

Internet Explorer 3.0 is really just a shell that serves as a wrapper for an ActiveX control that provides the bulk of the browser functionality. This control is called InternetExplorer, and you can use it to provide powerful browsing functionality in your VBA applications. Specifically, using the Automation techniques I described in Chapter 15, "Controlling Applications Via OLE Automation," you can use VBA to control just about everything associated with Internet Explorer:

- The position and dimensions of the window
- Whether or not the menu bar, toolbar, and status bar are displayed
- The current URL
- Sending the browser backward and forward between navigated URLs

This sounds a bit like the WebBrowser control from the preceding section. In fact, the WebBrowser control is a subset of the InternetExplorer object. Therefore, every property, method, and event that I described in the preceding section also applies to the InternetExplorer class, but you also get access to numerous other class members. This section discusses many of these extra features.

Setting References and Object Variables

If you haven't done so already, you first need to establish a reference to the object library that contains the Internet Explorer hierarchy. To reiterate, you do this by selecting Tools | References, activating the Microsoft Internet Controls library, and clicking OK. To view the members of the Internet Explorer class, open the Object Browser, select the SHDocVw library, and highlight InternetExplorer in the Classes list.

With that done, you can establish a connection to the Internet Explorer application by using code similar to the following (note that you must use late binding with Internet Explorer):

```
Dim ie As Object
Set ie = CreateObject("InternetExplorer.Application")
```

Internet Explorer Properties

As I've said, the InternetExplorer class contains not only the properties I mentioned earlier in connection with the WebBrowser control (such as `Busy`, `LocationName`, and `LocationURL`), but it also exposes quite a few more. Many of these properties are straightforward (such as `Height`, `Width`, `Top`, and `Left`), but here's a rundown of a few others:

`InternetExplorer``.FullName`: Returns the full pathname for the application that contains the specified *`InternetExplorer`* object.

`InternetExplorer``.FullScreen`: A `Boolean` value that toggles the specified *`InternetExplorer`* object between the normal window and a full-screen window in which the title bar, menu bar, toolbar, and status bar are hidden.

`InternetExplorer``.MenuBar`: A `Boolean` value that toggles the menu bar on and off for the specified *`InternetExplorer`* object.

`InternetExplorer``.Path`: Returns the full pathname for the specified *`InternetExplorer`* object.

`InternetExplorer``.StatusBar`: A `Boolean` value that toggles the status bar on and off for the specified *`InternetExplorer`* object.

InternetExplorer.StatusText: Returns or sets the status bar text for the specified *InternetExplorer* object.

InternetExplorer.ToolBar: A Boolean value that toggles the toolbar on and off for the specified *InternetExplorer* object.

InternetExplorer.Type: Returns a string that specifies the type name of the current document (such as Windows HTML Viewer) for the specified *InternetExplorer* object.

InternetExplorer.Visible: A Boolean value that toggles the specified *InternetExplorer* object between hidden and visible. Note that the InternetExplorer Automation object is hidden by default, so you must set this property to True to see the browser window.

Listing 20.6 presents a procedure that puts some of these properties to good use. An Object variable named ie is declared and then Set to the Internet Explorer Application object. The Navigate method displays a page, and then the toolbar, status bar, and menu bar are turned off. A Do...Loop checks the Busy property and loops while it's True. Then a MsgBox displays some information about the page and asks if you want to view it. If you click Yes, the browser is made visible and is activated; if you click No, the Quit method shuts down the browser.

Listing 20.6. A procedure that manipulates Internet Explorer via Automation using various members of the InternetExplorer class.

```
Sub AutomateInternetExplorer()
    Dim ie As Object
    Dim result As Integer
    '
    ' Set up the Automation object
    '
    Set ie = CreateObject("InternetExplorer.Application")
    '
    ' Navigate to a page and customize the browser window
    '
    ie.Navigate "http://www.microsoft.com/ie/"
    ie.Toolbar = False
    ie.StatusBar = False
    ie.MenuBar = False
    '
    ' Twiddle thumbs while the page loads
    '
    Do While ie.Busy
        DoEvents
    Loop
    '
    ' Display page info
    '
    result = MsgBox( _
        "Current URL:  " & ie.LocationURL & Chr(13) & _
        "Current Title: " & ie.LocationName & Chr(13) & _
        "Document type: " & ie.Type & Chr(13) & Chr(13) & _
        "Would you like to view this document?", _
        vbYesNo + vbQuestion)
    If result = vbYes Then
```


continues

Listing 20.6. continued

```
        '
        ' If Yes, make browser visible and activate it
        '
        ie.Visible = True
        AppActivate "Microsoft Internet Explorer"
    Else
        '
        ' If no, bail out
        '
        ie.Quit
    End If
    Set ie = Nothing
End Sub
```

Controlling Netscape Navigator Via Automation

Netscape Navigator also exposes various classes via Automation. However, unlike Internet Explorer's Automation interface, which is driven by the `Application` object, Navigator's main Automation interface only provides access to network data. In other words, all you can do with Navigator via Automation is open a hidden instance of the browser, connect to a remote data source (usually a Web page), and retrieve information about that source using the same protocols and mechanisms that are supported by Navigator (such as SSL and SOCKS).

Connecting to Navigator

As usual, when dealing with Automation, you begin by establishing a reference in your VBA project to the type library with which you want to work. For Navigator, select Tools | References to display the References dialog box. Click Browse and then open the \Netscape\Navigator\Program\ folder. Highlight the file named Netscape.tlb and click Open. To view the members of the Navigator class, open the Object Browser, select the Netscape library, and highlight CNetworkCX in the Classes list.

You can now establish a connection to Navigator via Automation by creating a new `Netscape.Network.1` object, as shown here:

```
Dim nav As Object
Set nav = CreateObject("Netscape.Network.1")
```

Methods of the `Netscape.Network.1` Object

The `Netscape.Network.1` object has many useful methods that let you perform tasks such as opening a page, reading the contents of a page, and finding out if a URL returns an error message (such as `404 Not Found`). Here's a summary of this object's methods:

`Object.BytesReady`: Uses the specified `Netscape.Network.1 Object` to return the number of bytes currently available to be downloaded (the `Read` method is described later).

`Object.Close`: Disconnects the currently active connection (the `Open` method is described later) and resets the specified `Netscape.Network.1 Object`.

`Object.GetContentEncoding`: Uses the specified `Netscape.Network.1 Object` to return the MIME encoding for the currently open document. The return value is useful for determining which application you should use to work with the retrieved data (if any). You should run this method only if the `Open` method was successful.

`Object.GetContentLength`: Uses the specified `Netscape.Network.1 Object` to return the total number of bytes in the currently opened document. If the return value is less than or equal to 0, no length was returned by the server.

`Object.GetContentType`: Uses the specified `Netscape.Network.1 Object` to return the MIME type for the currently open document.

`Object.GetErrorMessage`: Uses the specified `Netscape.Network.1 Object` to return the internal Netscape error message for the current document. (See also the `GetStatus` method, described later.)

`Object.GetExpires`: Uses the specified `Netscape.Network.1 Object` to return the date and time (as a string) that the currently open document is set to expire.

`Object.GetLastModified`: Uses the specified `Netscape.Network.1 Object` to return the data and time (as a string) that the currently open document was last modified.

`Object.GetServerStatus`: Uses the specified `Netscape.Network.1 Object` to return the error status that was reported by the server. (See `GetStatus`, described later.)

`Object.GetStatus`: Uses the specified `Netscape.Network.1 Object` to return the status of the current operation. Here's a list of the possible status codes:

Status	*What It Indicates*
0	Normal.
1	The user name was requested.
2	A password was requested.
256	Netscape is currently busy; attempt the operation again.
512	The server reported an error; use `GetServerStatus` to return the specific error code.
1024	An internal load error occurred, and the server was never contacted.
2048	Netscape has suggested an error message; use `GetErrorMessage` to return the error.

`Object`.`IsFinished`: Uses the specified `Netscape.Network.1` *`Object`* to determine whether or not the current `Read` operation is complete. (This is the same as if the `Read` method returned the value –1; this is described later.)

`Object`.`Open`: Uses the specified `Netscape.Network.1` *`Object`* to open a connection to a remote document. This method returns `True` if the operation was successful, and `False` if Navigator couldn't establish a connection. For the latter, use `GetStatus` to determine why the operation failed. Here's the syntax used by the `Open` method:

```
Object.Open(pURL, iMethod, pPostData, lPostDataSize, pPostHeaders)
```

`Object`	The `Netscape.Network.1` object you're working with.
`pURL`	The address of the page you want to retrieve.
`iMethod`	The method with which to retrieve the URL. Use `0` for GET, `1` for POST, and `3` for HEAD.
`pPostData`	The data to post to the server if ***`iMethod`*** is 1.
`lPostDataSize`	The length of ***`pPostData`*** in bytes.
`pPostHeaders`	A null-terminated string of characters that specifies additional headers to post to the server if ***`iMethod`*** is 1.

`Object`.`Read`: Uses the specified `Netscape.Network.1` *`Object`* to retrieve a remote document to which you've established a connection via the `Open` method. Here's the syntax:

```
Object.Read(pBuffer, iAmout)
```

`Object`	The `Netscape.Network.1` object you're working with.
`pBuffer`	A string buffer in which to store the retrieved information.
`iAmount`	The maximum amount of data to store in the buffer.

This method returns the number of bytes that were stored in the buffer. If `Read` returns 0, there was no data to be read, but this doesn't mean the operation is complete (in other words, there might be more data to come); if `Read` returns –1, there is no data left to retrieve.

Application: The Navigator Automator

To put these Navigator Automation techniques through their paces, I developed an application called the Navigator Automator, shown in Figure 20.6. When you enter a URL in the Location text box and click Read, the application establishes a connection to the page and then performs the following tasks:

- It displays various document statistics, including the date the document was last modified, the number of bytes, and so on.
- It reads the source code and displays it in the Document Source text box.
- It extracts the document's links and displays the URLs in the Document Links list box.

If you click the Check Links button, the application runs through the list of links and checks for errors.

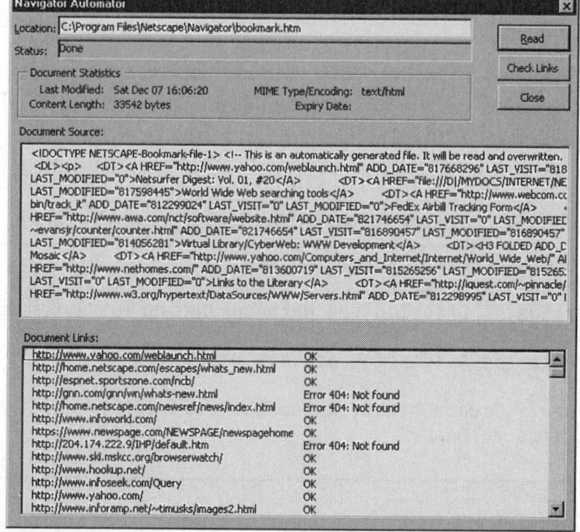

FIGURE 20.6.
The Navigator Automator is a VBA application that controls Netscape Navigator via Automation.

NOTE: NAVIGATOR AUTOMATOR IS ON THE CD

The Navigator Automator application is part of the VBA project in Chaptr20.doc. If you don't have Word, or if you would like to import the application into another program, you'll find the form file on the CD under the name NavAuto.frm.

The Navigator Automator form is named `frmNavAuto`, and it contains (among others) the following controls:

Name	*Type*	*Description*
`txtLocation`	Text box	Use this text box to enter the URL you want to work with.
`cmdRead`	Command button	Click this button to connect to the URL specified in the `txtLocation` text box.

continues

Name	*Type*	*Description*
`cmdCheckLinks`	Command button	Click this button to check the links contained in the list box.
`lblStatus`	Label	Displays the current status of the operation.
`txtSource`	Text box	Displays the data contained in the specified URL.
`lstLinks`	List box	Displays the URLs of the links contained in the document.

Listing 20.7 shows the event handler for the `Initialize` event. This code just creates the `Netscape.Network.1` Automation object that will be used throughout the application. Note that `nav` is a global variable defined at the top of the form module.

Listing 20.7. The `Initialize` event creates the `Netscape.Network.1` Automation object.

```
Private Sub UserForm_Initialize()
    On Error Resume Next
    lblStatus = "Creating the Netscape.Network.1 Automation object..."
    '
    ' Create the Automation object
    '
    Set nav = CreateObject("Netscape.Network.1")
    lblStatus = "Ready"
End Sub
```

Listing 20.8 shows the event handler for the Read button's `Click` event. Here's a summary of the various tasks performed by this procedure:

- The Location text box is checked to make sure it isn't empty.
- The `Open` method is invoked to establish a connection to the document. A `Do...Loop` checks `GetStatus` to make sure Navigator isn't busy and that the timeout threshold hasn't been passed.
- Another `Do...Loop` examines `GetServerStatus` and `GetStatus` to see the result of the `Open` method. Again, a timeout check is used to make sure this loop isn't infinite.
- If the connection is established without mishap, the procedure runs various methods (such as `GetLastModified` and `GetContentLength`) to return data about the document.
- The `Read` method loads the document data and stores it in the Document Source text box.
- Another `Do...Loop` examines the Document Source text and extracts the URLs of all the links. Each URL is added to the Document Links list box.

- If the connection isn't established, an error message is displayed in the Status label. For server errors, the code calls the `HTTPError` function to return a description of the error (see Listing 20.10).

Listing 20.8. This event handler opens a connection, gets the document stats, reads the HTML source, and extracts the links.

```
Private Sub cmdRead_Click()
    Dim connected As Boolean            ' True if connected OK
    Dim start As Long                   ' Starts the timeout timer
    Dim timeout As Integer              ' Max time for each operation
    Dim timedOut As Integer             ' True if operation timed out
    Dim currStatus As Integer           ' Holds GetStatus() result
    Dim currServerStatus As Integer     ' Holds GetServerStatus() result
    Dim buffer As String * 10000        ' Holds the data being read
    Dim length As Long                  ' The length of the data
    Dim result As Integer               ' Holds the Read return code
    Dim urlStart As Long                ' Link starting character position
    Dim urlEnd As Long                  ' Link ending character position
    Dim url As String                   ' The extracted URL
    Dim str As String                   ' A temporary string value
    timeout = 10
    '
    ' Clear the current data
    '
    txtSource = ""
    lstLinks.Clear

    With nav
        '
        ' Make sure the text box isn't empty
        '
        If txtLocation = "" Then
            Beep
            lblStatus = "Please enter a location!"
            txtLocation.SetFocus
            Exit Sub
        End If
        '
        ' Open the connection. Loop if Navigator is busy.
        '
        lblStatus = "Opening the connection..."
        start = Timer
        timedOut = False
        Do
            connected = .Open(txtLocation, 0, "", 0, "")
            If Timer - start > timeout Then
                timedOut = True
                Exit Do
            End If
        Loop While .GetStatus = 256
        '
        ' Get the current status. Loop while
        ' the server status is -1 (no status)
        '
```

continues

Listing 20.8. continued

```
If Not timedOut Then
    start = Timer
    Do
        currServerStatus = .GetServerStatus
        currStatus = .GetStatus
        If Timer - start > timeout Then
            timedOut = True
            Exit Do
        End If
    Loop While currServerStatus = -1
End If

If connected Then
    '
    ' Check for a timeout error
    '
    If timedOut Then
        '
        ' The operation timed out
        '
        lblStatus = "Operation timed out"
        .Close
        Exit Sub
    End If
    '
    ' Check Navigator status
    '
    If currStatus = 0 Then
        '
        ' Get the document statistics
        '
        lblStatus = "Connection opened successfully! Getting document stats
        ➥and links..."
        lblLastModified = Format(.GetLastModified, "mmm d, yyyy h:m AM/PM")
        length = .GetContentLength
        lblContentLength = length & " bytes"
        lblMIME = .GetContentType & .GetContentEncoding
        lblExpiryDate = Format(.GetExpires, "mmm d, yyyy h:m AM/PM")
        Me.Repaint
        '
        ' Read in the document data
        '
        If length > 10000 Or length = 0 Then length = 10000
        Do While .Read(buffer, length) >= 0
            txtSource = txtSource & buffer
        Loop
        Me.Repaint
        '
        ' Extract the links
        '
        str = txtSource
        '
        ' Find the first instance of the "<A HREF" tag
        '
        urlStart = InStr(str, "<A HREF=")
        Do While urlStart > 0
```

```
                '
                ' Lop off everything that comes before "<A HREF"
                '
                str = Mid$(str, urlStart + 9)
                '
                ' Find the quotation mark (") that ends the URL
                '
                urlEnd = InStr(str, Chr$(34))
                If urlEnd > 0 Then
                    '
                    ' Extract the URL and add it to the list
                    '
                    url = Left$(str, urlEnd - 1)
                    lstLinks.AddItem url
                End If
                '
                ' Find the next instance of the "<A HREF" tag
                '
                urlStart = InStr(urlEnd + 1, str, "<A HREF=")
            Loop
            lblStatus = "Done"
        ElseIf currStatus = 512 Then
            '
            ' A problem was reported by the server
            '
            lblStatus = "Error " & HTTPError(currServerStatus)
        Else
            lblStatus = "Non-server error: " & currStatus
        End If
    End If
    Me.Repaint
  End With
End Sub
```

Listing 20.9 shows the event handler for the Check Links button's `Click` event. Here's a summary of what happens in this procedure:

- A `For...Next` loop runs through each item in the Document Links list. The `url` variable stores the URL for each item. Note that this is a two-column list, so we have to specify row and column values in the `List` property.
- If a link begins with HTTP, a `Do...Loop` attempts to `Open` a connection to the URL. As before, we check to make sure Navigator isn't busy, and a timeout check prevents an infinite loop.
- Another `Do...Loop` checks `GetServerStatus` and `GetStatus` to see the result of the `Open` method.
- Depending on the result of this loop, the appropriate status message is displayed in the second column of the list. Again, the `HTTPError` function is invoked if a server error was reported.

Listing 20.9. This event handler runs when you click the Check Links button. It runs through the list of links and attempts to establish a connection for each link.

```
Private Sub cmdCheckLinks_Click()
    Dim i As Integer                 ' Counter
    Dim url As String                ' The URL to check
    Dim connected As Boolean         ' True if connected OK
    Dim start As Long                ' Starts the timeout timer
    Dim timeout As Integer           ' Max time for each operation
    Dim timedOut As Integer          ' True if operation timed out
    Dim currStatus As Integer        ' Holds GetStatus() result
    Dim currServerStatus As Integer  ' Holds GetServerStatus() result
    timeout = 10
    '
    ' Make sure there are some links to check
    '
    If lstLinks.ListCount = 0 Then
        lblStatus = "There are no links to check!"
        Beep
        Exit Sub
    End If
    '
    ' Run through the list of links
    '
    For i = 0 To lstLinks.ListCount - 1
        '
        ' Get the URL and make sure it's for a Web page
        '
        url = lstLinks.List(i, 0)
        If Left(url, 4) = "HTTP" Then
            lblStatus = "Checking link " & i & " of " & lstLinks.ListCount
            Me.Repaint
            '
            ' Open the connection. Loop if Navigator is busy.
            '
            start = Timer
            timedOut = False
            Do
                connected = nav.Open(url, 0, "", 0, "")
                If Timer - start > timeout Then
                    timedOut = True
                    Exit Do
                End If
            Loop While nav.GetStatus = 256
            '
            ' Get the current status. Loop while
            ' the server status is -1 (no status)
            '
            If Not timedOut Then
                start = Timer
                Do
                    currServerStatus = nav.GetServerStatus
                    currStatus = nav.GetStatus
                    If Timer - start > timeout Then
                        timedOut = True
                        Exit Do
                    End If
                Loop While currServerStatus = -1
```

```
            End If
            '
            ' Check for an error
            '
            If timedOut Then
                '
                ' The operation timed out
                '
                lstLinks.List(i, 1) = "Operation timed out"
            Else
                If currStatus = 0 Then
                    '
                    ' Link is OK
                    '
                    lstLinks.List(i, 1) = "OK"
                ElseIf currStatus = 512 Then
                    '
                    ' A problem was reported by the server
                    '
                    lstLinks.List(i, 1) = "Error " & HTTPError(currServerStatus)
                Else
                    lstLinks.List(i, 1) = "Non-server error: " & currStatus
                End If
            End If
            nav.Close
        Else
            lstLinks.List(i, 1) = "N/A"
        End If
    Next 'i
    lblStatus = "Done"
End Sub
```

Listing 20.10 shows the `HTTPError` function. This function is invoked whenever Navigator reports a 512 status code, which implies a server error. The server error (as given by `GetServerStatus`) is passed to the function (as the `errCode` argument), and a `Select Case` structure returns the appropriate error message.

Listing 20.10. This function accepts a `GetServerStatus` error code and returns a string description of the error.

```
Function HTTPError(errCode As Integer) As String
    Select Case errCode
        Case 204
            HTTPError = errCode & ": No content"
        Case 301
            HTTPError = errCode & ": Moved permanently"
        Case 302
            HTTPError = errCode & ": Moved temporarily"
        Case 400
            HTTPError = errCode & ": Bad request"
        Case 401
            HTTPError = errCode & ": Unauthorized"
```

continues

Listing 20.10. continued

```
        Case 403
            HTTPError = errCode & ": Forbidden"
        Case 404
            HTTPError = errCode & ": Not found"
        Case 500
            HTTPError = errCode & ": Internal server error"
        Case 501
            HTTPError = errCode & ": Not implemented"
        Case 502
            HTTPError = errCode & ": Bad gateway"
        Case 503
            HTTPError = errCode & ": Service unavailable"
        Case Else
            HTTPError = errCode & ": Unknown error"
    End Select
End Function
```

Listing 20.11 shows the event handler for the Close button's `Click` event. This procedure closes the Automation object, wipes out the nav object variable, and unloads the form.

Listing 20.11. This event handler closes the Automation object, discards the object variable, and unloads the form.

```
Private Sub cmdClose_Click()
    nav.Close
    Set nav = Nothing
    Unload Me
End Sub
```

Summary

This chapter ran through a few topics related to VBA Internet and intranet programming. I began by showing you how to work with the Hyperlink object that's new to Office 97. You learned how to add hyperlinks and how to manipulate their properties and methods. From there I showed you how to use the WebBrowser object to create a custom browser from scratch. I presented a full-featured sample application that utilized many of the properties and methods available with the WebBrowser object. We then turned our attention to Automation. In particular, you learned how to control Internet Explorer and Netscape Navigator via Automation. For the latter, I created an application that lets you read the data from a Web page, display the links available on that page, and check those links for errors.

Here's a list of chapters where you'll find related information:

- See Chapter 15, "Controlling Applications Via OLE Automation," to get a detailed explanation of Automation and how to use it in your VBA code.

- I discuss ActiveX controls and VBScript in Chapter 21, "Web Page Programming: ActiveX and VBScript."
- I discuss low-level file I/O in Chapter 26, "VBA Tips and Techniques." In particular, I show you how to use VBA to create HTML files on-the-fly.
- To learn more about HTML, see Appendix D, "An HTML Primer."

CHAPTER 21

Web Page Programming: ActiveX and VBScript

IN THIS CHAPTER

The essential is to excite the spectators. If that means playing Hamlet on a flying trapeze or in an aquarium, you do it.

—Orson Welles

As you may know, HTML forms are the Web equivalent of application dialog boxes. This is a reasonable analogy, because both forms and dialog boxes use various controls—text boxes, option buttons, lists, command buttons, and so on—to get information from the user. When running applications on their computers, however, few people think of the program's dialog boxes as being the interesting part. Instead, most folks would agree that it's the *application itself* that's interesting. In the end, dialog boxes are just a necessary evil for making the program do our bidding.

This helps explain why, in the end, Web-based forms aren't all that exciting. They're great for grabbing information from the user and for querying databases, but that's about the extent of it. No, to make your Web pages truly interesting, you need to give people *applications* to play with. This is where ActiveX comes in. ActiveX controls are miniprograms that turn an otherwise-lifeless Web page into a dynamic, interactive object. In other words, the page becomes an application.

With this sort of promise, it's no wonder that ActiveX is one of the hottest and most exciting areas of Web page development. If you're interested in leveraging this powerful technology for your Web pages, this chapter shows you several methods for getting the job done. You'll also be introduced to VBScript, the subset of VBA that lets you program Web-based ActiveX objects.

ActiveX: The <OBJECT> Tag

As with anything else you insert into a Web page, ActiveX controls are defined via HTML tags. In this case, the basic container tags for an ActiveX control are `<OBJECT>` and `</OBJECT>`. The `<OBJECT>` tag has quite a few attributes that control various aspects of the object, including the type of object, its location, the height and width, and more. Some of these attributes are listed in Table 21.1.

Table 21.1. A few attributes of the <OBJECT> tag.

Attribute	*Description*
`ALIGN=`*`alignment`*	Sets the alignment of the object within the page (*`alignment`* can be `LEFT`, `RIGHT`, or `CENTER`).
`BORDER=`*`n`*	If the object is a link, this attribute specifies the width of the border.
`CLASSID=`*`id`*	A value that identifies the object implementation.

Attribute	*Description*
`DATA=`*`path`*	Identifies data for the object.
`HEIGHT=`*`n`*	The suggested height of the object.
`HSPACE=`*`n`*	The horizontal "gutter." This is the space between the object and any text or images to the left or right of the object.
`ID=`*`ObjectName`*	A text string that identifies the object. This value is used by programs to refer to the object.
`NAME=`*`ControlName`*	The name of the object in a form. When the form is submitted, this value is sent along with the control's data.
`STANDBY=`*`message`*	Sets the message that appears while the object is loading.
`TYPE=`*`type`*	Specifies the Internet media type for data.
`USEMAP=`*`path`*	Specifies the image map to use with the object.
`VSPACE=`*`n`*	The vertical gutter. This is the space between the object and any text or images above or below the object.
`WIDTH=`*`n`*	The suggested width of the object.

For registered ActiveX controls, the syntax of the `CLASSID` attribute is as follows:

```
CLSID:class-identifier
```

Here, *`class-identifier`* is the object's `CLSID` as found in the Registry. To insert an ActiveMovie control object, for example, you could use the following `<OBJECT>` tag:

```
<OBJECT
    ID="ActiveMovie1"
    WIDTH=200
    HEIGHT=100
    CLASSID="CLSID:05589FA1-C356-11CE-BF01-00AA0055595A">
```

Most ActiveX objects also have a selection of properties. An ActiveMovie object, for example, has a `FileName` property that you can use to specify a video clip file. To set an object's properties, you include one or more `<PARAM>` tags between the `<OBJECT>` and `</OBJECT>` tags. For each `<PARAM>` tag, you specify a `NAME` attribute and a `VALUE` attribute. For example, the following sequence of tags defines an ActiveMovie object and sets its `FileName` property to `MyMovie.avi`:

```
<OBJECT
    ID="ActiveMovie1"
    WIDTH=200
    HEIGHT=100
    CLASSID="CLSID:05589FA1-C356-11CE-BF01-00AA0055595A">
<PARAM NAME="FileName" VALUE="MyMovie.avi">
</OBJECT>
```

Many ActiveX controls have quite a few properties, so your <OBJECT> definitions can get quite long. Here's some code that defines a Marquee (scrolling text) object:

```
<OBJECT
    ID="marquee1"
    ALIGN=CENTER
    CLASSID="clsid:1a4da210-2117-11cf-be21-0080c72edd2d"
    WIDTH=200
    HEIGHT=200>
<PARAM NAME="ScrollStyleX" VALUE="Circular">
<PARAM NAME="ScrollStyleY" VALUE="Circular">
<PARAM NAME="szURL" VALUE="marqcont.htm">
<PARAM NAME="ScrollDelay" VALUE=60>
<PARAM NAME="LoopsX" VALUE=-1>
<PARAM NAME="LoopsY" VALUE=-1>
<PARAM NAME="ScrollPixelsX" VALUE=0>
<PARAM NAME="ScrollPixelsY" VALUE=-3>
<PARAM NAME="DrawImmediately" VALUE=0>
<PARAM NAME="Whitespace" VALUE=0>
<PARAM NAME="PageFlippingOn" VALUE=0>
<PARAM NAME="Zoom" VALUE=100>
<PARAM NAME="WidthOfPage" VALUE=400>
</OBJECT>
```

NOTE: ACTIVEX AND NAVIGATOR

ActiveX controls work fine with Internet Explorer, but what about Netscape? For starters, users won't be able to work with ActiveX controls unless they've installed the ActiveX plug-in created for Netscape by NCompass (see `http://www.ncompasslabs.com/`). Second, at the time this book was written, Netscape didn't support the <OBJECT> tag. Instead, you use the `<EMBED SRC="Path">` tag, where *Path* is the pathname of the object. Netscape has promised to provide support for ActiveX in version 4 of the Navigator.

An Easier Way: The ActiveX Control Pad

At this point, you're probably wondering if ActiveX is worth the trouble. After all, who has the time (or the inclination) to track down CLSIDs for every object you use? And how are you supposed to know which properties are supported by which objects?

To solve these problems and encourage people to use ActiveX controls, Microsoft created a handy tool called the ActiveX Control Pad, included with Internet Explorer 3. You can also download the ActiveX Control Pad separately from Microsoft's Web site:

`http://www.microsoft.com/workshop/author/cpad/`

The idea behind the ActiveX Control Pad is to give you an easy, graphical way to insert ActiveX objects and adjust their properties. In fact, the ActiveX Control Pad works a lot like Word's Form Design mode. In other words, you just select the object you want to insert, use the mouse to size the object as needed, and display its properties sheet to set up the parameters to your liking. When you're done, ActiveX Control Pad inserts the <OBJECT> tag—complete with the correct CLSID—and any required <PARAM> tags. That's a big improvement over coding controls by hand, but the ActiveX Control Pad offers even more advantages:

- A separate component called the HTML Layout Control makes it easy to position ActiveX controls accurately. You can even save these layouts and reuse them in other Web pages.
- The ActiveX Control Pad is really just a text editor (albeit a powerful one), so you can tweak other HTML tags at will.
- You can use VBScript or JavaScript to control ActiveX objects programmatically. There is even a Script Wizard that you can use to get up to speed quickly.

Inserting ActiveX Controls

When you load the ActiveX Control Pad, you end up in a window like the one shown in Figure 21.1. As you can see, the Control Pad presents you with a new Web page that contains the basic HTML tags. You can use this file as a starting point if you want to work on a new page, or you can open an existing HTML document (by selecting File | Open). Either way, you add to the file by using any of the following techniques:

- Type text and HTML tags directly into the document window.
- Insert an ActiveX object.
- Insert an HTML layout.

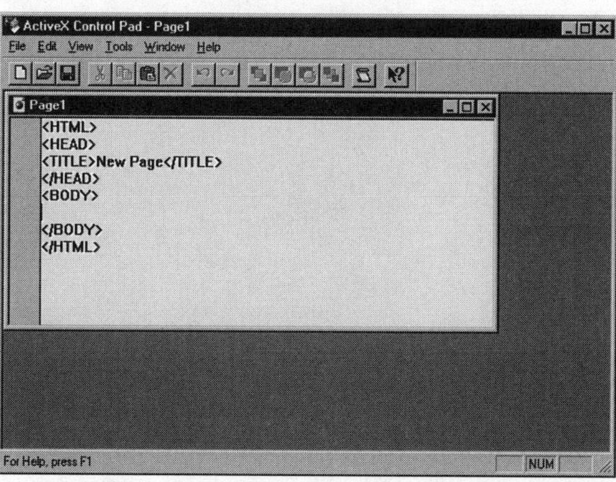

FIGURE 21.1.
The ActiveX Control Pad window.

I'll show you how to work with HTML layout files later in this chapter. The rest of this section shows you how to insert ActiveX controls.

To insert an ActiveX control, position the cursor where you want the control to appear, and then select Edit | Insert ActiveX Control. In the Insert ActiveX Control dialog box, shown in Figure 21.2, use the Control Type list to highlight the control you want to work with, and then click OK.

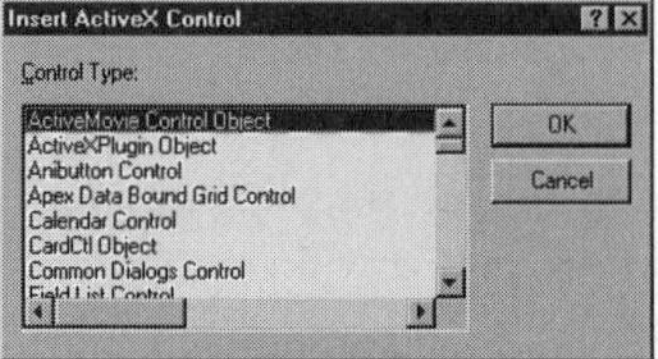

FIGURE 21.2.
Use this dialog box to choose the ActiveX control you want to insert.

When you insert the object, the ActiveX Control Editor appears, and the object's properties sheet is displayed, as shown in Figure 21.3. Each property shown corresponds to a `<PARAM>` tag for the object. All you have to do, however, is click a property and then enter the value you want in the text box near the top of the sheet. To apply the property, either click the Apply button or press Enter. When you're done, close the properties sheet to return to the ActiveX Control Editor window. From there, you can size the control to suit your needs. If you need to return to the properties sheet, double-click the control.

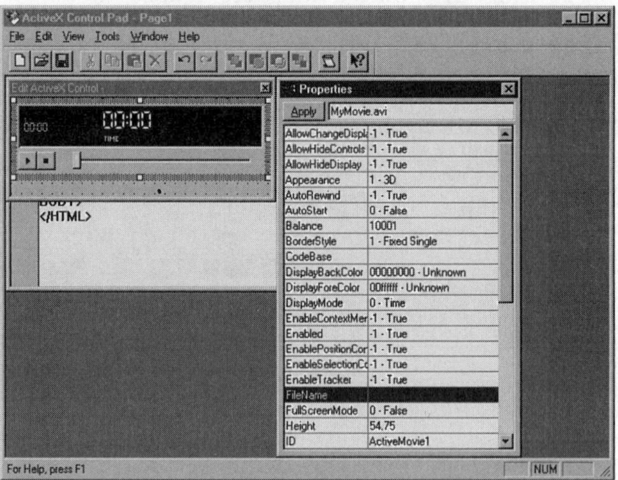

FIGURE 21.3.
The ActiveX Control Editor and properties sheet.

When all that's done, close the Editor window. The ActiveX Control Pad will insert the appropriate `<OBJECT>` and `<PARAM>` tags into the HTML file, as shown in Figure 21.4. If you need to make changes to the control, you have two choices:

- Move the cursor between the `<OBJECT>` and `</OBJECT>` tags and select Edit | Edit ActiveX Control.
- Click the Edit ActiveX Control button that appears to the left of the object's tags (see Figure 21.4).

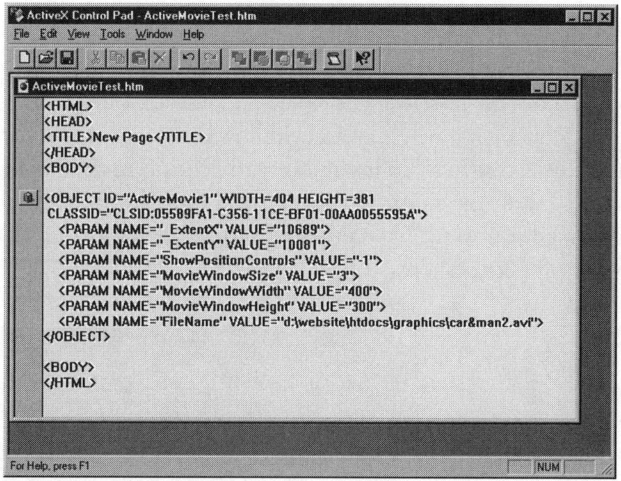

FIGURE 21.4.
The ActiveX Control Pad sets up the correct `<OBJECT>` *and* `<PARAM>` *tags automatically.*

Working with HTML Layouts

HTML gives you only the most rudimentary control over the layout of your Web pages: You can align things to the left, right, or center; you can use the `<PRE>` tag to make the browser honor white space; and you can use tables to align text and graphics. However, if you've ever worked with a page layout program, or if you've ever added graphical elements to a document or worksheet, you know that precise control over the placement of objects is crucial for getting the best results.

> **NOTE: LEARNING HTML**
>
> If you're not familiar with HTML, head for Appendix D, "An HTML Primer," to learn the basics.

Happily, there *is* a way to position your ActiveX controls with precision: by using HTML layouts. An HTML layout is actually an ActiveX control that acts as a container for other controls. The idea is that you insert ActiveX controls into the layout control and then use its fine-grained X- and Y-coordinate grid to position the controls with precision. Then you insert the layout control into your Web page. The browser will show the controls that are embedded within the layout exactly as you placed them.

The other advantage of working with layouts is that they save you from reinventing the wheel. For example, suppose that you need to repeat a particular arrangement of ActiveX controls over many pages. Instead of inserting each control into all these pages, you would create a single layout control that encompasses the ActiveX components you need, and then you would just insert this layout into each page.

Creating an HTML Layout

To help you create HTML layouts, the ActiveX Control Pad offers the HTML Layout Control window. To display it, select File | New HTML Layout (or press Ctrl-E). As you can see in Figure 21.5, you get a new Layout window along with a Toolbox that contains buttons for various ActiveX controls. To insert a control, click it in the Toolbox, move the mouse pointer to where you want the control to appear, and drag the mouse pointer to make the control the size and shape you want. To adjust the properties for a control, double-click the control to display the properties sheet.

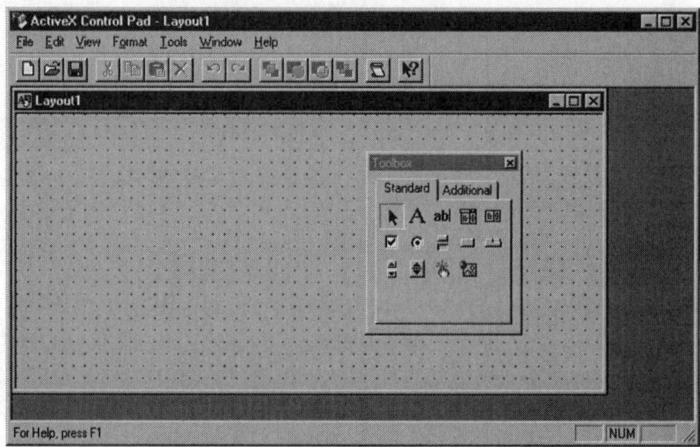

FIGURE 21.5.
Use the HTML Layout Control window to create an HTML layout.

The controls you insert are much like the graphic elements you add in other programs. This means that you use the same basic techniques to format and work with the controls:

- To select a control, click it.
- To select multiple controls, either hold down Ctrl and click each one, or use the mouse to drag a selection box around the controls.
- To move a control, place the mouse pointer over the control, hold down the left mouse button, and drag the mouse.
- To size a control, click it and then drag the selection handles.

The Format menu boasts a number of commands that come in handy for positioning and sizing multiple controls at once. Most of these commands perform the same function as the equivalent commands in the Visual Basic Editor, so I'll just review them quickly here:

Align: Use the cascade menu that appears to line up the controls relative to each other. For example, choosing Left aligns the selected objects on their left edges.

Make Same Size: The cascade menu commands that appear let you make the selected objects the same size. In other words, all the other objects are sized the same as whatever object currently has the focus. (The object that has the focus is the one with the white selection handles, as shown in Figure 21.6.)

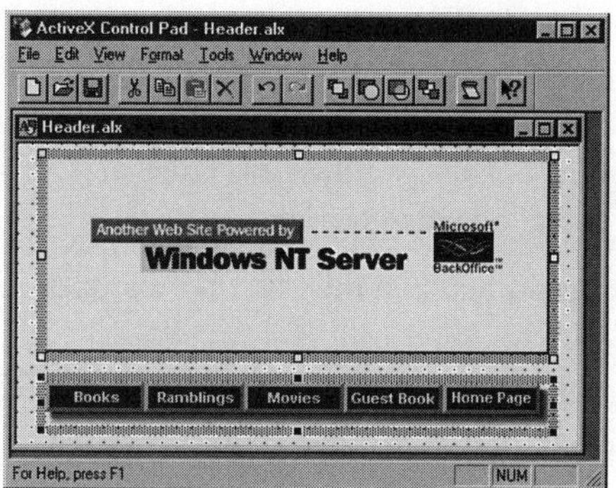

FIGURE 21.6.
The HTML Layout Control with a couple of objects added.

Size: In the cascade menu, select To Fit to size the selected objects to fit the data inside them. Select To Grid to size the objects to the nearest grid points.

Horizontal Spacing: The commands on this cascade menu determine the left and right spacing between the selected objects.

Vertical Spacing: The commands on this cascade menu determine the top and bottom spacing between the selected objects.

Snap to Grid: When this command is activated, you can only move and size the objects along the grid. For more precise control over each object, deactivate this command.

Another technique you can implement with an HTML layout control that's impossible with HTML tags is overlapping multiple objects. The Format menu also has a few commands for managing overlapped objects:

Send To Back: If the current object sits on top of another object, selecting this command will move it behind the object. If the object overlaps multiple objects, this command moves the object behind all the other objects.

Move Backward: If the current object sits on top of another object, selecting this command will move it behind the object.

Move Forward: If the current object is behind another object, selecting this command will move it in front of the object.

Bring To Front: If the current object is behind another object, selecting this command will move it in front of the object. If the object is overlapped by multiple objects, this command moves the object in front of all the other objects.

Inserting an HTML Layout

When you're done, save the layout object and then close the Layout window. The ActiveX Control Pad saves the data to an .ALX file. This is a text file that contains the `<OBJECT>` and `<PARAM>` tags for the controls you added to the layout.

To insert the layout control into your Web page, position the cursor where you want the control to appear and then select Edit | Insert HTML Layout. In the dialog box that appears, highlight the .ALX file and click Open. The ActiveX Control Pad inserts a new <OBJECT> tag that refers to the layout control, as shown in Figure 21.7. If you need to make changes to the layout, use either of the following techniques:

- Move the cursor between the <OBJECT> and </OBJECT> tags and select Edit | Edit HTML Layout.
- Click the Edit HTML Layout button that appears to the left of the layout's tags (see Figure 21.7).

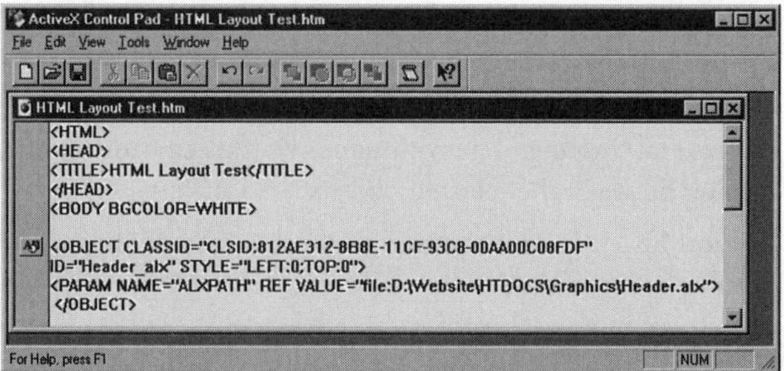

FIGURE 21.7.
An HTML layout is an ActiveX control with its own <OBJECT> *specification.*

Figure 21.8 shows how the layout appears when you display the page using Internet Explorer.

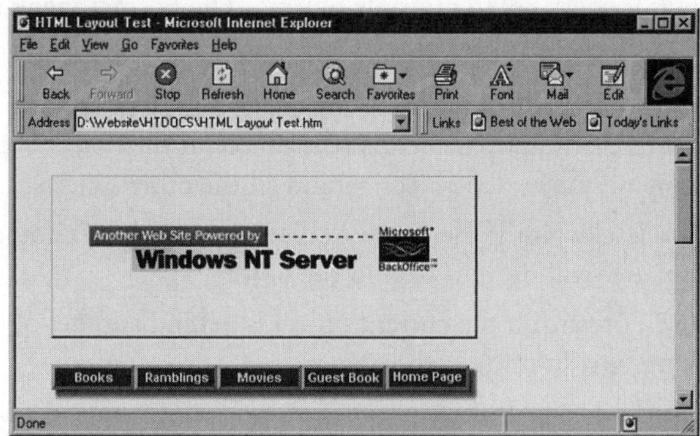

FIGURE 21.8.
When you open the page in a browser, the objects embedded in the layout are displayed exactly as you laid them out.

Setting HTML Layout Defaults

The ActiveX Control Pad has a few default settings for the HTML layout control. To modify these settings, select Tools | Options | HTML Layout. You'll see the HTML Layout Options dialog box, shown in Figure 21.9. Here's a rundown of the available controls:

Grid Settings: The spinners in this group determine the number of pixels between each grid marker. You can set the Vertical Spacing and Horizontal Spacing.

Show Grid: This check box toggles the grid on and off.

Snap To Grid: This check box toggles the Format | Snap To Grid command on and off.

Click OK to put the settings into effect.

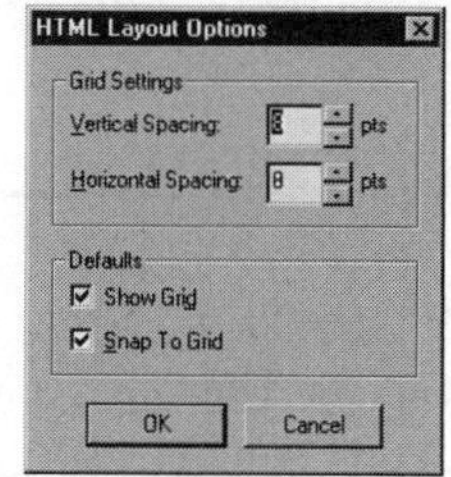

FIGURE 21.9.
Use this dialog box to set a few default options for the HTML Layout window.

Working with the Script Wizard

By themselves, ActiveX controls add an entirely new level of interaction to Web pages: animation, multimedia, games, even full-fledged applications. However, there is yet another level of interaction to be explored: communication between the controls themselves.

For example, you might want to keep one or more controls invisible until a video clip finishes playing. When the clip is done, you could display the controls. Similarly, you might want to keep a group of controls disabled until the user activates a particular check box or option button.

Another example involves validating form data before processing it. For instance, you might want to make sure that a particular field wasn't left blank, or you might want to check that a numeric field doesn't contain letters or other nonnumeric characters. One of the big problems with using HTML forms is that you usually have no way of validating the user's data *before* it gets to the server. The script can (and should) scour the submitted data for errors, but it can only report any problems to the user by displaying a separate page. This means that the user must go back to the form, make the necessary corrections, and submit the form all over again. It would be faster and more efficient if the form could somehow check the data before it's shipped out to the server.

For all of these situations and many more, Web page scripts are invaluable. A Web page script is a section of programming code inserted into a page by means of the `<SCRIPT>` tag. The tag specifies the script language you're using—which will either be VBScript (which I discuss later in this chapter) or JavaScript.

The idea is that you create procedures that run when a particular event occurs in conjunction with a particular object. For example, you can designate a procedure that will run when a video clip finishes playing, a check box is activated, or a form's submit button is clicked.

You now know more than enough VBA to handle VBScript without any trouble. However, in the same way that using an application's macro recorder can save coding time, so can the ActiveX

Control Pad's Script Wizard. As long as your needs aren't too sophisticated, you can use the Script Wizard to add simple script functionality to your Web pages. More than likely, however, you'll need to tweak the VBScript code by hand to set it up just the way you want.

As an example, let's see how you can use the Script Wizard to make one control respond to something that happens in another control. Begin by inserting two ActiveX controls into a Web page:

Microsoft Forms 2.0 CheckBox: Enter `Button Activator` in the `Caption` property and `False` in the `Value` property.

Microsoft Forms 2.0 CommandButton: Enter `Can't Click Me` in the `Caption` property and select 0-False in the `Enabled` property.

Figure 21.10 shows the resulting HTML file (with a couple of extra `<P>` tags thrown in to separate the controls).

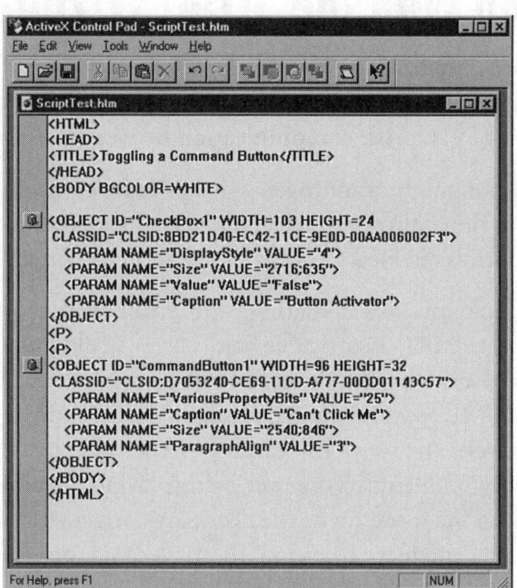

FIGURE 21.10.
An HTML page with an ActiveX check box and command button.

With your controls in place, crank up the Script Wizard by selecting Tools | Script Wizard. The top half of the Script Wizard window is divided into two sections, as shown in Figure 21.11:

Select an Event: This section displays a list of the objects associated with the Web page. Each of these objects has one or more events associated with it, such as `Click` (the user clicks the object) and `Change` (the user changes the object's value). To see these events, click the plus sign (+) beside the object.

Insert Actions: This section also displays a list of the page objects. In this case, though, each object has a list of the actions that can be performed on the object. Most of these actions involve changing the object's properties.

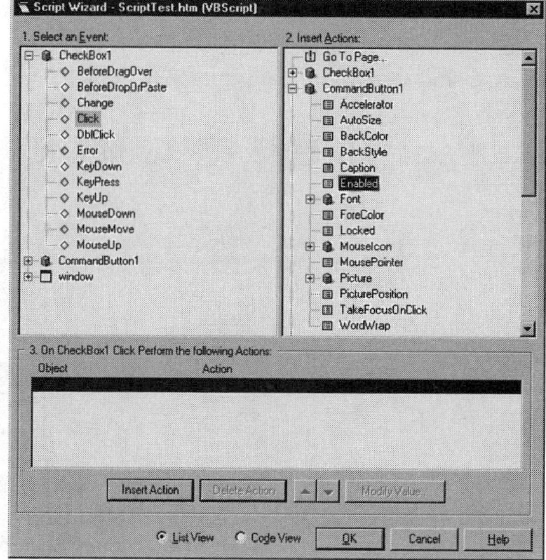

FIGURE 21.11.
The Script Wizard: A quick and dirty method of creating VBScript code.

You'll insert two actions:

1. Open the `CheckBox1` branch in the Select an Event list and highlight the `Click` event.
2. Open the `CommandButton1` branch in the Insert Action list and highlight `Enabled`.
3. Click Insert Action. The Script Wizard displays the dialog box shown in Figure 21.12, which prompts you for a new value. In other words, you should decide what value you want for `Enabled` when the user clicks the check box.

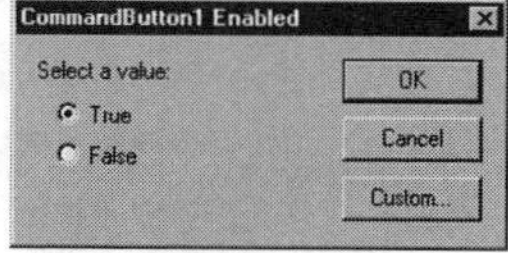

FIGURE 21.12.
Script Wizard will often prompt you for a new value.

4. Since you set up the command button with `Enabled` as `False`, activate `True` and click OK.
5. In the Insert Action list, highlight `Caption` and click Insert Action. This time, the Script Wizard prompts you to enter a text string. This will be the new caption after the user clicks the check box.
6. Type `Click Me` and click OK.

You should now see two actions in the bottom pane, as shown in Figure 21.13. Click OK to return to the ActiveX Control Pad window. As you can see in Figure 21.14, the Script Wizard has added a `<SCRIPT>` tag and inserted the VBScript programming code that corresponds to the actions you selected. (Note that if you need to make changes to your script, you can click the Edit Script button to the left of the script.) Save your work and load the page into Internet Explorer. When you click the check box object that you added to the page, the command button will become active, and the caption will change to "Click Me." Refresh the page to try it again.

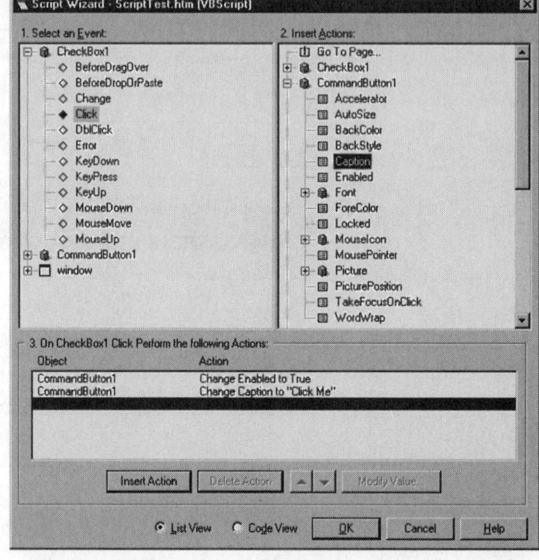

FIGURE 21.13.
Inserted actions appear in the bottom pane of the Script Wizard window.

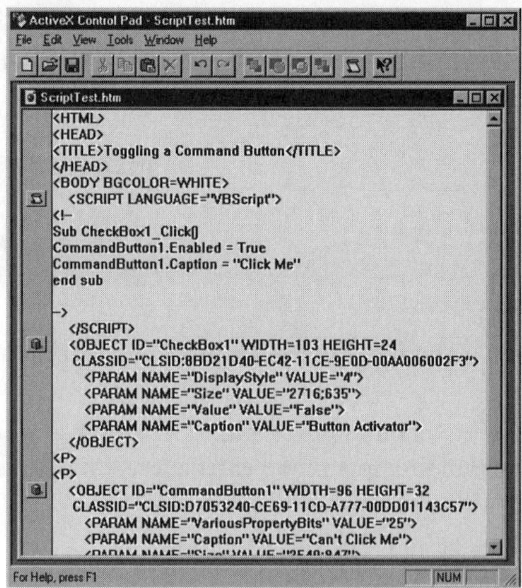

FIGURE 21.14.
The Script Wizard adds the programming code that corresponds to the actions you inserted.

NOTE: SWITCHING SCRIPTING LANGUAGES

The Script Wizard writes VBScript code by default. If you prefer to work with JavaScript, select Tools | Options | Script to display the Script Options dialog box. Activate the JavaScript option and click OK.

Programming Web Pages with VBScript

HTML lets you create increasingly interactive and dynamic pages—from links to forms to database queries to ActiveX controls. Now that you know VBA, you can put that knowledge to good use by building some client-side intelligence into your pages. In other words, you can insert snippets of VBA-like code into your pages; this code will run automatically on users' machines when they download your page.

The secret of this is an offshoot of the VBA language called *VBScript*. In a browser that understands how to run VBScript programs (such as Internet Explorer), you can implement programs to validate form data, customize pages based on, say, the current time or the browser being used, get the various objects on the page to communicate with each other, and much more. These *scripts* (as they're called) can be as simple as displaying a message box when the user clicks a page object, to full-fledged games and applications. The rest of this chapter introduces you to VBScript, outlines the differences between VBA and VBScript, runs through the object hierarchy you have at your disposal, and shows you how to implement VBScript code in your Web pages.

The Differences Between VBA and VBScript

VBScript is designed as a strict subset of VBA. In other words, all elements of VBScript are present in VBA, but some VBA elements aren't implemented in VBScript. In almost all cases, these language constructs were left out of VBScript for one or both of the following reasons:

- To make the scripts execute as quickly as possible: As you'll see, VBScript code is downloaded along with the rest of the HTML in a Web page, and the browser then interprets the script. Since in most cases the script exists to provide the user with a dynamic or interactive page, slow code interpretation would be counterproductive.
- To provide extra security: Since scripts are small programs that execute on a remote machine without user intervention, some security must be provided. After all, few people would want to use a VBScript-enhanced page if there were a possibility that the code could disrupt or crash their machine. For this reason, all VBA language constructs that would give the script access to the user's hard drive or operating system have been expunged from VBScript.

Table 21.2 summarizes the VBA language features that aren't present in VBScript.

Table 21.2. VBA language elements that aren't implemented in VBScript.

VBA Category	*Not in VBScript*
Arrays	Arrays declared with lower bound <> 0
	`Array` function
	`Option Base`
	`Private`, `Public`
Collection	`Add`, `Count`, `Item`, `Remove`
Conditional Compilation	`#Const`
	`#If...Then...#Else`
Control Flow	`DoEvents`
	`For Each...Next`
	`With...End With`
	`GoSub...Return`, `GoTo`
	`On Error GoTo`
	`On...GoSub`, `On...GoTo`
	Line numbers, line labels
Data Conversion	`CCur`, `CVar`, `CVDate`
	`Format`
	`Str`, `Val`
Data Types	All intrinsic data types except `Variant`
	`Type...End Type`
Date/Time	`Date` statement, `Time` statement
	`Timer`
DDE	`LinkExecute`, `LinkPoke`, `LinkRequest`, `LinkSend`
Debugging	`Debug.Print`
	`End`, `Stop`
Declaring Variables	`Declare`
	`Public`, `Private`, `Static`
	`New`
	`Const`
	Type-declaration characters
Error Handling	`Erl`
	`Error`
	`On Error...Resume`
	`Resume`, `Resume Next`
File I/O	All

VBA Category	*Not in VBScript*
Financial Functions	All

Object Manipulation	`CreateObject`
	`GetObject`
	`TypeOf`

Objects	Clipboard Collection
Operators	`Like`

Options	`Def`*`type`*
	`Option Base`
	`Option Compare`
	`Option Private Module`

Strings	Fixed-length strings
	`LSet`, `RSet`
	`Mid` statement
	`StrConv`

NOTE: YOU CAN'T SET THE DATE AND TIME

VBScript doesn't implement the `Date` and `Time` statements because they can be used to set the system date and time. If you just need to know the current date and time on the user's system, you can use the `Date` and `Time` functions (as well as other date/time functions, such as `Hour` and `Day`).

Other than the restrictions outlined in Table 21.2, the rest of the VBA universe is at your disposal. You can use `If...Then...Else` statements, `Do...Loop` structures, functions such as `MsgBox` and `Format`, and whatever else your code requires.

Not only that, but there's also a special object hierarchy for scripts that exposes numerous browser objects. Therefore, by using the properties, methods, and events associated with these objects, you gain a tremendous amount of control over how a browser looks and acts.

Attaching Scripts to a Page

Before you can add VBScript functionality to a Web page, you have to write the script and then insert the code directly into the page. Note that scripts aren't like, say, images, where you use a tag to point to an external file. No, with VBScript your statements are entered directly into the page and are completely visible to anyone who cares to look at the page's source code. (In other words, if you have an algorithm you want to patent, don't use it in a script!)

As you'll soon see, a script is just a chunk of text, so the tool you use to create your scripts is a matter of preference. Unfortunately, there is no VBScript equivalent of the Visual Basic Editor. The closest we have is the ActiveX Control Pad. As you saw earlier, this utility is handy for inserting ActiveX controls. Other than that, though, it's just a simple text editor.

An alternative would be to fire up an Office application and then switch to the Visual Basic Editor. You could start a new module and use it to write your script, which at least gives you the not-insignificant advantage of VBA's on-the-fly syntax checking and IntelliSense features. When your script is ready, you can copy it from the module and paste it into your page. For the latter, VBScript gives you two methods for inserting a script:

- The `<SCRIPT>` tag
- Adding the `LANGUAGE` attribute to a control

NOTE: THE SCRIPT DEBUGGER UTILITY

As this book was going to press, Microsoft released a new utility called Script Debugger for Internet Explorer. As its name implies, this utility lets you debug VBScript (or JavaScript) programs. You'll find this handy utility on Microsoft's Web site:

`http://www.microsoft.com/workshop/prog/scriptie/`

The Script Debugger operates much like the debugging environment that's available with the Visual Basic Editor. See Chapter 24, "Debugging VBA Procedures," to learn some basic debugging techniques.

The <SCRIPT> Tag

In Appendix D, I introduce you to various HTML tags. One of the things you'll learn is that many tags are *containers*. In other words, they require both a start and an end tag, like this:

```
<TITLE>My Home Sweet Home Page</TITLE>
```

Here, the `<TITLE>` tag tells the browser that the text that follows is the page title (to be displayed in the browser title bar), and the `</TITLE>` tag tells the browser that it has reached the end of the title text.

One way to incorporate VBScript into your pages is to use the `<SCRIPT>/</SCRIPT>` container, like so:

```
<SCRIPT LANGUAGE="language">
    Procedures go here
</SCRIPT>
```

The `LANGUAGE` attribute specifies the scripting language you're using. For VBScript, you use `<SCRIPT LANGUAGE="VBScript">`. (At the time this book was written, the only other scripting language supported was JavaScript, which uses the tag `<SCRIPT LANGUAGE="JScript">`.)

You enter your Sub and Function procedures between the <SCRIPT> and </SCRIPT> tags. When a VBScript-aware browser (such as Internet Explorer) encounters these tags, it begins processing (or *interpreting*) the script's commands immediately. Note that you can put the <SCRIPT> container inside the document's header or body.

Listing 21.1 shows a simple HTML file that includes the <SCRIPT> container (see WELCOME.HTM on the CD).

Listing 21.1. An HTML file with a <SCRIPT> tag.

```
<HTML>
<HEAD>
<TITLE>Our First Look at a VBScript Page</TITLE>
</HEAD>
<BODY>
<H3>Listing 21.1. An HTML file with a &lt;SCRIPT&gt; tag.</H3>
<SCRIPT LANGUAGE="VBScript">
Sub WelcomeMat
   MsgBox "Welcome to VBScript!"
End Sub
Call WelcomeMat
</SCRIPT>
</BODY>
</HTML>
```

As you can see, the <SCRIPT> container includes a Sub procedure named WelcomeMat. This simple procedure just invokes MsgBox to display a message. Since the Call WelcomeMat statement is outside of any procedure, it gets executed by the browser immediately. (These statements act somewhat like "OnLoad" event procedures.) Therefore, the message is displayed as soon as you open this page, as shown in Figure 21.15.

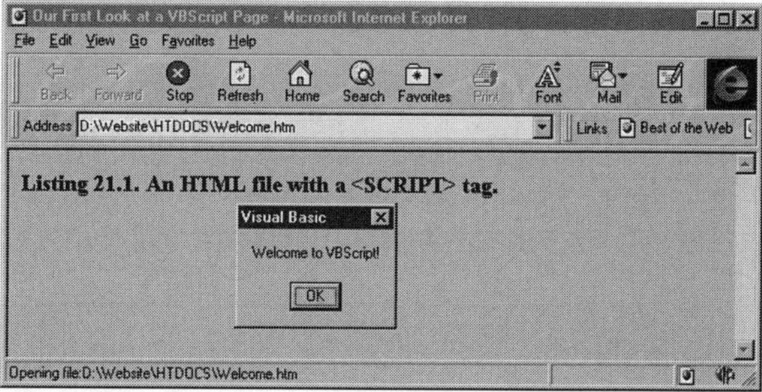

FIGURE 21.15.
The Web page that appears when you load the HTML file in Listing 21.1.

A Note About VBScript Event Procedures

Although it's perfectly acceptable to have regular Sub and Function procedures within the <SCRIPT> container, most of your pages will use *event procedures* instead. In other words, you'll include code to handle particular events, such as entering text in a form or clicking a button.

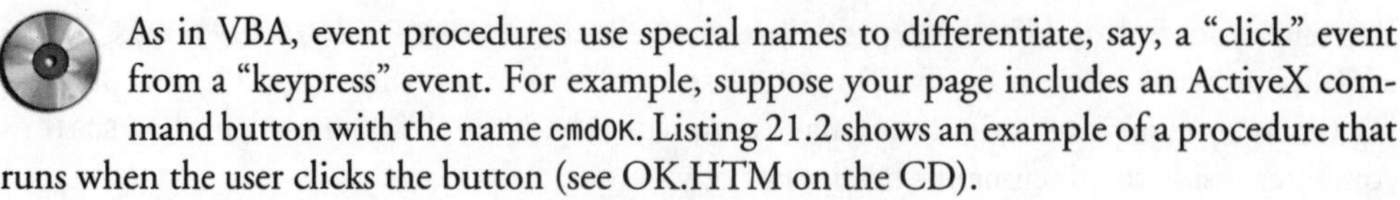

As in VBA, event procedures use special names to differentiate, say, a "click" event from a "keypress" event. For example, suppose your page includes an ActiveX command button with the name `cmdOK`. Listing 21.2 shows an example of a procedure that runs when the user clicks the button (see OK.HTM on the CD).

Listing 21.2. An example of an event procedure.

```
<HTML>
<HEAD>
<TITLE>An Event Procedure Example</TITLE>
</HEAD>
<BODY>
<SCRIPT LANGUAGE="VBScript">
Sub cmdOK_Click
    msgbox "Yup, you clicked OK!"
End Sub
</SCRIPT>
Click here:
<OBJECT ID="cmdOK" WIDTH=75 HEIGHT=25
 CLASSID="CLSID:D7053240-CE69-11CD-A777-00DD01143C57">
    <PARAM NAME="Caption" VALUE="OK">
    <PARAM NAME="Size" VALUE="1953;846">
    <PARAM NAME="FontCharSet" VALUE="0">
    <PARAM NAME="FontPitchAndFamily" VALUE="2">
    <PARAM NAME="ParagraphAlign" VALUE="3">
    <PARAM NAME="FontWeight" VALUE="0">
</OBJECT>
</BODY>
</HTML>
```

When you attach an underscore (_) and the type of event to the button's name, VBScript knows that you want to run this procedure each time the event occurs. This method doesn't work with regular HTML controls, however. For that, you need to specify the procedure to run when you define the control. I'll show you how to do this in the next section.

Using the LANGUAGE Attribute with a Control

Instead of defaulting to the standard procedure names for your event handlers, you can specify a procedure to run when you define the object. Doing so gives you the following advantages:

- You can set up event handlers for regular HTML form controls.
- You can specify the same procedure to be the event handler for multiple controls.
- You can use different scripting languages within the same page. For example, you could set up an event procedure in VBScript for one control and another event procedure in JavaScript for a different control.

The downside of this method is that it can't be used with objects inserted using the `<OBJECT>` tag.

To specify a procedure, you add both the LANGUAGE attribute and the appropriate event procedure attribute to the tag that defines the control. For example, consider the following <INPUT> tag for a command button:

```
<INPUT
    TYPE=BUTTON
    VALUE="Cancel"
    LANGUAGE="VBScript"
    ONCLICK="ProcessClick()">
```

The ONCLICK attribute specifies the procedure to run when the button is clicked, and the LANGUAGE attribute tells the browser which scripting language to expect.

The Scripting Object Hierarchy

Although it's mildly interesting to be able to make a Web page display a dialog box, the true fun occurs when you use VBScript to manipulate not only the various objects in the page, but also the browser itself! To accomplish all this, your VBScript code must interact with the *scripting object hierarchy*. This is an object model that defines the various items that VBScript can work with, as well as their properties, methods, and events.

Unlike the Office applications, which have dozens of objects to deal with, the scripting object model is relatively simple. It begins with a single top-level object called the Window object. Under the Window object are just six second-level objects:

Document: Represents the current document in the window.

Location: Represents the URL of the current document.

History: Represents the history list for the browser.

Frame: Represents an array of the frames in the current window.

Script: Represents the script being used.

Navigator: Represents the browser application (such as Internet Explorer) in which the Web page is being displayed.

The next few sections describe a few of these objects, as well as their most useful properties and methods.

The Window Object

The Window object represents the browser window and therefore serves as a container for the entire scripting object model. Note that VBScript assumes that the Window object is being referenced by default. Therefore, you rarely have to mention the Window object directly. For example, the statements `Window.name` and `name` are equivalent. This section examines some common properties and methods for this object.

Window Object Properties

The Window object properties govern various aspects of the window's appearance and how the window fits into the current frame setup:

`defaultStatus`: Determines the default text that appears in the browser's status bar (that is, the text that appears when the browser is waiting for input).

`name`: Returns the name of the window. You usually name a window while using frames (that is, by using the `NAME` attribute in the `<FRAME>` tag). You can also give a window a name by using the `open` method (see the next section) or by using the `TARGET` attribute in the `<A HREF>` tag.

`opener`: Returns a Window object that represents the window that opened the current window.

`parent`: Returns a Window object that represents the parent window of the current window. (The parent is the frame in which the current window resides.)

`self`: Returns a Window object that represents the current window.

`status`: Sets the text in the browser's status bar.

`top`: Returns a Window object that represents the topmost window in the current frame array.

Window Object Methods

You can use the Window object's methods to manipulate the browser window:

`alert`: Displays an alert box. This is similar to running `MsgBox` in VBA with the `vbExclamation` constant.

`close`: Closes the window.

`confirm`: Displays a dialog box with a message and OK and Cancel buttons (it's similar to using `MsgBox` in VBA with `vbOKCancel`):

```
return = confirm("Do you want to submit the form?")
```

If the user clicks OK, `confirm` returns `True`; if the user clicks Cancel, `confirm` returns `False`.

`navigate`: Navigates the window to a specified URL. For example, the following statement navigates to `http://www.mcp.com/`:

```
window.navigate "http://www.mcp.com/"
```

`open`: Opens a new window using the following syntax:

```
window.open(url, target, options)
```

url	A string specifying the URL to display in the new window.
target	The target name to use for the new window.

`options`	A comma-separated list of values that determines various properties of the new window:

`toolbar`	A Boolean value (`1` or `0`, `yes` or `no`) that determines whether the new window displays the toolbar.
`location`	A Boolean value (`1` or `0`, `yes` or `no`) that determines whether the new window displays the location box.
`status`	A Boolean value (`1` or `0`, `yes` or `no`) that determines whether the new window displays the status bar.
`menubar`	A Boolean value (`1` or `0`, `yes` or `no`) that determines whether the new window displays the menu bar.
`scrollbars`	A Boolean value (`1` or `0`, `yes` or `no`) that determines whether the new window displays the scrollbars.
`resizeable`	A Boolean value (`1` or `0`, `yes` or `no`) that determines whether the new window can be resized.
`width`	Sets the width of the new window in pixels.
`height`	Sets the height of the new window in pixels.
`top`	Sets the Y-coordinate position of the top of the window.
`left`	Sets the X-coordinate position of the left edge of the window.

Here's an example:

```
window.open "http://www.yahoo.com/", "Frame2", "toolbar=no, location=no"
```

`prompt`: Displays a dialog box to ask the user for input (similar to VBA's `InputBox` function). Here's the syntax:

```
prompt(prompt, default)
```

`prompt`	The prompt that appears in the dialog box.
`default`	The initial value that appears inside the text box.

Window Object Events

The Window object supports only two events:

`onLoad`: Fires when the contents of the window are loaded.

`onUnload`: Fires when the contents of the window are unloaded.

In both cases, you define the event handler within the <BODY> tag, like so:

```
<BODY onLoad="HiThere()" onUnload="Bye()">
<SCRIPT LANGUAGE="VBScript">
Sub HiThere()
    MsgBox "Welcome!"
End Sub
Sub Bye()
    MsgBox "So long!"
End Sub
</SCRIPT>
```

The Document Object

The Document object represents the Web page currently loaded into the browser. It also serves as a container for the objects inside the page, including the `Links` object (the collection of all the Link objects on the page), the `Forms` object (the collection of Form objects on the page), and the Location object.

Note that, unlike the Windows object, to work with the Document object properties and methods, you must precede the property with the `document` keyword (for example, `document.title`). The next two sections take you through some Document object properties and methods.

Document Object Properties

The Document object's properties let you customize the document display programmatically. This includes the background color, the link colors, the title of the document, and more.

`anchors`: Returns the `Anchors` object—the collection of all the anchors in the document. (Use `document.anchors.length` to determine the number of anchors in the document.)

`bgColor`: Returns or sets the color of the document's background. When setting this property (and any of the other color-related properties), you use a string value that consists of either a color name or an RGB value. For example, both of the following properties set the background color to white:

```
document.bgColor = "white"

document.bgColor = "#FFFFFF"
```

`fgColor`: Returns or sets the color of the document foreground (text).

`forms`: Returns the `Forms` object—the collection of all the forms in the document. For detailed information about the Forms object, see "How VBScript Interacts with Forms" later in this chapter.

`lastModified`: Returns a date string that corresponds to the date the document was last modified.

`linkColor`: Returns or sets the color of the document's links.

`links`: Returns the `Links` object—the collection of all the links in the document. Each member of this collection is a Link object, which has various properties that govern each link's URL (such as `href`, `protocol`, and `host`).

`location`: Returns the Location object. The properties of this object (such as `protocol`, `host`, and `pathname`) specify the various parts of the document's URL.

`title`: Returns the document's title (that is, the text between the `<TITLE>` and `</TITLE>` tags).

`vLinkColor`: Returns or sets the color of the document's visited links.

Document Object Methods

The Document object has only a few methods, and only one of them is particularly useful:

`write`: This method writes text into the document:

```
document.write text
```

Here, *`text`* is the string you want to insert. Here are a few things to bear in mind when using this handy method:

- The text is written at the point where the `write` method resides in the document.
- The `write` statement must be executed when the browser parses the script. Therefore, you insert the `write` method either by itself, outside of a procedure (yet still within the `<SCRIPT>` container, of course), or inside a procedure that is invoked by the `Call` statement.
- You can include HTML tags in the *`text`* argument. The browser will render them faithfully.

Listing 21.3 shows several examples of the `write` method (see WRITE.HTM on the CD).

Listing 21.3. Some examples of the `write` method.

```
<HTML>
<HEAD>
<TITLE>Document.Write Examples</TITLE>
</HEAD>
<BODY BGCOLOR=WHITE>
This line is part of the regular body text.
<P>
<SCRIPT LANGUAGE="VBScript">
' This line runs when the browser parses the script
Call WriteGreeting
Sub WriteGreeting
    Dim hr
    hr = Hour(Now)
    If hr < 12 Then
        document.write "Good morning!"
```

continues

Listing 21.3. continued

```
    ElseIf hr < 17 Then
        document.write "Good afternoon!"
    Else
        document.write "Good evening!"
    End If
End Sub
</SCRIPT>
<P>
Another line of body text.
<P>
<SCRIPT LANGUAGE="VBScript">
' These statements are executed at parse-time
document.write "You're visiting at "
document.write Time() & " on " & Date() & "."
</SCRIPT>
</BODY>
</HTML>
```

The first `<SCRIPT>` container uses a `Call` function to execute the `WriteGreeting` procedure during parse time. `WriteGreeting` checks the current hour and displays an appropriate greeting. The second `<SCRIPT>` container just has a couple of `write` methods. Again, these are executed at parse time. As you can see in Figure 21.16, the text specified by the `write` methods is displayed where the `write` statements occur in the HTML file.

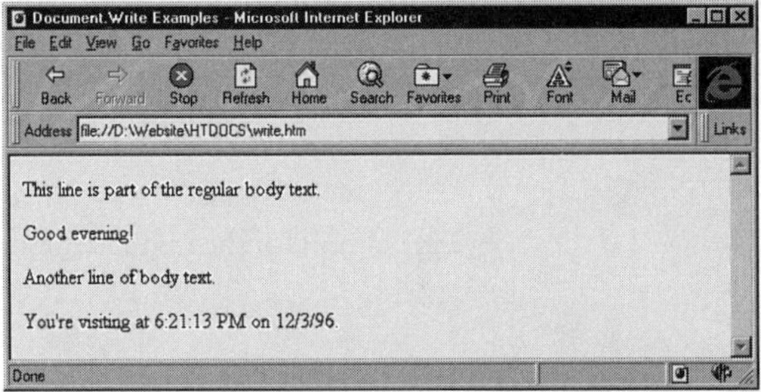

FIGURE 21.16.
The `write` method inserts text into a Web page.

> **NOTE: THE `WRITELN` METHOD**
>
> The Document object also has a `writeLn` method, which is identical to `write`, except that it includes a newline character at the end of the specified text. However, most browsers ignore newline characters, so this method works only if you precede it with a `<PRE>` tag.

The Navigator Object

The Navigator object provides you with information about which browser is being used to display the window. The Navigator object has four properties:

`appCodeName`: Returns the browser's code name (such as "Mozilla").

`appName`: Returns the browser's application name (such as "Microsoft Internet Explorer").

`appVersion`: Returns the browser's version number. Note that this usually contains the operating system as well:

```
2.0 (compatible; MSIE 3.0A; Windows 95)
```

`userAgent`: Returns the browser's user agent (usually the `appCodeName` combined with the `appVersion`).

How VBScript Interacts with Forms

HTML forms currently put a great deal of the processing burden on the server. Not only must the server dish out the form in the first place, but it must also validate the submitted data, massage the information, and return another Web page. Your VBScript code can help relieve at least a little of that burden by implementing one or both of the following:

- Validating the data before it gets sent to the server: As you'll see a bit later, form controls are just objects to VBScript. Therefore, your code can check the value of any field to see if it falls within the correct parameters. If it doesn't, VBScript can delay the submission until the user enters the correct data.
- Performing calculations or other functions within the page: Again, since VBScript can easily manipulate the contents of a field, it can assume some duties that would otherwise fall to the server. For example, if your form makes calculations, VBScript can perform these calculations on-the-fly without having to submit the form.

Since form and control manipulation is one of VBScript's strongest features, this section takes a close look at forms and how you can work with them from your scripts.

The Form Object

A Form object is a scripting object model representation of a Web page form, which means every object between (and including) the `<FORM>` and `</FORM>` tags. For pages with multiple forms, the `Forms` collection represents all the Form objects in the page.

To reference a Form object in your code, you have two choices:

- Use an index with the `Forms` object. For example, `document.forms(0)` refers to the first Form object in the page.
- Use the name of the form as defined by the `NAME` attribute in the `<FORM>` tag. For example, if a form has been set up with `<FORM NAME="MyForm">`, you could reference this form with the statement `document.MyForm`.

Form Properties

Most of the properties of the Form object correspond to the various attributes you can include in the `<FORM>` tag:

`action`: Returns or sets the URL that is used to submit the form. This is equivalent to the `ACTION` attribute in the `<FORM>` tag.

`encoding`: Returns or sets the form encoding (for example, `text/html`). This is equivalent to the `<FORM>` tag's `ENCTYPE` attribute.

`method`: Returns or sets the method used to submit the form. This is equivalent to the `METHOD` attribute in the `<FORM>` tag.

`target`: Sets the target window for the form output. This is identical to setting the `TARGET` attribute in the `<FORM>` tag.

The following statements use these properties to adjust how the form will be sent:

```
document.MyForm.action = "http://www.server.com/cgi-bin/process.exe"
document.MyForm.encoding = "text/html"
document.MyForm.method = "POST"
document.MyForm.target = "resultsWindow"
```

Submitting a Form

A form is sent to the server when the user clicks a "submit" button. In VBScript, you can send a form to the server any time you like by invoking the Form object's `submit` method.

Note, too, that Form objects also recognize the `onSubmit` event. This event is fired, naturally enough, whenever a form is submitted to the server. This lets you set up an event handler to process or check the form data before passing it along to the server. For example, the following statement specifies that VBScript should run the `ValidateIt` procedure whenever the user (or your script) attempts to submit the form:

```
document.MyForm.onsubmit = "ValidateIt()"
```

The problem with setting up an `onSubmit` event handler in this manner is that you have no way to bail out of the submission if there's an error or some other anomaly. If you would like the ability to cancel a submission, you must include the `return` keyword in the `onSubmit` specification:

```
document.MyForm.onsubmit = "return ValidateIt()"
```

Here, `ValidateIt` must be a Function procedure that returns a Boolean value (`True` or `False`). If the procedure returns `True`, the submission continues. However, if the procedure returns `False`, the submission is aborted and the user stays with the form.

Dealing with Form Controls

The Form object has an `elements` property that is a collection of all the controls inside the form. These controls include not only the standard HTML controls, but also any objects inserted with the `<OBJECT>` tag (such as ActiveX controls).

You can use the `elements` collection to refer to a control by its index number (where the first control is 0, the second control is 1, and so on). However, this method makes your code difficult to read. Instead, you should name each control, either by using the `NAME` attribute in an HTML control or by using the `ID` attribute in an `<OBJECT>` tag. For example, if you have a command button named `cmdOK` on a form named `MyForm`, you can reference this button as `document.MyForm.cmdOK`.

Control Properties

The various types of controls have their own set of properties, some of which are common among all controls, and some of which are unique to each control. Most of these properties are straightforward, so here's a quick run-through:

`checked`: For a check box or option button, this property returns or sets the state of the specified control (where `1` or `True` means the control is activated, and `0` or `False` means the control is deactivated). For example, you could use the following statements to toggle the state of a check box on or off:

```
Set cb = document.MyForm.CheckBox1
cb.checked = Not cb.checked
```

> **TIP: USE OBJECT VARIABLES FOR SHORTER CODE**
>
> In the `checked` example, notice how I `Set` a variable named `cb` to the check box object given by `document.MyForm.CheckBox1`. This is always a good idea if the object's reference is long-winded and you'll be referring to the object more than once.

`defaultChecked`: Returns or sets the default state of a check box or option button.

`defaultValue`: Returns or sets the default value of the control.

`form`: Returns the Form object in which the control resides.

`Length`: In a list (that is, a `<SELECT>` control), this property returns the number of items in the list.

`name`: Returns or sets the control name.

`value`: Returns or sets the value of the specified control.

`selectedIndex`: For a list, this property returns the selected item.

Control Methods

Here's a quick look at the various methods available for form controls, all of which are straightforward:

`blur`: Removes the focus from the specified control.

`click`: Clicks the control.

`focus`: Gives the specified control the focus.

`select`: Selects the contents of a `TEXT`, `TEXTAREA`, or `PASSWORD` control.

Control Events

You'll often need to set up event handlers for your forms. For example, you might want to trap a `RESET` button to ask the user if she's sure she wants to proceed. VBScript offers two methods for specifying an event handler for a particular control: You can reference a procedure using the control's `<INPUT>` tag, or you can create a `<SCRIPT>` tag that references the control.

For the first method, you include an ON*EVENT* attribute in the control's `<INPUT>` tag. Here, the *EVENT* part is the name of the event you want to trap. For the `Click` event, you would use the `ONCLICK` attribute, like so:

```
<INPUT TYPE=BUTTON NAME="cmdCalc" VALUE="Calculate" ONCLICK="DoIt">
<SCRIPT LANGUAGE="VBScript">
Sub DoIt
    Event handler code goes here.
End Sub
</SCRIPT>
```

In this case, the `DoIt` procedure executes whenever the user clicks the `cmdCalc` button.

For the second method, you add `FOR` and `EVENT` attributes to a separate `<SCRIPT>` tag. The `FOR` attribute specifies the name of the control, and the `EVENT` attribute specifies the event you want to trap. Here's an example:

```
<INPUT TYPE=BUTTON NAME="cmdCalc" VALUE="Calculate">
<SCRIPT FOR="cmdCalc" EVENT="onClick" LANGUAGE="VBScript">
    Event handler code goes here.
</SCRIPT>
```

The latter technique is preferred because it's both more efficient (two fewer lines) and more readable (you get more information about what the script does).

Here's a summary of the control events you can trap in this manner:

`onBlur`: Fires when the specified control loses the focus.

`onChange`: Fires when the value of the control changes.

`onClick`: Fires when the user clicks the control.

`onFocus`: Fires when the specified control gets the focus.

`onSelect`: Fires when the contents of a `TEXT`, `TEXTAREA`, or `PASSWORD` control are selected.

Example: A Mortgage Calculator

To finish our look at VBScript, let's check out a sample form that demonstrates both form validation and client-side processing. The form we'll be using is shown in Figure 21.17. As you can see, it's a simple calculator that, given various parameters such as house price and interest rate, figures out the monthly mortgage payment (among other things).

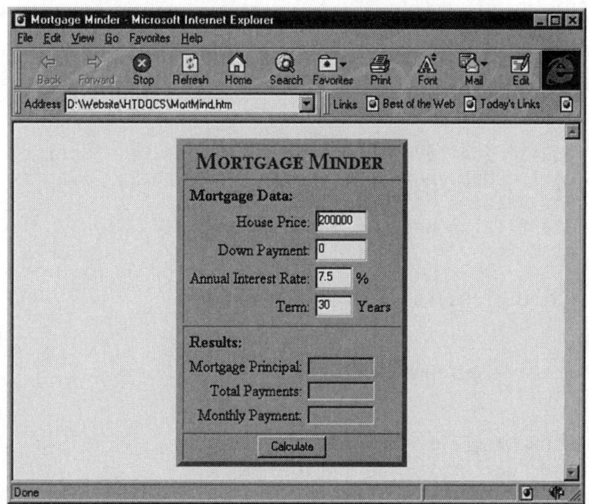

FIGURE 21.17.
The sample mortgage calculator that we'll be using.

The top part of the form consists of four HTML text boxes that you use to enter the mortgage data. The bottom half of the form contains three ActiveX Label controls that are used to display the results of the calculation. Thanks to VBScript, the form is set up to do the following:

- Recalculate every time you change a text box value and then navigate to another text box.
- Recalculate whenever you click the Calculate button.
- Prevent zero values from being entered into the text boxes.

Listing 21.4 gives you the complete HTML file for this application (see MORTMIND.HTM on the CD). Although this listing looks intimidatingly long, most of the code is needed just to display the form properly.

Listing 21.4. A form-based mortgage calculator with VBScript validation and calculations.

```
<HTML>
<HEAD>
<TITLE>Mortgage Minder</TITLE>
</HEAD>
<BODY BGCOLOR=WHITE>
<CENTER>
<FORM NAME="MortgageMinder">
<TABLE BORDER=5 BGCOLOR=SILVER CELLPADDING=2>
<TR><TD COLSPAN=2 ALIGN=CENTER>
<B><FONT SIZE=+2 COLOR=BLUE>M<FONT SIZE=+1>ORTGAGE <FONT SIZE=+2>M<FONT SIZE=+1>
➥INDER</FONT></B>
</TD></TR>
<TR><TD COLSPAN=2>
<TABLE BORDER=0 CELLPADDING=2>
<TR><TD COLSPAN=2><B>Mortgage Data:</B></TD>
<TR><TD ALIGN=RIGHT>House Price:</TD>
<TD><INPUT
    TYPE=TEXT
    NAME="Price"
    VALUE="200000"
    SIZE=7>
</TD></TR>
<SCRIPT FOR="Price" EVENT="onChange" LANGUAGE="VBScript">
    Set ctrl = document.MortgageMinder.Price
    If ctrl.Value = "" Then
        alert ("The House Price can't be 0!")
        ctrl.focus
    Else
        CalculatePayment()
    End If
</SCRIPT>
<TR><TD ALIGN=RIGHT>Down Payment:</TD>
<TD><INPUT
    TYPE=TEXT
    NAME="DownPayment"
    VALUE=0
    ONCHANGE="CalculatePayment()"
    SIZE=7>
</TD></TR>
<TR><TD ALIGN=RIGHT>Annual Interest Rate:</TD>
<TD><INPUT
    TYPE=TEXT
    NAME="InterestRate"
    VALUE="7.5"
    SIZE=4>
%
</TD></TR>
<SCRIPT FOR="InterestRate" EVENT="onChange" LANGUAGE="VBScript">
    Set ctrl = document.MortgageMinder.InterestRate
    If ctrl.Value = "" Then
        alert ("The Interest Rate can't be 0!")
        ctrl.focus
    Else
        CalculatePayment()
    End If
</SCRIPT>
<TR><TD ALIGN=RIGHT>Term:</TD>
<TD><INPUT
```

```
    TYPE=TEXT
    NAME="Term"
    VALUE="30"
    SIZE=4>
Years
</TD></TR>
<SCRIPT FOR="Term" EVENT="onChange" LANGUAGE="VBScript">
    Set ctrl = document.MortgageMinder.Term
    If ctrl.Value = "" Then
        alert ("The Term can't be 0!")
        ctrl.focus
    Else
        CalculatePayment()
    End If
</SCRIPT>
</TABLE></TD></TR>
<TR><TD>
<TABLE BORDER=0 CELLPADDING=2>
<TR><TD COLSPAN=2><B>Results:</B></TD>
<TR><TD ALIGN=RIGHT>Mortgage Principle:</TD>
<TD><OBJECT ID="Principle" WIDTH=71 HEIGHT=19
 CLASSID="CLSID:978C9E23-D4B0-11CE-BF2D-00AA003F40D0">
    <PARAM NAME="Size" VALUE="1870;494">
    <PARAM NAME="SpecialEffect" VALUE="2">
    <PARAM NAME="FontCharSet" VALUE="0">
    <PARAM NAME="FontPitchAndFamily" VALUE="2">
    <PARAM NAME="FontWeight" VALUE="0">
</OBJECT>
</TD><TR>
<TD ALIGN=RIGHT>Total Payments:</TD>
<TD><OBJECT ID="TotalPayments" WIDTH=71 HEIGHT=19
 CLASSID="CLSID:978C9E23-D4B0-11CE-BF2D-00AA003F40D0">
    <PARAM NAME="Size" VALUE="1870;494">
    <PARAM NAME="SpecialEffect" VALUE="2">
    <PARAM NAME="FontCharSet" VALUE="0">
    <PARAM NAME="FontPitchAndFamily" VALUE="2">
    <PARAM NAME="FontWeight" VALUE="0">
</OBJECT>
</TD></TR>
<TR><TD ALIGN=RIGHT>Monthly Payment:</TD>
<TD><OBJECT ID="Payment" WIDTH=71 HEIGHT=19
 CLASSID="CLSID:978C9E23-D4B0-11CE-BF2D-00AA003F40D0">
    <PARAM NAME="Size" VALUE="1870;494">
    <PARAM NAME="SpecialEffect" VALUE="2">
    <PARAM NAME="FontCharSet" VALUE="0">
    <PARAM NAME="FontPitchAndFamily" VALUE="2">
    <PARAM NAME="FontWeight" VALUE="0">
</OBJECT>
</TD></TR>
</TABLE>
<TR><TD ALIGN=CENTER COLSPAN=2>
<INPUT
    TYPE=BUTTON
    NAME="cmdCalc"
    VALUE="Calculate">
<SCRIPT FOR="cmdCalc" EVENT="onClick" LANGUAGE="VBScript">
    Set frm = document.MortgageMinder
    If frm.Price.Value = "" Then
```

continues

Listing 21.4. continued

```
        alert ("The House Price can't be 0!")
        frmPrice.focus
    ElseIf frm.InterestRate.Value = "" Then
        alert ("The Interest Rate can't be 0!")
        frm.InterestRate.focus
    ElseIf frm.Term.Value = "" Then
        alert ("The Term can't be 0!")
        frm.Term.focus
    Else
        CalculatePayment()
    End If
</SCRIPT>
</TD>
</TR>
</TD></TR>
</TABLE>
</FORM>
</TABLE>
<SCRIPT LANGUAGE="VBScript">
Sub CalculatePayment
    Set frmCalc = Document.MortgageMinder
    price = frmCalc.Price.Value
    dnpmt = frmCalc.DownPayment.Value
    prin = price - dnPmt
    intRate = (frmCalc.InterestRate.Value/100) / 12
    term = frmCalc.Term.Value * 12
    pmt = int((prin*intRate)/(1-(1+intRate)^(-1*term))*100)/100
    frmCalc.Principle.Caption = prin
    frmCalc.TotalPayments.Caption = term
    frmCalc.Payment.Caption = pmt
End Sub
</SCRIPT>
</BODY>
</HTML>
```

The first thing to notice is that each text box has its own `<SCRIPT>` container with the appropriate `FOR` attribute pointing to the control. For example, here are the definition and the event handler for the House Price text box:

```
<TR><TD ALIGN=RIGHT>House Price:</TD>
<TD><INPUT
    TYPE=TEXT
    NAME="Price"
    VALUE="200000"
    SIZE=7>
</TD></TR>
<SCRIPT FOR="Price" EVENT="onChange" LANGUAGE="VBScript">
    Set ctrl = document.MortgageMinder.Price
    If ctrl.Value = "" Then
        alert ("The House Price can't be 0!")
        ctrl.focus
    Else
        CalculatePayment()
    End If
</SCRIPT>
```

This is an `onChange` event handler, so it fires every time the user makes a change to the text box value. The event handler first checks to see if the field is empty. If it is, an `alert` box is displayed, and the focus is returned to the control. Otherwise, the `CalculatePayment` procedure (near the end of the listing) executes to recalculate the mortgage number.

The Calculate button also has an event handler that traps the `onClick` event. In this case, *every* field (except Down Payment) is checked for no value.

Finally, the `CalculatePayment` procedure, shown next, performs the nitty-gritty number crunching. First, the `Value` of each text box is stored in a variable (as well as the Form object). VBScript has no financial functions, so we have to use a formula to calculate the mortgage payment. When that's done, the calculations are stored in the ActiveX labels, and we're done.

```
<SCRIPT LANGUAGE="VBScript">
Sub CalculatePayment
    Set frmCalc = Document.MortgageMinder
    price = frmCalc.Price.Value
    dnpmt = frmCalc.DownPayment.Value
    prin = price - dnPmt
    intRate = (frmCalc.InterestRate.Value/100) / 12
    term = frmCalc.Term.Value * 12
    pmt = int((prin*intRate)/(1-(1+intRate)^(-1*term))*100)/100
    frmCalc.Principle.Caption = prin
    frmCalc.TotalPayments.Caption = term
    frmCalc.Payment.Caption = pmt
End Sub
</SCRIPT>
```

Summary

This chapter began by showing you how to work with the ActiveX Control Pad utility. To help you appreciate what a handy tool the ActiveX Control Pad is, I first went through the syntax of HTML's `<OBJECT>` tag with its ugly `CLASSID` attribute and `<PARAM>` tags. With that safely out of the way, you then learned the much more civilized procedure of using the ActiveX Control Pad to select a control, change its properties, and insert it into your Web page. You also learned about two other components of the ActiveX Control Pad: the HTML Layout control and the Script Wizard.

This chapter also showed you how to use VBScript, a subset of VBA. You first learned about some of the differences between the two languages, especially the elements in VBA that are missing from VBScript (such as the financial functions). I then showed you a couple of methods for inserting VBScript code into an HTML page. From there, we went on a tour of the scripting object hierarchy, including the Window, Document, Navigator, and Form objects. I closed by showing a sample form that demonstrated VBScript's validation and client-side processing capabilities.

Here's where you can find related information:

- The HTML Layout Control is similar to the user forms you work with in the Visual Basic Editor. See Chapter 11, "Working with Microsoft Forms," for details.
- To learn the basics of HTML, see Appendix D, "An HTML Primer."

CHAPTER 22

E-Mail and Groupware Programming with Outlook

IN THIS CHAPTER

It is interaction with others which teaches man all he knows.

—*Euripides*

Users of Office 95 had to rely on two separate tools to manage their electronic lives: Microsoft Exchange—the Windows 95 e-mail client—and Schedule+—the Office address book and time-management program. Although both applications were a large step up from sticky notes and postage stamps, the combination was never satisfying. Why? Well, let me count the ways:

- Although Windows 95's Exchange client was to be admired for its ability to combine multiple e-mail systems and faxing in a single Inbox, it was woefully lacking in features. Items such as message filtering and automatic signatures, although available for years in other clients, were nowhere to be found in Exchange. (However, the client that shipped with Exchange Server was a noticeable improvement.)
- Schedule+ had some interesting and useful features, but it suffered from a clunky interface. And its piggish use of system resources made you reluctant to leave it open all the time—usually a prerequisite for a scheduling tool!
- Exchange and Schedule+ didn't know how to work with each other. For example, they couldn't share a common address book or even exchange addresses via a common file format.
- Neither program was set up to properly handle the groupware services offered by Microsoft Exchange Server.

To solve these problems, Microsoft came up with a new program called Outlook to replace both the Exchange client and Schedule+. Not only does it combine the functionality of Exchange and Schedule+ in a single package, but it also includes a boatload of new features that turn it into a truly useful information management tool. This chapter takes you through a number of methods for taking advantage of Outlook's e-mail and groupware capabilities, on both a forms level and a programming level.

An Introduction to Outlook

In the never-ending quest to straighten out our lives, we've seen no shortage of software solutions, from personal organizers to contact managers to personal information managers. Now, with Outlook, we have yet another category of organizing software: the *desktop information manager*. As its name (but not its unfortunate "DIM" acronym) implies, this new category operates on a more general level than its predecessors. So, yes, you can use Outlook to store names and phone numbers and to set up appointments and remind you of birthdays. But Outlook also offers the following:

- E-mail features integrated throughout
- One-click access to a contact's Web site
- The ability to view and work with disk files and folders

- Full support of the groupware features found in Microsoft Exchange Server
- The ability to track your activities (including the files you work with and the phone calls you make)

Before we get to Outlook's programmable features, here's a quick look at each of the major components in Outlook:

Inbox: This is Outlook's e-mail client. Like Exchange, the Outlook client supports multiple e-mail systems, including Internet Mail, Microsoft Mail, Exchange Server, and the Microsoft Network. However, Outlook goes well beyond Exchange (the Windows 95 version, that is) by offering many advanced features, such as multiple views, message filtering and grouping, rules, and automatic signatures.

Calendar: This is Outlook's scheduling tool. It lets you define both one-time-only and recurring appointments and events. The interface is extremely flexible in that not only does it support the standard daily, weekly, and monthly views, but you can also view any number of days. Also, the new AutoDate feature lets you enter natural-language dates (such as `next Tuesday`) and have them translated into the correct dates. As with Schedule+, you can also have Outlook remind you of upcoming appointments. The Meeting Planner is a handy tool that takes much of the confusion and guesswork out of organizing a large meeting.

Contacts: This folder is a very powerful contacts database. You can track more than 100 fields, including e-mail addresses and Web sites. You can phone contacts using your modem, send e-mail messages, plan meetings, and even surf to Web sites, all within this folder.

Tasks: This is your Outlook "to do" list. Not only can you set up personal tasks, but you can also send task requests via e-mail to other people. If they accept these requests, each person's Tasks folder is updated automatically. For ongoing tasks, the other person can send you status reports that keep you apprised of his or her progress. (Again, Outlook updates the task's status automatically.)

Journal: This is one of Outlook's most interesting features. The Journal is a record of various tasks you've performed, such as sending an e-mail message, making a phone call, or submitting a meeting request. A timeline shows you when you performed each activity. You can also set up Journal to show you when you worked with Office documents and for how long.

Notes: This is Outlook's answer to sticky notes. A Note is a small window in which you enter some text, such as a scrap of conversation, a quotation, or an idea. These Notes are independent of the Outlook window, so you can keep them in view all the time.

Exchange Server support: Outlook fully supports the groupware tools in Exchange Server. This means that you can set up public folders for global contact lists and shared schedules. You also can create newsgroup-like folders in which messages are posted to the folder, not to individuals.

A Summary of Outlook's Programmable Features

When designing Outlook, one of Microsoft's goals was to give as many people as possible the ability to customize the program and take advantage of its dynamic properties. To accomplish this, the designers added many features that let users "program" Outlook without doing any programming (for details, see the next section):

- Changing the folder view
- Sorting messages
- Grouping messages
- Filtering messages
- Defining a custom view
- Using rules to process messages automatically
- Creating public folders

On a slightly higher level, you can gain even more control over Outlook's operation and appearance by getting your hands a little dirtier:

- Create custom forms by modifying any of Outlook's built-in forms (such as Message and Contact).
- Add VBScript code to a form in order to control the form programmatically.
- Incorporate Office 97 documents into Outlook's forms, and then use VBA macros embedded in these documents to control the operation of the form.
- Use Automation to control Outlook's objects from any VBA application.

I'll discuss each of these techniques in detail later in this chapter.

Customizing Outlook Without Programming

Before getting to some hard-core Outlook programming, let's take a quick look at a few features that let users customize and control Outlook without slinging code. Since the focus of this book is programming, the following descriptions are purposefully brief and deal only with the Inbox module. (Most of these techniques can be easily transferred to other modules, such as Calendar and Contacts.)

Changing the Folder View

When you're using the Inbox folder, you'll often need to work with multiple, related messages. For example, you might want to see all the messages from a particular correspondent, or you might want to work with all messages that have the same Subject line (even if there's a "RE:"

or "FW:" tacked on to the beginning). Outlook is particularly strong in this area because, as you'll see in the next few sections, it provides you with a seemingly endless number of ways to manipulate a message list.

We'll begin this section by looking at *views*. A view is just another way of looking at a message list. For example, the Unread Messages view tells Outlook to display only those messages that you haven't opened.

Outlook's default view is Messages with AutoPreview. This view displays each unread message by showing the header information (From, Subject, Received) followed by the first three lines of the message body. This is an excellent feature, but there are nine other predefined views that you might want to try out:

Messages: Displays each message on a single line that shows only the header information.

By Message Flag: Splits the folder into two panes. The top pane shows the messages you've flagged (and the type of flag you've set), and the bottom pane shows the unflagged messages. You also get an extra Message Flag column that tells you the type of flag. This is an example of a message *group*. See "Grouping Items" later in this chapter for more information on grouping.

Last Seven Days: Displays only those messages that you've received in the last week. This is an example of a message *filter*. See "Filtering Items" later in this chapter for more information on filters.

Flagged for Next Seven Days: This view filters the messages to show only those that have been flagged *and* whose flags are due within the next week. (A new Due By column tells you the due date of each flag.)

By Conversation Topic: This view groups the messages according to the "conversation" defined for each message. This applies only to Exchange Server and Microsoft Mail messages. For regular messages, the conversation is the same as the subject. For messages posted to public folders, you can define a topic that is separate from the subject line. See "Instant Groupware: Posting Messages to Public Folders" later in this chapter.

By Sender: This view groups the messages by the name of the person who sent each message.

Unread Messages: This view filters the messages to show only those that haven't yet been read (or marked as read).

Sent To: This view groups the messages by the name of the person to whom each message was sent.

Message Timeline: This unique view, shown in Figure 22.1, displays a timeline that lists the messages you've received underneath the time you received them. The View menu has three commands—Day, Week, and Month—that you can use to customize the timeline. Alternatively, use the following toolbar buttons:

Day (shows messages by day)

Week (shows messages by week)

Month (shows messages by month)

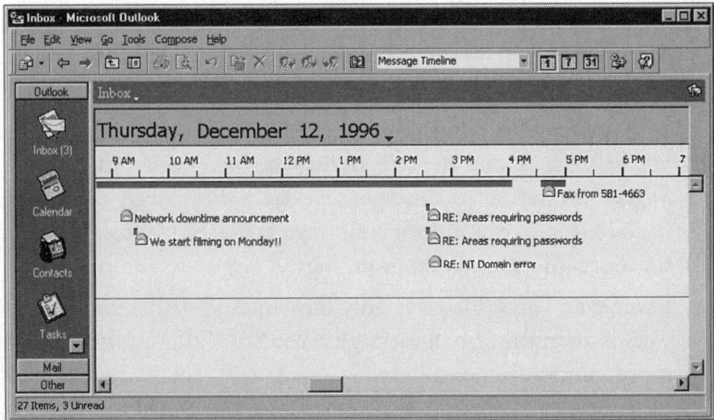

FIGURE 22.1.
The timeline view shows you when you received each message.

To change the view, Outlook gives you two methods:

- Select View | Current View, and then choose the view you want from the cascade menu that appears.

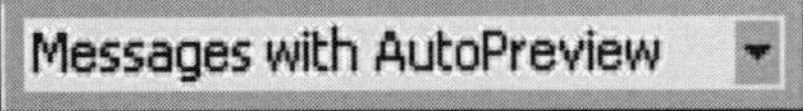

- Use the Current View drop-down list on the toolbar.

TIP: ACTIVATING AUTOPREVIEW

You can access the AutoPreview feature in any of the views, not just Messages by AutoPreview. Either activate the View | AutoPreview command or click the AutoPreview button on the toolbar.

NOTE: CREATING CUSTOM VIEWS

Outlook also lets you define your own views. I'll tell you how to do this after I show you how to sort, filter, and group messages (see the section "Defining a Custom View").

Sorting Items

By default, Outlook sorts the Inbox messages in descending order according to the values in the Received column. Similarly, messages in the Sent Items folder are sorted by the values in the Sent column. But you're free to sort the messages based on any displayed column. Here are the techniques you can use:

- Select View | Sort to display the Sort dialog box, shown in Figure 22.2. Use the Sort items by list to choose the first column you want to use for the sort, use Then by to select a second column, and so on. In each case, activate either Ascending or Descending. Click OK to put the sort order into effect.

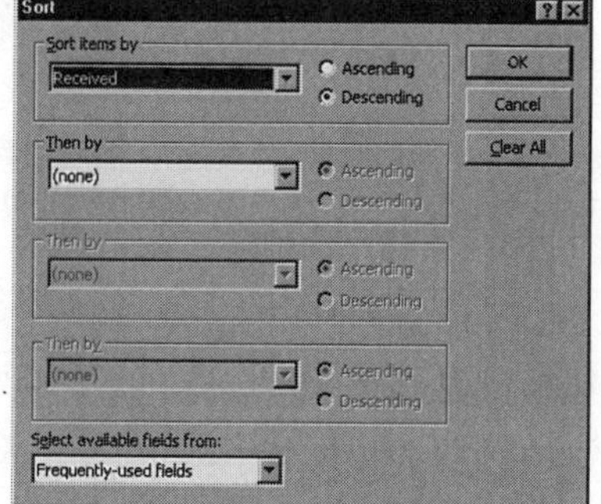

FIGURE 22.2.
Use this dialog box to sort your messages.

- Click the header for the column you want to use for the sort. An arrow appears beside the column name to tell you the direction of the sort (an up arrow for ascending and a down arrow for descending).
- Right-click the header of the column you want to use, and then select either Sort Ascending or Sort Descending from the context menu.

> **NOTE: SORT ORDERS ARE UNIQUE TO EACH FOLDER**
>
> The sort order you choose is unique to the current folder. This is convenient, because it lets you set up different sort orders for different folders.

Grouping Items

You saw earlier that Outlook comes with a few views that group related messages. For example, the By Sender view groups the messages by the name of the person who sent the message. As you can see in Figure 22.3, selecting this view transforms the message list into a display that's reminiscent of the outline views in Word or Excel. In other words, each "group" has a plus sign (+) button beside it. Clicking this plus sign reveals the members of the group.

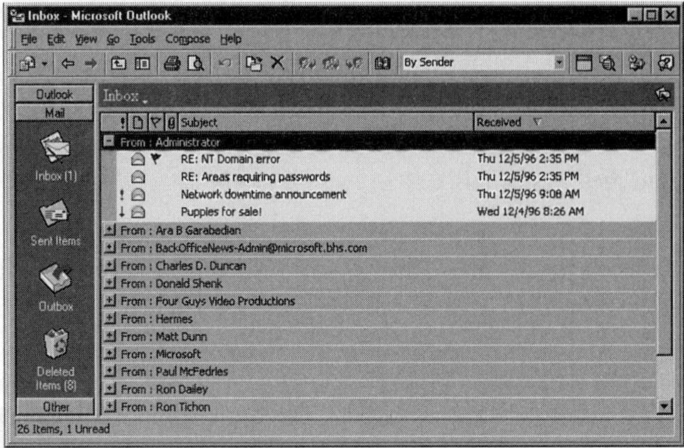

FIGURE 22.3.
The message list grouped by sender.

The big advantage of working with grouped messages is that Outlook treats them as a unit. This means that you can open, move, or delete all the messages in the group with a single operation.

Defining a New Grouping

Although some of the views group messages, they might not be the exact groupings you want to work with. No matter: Outlook is happy to let you define your own groupings. Just follow these steps:

1. Select View | Group By to display the Group By dialog box, shown in Figure 22.4.

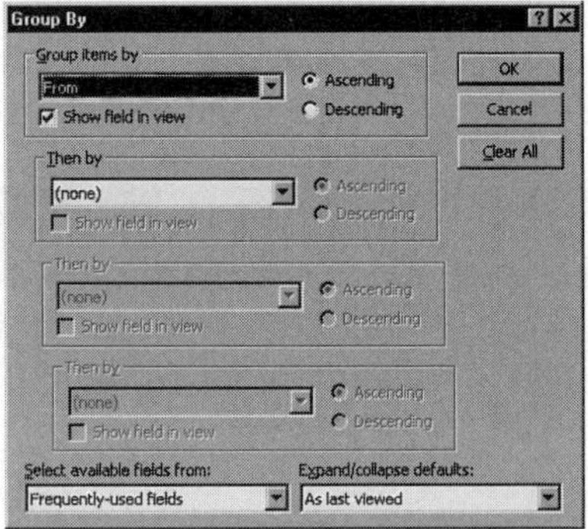

FIGURE 22.4.
Use the Group By dialog box to define a new grouping for the messages.

2. Use the Select available fields from list to choose the category from which you want to select your grouping fields.
3. Use the Group items by list to choose the first field you want to use for the grouping. If you want to include the field as a column, activate the Show field in view check box. You can also activate either Ascending or Descending to sort the groups on this field.

4. To create subgroups, use one or more of the Then by lists to select other fields.
5. The Expand/collapse defaults list determines whether the groupings are displayed expanded (each message in each group is shown) or collapsed (only the groups are shown). You can also choose As last viewed to display the groups as you last had them.
6. Click OK to put the grouping into effect.

Working with the Group By Box

When you group your messages, Outlook adds the Group By box just below the folder banner, as shown in Figure 22.5 (see the button labeled Subject). The button inside the Group By box tells you which field is being used for the grouping. (In Figure 22.5, this is the Subject button.) Here's a summary of the various techniques you can use with the Group By box to adjust your groupings:

- If you don't see the Group By box, either activate the View | Group By Box command or click the Group By Box button on the toolbar.

- Click the field button inside the Group By box to toggle the group sort order between ascending and descending. (In Figure 22.5, for example, you would click the Subject button.)
- To add an existing message list field to the grouping, drag the field's header into the Group By box.
- To add any other field to the Group By box, select View | Field Chooser to display the Field Chooser dialog box, and then drag the field you want to use into the Group By box.
- If you have multiple fields in the Group By box, you can change the subgroupings by dragging the field buttons left or right.
- To remove the grouping, either drag the field button outside the group box or right-click the field button and choose Don't Group By This Field.

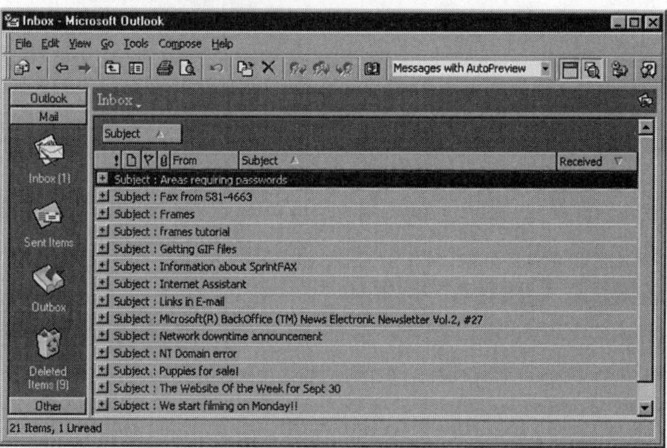

FIGURE 22.5.
You can use the Group By box to work with your groups.

Filtering Items

Grouping messages often makes them easier to deal with, but you're still working with *all* the messages inside the folder. To really knock a message list down to size, you need to *filter* the messages. When we looked at views earlier, you saw that certain views displayed only selected messages. For example, choosing the Last Seven Days view reduced the message list to just those missives that were received in the last week.

As with groups, Outlook makes it easy to design your own filters. You'll soon see that filtering is one of Outlook's most powerful (and potentially complex) features. Yes, you can perform simple filters on field values, but Outlook can take you far beyond these basic filters. For example, you can filter messages based on words or phrases in the subject or body.

To get started, select View | Filter. The Filter dialog box that appears, shown in Figure 22.6, contains three tabs:

Messages: Use the controls in this tab to set message-based criteria. For example, you can enter a word or phrase in the Search for the word(s) text box and select an item from the In drop-down list (for example, `subject field only`). Outlook will filter messages that contain the word or phrase in the chosen item.

More Choices: This tab lets you fine-tune your filter. For example, you can set up a case-sensitive filter by activating the Match case checkbox. You can also filter based on priority, importance, attachments, and size.

Advanced: This tab lets you set up sophisticated criteria for your filter. Use the Field list to choose a field, use the Condition list to select an operator (such as `contains` or `is empty`), and use the Value list to enter a criteria value. Click Add to List to add the criteria to the filter.

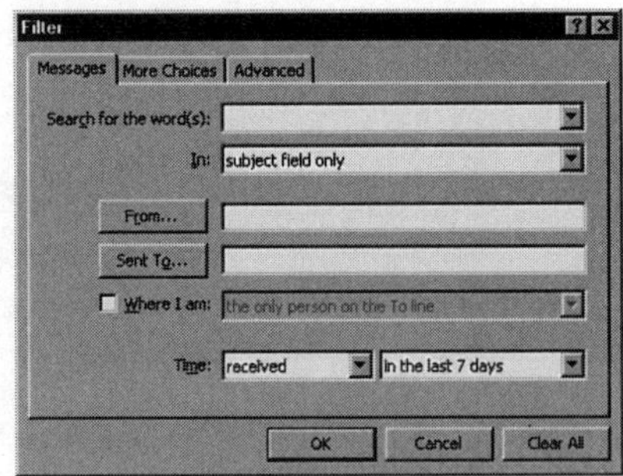

FIGURE 22.6.
Use the Filter dialog box to set up a custom message filter.

Defining a Custom View

If you go to a lot of work to set up a sort order, grouping, or filter, it seems a shame to have to repeat the process each time you want to use the same view. Happily, Outlook lets you avoid that drudgery by letting you save custom sorts, groupings, or filters. In fact, Outlook goes one better by letting you save *combinations* of these views. In other words, you can define a view that includes a sort order, a grouping, and a filter. And, for added convenience, these views are available along with Outlook's predefined views, so they're easy to implement.

Here are the steps to follow to create a custom view:

1. If you want to apply the view to only a specific folder, select the folder.
2. Select View | Define Views to display the Define Views for *Folder* dialog box (where *Folder* is the name of the current folder).
3. Click New. Outlook displays the Create a New View dialog box, shown in Figure 22.7.

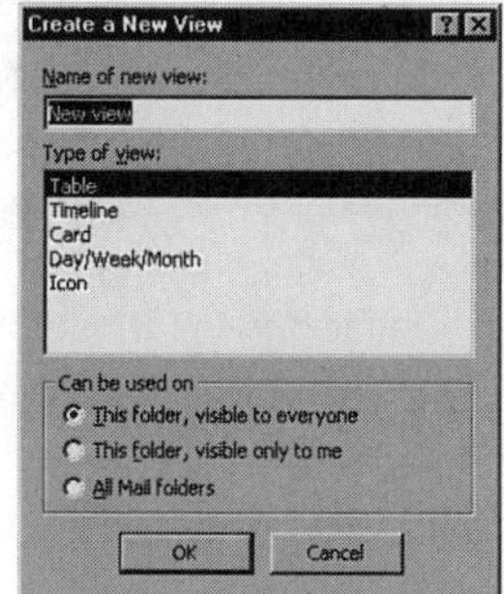

FIGURE 22.7.
Use this dialog box to name your view and choose the view type.

4. Use the Name of new view text box, enter a name for the view you'll be creating, and use the Type of view list to choose the view type. (For a mail folder, this will probably be Table, but feel free to try out some of the others.) Also, use the Can be used on group to select the folders to which the view will apply. Click OK to continue.
5. The View Summary dialog box, shown in Figure 22.8, contains various buttons that let you define the view specifics:

    Fields: Displays the Show Fields dialog box so that you can choose which fields to include in your view.

    Group By: Displays the Group By dialog box so that you can specify a grouping.

    Sort: Displays the Sort dialog box so that you can set up a sort order for the messages.

    Filter: Displays the Filter dialog box so that you can create a message filter for the view.

    Format: Displays the Format dialog box so that you can adjust the view's fonts and other formatting options.
6. Click OK to return to the Define Views dialog box.
7. If you'd like to switch to the new view right away, click Apply View. Otherwise, click Close to return to Outlook.

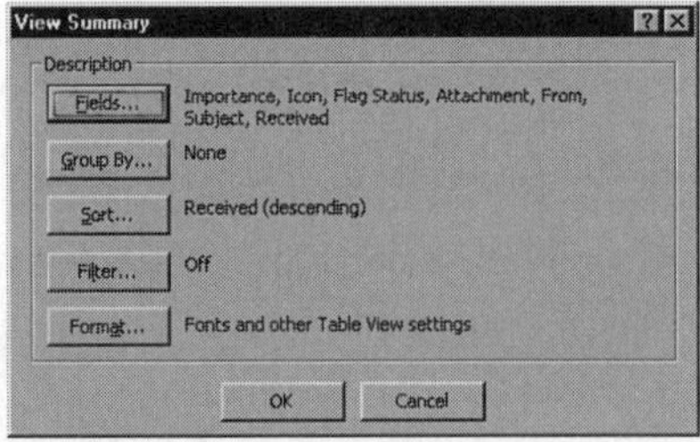

FIGURE 22.8.
Use the buttons in the View Summary dialog box to spell out the particulars of your custom view.

TIP: MODIFY AN EXISTING VIEW

If another view exists that's similar to the custom view you want to create, there's a method you can use to save some time. Rather than creating the new view from scratch, highlight the existing view in the Define Views dialog box, and then click Copy. In the Copy View dialog box that appears, enter a name for the new view and click OK. Outlook will then display the View Summary dialog box so that you can make your adjustments.

Using Rules to Process Messages Automatically

As e-mail becomes a ubiquitous feature on the business (and even home) landscape, you'll find that e-mail chores take up more and more of your time. And I'm not just talking about the three R's of e-mail: reading, 'riting, and responding. Basic e-mail maintenance—flagging, moving, deleting, and so on—also takes up large chunks of otherwise-productive time.

To help ease the e-mail time crunch, Outlook lets you set up "rules" that perform actions in response to specific events. Here are just a few of the things you can do with rules:

- Move an incoming message to a specific folder if the message contains a particular keyword in the subject or body, or if it's from a particular person.
- Automatically delete messages with a particular subject or from a particular person.
- Flag messages based on specific criteria (such as keywords in the subject line or body).
- Have Outlook notify you with a custom message if an important message arrives.
- Have copies of messages you send stored in a specific folder, depending on the recipient.

Clearly, rules are powerful tools that shouldn't be wielded lightly or without care. Fortunately, Outlook comes with an Inbox Assistant that makes the process of setting up and defining rules almost foolproof. (Note, however, that you can use the Inbox Assistant only if you've installed the Exchange Server information service.) To get started, select Tools | Inbox Assistant. In the Inbox Assistant dialog box that appears, click Add Rule. You'll see the Edit Rule dialog box, shown in Figure 22.9.

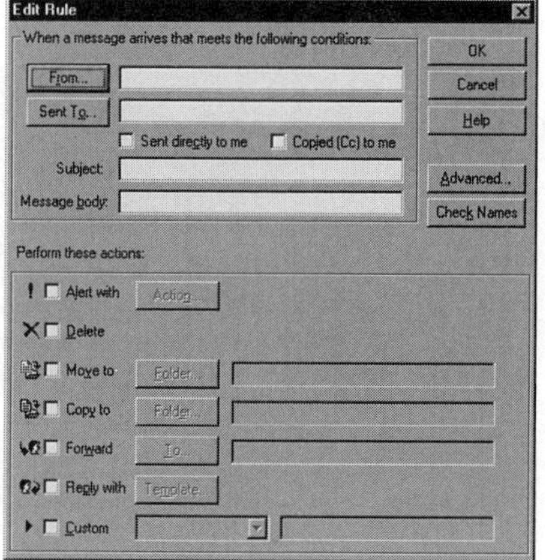

FIGURE 22.9.
Use the Edit Rule dialog box to define a rule.

Your first step is to define the criteria that will cause Outlook to invoke this rule—that is, the conditions an incoming message must meet in order to apply the rule to that message. That's the purpose of the controls in the group called When a message arrives that meets the following conditions:

> From: Use this control to specify one or more e-mail addresses (or click the From button to choose them from the address book). In this case, Outlook will invoke the rule for any message sent from one of these addresses.
>
> Sent To: Use this control to specify the addresses of the message recipients that will invoke the rule. You can also activate the Sent directly to me check box for messages in which your address is on the To line, and you can activate the Copied (Cc) to me check box for messages in which your address is on the Cc line.
>
> Subject: Use this text box to enter a word or phrase that must appear in the Subject line to invoke the rule.
>
> Message body: Use this text box to enter a word or phrase that must appear in the message body to invoke the rule.
>
> Advanced: Clicking this button displays the Advanced dialog box, shown in Figure 22.10. These options control advanced criteria such as the size of the message, the date it was received, the Importance and Sensitivity levels, and more.

Once you've determined *when* the rule will be invoked, you need to specify the *action* that Outlook will perform on the messages that satisfy these criteria. That's the job of the controls in the Perform these actions group:

> Alert with: Activate this check box to have Outlook display a message when the message arrives. Clicking the Action button displays the Alert Actions dialog box, shown in Figure 22.11. You can use this dialog box to specify the message and choose a sound to play.

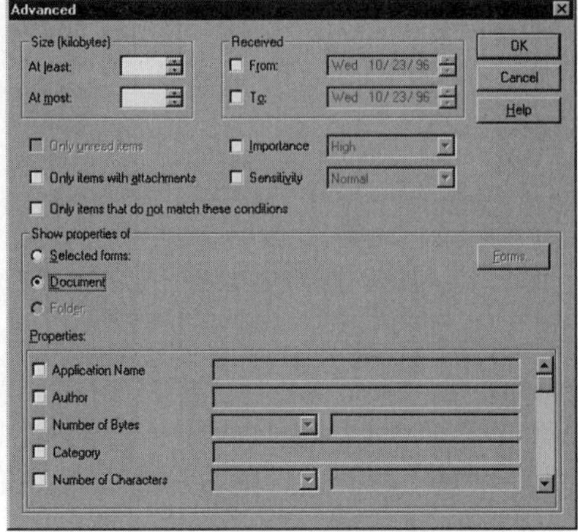

FIGURE 22.10.
Use the Advanced dialog box to set up sophisticated criteria for invoking the rule.

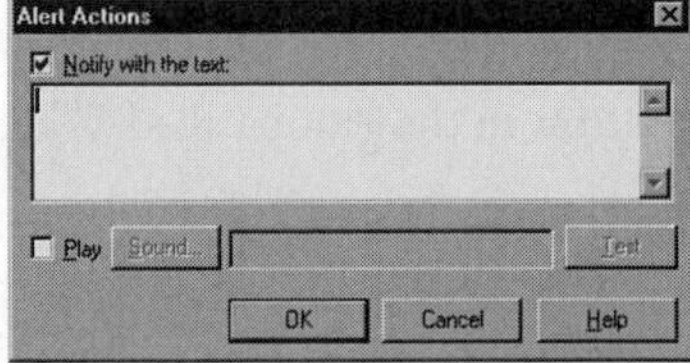

FIGURE 22.11.
Use the Alert Actions dialog box to specify a message to display and a sound to play when the message arrives.

Delete: Activate this check box to delete the message upon arrival.

Move to: Activate this check box to move the message to a folder you specify. You can either type the folder name or click Folder to choose the folder from a dialog box.

Copy to: Activate this check box to copy the message to the specified folder.

Forward: Activate this check box to forward the message. Use the text box to specify one or more recipients, or click the To button to choose names from the address book.

Reply with: Activate this check box to generate a reply message. Click Template to choose a different e-mail template for the reply.

Custom: Activate this check box to apply a custom action to the message (such as an action supplied by a third-party vendor).

When you're done, click OK to add the new rule to the Inbox Assistant, shown in Figure 22.12.

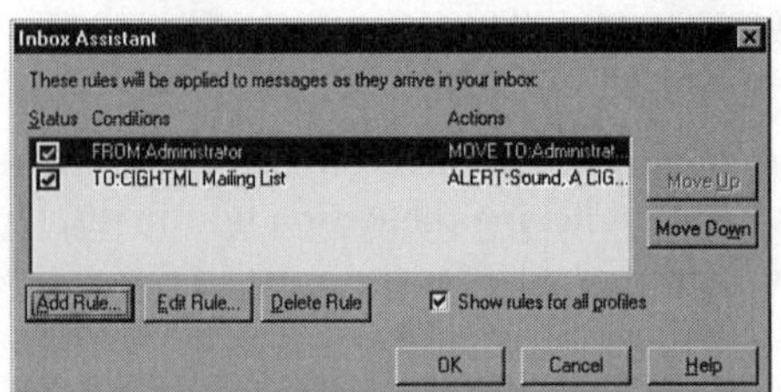

FIGURE 22.12.
The rules you've defined appear in the Inbox Assistant dialog box.

NOTE: RULE MAINTENANCE

You can use the Inbox Assistant dialog box to maintain your rules. For example, each rule you've defined has a checkbox beside it that toggles the rule on and off. You can change a rule by highlighting it and clicking Edit Rule. To get rid of a rule, highlight it and click Delete Rule.

Instant Groupware: Posting Messages to Public Folders

E-mail systems that operate under the aegis of Microsoft Exchange Server can have public folders that are accessible to each client on the system—assuming, that is, that these clients have installed Outlook's Microsoft Exchange Server information service. When you open the Folder List (by selecting View | Folder List), you'll see a folder named Public Folders. This is the Exchange Server container for all the public folders. In particular, this folder contains a subfolder named All Public Folders in which users can create new public folders. Figure 22.13 shows some examples.

FIGURE 22.13.
Exchange Server public folders are accessible to all clients on the network.

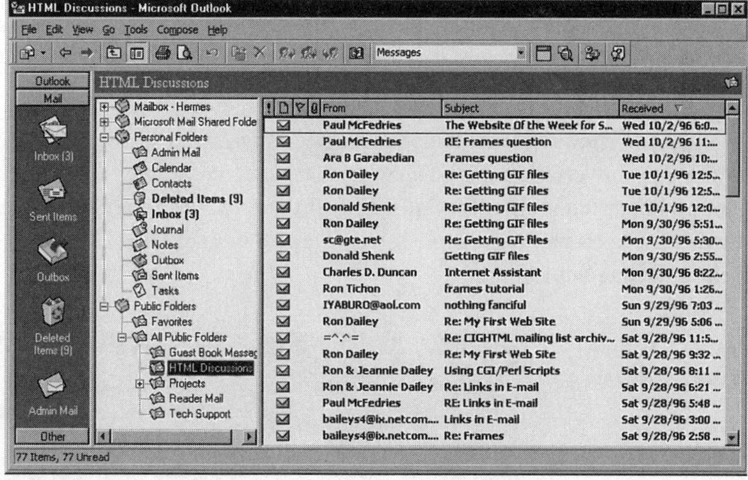

NOTE: MODIFYING ITEMS IN PUBLIC FOLDERS

When you're working with public folders and the messages they contain, the general rule is that you can modify only items that you created yourself. For example, if you create a public folder, only you can move, rename, or delete it. Similarly, you can modify messages in someone else's public folder only if you posted those messages yourself.

continues

continued

However, Outlook gives the owner of each public folder a mechanism for adjusting permissions and other properties. Right-click your folder and choose Properties from the context menu. The properties sheet that appears gives you numerous options for setting up user permissions, defining the operation of the folder, and more.

Public folders are a convenient way to share e-mail among a group of users, but they can act as more than just common storage areas. Specifically, you can use a public folder to set up "conversations" between users. In this sense, a public folder becomes more like a Usenet newsgroup. Instead of sending a message to one or more e-mail recipients, you "post" the message to the folder. Others can then read the message and post replies in the same folder. A group of related posts is called a *conversation.*

Posting a message is more or less the same as composing an e-mail message. Here are the differences:

- To post a new message to a public folder, display the folder and select Compose | New Post in This Folder (or press Ctrl-Shift-S). In the message composition window that appears, enter a subject and the message, and then click Post.
- To post a reply to a message in a public folder, highlight the message and then select Compose | Post Reply in This Folder. Again, enter a subject and the message, and then click Post.

Figure 22.14 shows a public folder with a few conversations going. In this example, I've switched to the By Conversation Topic view so that you can see how Outlook groups conversations. Notice, in particular, that Outlook differentiates between the Conversation field and the Subject field. This is handy, because it lets you post messages to a particular conversation, yet still write a unique Subject line.

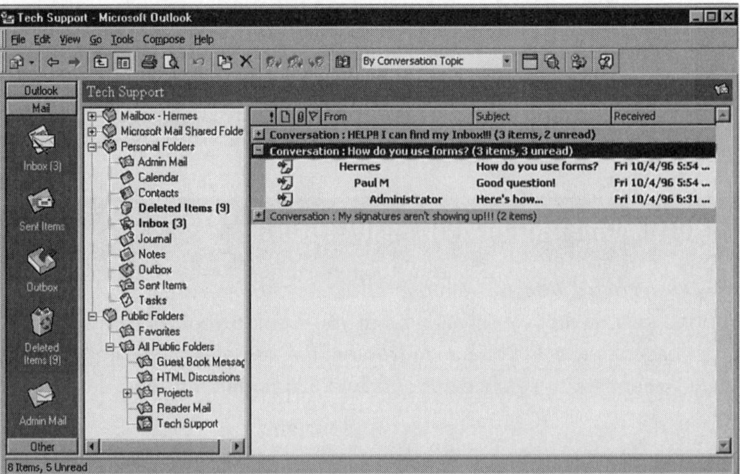

FIGURE 22.14.
A public folder with several ongoing conversations.

Public folders are useful for more than just e-mail. For example, if you'd like to give other people access to your schedule, Outlook lets you create public Calendar folders on Microsoft Exchange Server systems. This lets people on your network check your schedule to see when you're free or busy, which might help them schedule their own meetings and appointments.

Public Calendar folders (which, like e-mail folders, you create in the Public Folders area of your Exchange Server system) are set up by default as read-only for everyone but yourself. You can change this by setting permissions on the folder. (Highlight the folder and select File | Folder | Properties. In the properties sheet that appears, use the Permissions tab to modify the access privileges for the folder.)

Note, however, that you don't need to set up a public Calendar folder to use Outlook's group scheduling features. That's because rudimentary information about your schedule is "published" on the server as you enter and adjust appointments. This information includes the times of your appointments and whether you've designated that time as "free" or "busy." Outlook uses this so-called *free/busy information* when you're requesting or planning a meeting.

Creating Custom Outlook Forms

Much of what you do in Outlook—from writing an e-mail message to adding a contact to planning a meeting—involves working with a form. For example, selecting Compose | New Mail Message while working in a mail folder produces the Message form, shown in Figure 22.15. You fill in the fields and click Send, and Outlook creates and sends an e-mail message.

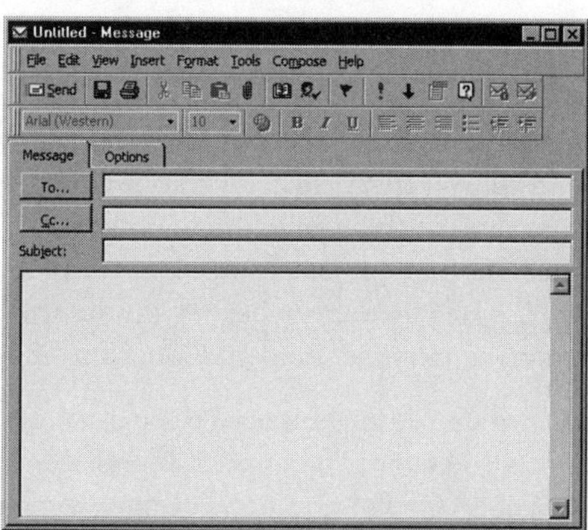

FIGURE 22.15.
Working with Outlook often involves working with forms.

If you need to design groupware or messaging applications in Outlook, the good news is that all of the built-in Outlook forms are completely customizable. You can remove fields you don't need, add new fields and controls, and even set up validation rules for any field. For example, Figure 22.16 shows a "phone message" form that was customized from the standard Outlook Message form. This new form still sends an e-mail message, but it now includes extra fields and controls that deal specifically with phone message data. Significantly, the new form inherits the underlying functionality of the original form, which in this case means that e-mail capabilities are built right into the new form.

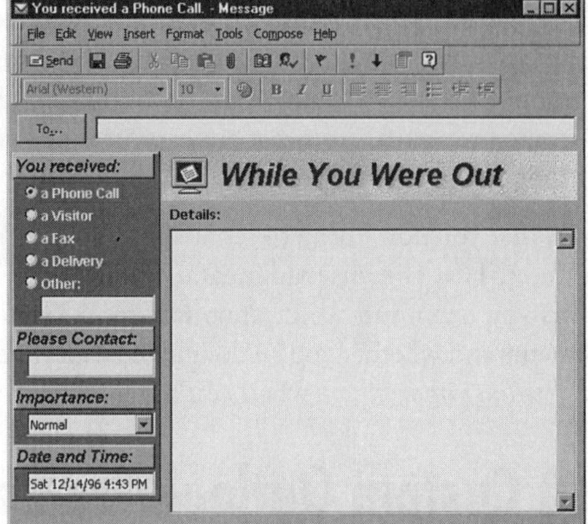

FIGURE 22.16.
A customized version of the Message form that e-mails a phone message.

Best of all, you already know how to use Outlook's Form Designer because it's almost identical to the forms module in the Visual Basic Editor (which I described in Chapter 11, "Working with Microsoft Forms"). The next few sections show you how to use the Forms Designer to create and work with custom forms.

Displaying the Forms Designer

Unlike the forms you create in the Visual Basic Editor, you don't start custom Outlook forms from scratch. Instead, you always begin with one of Outlook's built-in forms and modify it to suit your needs. So the first thing you need to decide is which of Outlook's standard forms you want to use as the basis for your new form. For example, if you'll be using your form to e-mail information, you'll probably want to begin with the standard Message form. Similarly, if you want to gather contact data, the standard Contact form is the place to start.

Once you've decided on a form, you need to open it. (Selecting File | New and then choosing a form from the cascade menu that appears is probably the easiest way to go.) With the form on-screen, select Tools | Design Outlook Form to switch to the Forms Designer window. Figure 22.17 shows the Forms Designer displaying a standard Message form.

NOTE: OFFICE DOCUMENT FORMS

Rather than customizing an existing Outlook form, you can wrap an Office document inside a form by selecting File | New | Office Document. You can then edit the document as needed.

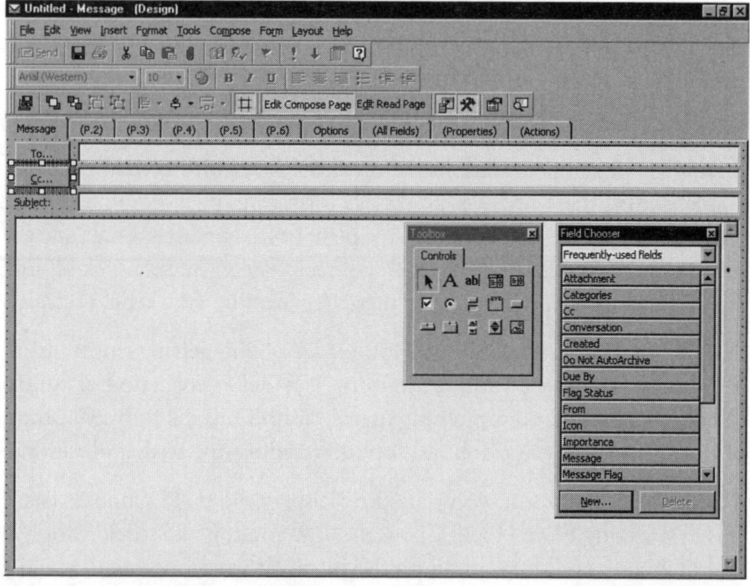

FIGURE 22.17.
Use the Forms Designer to customize any of Outlook's standard forms.

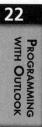

NOTE: SAVING THE CUSTOM FORM

Since it's likely that you'll want to reuse your custom form, you should save it to disk. Just select File | Save As and use the Save As dialog box to choose a location and name for the .OFT (Outlook Form Template) file. For easiest access to the file, make sure you save it in the \Microsoft Office\Templates\Outlook folder.

To use the file later, you have several choices:

- If you saved the file with the other Outlook templates, select New | File | Choose Template, choose the file from the Choose Template dialog box that appears, and click OK.
- If you saved the file in a different location, use Explorer to find the file and then double-click it.
- The .OFT file format is independent of Outlook in the sense that you can display these files without having an Outlook session running. So, for example, you can set up a link to an .OFT file in an intranet Web page. When the user clicks the link, the form appears.

Adding Fields and Controls

The bulk of the Forms Designer window is taken up by the design grid. As with user forms created in the Visual Basic Editor, you use this grid to lay out the fields and controls for the data you need. Note, however, that although you can use the terms "field" and "control" interchangeably in the Visual Basic Editor, they have specific meanings in the Forms Designer.

Working with Fields

A *field* is a predefined Outlook object that comes with certain characteristics built in. For example, adding the To field to a Message form gives you a command button and a text box. The command button lets users choose a recipient from the address book, and the text box either displays the chosen addresses or lets the user add recipient addresses by hand. Either way, when the user clicks the form's Send button, the message is sent to the To field recipients automatically.

This seems pretty standard until you realize you're getting this built-in functionality for free. Recall from Chapter 11 that a user form is a lifeless collection of controls until you add event handlers to make it do something useful. With Outlook, however, the event handlers are part of the package, so you can build sophisticated form-based applications with no coding.

To add fields to a form, you must first display the Field Chooser (see Figure 22.17). You do this by selecting Form | Field Chooser. Now you can add a field simply by dragging it from the Field Chooser and dropping it on the form. (If you don't see the field you want, try selecting a different field set using the drop-down list that appears at the top of the Field Chooser.)

When laying out your fields, keep these points in mind:

- The Forms Designer has a nice feature called AutoLayout that removes much of the drudgery of laying out fields. When you drop a field onto a form, AutoLayout checks to see if there is already a field above the one you just added. If there is, AutoLayout will automatically align the new field with the left side of the existing field. To take advantage of this convenience, make sure that the Layout | AutoLayout command is activated.
- The Layout menu is stuffed with many other layout-related commands and cascade menus that let you align and size fields, group and ungroup fields, work with the grid, and adjust the tab order. I covered all of these commands in Chapter 11.

Creating Custom Fields

The Forms Designer lets you create custom fields. The advantage here is that, once again, you can get some built-in functionality for free. For example, one of Outlook's most interesting features is its ability to accept natural-language entries in date and time fields and convert these entries into real dates and times. If today is October 7th, for example, entering `next week` in a date field will cause Outlook to enter October 14th as the date. If you create a custom date field, this AutoDate functionality is built right in.

Here are the steps to follow to create a custom field:

1. In the Field Chooser, click New to display the New Field dialog box, shown in Figure 22.18.

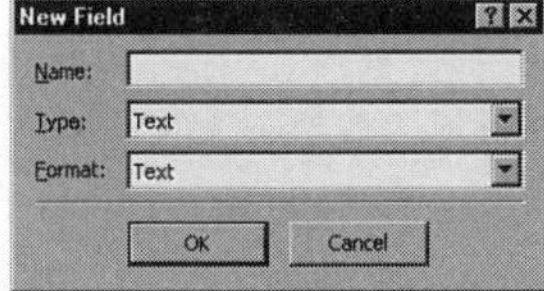

FIGURE 22.18.
Use the New Field dialog box to create a custom field object.

2. Use the Name text box to enter a name for the new field.
3. Use the Type drop-down list to choose the type of data that will be entered into the field.
4. Use the Format drop-down list to specify how you want the field data to appear.

NOTE: FORMULA FIELDS

If you choose either Combination or Formula in the Type list, the Format drop-down list changes to the Formula text box. You use combination fields to combine multiple fields into a single piece of data. You use formula fields to create expressions that return values.

In either case, click the new Edit button that appears and use the Formula Field dialog box to construct a formula. See the section titled "Validation Properties" to learn more about constructing formulas.

5. Click OK to create the field.

To use your custom field, select the User-defined fields item from the Field Chooser's drop-down list, and then add your field from there.

Working with Controls

A *control* can be one of the standard dialog box objects—such as a text box, label, check box, or list—or it can be an ActiveX control. Although you might get some built-in functionality with an ActiveX control, the standard dialog box controls are just empty shells that require some coding to bring to life. (See "Controlling Forms Via VBScript" later in this chapter.)

To work with controls, you use the same Control Toolbox that you learned about in Chapter 11 (see Figure 22.17). To display the Toolbox, activate the Form | Control Toolbox command. From here, you click the control you want and then drag within the form to define the object's size and shape.

If you want to use an ActiveX control or some other control installed on your system, move the mouse pointer into the Control Toolbox, right-click an empty area in the Controls tab, and click Custom Controls. In the Additional Control dialog box that appears, activate the check box beside each control you want to add to the Toolbox, and then click OK.

NOTE: TRYING OUT THE FORM

As you work with a custom form, keep in mind that you can "test drive" the form at any time by deactivating the Tools | Design Outlook Form command. This takes you out of the Forms Designer and displays the form as the user will see it.

Working with Object Properties

Once you've added a field or control to the form, you can customize the object's look and feel by working with its properties. To display the properties sheet for an object, either click the object and select Form | Properties, or right-click the object and select Properties from the shortcut menu. Figure 22.19 shows the dialog box that Outlook displays. The next three sections take you through each of the three tabs in this dialog box.

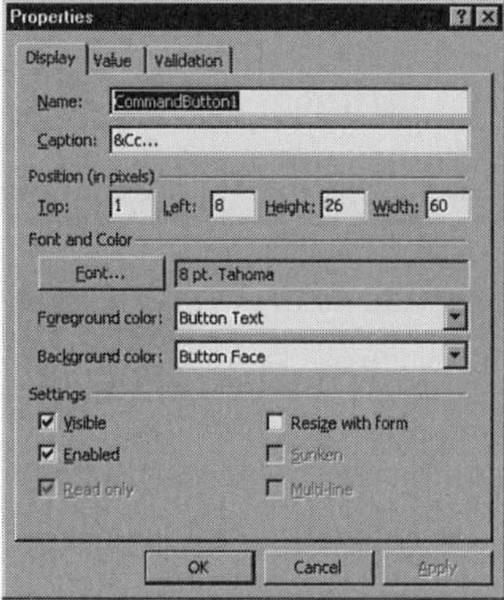

FIGURE 22.19.
Use this properties sheet to set up a field or control.

Display Properties

The Display tab contains various options for controlling the look of the field or control. Here's a summary:

Name: Assigns a name to the object.

Caption: Sets the text to display beside the object. This property is available only for certain controls (such as command buttons and check boxes. To assign an accelerator key to the object, place an ampersand (&) before the letter you want to use.

Position: Specifies the position and size of the object in pixels.

Font and Color: The Font button sets the font of the object text, and the two drop-down lists set the foreground and background colors.

Visible: Activate this check box to make the object visible to the user.

Enabled: Activate this check box to allow the user to work with the object.

Read only: Activate this check box to prevent the user from making changes to the object's contents. Note that this isn't the same as activating the Enabled check box. For example, if you make a recipient text box read-only, the user can still highlight the text and right-click the text to work with a displayed address.

Resize with form: Activate this check box to force Outlook to change the control's size (that is, the width) in relation to the current size of the form.

Sunken: Activate this check box to make the control appear as though it's sunken into the form.

Multi-line: Activate this check box to make a text box accept multiple lines of data.

Value Properties

The Value tab, shown in Figure 22.20, contains options that let you specify the type of data to display in a field or control and the initial value of the object. Here's the rundown:

Choose Field: Associates a field with the object. If the object isn't a built-in Outlook field, a New button also appears so that you can create a new field.

Type: Tells you the type of information that the object will show. This box is read-only.

Format: Specifies a format for the data.

Property to use: Specifies which of the object's properties Outlook will display in the field. For controls, this is usually set to the `Value` property.

Value: Determines the value displayed in the field, depending on what you specify in the Property to use option.

Set the initial value of this field to: Activate this check box to have Outlook enter an initial value into the field. You can enter a specific value into the text box provided, or you can click Edit to construct a formula (see the next section).

Calculate this formula when I compose a new form: Tells Outlook to display the initial value only when a new form is created based on this template.

Calculate this formula automatically: Tells Outlook to display the initial value whenever this form is displayed.

Validation Properties

In Chapter 11 you saw how you can use event handlers to examine the data the user entered into a control, and to validate the data. For example, you might want to check that a month value is between 1 and 12 or that a dollar amount is a positive number. Although coding event handlers is still the best way to validate data, the Validation tab, shown in Figure 22.21, gives you some quick-and-dirty options for checking input values:

A value is required for this field: Activate this check box to force the user to enter a value into the field. If the user fails to enter a value, Outlook displays an error message when the user attempts to close, save, or send the form.

Validate this field before closing the form: Activate this check box to have Outlook run a validation check on the field whenever the user attempts to close, save, or send the form. Use the two text boxes described next to set up the validation.

Validation Formula: Specifies the formula Outlook must use when validating the field data. Click Edit to construct a formula (described in a moment).

Display this message if the validation fails: Specifies a message to display to the user if the data he enters doesn't match the validation criterion. If you leave this text box blank, Outlook displays a generic `The data you entered for "Field" is not valid` message (where *Field* is the name of the field).

Include this field for Printing and Save As: Activate this check box to include the field when the user prints the form data or when he uses Save As to save the form under a different name.

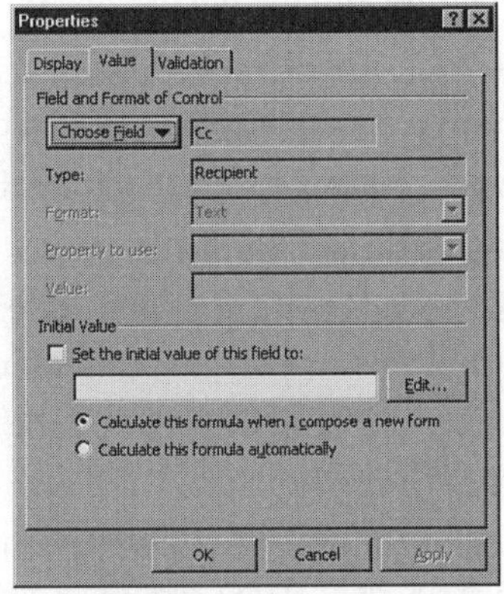

FIGURE 22.20.
Use the Value tab to specify the type of data that will be entered into the form.

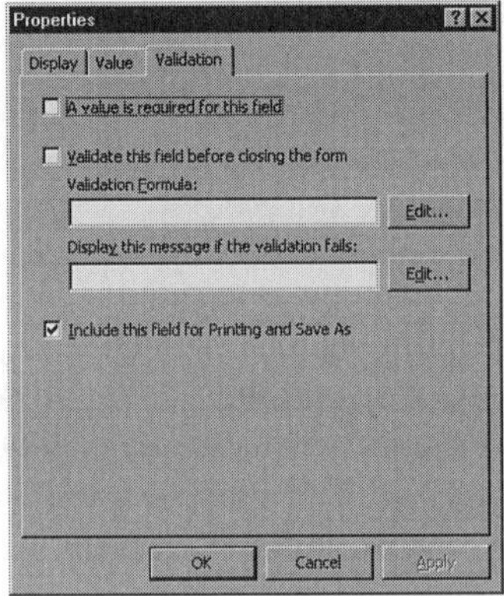

FIGURE 22.21.
Use the Validation tab to set various options for checking the data entered into the field.

You've seen in several places that Outlook lets you design a formula for use in a custom field, an initial field value, or a validation criterion. In each case, you click an Edit button to display a dialog box that lets you construct a formula, as shown in Figure 22.22. Here are the steps to follow to use this dialog box to build a formula:

1. Use the Formula text box to enter the expression you want to use. You do this by combining operands with the same arithmetic, comparison, and logical operators I outlined in Chapter 3, "Building VBA Expressions."
2. If you'd like to include a field in your expression, click the Field button, choose a Field category, and choose a field name.
3. If you'd like to include one of Outlook's built-in functions in your expression, click the Function button, choose a Function category, and choose a function name.
4. Click OK.

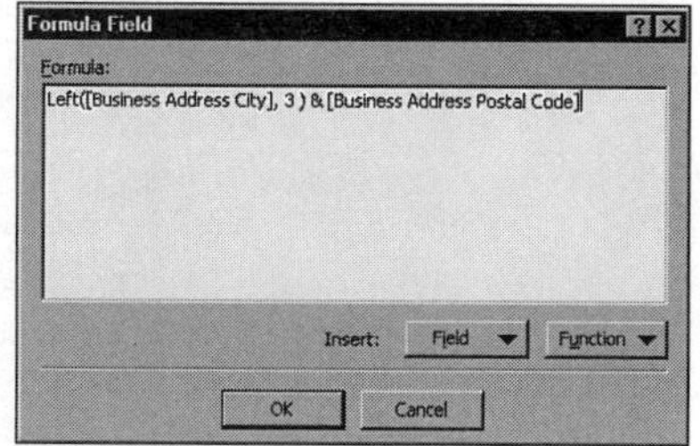

FIGURE 22.22.
Use the Formula Field dialog box to construct a formula to display in a custom field.

Advanced Properties

As you learned in Chapter 11, controls have a number of properties that you can set at design time. I covered many of these properties in the preceding sections, but by no means all of them. To see a complete list of the available properties, either click the object and select Form | Advanced Properties, or right-click the object and select Advanced Properties from the shortcut menu. Figure 22.23 shows an example of the properties sheet that appears (for a command button, in this case). As you can see, this window is identical to the Properties window that you're used to seeing in the Visual Basic Editor.

Working with Form Pages

Just below the toolbars, the Forms Designer displays a series of tabs. These tabs represent the pages that are part of the form, which the user can display by clicking a tab. When you're customizing a form, click a tab to add objects to and remove objects from the page. Here's a quick rundown of a few techniques you can use when working with these pages in the Forms Designer:

- The parentheses around a tab's name indicate that Outlook won't display the page when the user opens the form.
- To allow the user to display a page, click the page and then activate the Forms | Display This Page command. Deactivating this command will prevent Outlook from displaying the page.

- To change the name of the current page, select Forms | Rename Page, enter the new name in the Rename Page dialog box that appears, and click OK.
- To set a page's advanced properties, either click an empty section of the page and select Form | Advanced Properties, or right-click the page and select Advanced Properties from the shortcut menu.
- If you'd like to specify different layouts for filling in the form and for reading the sent form data, activate the Form | Separate Read Layout command. To switch between the compose and read layouts, click the Edit Compose Page and Edit Read Page buttons on the toolbar.

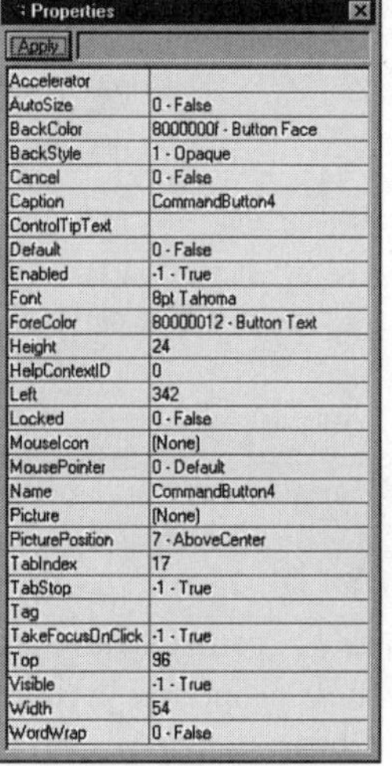

FIGURE 22.23.
The Advanced Properties command displays a complete list of the properties available for an object.

Setting Form Properties

So far, you've seen techniques for setting properties at the field, control, and page levels. However, the Forms Designer also defines a number of properties at the form level. To see these properties, activate the (Properties) page, as shown in Figure 22.24. Here's a summary of the available controls (note that the number of enabled controls depends on the type of form you're customizing):

Form Caption: Enter the form name that will be used when you publish the form in a forms library (see "Publishing a Form" later in this chapter).

Version: Enter the current version number of the form. Use this value to keep track of different versions of the form. Once you've published the form, the version number also appears when users highlight the form in the forms library.

Form Number: Enter a number for the form.

Category: Use this combo box to enter or select a category to use when publishing the form. As you'll see later, users can choose to view the forms in a forms library by category.

Sub-Category: Use this combo box to enter or select a subcategory to use when publishing the form. For example, if you're using Human Resources as the main category, you might use Personnel as a subcategory.

Always use Microsoft Word as the e-mail editor: For message forms, activate this check box to force any new messages based on this form to use WordMail as the editor. Click the Template button to select the default template that Word should load.

Contact: Click this button to specify the name of the person who should be contacted if a user has a question or comment about the form.

Description: Enter a description of the form.

Change Large Icon: Click this button to choose the icon to display when the user views the form templates in Large Icons view.

Change Small Icon: Click this button to choose the icon to display when the user views the form templates in Small Icons view.

Protect form design: If you activate this check box, Outlook displays the Password dialog box so that you can specify a password for the form's design. When the user selects Tools | Design Outlook Form, he must enter the correct password in order to view the form in the Forms Designer.

Save form definition with item: When this check box is activated, Outlook saves the entire form definition with every item that is created using the form. Deactivate this check box if you plan on publishing the form to a forms library. In this case, Outlook stores the form definition only in the library.

Use form only for responses: If you activate this check box, this form will be used only when the user is responding to a message.

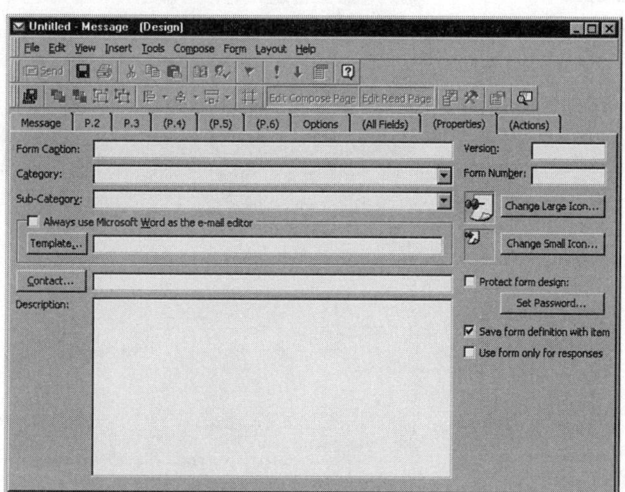

FIGURE 22.24.
Use the (Properties) page to set various form-level properties.

Specifying Form Actions

When someone receives a form, there are usually a number of actions he can take. With an e-mail message, for example, he can reply to the sender, reply to all the recipients, forward the message, and so on.

To specify the available actions for your custom form, activate the (Actions) page in the Form Designer. Figure 22.25 shows the default actions that are defined for a Message form. To create a new action, click the New button to display the Form Action Properties dialog box, shown in Figure 22.26, and then fill in the following information:

Action name: Enter the name of the action.

Form name: Use this combo box to specify the form that you want to appear when the user selects this action.

When responding: For messages, use this drop-down list to determine what you want Outlook to do with the original message.

Address form like a: Use this drop-down list to specify how you want addresses to appear in the new form.

Show action on: Activate this check box to give the user access to the action on both the menu tree and the toolbar or only on the menu.

This action will: Use these options to determine what happens when the user selects this action.

Subject prefix: For a message, use this text box to specify text that is added to the beginning of the Subject text.

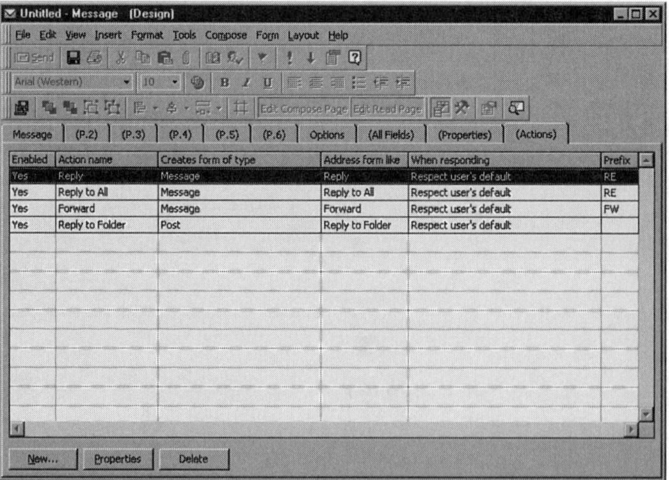

FIGURE 22.25.
The (Actions) page defines the available actions for a form.

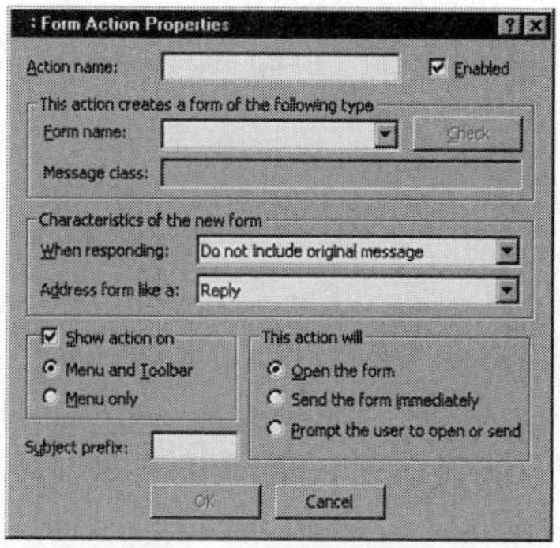

FIGURE 22.26.
Use this dialog box to define a custom action for your form.

When you're done, click OK to add your action. You can get rid of an existing action by selecting it and clicking Delete. To make changes to an existing action, select the action and click Properties.

Publishing a Form

Although others can still use your form if you save the .OFT file to a shared folder, it's more convenient to publish the folder to a public Exchange Server folder. Here are the steps to follow:

1. Select File | Publish Form As to display the Publish Form As dialog box, shown in Figure 22.27.

FIGURE 22.27.
Use this dialog box to specify a form name and a forms library.

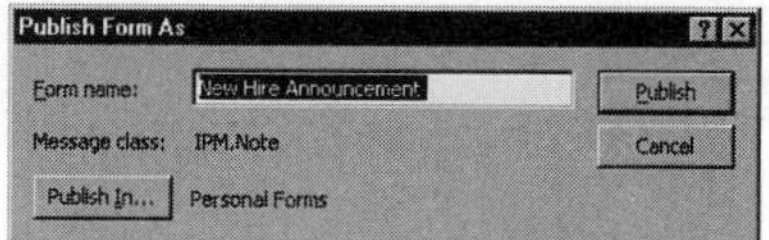

2. The text that appears in the Form name box is the same as the text you entered into the Form Caption box in the (Properties) page. Change the name if necessary.
3. By default, Outlook publishes custom forms in the forms library named Personal Forms. If you want to publish the form in a different location, click the Publish In button, and then use the Set Library To dialog box to choose either another forms library or a folder.
4. Click Publish.

Automation and the Outlook Object Model

As you've seen, Outlook has an amazing number of options for customizing objects without forging any code. These options were designed for end-users who lack programming skills, as well as for developers who need to get low-level applications up to speed quickly. However, this is a programming book, so I assume not only that you have programming skills, but also that you'll eventually need to create higher-level Outlook applications. So I'll spend the rest of this chapter showing you how to build programmability into Outlook, both indirectly (by using VBA to control Outlook's Automation interface) and directly (by using VBScript in a form).

Before we get down to the brass tacks of Outlook programming, however, we need to examine Outlook's object model. This will give you an idea of the kinds of objects you can manipulate and how you can manipulate them. Throughout the rest of this section, I'll introduce you to the object model and show you how to use this model to work with Outlook via Automation in your VBA applications.

NOTE: OUTLOOK AUTOMATION SETUP

As always when dealing with Automation, your first chore is to set up a reference to the required object library in your VBA project. In this case, highlight your project and select Tools | References in the Visual Basic Editor, activate the check box beside Microsoft Outlook 8.0 Object Library in the Available References list, and click OK.

Also note that this chapter assumes that you're familiar with Automation concepts. If you aren't, you might want to read Chapter 15, "Controlling Applications Via OLE Automation," before continuing.

The `Application` Object

The top-level object in the Outlook hierarchy is the `Application` object. You use this object to return information about the current Outlook session and to gain access to the rest of the Outlook hierarchy. To establish an Automation connection with this object, you use the `CreateObject` function. For example, the following statements establish an early binding connection to Outlook:

```
Dim ol As Outlook.Application
Set ol = CreateObject("Outlook.Application")
```

The `Application` object has four second-level objects:

Assistant: This is a property of the `Application` object, and it returns an Assistant object that represents the Microsoft Office Assistant. (This object is common to all the Microsoft Office application hierarchies.)

Explorer: This object references the window in which Outlook is displaying a folder's contents. See "The Explorer Object."

Inspector: This object references the window in which Outlook is displaying an item's contents. See "The Inspector Object."

NameSpace: This object acts as a sort of "abstract root" object for the Outlook application. See "The NameSpace Object."

The NameSpace Object

You use the NameSpace object to log on and off, return information about the current user, and more. To return a NameSpace object, you use the `GetNameSpace` method with the `MAPI` argument (which is the only argument currently supported by this method). Here's an example:


```
Dim ol As Outlook.Application
Dim ns As NameSpace
Set ol = CreateObject("Outlook.Application")
Set ns = ol.GetNameSpace("MAPI")
```

Logging On to a MAPI Session

Once you have the NameSpace object, you can log on to establish a MAPI session by invoking the `Logon` method:

NameSpace`.Logon(`*`Profile, Password, ShowDialog, NewSession`*`)`

NameSpace	The NameSpace object.
Profile	The name of the Outlook profile to use in the MAPI session.
Password	The password used with the profile.
ShowDialog	A `Boolean` value that determines whether or not Outlook displays the Logon dialog box. Use `True` to display the dialog box.
NewSession	A `Boolean` value that determines whether or not Outlook creates a new MAPI session. Set this argument to `True` to start a new session; use `False` to log on to the current session.

For example, the following statement logs on to a MAPI session using the `Windows Messaging Settings` profile (assuming that the current NameSpace is represented by a variable named `ns`):

```
ns.Logon "Windows Messaging Settings"
```

Logging Off a MAPI Session

When you've completed your labors in a MAPI session, you can log off by running the NameSpace object's `Logoff` method:

NameSpace`.Logoff`

NameSpace	The NameSpace object.

Working with MAPIFolder Objects

The NameSpace object also acts as a root folder for all the Outlook folders. This means you can use it to return a reference to a folder and then work with that folder. Note that in the Outlook object model, folders are MAPIFolder objects.

One way to return a MAPIFolder object is to use the `GetDefaultFolder` method, which returns the default folder for a given type in the current profile. Here's the syntax:

NameSpace`.GetDefaultFolder(`*`FolderTypeEnum`*`)`

NameSpace	The NameSpace object.
FolderTypeEnum	A constant that specifies the type of folder. You can use any of the following defined constants: `olFolderCalendar`, `olFolderContacts`, `olFolderDeletedItems`, `olFolderInbox`, `olFolderJournal`, `olFolderNotes`, `olFolderOutbox`, `olFolderSentMail`, and `olFolderTasks`.

Alternatively, you can use the `Folders` property to return a `Folders` object that represents all of the MAPIFolder objects in the namespace. To reference a specific folder, use `Folders(`*`Index`*`)`, where *`Index`* is either an integer value—where the first folder is 1—or the name of a folder—such as `Folders("Public Folders")`.

Listing 22.1 shows a procedure that enumerates the first- and second-level folders in the namespace. (The second-level folders are derived by using the `Folders` property of the MAPIFolder object. The name of each folder is displayed in the Visual Basic Editor's Immediate window (activate the View | Immediate Window command to see the results; check out Chapter 24, "Debugging VBA Procedures," for more information).

Listing 22.1. A procedure that enumerates the first- and second-level folders in the Outlook namespace.

```
Sub EnumerateFolders()
    Dim ol As Outlook.Application
    Dim ns As NameSpace
    Dim folder As MAPIFolder, subfolder As MAPIFolder
    '
    ' Establish a connection and log on
    '
    Set ol = CreateObject("Outlook.Application")
    Set ns = ol.GetNamespace("MAPI")
    ns.Logon
    '
    ' Run through the first-level folders
    '
    For Each folder In ns.Folders
        Debug.Print folder.Name
        '
        ' Run through the second-level folders, if any
        '
        If folder.Folders.Count > 1 Then
            For Each subfolder In folder.Folders
                Debug.Print "   " & subfolder.Name
```

```
            Next 'subfolder
        End If
    Next 'folder
    '
    ' Log off the session
    '
    ns.Logoff
    Set ol = Nothing
End Sub
```


NOTE: THIS CHAPTER'S CODE LISTINGS

The code listings for this chapter are, as usual, on the CD. I used Excel for this chapter, so the listings are in a workbook named Chaptr22.xls. If you don't have Excel, you can open Chaptr22.bas instead.

The Explorer Object

As I mentioned earlier, the Explorer object represents the window Outlook is using to display a folder's contents. There are two ways to return an Explorer object:

Application.`ActiveExplorer`: This method returns an Explorer object that represents the currently displayed window for the specified Outlook *`Application`* object. If no window is currently displayed, this method returns `Nothing`.

MAPIFolder.`GetExplorer`: This method returns an Explorer object that represents a new window for the specified *`MAPIFolder`*. Here's the syntax:

MAPIFolder`.GetDefaultFolder(`*DisplayMode*`)`

MAPIFolder	The MAPIFolder object.
DisplayMode	A constant that determines how the Explorer object will display the folder. You have the following choices:

DisplayMode	*Description*
`olFolderDisplayFolderOnly`	Displays only the folder contents and the folder banner.
`olFolderDisplayNoNavigation`	Displays the folder contents and the folder banner without access to the folder list.
`olFolderDisplayNormal`	Displays the folder contents, folder banner, and Outlook bar.

Here are some Explorer object properties and methods:

> *Explorer*.CommandBars: Returns the CommandBars collection, which represents the CommandBar objects associated with the specified *Explorer* object. (See Chapter 12, "Creating Custom Menus and Toolbars," to learn more about command bars.)
>
> *Explorer*.CurrentFolder: Returns or sets a MAPIFolder object that represents the folder associated with the specified *Explorer* object.
>
> *Explorer*.Close: Closes the window associated with the specified *Explorer* object.
>
> *Explorer*.Display: Displays the window associated with the specified *Explorer* object.

Listing 22.2 shows a procedure that checks for an existing Explorer object and creates a new Explorer if one doesn't exist (that is, if the ActiveExplorer method returns Nothing).

Listing 22.2. A procedure that logs on to a MAPI session and then displays an Explorer object.

```
Sub DisplayDefaultInboxFolder()
    Dim ol As Outlook.Application
    Dim ns As NameSpace
    Dim folder As MAPIFolder
    Dim exp As Explorer
    '
    ' Establish a connection and log on
    '
    Set ol = CreateObject("Outlook.Application")
    Set ns = ol.GetNamespace("MAPI")
    ns.Logon
    '
    ' Get the default Inbox folder and set the Explorer
    '
    Set folder = ns.GetDefaultFolder(olFolderInbox)
    Set exp = ol.ActiveExplorer
    '
    ' If no folder is displayed, create a new one and display it
    '
    If exp Is Nothing Then
        Set exp = folder.GetExplorer(olFolderDisplayNoNavigation)
        exp.Display
    End If
    Set ol = Nothing
End Sub
```

The Inspector Object

When you open an Outlook item (such as an e-mail message or a contact), the window in which the item appears is an Inspector object. As with the Explorer object, there are two ways to return an Inspector object:

> *Application*.ActiveInspector: This method returns an Inspector object that represents the currently displayed item window for the specified Outlook *Application* object. If no window is currently displayed, this method returns Nothing.

`Item.GetExplorer`: This property returns an Explorer object that represents a new window for the specified `Item`. (See the next section for details.)

The properties and methods of the Inspector object are similar to those of the Explorer object. Here's a summary of a few of the most useful members of this class:

`Inspector.CommandBars`: Returns the `CommandBars` collection, which represents the CommandBar objects associated with the specified `Inspector` object.

`Inspector.CurrentItem`: Returns or sets an Item object that represents the item associated with the specified `Inspector` object.

`Inspector.ModifiedFormPages`: Returns a `Pages` object that represents the various tabs in the specified `Inspector` object.

`Inspector.Close`: Closes the window associated with the specified `Inspector` object.

`Inspector.Display`: Displays the window associated with the specified `Inspector` object.

`Inspector.HideFormPage`: Hides a form page in the specified *Inspector* object. Here's the syntax:

```
Inspector.HideFormPage(PageName)
```

`Inspector`	The Inspector object you want to work with.
`PageName`	The name of the page you want to hide.

`Inspector.IsWordMail`: Returns `True` if the specified `Inspector` object uses WordMail; returns `False` otherwise.

`Inspector.SetCurrentFormPage`: Displays a page in the specified `Inspector` object:

```
Inspector.SetCurrentFormPage(PageName)
```

`Inspector`	The Inspector object you want to work with.
`PageName`	The name of the page you want to display.

`Inspector.ShowFormPage`: Makes a previously hidden page visible in the specified `Inspector` object. Here's the syntax:

```
Inspector.ShowFormPage(PageName)
```

`Inspector`	The Inspector object you want to work with.
`PageName`	The name of the page you want to show.

Working with Item Objects

Once you've logged on to a MAPI session and have referenced the MAPIFolder object you want to work with, you can use the `Items` collection to deal with the various items in the folder. This section discusses the various types of items available and shows you how to create new ones.

Types of Item Objects

Depending on the type of folder you're using, the `Items` collection will contain one or more of the objects listed in Table 22.1. In each case, you can return an item by using `Items(Index)`, where *`Index`* is either an integer (where the first item in the folder is 1) or a value from the default property listed in Table 22.1.

Table 22.1. Outlook's item object types.

Item	*Default Property*	*Description*
AppointmentItem	`Subject`	This object represents an appointment or meeting in a Calendar folder.
ContactItem	`FullName`	This object represents a contact in a Contacts folder.
JournalItem	`Subject`	This object represents a journal entry in a Journal folder.
MailItem	`Subject`	This object represents a mail message in an Inbox folder. (Note that the Inbox folder type represents any mail folder, not just the Inbox folder.)
NoteItem	`Subject`	This object represents a note in a Notes folder.
TaskItem	`Subject`	This object represents a task in a Tasks folder.

NOTE: RETURNING AN ITEM'S TYPE

Table 22.1 lists the main item types, but there are also five other types you'll come across: MeetingRequestItem, PostItem, RemoteItem, ReportItem, and TaskRequestItem. Since these types often coexist with other types in a single folder, you often need to know what type of item you're dealing with. To find this out, use the `TypeName(Item)` function, where *`Item`* is the item object you're working with.

A Closer Look at MailItem Objects

Each of the item object types listed in Table 22.1 has dozens of properties and methods, which is a reflection of the tremendous attention to detail that characterizes the Outlook product. Rather than going through each property and method for each item object (which would probably double the size of this book), I'll use this section to examine the object you'll probably use the most in your VBA applications: the MailItem object.

MailItem Object Properties

The MailItem property boasts more than 60 different properties that cover everything from the message recipients to the assigned sensitivity. Here's a list of the most useful MailItem properties:

`MailItem.AlternateRecipientAllowed`: Returns `True` if the specified `MailItem` can be forwarded; returns `False` otherwise. You can also set this property.

`MailItem.Attachments`: Returns the `Attachments` object—the collection of all attached files—for the specified `MailItem`. Use the `Attachments` object's `Add` method to add an attachment to a message:

```
mItem.Attachments.Add "C:\My Documents\Memo.doc"
```

`MailItem.BCC`: Returns the display names (separated by semicolons) of the addresses listed as blind courtesy copy recipients for the specified `MailItem`. See the description of the `Recipients` property to learn how to add e-mail addresses to a message.

`MailItem.Body`: Returns or sets the body text for the specified `MailItem`.

`MailItem.CC`: Returns the display names (separated by semicolons) of the addresses listed as courtesy copy recipients for the specified `MailItem`. See the description of the `Recipients` property to learn how to add e-mail addresses to a message.

`MailItem.ConversationIndex`: Returns the index of the conversation thread associated with the specified `MailItem`.

`MailItem.ConversationTopic`: Returns the topic of the conversation thread associated with the specified `MailItem`.

`MailItem.CreationTime`: Returns the date and time that the specified `MailItem` was created.

`MailItem.DeferredDeliveryTime`: Returns or sets the date and time that the specified `MailItem` is to be delivered.

`MailItem.ExpiryTime`: Returns or sets the date and time that the specified `MailItem` is to expire.

`MailItem.Importance`: Returns or sets the importance level for the specified `MailItem`. This property can be one of the following constants: `olImportanceHigh`, `olImportanceLow`, or `olImportanceNormal`.

`MailItem.ReadReceiptRequested`: Returns `True` if the sender has requested a read receipt for the specified `MailItem`; returns `False` otherwise.

`MailItem.ReceivedTime`: Returns or sets the date and time that the specified `MailItem` was received.

`MailItem.Recipients`: Returns a `Recipients` object—the collection of recipients—for the specified `MailItem`. You use the `Recipients` object's `Add` method to add new recipients to a message:

MailItem`.Recipients.Add(`***Name***`)`

MailItem	The message to which you want to add the recipient.
Name	The recipient's e-mail address. If the recipient is in the address book, you can just use the display name.

To determine the message line to which the recipient will be added (To, Cc, or Bcc), set the `Type` property of the new recipient. Use `olTo` for the To line, `olCC` for the Cc line, or `olBCC` for the Bcc line. For example, assuming that `newMessage` is an object variable that represents a MailItem, the following statements add two recipients—one on the To line and one on the Cc line:

```
newMessage.Recipients.Add("Biff").Type = olTo
newMessage.Recipients.Add("bob@weave.com").Type = olCC
```

MailItem`.SaveSentMessageFolder`: Returns or sets the MAPIFolder object in which a copy of the specified *MailItem* will be saved once it has been sent.

MailItem`.SenderName`: Returns the display name of the sender of the specified *MailItem*.

MailItem`.Sensitivity`: Returns or sets the sensitivity level of the specified *MailItem*. This property can be one of the following constants: `olConfidential`, `olNormal`, `olPersonal`, or `olPrivate`.

MailItem`.SentOn`: Returns the date and time that the specified *MailItem* was sent.

MailItem`.Size`: Returns the size of the specified *MailItem* in bytes.

MailItem`.Subject`: Returns or sets the subject line of the specified *MailItem*.

MailItem`.To`: Returns the display names (separated by semicolons) of the addresses listed in the To line of the specified *MailItem*. See the discussion of the `Recipients` property to learn how to add e-mail addresses to a message.

MailItem`.UnRead`: Returns `True` if the specified *MailItem* has not been read; returns `False` otherwise. You can also set this property.

MailItem`.VotingOptions`: Returns or sets the voting options (separated by semicolons) for the specified *MailItem*.

MailItem`.VotingResponse`: Returns or sets the voting response for the specified *MailItem*.

Listing 22.3 shows a procedure that logs on to a MAPI session, runs through the items in the default Inbox folder, and records the `SenderName`, `Subject`, `Size`, `ReceivedTime`, and the first 100 characters of the `Body` onto a worksheet. (Note the use of VBA's `TypeName` function, described earlier, which makes sure that we only work with MailItem objects.)

Listing 22.3. A procedure that reads Inbox data into a worksheet.

```
Sub ReadInboxData()
    Dim ol As Outlook.Application
    Dim ns As NameSpace
    Dim folder As MAPIFolder
```

```
    Dim ws As Worksheet
    Dim i As Integer
    '
    ' Establish a connection and log on
    '
    Set ol = CreateObject("Outlook.Application")
    Set ns = ol.GetNamespace("MAPI")
    ns.Logon
    '
    ' Get the default Inbox folder and
    ' set the Receive Mail worksheet
    '
    Set folder = ns.GetDefaultFolder(olFolderInbox)
    Set ws = Worksheets("Receive Mail")
    '
    ' Run through each item in the Inbox
    '
    For i = 1 To folder.Items.Count
        '
        ' Make sure we only grab MailItems
        '
        If TypeName(folder.Items(i)) = "MailItem" Then
            With folder.Items(i)
                '
                ' Record the sender, subject, size,
                ' received time, and some of the body
                '
                ws.[A1].Offset(i, 0) = .SenderName
                ws.[A1].Offset(i, 1) = .Subject
                ws.[A1].Offset(i, 2) = .Size
                ws.[A1].Offset(i, 3) = .ReceivedTime
                ws.[A1].Offset(i, 4) = Left(.Body, 100)
            End With
        End If
    Next 'i
    '
    ' Log off the session
    '
    ns.Logoff
    Set ol = Nothing
End Sub
```


Creating a New MailItem Object

When you need to send an e-mail message, you first need to create a new MailItem object. You do this by invoking the `Application` object's `CreateItem` method:

`Application``.CreateItem(`***`ItemType`***`)`

`Application`	An Outlook `Application` object.
`ItemType`	A constant that specifies the type of item you want to create. For a MailItem, use `olMailItem`. The other constant values you can use are `olAppointmentItem`, `olContactItem`, `olJournalItem`, `olNoteItem`, `olPostItem`, and `olTaskItem`.

Listing 22.4 shows a sample procedure that creates a new MailItem object; uses data from an Excel worksheet to set the MailItem object's recipient, subject, and body; and sends the message.

Listing 22.4. A procedure that uses worksheet data to send an e-mail message.

```
Sub SendFromWorksheet()
    Dim ol As Outlook.Application
    Dim ns As NameSpace
    Dim ws As Worksheet
    Dim newMessage As MailItem
    '
    ' Establish a connection and log on
    '
    Set ol = CreateObject("Outlook.Application")
    Set ns = ol.GetNamespace("MAPI")
    ns.Logon
    '
    ' Data is in the Send mail worksheet
    '
    Set ws = Worksheets("Send Mail")
    '
    ' Create the new MailItem
    '
    Set newMessage = ol.CreateItem(olMailItem)
    '
    ' Specify the recipient, subject, and body
    ' and then send the message
    '
    With newMessage
        .Recipients.Add ws.[B2]
        .Subject = ws.[B3]
        .Body = ws.[B4]
        .Send
    End With
    '
    ' Log off the session
    '
    ns.Logoff
    Set ol = Nothing
End Sub
```

MailItem Object Methods

With the methods available to the MailItem object, you can send messages, reply to and forward messages, move messages to a different folder, and more. Here's a summary of some of the MailItem object methods:

MailItem.Close: Closes the Inspector object in which the specified *MailItem* object is displayed. This method uses the following syntax:

***MailItem*.Close(*SaveMode*)**

MailItem The MailItem object you want to work with.

SaveMode	A constant that determines how the Inspector is closed:	
	`olDiscard`	Closes the Inspector without saving changes.
	`olPromptForSave`	Prompts the user to save changes.
	`olSave`	Saves changes automatically.

`MailItem.Copy`: Creates a copy of the specified `MailItem` object.

`MailItem.Delete`: Deletes the specified `MailItem` object.

`MailItem.Display`: Displays the specified `MailItem` object in a new Inspector using the following syntax:

```
MailItem.Display(Modal)
```

MailItem	The MailItem object you want to work with.
Modal	Use `True` to make the Inspector a modal window; use `False` for a nonmodal window.

`MailItem.Forward`: Forwards the specified `MailItem` object. This method returns a new MailItem object that represents the message to be forwarded.

`MailItem.Move`: Moves the specified `MailItem` object to a different folder using the following syntax:

```
MailItem.Move(DestFldr)
```

MailItem	The MailItem object you want to work with.
DestFldr	The MAPIFolder object to which you want to move the message.

`MailItem.PrintOut`: Prints the specified `MailItem` object.

`MailItem.Reply`: Replies to the sender of the specified `MailItem` object. This method returns a new `MailItem` object that represents the reply to be sent.

`MailItem.ReplyAll`: Replies to all the recipients of the specified `MailItem` object. This method returns a new `MailItem` object that represents the reply to be sent.

`MailItem.Save`: Saves the specified `MailItem` object.

`MailItem.SaveAs`: Saves the specified `MailItem` object under a different name or path using the following syntax:

```
MailItem.SaveAs(Path, Type)
```

MailItem	The MailItem object you want to work with.	
Path	The path to which you want to save the MailItem.	
Type	A constant that specifies the file type you want to use:	
	`olDoc`	Word format (*.doc)
	`olMsg`	Message format (*.msg)

`olRTF`	Rich text format (*.rtf)
`olTemplate`	Outlook template format (*.oft)
`olTxt`	Text-only format (*.txt)

`MailItem``.Send`: Sends the specified *`MailItem`* object.

Controlling Forms Via VBScript

When I showed you how to work with VBScript in the preceding chapter, the context for our code was a Web page. In particular, you saw that many of the advantages that VBScript brings to the table are realized when you're working with an HTML form embedded in a Web page. These advantages included the ability to produce dynamic forms that respond to events and to validate form data before submission to a server.

However, VBScript is no one-trick pony. You can realize the same advantages that VBScript applies to Web forms when you're working with Outlook forms. That's because Microsoft designed Outlook forms to handle VBScript procedures that can work directly with form objects and respond to form events. This lets you add dynamic characteristics to your forms and allows you to go well beyond the relatively simple validation features that are implemented as object properties (and that we discussed earlier in this chapter). This section shows you how to implement VBScript in your custom Outlook forms.

Adding Scripts to a Form

To let you attach scripts to a form, the Forms Designer has a Script Editor feature. This is a simple text editor in which you write your VBScript event handlers, functions, and procedures. To open the Script Editor, make sure you're in the Forms Designer, and then select Form | View Code. Figure 22.28 shows the Script Designer window with some VBScript code already added.

Bear in mind that the Script Editor doesn't have the fancy IntelliSense features that you might have grown to depend on in the Visual Basic Editor. There are no syntax colors, no popup hints, no case adjustments, and no automatic syntax checks. If you'd prefer to have these features around in order to keep your code on the straight and narrow, you might consider building your VBScripts in the Visual Basic Editor and then transferring them to the Script Editor when you're ready to try them. If you go this route, however, make sure you use only the language elements that are part of the VBScript subset. (I reviewed the differences between VBScript and VBA in Chapter 21, "Web Page Programming: ActiveX and VBScript.")

VBScript and the Form Object

Since your VBScripts exist at the form level, it makes sense that they'll spend much of their time manipulating either the form itself or one of the fields or controls defined on the form. This section examines how VBScript interacts with the form. I'll discuss fields and controls a bit later.

FIGURE 22.28.
Use the Form Designer's Script Editor to create your VBScript procedures.

```
' This event handler runs whenever the user reads the item. The procedure updates the
' custom ReadCounter property, which monitors the number of times the item has been read.
'
Function Item_Read()
    '
    ' Increment the current value
    '
    Item.UserProperties.Item("ReadCounter").Value = _
        Item.UserProperties.Item("ReadCounter").Value + 1
    '
    ' Save now to avoid the user being prompted to save changes unnecessarily
    '
    Item.Save
End Function
'
' This event handler fires when the item is opened. The procedure displays the number
' of times the item has been read.
'
Function Item_Open()
    '
    ' Don't display the message if we've just created the item (i.e., the ReadCounter
    ' property is still 0).
    '
    If Item.UserProperties.Item("ReadCounter").Value <> 0 Then
        MsgBox "This item has been read " & _
               Item.UserProperties.Item("ReadCounter").Value & _
               " times."
    End If
End Function
```

In all your VBScript procedures, you use the `Item` keyword to reference the form object. This makes sense, because a form is really a particular variation on the Outlook item theme, be it a MailItem, ContactItem, or whatever. Therefore, all of the properties and methods that are native to the type of item you're working with are fair game inside your VBScript routines. In a MailItem form, for example, `Item.Save` saves the form, `Item.Send` sends the form, and `Item.Close` closes the form.

Form Events

The `Item` keyword gives you access not only to a form's properties and methods, but also to any one of the many events that are associated with the item. Most item events are common to all the item types. They cover actions such as reading the item, sending the item, and closing the item.

To add an event handler stub procedure to the Script Editor, select Script | Event to display the Events dialog box, shown in Figure 22.29. Highlight the event you want to work with, and then click Add.

FIGURE 22.29.
Use the Events dialog box to select the event you want to handle.

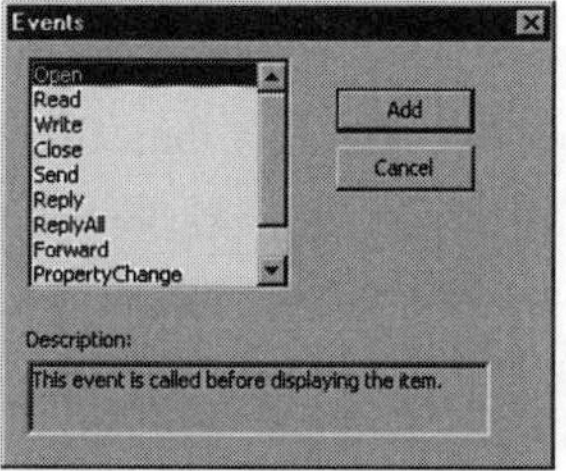

The Script Editor inserts a stub procedure with the following general structure:

```
Function Item_Event(Arguments)
End Function
```

Here, `Event` is the name of the event you highlighted, and `Arguments` is a set of one or more arguments that are passed to the procedure. (Note that many of the event handlers have no arguments at all.) As usual with these procedure stubs, you define the event handler by adding code between the `Function` and `End Function` statements.

Here's a rundown of the various events you can trap:

`Close`: This event fires when the user closes the item or when your code invokes the `Close` method.

TIP: CANCELING EVENTS

All of Outlook's event handlers are implemented as Function procedures. This means that you can cancel any event by setting the function's return value to `False`. To cancel the `Close` event, for example, you would add the following statement to the event handler:

```
Item_Close = False
```

`CustomAction`: This event fires when the user or your code runs a custom action. This procedure uses the following syntax:

```
Item_CustomAction(ByVal Action, ByVal NewItem)
```

Action	The custom action.
NewItem	The new item that is created in response to the custom action.

`CustomPropertyChange`: This event fires when the user or your code changes the value of a custom control. Here's the syntax:

```
Item_CustomPropertyChange(ByVal Name)
```

Name	The name of the custom property.

I'll discuss custom properties in more detail when I discuss working with controls in your VBScript procedures. See the next section.

`Forward`: This event fires when the user forwards the item or when your code invokes the `Forward` method. Here's the syntax:

```
Item_Forward(ByVal ForwardItem)
```

ForwardItem	The new item that will be forwarded.

`Open`: This event fires when the user opens the item. Note that this event fires after the `Read` event (discussed in a moment).

`PropertyChange`: This event fires when the user or your code changes the value of a standard item property (such as `Subject` or `To`). Here's the syntax:

```
Item_PropertyChange(ByVal Name)
```

Name	The name of the property.

`Read`: This event fires when the user displays the item for editing in an Inspector or displays the item in a view that allows in-cell editing. This event fires before the `Open` event.

`Reply`: This event fires when the user replies to the item or when your code invokes the `Reply` method. Here's the syntax:

```
Item_Reply(ByVal Response)
```

Response	The new reply item.

`ReplyAll`: This event fires when the user replies to all or when your code invokes the `ReplyAll` method. Here's the syntax:

```
Item_ReplyAll(ByVal Response)
```

Response	The new reply item.

`Send`: This event fires when the user sends the item or when your code invokes the `Send` method.

`Write`: This event fires when the user saves the item or when your code invokes the `Save` or `SaveAs` method.

Working with Controls (Custom Properties)

As you've seen, working with an item's standard properties is straightforward. You can either return or set the `Item` object's properties, or you can trap changes to the standard properties by writing a handler for the `PropertyChange` event. (For the latter, the event handler passes the name of the property, so you could set up a series of `If...Then` statements or even a `Select Case` structure to handle the various possibilities.)

However, you can also define custom properties for an item. These properties generally are nonfield controls—such as text boxes and check boxes—that you add to the form using the Control Toolbox. To define the control as a custom property of the form, follow these steps:

1. Click the control and select Form | Properties.
2. In the Properties dialog box that appears, activate the Value tab.
3. Click New to display the New Field dialog box, shown in Figure 22.30.

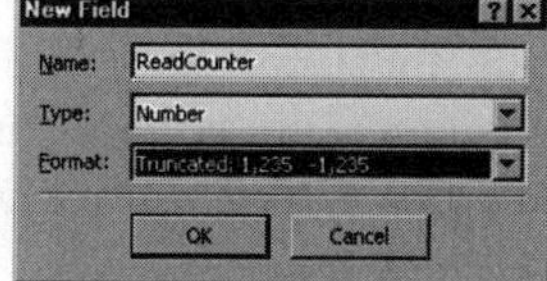

FIGURE 22.30.
Use the New Field dialog box to define the particulars of a custom property.

4. Use the Name text box to enter a name for the custom property.
5. Use the Type and Format lists to select a data type and data format for the property.
6. Click OK to return to the Properties dialog box.
7. If you also want to trap events for the control, activate the Display tab and enter a meaningful name for the control in the Name text box. (Note that this is only the name of the control; the name you entered in step 4 is the name of the custom property.)
8. Click OK.

With the custom property now defined, it becomes a UserProperty object for the item. `UserProperties` is the collection of all UserProperty objects in an item. You use this collection to reference a specific custom property, like so:

```
Item.UserProperties.Item("Name")
```

Here, *`Name`* is the name you specified for the custom property (in step 4).

For example, the following statement returns the value of the `ReadCounter` custom property:

```
Item.UserProperties.Item("ReadCounter").Value
```

Also recall that you can trap a change to any custom property by setting up a handler for the Item object's `CustomPropertyChange` event. Again, the event handler passes the name of the property so that your code can test for different properties.

Finally, you can also trap certain events for custom controls. If you add a command button or a check box, for example, you can trap the `Click` event. To do this, create a stub procedure with the following structure:

```
Sub ControlName_Event()
End Sub
```

Here, *`ControlName`* is the name of the control (see step 7 in the preceding procedure), and *`Event`* is the event you want to trap. The following example traps the `Click` event for a command button:

```
Sub CommandButton1_Click()
   [event handler code goes here]
End Sub
```

Summary

This chapter showed you various methods for setting up groupware and e-mail applications with Outlook. After a brief introduction to Outlook and its programmable features, I showed you a number of techniques for customizing Outlook without having to resort to code. These techniques included changing the view, sorting, grouping, filtering, custom views, and rules. From there, I showed you how to create custom Outlook forms, including working with fields and controls; setting object properties; manipulating form pages, properties, and actions; and publishing the form.

With the nonprogramming features out of the way, I turned your attention to programming Outlook. We began with a look at the Outlook object model and how to access it via Automation. In particular, we took a close look at the MailItem object and how to use it to read and send e-mail messages. I finished with a look at how to create dynamic Outlook forms by adding VBScript event handlers and procedures.

For related information, check out the following chapters:

- For a complete look at VBA's Automation techniques, head for Chapter 15, "Controlling Applications Via OLE Automation."
- To learn more about VBScript, see Chapter 21, "Web Page Programming: ActiveX and VBScript."
- I use Outlook to send batch e-mail messages in the E-Mail Merge application that's discussed in Chapter 29, "Access and Outlook: E-Mail Merge."

IN THIS PART

Unleashing Advanced VBA Programming

CHAPTER 23

Trapping Program Errors

IN THIS CHAPTER

If you want a place in the sun, you've got to expect a few blisters.

—*Abigail Van Buren*

In Chapter 5, "Controlling Your VBA Code," I showed you how to use `If...Then` and other control structures to add "intelligence" to your VBA programs. You'll notice, however, that whenever people write about coding programs for decision-making and other "smart" things, they always put words such as "intelligence" and "smart" in quotation marks (as I'm doing now). Why? Well, the cynics in the crowd (and those who've suffered through a few too many general protection faults) would say it's because using the words *intelligence* and *program* in the same sentence borders on the oxymoronic. However, the more common reason is the obvious fact that these techniques don't make your procedures truly intelligent; they just make them seem that way to the user.

In the end, programs are really pretty dumb. After all, they can only do what you, the programmer, tell them to do. For example, if you tell a program to copy a file to a nonexistent disk, the dim brute just doesn't have the smarts to pull back from the abyss.

In Chapter 24, "Debugging VBA Procedures," I'll show you quite a few techniques that will prove invaluable for stomping on program bugs, so that hopefully you'll be able to ship problem-free applications. However, a deep paranoia about potential program problems should be your alliterative frame of mind whenever you create an application. In other words, *always* assume that something, somewhere, at some time can and will go wrong (think of this as a kind of "Murphy's Law of Coding"). After all, you might have tested your code thoroughly on *your* system, but you never know what strange combination of hardware and software it's likely to find out in the cold, cruel world. Similarly, you don't have all that much control over how a user interacts with your program. For example, the user might supply an invalid argument for a function or forget to insert a floppy disk for a backup operation.

Given this heightened (enlightened?) state of paranoia, you must code your applications to allow for potential errors, no matter how obscure. A properly designed program doesn't leave the user out in the cold if an error rears its ugly head. Instead, you need to install code that *traps* these errors and either fixes the problem (if possible), alerts the user to the error so that she can fix it (such as by inserting a disk in a floppy drive), or reports a meaningful explanation of what went wrong so that the user can give you feedback. To that end, this chapter takes you through VBA's error-trapping techniques.

A Basic Error-Trapping Strategy

For many programmers, adding error-trapping code to a procedure can usually be found near the bottom of their to-do lists (probably just before adding comments to a procedure!). That's because error-trapping code isn't even remotely glamorous, and the optimistic (some would say foolhardy) programmer assumes it will never be needed.

That's a shame, because setting up a bare-bones error trap takes very little time. Even a more sophisticated trap can be reused in other procedures, so you really only have a one-time expenditure of energy. To help you get started down this crucial path toward good program hygiene, this section presents a basic strategy for writing and implementing error-trapping code. This strategy will unfold in four parts:

- Setting the error trap
- Coding the error handler
- Resuming program execution
- Disabling the error trap

Setting the Trap

In the simplest error-trapping case, VBA offers what I call the "never mind" statement:

```
On Error Resume Next
```

When inserted within a procedure, this statement tells VBA to bypass any line in the procedure that generates an error and to resume execution with the line that immediately follows the offending statement. No error message is displayed, so the user remains blissfully unaware that anything untoward has occurred. There are three things to note about implementing this statement:

- The trap applies to any executable statement that occurs *after* the `On Error Resume Next` statement.
- The trap also applies to any executable statement within each procedure that is called by the procedure containing the `On Error Resume Next` statement.
- The trap is disabled when the procedure ends.

Since the `On Error Resume Next` statement does nothing to resolve whatever caused the error, and since skipping the offending statement might cause further errors, this error trap is used only rarely.

To set a true error trap, use the `On Error GoTo` statement instead:

```
On Error GoTo line
```

Here, *`line`* is a line label, which is a statement that is used to mark a spot within a procedure (line labels aren't executable). The idea is that, if an error occurs, the procedure containing the `On Error GoTo` statement will branch immediately to the first statement after the line label. This statement should be the beginning of the *error handler* code that processes the error in some way (see the next section). Here's the general structure that sets up a procedure to trap and handle an error:

```
Sub Whatever()
    On Error GoTo ErrorHandler
    [regular procedure statements go here]
    '
    ' If no error occurs, bypass the error handler
    '
    Exit Sub
    '
    ' If an occurs, the code will branch here
    '
ErrorHandler:
    [error handler code goes here]
End Sub
```

Here are some notes about this structure:

- To ensure that all statements are protected, place the `On Error GoTo` statement at the top of the procedure.
- The last statement before the error handler line label should be `Exit Sub` (or `Exit Function` if you're working with a Function procedure). This ensures that the procedure bypasses the error handler if no error occurs.
- The line label is a string—without spaces or periods—followed by a colon (:) at the end to tell VBA that it's just a label and should not be executed.

Coding the Error Handler

The `On Error GoTo` statement serves as the mechanism by which errors are trapped, but the nitty-gritty of the trap is the error handler. The handler is a group of statements designed to process the error, either by displaying a message to the user or by resolving whatever problem raised the error.

The simplest error handler just displays a message that tells the user that a problem occurred. Listings 23.1 and 23.2 provide an example. Listing 23.1 uses a couple of `InputBox` functions to get two numbers from the user: a dividend and a divisor. With these values in hand, the procedure calls the `Divide` function, as shown in Listing 23.2.

NOTE: THIS CHAPTER'S CODE LISTINGS

To examine this chapter's code, open the Excel worksheet named Chaptr23.xls on the CD. To examine the code without using Excel, open the file named Chaptr23.bas.

Listing 23.1. The `GetNumbers` procedure prompts the user for a dividend and a divisor.

```
Sub GetNumbers()
    Dim done As Boolean
    Dim divisor As Variant
    Dim dividend As Variant
    '
    ' Prompt user for dividend and divisor.
    '
    done = False
    Do While Not done
        dividend = InputBox("Enter the dividend:", "Divider")
        divisor = InputBox("Enter the divisor:", "Divider")
        done = Divide(dividend, divisor)
    Loop
End Sub
```

The purpose of the `Divide` function, shown in Listing 23.2, is to divide the `dividend` argument by the `divisor` argument. To trap a "division by zero" error, an `On Error GoTo` statement tells VBA to branch to the `DivByZeroHandler` label. The division is performed, and, if all goes well, a `MsgBox` displays the result. However, if the `divisor` value is 0, an error will occur, and the code will branch to the `DivByZeroHandler` label. This error handler displays a message and asks the user if he wants to try again. The function's return value is set according to the user's choice.

Listing 23.2. The `Divide` function divides the dividend by the divisor. This function traps "division by zero" errors.

```
Function Divide(dividend, divisor) As Boolean
    Dim msg As String
    Dim result As Single
    '
    ' Set the trap
    '
    On Error GoTo DivByZeroHandler
    '
    ' Perform the division
    '
    result = dividend / divisor
    '
    ' If it went okay, display the result
    '
    msg = dividend & _
          " divided by " & _
          divisor & _
          " equals " & _
          result
    MsgBox msg
    '
    ' Set the return value and bypass the error handler
    '
    Divide = True
    Exit Function
```

continues

Listing 23.2. continued

```
    '
    ' Code branches here if an error occurs
    '
DivByZeroHandler:
    '
    ' Display the error message
    '
    result = MsgBox("You entered 0 as the divisor! Try again?", _
                    vbYesNo + vbQuestion, _
                    "Divider")
    '
    ' Return the user's choice
    '
    If result = vbYes Then
        Divide = False
    Else
        Divide = True
    End If
End Function
```

In this example, setting up the error handler was no problem, because the potential error—division by zero—was a fairly obvious one. (Also note that in a production application you would confirm a nonzero divisor as soon as the user entered the value rather than wait for the division to occur.) In practice, however, your error handlers will require a more sophisticated approach that tests for multiple error types. For this you need to know about error numbers. I'll discuss those later in this chapter, in the section "`Err` Object Properties."

Resuming Program Execution

In Listing 23.2, the error message displayed to the user asks if he wants to input the values again, and an `If...Then` tests the response and sets the function's return value accordingly. This example is a bit contrived, because your errors won't necessarily occur inside a Function procedure or loop. However, you'll often still need to give the user a choice of continuing with the program or bailing out. To do this, you can add one or more `Resume` statements to your error handlers. VBA defines three varieties of `Resume` statement:

`Resume`	Tells VBA to resume program execution at the same statement that caused the error.
`Resume Next`	Tells VBA to resume program execution at the first executable statement after the statement that caused the error.
`Resume` *`line`*	Tells VBA to resume program execution at the label specified by *`line`*.

Listing 23.3 shows an example. The `BackUpToFloppy` procedure is designed to get a drive letter from the user and then save the active workbook to that drive. If a problem occurs (such as having no disk in the drive), the routine displays an error message and gives the user the option of trying again or quitting.

Listing 23.3. This procedure backs up the active workbook to a drive specified by the user and traps any errors (such as having no disk in the drive).

```
Sub BackUpToFloppy()
    Dim backupDrive As String
    Dim backupName As String
    Dim msg As String
    Dim done As Boolean
    Dim result As Integer
    '
    ' Define the location of the error handler
    '
    On Error GoTo ErrorHandler
    '
    ' Initialize some variables and then loop
    '
    Application.DisplayAlerts = False
    done = False
    backupDrive = "A:"
    While Not done
        '
        ' Get the drive to use for the backup
        '
        backupDrive = InputBox( _
            Prompt:="Enter the drive letter for the backup:", _
            Title:="Backup", _
            Default:=backupDrive)
        '
        ' Check to see if OK was selected
        '
        If backupDrive <> "" Then
            '
            ' Make sure the backup drive contains a colon (:)
            '
            If InStr(backupDrive, ":") = 0 Then
                backupDrive = Left(backupDrive, 1) & ":"
            End If
            '
            ' First, save the file
            '
            ActiveWorkbook.Save
            '
            ' Assume the backup will be successful,
            ' so set done to True to exit the loop
            '
            done = True
            '
            ' Concatenate drive letter and workbook name
            '
            backupName = backupDrive & ActiveWorkbook.Name
            '
            ' Make a copy on the specified drive
            '
            ActiveWorkbook.SaveCopyAs FileName:=backupName
        Else
            Exit Sub
        End If
```

continues

Listing 23.3. continued

```
    Wend
    '
    ' Bypass the error handler
    '
    Exit Sub
    '
    ' Code branches here if an error occurs
    '
ErrorHandler:
    msg = "An error has occurred!" & Chr(13) & Chr(13) & _
          "Select Abort to bail out, Retry to re-enter the drive" & Chr(13) & _
          "letter, or Ignore to attempt the backup again."
    result = MsgBox(msg, vbExclamation + vbAbortRetryIgnore)
    Select Case result
        Case vbAbort
            done = True
        Case vbRetry
            done = False
            Resume Next
        Case vbIgnore
            Resume
    End Select
End Sub
```

The bulk of the procedure asks the user for a drive letter, saves the workbook, concatenates the drive letter and workbook name, and saves a copy of the workbook on the specified drive.

The error routine is set up with the following statement at the top of the procedure:

```
On Error GoTo ErrorHandler
```

If an error occurs, the procedure jumps to the `ErrorHandler` label. The error handler's `MsgBox` function gives the user three choices (see Figure 23.1), which get processed by the subsequent `Select Case` structure:

Abort — Selecting this option (`Case vbAbort`) bails out of the `While...Wend` loop by setting the `done` variable to `True`.

Retry — Selecting this option (`Case vbRetry`) means the user wants to reenter the drive letter. The `done` variable is set to `False`, and then the `Resume Next` statement is run. If the error occurs during the `SaveCopyAs` method, the next statement is `Wend`, so the procedure just loops back (because we set `done` to `False`) and runs the `InputBox` function again.

Ignore — Selecting this option (`Case vbIgnore`) means the user wants to attempt the backup again. For example, if the user forgot to insert a disk in the drive, or if the drive door wasn't closed, the user would fix the problem and then select this option. In this case, the error handler runs the `Resume` statement to retry the `SaveCopyAs` method (or whatever).

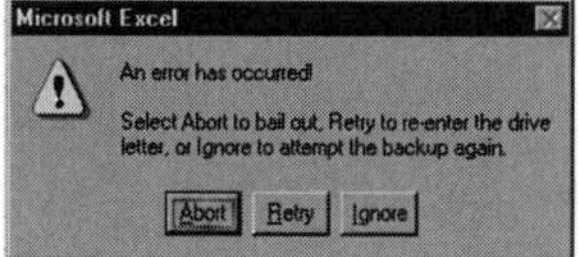

FIGURE 23.1.
If an error occurs, the error handler displays this dialog box.

Disabling the Trap

Under normal circumstances, an error trap set by the `On Error GoTo` statement is disabled automatically when the procedure containing the statement is finished executing. However, there might be times when you want to disable an error trap before the end of a procedure. For example, when you're testing a procedure, you might want to enable the trap for only part of the code and let VBA generate its normal runtime errors for the rest of the procedure.

To disable an error trap at any time during a procedure, even within an error handler, use the following statement:

```
On Error GoTo 0
```

Working with the `Err` Object

The problem with the error traps we've set so far is a lack of information. For example, the `Divide` function (in Listing 23.2) assumes that any error that occurs is a result of an attempted division by zero. However, there are two other runtime error possibilities:

Overflow: This error is raised if *both* the dividend and divisor are 0.

Type mismatch: This error is raised if either value is nonnumeric.

It's likely that you'll want your error handler to treat these errors differently. For example, a division by 0 error requires only that the divisor be reentered, but an overflow error requires that both the dividend and the divisor be reentered.

To handle different errors, VBA provides the `Err` object, which holds information about any runtime errors that occur. You can use the properties of this object to get specific error numbers and descriptions, and you can use the methods of this object to control errors programmatically.

`Err` Object Properties

The `Err` object has a number of properties, but the following three are the ones you'll use most often:

`Err.Description`: Returns the error description.

`Err.Number`: Returns the error number.

`Err.Source`: Returns the name of the project in which the error occurred.

For example, Listing 23.4 shows a procedure that attempts to divide two numbers. The Err object is used in two places within the error handler:

- The error message displayed to the user contains both Err.Number and Err.Description.
- A Select Case structure examines Err.Number to allow the handler to perform different actions depending on the error.

Listing 23.4. This procedure divides two numbers. It traps three specific errors: division by zero, overflow, and type mismatch.

```
Sub DivideNumbers()
    '
    ' Set the trap
    '
    On Error GoTo DivByZeroHandler
    '
    ' Declare variables
    '
    Dim divisor As Variant
    Dim dividend As Variant
    Dim result As Single
    Dim msg As String
    '
    ' Prompt user for the dividend
    '
GetDividendAndDivisor:
    dividend = InputBox("Enter the dividend:", "Divider")
    If dividend = "" Then Exit Sub
    '
    ' Prompt user for the divisor
    '
GetDivisorOnly:
    divisor = InputBox("Enter the divisor:", "Divider")
    If divisor = "" Then Exit Sub
    '
    ' Perform the division
    '
    result = dividend / divisor
    '
    ' If it went okay, display the result
    '
    msg = dividend & _
          " divided by " & _
          divisor & _
          " equals " & _
          result
    MsgBox msg
    '
    ' Bypass the error handler
    '
    Exit Sub
    '
    ' Code branches here if an error occurs
    '
```

```
DivByZeroHandler:
    '
    ' Display the error message
    '
    msg = "An error occurred!" & Chr(13) & Chr(13) & _
          "Error number:  " & Err.Number & Chr(13) & _
          "Error message: " & Err.Description
    MsgBox msg, vbOKOnly + vbCritical
    '
    ' Check the error number
    '
    Select Case Err.Number
        '
        ' Division by zero
        '
        Case 11
            Resume GetDivisorOnly
        '
        ' Overflow
        '
        Case 6
            Resume GetDividendAndDivisor
        '
        ' Type mismatch
        '
        Case 13
            If Not IsNumeric(dividend) Then
                Resume GetDividendAndDivisor
            Else
                Resume GetDivisorOnly
            End If
        '
        ' Anything else, just quit
        '
        Case Else
            Exit Sub
    End Select
End Sub
```


Err Object Methods

The `Err` object also comes equipped with a couple of methods you can use:

`Err.Clear`: This method resets all of the `Err` object's properties. (In other words, numeric properties are set to 0, and string properties are set to the null string.) Note that this method is invoked automatically whenever your code runs any of the following statements:

```
Exit Function

Exit Property

Exit Sub

On Error GoTo 0
```

```
On Error GoTo line
On Error Resume Next
Resume
Resume line
Resume Next
```

`Err.Raise`: This method generates a runtime error. You normally use this method during debugging to create an error on purpose and thus check to see that your error handler is operating correctly. In this case, you need only use the following simplified syntax:

```
Err.Raise Number
```

Number	The number of the error you want to raise.

(This method also has a few other parameters that let you define your own errors for use in, say, a custom class object. See the VBA Help file for details.)

Trappable VBA Errors

VBA has dozens of trappable errors. They are all described in Table 23.1.

Table 23.1. VBA's trappable errors.

Number	*Description*
3	Return without `GoSub`
5	Invalid procedure call
6	Overflow
7	Out of memory
9	Subscript out of range
10	This array is fixed or temporarily locked
11	Division by zero
13	Type mismatch
14	Out of string space
16	Expression too complex
17	Can't perform requested operation
18	User interrupt occurred
20	Resume without error
28	Out of stack space

Number	*Description*
35	Sub, Function, or Property not defined
47	Too many DLL application clients
48	Error in loading DLL
49	Bad DLL calling convention
51	Internal error
52	Bad filename or number
53	File not found
54	Bad file mode
55	File already open
57	Device I/O error
58	File already exists
59	Bad record length
61	Disk full
62	Input past end of file
63	Bad record number
67	Too many files
68	Device unavailable
70	Permission denied
71	Disk not ready
74	Can't rename with different drive
75	Path/file access error
76	Path not found
91	Object variable or `With` block variable not set
92	`For` loop not initialized
93	Invalid pattern string
94	Invalid use of Null
97	Can't call Friend procedure on an object that is not an instance of the defining class
298	System DLL could not be loaded
320	Can't use character device names in specified filenames
321	Invalid file format
322	Can't create necessary temporary file

continues

Table 23.1. continued

Number	Description
325	Invalid format in resource file
327	Data value named not found
328	Illegal parameter; can't write arrays
335	Could not access system registry
336	ActiveX component not correctly registered
337	ActiveX component not found
338	ActiveX component did not run correctly
360	Object already loaded
361	Can't load or unload this object
363	ActiveX control specified not found
364	Object was unloaded
365	Unable to unload within this context
368	The specified file is out of date. This program requires a later version.
371	The specified object can't be used as an owner form for `Show`
380	Invalid property value
381	Invalid property-array index
382	`Property Set` can't be executed at runtime
383	`Property Set` can't be used with a read-only property
385	Need property-array index
387	`Property Set` not permitted
393	`Property Get` can't be executed at runtime
394	`Property Get` can't be executed on write-only property
400	Form already displayed; can't show modally
402	Code must close topmost modal form first
419	Permission to use object denied
422	Property not found
423	Property or method not found
424	Object required
425	Invalid object use
429	ActiveX component can't create object or return reference to this object
430	Class doesn't support Automation

Number	*Description*
432	Filename or class name not found during Automation operation
438	Object doesn't support this property or method
440	Automation error
442	Connection to type library or object library for remote process has been lost
443	Automation object doesn't have a default value
445	Object doesn't support this action
446	Object doesn't support named arguments
447	Object doesn't support current locale setting
448	Named argument not found
449	Argument not optional, or invalid property assignment
450	Wrong number of arguments, or invalid property assignment
451	Object not a collection
452	Invalid ordinal
453	Specified DLL function not found
454	Code resource not found
455	Code resource lock error
457	This key is already associated with an element of this collection
458	Variable uses a type not supported in Visual Basic
459	This component doesn't support events
460	Invalid Clipboard format
461	Specified format doesn't match format of data
480	Can't create AutoRedraw image
481	Invalid picture
482	Printer error
483	Printer driver doesn't support the specified property
484	Problem getting printer information from the system. Make sure the printer is set up correctly.
485	Invalid picture type
486	Can't print form image to this type of printer
520	Can't empty Clipboard
521	Can't open Clipboard

continues

Table 23.1. continued

Number	Description
735	Can't save file to TEMP directory
744	Search text not found
746	Replacements too long
31001	Out of memory
31004	No object
31018	Class is not set
31027	Unable to activate object
31032	Unable to create embedded object
31036	Error saving to file
31037	Error loading from file

Summary

This chapter showed you how to lay traps for those pesky errors that are inevitable in any reasonably-sized program. Much of this chapter was devoted to explaining the particulars of a four-pronged error-trapping strategy: set the trap with `On Error GoTo`, code the error handler, use one of the `Resume` statements to continue the program, and disable the trap (if necessary) with `On Error GoTo 0`. You also learned about the properties and methods of the `Err` object, including the useful `Number` and `Description` properties.

Here's a list of chapters where you'll find related information:

- An important part of trapping errors is letting the user know what's happening and, possibly, giving him some kind of clue how to fix the problem. Basic user interaction techniques are indispensable here, and I showed you quite a few in Chapter 10, "Interacting with the User."
- I mentioned that you can use the `Raise` method to set up your own errors for custom classes. To learn more about classes, see Chapter 16, "Rolling Your Own Objects with Class Modules."
- You can eliminate many trappable errors by making sure your code is as bug-free as possible. Chapter 24, "Debugging VBA Procedures," shows you a number of methods for fumigating your procedures.

CHAPTER 24

Debugging VBA Procedures

IN THIS CHAPTER

If debugging is the process of removing bugs, then programming must be the process of putting them in.

—Dykstra

It's usually easy to get short Sub and Function procedures up and running. However, as your code grows larger and more complex, errors inevitably creep in. As you learned in the preceding chapter, you can trap those errors to avoid having the user deal with them in their raw state, but it's obviously better to stamp them out before you ship your application.

Many of the bugs that creep into your code will be simple syntax problems you can fix easily, but others will be more subtle and harder to find. For the latter—whether the errors are incorrect values being returned by functions or problems with the overall logic of a procedure—you'll need to be able to look "inside" your code to scope out what's wrong. The good news is that VBA gives you several reasonably sophisticated debugging tools that can remove some of the burden of program problem solving. This chapter looks at these tools and shows you how to use them to help recover from most programming errors.

NOTE: THE "BUG" IN DEBUGGING

A *bug* is a logical or syntactical error in a computer program. The term descends from the earliest days of room-size computers, when problems occasionally were traced to insects getting stuck between vacuum tubes (although such stories always sound somewhat apocryphal to me).

A Basic Strategy for Debugging

Debugging, like most computer skills, involves no great secrets. In fact, all debugging is usually a matter of taking a good, hard, dispassionate look at your code. Although there are no set-in-stone techniques for solving programming problems, you can formulate a basic strategy that will get you started.

When a problem occurs, the first thing you need to determine is what kind of error you're dealing with. There are four basic types: syntax errors, compile errors, runtime errors, and logic errors.

Syntax Errors

These errors arise from misspelled or missing keywords and incorrect punctuation. VBA catches most (but not all) of these errors when you enter your statements. Note, too, that the Visual Basic Editor uses a red font to display any statements that contain syntax errors.

Syntax errors are flagged right away by VBA, which means that you just have to read the error message and then clean up the offending statement. Unfortunately, not all of VBA's error messages are helpful. For example, one common syntax error is to forget to include a closing quotation mark in a string. When this happens, VBA reports the following unhelpful message:

```
Expected: list separator or )
```

Compile Errors

When you try to run a procedure, VBA takes a quick look at the code to make sure things look right. If it sees a problem (such as an `If...Then` statement without a corresponding `End If`), it highlights the statement where the problem has occurred and displays an error message.

Fixing compile errors is also usually straightforward. Read the error message and see where VBA has highlighted the code. Doing so almost always gives you enough information to fix the problem.

Runtime Errors

These errors occur during the execution of a procedure. They generally mean that VBA has stumbled upon a statement that it can't figure out. It might be a formula attempting to divide by zero or using a property or method with the wrong object.

Runtime errors produce a dialog box such as the one shown in Figure 24.1. These error messages usually are a little more vague than the ones you see for syntax and compile errors. It often helps to see the statement where the offense has occurred. You can do this by clicking the Debug button. This activates the module and places the insertion point on the line where the error has occurred. If you still can't see the problem, you need to rerun the procedure and pause at or near the point in which the error occurs. This lets you examine the state of the program when it tries to execute the statement. These techniques are explained later in this chapter.

FIGURE 24.1.
A typical runtime error message.

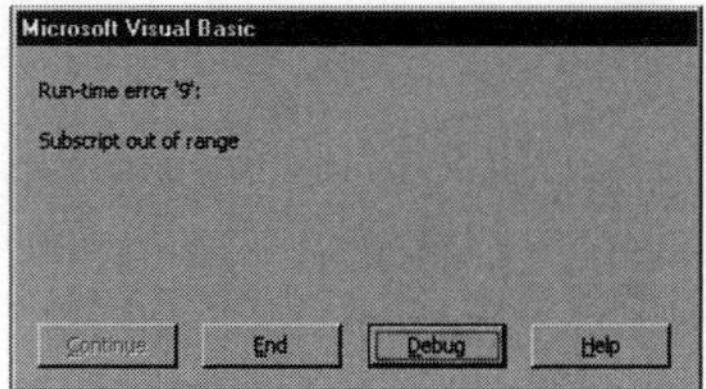

Logic Errors

If your code zigs instead of zags, the cause is usually a flaw in the logic of your procedure. It might be a loop that never ends or a `Select Case` that doesn't select anything.

Logic errors are the toughest to pin down, because you don't get any error messages to give you clues about what went wrong and where. To help, VBA lets you trace through a procedure one statement at a time. This allows you to watch the flow of the procedure and see if the code does what you want it to do. You can also keep an eye on the values of individual variables and properties to make sure they're behaving as expected.

Pausing a Procedure

Pausing a procedure in midstream lets you see certain elements, such as the current values of variables and properties. It also lets you execute program code one statement at a time so that you can monitor the flow of a procedure.

When you pause a procedure, VBA enters *break mode,* which means it displays the code window, highlights the current statement (the one that VBA will execute next) in yellow, and displays a yellow arrow in the Margin Indicator Bar that points to the current statement. See Figure 24.2.

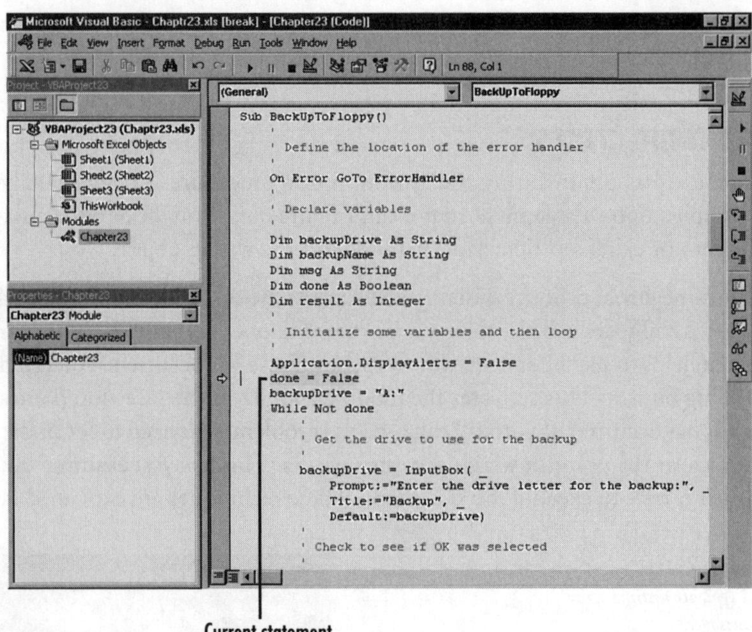

FIGURE 24.2.
VBA displays the Debug window when you enter break mode.

Entering Break Mode

VBA gives you no less than five ways to enter break mode:

- From a runtime error dialog box
- By pressing F8 at the beginning of a procedure
- By pressing Esc or Ctrl-Break while a procedure is running
- By setting breakpoints
- By using a `Stop` statement

Entering Break Mode from an Error Dialog Box

When a runtime error occurs, the dialog box that appears only tells you the error number and the error description. It doesn't tell you where the error occurred. Instead of scouring your code for possible bugs, you should click the Debug button to enter break mode. This will take you directly to the line that caused the error so that you can investigate the problem immediately.

Entering Break Mode at the Beginning of a Procedure

If you're not sure where to look for the cause of an error, you can start the procedure in break mode. Place the insertion point anywhere inside the procedure, and then use any of the following methods:

- Select Run | Step Into.
- Press F8.
- Click the Step Into button on the Debug toolbar. (If you don't see the Debug toolbar on-screen, activate View | Toolbars | Debug.)

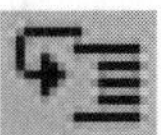

No matter which method you use, VBA enters break mode and highlights the `Sub` statement.

Entering Break Mode by Pressing the Esc Key

If your procedure isn't producing an error but appears to be behaving strangely, you can enter break mode by selecting Run | Break or by clicking the Break button on the Debug toolbar while the procedure is running. VBA pauses on whatever statement it was about to execute.

Alternatively, you can press Ctrl-Break to display the dialog box shown in Figure 24.3. Click Debug to put VBA into break mode.

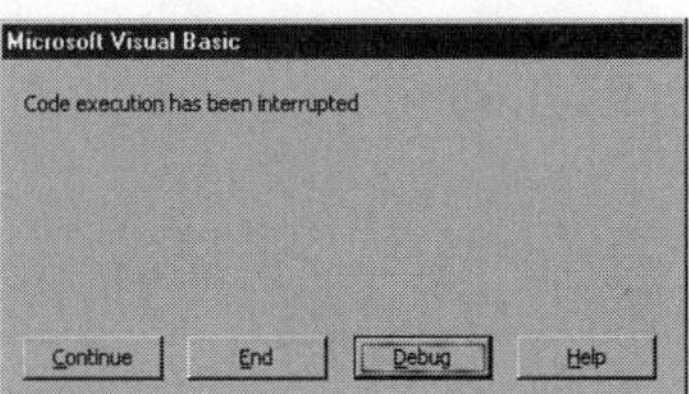

FIGURE 24.3.
This dialog box appears if you press Ctrl-Break while a procedure is running.

Setting a Breakpoint

If you know approximately where an error or logic flaw is occurring, you can enter break mode at a specific statement in the procedure by setting up a *breakpoint.*

To do this, first activate the module containing the procedure you want to run. Then move the insertion point to the statement where you want to enter break mode. VBA will run every line of code up to, but not including, this statement. Now use any of the following techniques to set the breakpoint:

- Select Debug | Toggle Breakpoint.
- Press F9.

- Click the Toggle Breakpoint button on the Debug toolbar.

As shown in Figure 24.4, VBA highlights the entire line in red and adds a breakpoint indicator in the Margin Indicator Bar.

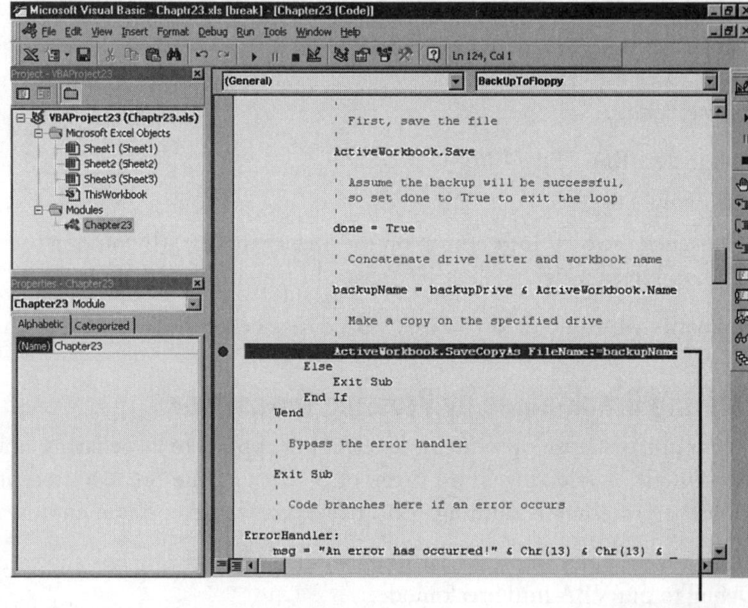

FIGURE 24.4.
When you set a breakpoint, VBA highlights the entire line in red.

NOTE: REMOVING BREAKPOINTS

The methods that set a breakpoint are toggles, so you can remove a breakpoint by placing the insertion point on the same line and running any of the breakpoint methods.

To remove all the breakpoints in the module, select Debug | Clear All Breakpoints or press Ctrl-Shift-F9.

Entering Break Mode Using a `Stop` Statement

When developing your applications, you'll often test the robustness of a procedure by sending it various test values or by trying it out under different conditions. In many cases, you'll want to enter break mode to make sure things look okay. You could set breakpoints at specific statements, but you lose them if you close the file. For something a little more permanent, you can include a `Stop` statement in a procedure. VBA automatically enters break mode whenever it encounters a `Stop` statement.

Figure 24.5 shows the `BackUpToFloppy` procedure with a `Stop` statement inserted just before the statement that runs the `SaveCopyAs` method.

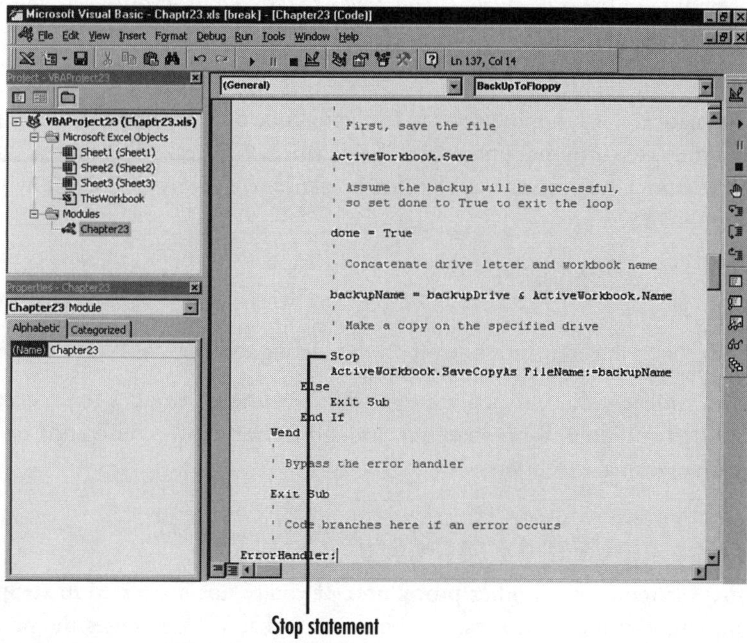

FIGURE 24.5.
You can insert `Stop` *statements to enter break mode at specific procedure locations.*

Exiting Break Mode

To exit break mode, you can use either of the following methods:

- Resume normal program execution by selecting Run | Continue, by pressing F5, or by clicking the Continue button on the Debug toolbar.

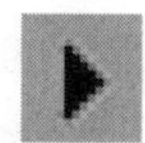

- End the procedure by selecting Run | Reset or by clicking on the Debug toolbar's Reset button.

Stepping Through a Procedure

One of the most common (and most useful) debugging techniques is to step through the code one statement at a time. This lets you get a feel for the program flow to make sure that things such as loops and procedure calls are executing properly. You can use three techniques:

- Stepping into a procedure
- Stepping over a procedure
- Stepping to a cursor position

Stepping Into a Procedure

Stepping into a procedure means you execute one line at a time (in break mode), starting at the beginning of the procedure. If you haven't started a procedure yet, you step into it using any of the techniques described in the section "Entering Break Mode at the Beginning of a Procedure."

Alternatively, you might prefer to run your code until it's about to call a particular procedure, and then step into that procedure. To do this, set a breakpoint on the statement that calls the procedure. Once your code hits that breakpoint, use any of the following techniques to step into the procedure:

- Select Debug | Step Into.
- Press F8.

- Click the Step Into button on the Debug toolbar.

Once you're inside the procedure, use these same techniques to execute the procedure code one line at a time. Keep stepping through until the procedure ends or until you're ready to resume normal execution.

Stepping Over a Procedure

Some statements call other procedures. If you're not interested in stepping through a called procedure, you can step over it. This means that VBA executes the procedure normally and then resumes break mode at the next statement *after* the procedure call. To step over a procedure, first either step into the procedure until you come to the procedure call you want to step over, or set a breakpoint on the procedure call and run the application. Once you're in break mode, you can step over the procedure using any of the following techniques:

- Select Debug | Step Over.
- Press Shift-F8.
- Click the Step Over button on the Debug toolbar.

TIP: STEPPING OVER SEVERAL STATEMENTS

VBA5.0

Instead of stepping over an entire procedure, you might need to step over only a few statements. To do this, enter break mode, place the insertion point inside the line where you want to reenter break mode, and select Debug | Run To Cursor (or press Ctrl-F8).

Stepping Out of a Procedure

I'm always accidentally stepping into procedures I'd rather step over. If the procedure is short, I just step through it until I'm back in the original procedure. If it's long, however, I don't want to waste time going through every line. Instead, I invoke the Step Out feature using any of these methods:

- Select Debug | Step Out.
- Press Ctrl-Shift-F8.
- Click the Step Out button on the Debug toolbar.

VBA executes the rest of the procedure and then reenters break mode at the first line after the procedure call.

Monitoring Procedure Values

Many runtime and logic errors are the result of (or, in some cases, can result in) variables or properties assuming unexpected values. If your procedure uses or changes these elements in several places, you'll need to enter break mode and monitor the values of these elements to see where things go awry. The Visual Basic Editor offers a number of methods for monitoring values, and I discuss them in the next few sections.

Using the Locals Window

VBA 5.0

Most of the values you'll want to monitor will be variables. Although watch expressions (discussed in the next section) are best if you want to keep an eye on only one or two variables, the Visual Basic Editor gives you an easy method to use if you want to monitor *all* the variables in any procedure. This method makes use of a special VBA window called the Locals window (which is new to VBA 5.0). You can display this window using either of these techniques:

- Activate View | Locals Window.
- Click the Locals Window button on the Debug toolbar.

When your procedure enters break mode, the Locals window displays a line for each declared variable in the current procedure. As you can see in Figure 24.6, each line shows the variable name, its current value, and its type. The top line is the name of the module. If you click the plus sign (+) to the left of the module name, you'll see a list of the module-level (global) variables.

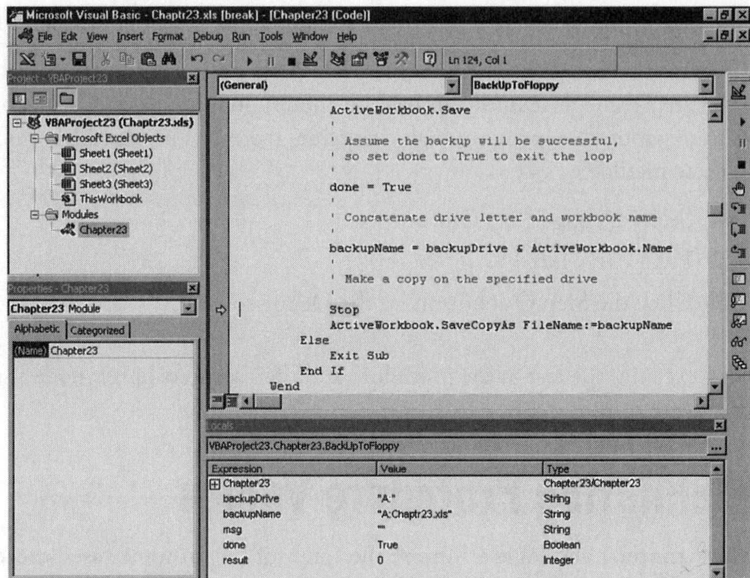

FIGURE 24.6.
Use the Locals window to keep track of the current value of all your variables.

Adding a Watch Expression

Besides monitoring variable values, VBA also lets you monitor the results of any expression or the current value of an object property. To do this, you need to set up *watch expressions* that define what you want to monitor. These watch expressions appear in the Watch window, which you can display by using either of the following methods:

- Activate View | Watch Window.
- Click the Watch Window button on the Debug toolbar.

To add a watch expression, follow these steps:

1. If the expression exists inside the procedure (for example, an object property), select the expression as follows:

   For single-word expressions, place the insertion point anywhere inside the word.

   For more complex expressions, highlight the entire expression.
2. Select Debug | Add Watch to display the Add Watch dialog box, shown in Figure 24.7.
3. If the expression you want to monitor isn't already shown in the Expression text box, enter the expression. You can enter a variable name, a property, a user-defined function name, or any other valid VBA expression.
4. Use the Context group to specify the context of the variable (that is, where the variable is used). You enter the Procedure and the Module.

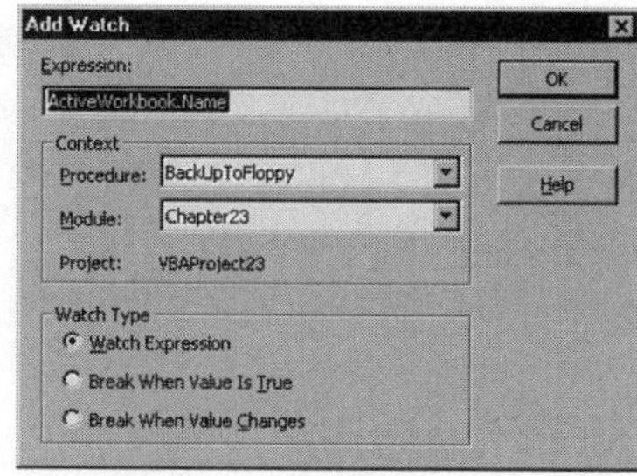

FIGURE 24.7.
Use the Add Watch dialog box to add watch expressions.

5. Use the Watch Type group to specify how VBA watches the expression:

Watch Expression	Displays the expression in the Watch window when you enter break mode.
Break When Value Is True	Tells VBA to automatically enter break mode when the expression value becomes True (or nonzero).
Break When Value Changes	Automatically enters break mode whenever the value of the expression changes.

6. Click OK.

Once you've added a watch expression, you monitor it by entering break mode and examining the expression in the Watch window, as shown in Figure 24.8.

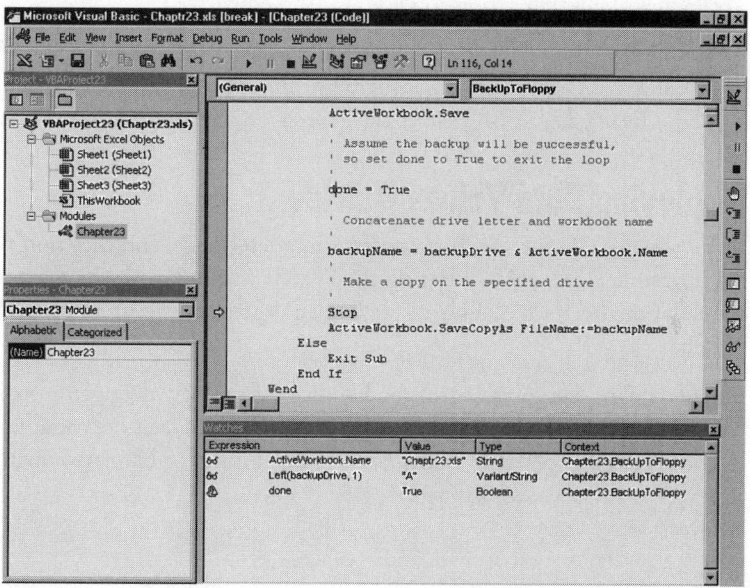

FIGURE 24.8.
The Watch window with a couple of watch expressions.

TIP: YOU CAN ADD WATCH EXPRESSIONS IN DEBUG MODE

The Debug | Add Watch command is available when you're in break mode, so you can add more watch expressions if necessary.

Editing a Watch Expression

You can make changes to a watch expression while in break mode. Follow these steps:

1. Select the Watch window by clicking it or by selecting View | Watch Window.
2. Click the watch expression you want to edit.
3. Select Debug | Edit Watch, press Ctrl-W, or double-click the watch expression. VBA displays the Edit Watch dialog box.
4. Make your changes to the watch expression.
5. Click OK to return to the Debug window.

Deleting a Watch Expression

To delete a watch expression you no longer need to monitor, follow these steps:

1. Select the Watch window by clicking it or by selecting View | Watch Window.
2. Click the watch expression you want to edit.
3. Select Debug | Edit Watch or press Ctrl-W to display the Edit Watch dialog box.
4. Click the Delete button, or highlight the expression in the Watch window and press the Delete key. VBA deletes the expression and returns you to the Debug window.

Displaying Data Values Quickly

Many variables, properties, and expressions are set once, and they don't change for the rest of the procedure. To avoid cluttering the Watch window with these expressions, VBA offers a couple of methods for quickly displaying an expression's current value: Data Tips and Quick Watch.

VBA 5.0

The Data Tips feature is one of the handiest of the new debugging tools in VBA 5.0. When you're in break mode, simply move the mouse pointer over the variable or property you want to know the value of. After a brief pause, VBA displays a banner showing the current value of the expression, as shown in Figure 24.9.

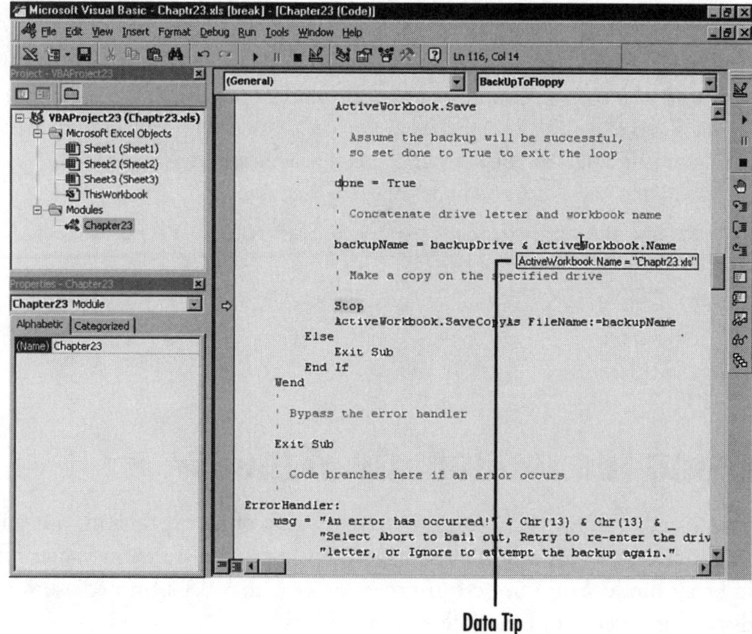

FIGURE 24.9.
VBA 5.0 displays Data Tips when you hover the mouse pointer over an expression in break mode.

The Quick Watch feature displays a dialog box that shows the expression, its current context, and its current value. To try this, enter break mode and then either place the insertion point inside the expression you want to display or highlight the expression. Then use any of the following techniques to display a Quick Watch dialog box like the one shown in Figure 24.10:

- Select Debug | Quick Watch.
- Press Shift-F9.
- Click the Quick Watch button on the Debug toolbar.

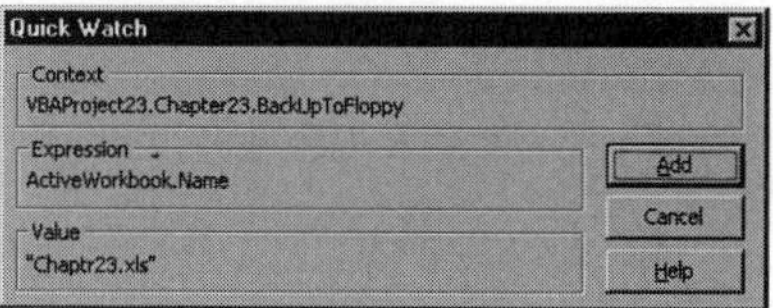

FIGURE 24.10.
Use the Quick Watch dialog box to quickly display the value of an expression.

If you want to add the expression to the Watch window, click the Add button. To return to break mode without adding the expression, click Cancel.

TIP: DISPLAY THE CALL STACK

In VBA, the *call stack* is a list of the active procedure calls. The current procedure appears at the top of the list, the procedure that called the current procedure appears on the next line, and so on. The call stack is a useful tool for tracing the execution of your code. To display the call stack, use either of these techniques:

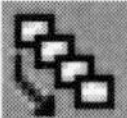

- In break mode, select View | Call Stack, press Ctrl-L, or click the Call Stack button on the Debug toolbar.
- In the Locals window, click the ellipsis (...) button that appears just below the Close button.

Using the Immediate Window

The Watch window tells you the current value of an expression, but you'll often need more information than this. You also might want to plug in different values for an expression while in break mode. You can perform these tasks with VBA's Immediate window, which you can display using either of the following methods:

- Activate View | Immediate Window.
- Click the Immediate Window button on the Debug toolbar.

Printing Data in the Immediate Window

You can use the `Print` method of the special `Debug` object to print text and expression values in the Immediate window. There are two ways to do this:

- By running the `Print` method from the procedure
- By entering the `Print` method directly into the Immediate window

The `Print` method uses the following syntax:

```
Debug.Print OutputList
```

`OutputList` An expression or list of expressions to print in the Immediate window.
If you omit *`OutputList`*, a blank line is printed.

Here are a few notes to keep in mind when using this method:

- Use `Spc(`*`n`*`)` in *`OutputList`* to print *n* space characters.
- Use `Tab(`*`n`*`)` in *`OutputList`* to print *n* tab characters.
- Separate multiple expressions with either a space or a semicolon.

Running the `Print` Method from a Procedure

If you know that a variable or expression changes at a certain place in your code, enter a `Debug.Print` statement at that spot. When you enter break mode, the *`OutputList`* expressions appear in the Immediate window. For example, Figure 24.11 shows a procedure in break mode. The information displayed in the Immediate window was generated by the following statement:

```
Debug.Print "The backup filename is "; backupName
```

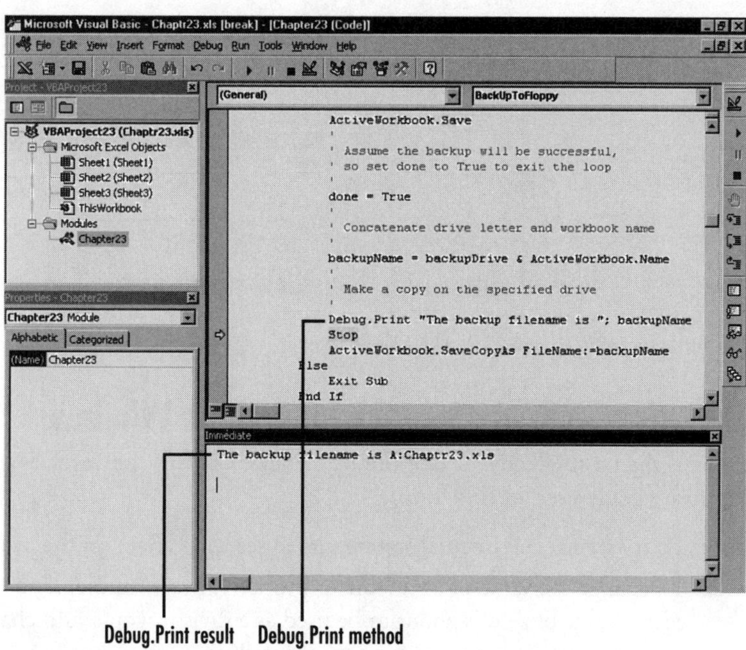

FIGURE 24.11.
Use `Debug.Print` *in your code to display information in the Immediate window.*

Running the `Print` Method in the Immediate Window

You can also use the `Print` method directly in the Immediate window to display information. Note that when you're in break mode you don't need to specify the `Debug` object.

Figure 24.12 shows a couple of examples. In the first line, I typed `print backupdrive` and pressed Enter. VBA responded with `A:`. In the second example, I typed `? backupname` (`?` is the short form of the `Print` method), and VBA responded with `A:Chaptr23.xls`.

FIGURE 24.12.
You can enter `Print` *statements directly in the Immediate window. Note the use of the question mark (?) as a short form of the* `Print` *method.*

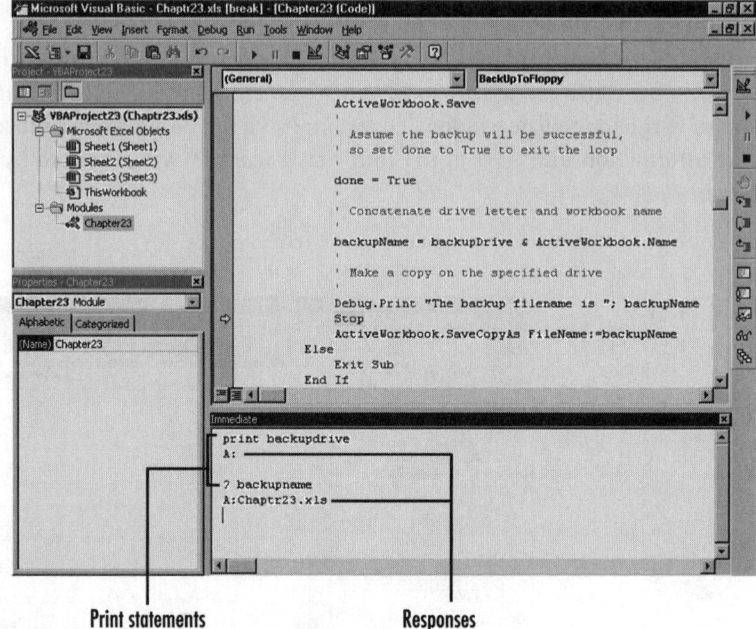

Executing Statements in the Immediate Window

Perhaps the most effective use of the Immediate window, however, is to execute statements. There are many uses for this feature:

- To try some experimental statements to see their effect on the procedure.
- To change the value of a variable or property. For example, if you see that a variable with a value of zero is about to be used as a divisor, you could change that variable to a nonzero value to avoid crashing the procedure.
- To run other procedures or user-defined functions to see if they operate properly under the current conditions.

You enter statements in the Immediate window just as you do in the module itself. For example, entering the following statement in the Immediate window changes the value of the `backupName` variable:

```
backupName = "B:Chaptr23.xls"
```

TIP: RUN MULTIPLE STATEMENTS

You can execute multiple statements in the Immediate window by separating each statement with a colon. For example, you can test a `For...Next` loop by entering a statement similar to the following:

```
For i=1 To 10:Print i^2:Next
```

Debugging Tips

Debugging your procedures can be a frustrating job—even during the best of times. Here are a few tips to keep in mind when tracking down programming problems.

Indent Your Code for Readability

VBA code is immeasurably more readable when you indent your control structures. Readable code is that much easier to trace and decipher, so your debugging efforts have one less hurdle to negotiate. Indenting code is a simple matter of pressing Tab an appropriate number of times at the beginning of a statement.

It helps if VBA's automatic indentation feature is enabled. To check this, select Tools | Options to display the Options dialog box, select the Editor tab, and activate the Auto Indent check box.

NOTE: SETTING THE TAB WIDTH

By default, VBA moves the insertion point four spaces to the right when you press the Tab key. You can change this default by entering a new value in the Tab Width text box in the Editor tab of the Options dialog box.

Turn on Syntax Checking

VBA's automatic syntax checking is a real time-saver. To make sure this option is turned on, activate the Auto Syntax Check check box in the Editor tab of the Options dialog box.

Require Variable Declarations

To avoid errors caused by using variables improperly, you should always declare your procedure variables. To make VBA display an error if you don't declare a variable, add the following statement to the top of the module:

```
Option Explicit
```

> **TIP: REQUIRING VARIABLE DECLARATIONS**
>
> To have VBA include the `Option Explicit` statement in every new module, activate the Require Variable Declaration check box in the Editor tab of the Options dialog box.

Break Down Complex Procedures

Don't try to solve all your problems at once. If you have a large procedure that isn't working right, test it in small chunks to try and narrow down the problem. To test a piece of a procedure, add an `Exit Sub` statement after the last line of the code you want to test.

Enter VBA Keywords in Lowercase

If you always enter keywords in lowercase letters, you can easily detect a problem when you see that VBA doesn't change the word to its normal case when you enter the line.

What to Do When a Procedure Refuses to Run

If your procedure refuses to run, check the following:

- Make sure the document containing the module is open.
- If you're trying to run the procedure by pressing a shortcut key, make sure the shortcut key has been defined.
- Check to see whether another procedure has the same shortcut key. If one does and it appears earlier in the Macro dialog box list, your procedure won't run. You'll need to change the shortcut key for one of the procedures.
- Make sure that another open module doesn't have a procedure with the same name.

Comment Out Problem Statements

If a particular statement is giving you problems, you can temporarily deactivate it by placing an apostrophe at the beginning of the line. This tells VBA to treat the line as a comment.

VBA 5.0 Don't forget that VBA 5.0 has a new Comment Block feature that will comment out multiple statements at once. To use this feature, select the statements you want to work with and then click the following buttons on the Edit toolbar:

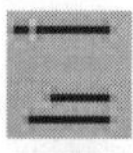 Comment Block

 Uncomment Block

Break Up Long Statements

One of the most complicated aspects of procedure debugging is making sense out of long statements (especially formulas). The Immediate window can help (you can use it to print parts of the statement), but it's usually best to keep your statements as short as possible. Once you get things working properly, you can often recombine statements for more efficient code.

Use Excel's Range Names Whenever Possible

In Excel, procedures are much easier to read and debug if you use range names in place of cell references. Not only is a name such as Expenses!Summary more comprehensible than Expenses!A1:F10, it's safer, too. If you add rows or columns to the Summary range, the name's reference changes as well. With cell addresses, you have to adjust the references yourself.

Take Advantage of User-Defined Constants

If your procedure uses constant values in several different statements, you can give yourself one less debugging chore by creating a user-defined constant for the value (see Chapter 2, "Understanding Variables"). This gives you three important advantages:

- It ensures that you don't enter the wrong value in a statement.
- It's easier to change the value, because you have to change only the constant declaration.
- Your procedures will be easier to understand.

Summary

This chapter showed you how to use VBA's debugging facilities to weed out errors in your code. You learned a basic debugging strategy, how to pause and step through a procedure, and how to use breakpoints, watch expressions, and the Immediate window. Here are some places to go to find related information:

- The best way to stamp out bugs in your VBA code is to become familiar with the basic building blocks of VBA programming. These basics were covered in Part I, "Introducing VBA."
- To help avoid errors caused by your users, you should set up your application's interface to minimize the possibility of improper data entry and to make it as easy as possible for users to work with the program. Creating a custom user interface is the subject of Part III, "Unleashing VBA User Interface Design."
- If an error *does* occur in your application, you should trap it and give the user an explanation of what went wrong. To learn how to work with VBA's error-trapping features, see Chapter 23, "Trapping Program Errors."

CHAPTER 25

Programming the Windows API

IN THIS CHAPTER

A good workman can use any kind of tool.

—François Rabelais

With a couple of dozen chapters under your belt, you're in a great position to appreciate the power and flexibility of VBA. For one thing, the programming language is a robust system that includes all the structures, statements, and functions you need to build quality applications. Throw in the ability to manipulate application objects, work with Data Access Objects, create custom classes, and interact with Automation interfaces, and add to the mix external tools such as the user forms designer and integrated debugger, and you've got yourself a programming environment that's both powerful and easy to use.

However, you might have come across a few hurdles that VBA just can't leap. For example, you might need to display a user form that takes up the entire screen, but user forms can't be maximized, and VBA gives you no way to determine the current screen dimensions. Similarly, before copying a file, you might need to know how much free space is on the disk, but VBA has no function or method that will tell you. Or what if you need to know the path in which Windows is installed? Again, VBA draws a blank.

To overcome these and many other VBA limitations, you can access a powerful—and very fast—library of routines called the Windows 32-bit Application Programming Interface (known more familiarly as the Win32 API, or sometimes just Win32). This chapter introduces you to the Win32 API, shows you how to access its routines from within your VBA applications, and runs through a few examples.

Understanding the Win32 API

The Win32 API is a collection of more than 1,500 Sub and Function procedures that provide access to many Windows services. These procedures reside in a series of *dynamic link libraries* (DLLs) that form the core of the Windows 95 and Windows NT operating systems. (Most of the Win32 API can be found in just three files: GDI32.dll, Kernel32.dll, and User32.dll.) Windows programs use these routines for such basic services as creating windows; opening, reading, and writing files; editing Registry entries; and much more. In fact, your VBA procedures make extensive use of the Win32 API, although the underlying mechanism is hidden from you. When you display a user form, create a menu, use `Shell` to start a program, and so on, VBA translates these actions into calls to the Win32 API behind the scenes.

Declaring Win32 API Procedures

Since the Win32 API exists in files that are external to the VBA environment, you must specify a function and its DLL before you can use the function in your code. This is not unlike Automation, in which you have to set up a reference to an external object library before you can use the library's objects. With API functions, however, you create a "reference" by setting up a *declaration* for the function. This declaration must provide the following information:

- The name of the Function or Sub procedure.
- The DLL in which the procedure resides.
- The arguments (and their data types) used by the procedure.
- The data type of the value that is returned by the procedure (Function procedure only).

To accomplish this, VBA provides the `Declare` statement. This statement must be placed at the module level, and you use one of the following syntaxes, depending on whether you want to work with a Sub or Function procedure:

```
Declare Sub Name Lib "LibName" Alias "AliasName" (ArgList)

Declare Function Name Lib "LibName" Alias "AliasName" (ArgList) As Type
```

Name	The name of the Sub or Function procedure you want to use. (Note that these names are case-sensitive.)
LibName	The name of the DLL file in which the procedure can be found (for example, kernel32).
AliasName	An alternative name for the procedure.
ArgList	A list of arguments (along with their respective data types) that are passed to the procedure.
Type	The data type of the value returned by a Function procedure.

For example, the following statement declares a function named `Beep` from the kernel32 DLL:

```
Declare Function Beep Lib "kernel32" Alias "Beep" (ByVal dwFreq As Long, ByVal
➥dwDuration As Long) As Long
```

As you can see, these `Declare` statements can be quite complex (and `Beep` is one of the simpler functions!). Fortunately, you'll never have to type in a Win32 API declaration, because you'll find a complete list of the appropriate `Declare` statements on this book's CD in the file named Win32API.txt. Just load the file into a word processor or text editor, search for the procedure name you need, and paste the entire `Declare` statement into your code.

CAUTION: DON'T USE WIN32 FUNCTIONS IN WIN16

This chapter assumes that you'll be using API functions in 32-bit environments. If you're building an application for use in a 16-bit environment (an Excel 5 application, for example), these API functions will fail for any of the following reasons:

- Win32 procedures use different library calls (for example, `user32` in Win32 versus `user` in Win16).
- Many Win32 argument and function data types have been changed to `Long` to accommodate the 32-bit data values. The corresponding arguments in the Win16 API mostly use `Integer` data types.
- Many Win32 procedures aren't available in the Win16 API.

For your 16-bit applications, use the `Declare` and `Const` statements from the file named Win16API.txt on the CD.

If your application must run in both 16-bit and 32-bit environments, you'll need to use VBA's conditional compilation feature to avoid problems. See the next chapter for details.

Using Constants with API Procedures

Although many of the Win32 API procedures will accept any value in their arguments (within the limits of the argument data types, of course), you'll often have to specify a constant value. In these cases, the API defines one or more constants that you can plug in. However, the Win32API.txt file I mentioned earlier comes with a number of `Const` statements that set up VBA constants you can use.

For example, the Win32 API has a `ShowWindow` function that lets you maximize, minimize, or restore any open window. Here's the syntax:

```
Declare Function ShowWindow Lib "user32" (ByVal hwnd As Long, ByVal nCmdShow As
➥Long) As Long
```

hwnd	A handle that points to the window you want to work with. (I'll explain how you get a window's handle in a moment.)
nCmdShow	A constant value that determines how you want to show the window.

Here's the constant definition from Win32API.txt that controls minimizing a window:

```
Public Const SW_MINIMIZE = 6
```

Listing 25.1 shows an example, as well as some of the other constants accepted by the `ShowWindow` function. Here, I've declared two Win32 API functions at the module level: `ShowWindow` and `FindWindow`. The latter is used to locate an open window based on its title bar text:

```
Declare Function FindWindow Lib "user32" Alias "FindWindowA" (ByVal lpClassName
➥As String, ByVal lpWindowName As String) As Long
```

lpClassName	The class name of the window (use `vbNullString`).
lpWindowName	The title bar text of the window you want to find.

If `FindWindow` locates the window, it returns a handle to the window that you can then pass to the `ShowWindow` function; otherwise, `FindWindow` returns 0. In this case, if `FindWindow` locates the window, `ShowWindow` is called, and the window is minimized.

Listing 25.1. In this example, the ShowWindow API function accepts several constants.

```
' Declare the Win32 API functions
'
Declare Function ShowWindow Lib "user32" (ByVal hwnd As Long, ByVal nCmdShow As
➥Long) As Long
Declare Function FindWindow Lib "user32" Alias "FindWindowA" (ByVal lpClassName
➥As String, ByVal lpWindowName As String) As Long
'
' Set up the constants
'
Public Const SW_NORMAL = 1
Public Const SW_MAXIMIZE = 3
Public Const SW_MINIMIZE = 6
Public Const SW_RESTORE = 9
Sub WindowTest()
    Dim hInst As Long
    '
    ' Look for the window of the current application
    '
    hInst = FindWindow(vbNullString, Application.Caption)
    If Not IsNull(hInst) Then
        '
        ' If we found it, minimize it
        '
        ShowWindow hInst, SW_MINIMIZE
    End If
End Sub
```

NOTE: THIS CHAPTER'S CODE LISTINGS

To get the code listings for this chapter, open the file named Chaptr25.xls on the CD. In case you don't have Excel, you'll find the listings in separate .BAS files (for example, Listing_25_1.bas).

Using Type Definitions with API Procedures

In Chapter 2, "Understanding Variables," I showed you how to use the `Type...End Type` structure to create user-defined data types. As you work with the Win32 API, you'll see that it makes extensive use of these type definitions. For example, consider the syntax of the `GetVersionEx` API function:

```
Declare Function GetVersionEx Lib "kernel32" Alias "GetVersionExA"
➥(lpVersionInformation As OSVERSIONINFO) As Long
```

lpVersionInformation	A variable that returns information about the Windows version.

Notice that the ***lpVersionInformation*** argument is defined to be of data type `OSVERSIONINFO`. These all-uppercase data types tell you that you're dealing with a type definition, which you'll also find in the Win32API.txt file. Here's the type definition for `OSVERSIONINFO`:

```
Type OSVERSIONINFO
    dwOSVersionInfoSize As Long
    dwMajorVersion As Long
    dwMinorVersion As Long
    dwBuildNumber As Long
    dwPlatformId As Long
    szCSDVersion As String * 128
End Type
```

The idea here is that you include this type definition in your code, declare a new variable to be of this type, and pass this new variable to the `GetVersionEx` function. The variable is passed by reference, so your program will be able to access any modifications made to the variable's members. In particular, the members `dwMajorVersion`, `dwMinorVersion`, `dwBuildNumber`, and `dwPlatformID` will return information about the Windows version. Listing 25.2 shows a procedure that uses `GetVersionEx` to return this data and then displays it in a dialog box like the one shown in Figure 25.1.

NOTE: WATCH OUT FOR "SIZE" MEMBERS

Notice that the first member of the `OSVERSIONINFO` type definition is `dwOSVersionInfoSize`. This member represents the size of the type definition structure. You'll see these "`Size`" members quite often in the Win32 API. To handle this kind of member correctly, make sure you set the value of this member to the length of the structure. Use `Len(`*`var`*`)`, where *var* is the variable name you used when you declared an instance of the type definition (see Listing 25.2 for an example).

Listing 25.2. This example uses the `GetVersionEx` API function, which accepts an argument that uses a custom type definition.

```
' The type definition
'
Type OSVERSIONINFO
    dwOSVersionInfoSize As Long
    dwMajorVersion As Long
    dwMinorVersion As Long
    dwBuildNumber As Long
    dwPlatformId As Long
    szCSDVersion As String * 128
End Type
'
' Declare the function
'
Declare Function GetVersionEx Lib "kernel32" Alias "GetVersionExA"
➥(lpVersionInformation As OSVERSIONINFO) As Long
'
' Constants used with OSVERSIONINFO.dwPlatformId
'
Public Const VER_PLATFORM_WIN32s = 0
Public Const VER_PLATFORM_WIN32_WINDOWS = 1
Public Const VER_PLATFORM_WIN32_NT = 2
Sub GetWinVer()
    Dim os As OSVERSIONINFO
    Dim msg As String

    os.dwOSVersionInfoSize = Len(os)
    GetVersionEx os

    msg = "Major Version: " & os.dwMajorVersion & Chr(13) & _
          "Minor Version: " & os.dwMinorVersion & Chr(13) & _
          "Build Number: " & os.dwBuildNumber & Chr(13) & _
          "Platform ID: "
    Select Case os.dwPlatformId
        Case VER_PLATFORM_WIN32s
            msg = msg & "Win32s"
        Case VER_PLATFORM_WIN32_WINDOWS
            msg = msg & "Windows"
        Case VER_PLATFORM_WIN32_NT
            msg = msg & "Windows NT"
    End Select
    MsgBox msg, vbOKOnly + vbInformation, "Windows Version"
End Sub
```

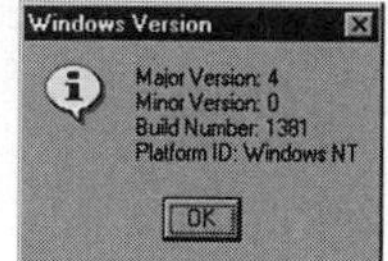

FIGURE 25.1.
The dialog box displayed by the `GetWinVer` *procedure in Listing 25.2.*

Some Cautionary Notes

Before we get too involved in the intricacies of the Win32 API, you should know that you're dealing with fire when you use these functions. One false move (even just a mistaken argument), and you could crash the VBA application with a General Protection Fault, and possibly even render Windows itself unstable. For this reason, make sure you save your work constantly as you program with the Win32 API. To help you avoid crashes, here are a few things to keep in mind as you work with API functions:

- Always copy the `Declare`, `Type...End Type`, and `Const` statements from Win32API.txt. If you try to type them by hand, you're only asking for trouble.
- Make sure that the variables you use in your procedure have the same data types as the arguments specified in the `Declare` statement.
- If you plan on storing the result of an API function in a variable, make sure that variable is declared with the same data type as the function.
- Whenever a Win32 API procedure requires a string, initialize the string with a specific length, which should be at least 256 bytes:

```
Dim strBuffer * 256
```

- Make sure you always use `Option Explicit` in conjunction with API procedures. This ensures that none of the variables you pass to these procedures are using the default `Variant` data type.

Win32 API Examples

I mentioned earlier that the Win32 API has more than 1,500 Sub and Function procedures. However, the vast majority of these procedures are highly technical and are of interest only to C/C++ developers. That still leaves quite a few that could come in handy in your VBA applications. I'll spend the rest of this chapter looking at examples of these procedures.

NOTE: MORE WIN32 INFO

The examples in this section represent only the tiniest fraction of the available API functions. If you're interested in learning more about the Win32 API and seeing even more of the functions at work, you might want to get a copy of *32-Bit Programming* (Sams Publishing, 1995).

Beeping the Speaker

VBA provides you with a simple `Beep` statement that you can use to get the user's attention. Unfortunately, `Beep` produces only a single sound. This isn't a problem most of the time, but there are situations in which you might need something different. For example, you usually want to beep the speaker at the end of a long operation in order to bring the user's attention back to the screen. But what if an error occurs during the operation? It would be nice to have a different sound to go with your error message.

If you're working with Windows NT, use Win32's `Beep` function to get different sounds:

```
Declare Function Beep Lib "kernel32" (ByVal dwFreq As Long, ByVal dwDuration As
➥Long) As Long
```

dwFreq	The frequency of the sound you want in hertz. You can use any value between 37 and 32767.
dwDuration	The length of the sound in milliseconds.

Note that in Windows 95, both arguments are ignored, so invoking this function only produces the default sound event (which is the same thing as VBA's `Beep` statement). To get different sounds in Windows 95, use the `MessageBeep` function instead:

```
Declare Function MessageBeep Lib "user32" (ByVal wType As Long) As Long
```

wType A constant that determines which of Windows' sound events is played:

wType	*Associated Event*
0	Default sound
16	Critical Stop
32	Question
48	Exclamation
64	Asterisk

Here are the defined constants from Win32API.txt:

```
Public Const MB_ICONHAND = &H10&
Public Const MB_ICONQUESTION = &H20&
Public Const MB_ICONEXCLAMATION = &H30&
Public Const MB_ICONASTERISK = &H40&
```

Note, however, that these constants produce different sounds only if the Windows 95 system has defined different sound files for the events just listed. To change the sound files associated with these events, select Start | Settings | Control Panel and then double-click Control Panel's Sounds icon. Using the Sounds Properties dialog box, shown in Figure 25.2, you can associate sound files with various events.

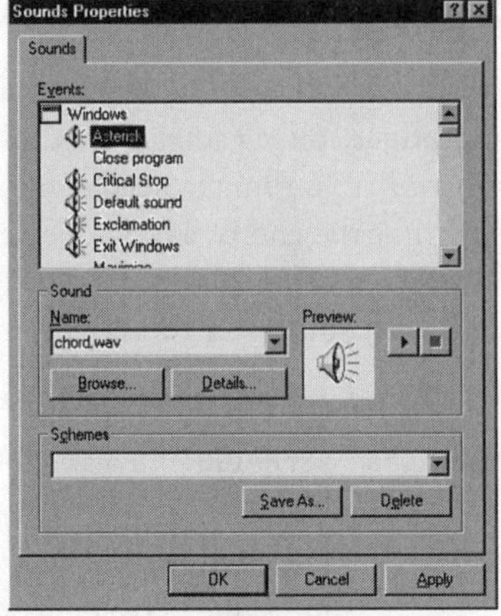

FIGURE 25.2.
Use this dialog box to associate sound files with different Windows 95 events.

TIP: MODIFY THE REGISTRY VIA VBA

The sound files associated with each event are stored in the Windows 95 Registry. I'll show you how to modify Registry settings programmatically later in this chapter, in the section "Working with the Registry."

Listing 25.3 presents two procedures. The `BeepTest` procedure uses Win32's `Beep` function to play a series of tones, and the `MessageBeepTest` procedure tries out the various `MessageBeep` constants.

Listing 25.3. Using the Beep and MessageBeep API functions to control the speaker.

```
Declare Function Beep Lib "kernel32" (ByVal dwFreq As Long, ByVal dwDuration As
➥Long) As Long
Declare Function MessageBeep Lib "user32" (ByVal wType As Long) As Long
'
' This procedure works in Windows NT.
'
Sub BeepTest()
    Dim i As Integer
    For i = 100 To 2000 Step 100
        Beep i, 50
    Next 'i
End Sub
'
' This procedure works in Windows 95.
'
```

```
Sub MessageBeepTest()
    Dim i As Integer
    For i = 0 To 64 Step 16
        MessageBeep i
        Application.Wait Now + TimeValue("00:00:02")
    Next 'i
End Sub
```

Returning Windows' Folders

The Win32 API has four functions that return information about the folders that Windows uses: `GetWindowsDirectory`, `GetSystemDirectory`, `GetTempPath`, and `GetCurrentDirectory`.

You use the `GetWindowsDirectory` function to return the folder in which Windows was installed:

```
Declare Function GetWindowsDirectory Lib "kernel32" Alias "GetWindowsDirectoryA"
➥(ByVal lpBuffer As String, ByVal nSize As Long) As Long
```

lpBuffer	A `String` variable in which the pathname will be returned.
nSize	The length of the ***lpBuffer*** variable.

Many API functions require this argument combination (that is, a string buffer and the length of that buffer). The basic technique for these kinds of API functions is to declare a `String` variable with a specific size and then use VBA's `Len` function to pass the length of the string to the API function. Here's an example:

```
Dim strBuffer As String * 256
GetWindowsDirectory(strBuffer, Len(strBuffer))
```

In this case, the Windows folder will be stored in the `strBuffer` variable. Note that this API function (and the others we'll be examining in this section) returns 0 if the function isn't successful, so your code should test the function's return value. (If the function is successful, it returns the length of the returned pathname.)

You use the `GetSystemDirectory` function to return the pathname of Windows' System folder:

```
Declare Function GetSystemDirectory Lib "kernel32" Alias "GetSystemDirectoryA"
➥(ByVal lpBuffer As String, ByVal nSize As Long) As Long
```

lpBuffer	A `String` variable in which the pathname will be returned.
nSize	The length of the ***lpBuffer*** variable.

The `GetTempPath` function returns the pathname of the folder that Windows uses for its temporary files. Here's the syntax (note that the positions of the buffer length and the buffer variable are reversed):

```
Declare Function GetTempPath Lib "kernel32" Alias "GetTempPathA" (ByVal
➥nBufferLength As Long, ByVal lpBuffer As String) As Long
```

nBufferLength	The length of the ***lpBuffer*** variable.
lpBuffer	A `String` variable in which the pathname will be returned.

The GetCurrentDirectory function returns the pathname of the current Windows folder. Here's the syntax (again, the positions of the buffer length and the buffer variable are reversed):

```
Declare Function GetCurrentDirectory Lib "kernel32" Alias "GetCurrentDirectoryA"
➥(ByVal nBufferLength As Long, ByVal lpBuffer As String) As Long
```

nBufferLength	The length of the ***lpBuffer*** variable.
lpBuffer	A String variable in which the pathname will be returned.

NOTE: SETTING THE CURRENT DIRECTORY

If you need to set the current Windows directory, use Win32's SetCurrentDirectory function:

```
Declare Function SetCurrentDirectory Lib "kernel32" Alias
➥"SetCurrentDirectoryA" (ByVal lpPathName As String) As Long
```

lpPathName	A String variable that specifies the new path.

Listing 25.4 shows the WinDirInfo procedure that runs all four of these functions and prints the results in the Immediate window, as shown in Figure 25.3. (See Chapter 24, "Debugging VBA Procedures," for details on the Immediate window and the Debug.Print method.)

Listing 25.4. A procedure that uses several Win32 API functions to return the pathnames of various Windows folders.

```
Declare Function GetWindowsDirectory Lib "kernel32" Alias "GetWindowsDirectoryA"
➥(ByVal lpBuffer As String, ByVal nSize As Long) As Long
Declare Function GetSystemDirectory Lib "kernel32" Alias "GetSystemDirectoryA"
➥(ByVal lpBuffer As String, ByVal nSize As Long) As Long
Declare Function GetTempPath Lib "kernel32" Alias "GetTempPathA" (ByVal
➥nBufferLength As Long, ByVal lpBuffer As String) As Long
Declare Function SetCurrentDirectory Lib "kernel32" Alias "SetCurrentDirectoryA"
➥(ByVal lpPathName As String) As Long
Declare Function GetCurrentDirectory Lib "kernel32" Alias "GetCurrentDirectoryA"
➥(ByVal nBufferLength As Long, ByVal lpBuffer As String) As Long
Sub WinDirInfo()
    Dim strBuffer As String * 256
    Dim retVal As Long
    '
    ' Get the main Windows folder
    '
    retVal = GetWindowsDirectory(strBuffer, Len(strBuffer))
    If retVal <> 0 Then
        Debug.Print "Main Windows folder: "; strBuffer
    End If
    '
    ' Get the Windows system folder
    '
    strBuffer = ""
```

```
    retVal = GetSystemDirectory(strBuffer, Len(strBuffer))
    If retVal <> 0 Then
        Debug.Print "Windows system folder: "; strBuffer
    End If
    '
    ' Get the folder for temporary files
    '
    strBuffer = ""
    retVal = GetTempPath(Len(strBuffer), strBuffer)
    If retVal <> 0 Then
        Debug.Print "Windows temporary folder: "; strBuffer
    End If
    '
    ' Get the current folder
    '
    strBuffer = ""
    retVal = GetCurrentDirectory(Len(strBuffer), strBuffer)
    If retVal <> 0 Then
        Debug.Print "Windows current folder: "; strBuffer
    End If
End Sub
```

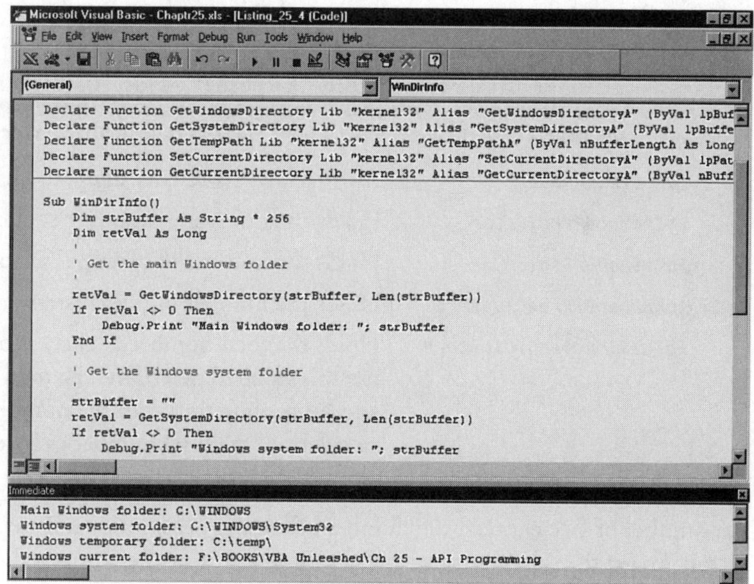

FIGURE 25.3.
The output of the `WinDirInfo` *procedure.*

In practice, you'll probably want to use the results of these functions to locate or store files. So you should note that, in each case, the `strBuffer` variable is 256 characters long, even if the returned path is less than that. If you only want to deal with the path, you can avoid the white space in the string by taking advantage of the fact that each function, if successful, returns the length of the pathname. This means that you can use VBA's `Left$` function to return just the pathname. For example, the following statements get the main Windows folder and then use the returned values to derive the pathname of the Media subfolder:

```
retVal = GetSystemDirectory(strBuffer, Len(strBuffer))
mediaFolder = Left$(strBuffer, retVal) & "\Media\"
```

Returning Disk Drive Information

This section examines two API functions that return information about the disk drives on a system: `GetDiskFreeSpace` and `GetDriveType`.

Determining the Number of Bytes Free

If your VBA procedures create, copy, move, or back up files, you'll probably want to know how much disk real estate you have to work with. For example, if your program is going to back up a document to a floppy disk, you should check to see how many free bytes the disk has before performing the operation. You can do that by invoking Win32's `GetDiskFreeSpace` function:

```
Declare Function GetDiskFreeSpace Lib "kernel32" Alias "GetDiskFreeSpaceA" (ByVal
➥lpRootPathName As String, lpSectorsPerCluster As Long, lpBytesPerSector
➥As Long, lpNumberOfFreeClusters As Long, lpTotalNumberOfClusters As Long) As Long
```

lpRootPathName	A string that represents any path on the disk.
lpSectorsPerCluster	Holds the number of sectors per cluster.
lpBytesPerSector	Holds the number of bytes per sector.
lpNumberOfFreeClusters	Holds the number of free clusters on the disk.
lpTotalNumberOfClusters	Holds the total number of clusters on the disk. You can use this value to determine the total capacity of the disk and, in conjunction with the number-of-bytes-free calculation, the total number of bytes used on the disk.

The `GetDiskFreeSpace` function works by returning three values (among others) about a disk: the number of free clusters, the number of sectors per cluster, and the number of bytes per sector. To get the total free space in bytes, you multiply these three values together.

NOTE: DETERMINING FILE SIZE

If you're moving or copying a file to a drive, it doesn't help to know how much free space exists on the drive if you don't know the size of the file. You can determine this by using VBA's `FileLen(pathname)` function, where *pathname* is the path and filename of the file. I'll talk more about VBA's low-level file functions in the next chapter.

Listing 25.5 shows a procedure that puts this function through its paces by checking the amount of free space on the floppy disk in drive A. (There is no error-trapping code in the `GetBytesFree` procedure, so be sure to place a formatted disk in the drive before you run this example.)

Listing 25.5. A procedure that determines the number of bytes available on a disk.

```
Declare Function GetDiskFreeSpace Lib "kernel32" Alias "GetDiskFreeSpaceA" (ByVal
➥lpRootPathName As String, lpSectorsPerCluster As Long, lpBytesPerSector As
➥Long, lpNumberOfFreeClusters As Long, lpTotalNumberOfClusters As Long)
➥As Long
Sub GetBytesFree()
    Dim lpSectorsPerCluster As Long
    Dim lpBytesPerSector As Long
    Dim lpNumberOfFreeClusters As Long
    Dim lpTotalNumberOfClusters As Long
    Dim retVal As Long

    retVal = GetDiskFreeSpace("A:\", lpSectorsPerCluster, lpBytesPerSector,
    ➥lpNumberOfFreeClusters, lpTotalNumberOfClusters)
    If retVal <> 0 Then
        Debug.Print "Sectors per cluster: "; lpSectorsPerCluster
        Debug.Print "Bytes per sector: "; lpBytesPerSector
        Debug.Print "Free clusters: "; lpNumberOfFreeClusters
        Debug.Print "Bytes free: "; lpSectorsPerCluster * lpBytesPerSector *
        ➥lpNumberOfFreeClusters
    End If
End Sub
```

Getting the Drive Type

During file operations, it's also important to know the type of disk drive you're dealing with. For example, if your code lets the user choose the drive for a copy or move operation, you'll want to make sure she doesn't choose a CD-ROM drive. To determine the drive type, the Win32 API offers the `GetDriveType` function:

```
Declare Function GetDriveType Lib "kernel32" Alias "GetDriveTypeA" (ByVal ndrive
➥As String) As Long
```

nDrive	A `String` variable that specifies the path of the root directory on the drive.

`GetDriveType` returns one of the following values:

Return Value	*Meaning*
0	The drive type couldn't be determined.
1	The drive doesn't have a root directory.
2	The drive is removable (such as a floppy disk drive).
3	The drive is fixed (such as a hard disk drive).
4	The drive is a network drive.
5	The drive is a CD-ROM drive.
6	The drive is a RAM disk.

Listing 25.6 shows the `DetermineDriveType` procedure, which prompts you for a drive root and then uses `GetDriveType` to return the drive type. A `Select Case` structure is used to translate the returned value into a message.

Listing 25.6. A procedure that determines the drive type.

```
Declare Function GetDriveType Lib "kernel32" Alias "GetDriveTypeA" (ByVal ndrive
➥As String) As Long
Public Const DRIVE_REMOVABLE = 2
Public Const DRIVE_FIXED = 3
Public Const DRIVE_REMOTE = 4
Public Const DRIVE_CDROM = 5
Public Const DRIVE_RAMDISK = 6
Sub DetermineDriveType()
    Dim ndrive As String
    Dim done As Boolean
    Dim retVal As Long
    done = False
    '
    ' Loop until Cancel is clicked
    '
    While Not done
        '
        ' Get the drive root
        '
        ndrive = InputBox("Enter the root address of the drive:")
```

```
        If ndrive <> "" Then
            '
            ' Get the drive type
            '
            retVal = GetDriveType(ndrive)
            '
            ' Translate the return value
            '
            Select Case retVal
                Case 0
                    MsgBox "Can't determine the drive type!"
                Case 1
                    MsgBox "Root directory does not exist!"
                Case DRIVE_REMOVABLE
                    MsgBox Left(ndrive, 2) & " is a removable drive."
                Case DRIVE_FIXED
                    MsgBox Left(ndrive, 2) & " is a fixed drive."
                Case DRIVE_REMOTE
                    MsgBox Left(ndrive, 2) & " is a network drive."
                Case DRIVE_CDROM
                    MsgBox Left(ndrive, 2) & " is a CD-ROM drive."
                Case DRIVE_RAMDISK
                    MsgBox Left(ndrive, 2) & " is a RAM disk."
            End Select
        Else
            done = True
        End If
    Wend
End Sub
```

Getting System Metrics

In Windows, system *metrics* are the dimensions (height and width) of the various display elements, including the screen, the scroll bars, the icons, the title bar, and so on. The `GetSystemMetrics` API function returns the values for all of Windows' system metrics, as well as some configuration information. Here's the syntax:

```
Declare Function GetSystemMetrics Lib "user32" (ByVal nIndex As Long) As Long
```

nIndex A constant that determines the metric information you want returned.

The value returned by the function is the metric you asked for. Listing 25.7 shows the various constants that `GetSystemMetrics` accepts. The `RunThroughMetrics` procedure sends each of these constants—as well as the constant name and a description—to a procedure named `GetMetric`. This procedure calls `GetSystemMetrics` and displays the results in the Immediate window.

Listing 25.7. This example polls the GetSystemMetrics API function.

```
Declare Function GetSystemMetrics Lib "user32" (ByVal nIndex As Long) As Long
'
' Constants for GetSystemMetrics
'
Private Const SM_CXSCREEN = 0
Private Const SM_CYSCREEN = 1
Private Const SM_CXVSCROLL = 2
Private Const SM_CYHSCROLL = 3
Private Const SM_CYCAPTION = 4
Private Const SM_CXBORDER = 5
Private Const SM_CYBORDER = 6
Private Const SM_CXDLGFRAME = 7
Private Const SM_CYDLGFRAME = 8
Private Const SM_CYVTHUMB = 9
Private Const SM_CXHTHUMB = 10
Private Const SM_CXICON = 11
Private Const SM_CYICON = 12
Private Const SM_CXCURSOR = 13
Private Const SM_CYCURSOR = 14
Private Const SM_CYMENU = 15
Private Const SM_CXFULLSCREEN = 16
Private Const SM_CYFULLSCREEN = 17
Private Const SM_CYKANJIWINDOW = 18
Private Const SM_MOUSEPRESENT = 19
Private Const SM_CYVSCROLL = 20
Private Const SM_CXHSCROLL = 21
Private Const SM_DEBUG = 22
Private Const SM_SWAPBUTTON = 23
Private Const SM_RESERVED1 = 24
Private Const SM_RESERVED2 = 25
Private Const SM_RESERVED3 = 26
Private Const SM_RESERVED4 = 27
Private Const SM_CXMIN = 28
Private Const SM_CYMIN = 29
Private Const SM_CXSIZE = 30
Private Const SM_CYSIZE = 31
Private Const SM_CXFRAME = 32
Private Const SM_CYFRAME = 33
Private Const SM_CXMINTRACK = 34
Private Const SM_CYMINTRACK = 35
Private Const SM_CXDOUBLECLK = 36
Private Const SM_CYDOUBLECLK = 37
Private Const SM_CXICONSPACING = 38
Private Const SM_CYICONSPACING = 39
Private Const SM_MENUDROPALIGNMENT = 40
Private Const SM_PENWINDOWS = 41
Private Const SM_DBCSENABLED = 42
Private Const SM_CMOUSEBUTTONS = 43
'
' This procedure accepts a constant value, the constant name,
' and a decription of the metric, and displays the results in
' the Immediate window.
'
```

```
Sub GetMetric(nIndex As Long, constantName As String, metricDesc As String)
    Dim retVal As Long
    retVal = GetSystemMetrics(nIndex)
    Debug.Print metricDesc; Tab(35); constantName; Tab; retVal
End Sub
'
' This procedure runs through each of the available metrics.
'
Sub RunThroughMetrics()
    GetMetric SM_CXSCREEN, "SM_CXSCREEN", "Screen width in pixels"
    GetMetric SM_CYSCREEN, "SM_CYSCREEN", "Screen height in pixels"
    GetMetric SM_CXVSCROLL, "SM_CXVSCROLL", "Vertical scroll arrow width"
    GetMetric SM_CYHSCROLL, "SM_CYHSCROLL", "Horizontal scroll arrow height"
    GetMetric SM_CYCAPTION, "SM_CYCAPTION", "Caption bar height"
    GetMetric SM_CXBORDER, "SM_CXBORDER", "Window border width"
    GetMetric SM_CYBORDER, "SM_CYBORDER", "Window border height"
    GetMetric SM_CXDLGFRAME, "SM_CXDLGFRAME", "Dialog window frame width"
    GetMetric SM_CYDLGFRAME, "SM_CYDLGFRAME", "Dialog window frame height"
    GetMetric SM_CYVTHUMB, "SM_CYVTHUMB", "Vertical scroll thumb height"
    GetMetric SM_CXHTHUMB, "SM_CXHTHUMB", "Horizontal scroll thumb width"
    GetMetric SM_CXICON, "SM_CXICON", "Icon width"
    GetMetric SM_CYICON, "SM_CYICON", "Icon height"
    GetMetric SM_CXCURSOR, "SM_CXCURSOR", "Cursor width"
    GetMetric SM_CYCURSOR, "SM_CYCURSOR", "Cursor height"
    GetMetric SM_CYMENU, "SM_CYMENU", "Menu bar height"
    GetMetric SM_CXFULLSCREEN, "SM_CXFULLSCREEN", "Full screen client area width"
    GetMetric SM_CYFULLSCREEN, "SM_CYFULLSCREEN", "Full screen client area height"
    GetMetric SM_CYKANJIWINDOW, "SM_CYKANJIWINDOW", "Kanji window height"
    GetMetric SM_MOUSEPRESENT, "SM_MOUSEPRESENT", "Mouse present flag"
    GetMetric SM_CYVSCROLL, "SM_CYVSCROLL", "Vertical scroll arrow height"
    GetMetric SM_CXHSCROLL, "SM_CXHSCROLL", "Horizontal scroll arrow width"
    GetMetric SM_DEBUG, "SM_DEBUG", "Debug version flag"
    GetMetric SM_SWAPBUTTON, "SM_SWAPBUTTON", "Mouse buttons swapped flag"
    GetMetric SM_CXMIN, "SM_CXMIN", "Minimum window width"
    GetMetric SM_CYMIN, "SM_CYMIN", "Minimum window height"
    GetMetric SM_CXSIZE, "SM_CXSIZE", "Minimize/Maximize icon width"
    GetMetric SM_CYSIZE, "SM_CYSIZE", "Minimize/Maximize icon height"
    GetMetric SM_CXFRAME, "SM_CXFRAME", "Window frame width"
    GetMetric SM_CYFRAME, "SM_CYFRAME", "Window frame height"
    GetMetric SM_CXMINTRACK, "SM_CXMINTRACK", "Minimum window tracking width"
    GetMetric SM_CYMINTRACK, "SM_CYMINTRACK", "Minimum window tracking height"
    GetMetric SM_CXDOUBLECLK, "SM_CXDOUBLECLK", "Double click x tolerance (3.1)"
    GetMetric SM_CYDOUBLECLK, "SM_CYDOUBLECLK", "Double click y tolerance (3.1)"
    GetMetric SM_CXICONSPACING, "SM_CXICONSPACING", "Horizontal icon spacing (3.1)"
    GetMetric SM_CYICONSPACING, "SM_CYICONSPACING", "Vertical icon spacing (3.1)"
    GetMetric SM_MENUDROPALIGNMENT, "SM_MENUDROPALIGNMENT", "Left or right menu
    ➥drop (3.1)"
    GetMetric SM_PENWINDOWS, "SM_PENWINDOWS", "Pen extensions installed (3.1)"
    GetMetric SM_DBCSENABLED, "SM_DBCSENABLED", "DBCS version of USER32 installed"
    GetMetric SM_CMOUSEBUTTONS, "SM_CMOUSEBUTTONS", "Number of buttons on mouse"
End Sub
```

Exiting Windows from VBA

For beginning users, it's often desirable to hide as much of the surrounding interface as possible. For example, if you're building an Excel application, you might want to boot Windows directly into the application so that the user never has to bother with Windows at all. For these kinds of situations, the API has an `ExitWindowsEx` function that lets you shut down Windows from your VBA procedures:

```
Declare Function ExitWindowsEx Lib "user32" Alias "ExitWindowsEx" (ByVal uFlags As
➥Long, ByVal dwReserved As Long) As Long
```

uFlags	A constant that determines whether Windows shuts down the computer, reboots the computer, or logs off.
dwReserved	This argument is ignored.

There are several constants you can use with this function, but the following three are the most useful:

uFlags *Value*	*Meaning*
`EWX_LOGOFF` (or 0)	Shuts down all running programs and logs the user off the system.
`EWX_SHUTDOWN` (or 1)	Shuts down all running programs and tells the user when it's safe to turn off the system.
`EWX_REBOOT` (or 2)	Shuts down all running programs and then reboots the system.

This function returns 0 if the shutdown was unsuccessful.

To demonstrate this function, I built a user form named VBAShutDown, shown in Figure 25.4. Listing 25.8 shows the `Declare` and constant definitions (see the module named Listing_25_8) as well as the `Click` event handler for the OK button. This handler examines the values of the option buttons and then runs `ExitWindowsEx` with the appropriate argument.

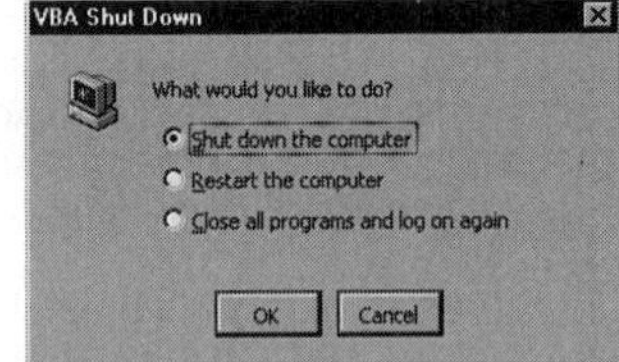

FIGURE 25.4.
Running the VBAShutDown user form displays this dialog box.

Listing 25.8. Declares the ExitWindows function as Public and then runs the VBAShutDown user form.

```
Public Declare Function ExitWindowsEx Lib "user32" (ByVal uFlags As Long, ByVal
➥dwReserved As Long) As Long
Public Const EWX_LOGOFF = 0
Public Const EWX_SHUTDOWN = 1
Public Const EWX_REBOOT = 2
Sub ShutDownFromExcel()
    VBAShutDown.Show
    Set VBAShutDown = Nothing
End Sub
'
' The event handler for the OK button's Click event.
'
Private Sub cmdOK_Click()
    Dim dwReserved As Long
    Dim retVal As Long
    '
    ' Exit Windows according to the option selected
    '
    If optShutDown = True Then
        retVal = ExitWindowsEx(EWX_SHUTDOWN, dwReserved)
    ElseIf optRestart = True Then
        retVal = ExitWindowsEx(EWX_REBOOT, dwReserved)
    Else
        retVal = ExitWindowsEx(EWX_LOGOFF, dwReserved)
    End If
End Sub
```

A Better Way to Handle DoEvents

In Windows 3.1, if you began a long procedure while running VBA, the user would normally see the hourglass icon, and she wouldn't be able to perform any other tasks until your procedure completed its chores. Here's an example of a procedure fragment that would prevent the user from doing anything else:

```
For i = 1 To 25000
    Application.StatusBar = "Number " & i
Next i
```

To keep this from happening, VBA provided the `DoEvents` statement, which served to yield execution to the operating system so that it could process any pending system events, such as mouse movements or keystrokes. Adding this statement to the `For...Next` loop just shown lets the user interact with the system while the loop runs its course:

```
For i = 1 To 25000
    Application.StatusBar = "Number " & I
    DoEvents
Next i
```

Windows 95 and Windows NT are preemptive multitasking environments, so there's less need for `DoEvents`. However, certain operations still tend to monopolize the system, so you might still need `DoEvents` statements in your code.

The problem with `DoEvents` is that it's extremely slow. When you run this statement, it tells Windows to check its list of possible events to see if any are pending. This is wasteful if there are no messages in the event queue and, since there usually are no messages waiting, `DoEvents` is needlessly slow.

To improve the performance of your procedures that use `DoEvents`, you can use Win32's `GetQueueStatus` function to see if there are any events waiting in the message queue. If there are, *then* your code can run `DoEvents`. Here's the `GetQueueStatus` syntax:

```
Declare Function GetQueueStatus Lib "user32" (ByVal fuFlags As Long) As Long
```

fuFlags This argument is a constant that specifies the type of messages to look for in the queue. For our purposes, there are five constants that look for user input messages:

`QS_KEY`	All keyboard input
`QS_MOUSEMOVE`	Mouse movements
`QS_MOUSEBUTTON`	Mouse clicks
`QS_MOUSE`	All mouse input
`QS_INPUT`	All mouse and keyboard input

If no messages are waiting in the queue, the function returns 0. How does this help your code? Well, if there are no events waiting to be processed, there's no point in running the `DoEvents` statement. So your code can simply check the return value of `GetQueueStatus` and invoke `DoEvents` only when an event is pending.

Listing 25.9 shows a procedure designed to demonstrate the difference that the `GetQueueStatus` function can make in application performance. This procedure consists mostly of two `For...Next` loops. The first loop just calls `DoEvents`, and the second loop checks `GetQueueStatus` and runs `DoEvents` only if an event is in the queue. Each loop is timed, and `Debug.Print` statements show the results in the Immediate window. As you can see in Figure 25.5, the results are astounding: The first loop took over 20 seconds, and the second loop took only about half a second. (Your mileage may vary. If you're using a relatively slow system, you might want to reduce the size of the loops.)

Listing 25.9. This example compares application performance using `DoEvents` by itself and using the `GetQueueStatus` API function.

```
Declare Function GetQueueStatus Lib "user32" (ByVal fuFlags As Long) As Long
Public Const QS_KEY = &H1
Public Const QS_MOUSEMOVE = &H2
Public Const QS_MOUSEBUTTON = &H4
```

```
Public Const QS_MOUSE = (QS_MOUSEMOVE Or QS_MOUSEBUTTON)
Public Const QS_INPUT = (QS_MOUSE Or QS_KEY)
Sub DoEventsTester()
    Dim i As Long
    Dim start As Long
    '
    ' Get the current Timer value and start the "DoEvents only" loop
    '
    start = Timer
    For i = 1 To 100000
        DoEvents
    Next 'i
    '
    ' Display the results
    '
    Debug.Print "With DoEvents by itself: "; Timer - start; " seconds"
    '
    ' Get the current Timer value and start the "GetQueueStatus" loop
    '
    start = Timer
    For i = 1 To 100000
        If GetQueueStatus(QS_INPUT) <> 0 Then DoEvents
    Next 'i
    '
    ' Display the results
    '
    Debug.Print "With GetQueueStatus check: "; Timer - start; " seconds"
End Sub
```

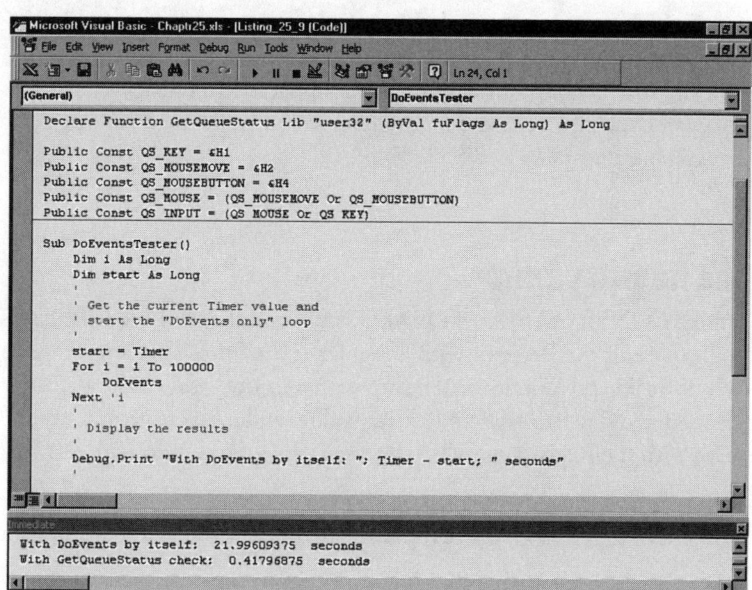

FIGURE 25.5.
The procedure results show that `GetQueueStatus` *makes a huge difference in application speed.*

Working with the Registry

When you change the desktop wallpaper using Control Panel's Display icon, the next time you start your computer, how does Windows 95 know which wallpaper you selected? If you change your video display driver, how does Windows 95 know to use that driver at startup and not the original driver loaded during Setup? In other words, how does Windows 95 "remember" the various settings and options that you've selected yourself or that are appropriate for your system?

The secret of Windows 95's prodigious memory is the Registry—a central repository that Windows 95 uses to store anything and everything that applies to the configuration of your system. This includes hardware settings, object properties, operating system settings, and application options.

However, the Registry isn't a tool wielded only by Windows. Most 32-bit applications make use of the Registry as a place to store setup options, customization values selected by the user, and much more. The good news is that not only can your VBA applications read the current value of any Registry setting, but they can also use the Registry as a storage area. This lets you keep track of program settings, recently used files, and any other configuration data that you'd like to save between sessions. This section shows you how to use the Win32 API to manipulate the Registry from within your applications.

NOTE: VBA'S REGISTRY STATEMENTS

If you're interested only in storing your application's settings in the Registry, VBA offers several statements that are much easier to use than the API functions. I'll show you how to use these statements in Chapter 26.

The Registry Editor

Unlike CONFIG.SYS, AUTOEXEC.BAT, and the .INI files, the Registry files are binary, so you can't edit the Registry with a regular text editor. That's not a problem, though, because Windows 95 and Windows NT ship with a utility—called the Registry Editor—that lets you view, edit, and delete existing Registry values and even create new ones. Before learning how to work with the Registry via VBA, let's see what you can do with the Registry Editor.

As you can imagine, the Registry Editor is a powerful tool, and it's not something to be wielded lightly. For that reason, the Setup program doesn't install a shortcut for the Registry Editor on any of the Start menus. To crank up the Registry Editor, you must use one of the following techniques:

- In Windows 95, select Start | Run, type `regedit` in the Run dialog box, and click OK.
- In Windows NT, select Start | Run, type `regedt32` in the Run dialog box, and click OK.

When the Registry Editor loads, you'll see a window similar to the one shown in Figure 25.6 (this is the NT version of the Registry Editor).

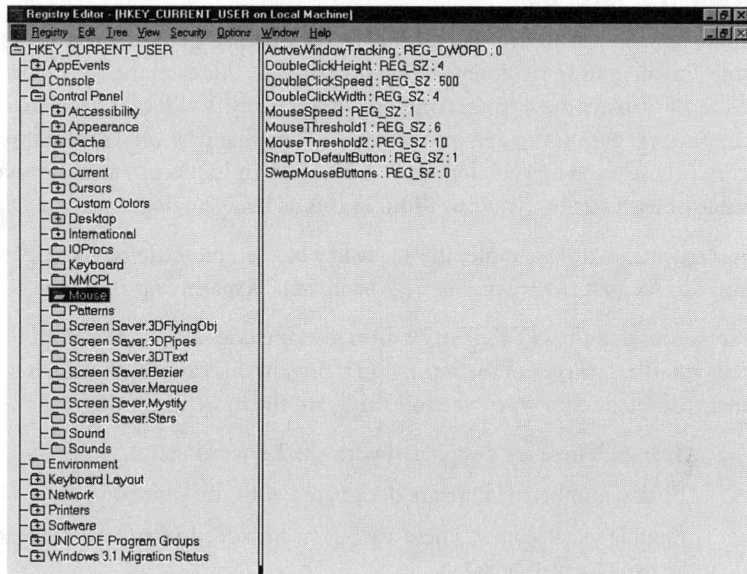

FIGURE 25.6.
The Windows NT Registry Editor.

Examining the Structure of the Registry

The Registry Editor window looks a lot like the Explorer window, and it works basically the same. The left side of the Registry Editor window is similar to Explorer's Folders pane, except that rather than folders, you see *keys*. For lack of a better phrase, I'll call the left pane the *Keys pane.*

Navigating the Keys Pane

The Keys pane, like Explorer's Folders pane, is organized in a treelike hierarchy. At the root level are several special keys called *handles,* whose names all start with HKEY:

- Windows 95 has six handles, and they're all accessible via the Keys pane.
- Windows NT has five handles, and they're accessible via the Window menu (in other words, NT displays each handle in its own window).

These keys are referred to collectively as the Registry's *root keys.* They all contain subkeys, which you can display by clicking the plus sign (+) to the left of each key (in NT, you need to double-click the plus sign). When you open a key, the plus sign changes to a minus sign (–). To close a key, click the minus sign (in NT, double-click it).

You'll often have to drill down several levels to get to the key you want. For example, Figure 25.6 shows the Registry Editor after I've opened the `HKEY_CURRENT_USER` key and then opened the `Control Panel` subkey.

Registry Settings

If the left side of the Registry Editor window is analogous to Explorer's Folder pane, the right side is analogous to Explorer's Contents pane. In this case, the right side of the Registry Editor window displays the settings contained in each key (so I'll call it the *Settings pane*). Each line in the Settings pane is divided into two areas. The first part shows the name of each setting in the currently selected key (analogous to a filename in Explorer), and the second part tells you the value of each setting (you can think of this as being analogous to the contents of a file).

In Figure 25.6, for example, the `Mouse` key has several settings. On the third line, for example, you can see that the setting name is `DoubleClickSpeed`, and the value is 500.

Note, too, that the NT Registry Editor also includes `REG_SZ` as part of the setting's value. This tells you the data type of the settings (a string, in this case). Although Registry key settings have many different data types, the following are the most common:

Strings: These are designated with the keyword `REG_SZ`.

Binary numbers: These are designated with the keyword `REG_BINARY`.

Double word values: These are 32-bit hexadecimal values arranged as eight digits. The keyword is `REG_DWORD`.

The Registry's Root Keys

The root keys are your Registry starting points, so you'll need to become familiar with what kinds of data each key holds. The next few sections summarize the contents of each key.

The HKEY_CLASSES_ROOT Key

The `HKEY_CLASSES_ROOT` key contains the same data that the Windows 3.1 Registry showed: file extensions and their associations, as well as applications and their OLE and DDE (Dynamic Data Exchange) information. There are also keys related to shortcuts and other interface features.

The top part of this key contains subkeys for various file extensions. You'll see `.bmp` for .BMP (Paint) files, `.doc` for .DOC (WordPad) files, and so on. In each of these subkeys, the `Default` setting (in Windows 95) or the `<No Name>` setting (in Windows NT) tells you the name of the registered file type associated with the extension. For example, if you highlight the `.txt` subkey, you'll see that it's associated with the `txtfile` file type.

These registered file types appear as subkeys later in the `HKEY_CLASSES_ROOT` branch. If you scroll down, you'll eventually come across the `txtfile` subkey. The Registry keeps track of various settings for each registered file type. In particular, the `shell` subkey tells you the actions associated with this file type.

The `HKEY_CLASSES_ROOT` key is actually a copy (or an *alias,* as these copied keys are called) of the following `HKEY_LOCAL_MACHINE` key:

```
HKEY_LOCAL_MACHINE\SOFTWARE\Classes
```

The Registry creates an alias for `HKEY_CLASSES_ROOT` to make these keys easier for applications to access and to improve compatibility with Windows 3.1 programs.

The HKEY_CURRENT_USER Key

If you've set up multiple user profiles on your computer, the `HKEY_CURRENT_USER` key contains data that applies to the user who's currently logged on. (If you don't have multiple user profiles, `HKEY_CURRENT_USER` is the same as `HKEY_USERS`.)

`HKEY_CURRENT_USER` contains user-specific settings for Control Panel options, network connections, applications, and more. Note that `HKEY_CURRENT_USER` is an alias for the subkey of `HKEY_USERS` that corresponds to the current user. For example, if the current user is Biff, `HKEY_CURRENT_USER` is the same as `HKEY_USERS\Biff`.

Here's a summary of some of the settings contained in the various `HKEY_CURRENT_USER` subkeys (the availability of these settings varies between Windows 95 and Windows NT):

`AppEvents`: Sound files that play when particular system events occur (such as the maximizing of a window).

`Control Panel`: Settings related to certain Control Panel icons.

`InstallLocationsMRU`: A list of the drives and folders that were most recently used (MRU) to install software or drivers.

`Keyboard Layout`: The keyboard layout as selected via Control Panel's Keyboard icon.

`Network`: Settings related to mapped network drives.

`RemoteAccess`: Settings related to Dial-Up Networking.

`Software`: User-specific settings related to installed applications. Most 32-bit programs use this key to save their user-specific settings instead of using WIN.INI or private .INIs.

The HKEY_LOCAL_MACHINE Key

The HKEY_LOCAL_MACHINE key contains non-user–specific configuration data for your system's hardware and applications. Let's run through the various HKEY_LOCAL_MACHINE subkeys:

Config: Contains subkeys for each hardware profile defined on your system. The subkey name is a unique identifier assigned to each profile (for example, 0001). To find out which profile is current, you have to head to the following subkey:

HKEY_LOCAL_MACHINE\System\CurrentControlSet\control\IDConfigDB

The CurrentConfig setting gives you the identifier of the current profile. The names of each profile are stored in the various "FriendlyName" settings (for example, FriendlyName0001). The current configuration is aliased by the HKEY_CURRENT_CONFIG key (see the section "The HKEY_CURRENT_CONFIG Key" a bit later).

Enum: Contains the data gathered by the Windows 95 bus enumerators. Enum contains subkeys for each hardware class, and each hardware class has subkeys for the installed devices in that class. Each device subkey has various settings related to the device, including its description, its driver, and its hardware ID.

Hardware: Contains subkeys related to serial ports and modems (used by HyperTerminal), as well as the floating-point processor.

Network: Contains a Logon subkey with various settings related to the network logon, including the user name and whether or not the logon was validated by a network server.

Security: Contains a Provider subkey that specifies the domain under which network security is administered.

SOFTWARE: Contains computer-specific settings related to installed applications. Most 32-bit programs use this key to save their computer-specific settings instead of using WIN.INI or private .INIs. The Classes subkey is aliased by the HKEY_CLASSES_ROOT key. The Microsoft subkey contains settings related to Windows 95 (as well as any other Microsoft products you have installed on your computer).

System: Contains subkeys and settings related to Windows 95 startup, including the following ones in the CurrentControlSet\control subkey: installable file systems (the FileSystem subkey), a list of the installed Windows 95 files (the InstalledFiles subkey), printers (the Print subkey), the time zone (the TimeZoneInformation subkey), and a list of the drivers loaded from VMM32.VXD (the VMM32Files subkey).

The HKEY_USERS Key

The HKEY_USERS key contains settings for Control Panel options, network connections, applications, and more. If you haven't enabled user profiles on your machine, HKEY_USERS has only one subkey, .Default, which contains the same settings as HKEY_CURRENT_USER.

If you have enabled user profiles, HKEY_USERS always has two subkeys: the .Default subkey, and a key for the current user. The settings in the .Default subkey are applied to users logging in for the first time, and the subkey for the current user is the same as HKEY_CURRENT_USER.

The HKEY_CURRENT_CONFIG Key

In Windows 95, the HKEY_CURRENT_CONFIG key contains settings for the current hardware profile. If your machine uses only one hardware profile, HKEY_CURRENT_CONFIG is an alias for HKEY_LOCAL_MACHINE\Config\0001. If your machine uses multiple hardware profiles, HKEY_CURRENT_CONFIG is an alias for HKEY_LOCAL_MACHINE\Config*CurrentConfig*, in which *CurrentConfig* is the numeric identifier of the current hardware profile. This identifier is given by the CurrentConfig setting in the following key:

```
HKEY_LOCAL_MACHINE\System\CurrentControlSet\control\IDConfigDB
```

As with HKEY_CLASSES_ROOT, the HKEY_CURRENT_CONFIG alias makes it easier for applications to access the settings in this key.

The Registry and the Win32 API

Now that you're up to speed on the ins and outs of the Registry, it's time to put this knowledge to work and learn how to work with the Registry within your VBA applications. The Win32 API has many different Registry-related functions, but here are the four you'll use the most:

RegOpenKeyEx: Opens a Registry key.

RegQueryValueEx: Gets the current value of a Registry setting.

RegSetValueEx: Sets the value of a Registry setting.

RegCloseKey: Closes a Registry key.

The next four sections show you how to use each function.

Opening a Registry Key

Before you can work with a Registry setting, you must open the key in which it resides. You do that by running Win32's RegOpenKeyEx function:

```
Declare Function RegOpenKeyEx Lib "advapi32.dll" Alias "RegOpenKeyExA" (ByVal hKey
➥As Long, ByVal lpSubKey As String, ByVal ulOptions As Long, ByVal
➥samDesired As Long, phkResult As Long) As Long
```

hKey The handle of a currently open key, or one of the following constants:

`HKEY_CLASSES_ROOT`

`HKEY_CURRENT_USER`

`HKEY_LOCAL_MACHINE`

`HKEY_USERS`

lpSubKey A `String` that specifies the subkey you want to open.

ulOptions This is a reserved value that must always be set to 0.

samDesired One or more constants that determine the security access you have to the open key:

Value	*Meaning*
KEY_ALL_ACCESS	A combination of KEY_QUERY_VALUE, KEY_ENUMERATE_SUB_KEYS, KEY_NOTIFY, KEY_CREATE_SUB_KEY, KEY_CREATE_LINK, and KEY_SET_VALUE access.
KEY_CREATE_LINK	Permission to create a symbolic link.
KEY_CREATE_SUB_KEY	Permission to create subkeys.
KEY_ENUMERATE_SUB_KEYS	Permission to enumerate subkeys.
KEY_EXECUTE	Permission for read access.
KEY_NOTIFY	Permission for change notification.
KEY_QUERY_VALUE	Permission to query subkey data.
KEY_READ	A combination of KEY_QUERY_VALUE, KEY_ENUMERATE_SUB_KEYS, and KEY_NOTIFY access.

Value	*Meaning*
`KEY_SET_VALUE`	Permission to set subkey data.
`KEY_WRITE`	A combination of `KEY_SET_VALUE` and `KEY_CREATE_SUB_KEY` access.

phkResult A `Long` value that provides a handle to the opened key. You use this handle to reference the key in subsequent operations.

If the function succeeds, the return value is `ERROR_SUCCESS`. For example, suppose you want to work with a setting in the following key (Windows 95 only):

```
HKEY_CURRENT_USER\AppEvents\Schemes\Apps\.Default\.Default\.Current
```

Here's a procedure fragment that gives you an overview of how you would use `RegOpenKeyEx` to open this key:

```
Dim hResult As Long
Dim retVal As Long
strSubKey = "AppEvents\Schemes\Apps\.Default\.Default\.Current"
retVal = RegOpenKeyEx(HKEY_CURRENT_USER, strSubKey, 0&, KEY_ALL_ACCESS, hResult)
If retVal = ERROR_SUCCESS Then
    [do something with the key via the hResult handle]
Else
    [display an error message, or whatever]
End If
```

Closing a Registry Key

Before examining how you work with an open Registry key, let's see how you close an open key so we can tackle some useful examples in the next few sections. To close an open key, use the `RegCloseKey` API function:

```
Declare Function RegCloseKey Lib "advapi32.dll" (ByVal hKey As Long) As Long
```

hKey The handle of the key you want to close.

For example, the following statement uses the `hResult` handle to close an open key:

```
retVal = RegCloseKey(hResult)
```

Again, if this function is successful, it returns `ERROR_SUCCESS`.

Querying a Registry Value

Once you've got your open Registry key, you can "query" the value of any setting within that key. You do this by invoking Win32's `RegQueryValueEx` function:

```
Declare Function RegQueryValueEx Lib "advapi32.dll" Alias "RegQueryValueExA" (ByVal
➥hKey As Long, ByVal lpValueName As String, ByVal lpReserved As Long,
➥lpType As Long, lpData As Any, lpcbData As Long) As Long
```

hKey	The handle of the key opened with `RegOpenKeyEx`.
lpValueName	A `String` that specifies the name of the setting you want to work with.
lpReserved	A reserved value that must always be set to 0.
lpType	A variable that returns the data type of the retrieved value (for example, `REG_SZ` or `REG_DWORD`).
lpData	A variable that will store the returned value. Note that if you use a `String` variable, you have to pass it by value, like so: `ByVal lpData As Any`
lpcbData	The size, in bytes, of the ***`lpData`*** buffer.

As with the other Registry functions, if the function succeeds, the return value is `ERROR_SUCCESS`. Note, too, that the key identified by ***`hKey`*** must have been opened with at least `KEY_QUERY_VALUE` access.

As an example, let's see how you can use this function to determine whether or not a user is running the Windows 95 OEM Service Release 2 (OSR2). You can find out the Windows 95 version by right-clicking My Computer and then choosing Properties to display the System Properties dialog box. The original Windows 95 lists its version number as 4.00.95A, and the OSR2 release displays 4.00.95B.

The letter at the end is the Windows 95 "subversion." It's stored in the Registry in the following subkey:

```
HKEY_LOCAL_MACHINE\SOFTWARE\Microsoft\Windows\CurrentVersion
```

The setting is named `SubVersionNumber`. Listing 25.10 shows a procedure designed to extract this setting so that you can tell which version of Windows 95 you're dealing with. After declaring the API functions and initializing a ridiculous number of constants, this procedure performs the following tasks:

- The subkey that contains the `SubVersionNumber` setting is opened.
- The variables required for the `RegQueryValueEx` function are initialized, including the `strSetting` variable, which holds the name of the setting.
- `RegQueryValueEx` is run to get the value of the `SubVersionNumber` setting.
- A message is displayed that contains the Windows 95 version.

Listing 25.10. Using Win32 API functions to read the Windows 95 subversion from the Registry.

```
Declare Function RegOpenKeyEx Lib "advapi32.dll" Alias "RegOpenKeyExA" (ByVal hKey
➥As Long, ByVal lpSubKey As String, ByVal ulOptions As Long, ByVal
➥samDesired As Long, phkResult As Long) As Long
Declare Function RegQueryValueEx Lib "advapi32.dll" Alias "RegQueryValueExA" (ByVal
➥hKey As Long, ByVal lpValueName As String, ByVal lpReserved As Long, lpType
➥As Long, ByVal lpData As Any, lpcbData As Long) As Long
Declare Function RegCloseKey Lib "advapi32.dll" (ByVal hKey As Long) As Long
'
' You may not need all these variables!
'
Public Const DELETE = &H10000
Public Const READ_CONTROL = &H20000
Public Const WRITE_DAC = &H40000
Public Const WRITE_OWNER = &H80000
Public Const SYNCHRONIZE = &H100000
Public Const STANDARD_RIGHTS_READ = (READ_CONTROL)
Public Const STANDARD_RIGHTS_WRITE = (READ_CONTROL)
Public Const STANDARD_RIGHTS_EXECUTE = (READ_CONTROL)
Public Const STANDARD_RIGHTS_REQUIRED = &HF0000
Public Const STANDARD_RIGHTS_ALL = &H1F0000
Public Const KEY_QUERY_VALUE = &H1
Public Const KEY_SET_VALUE = &H2
Public Const KEY_CREATE_SUB_KEY = &H4
Public Const KEY_ENUMERATE_SUB_KEYS = &H8
Public Const KEY_NOTIFY = &H10
Public Const KEY_CREATE_LINK = &H20
Public Const KEY_READ = ((STANDARD_RIGHTS_READ Or KEY_QUERY_VALUE Or
➥KEY_ENUMERATE_SUB_KEYS Or KEY_NOTIFY) And (Not SYNCHRONIZE))
Public Const KEY_WRITE = ((STANDARD_RIGHTS_WRITE Or KEY_SET_VALUE Or
➥KEY_CREATE_SUB_KEY) And (Not SYNCHRONIZE))
Public Const KEY_EXECUTE = (KEY_READ)
Public Const KEY_ALL_ACCESS = ((STANDARD_RIGHTS_ALL Or KEY_QUERY_VALUE Or
➥KEY_SET_VALUE Or KEY_CREATE_SUB_KEY Or KEY_ENUMERATE_SUB_KEYS Or
➥KEY_NOTIFY Or KEY_CREATE_LINK) And (Not SYNCHRONIZE))
Public Const ERROR_SUCCESS = 0&
Public Const HKEY_CLASSES_ROOT = &H80000000
Public Const HKEY_CURRENT_USER = &H80000001
Public Const HKEY_LOCAL_MACHINE = &H80000002
Public Const HKEY_USERS = &H80000003
Public Const REG_SZ = 1
Public Const REG_BINARY = 3
Public Const REG_DWORD = 4
Sub GetWin95SubVersion()
    Dim strSubKey As String
    Dim strSetting As String
    Dim strData As String * 256
    Dim lngType As Long
    Dim lngDataLen As Long
    Dim hResult As Long
    Dim retval As Long
    '
    ' Specify the subkey
    '
    strSubKey = "SOFTWARE\Microsoft\Windows\CurrentVersion"
```

continues

Listing 25.10. continued

```
    '
    ' Open the subkey
    '
    retval = RegOpenKeyEx(HKEY_LOCAL_MACHINE, strSubKey, 0&, KEY_QUERY_VALUE,
    ➥hResult)
    '
    ' Did it work?
    '
    If retVal = ERROR_SUCCESS Then
        '
        ' Specify the setting name
        '
        strSetting = "SubVersionNumber"
        '
        ' Initialize the buffer length variable
        '
        lngDataLen = Len(strData)
        '
        ' Make sure we've got a good handle
        '
        If hResult <> 0 Then
            '
            ' Get the setting's value
            '
            retVal = RegQueryValueEx(hResult, strSetting, 0&, lngType, strData,
            ➥lngDataLen)
            '
            ' Everything okay?
            '
            If retVal = ERROR_SUCCESS Then
                '
                ' Test the returned string
                '
                If UCase$(Left$(strData, 1)) = "A" Then
                    MsgBox "You're running regular Windows 95."
                Else
                    MsgBox "You're running Windows 95 OSR2."
                End If
            End If
        End If
        '
        ' Close the key
        '
        retVal = RegCloseKey(hResult)
    Else
        MsgBox "Error opening key: " & retVal
    End If
End Sub
```

You might be wondering how you use `RegQueryValueEx` to return the current value of a `(Default)` or `<No Name>` setting. For these types of settings, you pass a null buffer to the

RegQueryValueEx function. For example, the following procedure fragment returns the name of the file that produces the default beep sound in the current sound scheme:

```
strSubKey = "AppEvents\Schemes\Apps\.Default\.Default\.Current"
retVal = RegOpenKeyEx(HKEY_CURRENT_USER, strSubKey, 0&, KEY_QUERY_VALUE, hResult)
strSetting = ""
lngDataLen = Len(strData)
retVal = RegQueryValueEx(hResult, strSetting, 0&, lngType, strData, lngDataLen)
```

Setting a Registry Value

Rather than just reading the value of a Registry setting, you might need your code to change the value. For example, earlier I told you that you can use the MessageBeep API function to play the different event sounds. Rather than trust that the user has set these sounds to something other than the default beep, you can set the sounds programmatically. The secret of this is the RegSetValueEx API function:

```
Declare Function RegSetValueEx Lib "advapi32.dll" Alias "RegSetValueExA" (ByVal
➥hKey As Long, ByVal lpValueName As String, ByVal Reserved As Long, ByVal
➥dwType As Long, lpData As Any, ByVal cbData As Long) As Long
```

hKey	The handle of the key opened with RegOpenKeyEx.
lpValueName	A String that specifies the name of the setting you want to change.
Reserved	A reserved value that must always be set to 0.
dwType	A constant that specifies the data type of the setting (for example, REG_SZ or REG_DWORD).
lpData	A variable that contains the new value. Note that if you use a String variable, you have to pass it by value, like so: ByVal ***lpData*** As Any
cbData	The size, in bytes, of the ***lpData*** buffer.

As usual, the function returns ERROR_SUCCESS if it's successful. Also, make sure you open the key identified by ***hKey*** with at least KEY_SET_VALUE access.

As an example, Listing 25.11 shows a procedure that changes the value of the default beep. The appropriate subkey is opened, and then the GetWindowsDirectory API function is brought back in order to construct the path to the Media subfolder. With this path in hand, the strData variable is set to a file called The Microsoft Sound.wav. Then RegSetValueEx modifies the Registry setting, and MessageBeep plays the new sound.

Listing 25.11. Using Win32 API functions to change the default beep in the Registry.

```
Declare Function RegOpenKeyEx Lib "advapi32.dll" Alias "RegOpenKeyExA" (ByVal hKey
➥As Long, ByVal lpSubKey As String, ByVal ulOptions As Long, ByVal
➥samDesired As Long, phkResult As Long) As Long
Declare Function RegCloseKey Lib "advapi32.dll" (ByVal hKey As Long) As Long
Declare Function RegSetValueEx Lib "advapi32.dll" Alias "RegSetValueExA" (ByVal
➥hKey As Long, ByVal lpValueName As String, ByVal Reserved As Long, ByVal
➥dwType As Long, ByVal lpData As Any, ByVal cbData As Long) As Long
Declare Function GetWindowsDirectory Lib "kernel32" Alias "GetWindowsDirectoryA"
➥(ByVal lpBuffer As String, ByVal nSize As Long) As Long
Declare Function MessageBeep Lib "user32" (ByVal wType As Long) As Long
Sub ChangeDefaultSound()
    Dim strSubKey As String
    Dim strSetting As String
    Dim strData As String
    Dim strWinDir As String * 256
    Dim lngType As Long
    Dim lngDataLen As Long
    Dim hResult As Long
    Dim retval As Long
    '
    ' Specify the subkey
    '
    strSubKey = "AppEvents\Schemes\Apps\.Default\.Default\.Current"
    '
    ' Open the subkey
    '
    retval = RegOpenKeyEx(HKEY_CURRENT_USER, strSubKey, 0&, KEY_SET_VALUE, hResult)
    '
    ' Did it work?
    '
    If retval = ERROR_SUCCESS Then
        '
        ' Get the main Windows folder (assume it works)
        '
        retval = GetWindowsDirectory(strWinDir, Len(strWinDir))
        '
        ' We're changing a default setting, so send the null string
        '
        strSetting = ""
        '
        ' Store the new value in the buffer
        '
        strData = Left$(strWinDir, retval) & "\Media\The Microsoft Sound.wav"
        lngDataLen = Len(strData)
        '
        ' Make sure we've got a good handle
        '
        If hResult <> 0 Then
            '
            ' Set the value
            '
            retval = RegSetValueEx(hResult, strSetting, 0&, REG_SZ, strData,
            ➥lngDataLen)
            '
            ' If everything's okay, play the new sound
            '
```

```
            If retval = ERROR_SUCCESS Then
                MessageBeep 0
            End If
        End If
        '
        ' Close the key
        '
        retval = RegCloseKey(hResult)
    Else
        MsgBox "Error opening key: " & retval
    End If
End Sub
```

Summary

This chapter showed you how to tap into the power of the Win32 API. After a brief overview of Win32, I showed you how to declare the API Sub and Function procedures in your VBA modules, including how to use constants and type definitions and how to avoid problems. The rest of this chapter examined a few API examples.

For some related information, check out the following chapters:

- The procedures in this chapter made extensive use of the `Debug.Print` statement and the Immediate window. I showed you how to work with these VBA elements in Chapter 24, "Debugging VBA Procedures."
- The Win32 API has functions that let you read and save Registry entries. However, VBA 5.0 now has built-in functions for handling these duties. I'll tell you how to use them in Chapter 26, "VBA Tips and Techniques."

- Chapter 26 is also the place to go for information on VBA's low-level file functions.
- I use the `GetDriveType` and `GetDiskFreeSpace` API functions in Chapter 28, "Making Backups as You Work."

CHAPTER 26

VBA Tips and Techniques

IN THIS CHAPTER

We never stop investigating. We are never satisfied that we know enough to get by. Every question we answer leads on to another question. This has become the greatest survival trick of our species.

—Desmond Morris

Although I've labeled this a "Tips and Techniques" chapter, it's more like a hodgepodge of miscellaneous VBA ideas and methods that simply didn't fit anywhere else in the book. Although you can write powerful and useful VBA applications without using any of the techniques I've outlined in this chapter (with the possible exception of the section "Tips for Faster Procedures"), they're indispensable when you *do* need them. For example, if you'll be coding for 16-bit and 32-bit versions of Excel, the compiler directives will prove most useful. Similarly, any time you need to store user choices or program parameters, the Registry is the ideal place to do so. And although low-level file I/O sounds hopelessly arcane, you'll be pleasantly surprised at just how often this crucial skill comes in handy. This chapter covers all of these techniques and much more.

Conditional Compilation in VBA

VBA's `If...Then...Else` statement is normally used to check a particular condition and then run a different set of statements depending on the result. In most cases, the condition you check will be a local one: the current value of a variable, the return value of a function, the current time, and so on. However, what if you have a condition to check that is more global in scope? Here are some examples:

- You might need to run different sets of statements depending on the customer or department using your application. For example, if Marketing is using the application, open the Marketing database, but if Accounting is using the application, open the Accounting database instead.
- You might need to run certain statements only if you're testing and debugging your code. For example, while testing the application, you might sprinkle `Debug.Print` statements throughout the code to check certain values (see Chapter 24, "Debugging VBA Procedures"). However, you don't want these statements to execute when the application is finalized.
- You might need to code for both 32-bit and 16-bit environments if you're using API functions (see Chapter 25, "Programming the Windows API"). If you're in a 32-bit environment, you'll want to run a particular Win32 function, but if you're in a 16-bit environment, you'll want to run the corresponding Win16 function.

I describe these scenarios as "global" because you'll probably have to test for them throughout your code. For example, suppose you're building an application that will be used by multiple departments. At different points in your code, you'll need to test for a particular department in order to perform actions specific to that department: open a document, display a form, customize a `MsgBox` statement, and so on.

One way to handle this would be to set up a module-level constant that holds the name of the department (to continue the example). Your code could then test for the value of the constant using `If...Then...Else` statements, like so:

```
Const DEPT = "Marketing"
Sub Procedure1()
    If DEPT = "Marketing" Then
        [Put Marketing-specific code here]
    ElseIf DEPT = "Accounting" Then
        [Put Accounting-specific code here]
    [etc.]
    End If
End Sub
```

When the application is done, you set the `DEPT` constant equal to `Marketing` and then distribute the file to the Marketing department. You then change `DEPT` to `Accounting` and distribute the application to the Accounting department, and so on. This approach works quite nicely, and it's relatively easy to apply it to the other scenarios just listed.

There is one problem, however: When VBA compiles your code (that is, when it converts the code into the format VBA uses to execute the statements), it compiles *all* of the code. So even if you've specified a particular value for your global constant, VBA still compiles the code that will never be executed. This isn't a catastrophe for small applications, but larger applications might end up with thousands of lines of "redundant" code. When compiled, these files will be much larger than they need to be, which means that they consume more memory and disk space, and they'll run slower.

VBA 5.0

Creating separate, department-specific (or whatever) applications would solve this problem, but your application will be much harder to maintain. So what's the solution? Use the *conditional compilation* feature that's new in VBA 5.0. With conditional compilation, you still set up conditions in your code by using a global constant and a series of tests. However, VBA will compile only the code that satisfies the condition. If you set the constant equal to "Marketing," for example, VBA will compile only the Marketing-specific statements and will ignore everything else.

Setting Up Your Application for Conditional Compilation

VBA 5.0

Enabling conditional compilation in your code involves using the two *compiler directives* that are new to VBA 5.0: `#Const` and `#If...Then`.

You use the `#Const` compiler directive to declare a module-level conditional compilation constant. As before, you set the value of this constant according to the scenario you want to use and then test the value of this constant throughout your code. This directive is identical to the regular `Const` statement (described in Chapter 2, "Understanding Variables"), except that it includes the leading number sign (#), which identifies it as a compiler directive. Here's an example:

```
#Const DEPT = "Marketing"
```

NOTE: #CONST SCOPE

Unfortunately, `#Const` compiler directives can be declared only with module-level scope. You can't add the `Public` keyword to make the constant available to all the modules in your project.

To test your conditional compilation constant, you use the `#If...Then` compiler directive:

```
#If CONSTANT = Value1 Then
    [If statements go here]
#ElseIf CONSTANT = Value2 Then
    [ElseIf statements go here]
etc.
#Else
    [Else statements go here]
#End If
```

Listing 26.1 shows a sample procedure that sets up conditional compilation and displays a welcome message, depending on the value of the `DEPT` constant.

Listing 26.1. A simple example of conditional compilation.

```
#Const DEPT = "Marketing"
Sub Main()
    #If DEPT = "Marketing" Then
        MsgBox "Welcome to the Marketing application!"
    #ElseIf DEPT = "Accounting" Then
        MsgBox "Welcome to the Accounting application!"
    #Else
        MsgBox "Welcome to the application!"
    #End If
End Sub
```

NOTE: THIS CHAPTER'S CODE LISTINGS

```
#Const APPLICATION = "Excel"
#If APPLICATION = "Excel" Then
    MsgBox "Code listings are on the CD in the file named Chaptr26.xls"
#Else
     MsgBox "Code listings are on the CD in the file named Chaptr26.bas"
#End If
```

Conditional Compilation for Debugging

Conditional compilation can be easily adapted to any scenario in which you need to run different statements depending on a global condition. In the examples cited earlier, you could set up conditional compilation for debugging code by declaring a constant that takes on a Boolean value, like so:

```
#Const DEBUGMODE = True
Sub Procedure1()
    #If DEBUGMODE Then
        Debug.Print something
    #End If
End Sub
```

When you're testing your application, keep the `DEBUGMODE` constant set to `True` and use `#If DEBUGMODE Then` tests to add debugging code throughout your application. When you're ready to distribute the project, set `DEBUGMODE` to `False`.

Conditional Compilation for Win32 and Win16

Of the scenarios mentioned earlier, the one that isn't quite straightforward is testing for a 32-bit versus a 16-bit environment. Yes, it's possible to declare an appropriate `#Const` directive:

```
#Const OS = "32-Bit"
```

However, in order for this to work properly, you have to be certain about the user's system. For example, suppose your application uses API calls and you've set up conditional compilation to use 32-bit functions if the `OS` constant equals `32-bit`. If a 16-bit user somehow gets ahold of the application, not only will your program fail, but it might also crash the user's machine.

To be certain that 32-bit API functions are called only in 32-bit environments, and that 16-bit API functions are called only in 16-bit environments, VBA provides two built-in constants:

`Win16`: This constant is `True` if the code is running in a 16-bit environment.

`Win32`: This constant is `True` if the code is running in a 32-bit environment.

For example, the Win32 API uses a function called `GetVersionEx` to return information about the current Windows version (see the preceding chapter for details):

```
Declare Function GetVersionEx Lib "kernel32" Alias "GetVersionExA"
➥(lpVersionInformation As OSVERSIONINFO) As Long
```

However, the Win16 API uses a function called `GetVersion`:

```
Declare Function GetVersion Lib "kernel" () As Long
```

To run these functions properly, you must do two things:

- Use `#If...Then` at the module level to set up conditional compilation for the `Declare` statements as well as any `Const` and `Type...End Type` statements associated with the function.
- Use `#If...Then` at the procedure level to run the function that's appropriate for the environment.

Listing 26.2 shows an example. At the module level, I use `#If Win32 Then` to check for a 32-bit environment. If `Win32` is `True`, `GetVersionEx` is declared, and its associated `Type...End Type` and `Const` statements are also declared. Otherwise, Win16's `GetVersion` function is declared. I also use `#If Win32 Then` in the procedure to set up and run the appropriate function.

Listing 26.2. A revised version of `GetWinVer` that uses conditional compilation to differentiate between a Win32 call and a Win16 call.

```
#If Win32 Then
    Declare Function GetVersionEx Lib "kernel32" Alias "GetVersionExA"
    ➥(lpVersionInformation As OSVERSIONINFO) As Long
    Type OSVERSIONINFO
        dwOSVersionInfoSize As Long
        dwMajorVersion As Long
        dwMinorVersion As Long
        dwBuildNumber As Long
        dwPlatformId As Long
        szCSDVersion As String * 128
    End Type
    Public Const VER_PLATFORM_WIN32s = 0
    Public Const VER_PLATFORM_WIN32_WINDOWS = 1
    Public Const VER_PLATFORM_WIN32_NT = 2
#Else
    Declare Function GetVersion Lib "kernel" () As Long
#End If
Sub GetWinVer2()
    Dim os As OSVERSIONINFO
    Dim msg As String

    #If Win32 Then
        os.dwOSVersionInfoSize = Len(os)
        GetVersionEx os

        msg = "Major Version: " & os.dwMajorVersion & Chr(13) & _
              "Minor Version: " & os.dwMinorVersion & Chr(13) & _
            "Build Number: " & os.dwBuildNumber & Chr(13) & _
            "Platform ID: "
        Select Case os.dwPlatformId
            Case VER_PLATFORM_WIN32s
                msg = msg & "Win32s"
            Case VER_PLATFORM_WIN32_WINDOWS
                msg = msg & "Windows"
            Case VER_PLATFORM_WIN32_NT
                msg = msg & "Windows NT"
        End Select
    #Else
        msg = "Windows Version: " & GetVersion
    #End If
    MsgBox msg, vbOKOnly + vbInformation, "Windows Version"
End Sub
```

Saving Application Settings in the Registry

VBA 5.0

The preceding chapter showed you how to use Win32 function calls to return and set values throughout the Windows Registry. However, if you're only interested in using the Registry to store settings between sessions of your application, VBA provides several statements that are much easier to use than the API calls. The next few sections show you how to use these statements to store, read, and delete application-specific Registry settings.

Storing Settings in the Registry

To store a setting in the Registry, use the `SaveSetting` statement:

```
SaveSetting appname, section, key, setting
```

appname	The name you want to use to identify your application in the Registry.
section	The section in which to store the value. This will be a subkey of the ***appname*** key.
key	The name of the key setting that you want to store.
setting	The value to which ***key*** is being set.

When you run this statement, VBA creates a new key in the Registry, as follows:

```
\HKEY_CURRENT_USER\Software\VB and VBA Program Settings\appname\section\
```

The ***key*** setting is added to this subkey, and its value is set to ***setting***. For example, consider the following statement:

```
SaveSetting "VBA Unleashed", "Chapter 26", "Test", "OK"
```

Figure 26.1 shows how the new setting appears in the Windows 95 Registry Editor.

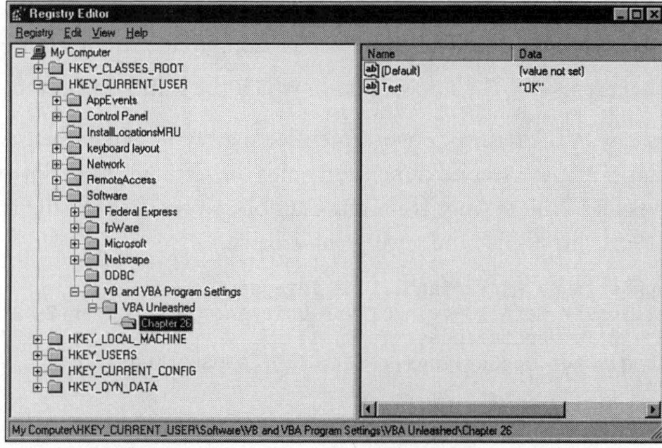

FIGURE 26.1.
Use the `SaveSetting` *statement to store application settings in the Registry.*

NOTE: WORKING WITH .INI FILES IN 16-BIT WINDOWS

The `SaveSetting` statement, as well as all the other statements I tell you about in this section, do double duty in 16-bit Windows. In other words, instead of working with Registry settings, they work with settings in an .INI file. In this case, you use the ***appname*** argument to specify the name of the .INI file, and the rest of the arguments specify the section, key, and value in the .INI file, as follows:

```
[section]
key=setting
```

Reading Settings from the Registry

Once you've stored a value in the Registry, reading it is a simple matter of invoking the `GetSetting` statement:

```
GetSetting(appname, section, key, default)
```

appname	The name you're using to identify your application in the Registry.
section	The section in which the value is stored.
key	The name of the key setting that you want to retrieve.
default	The value to be returned if ***key*** doesn't exist or isn't set.

To retrieve the value stored in the example shown earlier, you would use a statement similar to the following:

```
currValue = GetSetting("VBA Unleashed", "Chapter 26", "Test")
```

Rather than reading a single setting at a time, VBA lets you retrieve every setting in a particular section with a single call to the `GetAllSettings` function:

```
GetAllSettings(appname, section)
```

appname	The name you're using to identify your application in the Registry.
section	The section in which the values are stored.

In this case, VBA returns a two-dimensional array in which the first dimension holds the setting names and the second dimension holds the setting values. For example, the following code retrieves all of the settings from our example, stores them in the `appSettings` array, and uses `Debug.Print` to display the setting/value pairs:

```
Dim appSettings As Variant, i As Integer
appSettings = GetAllSettings("VBA Unleashed", "Chapter 26")
For i = 0 To Ubound(appSettings, 1)
   Debug.Print appSettings(i, 0); "="; appSettings(i, 1)
Next 'i
```

Deleting Settings from the Registry

If you no longer need to track a particular key setting, use the `DeleteSetting` statement to remove the setting from the Registry:

```
DeleteSetting appname, section, key
```

appname	The name you're using to identify your application in the Registry.
section	The section in which the key value is stored.
key	The name of the key setting that you want to delete. If you omit *key*, VBA deletes the entire ***appname\section*** subkey.

To delete the `Test` key setting used in the earlier examples, you would use the following statement:

```
DeleteSetting "VBA Unleashed", "Chapter 26", "Test"
```

An Example: Tracking File Usage

Let's work through a concrete example of these Registry statements. Suppose you'd like to track the number of times a particular document has been opened, as well as the last date and time the file was opened. Listing 26.3 shows an event handler for the `Open` event in the Chaptr26.xls workbook. This procedure creates the following subkey:

```
\HKEY_CURRENT_USER\Software\VB and VBA Program Settings\VBA Unleashed\Chapter 26\
```

Within this subkey, three settings are stored:

`NumberOfAccess`: Holds the number of times that the file has been opened.

`LastAccessDate`: Holds the date that the file was last opened.

`LastAccessTime`: Holds the time that the file was last opened.

This procedure performs the following chores:

- It first uses `GetSetting` to return the `NumberOfAccess` value, with a default of 0.
- If the returned value is 0, this means that the setting doesn't exist, so this must be the first time the user has opened the file. In this case, a welcome message is displayed, and the `numAccesses` variable is set to 1.
- Otherwise, the `LastAccessDate` and `LastAccessTime` settings are retrieved, and a different welcome message—showing the Registry settings—is displayed.
- Three `SaveSettings` statements update the Registry values.

Note, too, that you can run the `RemoveChapter26Settings` procedure to clear the Registry entries.

Listing 26.3. The event handler for the Chaptr26.xls workbook's Open event. This procedure uses the Registry to store the number of times this file has been opened, as well as the last date and time it was opened.

```
Private Sub Workbook_Open()
    Dim numAccesses As Integer
    Dim lastAccessDate As Date
    Dim lastAccessTime As Date
    Dim msg As String
    '
    ' Get the number of accesses from the Registry
    '
    numAccesses = GetSetting("VBA Unleashed", "Chapter 26", "NumberOfAccesses", 0)
    If numAccesses = 0 Then
        '
        ' This is the first time this file has been opened
        '
        MsgBox "Welcome to the Chapter 26 code listings!" & Chr(13) & Chr(13) & _
               "This is the first time you have opened this file." & Chr(13) & _
               "The Registry settings will now be created."
        numAccesses = 1
    Else
        '
        ' The file has been opened more than once. Get the last date and time.
        '
        lastAccessDate = CDate(GetSetting("VBA Unleashed", "Chapter 26",
        ➥"LastAccessDate"))
        lastAccessTime = CDate(GetSetting("VBA Unleashed", "Chapter 26",
        ➥"LastAccessTime"))
        msg = "Welcome to the Chapter 26 code listings!" & _
              Chr(13) & Chr(13) & _
             "You have opened this file " & numAccesses & " times." & _
             Chr(13) & _
             "You last opened this file on " & lastAccessDate & " at " &
             ➥lastAccessTime
        MsgBox msg, vbOKOnly + vbInformation, "VBA Unleashed"
    End If
    '
    ' Update the settings
    '
    SaveSetting "VBA Unleashed", "Chapter 26", "NumberOfAccesses", numAccesses + 1
    SaveSetting "VBA Unleashed", "Chapter 26", "LastAccessDate", Date
    SaveSetting "VBA Unleashed", "Chapter 26", "LastAccessTime", Time
End Sub
Sub RemoveChapter26Setting()
    DeleteSetting "VBA Unleashed", "Chapter 26"
End Sub
```

Reading All the Section Settings

Rather than just reading one setting at a time, VBA lets you retrieve every setting in a given section by using the `GetAllSettings` statement:

`GetAllSettings(`***`appname`***`,` ***`section`***`)`

appname	The name you're using to identify your application in the Registry.
section	The section in which the values are stored.

In this case, VBA returns a two-dimensional array of values in which the first index is the name of the key setting and the second index is the current value of the setting. Listing 26.4 shows a procedure that returns all of the `Chapter 26` subkey settings created in the preceding section.

Listing 26.4. This procedure uses `GetAllSettings` to return every setting in the `Chapter 26` subkey and then prints the setting names and values.

```
Sub GetAllChapter26Settings()
    Dim ch26Settings As Variant
    Dim i As Integer
    '
    ' Get the settings
    '
    ch26Settings = GetAllSettings("VBA Unleashed", "Chapter 26")
    '
    ' Run through the key settings, displaying the name and value
    '
    For i = 0 To UBound(ch26Settings, 1)
        Debug.Print ch26Settings(i, 0); ": "; ch26Settings(i, 1)
    Next 'i
End Sub
```

Accessing the File System Through VBA

If your applications need to work with the file system, VBA boasts quite a few features that make it easy. These features include a number of statements that return information about files and folders, as well as a number of functions with which you can manipulate files and folders. There are also powerful functions that give you direct access to files. This section examines all of VBA's file-related statements and functions.

Returning File and Folder Information

If you need information about the file system—whether it's the name of the current directory, whether or not a particular file exists, or a file's date and time stamp—VBA has a function that can do the job. The next few sections look at five VBA functions that return file system data: `CurDir`, `Dir`, `FileDateTime`, `FileLen`, and `GetAttr`.

The CurDir Function

If you need to know the name of the active folder on a specific drive, use either the `CurDir` or the `CurDir$` function:

```
CurDir(drive)
```

```
CurDir$(drive)
```

drive	The disk drive you want to work with. If you omit *drive*, VBA uses the current drive.

The `CurDir` function returns the path as a `Variant`, and the `CurDir$` function returns the path as a `String`. For example, the following statements display the current folder on drive D and the letter of the current drive:

```
MsgBox "Current folder on drive D is " & CurDir$("D")
MsgBox "The current drive is " & Left(CurDir$, 1)
```

To change the current drive and folder, see the descriptions of the `ChDrive` and `ChDir` statements later in this chapter.

The Dir Function

To return the name of a file or folder, use the `Dir` function:

```
Dir(Pathname, Attributes)
```

Pathname	A `String` value that gives the file or folder specification. Note that you can use the standard wildcard characters—`?` for single characters and `*` for multiple characters.
Attributes	One or more constants that specify the file attributes:

Constant	*Attribute*
`vbNormal` (or 0)	Normal
`vbHidden` (or 2)	Hidden
`vbSystem` (or 4)	System
`vbVolume` (or 8)	Volume label
`vbDirectory` (or 16)	Folder

If `Dir` is unsuccessful—that is, if no such file or folder exists—it returns the null string (`""`). This is a handy way to check for the existence of a file. For example, the following procedure fragment checks to see if C:\Config.sys exists. If it does, the file is loaded into Notepad:

```
If Dir("C:\Config.sys") <> "" Then
    Shell "Notepad C:\Config.sys"
End If
```

If `Dir` is successful, it returns the first file or folder name that matches the ***Pathname*** file specification. To return the next file or folder name that matches the specification, you call `Dir` again, but this time without any arguments. Listing 26.5 shows a procedure that utilizes this technique to store the names of all the files from C:\ in a worksheet. After a bit of preparation, the procedure runs `Dir("C:\", vbNormal)` to return the first file. Then a `Do While` loop runs `Dir` until there are no more filenames to return. Along the way, the filenames are stored in a worksheet. Then, when all is said and done, the filenames are sorted. At this point, you could use the sorted list to populate a list box or some other control.

Listing 26.5. This procedure reads all the filenames from the root folder of drive C, stores them in Sheet1, and sorts them by name.

```
Sub GetFilenames()
    Dim i As Integer
    i = 0
    '
    ' Start at cell A1
    '
    With Worksheets("Sheet1").[A1]
        '
        ' Clear the current values, if any
        '
        .CurrentRegion.Clear
        '
        ' Get the initial file and store it in A1
        '
        .Value = UCase$(Dir("C:\", vbNormal))
        '
        ' Get the rest of the files and store them in Column A
        '
        Do While .Offset(i, 0) <> ""
            i = i + 1
            .Offset(i, 0) = UCase$(Dir)
        Loop
        '
        ' Sort the filenames
        '
        .Sort Key1:=Worksheets("Sheet1").Columns("A")
    End With
End Sub
```

The `FileDateTime` Function

If you need to know when a file was last modified, use the `FileDateTime` function:

`FileDateTime(`***`Pathname`***`)`

Pathname	A string that specifies the file you want to work with (including, optionally, the drive and folder where the file resides).

If successful, FileDateTime returns a Variant date expression that holds the date and time stamp for the specified file.

The FileLen Function

The preceding chapter showed you how to use the Win32 API to calculate the amount of free space on a disk. I mentioned that if you need to know the size of a file (to see if it will fit on the disk, for example), you should use the FileLen function:

```
FileLen(Pathname)
```

Pathname	A string that specifies the file you want to work with (including, optionally, the drive and folder where the file resides).

The FileLen function returns a Long value that tells you the number of bytes in the specified file. (On the odd chance that the file is already open, FileLen returns the size of the file when it was last saved.)

To help you try this function, Listing 26.6 presents the GetFolderUsage procedure, which calculates the total disk space used by the files in a folder. This procedure prompts you for a folder name and then uses the Dir function to return the filenames in that folder. For each filename, the FileLen function returns the number of bytes, and a running total is kept in the totalBytes variable.

Listing 26.6. This procedure combines Dir and FileLen to determine the number of bytes used by the files in a folder.

```
Sub GetFolderUsage()
    Dim folder As String
    Dim filename As String
    Dim totalBytes As Long
    '
    ' Get the folder name
    '
    folder = InputBox("Enter the folder name:", "Bytes Used in Folder")
    '
    ' See if the user clicked Cancel
    '
    If folder <> "" Then
        '
        ' Make sure there's a backslash at the end
        '
        If Right(folder, 1) <> "\" Then
            folder = folder & "\"
        End If
        '
        ' Get the first filename
        '
        filename = Dir(folder, vbNormal)
        totalBytes = 0
```

```
        '
        ' Loop through the rest of the files
        '
        Do While filename <> ""
            '
            ' Update the total number of bytes
            '
            totalBytes = totalBytes + FileLen(folder & filename)
            '
            ' Get the next filename
            '
            filename = Dir
        Loop
        '
        ' Display the total
        '
        MsgBox "The folder " & folder & " uses " & totalBytes & " bytes."
    End If
End Sub
```

The GetAttr Function

As you may know, each file and folder has a set of attributes that indicate its status on the system (such as read-only or hidden). You can test for these attributes by using the `GetAttr` function:

`GetAttr(`***`Pathname`***`)`

`Pathname` A string that specifies the file or folder you want to work with.

The return value is an integer that represents the sum of one or more of the following constants:

Constant	*Value*	*Attribute*
`vbReadOnly`	1	Read-only (the object can't be modified)
`vbHidden`	2	Hidden (the object isn't visible in the normal Explorer view)
`vbSystem`	4	System (the object is a system file)
`vbDirectory`	16	Directory (the object is a folder)
`vbArchive`	32	Archive (the object has been modified since it was last backed up)

To test for any of these attributes, you use the `And` operator to compare the result of the `GetAttr` function with the appropriate constant (this is known in the trade as a *bitwise comparison*). For example, if the following statement returns a nonzero value, the object given by `path` is read-only:

```
GetAttr(path) And vbReadOnly
```

In Listing 26.7, the `GetAttributes` procedure prompts you for a filename (using Excel's `GetOpenFilename` method), uses `GetAttr` to return the file's attributes, and performs several bitwise comparisons to determine all of the file's attributes.

Listing 26.7. A procedure that prompts for a filename and then returns the attributes of the selected file.

```
Sub GetAttributes()
    Dim pathname As String
    Dim attr As Integer
    Dim msg As String
    '
    ' Get the filename
    '
    pathname = Application.GetOpenFilename("All Files (*.*), *.*")
    '
    ' Check to see if Cancel was clicked
    '
    If pathname <> "" Then
        '
        ' Get the file's attributes
        '
        attr = GetAttr(pathname)
        msg = "Attributes for " & pathname & ":" & Chr(13)
        '
        ' Determine the file's attributes and display them
        '
        If attr And vbReadOnly Then msg = msg & Chr(13) & "Read-Only"
        If attr And vbHidden Then msg = msg & Chr(13) & "Hidden"
        If attr And vbSystem Then msg = msg & Chr(13) & "System"
        If attr And vbDirectory Then msg = msg & Chr(13) & "Directory"
        If attr And vbArchive Then msg = msg & Chr(13) & "Archive"
        MsgBox msg
    End If
End Sub
```

Manipulating Files and Folders

Besides just finding out file system information, VBA also lets you manipulate various aspects of the file system, including changing the current drive and folder, creating new folders, and deleting and renaming files and folders. The next few sections take you through each of VBA's file system manipulation statements.

The ChDir Statement

To change a drive's default folder, use the `ChDir` statement:

`ChDir` ***`Path`***

`Path`	A string that specifies the new default folder.

If the ***Path*** parameter doesn't include a drive designator, VBA changes the folder on whatever drive is current. If ***Path*** does include a drive, VBA changes the default folder on that drive, but it doesn't change the current drive. For example, if the current drive is C and you run `ChDir D:\`, the default folder is changed on drive D, but drive C remains the current drive.

The ChDrive Statement

To change the default drive, use the `ChDrive` statement:

```
ChDrive Drive
```

Drive — A string that specifies the letter of the new default drive.

For example, the following statement changes the default drive to E:

```
ChDrive "E"
```

The FileCopy Statement

If you need to copy a disk file from one location to another, use VBA's `FileCopy` statement:

```
FileCopy(Source, Destination)
```

Source — A `String` value that specifies the name of the file you want to copy (including, optionally, the drive and folder in which the file resides).

Destination — A `String` value that specifies the name of the destination file (including, optionally, the drive and folder).

The following statements set the ***Source*** variable to a filename, set the ***Destination*** variable to a filename on a network drive, and use `FileCopy` to copy the file:

```
source = "C:\My Documents\Letter.doc"
destination = "\\Server\pub\users\biff\Letter.doc"
FileCopy source, destination
```

The Kill Statement

When you need to delete files from the system, use the aptly-named `Kill` statement:

```
Kill Pathname
```

Pathname — A `String` value that specifies the name of the file you want to delete (including, optionally, the drive and folder in which the file resides).

You can use the `?` and `*` wildcard characters in the ***Pathname*** argument to delete multiple files. Note that the `Kill` statement generates an error if the specified file is open or doesn't exist. To avoid the latter error, first use the `Dir` function to see if the file exists:

```
If Dir("C:\Garbage.txt") <> "" Then
    Kill "C:\Garbage.txt"
End If
```

The MkDir Statement

If your application requires a new folder in which to store files, you can use the MkDir statement to create the folder:

```
MkDir Path
```

Path	A string that specifies the new folder. If you don't include the drive letter, VBA creates the folder on the current drive.

The following statement creates a new Backup folder on drive C:

```
MkDir "C:\Backup"
```

The Name Statement

You can rename a file or folder by running the Name statement:

```
Name oldpathname As newpathname
```

oldpathname	A String value that specifies the pathname of the folder or file you want to rename. (Wildcards are not supported.)
newpathname	A String value that specifies the new name of the folder or file. If you change the path but not the name of the file, VBA moves the file to the new location.

The Name statement generates an error if the specified file is open or doesn't exist.

The RmDir Statement

To let you delete a folder you no longer need, VBA offers the RmDir statement:

```
RmDir Path
```

Path	A string that specifies the folder you want to delete. If you don't include the drive letter, VBA deletes the folder from the current drive.

Note that RmDir will raise an error if the folder you specify still contains files. Your code should check to see if a folder contains files and, if it does, it should first use Kill to delete the files and then use RmDir to delete the folder. Listing 26.8 shows a procedure that does exactly that. After getting the name of the folder to delete, the procedure uses Dir to loop through the folder's files. (You might want to modify this code to check for subfolders as well.) If the folder contains files, the total is reported to the user, who then has the option of canceling the deletion. If the user elects to proceed, Kill is used to delete each file, and then RmDir deletes the folder.

Listing 26.8. This procedure deletes a folder. If the folder contains files, the procedure first deletes the files.

```
Sub DeleteFolder()
    Dim folder As String
    Dim filename As String
    Dim totalFiles As Integer
    '
    ' Get the folder name
    '
    folder = InputBox("Enter the name of the folder to delete:")
    '
    ' See if the user clicked Cancel
    '
    If folder <> "" Then
        '
        ' Make sure there's a backslash at the end
        '
        If Right(folder, 1) <> "\" Then
            folder = folder & "\"
        End If
        '
        ' Get the first filename
        '
        filename = Dir(folder, vbNormal)
        '
        ' Bail out if the folder doesn't exist
        '
        If filename = "" Then
            MsgBox "Folder doesn't exist!"
            Exit Sub
        End If
        '
        ' Loop through the rest to get the file total
        '
        totalFiles = 0
        Do While filename <> ""
            '
            ' Update the total number of files
            '
            totalFiles = totalFiles + 1
            '
            ' Get the next filename
            '
            filename = Dir
        Loop
        '
        ' Check the total
        '
        If totalFiles > 0 Then
            '
            ' If there are files, let the user know
            '
            If MsgBox("The folder " & folder & " contains " & _
                totalFiles & " files." & Chr(13) & _
                    "Are you sure you want to delete it?", _
                vbOKCancel + vbQuestion) = vbCancel Then
                Exit Sub
            End If
```

continues

Listing 26.8. continued

```
            '
            ' Get the first filename
            '
            filename = Dir(folder, vbNormal)
            '
            ' Loop through and Kill the rest of the files
            '
            Do While filename <> ""
                Kill folder & filename
                '
                ' Get the next filename
                '
                filename = Dir
            Loop
        End If
        '
        ' Delete the folder
        '
        RmDir folder
    End If
End Sub
```

The SetAttr Statement

Earlier you saw how to use the `GetAttr` function to return the attributes of a file or folder. However, you can also set these attributes by invoking the `SetAttr` statement:

`SetAttr` ***`Pathname`***`,` ***`Attributes`***

`Pathname`	A string that specifies the file or folder you want to work with.
`Attributes`	One or more constants that specify the attributes you want to set.

The constants recognized by VBA are the same as those outlined earlier for the `GetAttr` function (except that you can set the `Directory` attribute): `vbReadOnly`, `vbHidden`, `vbSystem`, and `vbArchive`. Note that this statement produces an error if you attempt to set the attributes of an open file.

Low-Level File I/O

When you work with a file in an application, you never work with the file directly. Instead, you use the application's interface to make changes to the file. For example, if you type some text, the application displays the text on-screen, but the physical act of storing in the file the bytes that represent each character is something that goes on behind the scenes.

This is the optimal arrangement the vast majority of the time, but there might be situations when you need more direct contact with your data:

- You might want to examine the contents of a file in order to see if a particular value is present in the file.
- You might need to read the contents of a text file into a text box control.
- You might need to extract certain values from a file and store them in a list box or database.
- You might need to write values to a file in a particular sequence.

For these and many other related scenarios, you need turn to the VBA features that give you direct access to the contents of any file. This process is known as *low-level file I/O* (input/out put), and it's the subject of the next few sections.

Opening a Disk File

All VBA-enabled applications have some sort of `Open` method that you can use to open documents within the application. However, these methods generally do nothing more than open a document within the application's interface. If you want direct access to a file, you need to turn to VBA's `Open` statement:

```
Open pathname For mode Access access lock As #filenumber Len=reclength
```

pathname	A string that specifies the file you want to open (including, optionally, the drive and folder).
mode	A keyword that determines how the file is opened (that is, the file mode). VBA accepts the following ***mode*** keywords: `Append`, `Binary`, `Input`, `Output`, and `Random` (see the next section for details).
access	A keyword that determines the file's read and write permissions. VBA accepts the following *access* keywords: `Shared`, `Lock Read`, `Lock Write`, and `Lock Read Write` (see "The Lock Permissions").
lock	A keyword that determines the file permissions for other processes. VBA accepts the following *lock* keywords: `Read`, `Write`, and `Read Write` (see "The Access Permissions").
filenumber	The file handle that you use to refer to the opened file in subsequent I/O operations (see "The File Handle").
reclength	An integer that specifies the size of the records in the file (see "The Record Length").

Because of the complexity of the `Open` statement, I'll spend the next few sections examining each parameter in more detail.

The File Mode

The **mode** parameter tells VBA how you want the file opened. This parameter can be any of the following keywords:

mode	*Description*
`Append`	Open text files in this mode when you want to write data to the end of the file.
`Binary`	Use this mode to access nontext data on a byte-by-byte basis.
`Input`	Use this mode to read data from text files sequentially. (In other words, you start at the beginning of the file and read the data in the order it appears in the file.)
`Output`	Use this mode to write data to text files sequentially. Note that text written to a file opened in this mode will overwrite any existing text.
`Random`	Open the file in this mode when the data in the file is arranged in fixed-size records containing one or more fields.

The file mode is the most important of the `Open` statement parameters because it determines how you can work with a file after it's opened. The five modes can be categorized into three different file access types:

- Sequential file access (the `Append`, `Input`, and `Output` modes) is used only with text files in which the data isn't arranged in any special order.
- Random file access (the `Random` mode) is used with text files in which the data is arranged into fixed-length records consisting of comma-separated fields.
- Binary file access (the `Binary` mode) is used with nontext files (such as graphics files or when you need to store data as efficiently as possible).

Understanding these file access types is crucial for performing successful low-level file I/O operations, so I'll explain each type in more detail later in this section.

The Access Permissions

The `access` parameter determines the permissions you have on the file. It accepts the following keywords:

`access`	*Description*
`Read`	Opens the file as read-only. You can't write new data to the file.
`Write`	Opens the file as write-only. You can't read data from the file.
`Read Write`	Opens the file with both read and write permission. Note that you can use this parameter only if the **mode** parameter is `Append`, `Binary`, or `Random`.

The Lock Permissions

The `lock` parameter controls the access that other processes have over a file you've opened. In a network environment, this parameter determines the access other users have to the file. Here are your choices:

lock	*Description*
`Shared`	Other processes can both read from and write to the file.
`Lock Read`	Other processes can't read from the file.
`Lock Write`	Other processes can't write to the file.
`Lock Read Write`	Other processes can't read from or write to the file.

The File Handle

All opened files have a *file handle,* which is a unique integer value by which you refer to the file in subsequent operations. To ensure that this handle is unique, VBA provides the `FreeFile` function, which returns an unused file handle. Here's the syntax:

```
FreeFile(rangenumber)
```

`rangenumber`	Determines the range of numbers from which the file handle is chosen. Use 0 to return a handle in the range 1 to 255; use 1 to return a handle in the range 256 to 511.

For example, the following statements generate an unused file handle, use that handle to open a file, and use it again to close the file:

```
fn = FreeFile
Open "C:\Config.sys" For Input Access Read As #fn
[Statements that work with the file go here]
Close #fn
```

NOTE: THE CLOSE AND RESET STATEMENTS

You use the `Close` statement to close one or more files that were opened using the `Open` statement. The syntax is `Close(`*`filenumberlist`*`)`, where *`filenumberlist`* is a comma-separated list of file handles, as in this example:

```
Close #fn1, #fn2
```

Alternatively, you can run the `Reset` statement to close all open files.

The Record Length

For files opened in random mode, you use the `reclength` parameter to specify the size of each record in bytes. Note that this number must be less than or equal to 32,767 (bytes). See "Understanding Random File Access" for more information.

Understanding Sequential File Access

As I mentioned earlier, you use sequential file access when you need to read data from or write data to text files in which the data is stored without structure. Sequential file access, therefore, is the ideal method for working with configuration files, error logs, HTML files, and pure-text files. This access method is called "sequential" because you can only work with the data in a linear fashion. When reading file data, for example, you start at the beginning of the file and work sequentially through the characters or lines in the file.

Although three different sequential access file modes are available, the methodology you apply is basically the same in all cases:

1. Use `FreeFile` to get the next available file handle.
2. Use this handle to open the file in `Append`, `Input`, or `Output` mode.
3. Read data from the file or write data to the file (or both).
4. Close the file using the `Close #filenumber` method, where ***`filenumber`*** is the handle of the opened file.

Reading Sequential File Data

To read the contents of a text file, open the file using the `Input` file mode and then use either the `Line Input #` statement or the `Input` function to get the data.

Reading One Line at a Time

The `Line Input #` statement reads the file data one line at a time and stores each line in a variable. Here's the syntax:

```
Line Input #filenumber, varname
```

`filenumber`	The handle of the file you're working with.
`varname`	The `String` (or `Variant`) variable in which you want to store the line.

The `Line Input #` statement works by reading the characters in the file one at a time until it stumbles upon either a carriage return character or a carriage return/line feed combination. The statement ignores these control characters and returns the text in the specified variable.

Bear in mind that the `Line Input #` statement generates an error if you attempt to read past the last character in the file. To prevent this from happening, use the `EOF` function to test for the end of the file:

```
EOF(filenumber)
```

`filenumber`	The handle of the file you're working with.

The `EOF` function returns `True` after the last line of data has been read, so your code can test this value to ensure that it doesn't go past the end of the file.

Listing 26.9 shows a procedure that puts all of these concepts to the test. The purpose of the `GetRUNLine` procedure is to examine the Win.ini file, extract the `RUN=` line, and display it. Here's what happens:

- `FreeFile` returns a free file handle and stores it in `fn`.
- The path to Win.ini is stored in the `winINI` variable, and `Dir` checks to make sure the file exists. (Note that you might need to alter this path if your main Windows directory is something other than C:\Windows.)

> **NOTE: RETURNING THE WINDOWS DIRECTORY**
>
> The `GetRUNLine` procedure would be an excellent place to use the `GetWindowsDirectory` API function I told you about in the preceding chapter. Since Win.ini is always stored in the main Windows directory, you could use the result of `GetWindowsDirectory` to ensure that you're using the correct path when looking for Win.ini.

- Win.ini is opened using `Input` mode.
- A `Do While` loop is set up to monitor `EOF(fn)` and to make sure we don't read past the end of the file.
- `Line Input #` stores each line in the `str` variable, and then this variable is examined to see if it begins with `RUN`. When this line is found, the procedure exits the loop.
- A message is displayed that shows the line (if it was found, that is).

Listing 26.9. This procedure opens Win.ini for input, reads the lines until the RUN= line is found, and then displays the line.

```
Sub GetRUNLine()
    Dim fn As Integer
    Dim winINI As String
    Dim str As String
    Dim lineExists As Boolean
    '
    ' Get the next free file handle
    '
    fn = FreeFile
    '
    ' Make sure WIN.INI exists
    '
    winINI = "C:\Windows\Win.ini"
    If Dir(winINI) <> "" Then
        '
        ' If it does, open it
        '
        Open winINI For Input As #fn
```

continues

Listing 26.9. continued

```
    '
    ' Read the file line-by-line until the end
    '
    lineExists = False
    Do While Not EOF(fn)
        '
        ' Store each line in the str variable
        '
        Line Input #fn, str
        '
        ' Check the beginning of each line for "RUN"
        '
        If Left(UCase$(str), 3) = "RUN" Then
            '
            ' If we find it, bail out of the loop
            '
            lineExists = True
            Exit Do
        End If
    Loop
    '
    ' Close the file
    '
    Close #fn
    '
    ' Display the message
    '
    If lineExists Then
        MsgBox "Here's the RUN= line from WIN.INI:" & _
               Chr(13) & Chr(13) & str
    Else
        MsgBox "The RUN line was not found!"
    End If
  End If
End Sub
```

Reading Characters

Instead of reading entire lines, you might prefer just to read a particular number of characters at a time. To do this, use the `Input` function:

`Input(`***`number`***`, `***`#filenumber`***`)`

number	The number of characters you want to read.
filenumber	The handle of the file you're working with.

For example, the following procedure fragment assumes that a file has been opened with the handle stored in `fn`. The code loops through the entire file one character at a time, checks each character to see if it's the letter E, and increments a counter if it is.

```
counter = 0
Do While Not EOF(fn)
```

```
    currChar = Input(1, #fn)
    If UCase$(currChar) = "E" Then
        counter = counter + 1
    End If
Loop
MsgBox "The letter E appears " & counter & " times in the file."
```

You'll often need to read in the entire contents of a text file. For example, you might want to display a text file in a text box on a user form. Rather than reading individual characters within a `Do While Not EOF()` structure, you can read the whole file in a single statement by taking advantage of the `LOF` function. `LOF` (length of file) returns the number of bytes in a file, which in a text file is the same as the number of characters:

```
LOF(filenumber)
```

filenumber	The handle of the file you're working with.

Given this, you can read the entire contents of a text file with a statement similar to this:

```
txtVar = Input(LOF(fn), #fn)
```

To put this handy technique to the test, I built a user form named `frmInput`, shown in Figure 26.2. You either enter the pathname of a text file in the top text box or click Browse to select a file from the Open dialog box. Either way, the contents of the file are displayed in the larger text box.

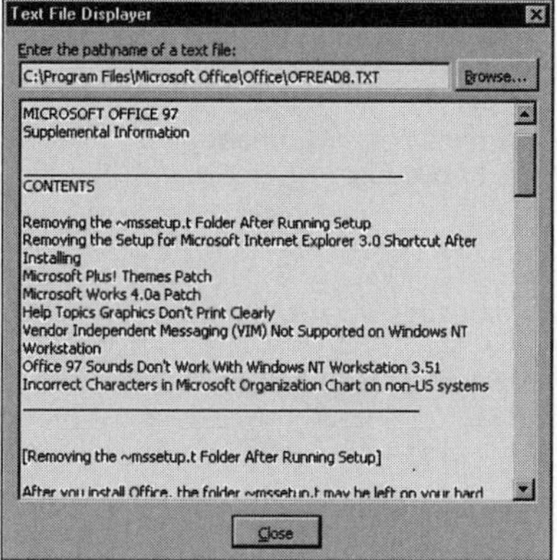

FIGURE 26.2.
This user form reads and displays the entire contents of a text file.

Listing 26.10 shows the event handlers and procedures that support this user form. Here's a quick summary:

`cmdBrowse_Click`: This is the `Click` event handler for the Browse button. It uses Excel's `GetOpenFilename` function to get the name of a file to open. The event handler calls `ReadFileContents` to input the file's text.

`cmdPathName_BeforeUpdate`: This is the `BeforeUpdate` event handler for the `cmdPathName` text box (the one at the top of the form). This procedure checks to make sure the specified file exists and, if it does, calls the `ReadFileContents` procedure to input the file's text.

`ReadFileContents`: This is the procedure that handles the nitty-gritty of inputting the file text. It gets a free file handle, opens the specified file in input mode, and uses the `Input` function combined with the `LOF` function to read the entire file text into the `txtContents` text box.

Listing 26.10. Support procedures for displaying a text file in a form text box.

```
' This is the Click event handler for the Browse button.
'
Private Sub cmdBrowse_Click()
    Dim strFileName As Variant
    '
    ' Get the name of a text file
    '
    strFileName = Application.GetOpenFilename("Text Files (*.txt; *.bas; *.bat;
    ➥*.ini), *.txt; *.bas; *.bat; *.ini")
    '
    ' Was Cancel clicked?
    '
    If strFileName <> False Then
        '
        ' If not, clear the text box and read the file contents
        '
        txtPathName = strFileName
        txtContents = ""
        ReadFileContents (strFileName)
        txtContents.SetFocus
    End If
End Sub
'
' This is the BeforeUpdate event handler for the "path" text box
'
Private Sub txtPathName_BeforeUpdate(ByVal Cancel As MSForms.ReturnBoolean)
    '
    ' Does the file exist?
    '
    If txtPathName <> "" Then
        If Dir(txtPathName) <> "" Then
            '
            ' If so, clear the text box and read the file contents
            '
            txtContents = ""
            ReadFileContents (txtPathName)
            txtContents.SetFocus
        Else
            '
            ' If not, display an error message and cancel the update
            '
            If MsgBox("The filename you entered doesn't exist!", vbRetryCancel)
            ➥= vbCancel Then
                txtPathName = ""
```

```
            End If
            Cancel = True
        End If
    End If
End Sub
'
' This procedure reads the file contents into the text box
'
Sub ReadFileContents(strName As String)
    Dim fn As Integer
    '
    ' Get the next free file handle
    '
    fn = FreeFile
    '
    ' Open the file for input
    '
    Open strName For Input As #fn
    '
    ' Use LOF to read the entire contents into the text box
    '
    txtContents = Input(LOF(fn), #fn)
    '
    ' Close the file
    '
    Close #fn
End Sub
```

Reading Multiple Data Items into Variables

Many text files contain a number of data items on each line of text. For example, if you download a daily stock price history, you'll usually get a text file with a line for each day containing data similar to this:

```
960102,87.8750,89.7500,87.3750,89.7500,3611200
```

In this case, the numbers represent the date, open, high, low, close, and volume for that day's trading, and each piece of data is separated by a comma.

It would certainly be possible to use `Line Input #` to read in these data lines, but if you need to work with the individual data items, you have to write a procedure that will parse the data. Instead of going to all that trouble, it's better to read the items directly into variables. You can do so by using the `Input #` statement:

```
Input #filenumber, varlist
```

filenumber	The handle of the file you're working with.
varlist	A comma-separated list of the variables you want to use to store the data items. You must specify one variable for each item of data, and the variable data types must match the data types of the items.

For the stock quote example, you could create a user-defined data type in which each member represents an item in the quote:

```
Type Quote
    qDate As String
    qOpen As Single
    qHigh As Single
    qLow As Single
    qClose As Single
    qVolume As Long
End Type
```

Listing 26.11 shows a procedure that uses this structure to read data from a file of stock quotes. For sample data, I've included a file named MSFT.txt on the CD. Note that the code in Listing 26.11 assumes that this file resides in the same folder as the Chaptr26.xls workbook.

The procedure opens MSFT.txt for input and then sets up a `Do While` loop to run through the entire file. Along the way, the `Input #` statement is used to store each data item in the members of the `Quote` type definition (which was instanced in the `q` variable near the top of the procedure). The procedure then writes each item to the Stock Quotes worksheet. (Note, too, that the procedure modifies the `qDate` member to convert it from the YYMMDD format supplied in the text file to the standard MM/DD/YY date format.)

Listing 26.11. This procedure opens MSFT.TXT (supplied on the CD) for input and reads the line items into variables.

```
Sub ReadStockQuotes()
    Dim fn As Integer
    Dim i As Integer
    Dim q As Quote
    '
    ' Get a free handle and then open MSFT.txt (the code
    ' assumes this file is in the workbook's folder)
    '
    fn = FreeFile
    Open ThisWorkbook.Path & "\MSFT.txt" For Input As #fn
    i = 1
    With Worksheets("Stock Quotes").[A1]
        '
        ' Clear any existing quotes
        '
        .CurrentRegion.Offset(1).Clear
        '
        ' Loop through the entire file
        '
        Do While Not EOF(fn)
            '
            ' Read the data into the Quote structure
            '
            Input #fn, q.qDate, q.qOpen, q.qHigh, q.qLow, q.qClose, q.qVolume
            '
            ' Write it to the Stock Quotes worksheet
            '
```

```
            .Offset(i, 0) = CDate(Mid(q.qDate, 3, 2) & "/" & Right(q.qDate, 2) &
            ➥"/" & Left(q.qDate, 2))
            .Offset(i, 1) = q.qOpen
            .Offset(i, 2) = q.qHigh
            .Offset(i, 3) = q.qLow
            .Offset(i, 4) = q.qClose
            .Offset(i, 5) = q.qVolume
            i = i + 1
        Loop
    End With
    '
    ' Close the file
    '
    Close #fn
End Sub
```

Writing Sequential File Data

Depending on the file mode you used in the `Open` statement, you can also write sequential data to an open file. You have two choices:

`Append`: Use this mode when you need to add data to the end of an existing file. The data that is currently in the file isn't altered in any way.

`Output`: When you open an existing file in `Output` mode, all file data is replaced as soon as you write anything to the file. Therefore, you should open an existing file in `Output` mode only when you're sure you want to completely rewrite the file. On the other hand, if the file you open in `Output` mode does *not* exist, VBA creates a brand new file.

Once you've settled on a sequential access mode, you can use either the `Print #` statement or the `Write #` statement to send text to the file.

The `Print #` Statement

The `Print #` statement is designed to write display-formatted data to an open sequential file:

```
Print #filenumber, outputlist
```

`filenumber` The handle of the file you're working with.

`outputlist` The text data you want to write to the file. The data is written as is, without any extra delimiting characters. If you omit *`outputlist`*, VBA writes a blank line to the file.

In the simplest case, the *`outputlist`* argument is a single text string or a variable containing `String`, `Date`, `Boolean`, or numeric data. With each call to the `Print #` statement, VBA writes a single line to the open file.

For example, earlier I showed you how to read the contents of a text file into a text box (see Listing 26.10). If you then used the text box to make changes to the contents, you could use `Print #` to save the changes back to the file. To test this, I created a copy of `frmInput`, named it `frmInput2`, and added a Save button. Listing 26.12 shows the `Click` event handler for the Save button. In this procedure, I reopen the file in `Output` mode and then use `Print #` to write the contents of the text box to the file.

Listing 26.12. The Save button's `Click` event handler writes the data back to the file.

```
Private Sub cmdSave_Click()
    Dim fn As Integer
    '
    ' Get the next free file handle
    '
    fn = FreeFile
    '
    ' Open the file for output
    '
    Open txtPathName For Output As #fn
    '
    ' Print the text box contents to the open file
    '
    Print #fn, txtContents
    '
    ' Close the file
    '
    Close #fn
End Sub
```

This is the most common way that `Print #` is utilized, but it's also possible to specify multiple variables or expressions as part of the *`outputlist`* argument. Here are a few notes to keep in mind when using this method:

- Use `Spc(`*`n`*`)` in *`outputlist`* to print *n* space characters.
- Use `Tab(`*`n`*`)` in *`outputlist`* to print *n* tab characters.
- Separate multiple expressions with either a space or a semicolon.

The `Write #` Statement

You learned earlier that the `Input #` statement is useful for reading comma-delimited data items into variables. You can also output data in the comma-delimited format by using the `Write #` statement:

```
Write #filenumber, outputlist
```

`filenumber`	The handle of the file you're working with.
`outputlist`	A comma-separated list of the variables you want to send to the file. If you omit *`outputlist`*, VBA writes a blank line to the file.

The `Write #` statement records the data with commas separating each item and with quotation marks around strings.

Understanding Random File Access

Sequential file access is the only way to go if the file you're reading or the data you're writing has no fixed, internal structure. However, there are plenty of situations in which the data does have a fixed structure. A simple database, for example, might have fixed field sizes.

If you know the internal structure of a file, you can achieve greater flexibility in working with the file if you open it using random access. This mode lets you directly read and write any record in the file. For example, you can ask VBA to read the tenth record. Unlike sequential access, where you would have to read the first nine records before you could read the tenth, random access lets you move directly to the tenth record and read it.

This is possible because of the fixed record sizes that random access files use. For example, suppose each record in the file is 10 bytes long. If you let VBA know this length, it can automatically assume that the first record starts at byte 1, the second starts at byte 11, and so on. To get the tenth record, VBA merely skips to the ninety-first byte and reads 10 bytes from there.

Alerting VBA to the record length in a random access file is the job of the `Open` statement's `Len` parameter. For example, if a file named data.db has 10-byte records, you'd open it with the following statement (assuming that `fn` is a free file handle):

```
Open "data.db" For Random As #fn Len = 10
```

To make random access files easier to work with, many programmers set up a user-defined data type with the following characteristics:

- Each member corresponds to a field in the file's records.
- Each member's data type is identical the data type used in the corresponding field.
- The size of each member is identical to the size of each corresponding field.

For example, the records in a simple employee database that tracks each person's first name, last name, age, and start date could be represented by the following type definition:

```
Type Employee
    first As String
    last As String
    age As Integer
    start As Date
End Type
```

In the following statements, this structure is instanced in a variable named `emp`, and the `Open` statement uses `Len(emp)` to specify the size of the records:

```
Dim emp As Employee
Open "employee.db" For Random As #fn Len = Len(emp)
```

Reading Random Access Records

Once you have a random access file opened, you can read any record by using the `Get` statement:

```
Get #filenumber, recnumber, varname
```

filenumber	The handle of the file you're working with.
recnumber	The record number you want to retrieve. If you omit the record number, VBA retrieves either the first record or the record immediately following the one retrieved by the last `Get` or `Put` statement.
varname	The variable in which the record data is stored.

For example, the following statement reads the tenth record into the `emp` variable:

```
Get #fn, 10, emp
```

Writing Random Access Records

When you want to write data to a random access file, use the `Put` statement:

```
Put #filenumber, recnumber, varname
```

filenumber	The handle of the file you're working with.
recnumber	The record number to which you want to record the data. If you omit the record number, VBA uses either the first record or the record immediately following the one retrieved by the last `Get` or `Put` statement.
varname	The variable containing the data you want to store in the record.

For example, the following statement writes the contents of the `emp` variable into the tenth record:

```
Put #fn, 10, emp
```

Working with Record Numbers

To return the number of the last record that was read from or written to the file, use the `LOC` function:

```
LOC(filenumber)
```

filenumber	The handle of the file you're working with.

Similarly, you can move the file pointer to a particular record by using the `Seek` statement:

```
Seek #filenumber, position
```

filenumber	The handle of the file you're working with.
position	The record number to which you want to move.

For example, the following statement moves the pointer to the fifteenth record:

```
Seek #fn, 15
```

Locking and Unlocking Records

You can control access to all or part of a random access file after it has been opened by using the `Lock` and `Unlock` statements. To restrict access to a file, use the `Lock` statement:

```
Lock #filenumber, recordrange
```

filenumber	The handle of the file you're working with.
recordrange	The record or range of records you want to lock. If you enter a single number, VBA locks that record number. To lock a range of records, use the syntax *start* `To` *end*, where *start* is the first record number you want to lock and *end* is the last record number you want to lock. If you omit this argument, VBA locks the entire file.

When you've finished working with the locked data, you can give other processes access to the data by running the `Unlock` statement:

```
Unlock #filenumber, recordrange
```

filenumber	The handle of the file you're working with.
recordrange	The record or range of records that you want to unlock. Note that you must use the same number or range that you used in the `Lock` statement.

For example, the following statements open a random access file, lock the tenth record, and read the tenth record into the `emp` variable. The data is then modified and written back to the file, and the record is unlocked.

```
Dim emp As Employee
Open "employee.db" For Random As #fn Len = Len(emp)
Lock #fn, 10
Get #fn, 10, emp
emp.Age = 40
Put #fn, 10, emp
Unlock #fn, 10
Close #fn
```

Understanding Binary File Access

Binary file access is similar to random access. The difference lies in how the file data is treated. Whereas random access treats a file as a collection of records, binary access sees any file as a collection of bytes. Therefore, although you use the same statements to work with binary files that you use to work with random files (that is, `Get`, `Put`, `LOC`, and `Seek`), you always work with byte positions within the file. So, for example, the following statement retrieves the tenth byte in an open file:

```
Get #fn, 10, var
```

NOTE: BINARY MODE IN ACTION

In Chapter 28, "Making Backups as You Work," I use Binary access mode to make copies of documents.

Tips for Faster Procedures

Short procedures usually are over in the blink of an eye. However, the longer your procedures get, and the more they interact with application objects, the more time they take to complete their tasks. For these more complex routines, you need to start thinking not only about *what* the procedure does, but *how* it does it. The more efficient you can make your code, the faster the procedure will execute. This section gives you a few tips for writing efficient code that runs quickly.

Turn Off Screen Updating

One of the biggest drags on procedure performance is the constant screen updating that occurs. If your procedure uses many statements that format text, enter formulas, or cut and copy data, the procedure will spend most of its time updating the screen to show the results of these operations. This not only slows everything down, but it also looks unprofessional. It's much nicer when the procedure performs all its chores behind the scenes and then presents the user with the finished product at the end of the procedure.

You can do this with the `Application` object's `ScreenUpdating` property. Set `ScreenUpdating` to `False` to turn off screen updates, and set it back to `True` to resume updating.

Hide Your Documents

If your procedure does a lot of switching between documents, you can speed things up by hiding the documents (or Excel worksheets) while you work with them. To do this, set the document's `Visible` property to `False`. You can work with hidden documents normally, and when your procedure is done, you can set `Visible` to `True` to display the results to the user.

CAUTION: HIDDEN DOCUMENTS ARE INACTIVE

As soon as you've hidden an active document or an Excel worksheet, VBA deactivates it. Therefore, if your procedures reference the active document, you need to activate the document (using the `Activate` method) right after hiding it.

Don't Select Data Unless You Have To

Two of VBA's slowest methods are `Activate` and `Select`, so you should use them sparingly. In the majority of cases, you can indirectly work with ranges, worksheets, text, and other data. In Excel, for example, you can work with a Range object by referencing it as an argument in the `Range` method (or in any other VBA statement that returns a Range object) and the `Worksheets` collection.

In Excel, Don't Recalculate Until You Have To

As you know, manual calculation mode prevents Excel from recalculating a worksheet until you say so. This saves you time when you're using sheets with complicated models—models in which you don't necessarily want to see a recalculation every time you change a variable.

You can get the same benefits in your procedures by using the `Application` object's `Calculation` property. Place Excel in manual calculation mode (as described earlier in this chapter) and then, when you need to update your formula results, use the `Calculate` method.

Optimize Your Loops

One of the cornerstones of efficient programming is loop optimization. Because a procedure might run the code inside a loop hundreds or even thousands of times, a minor improvement in loop efficiency can result in considerably reduced execution times.

When analyzing your loops, make sure that you're particularly ruthless about applying the preceding tips. One `Select` method is slow; a thousand will drive you crazy.

Also, weed out from your loops any statements that return the same value each time. For example, consider the following procedure fragment:

```
For i = 1 To 50000
   Application.StatusBar = "The value is " & Worksheets("Sheet1").[A1].Value
Next i
```

The idea of this somewhat useless code is to loop 50,000 times, each time displaying in the status bar the contents of cell A1 in the Sheet1 worksheet. The value in cell A1 never changes, but it takes time for Excel to get the value, slowing the loop considerably. A better approach would be the following:

```
currCell = Worksheets("Sheet1").[A1].Value
For i = 1 To 50000
    Application.StatusBar = "The value is: " & currCell
Next I
```

Transferring the unchanging `currCell` calculation outside the loop and assigning it to a variable means that the procedure has to call the function only once.

To test the difference, Listing 26.13 shows the `TimingTest` procedure. This procedure uses the `Timer` function (which returns the number of seconds since midnight) to time two `For...Next` loops. The first loop is unoptimized, and the second is optimized. On my system, the unoptimized loop takes about 17 seconds, and the optimized loop takes only 7 seconds—well under half the time.

Listing 26.13. A procedure that tests the difference between an optimized and an unoptimized loop.

```
Sub TimingTest()
    Dim i As Long, currCell As Variant
    Dim start1 As Long, finish1 As Long
    Dim start2 As Long, finish2 As Long
    '
    ' Start timing the unoptimized loop
    '
    start1 = Timer
    For i = 1 To 50000
        Application.StatusBar = "The value is " & Worksheets("Sheet1").[A1].Value
    Next i
    finish1 = Timer
    '
    ' Start timing the optimized loop
    '
    start2 = Timer
    currCell = Worksheets("Sheet1").[A1].Value
    For i = 1 To 50000
        Application.StatusBar = "The value is " & currCell
    Next i
    finish2 = Timer
    MsgBox "The first loop took " & finish1 - start1 & " seconds." & _
           Chr(13) & _
           "The second loop took " & finish2 - start2 & " seconds."
    Application.StatusBar = False
End Sub
```

Summary

This chapter closed out Part VII by examining a grab bag of useful VBA tips and techniques. I began by showing you the conditional compilation features that are new to VBA 5.0, including `#Const` and the `#If...Then` structure. From there, you learned a few easy methods for storing, reading, and deleting application-specific Registry settings. I then turned your attention to working with the file system through VBA. I took you through a long list of functions and statements that manipulate and return information about files and folders. To finish, we took a long look at VBA's powerful low-level file I/O capabilities.

Here's a list of chapters where you'll find related information:

- Conditional compilation is useful when debugging procedures. See Chapter 24, "Debugging VBA Procedures," for more information on VBA's debugging features.
- For more general methods for working with the Registry, see Chapter 25, "Programming the Windows API."
- Turn to Chapter 28, "Making Backups as You Work," for an example that uses Binary access mode to copy the contents of one file to another.

VIII

PART

IN THIS PART

Unleashing VBA Applications

CHAPTER 27

A Check Book Application

IN THIS CHAPTER

It is better that a man should tyrannize over his bank balance than over his fellow-citizens, and whilst the former is sometimes denounced as being but a means to the latter, sometimes at least it is an alternative.

—*John Maynard Keynes*

If you've ever wondered where all your money goes, this chapter's for you. Here we'll look at a check book application—called, appropriately enough, Check Book—that lets you record all the financial activity from a bank account into an Excel worksheet. You can use Check Book to record checks, deposits, withdrawals, ATM (automated teller machine) transactions, bank charges, and more. You can categorize each transaction so that you can see how much you're spending on clothing, groceries, and entertainment. This application even keeps a running balance for the account so that you know how much money you have before you write a check.

Using Check Book

You'll find the Check Book application in the file named Check Book.xls on this book's CD. When you open this workbook, you'll see the Register worksheet. (Figure 27.1 shows the worksheet with a few transactions already filled in.) This worksheet is similar to the paper check register you're familiar with, and it's where you enter the information for each transaction. You have the following fields:

Rec: The record number of the transaction. If you use the custom dialog boxes, this field is incremented automatically.

Date: The date of the transaction.

Chk Num: The check number (if the transaction is a check).

Payee/Description: If the transaction is a check, use this field to enter the name of the payee. For deposits or withdrawals, enter a short description.

Category: The application comes with more than 50 predefined income and expense categories that cover interest income, salary, clothing, utilities, and more. The dialog boxes list all the categories in drop-down list boxes; therefore, you can easily select the category you want from the list.

Debit: Cash outflows are placed in this column. Although the numbers are formatted to appear in red with parentheses around them, they are *not* negative numbers.

Credit: Cash inflows are placed in this column.

The ✓ column is used to indicate transactions that have cleared the bank (that is, transactions that appear on your bank statement). Normally the check marks are added by the Reconciliation feature, but you can enter a check mark yourself by pressing Ctrl-Shift-K or Alt-0252. (You must use the keyboard's numeric keypad to enter the numbers.)

Balance: The running balance in the account. With the exception of cell I2, which contains the formula `=G2-F2`, the cells in this column contain the following formula:

```
=Balance
```

This is a named formula that computes the balance at the time of the highlighted transaction. This is a relative reference formula, so its definition changes with each cell. For example, here is the formula when cell I3 is selected:

```
=I2 + G3 - F3
```

This translates as follows: take the previous Balance amount, add the current Credit amount, and subtract the current Debit amount.

Rec	Date	Chk Num	Payee/Description	Category	Debit	Credit	✓	Balance
1	1/22/97		Starting Balance			5,000.00	✓	5,000.00
2	1/23/97	1	Ma Bell	Phone - L. Dist	(87.25)			4,912.75
3	1/24/97	2	Accountant	L&P Fees	(750.00)			4,162.75
4	1/24/97		Birthday presents	Gifts	(250.00)			3,912.75
5	1/24/97		Paycheck	Salary		1,237.45		5,150.20
6	1/25/97	3	Eaton's	Clothing	(149.37)			5,000.83
7	1/25/97		Food City	Groceries	(87.50)			4,913.33
8	1/26/97		Texaco	Auto - Fuel	(25.00)			4,888.33
9	1/28/97	4	Hockey tickets	Entertainment	(145.00)			4,743.33
10	1/31/97		Last National Bank	Interest		22.87		4,766.20
11	1/31/97		Last National Bank	Bank Charge	(12.50)			4,753.70
12	2/1/97		Furnace repair	Repairs	(379.88)			4,373.82
13	2/5/97		Clascom Computers	Comp Software	(129.95)			4,243.87
14	2/6/97	5	VISA	Miscellaneous	(389.75)			3,854.12
15	2/7/97		Paycheck	Salary		1,237.45		5,091.57

FIGURE 27.1.
The Check Book worksheet.

Entering Account Information

When you first open Check Book, you need to give the application some basic information about the bank account, such as the name of the bank and the account number. This information, which appears in the transaction dialog boxes, can be handy if you're using the application for more than one account. You can also add or delete categories for the account.

Entering Basic Account Data

This procedure shows you how to enter basic account data:

1. Select Data | Check Book | Account Information or click the Account Information button on the Check Book toolbar. The Account Information dialog box, shown in Figure 27.2, appears.

2. In the Bank text box, enter the name of the bank for this account.
3. In the Account Number text box, enter the account number.

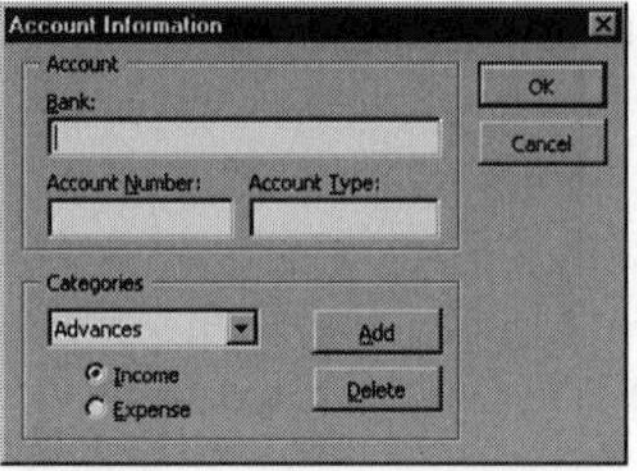

FIGURE 27.2.
Use the Account Information dialog box to enter basic information about your account.

4. In the Account Type text box, enter the type of account (for example, checking or savings).
5. Click OK.

Adding Check Book Categories

As I mentioned earlier, the Check Book application comes with dozens of predefined categories for your transactions. However, this list is by no means exhaustive, so you might like to add some categories. The following procedure shows you how to do so:

1. Display the Account Information dialog box as just described.
2. Select a type for the new category (Income or Expense).
3. In the Categories combo box, enter a name for the category. You can enter up to 255 characters, but only about 15 or so will appear in the Register worksheet's Category column.
4. Click the Add button. Check Book adds the new category and displays a message.
5. Click OK to return to the Account Information dialog box.
6. To add other categories, repeat steps 2 through 5.
7. When you're done, click OK.

Deleting Check Book Categories

To keep the category list manageable, you can delete categories you'll never use by following these steps:

1. Display the Account Information dialog box as described earlier.
2. In the Categories group, activate the type of category you want to delete (Income or Expense).
3. Select the category from the Categories drop-down list.
4. Click the Delete button. Check Book asks you whether you're sure you want to delete the category.
5. Click Yes to proceed with the deletion.

6. Repeat steps 2 through 5 to delete other categories.
7. When you've finished deleting, click OK.

Entering a Starting Balance

Before processing any transactions, you should enter a starting balance in the first row of the register. You can enter either the current balance in the account or the balance on your last bank statement. If you choose the latter, you'll also have to enter any subsequent transactions that have transpired since the date of the last statement. You need to enter two things:

- In row 2, enter the appropriate date in the Date field. If you're using the balance from your last statement, enter the statement date.
- If the account has a positive balance, enter the amount in the Credit field. Otherwise, enter the amount in the Debit field (remember to enter the debit balance as a positive number). The Balance field automatically lists the new balance.

Recording Checks

If you can write checks on your account, follow these steps to record checks in the Check Book register:

1. Select Data | Check Book | Record Check or click the Record Check button on the Check Book toolbar. Check Book displays the Check dialog box, shown in Figure 27.3.

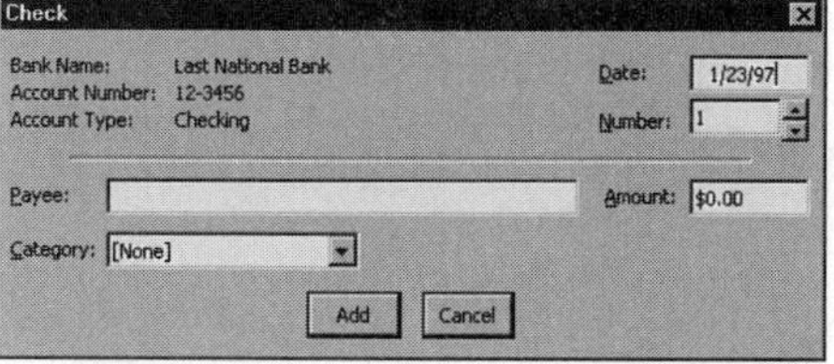

FIGURE 27.3.
Use the Check dialog box to record a check transaction.

2. Enter the check date in the Date text box. You can use any Excel data format, but the Date field is formatted as *mm/dd/yy*.
3. Enter the check number in the Number spinner.
4. Use the Payee text box to enter the name of the person or company to whom the check is payable.
5. In the Amount text box, enter the check amount.
6. Select a category from the Category drop-down list. If you don't want to use a category for this transaction, select [None].
7. Click the Add button. Check Book records the check and displays a fresh Check dialog box.

8. Repeat steps 2 through 7 to record other checks.
9. Click Close to return to the register.

Recording Withdrawals

When you withdraw money from the account, follow these steps to record the withdrawal:

1. Select Data | Check Book | Record Withdrawal or click the Record Withdrawal button on the Check Book toolbar. The Withdrawal Slip dialog box appears, as shown in Figure 27.4.

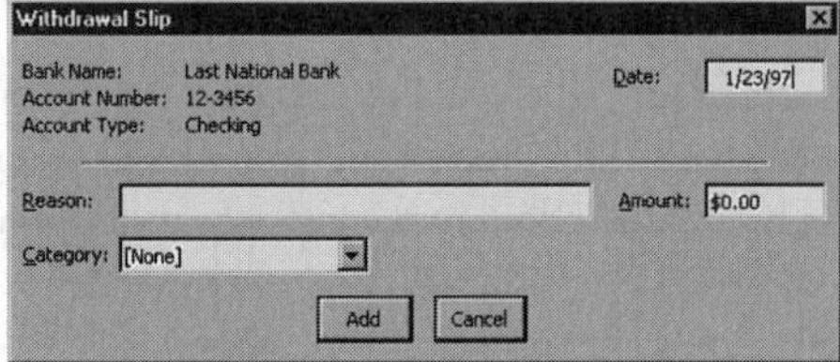

FIGURE 27.4.
Use the Withdrawal Slip dialog box to record withdrawals from your account.

2. Enter the withdrawal date in the Date text box.
3. Enter a reason for the withdrawal in the Reason text box.
4. In the Amount text box, enter the amount of the withdrawal.
5. Select a category from the Category drop-down list (or select [None]).
6. Click the Add button. Check Book records the withdrawal and displays a fresh Withdrawal Slip dialog box.
7. Repeat steps 2 through 6 to record other withdrawals.
8. Click Close to return to the register.

Recording Deposits

Here is how you record deposits to your account:

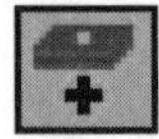

1. Select Data | Check Book | Record Deposit or click the Record Deposit button on the Check Book toolbar. Check Book displays the Deposit Slip dialog box, shown in Figure 27.5.

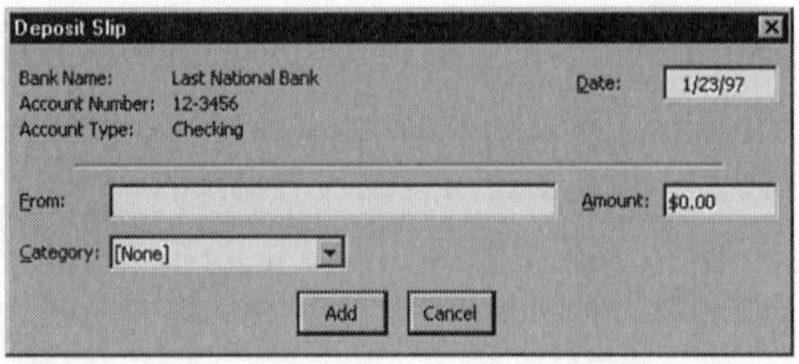

FIGURE 27.5.
Use the Deposit Slip dialog box to record deposits to the account.

2. Enter the date of the deposit in the Date text box.
3. In the From text box, enter the source of the deposit.
4. Enter the deposit amount in the Amount text box.
5. Select a category from the Category drop-down list (or select [None]).
6. Click the Add button. Check Book records the deposit and displays a fresh Deposit Slip dialog box.
7. To record other deposits, repeat steps 2 through 6.
8. Click Close to return to the register.

Balancing the Check Book

The Check Book application includes a Reconciliation feature that lets you balance the account by reconciling the Check Book register with your bank statement. You give the application the date and balance of your last statement and the date and balance of your current statement. Check Book then extracts the transactions you entered between those dates (and any older, uncleared transactions), and you check them off (one by one) with your statement.

Figure 27.6 shows the screen you'll be using. The area on the left shows the statement data. The Difference field is the value to watch. The area on the right displays the uncleared transactions that have occurred before or on the current statement date. You use the ✓ field to check off these transactions with the corresponding items on the new statement. If all goes well, the two transaction lists will be identical, and the Difference field will show 0.00. You've balanced the account!

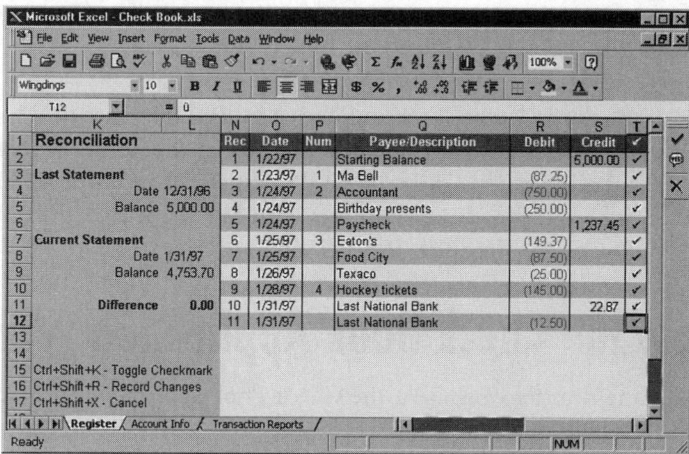

FIGURE 27.6.
The Reconciliation screen lets you compare your transactions with the bank statement.

If the Difference field isn't 0.00, you need to look for the discrepancy. You might have missed a transaction, or you might have entered the wrong amount. If you find the problem, cancel the reconciliation, fix (or add) the transaction, and try again.

The following procedure takes you through the necessary steps for completing the reconciliation:

1. With your statement in hand, enter any new bank charges or interest payments that appear in the statement.
2. Select Data | Check Book | Reconciliation or click the Reconciliation button on the Check Book toolbar. The Reconciliation dialog box appears, as shown in Figure 27.7.

FIGURE 27.7.
Use this dialog box to enter the date and balance on your current bank statement.

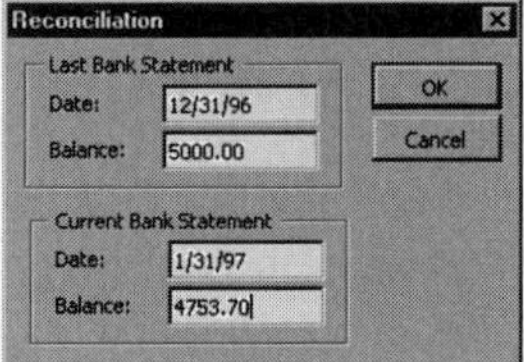

3. The Last Bank Statement group displays the information from the last reconciliation. (Or, if this is your first reconciliation, it shows the date and amount of your starting balance.) Edit this data if it's incorrect.
4. In the Current Bank Statement group, use the Date text box to enter the statement date and the Balance text box to enter the final balance on the statement.
5. Click OK. The Reconciliation dialog box, shown in Figure 27.7, appears.

6. In the ✓ field, enter check marks for each transaction that appears on the statement. To enter a check mark, press Ctrl-Shift-K or Alt-0252 (make sure you use the keyboard's numeric keypad to enter the numbers), or click the Toggle Check Mark button on the Reconcile toolbar.

7. If the reconciliation is successful (that is, the Difference field is 0), press Ctrl-Shift-R or click the Record Reconciliation button on the Reconcile toolbar to record the changes in the register. If you need to cancel the reconciliation and return to the register to make adjustments, press Ctrl-Shift-X or click the Cancel Reconciliation button on the Reconcile toolbar.

How the Check Book Application Works

Besides the Register worksheet, the Check Book application includes two other sheets that perform behind-the-scenes duties:

Account Info: This is the sheet where your account information, including the income and expense categories, is stored.

Transaction Reports: This worksheet contains two pivot tables. The Income Report pivot table shows the categories and the sum of the Credit field. This table is sorted in descending order by Sum of Credit so that the income categories appear at the top. The Expense Report pivot table shows the categories and the sum of the Debit field. This table is sorted in descending order by Sum of Debit so that the expense categories appear at the top.

NOTE: REFRESHING THE PIVOT TABLES

To update either pivot table, select a cell inside the table and then select Data | Refresh Data. Both tables were built using the Register range name (which refers to the transactions in the check book register), so a simple refresh will do the job.

The Check Book project also includes three user forms:

frmTransaction: Contains the basic layout of the dialog boxes used for the transactions. Properties such as the dialog box title are modified within the procedures.

frmAcctInfo: Defines the layout of the Account Information dialog box.

frmReconciliation: The user form for the Reconciliation dialog box.

Finally, the real meat of the Check Book application is the various procedures that display the dialog boxes and record the data. Here's a summary of the three modules you'll find in the project:

Transactions: Contains the VBA procedures that support the three Check Book transactions: recording checks, withdrawals, and deposits.

Miscellaneous: Contains just two procedures: one for displaying the Account Information dialog box, and one for toggling the ✓ character on and off.

Reconciliation: Contains the VBA procedures used by the Reconciliation feature.

Understanding the Account Info Worksheet

Figure 27.8 shows the Account Info worksheet. Many of the procedures (which you'll be looking at later) refer to cells or ranges on this sheet, so it's important to understand how the sheet is set up. The worksheet is divided into four areas: Account Data, Reconciliation Data, Income Categories, and Expense Categories.

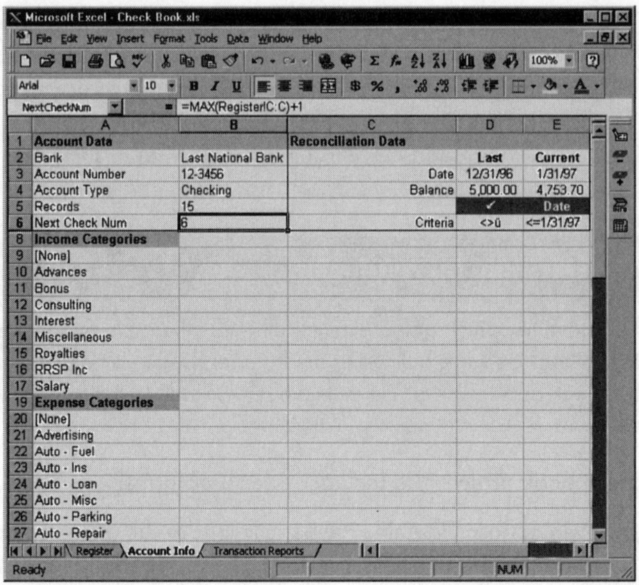

FIGURE 27.8.
The Account Info worksheet.

The Account Data Area

The Account Data area contains the account information and data that applies to the Register worksheet. Here's a summary of the cells, their names, and their descriptions:

Cell	*Name*	*Description*
B2	Bank	The name of the bank, as entered into the Account Information dialog box.
B3	AccountNumber	The account number from the Account Information dialog box.
B4	AccountType	The type of account from the Account Information dialog box.
B5	Records	The number of records (transactions) in the Register worksheet. The range of transactions is named Register; therefore, the value in this cell is given by the formula `=ROWS(Register-1)`. (You have to subtract 1 because the Register range includes the column headings.)
B6	NextCheckNum	The next likely check number you'll be using. This is given by the formula `=MAX(Register!C:C)+1`. (Column C is the Chk Num column in the Register worksheet.)

The Reconciliation Data Area

This area holds data used by the Reconciliation feature. It contains the following ranges and names:

Range	*Name*	*Description*
D3	LastDate	The date of the last bank statement.
D4	LastBalance	The balance on the last statement.
E3	CurrentDate	The date of the current statement.
E4	CurrentBalance	The balance on the current statement.
D5:E6	Criteria	The criteria range used to extract the transactions for the reconciliation. The ✓ field selects the uncleared transactions. (The ✓ character is the normal text representation of the ANSI 252 character used to create a check mark.) The Date field selects transactions that were entered on or before the `CurrentDate`.

The Income Categories Area

This area holds the list of income categories that appear in the Deposit Slip dialog box (or when you select the Income option in the Account Information dialog box).

The Expense Categories Area

This area holds the list of expense categories that appear in the Check and Withdrawal Slip dialog boxes (or when you select the Expense option in the Account Information dialog box).

The Transaction Procedures

The Transaction module contains a number of procedures that set up the application, display the transaction dialog boxes, and process the results. The next few sections discuss the procedures related to the transaction dialog boxes.

> **NOTE: THE WORKBOOK'S EVENT HANDLERS**
>
> Although I won't discuss them here, the Check Book workbook contains several event handlers that are used to manipulate the Check Book's menu commands and toolbars. For example, the event handler for the workbook's `Open` event adds the Data | Check Book command and performs a few other initialization chores. I showed you how to work with menus and toolbars in VBA in Chapter 12, "Creating Custom Menus and Toolbars."

A Tour of the Transaction Form

To understand the transaction procedures, you have to know a bit about the underlying form, which is named `frmTransaction` in the project. Here's a summary of the various fields that are manipulated by the procedures:

Control Name	*Control Type*	*Description*
`lblBankName`	Label	Displays the name of the bank.
`lblAcctNum`	Label	Displays the account number.
`lblAcctType`	Label	Displays the account type.
`txtDate`	Text box	Accepts the date of the transaction.
`txtNumber`	Text box	Accepts the check number of the transaction (checks only).
`spnNumber`	Spin box	Increments or decrements the check number (checks only).
`txtPayee`	Text box	Accepts the payee or description of the transaction.
`txtAmount`	Text box	Accepts the amount of the transaction.
`cboCategory`	Combo box	Holds the expense categories for checks and withdrawals, and the income categories for deposits.
`cmdAdd`	Command button	Records the transaction.
`cmdCancel`	Command button	Cancels the transaction.

Recording a Check

When you use the Record Check command, Check Book runs the `RecordCheck` procedure, shown in Listing 27.1. This procedure reads the current value of the `NextCheckNum` cell into the `txtNumber` text box, stores the same value in the `spnNumber` spin box (to start them off synchronized), and initializes the `cboCategory` combo box to the Expenses range. With these chores complete, the `Show` method displays the form.

Listing 27.1. This procedure sets up and displays the Check dialog box.

```
Sub RecordCheck()
    '
    ' Initialize dialog box controls for recording a check
    '
    With frmTransaction
        .txtNumber = Range("NextCheckNum")
        .spnNumber = .txtNumber
        .cboCategory.RowSource = "Expenses"
        '
        ' Show the dialog box
        '
```

```
        .Show
        Set frmTransaction = Nothing
    End With
End Sub
```

Recording a Withdrawal

Recording a withdrawal is handled by the `RecordWithdrawal` procedure. As you can see in Listing 27.2, this procedure is similar to `RecordCheck`. However, `RecordWithdrawal` uses a few extra statements to customize the form so that it appears like the Withdrawal Slip dialog box you saw in Figure 27.4:

- The form's `Caption` property is set to `Withdrawal Slip`.
- The label that appears as Payee in the Check dialog box is changed to Reason, and the accelerator key of the associated label is set to `R`.
- The label, text box, and spinner associated with the Number option are hidden.

Listing 27.2. This procedure sets up and displays the Withdrawal dialog box.

```
Sub RecordWithdrawal()
    '
    ' Initialize dialog box controls for recording a withdrawal
    '
    With frmTransaction
        .Caption = "Withdrawal Slip"
        .lblPayee = "Reason:"
        .lblPayee.Accelerator = "R"
        .lblNumber.Visible = False
        .txtNumber.Visible = False
        .spnNumber.Visible = False
        .cboCategory.RowSource = "Expenses"
        '
        ' Show the dialog box
        '
        .Show
        Set frmTransaction = Nothing
    End With
End Sub
```

Recording a Deposit

As you might expect, the procedure for recording a deposit—`RecordDeposit`, shown in Listing 27.3—is similar to that for recording a check or a withdrawal. Here are a few of the form properties that get changed in this procedure:

- The title of the dialog box is set to `Deposit Slip`.
- The label that appears as Payee in the Check dialog box and Reason in the Withdrawal Slip dialog box is set to From.

- The label, text box, and spinner associated with the Number option are hidden.
- The RowSource property of the combo box is set to the Income range on the Account Info worksheet.

Listing 27.3. This procedure sets up and displays the Deposit dialog box.

```
Sub RecordDeposit()
    '
    ' Initialize dialog box controls for recording a deposit
    '
    With frmTransaction
        .Caption = "Deposit Slip"
        .lblPayee = "From:"
        .lblPayee.Accelerator = "F"
        .lblNumber.Visible = False
        .txtNumber.Visible = False
        .spnNumber.Visible = False
        .cboCategory.RowSource = "Income"
        '
        ' Show the dialog box
        '
        .Show
        Set frmTransaction = Nothing
    End With
End Sub
```

The Activate Event Handler for the Transaction Form

Once your code invokes the Show method, you have two opportunities to run commands before the form appears on-screen:

The Initialize event: This event fires as soon as your code mentions the form. For example, this event fires when VBA runs the With frmTransaction statement in Listings 27.1, 27.2, and 27.3.

The Activate event: This event fires whenever the form gets the focus within the container application. However, user forms are always modal, so the Activate event will fire only once, just before the form appears on-screen.

In our case, we still have a few chores to perform before displaying the dialog box to the user. However, we can't use the Initialize event because, as I mentioned, it fires on the With frmTransaction statement, which occurs before we've had a chance to make our transaction-specific customizations. So we use the Activate event instead, as you can see in Listing 27.4. This procedure completes the setup tasks by loading the bank and account data, displaying the current date, and initializing the Amount and Category fields.

Listing 27.4. The event handler for the form's `Activate` event.

```
Private Sub UserForm_Activate()
    '
    ' Initialize some of the dialog box controls
    '
    lblBankName = Range("Bank")
    lblAcctNum = Range("AccountNumber")
    lblAcctType = Range("AccountType")
    txtDate = Format(Now, "m/d/yy")
    txtAmount = Format("0", "Currency")
    cboCategory.ListIndex = 0
    txtDate.SetFocus
End Sub
```


The Form's Event Handlers

As you work with the form, several event handlers lie in wait for particular events to fire. I'll describe these event handlers in this section.

For starters, we want to monitor the value in the `txtNumber` text box to make sure that it's a numeric value and to keep the value of the `spnNumber` spin box synchronized. To do this, the form traps the `BeforeUpdate` event for the text box, as shown in Listing 27.5. This event fires when the user changes the text box value and then leaves the field. If the text box isn't blank, the `IsNumeric` function checks to make sure it contains a number. If it doesn't, an error message is displayed, and the update is canceled. If the field does contain a number, the value of the spin box is set to the same number.

Listing 27.5. The `BeforeUpdate` event handler for the Check form's Number text box.

```
Private Sub txtNumber_BeforeUpdate(ByVal Cancel As MSForms.ReturnBoolean)
    If txtNumber <> "" Then
        If Not IsNumeric(txtNumber) Then
            MsgBox Prompt:="Please enter a numeric check number.", _
                   Title:="Check Book"
            Cancel = True
        Else
            spnNumber = txtNumber
        End If
    Else
        spnNumber = 0
    End If
End Sub
```

To keep the text box and the spin box values in sync, the application also traps the `Change` event for the spin box, as shown in Listing 27.6. In this case, the value of the text box is updated to the new value of the spin box.

Listing 27.6. The Change event handler for the Check form's Number spinner.

```
Private Sub spnNumber_Change()
    txtNumber = spnNumber
End Sub
```

Finally, the application also monitors the value of the Amount field (the `txtAmount` text box). Again, the `BeforeUpdate` event is trapped, and the text box is checked for a nonnumeric value, as shown in Listing 27.7. If the field contains a number, the `Format` function displays the number using the `Currency` format.

Listing 27.7. The BeforeUpdate event handler for the form's Amount text box.

```
Private Sub txtAmount_BeforeUpdate(ByVal Cancel As MSForms.ReturnBoolean)
    If txtAmount <> "" And Not IsNumeric(txtAmount) Then
        MsgBox Prompt:="Please enter a number for the amount.", _
               Title:="Check Book"
        Cancel = True
    Else
        txtAmount = Format(txtAmount, "Currency")
    End If
End Sub
```

The Event Handler for Adding a Transaction

In each transaction dialog box, when you click the Add button, Check Book records the information in the Register and then displays a fresh dialog box for the next transaction. This process is controlled by `cmdAdd_Click`—the event handler for the Add button's `Click` event, shown in Listing 27.8.

Listing 27.8. The Add button event handler.

```
Private Sub cmdAdd_Click()
    Dim regTopRow                 ' Top row of the Register range
    Dim regRows                   ' Total rows in the Register range
    Dim regNewRow As Integer      ' Row where new transaction will be added

    Application.ScreenUpdating = False
    With Range("Register")
        '
        ' Figure out the new row for the transaction
        '
        regTopRow = .Row
        regRows = .Rows.Count
        regNewRow = regTopRow + regRows
        '
        ' Enter universal transaction data in Register
        '
        .Cells(regNewRow, 1) = Range("Register").Rows.Count
        .Cells(regNewRow, 2) = CDate(txtDate)
```

```
        .Cells(regNewRow, 4) = txtPayee
        .Cells(regNewRow, 5) = cboCategory.Value
        .Cells(regNewRow, 9) = "=Balance"
        '
        ' Get rid of the dollar sign
        '
        txtAmount = Right(txtAmount, Len(txtAmount) - 1)
        '
        ' Enter transaction-specific data in Register
        '
        Select Case frmTransaction.Caption
            Case "Check"
                .Cells(regNewRow, 3) = CCur(txtNumber)
                .Cells(regNewRow, 6) = CCur(txtAmount)
            Case "Withdrawal Slip"
                .Cells(regNewRow, 6) = CCur(txtAmount)
            Case "Deposit Slip"
                .Cells(regNewRow, 7) = CCur(txtAmount)
        End Select
        '
        ' Redefine Register range name
        '
        Names.Add Name:="Register", _
              RefersTo:=.Resize(Range("Records") + 2)
    End With
    '
    ' Restart the With structure since we redefined Register
    '
    With Range("Register")
        '
        ' Shade odd record numbers
        '
        If Range("Records") Mod 2 = 1 Then
            With .Resize(1).Offset(.Rows.Count - 1)
                .Interior.Pattern = xlSolid
                .Interior.ColorIndex = 15
            End With
        Else
            With .Resize(1).Offset(.Rows.Count - 1)
                .Interior.Pattern = xlSolid
                .Interior.ColorIndex = 2
            End With
        End If
    End With
    '
    ' Reset Payee and amount
    '
    txtPayee = ""
    txtAmount = Format("0", "Currency")
    txtNumber = Range("NextCheckNum")
    spnNumber = txtNumber
    txtDate.SetFocus
    '
    ' Select the first cell of the new transaction
    '
    Cells(regNewRow, 1).Select
```

continues

Listing 27.8. continued

```
    '
    ' Change Cancel button caption to "Close" and
    ' turn screen updating back on
    '
    cmdCancel.Caption = "Close"
    Application.ScreenUpdating = True
End Sub
```

The bulk of the procedure runs within the `With Range("Register")` structure. First, the total number of rows in the range is stored in the `regRows` variable, and then the row number in which the new transaction will appear is calculated by adding the first row (the `Row` property, which is stored in the `regTopRow` variable) and `regRows`.

Then several `Cells` methods are called to enter the "universal" transaction data into the worksheet cells. (By "universal," I mean the data that is common to all three types of transactions.) The `Cells` methods return the cells in the new transaction row, and their values are set to the appropriate dialog box fields. Also, the `=Balance` formula is entered into the Balance field (column 9).

To handle the differences between checks, withdrawals, and deposits, a `Select Case` statement is used:

- For a check, a check number is entered, and the amount is entered in the Debit field (column 6). Note the use of the `CCur` conversion function to convert the text values into `Currency` data.
- For a withdrawal, the amount is entered in the Debit field (column 6).
- For a deposit, the amount is entered into the Credit field (column 7).

When that's done, the Register range name is redefined by using the `Names` object's `Add` method. The new range is calculated by using the `Resize` method to increase the number of rows in the Register range. The number of rows is determined by the following formula:

```
Range("Records") + 2
```

The Records cell, you'll recall, contains the number of transactions in the Check Book register. This number is one less than the number of rows in Register, and because you're adding a row for the new transaction, you have to add 2 to the Records value.

Since we've just renamed the Register range, the `With` structure we're in is no longer valid, so the procedure shuts it down using `End With` and then starts a new `With Range ("Register")` structure.

The Register worksheet uses shading on odd-numbered transactions to aid readability. The next section adds this shading automatically. It first checks to see if the new record number is odd using the following statement:

```
If Range("Records") Mod 2 = 1
```

VBA's `Mod` operator returns the remainder when you divide the number to the left of `Mod` by the number to the right of `Mod`. In this example, the procedure divides the value in the Records range by 2. If the remainder equals 1, the number is odd, so you need to shade the transaction. A combination of the `Resize` and `Offset` methods returns the transaction. Then the `Interior` property is set to a solid pattern (the `xlSolid` constant), and the color is set to gray (15). If the record isn't odd, the application colors the transaction cells white (`ColorIndex 2`) instead.

The final `With` statement resets the dialog box controls for the next transaction. The Payee/Reason/From control (`txtPayee`) is cleared, the Amount text box (`txtAmount`) is set to 0, and the Number text box and spinner are set to the new value in the NextCheckNum range. (This value is automatically updated when you add a transaction. (See the section "Understanding the Account Info Worksheet" earlier in this chapter.)

Also note that the caption of the `cmdCancel` button is set to Close (it appears initially as Cancel). This is standard practice for this kind of dialog box. A Cancel button is supposed to exit a dialog box without doing anything. By clicking Add, you've done something (added a transaction), so you can no longer "cancel" the dialog box; you can only "close" it.

The Account Information Procedures

The Check Box project uses several procedures to display and process the Account Information dialog box. The bulk of these procedures are form event handlers. We'll examine these routines in this section.

Examining the Account Information Form

Before getting to the procedures, it will help to know the details of the Account Information dialog box. The underlying form is named `frmAcctInfo` in the project, and it uses the following controls:

Control Name	*Control Type*	*Description*
`txtBankName`	Text box	Accepts the name of the bank.
`txtAcctNum`	Text box	Accepts the account number.
`txtAcctType`	Text box	Accepts the account type.
`txtDate`	Text box	Accepts the date of the transaction.
`cboCategory`	Combo box	Holds the expense and income categories.
`optIncome`	Option button	When activated, loads the income categories into the combo box.
`optExpenses`	Option button	When activated, loads the expense categories into the combo box.

continues

Control Name	*Control Type*	*Description*
`cmdAdd`	Command button	Adds the displayed category.
`cmdDelete`	Command button	Deletes the displayed category.
`cmdOK`	Command button	Puts the bank and account changes into effect.
`cmdCancel`	Command button	Cancels the dialog box.

Displaying the Account Information Dialog Box

When you run the Account Information command, the application calls the `DisplayAcctInfoForm` procedure (located in the Miscellaneous module), which does nothing more than invoke the form's `Show` method. This sets off the form's `Initialize` event, however, which is trapped by the event handler shown in Listing 27.9. This procedure initializes some of the dialog box controls: the three text boxes are assigned the account information data from the Account Info worksheet, and the combo box is initialized to contain the items from the Income range.

Listing 27.9. This procedure sets up and displays the Account Information dialog box.

```
Private Sub UserForm_Initialize()
    '
    ' Initialize Account Information dialog box
    '
    txtBankName = Range("Bank")
    txtAcctNum = Range("AccountNumber")
    txtAcctType = Range("AccountType")
    cboCategory.RowSource = "Income"
    cboCategory.ListIndex = 1
End Sub
```

The Event Handlers for the Option Buttons

The `optIncome_Click` and `optExpense_Click` event handlers are shown in Listing 27.10. The `optIncome_Click` procedure runs whenever you activate the Income option button. This routine modifies the `RowSource` property of the combo box to point to the Income range on the Account Info worksheet and the `LinkedCell` property to point to the IncomeLink cell. The `Value` is set to 1 to bypass the [None] item.

The `optExpense_Click` procedure is similar to the `optIncome_Click` procedure. When you activate the Expenses button, the event handler changes the `RowSource` property to the Expenses range and selects the second item.

Listing 27.10. The Click event handlers for the Income and Expense option buttons.

```
Private Sub optIncome_Click()
    cboCategory.RowSource = "Income"
    cboCategory.ListIndex = 1
End Sub
Private Sub optExpense_Click()
    cboCategory.RowSource = "Expenses"
    cboCategory.ListIndex = 1
End Sub
```


Adding a Category

When you click the Add button to add a category, Check Book runs the `cmdAdd_Click` event handler, shown in Listing 27.11. The procedure begins by declaring three variables: `newCategory` is the name of the new category, `rowNum` is the worksheet row number in which the new category will be inserted, and `catType` is the type of category (income or expense).

The `newCategory` variable is set to the `Value` property of the combo box. Then an `If` statement checks to see which type of category you're adding:

- In an income category (`optIncome` is `True`), `rowNum` is assigned a row within the Income range. (The actual location within the Income range isn't important, because you'll be sorting the range later.) Then an entire row is inserted at `Cells(rowNum,1)`, `newCategory` is placed in the cell, and the Income range is sorted to keep things in alphabetical order.
- In an expense category, the process is similar. The new row is set within the Expenses range, the new category is inserted, and Expenses is sorted.

The procedure ends by displaying a `MsgBox` function telling the user that the new category has been added.

Listing 27.11. The Click event handler for the Add command button.

```
Private Sub cmdAdd_Click()
    Dim newCategory, rowNum As Integer, catType As String
    Application.ScreenUpdating = False

    newCategory = cboCategory.Value
    '
    ' Determine if category is Income or Expense
    '
    If optIncome Then
        catType = "Income"
        rowNum = Range("Income").Row + 1
        With Worksheets("Account Info")
            .Cells(rowNum, 1).EntireRow.Insert
            .Cells(rowNum, 1).Value = newCategory
            .Range("Income").Sort Key1:=.Cells(rowNum, 1)
        End With
```

continues

Listing 27.11. continued

```
    Else
        catType = "Expense"
        rowNum = Range("Expenses").Row + 1
        With Worksheets("Account Info")
            .Cells(rowNum, 1).EntireRow.Insert
            .Cells(rowNum, 1).Value = newCategory
            .Range("Expenses").Sort Key1:=.Cells(rowNum, 1)
        End With
    End If

    MsgBox Prompt:="'" & newCategory & "' has been added " & _
           "to the list of " & catType & " categories.", _
           Buttons:=vbOKOnly + vbInformation, _
           Title:="Add Category"
    cboCategory.SetFocus
End Sub
```

Deleting a Category

The `cmdDelete_Click` procedure is shown in Listing 27.12. Check Book runs this event handler when you click the Delete button to delete a category.

The code first checks to make sure that an item in the list is selected. We have to insist upon this, because we'll need the value of the `ListIndex` property later (it's stored in the `currItem` variable). If no item is selected, `ListIndex` returns –1, which will throw off our calculations.

The category selected for deletion is given by the `Value` property of the combo box and is stored in the `categoryToDelete` variable. Then the `rowNum` variable is set to the worksheet row number that contains the category we'll be deleting. This value is calculated by adding `currItem`—which holds the `ListIndex` value—to the starting row number of either the Income or the Expenses range. (Now you see why we had to insist that a value be selected in the list.)

The procedure then checks to make sure you don't select the [None] item. The [None] item shouldn't be deleted, because you need it for entering transactions that don't have categories. If [None] is selected, the `alertMsg` and `alertButtons` variables are set up to display an appropriate message. Otherwise, these variables are set up to display a confirmation message.

In either case, a `MsgBox` function displays the constructed message, and the result is stored in the `response` variable. If you're deleting a legitimate category, the `response` variable is checked with an `If` statement. If `response` equals `vbYes`, the category's row is deleted.

Listing 27.12. The `Click` event handler for the Delete command button.

```
Sub cmdDelete_Click()
    Dim rowNum As Integer            ' The worksheet row to delete
    Dim categoryToDelete As String   ' The name of the category to delete
    Dim currItem As Integer          ' The item number of the category
```

```
    Dim alertMsg As String, alertButtons As Integer, response As Integer
    '
    ' Make sure an item is selected
    '
    currItem = cboCategory.ListIndex
    If currItem = -1 Then
        alertMsg = "No item is currently highlighted in the Category list." & _
                   Chr(13) & "Please select an item and try again."
        alertButtons = vbOKOnly + vbExclamation
        MsgBox alertMsg, alertButtons, "Check Book"
        cboCategory.SetFocus
        Exit Sub
    End If
    '
    ' Determine if category is Income or Expense
    '
    categoryToDelete = cboCategory.Value
    If optIncome Then
        rowNum = Range("Income").Row + currItem
    Else
        rowNum = Range("Expenses").Row + currItem
    End If
    '
    ' Check for [None] selected
    '
    If categoryToDelete = "[None]" Then
        alertMsg = "Can't delete the [None] category!"
        alertButtons = vbOKOnly + vbExclamation
    Else
        alertMsg = "Are you sure you want to delete the" & _
                   " " & categoryToDelete & " " & "category?"
        alertButtons = vbYesNo + vbQuestion
    End If
    '
    ' Ask for confirmation
    '
    response = MsgBox(Prompt:=alertMsg, _
                      Buttons:=alertButtons, _
                      Title:="Delete Category")
    '
    ' If user clicked Yes, delete the category
    '
    If response = vbYes Then
        Worksheets("Account Info").Cells(rowNum, 1).EntireRow.Delete
        cboCategory.ListIndex = currItem - 1
    End If

End Sub
```

Writing the Bank and Account Data

When you click the OK button, the application writes the values in the Bank, Account Number, and Account Type text boxes to the corresponding cells in the Account Info worksheet. These tasks are performed by the OK button's `Click` event handler, shown in Listing 27.13.

27

A CHECK BOOK APPLICATION

Listing 27.13. The Click event handler for the OK command button.

```
Private Sub cmdOK_Click()
    Range("Bank") = txtBankName
    Range("AccountNumber") = txtAcctNum
    Range("AccountType") = txtAcctType
    Unload Me
End Sub
```

The Reconciliation Procedures

The Reconciliation module contains several procedures that support the Check Book's Reconciliation feature. This section takes a look at these procedures.

The Reconciliation Form

Before we get to the procedures, it will help you to know the details of the Reconciliation dialog box. The underlying form is named `frmAcctInfo` in the project, and it uses the following controls:

Control Name	*Control Type*	*Description*
`txtLastDate`	Text box	The date of the last bank statement.
`txtLastBalance`	Text box	The account balance on the last bank statement.
`txtCurrDate`	Text box	The date of the current bank statement.
`txtCurrBalance`	Text box	The account balance on the current bank statement.
`cmdOK`	Command button	Starts the reconciliation.
`cmdCancel`	Command button	Cancels the reconciliation.

Displaying the Reconciliation Dialog Box

When you run the Reconciliation command, the application calls the `DisplayReconciliationForm` procedure, which resides in the Reconciliation module. This procedure simply runs the form's `Show` method.

The subsequent `Initialize` event is trapped by the event handler shown in Listing 27.14. The initialization statements read the appropriate cells from the Account Info worksheet for the Last Bank Statement controls, and display default data for the Current Bank Statement controls.

Listing 27.14. The `Initialize` event handler for the form.

```
Private Sub UserForm_Initialize()
    '
    ' Initialize the dialog box controls and then show the dialog box
    '
    txtLastDate = Range("LastDate")
    txtLastBalance = Range("LastBalance")
    txtCurrDate = ""
    txtCurrBalance = 0
End Sub
```


If you click OK, VBA runs the event handler shown in Listing 27.15. This procedure records the new data in Account Info, and then the `SetUpReconciliation` procedure (explained in the next section) is called to run the reconciliation.

Listing 27.15. The `Click` event handler for the OK command button.

```
Private Sub cmdOK_Click()
    Range("LastDate") = CDate(txtLastDate)
    Range("LastBalance") = CCur(txtLastBalance)
    Range("CurrentDate") = CDate(txtCurrDate)
    Range("CurrentBalance") = CCur(txtCurrBalance)
    SetUpReconciliation
    Unload Me
End Sub
```

Setting Up the Reconciliation Screen

As you'll soon see, Check Book creates the reconciliation transactions by extracting them from the Register (based on the values in the Account Info worksheet's Criteria range). However, Excel doesn't let you extract list records to a different worksheet, so the Reconciliation area must reside on the Register worksheet. I've placed the Reconciliation area to the right of the Register range, starting in column K. The problem with this arrangement is that rows might accidentally get deleted if you're performing maintenance within the register.

To guard against this possibility, the `SetUpReconciliation` procedure reconstructs the entire Reconciliation screen from scratch (see Listing 27.16, shown in a moment). The first statement turns off screen updating. Then a `With` statement adds and formats the labels and data used in the Reconciliation screen. A cell named Reconciliation (cell K1 in the Register worksheet) is the starting point, and the rest of the statements use either `Resize` or `Offset` to enter and format the cell values.

Most of the statements are straightforward, but one in particular might create a few furrows in your brow. Toward the end of the `With` statement, you'll see the following (take a deep breath):

```
With .Offset(10,1).FormulaArray = "=CurrentBalance-LastBalance-
➥SUM(IF(NOT(ISBLANK(Checkmarks)),Credits-Debits,0))"
```

This is the array formula that appears in the Difference cell in the Reconciliation screen (L11). `CurrentBalance` and `LastBalance` are the balances from the Account Info sheet. The Checkmarks name refers to the range of cells under the ✓ column in the extracted reconciliation transactions. Similarly, Credits refers to the range of cells under the Credit column, and Debits refers to the cells under the Debit column. The `IF()` part of the formula translates to the following:

> For each reconciliation transaction, if the ✓ field isn't blank (that is, it contains a check mark), return the difference between the Credit value and the Debit value; otherwise, return `0`.

The `SUM()` function adds up all these values.

Next, `SetUpReconciliation` sets up the new reconciliation transactions. The `With` statement—`With(Range("FirstCheckmark")`—uses the cell FirstCheckmark as the starting point (cell T2). The old transactions are cleared by first offsetting the CurrentRegion (the transactions plus the column headings) by one row (to move it off the headings) and by using the `Clear` method.

The `AdvancedFilter` method is used to extract the transactions. Notice how the `xlFilterCopy` constant is used to tell Excel to extract the records to a different location. The new location is governed by the `CopyToRange` named variable, which in this case is the Extract range (this is the range of column headings in the Reconciliation screen—N1:T1).

The next few statements redefine the Checkmarks, Credits, and Debits names used in the Difference formula, as well as the RecNums name you'll use later on. The size of each range is determined by the number of extracted transactions, and that value is stored in the `totalTrans` variable.

The rest of the procedure hides the Check Book toolbar, displays the Reconcile toolbar, and sets up the shortcut keys for recording or canceling the reconciliation.

Listing 27.16. A procedure that sets up the Reconcilation area in the Register worksheet.

```
Sub SetUpReconciliation()
    Dim totalTrans As Integer
    Application.ScreenUpdating = False
    '
    ' Add and format reconciliation labels and data
    '
    With Range("Reconciliation")
        With .Resize(20, 2)
            .Clear
            .Interior.Pattern = xlSolid
            .Interior.ColorIndex = 15
            .BorderAround
```

```
        End With
        .Value = "Reconciliation"
        .Font.Bold = True
        .Font.Size = 12
        .Offset(2, 0).Value = "Last Statement"
        .Offset(2, 0).Font.Bold = True
        .Offset(3, 0).Value = "Date"
        .Offset(3, 0).HorizontalAlignment = xlRight
        .Offset(3, 1).Value = Range("LastDate")
        .Offset(3, 1).NumberFormat = "m/d/yy"
        .Offset(4, 0).Value = "Balance"
        .Offset(4, 0).HorizontalAlignment = xlRight
        .Offset(4, 1).Value = Range("LastBalance")
        .Offset(4, 1).NumberFormat = "#,##0.00_);[Red](#,##0.00)"
        .Offset(6, 0).Value = "Current Statement"
        .Offset(6, 0).Font.Bold = True
        .Offset(7, 0).Value = "Date"
        .Offset(7, 0).HorizontalAlignment = xlRight
        .Offset(7, 1).Value = Range("CurrentDate")
        .Offset(7, 1).NumberFormat = "m/d/yy"
        .Offset(8, 0).Value = "Balance"
        .Offset(8, 0).HorizontalAlignment = xlRight
        .Offset(8, 1).Value = Range("CurrentBalance")
        .Offset(8, 1).NumberFormat = "#,##0.00_);[Red](#,##0.00)"
        With .Offset(10, 0)
            .Value = "Difference"
            .HorizontalAlignment = xlRight
            .Font.Bold = True
        End With
        With .Offset(10, 1)
            .FormulaArray = "=CurrentBalance-LastBalance-SUM(IF(NOT(ISBLANK
            ➥(Checkmarks)),Credits-Debits,0))"
            .NumberFormat = "#,##0.00_);[Red](#,##0.00)"
            .Font.Bold = True
        End With
        .Offset(14, 0).Value = "Ctrl+Shift+K - Toggle Checkmark"
        .Offset(15, 0).Value = "Ctrl+Shift+R - Record Changes"
        .Offset(16, 0).Value = "Ctrl+Shift+X - Cancel"
    End With
    '
    ' Display Reconciliation area
    '
    Application.Goto Reference:=Range("Reconciliation"), Scroll:=True
    '
    ' Set up new reconciliation
    '
    With Range("FirstCheckmark")
        '
        ' Clear the current transactions
        '
        .CurrentRegion.Offset(1, 0).Clear
        '
        ' Extract the new ones
        '
        Range("Register").AdvancedFilter _
            Action:=xlFilterCopy, _
            CriteriaRange:=Range("Criteria"), _
            CopyToRange:=Range("Extract")
```

continues

Listing 27.16. continued

```
        '
        ' Make sure there are transactions in the reconciliation
        '
        If Range("FirstRec") = "" Then
            MsgBox Prompt:="No transactions to reconcile!", _
                   Buttons:=vbOKOnly, _
                   Title:="Check Book"
            EndReconciliation
            Exit Sub
        End If
        '
        ' Redefine the ranges used by the Difference formula
        '
        totalTrans = .CurrentRegion.Rows.Count - 1
        Names.Add Name:="Checkmarks", RefersToR1C1:=.Resize(totalTrans)
        Names.Add Name:="Credits", RefersToR1C1:=.Offset(0, -1).Resize(totalTrans)
        Names.Add Name:="Debits", RefersToR1C1:=.Offset(0, -2).Resize(totalTrans)
        Names.Add Name:="RecNums", RefersToR1C1:=.Offset(0, -6).Resize(totalTrans)
        .Select
    End With
    '
    ' Set up toolbars
    '
    Application.CommandBars("Check Book").Visible = False
    With Application.CommandBars("Reconcile")
        .Top = 0
        .Visible = True
        .Position = msoBarRight
    End With
    '
    ' Set up shortcut keys for recording and canceling
    '
    Application.OnKey Key:="^+r", Procedure:="RecordReconciliation"
    Application.OnKey Key:="^+x", Procedure:="EndReconciliation"
End Sub
```

Recording the Reconciliation

When you record the reconciliation, the `RecordReconciliation` procedure, shown in Listing 27.17, is executed. The job of the `For Each...Next` loop is to copy the contents of the Reconciliation screen's ✓ field into the corresponding field in the Register range. The RecNums name refers to the range of cells below the Rec column. Each loop through these cells (each cell is named `recCell`) does three things:

1. The contents of the ✓ field (offset from `recCell` by six columns) are stored in `checkCell`.
2. The `MATCH()` worksheet function looks for the record number (the Value of `recCell`) in column A (the Rec column of the Register). The result is the row number of the transaction, which is stored in `registerRow`.

3. checkCell is stored in the ✓ field of the Register range. (The CheckField name refers to the column heading of the field.)

The next four statements record the statement data in the Account Info worksheet: CurrentDate is moved to LastDate and cleared, and CurrentBalance is moved to LastBalance and set to 0. The final statement calls the EndReconciliation procedure (discussed after Listing 27.17).

Listing 27.17. A procedure that records the reconciliation changes.

```
Sub RecordReconciliation()
    Dim registerRow As Integer, recCell As Range, checkCell As Variant
    '
    ' Record check marks
    '
    For Each recCell In Range("RecNums")
        checkCell = recCell.Offset(0, 6).Value
        registerRow = Application.Match(recCell.Value, [a1].EntireColumn, 0)
        Cells(registerRow, Range("CheckField").Column).Value = checkCell
    Next recCell
    '
    ' Record statement data
    '
    Range("LastDate").Value = Range("CurrentDate")
    Range("CurrentDate") = ""
    Range("LastBalance").Value = Range("CurrentBalance")
    Range("CurrentBalance") = 0
    '
    ' End it all
    '
    EndReconciliation
End Sub
```


Ending the Reconciliation

The EndReconciliation procedure, shown in Listing 27.18, performs several tasks that reset the Register worksheet: The Check Book toolbar is displayed, the Reconcile toolbar is hidden, the first cell of the Register range is selected, and the Ctrl-Shift-R and Ctrl-Shift-K shortcut keys are reset.

Listing 27.18. A procedure that ends the reconciliation.

```
Sub EndReconciliation()
    Application.CommandBars("Check Book").Visible = True
    Application.CommandBars("Reconcile").Visible = False
    Cells(Range("Register").Row + 1, 1).Select
    Application.OnKey Key:="^+r"
    Application.OnKey Key:="^+x"
End Sub
```

Summary

This chapter began Part VIII by taking you through the Check Book application. I showed you how this application works, and then I took you behind the scenes to see the procedures and other plumbing that make up the guts of the application. Here are some other chapters to read for related information:

- I cover Range objects and other elements of the Excel object model in Chapter 7, "Manipulating Excel with VBA."
- To get the full scoop on custom forms, see Chapter 11, "Working with Microsoft Forms."
- To learn how to manipulate menus and toolbars, head for Chapter 12, "Creating Custom Menus and Toolbars."
- I showed you how to work with Excel lists via VBA in Chapter 17, "Using VBA to Work with Excel Lists."

CHAPTER 28

Making Backups as You Work

IN THIS CHAPTER

In skating over thin ice, our safety is in our speed.

—*Ralph Waldo Emerson*

The documents you create are precious and, in most cases, irreplaceable. Hopefully, you already have a backup strategy in place where you're doing a full backup once a month or so and an incremental backup every couple of days. But even such an ambitious strategy has its drawbacks. If you backed up yesterday and your hard disk crashes today, you'll lose at least a full day's work (and that's a best-case scenario).

My credo is that you can never back up too often. Of course, you don't want to be cranking up your backup software every five minutes, but if you set things up right, you won't have to. In this chapter, I'll take you through a project named Backup that lets you make quick backups as you work. You never have to leave the friendly confines of your main application, and everything takes only a few seconds. You can even have Backup remind you to back up your data.

Using the Backup Application

Before lifting the hood to get a look at the engine that drives the Backup application, let's take the program for a spin around the block so that you can see what it can do.

The Backup project is part of the Chaptr28.xls workbook. (As you'll see later, Backup can be easily modified to work with other VBA-enabled applications.) Once you have this file open, you start Backup by launching the `ShowBackup` procedure, which you'll find in the Backup module (it's the only procedure in the module). Figure 28.1 shows the form that appears.

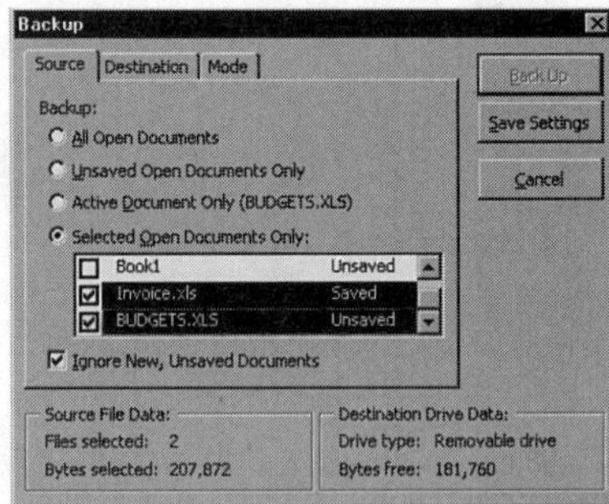

FIGURE 28.1.
Use the Backup form to back up some or all of your open documents.

Backing up involves four steps:

1. Select the documents you want to back up.
2. Select the destination for the backed-up files.
3. Select the backup mode.

4. Start the backup by clicking the Back Up button. (Alternatively, you can save the form's current settings without performing a backup by clicking the Save Settings button.)

The next three sections expand upon steps 1 through 3.

Selecting the Files to Back Up

Backup's Source tab displays a list of the application's currently open documents. When choosing the documents you want backed up, you have four options:

All Open Documents: Activate this option to back up each of the open documents.

Unsaved Open Documents Only: Activate this option to back up only documents that have unsaved changes. Note that the list box tells you which documents are unsaved.

Active Document Only: Activate this option to back up only the file that is currently active.

Selected Open Documents Only: Activate this option, and then activate the check boxes beside the documents you want to back up.

Also note that you can eliminate new, unsaved documents from these selections by activating the Ignore New, Unsaved Documents check box.

As you choose your documents, the Source File Data group shows you the number of files you've selected and the total number of bytes to be backed up.

Selecting the Backup Destination

Once you know which files you want to work with, the next step is to select where you want the files backed up to. You do this using the Destination tab, shown in Figure 28.2. Use the Back Up To combo box to either enter a folder path or select a path from the list (Backup keeps track of the last 10 paths you used).

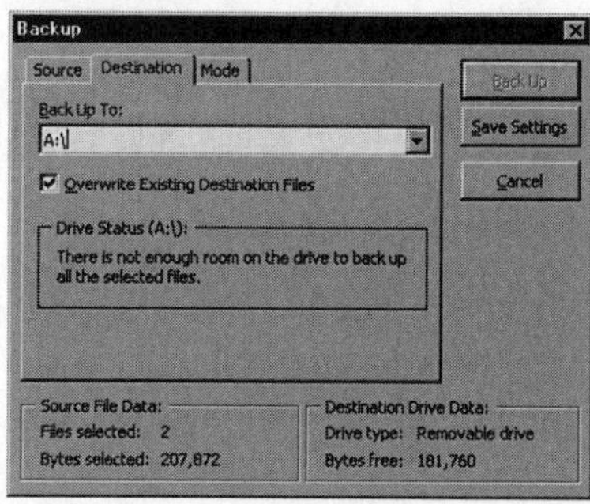

FIGURE 28.2.
Use the Destination tab to enter a location for the backed-up files.

After you enter or select a path, Backup displays the drive type and available disk space in the Destination Drive Data group. (If you type in the folder name, you have to exit the combo box to update the drive data.) If the amount of free space on the selected drive is less than the number of bytes selected for the backup, as in Figure 28.2, the Drive Status box lets you know, and the Back Up button becomes disabled.

In addition, you can specify that it's okay for Backup to overwrite files in the destination folder by activating the Overwrite Existing Destination Files check box. If you deactivate this check box, Backup will prompt you for a new destination name if a file with the same name already exists in the selected folder.

Setting the Backup Mode

Your final chore is to use the Mode tab, shown in Figure 28.3, to specify which of Backup's two modes you want to use:

- Manual: With this mode, the selected files are backed up, and then the Backup form is unloaded. To perform another backup, you have to redisplay the Backup form manually.
- Reminder: With this mode, the selected files are backed up, and the Backup form is redisplayed after a specified interval. This interval is determined by the three text boxes below the Reminder option button.

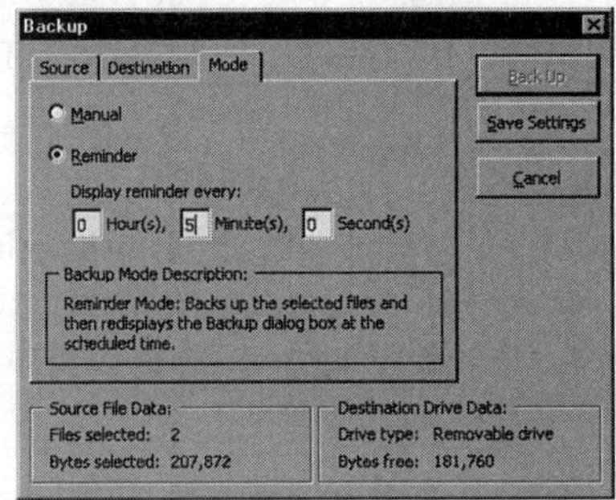

FIGURE 28.3.
Use the Mode tab to determine which Backup mode you want to use.

Understanding the Backup Application

The Backup project consists of just two objects:

- The frmBackup form: This is the Backup form you saw in the figures. Besides constituting the application's interface, you'll also find the bulk of the Backup procedures in this form's code window.
- The Backup module: This module contains only a single procedure—the `ShowBackup` procedure, which launches the application—as well as some API `Declare` statements and a few `Public` constants.

> **NOTE: INFO ON THE WIN32 API**
>
> This project uses a few calls to the Win32 API (Application Programming Interface). If you're not familiar with how these calls work, you might want to take a quick look at Chapter 25, "Programming the Windows API."

Backup is designed to be a generic backup component that you can use in any VBA-enabled application. To that end, this book's CD includes Backup.frm and Backup.bas, exported versions of the two objects just mentioned. If you import these files into another application, the only modifications you'll need to make concern the collection of open documents. In Excel, this is the `Workbooks` collection. To use this project with Word, for example, you'd modify all references to `Workbooks` so that they read `Documents`.

Backup and the Registry

As we work through the Backup code, you'll see that I make extensive use of the Windows Registry for storing settings and data. These settings are stored in the following key:

```
HKEY_CURRENT_USER\Software\VB and VBA Program Settings\VBA Unleashed\Backup\
```

Here's a quick summary of the data stored in this key:

`BackupFilter`: This setting stores a value that represents the currently selected option button in the Source tab.

`BackupMode`: This setting stores a value that represents the currently selected option button in the Mode tab.

`IgnoreNewAndUnsaved`: This setting stores the current state of the Ignore New, Unsaved Documents check box.

`IntervalHours`: This setting stores the current value of the Hour(s) text box in the Mode tab.

`IntervalMinutes`: This setting stores the current value of the Minute(s) text box in the Mode tab.

`IntervalSeconds`: This setting stores the current value of the Second(s) text box in the Mode tab.

`MRUFolder`*n*: These settings (`MRUFolder0`, `MRUFolder1`, and so on) represent the last 10 destination folders that you've entered into the Back Up To combo box. (MRU stands for "most recently used.")

`NextReminder`: This setting stores the time that the next reminder will be displayed.

`OverwriteDestFiles`: This setting stores the current state of the Overwrite Existing Destination Files check box.

`SelectedDocuments`: This setting is a string that holds the filenames of the documents that were selected in the Source tab. This setting is saved only if the Selected Open Documents Only option button is activated.

> **NOTE: VBA'S REGISTRY TOOLS**
>
> I use VBA's `SaveSetting` statement and `GetSetting` function to store and retrieve the values in the Registry. See Chapter 26, "VBA Tips and Techniques," to learn how to use these features.

A Tour of the Backup Form

The Backup form's code window is crammed with no less than 25 Sub and Function procedures. To help you make sense of all this verbiage, this section examines the Backup form and its controls and runs through the code as I introduce you to each form element.

Initializing the Form

The form's `Initialize` event handler is a long procedure that performs many tasks to get the form ready for action. Listing 28.1 shows the entire procedure. I'll explain the various parts after the listing.

Listing 28.1. The event handler for the Backup form's `Initialize` event.

```
' Global variables
'
Dim currDestDrive As String ' Holds the current destination disk drive
Dim initializing As Boolean ' True during the Initialize event
Dim nextReminder As Date    ' The time of the next scheduled reminder
Dim arrDocs() As BackupDoc  ' This array holds info for all the open documents
'
' Use the Initialize event handler to
' set up the form each time it's displayed
'
Private Sub UserForm_Initialize()
    Dim doc As Workbook ' Loop object
    Dim i As Integer    ' Counter
    Dim str As String   ' Temporary string variable

    initializing = True
    '
    ' Build the list of recently used folders
    '
    With cboDestination
        For i = 0 To 9
            str = GetSetting("VBA Unleashed", "Backup", "MRUFolder" & i, "")
            If str <> "" Then .AddItem str
        Next 'i
```

```
        If .ListCount > 0 Then .ListIndex = 0
    End With
    '
    ' Create the document array
    '
    ReDim arrDocs(Workbooks.Count)
    i = 0
    For Each doc In Workbooks
        arrDocs(i).Name = doc.Name
        arrDocs(i).Path = doc.Path
        '
        ' Make sure we're not dealing with a new, unsaved file
        '
        If doc.Path <> "" Then
            If doc.Saved = True Then
                arrDocs(i).State = "Saved"
            Else
                arrDocs(i).State = "Unsaved"
            End If
            arrDocs(i).Size = FileLen(doc.FullName)
        Else
            arrDocs(i).State = "Unsaved"
            arrDocs(i).Size = 0
        End If
        i = i + 1
    Next 'doc
    '
    ' Build the document list
    '
    Call BuildDocList()
    '
    ' Now that we have the documents list, get the setting
    ' that determines which documents are selected. Activating
    ' an option will fire that option's Click event.
    '
    str = GetSetting("VBA Unleashed", "Backup", "BackupFilter", "All")
    Select Case str
        Case "All"
            optAll = True
        Case "Unsaved"
            optUnsaved = True
        Case "Active"
            optActive = True
        Case "Selected"
            optSelected = True
            lstDocs.Enabled = True
            Call ParseSelectedFiles
    End Select
    '
    ' Get the check box values from the Registry
    '
    chkIgnoreNew = GetSetting("VBA Unleashed", "Backup", "IgnoreNewAndUnsaved",
➥True)
    chkOverwrite = GetSetting("VBA Unleashed", "Backup", "OverwriteDestFiles", True)
    '
    ' Set the Backup Mode option
    '
```

continues

Listing 28.1. continued

```
    If GetSetting("VBA Unleashed", "Backup", "BackupMode", "Manual") = "Manual"
    ➥Then
        optManual = True
    Else
        optReminder = True
    End If
    '
    ' Get the Reminder interval settings
    '
    txtIntervalHours = GetSetting("VBA Unleashed", "Backup", "IntervalHours", "0")
    txtIntervalMinutes = GetSetting("VBA Unleashed", "Backup", "IntervalMinutes",
    ➥"30")
    txtIntervalSeconds = GetSetting("VBA Unleashed", "Backup", "IntervalSeconds",
    ➥"0")
    nextReminder = TimeValue(GetSetting("VBA Unleashed", "Backup", "NextReminder",
    ➥"12:00:00 AM"))
    '
    ' Finished initialization, so display data
    '
    initializing = False
    Call DisplayDestinationData
End Sub
```

To help you get a feel for what's happening in this lengthy routine, let's break it up into manageable chunks and examine each one separately.

For starters, the top of the code window defines several global variables:

```
Dim currDestDrive As String ' Holds the current destination disk drive
Dim initializing As Boolean ' True during the Initialize event
Dim nextReminder As Date    ' The time of the next scheduled reminder
Dim arrDocs() As BackupDoc  ' This array holds info for all the open documents
```

The `currDestDrive` variable keeps track of the disk drive selected for the destination. You saw earlier that Backup displays the drive type and free space for the selected destination. Since it can sometimes take a while to glean this information from a drive (especially a floppy or network drive), tracking the current drive prevents you from requerying the same drive (if you change the destination folder from A:\ to A:\Backup, for example).

The `initializing` variable is a `Boolean` value that is set to `True` while the `Initialize` event handler is running. This lets you avoid some unnecessary work during the `Initialize` event. For example, adding items to a list box forces that list's `Click` event to fire. To avoid running the full `Click` event handler, you can test the value of `initializing`.

The `nextReminder` variable stores the time that the next reminder is scheduled to appear. We'll need this value in case we want to cancel a pending reminder (if we switch to Manual mode, for example.)

The `arrDocs` variable is an array that is used to hold the list of open documents. The array elements are declared as `BackupDoc` types, which is a custom type that's defined in the Backup module:

```
Type BackupDoc
    Name As String
    Path As String
    State As String
    Size As Long
    Selected As Boolean
End Type
```

This type stores the following information for each document:

`Name`: The document's filename.

`Path`: The document's pathname (drive and folder).

`State`: Whether the document is Saved or Unsaved.

`Size`: The document's file size, in bytes.

`Selected`: Whether or not the document is selected for backup.

NOTE: TYPE MEMBERS AS PROPERTIES

For simplicity, I'll refer to the elements in the `BackupDoc` type as "properties" of each document. Although it's true that, in a sense, these type members are custom properties of each document, always remember that these are not intrinsic object properties.

The `Initialize` event handler begins by declaring a few "worker bee" variables for loops, counters, and so on, and then `initializing` is set to `True`. With that out of the way, the procedure builds the list of recently used destination folders:

```
With cboDestination
    For i = 0 To 9
        str = GetSetting("VBA Unleashed", "Backup", "MRUFolder" & i, "")
        If str <> "" Then .AddItem str
    Next 'i
    If .ListCount > 0 Then .ListIndex = 0
End With
```

Here, `cboDestination` is the Back Up To combo box on the Destination tab. A `For...Next` loop uses `GetSetting` to read the `MRUFolder`*n* settings from the Registry, and the `AddItem` method adds the values to the list.

Next, the procedure creates the array of open documents:

```
ReDim arrDocs(Workbooks.Count)
i = 0
For Each doc In Workbooks
    arrDocs(i).Name = doc.Name
    arrDocs(i).Path = doc.Path
    '
    ' Make sure we're not dealing with a new, unsaved file
    '
    If doc.Path <> "" Then
        If doc.Saved = True Then
            arrDocs(i).State = "Saved"
```

```
            Else
                arrDocs(i).State = "Unsaved"
            End If
            arrDocs(i).Size = FileLen(doc.FullName)
        Else
            arrDocs(i).State = "Unsaved"
            arrDocs(i).Size = 0
        End If
        i = i + 1
    Next 'doc
```

The `arrDocs` array is redimensioned to `Workbooks.Count`, and then a `For Each...Next` loop runs through the `Workbooks` collection. Along the way, the code branches, depending on whether a document is a new, unsaved file. If it is—that is, if its `Path` property returns the null string—`State` is set to `Unsaved` and `Size` is set to 0; otherwise, these values are derived from the document's `Saved` and `Size` properties.

With the array of open documents constructed, the `Initialize` event handler then calls the `BuildDocList` procedure, which puts together the list of documents that appears on the Source tab. (I'll explain this procedure in the section "Backup's Support Procedures.") Then another call to `GetSetting` retrieves the `BackupFilter` value, which is used to activate the appropriate Source tab option button:

```
    Call BuildDocList()
    '
    ' Now that we have the documents list, get the setting
    ' that determines which documents are selected. Activating
    ' an option will fire that option's Click event.
    '
    str = GetSetting("VBA Unleashed", "Backup", "BackupFilter", "All")
    Select Case str
        Case "All"
            optAll = True
        Case "Unsaved"
            optUnsaved = True
        Case "Active"
            optActive = True
        Case "Selected"
            optSelected = True
            lstDocs.Enabled = True
            Call ParseSelectedFiles
    End Select
```

Also note that the `Selected` case also calls the `ParseSelectedFiles` procedure, which extracts the filenames from the Registry's `SelectedDocuments` setting (again, this procedure is explained in the section "Backup's Support Procedures").

The rest of the event handler uses `GetSetting` to retrieve settings and set up the form accordingly:

```
    ' Get the check box values from the Registry
    '
    chkIgnoreNew = GetSetting("VBA Unleashed", "Backup", "IgnoreNewAndUnsaved",
    ➥True)
    chkOverwrite = GetSetting("VBA Unleashed", "Backup", "OverwriteDestFiles", True)
```

```
    '
    ' Set the Backup Mode option
    '
    If GetSetting("VBA Unleashed", "Backup", "BackupMode", "Manual") = "Manual"
    ➥Then
        optManual = True
    Else
        optReminder = True
    End If
    '
    ' Get the Reminder interval settings
    '
    txtIntervalHours = GetSetting("VBA Unleashed", "Backup", "IntervalHours", "0")
    txtIntervalMinutes = GetSetting("VBA Unleashed", "Backup", "IntervalMinutes",
    ➥"30")
    txtIntervalSeconds = GetSetting("VBA Unleashed", "Backup", "IntervalSeconds",
    ➥"0")
    nextReminder = TimeValue(GetSetting("VBA Unleashed", "Backup", "NextReminder",
    ➥"12:00:00 AM"))
    '
    ' Finished initializing, so display data
    '
    initializing = False
    Call DisplayDestinationData
End Sub
```

The last statement is a call to the `DisplayDestinationData` procedure, which I'll explain later.

The Source Tab

With the Backup form now initialized and presented on-screen, we need code to process the user's interaction with the various controls. In this section, I'll show you the event handlers for the controls on the Source tab (see Figure 28.1).

The All Open Documents Option

The All Open Documents option button is named `optAll`, and its `Click` event handler appears in Listing 28.2. When this option is activated, we want to select every document in the list box. To that end, this procedure runs through the array of open documents and sets each member's `Selected` property to `True`. It then disables the list box (the list is enabled only when the Selected Open Documents Only option is activated) and calls `BuildDocList` to redisplay the list box.

Note, too, that if the Ignore New, Unsaved Documents check box (`chkIgnoreNew`) is activated, the procedure skips any array items in which the `Path` property is the null string.

Listing 28.2. The `Click` event handler for the All Open Documents option button.

```
Private Sub optAll_Click()
    Dim i As Integer     ' Counter
    '
    ' Set Selected property to True for all documents.
    '
```

continues

Listing 28.2. continued

```
    For i = 0 To UBound(arrDocs) - 1
        '
        ' Check to see if the "Ignore New, Unsaved
        ' Documents" check box is activated.
        '
        If chkIgnoreNew Then
            If arrDocs(i).Path <> "" Then
                arrDocs(i).Selected = True
            End If
        Else
            arrDocs(i).Selected = True
        End If
    Next 'i
    '
    ' Disable and rebuild the list
    '
    lstDocs.Enabled = False
    Call BuildDocList()
End Sub
```

The Unsaved Open Documents Only Option

The Unsaved Open Documents Only option button is named `optUnsaved`. Activating this option means that we want to select only documents that have unsaved changes. Listing 28.3 shows the button's `Click` event handler that accomplishes this. Again, the procedure runs through the array of open documents. This time, it checks the `State` value and, if it equals `Unsaved`, the procedure sets the document's `Selected` property to `True`. As before, allowances are made, depending on whether new, unsaved documents are to be ignored.

Listing 28.3. The `Click` event handler for the Unsaved Open Documents Only option button.

```
Private Sub optUnsaved_Click()
    Dim i As Integer     ' Counter
    '
    ' Set Selected property to True for all documents
    ' that have State = "Unsaved"
    '
    For i = 0 To UBound(arrDocs) - 1
        With arrDocs(i)
            If .State = "Unsaved" Then
                '
                ' Check to see if the "Ignore New,
                ' Unsaved Documents" check box is activated.
                '
                If chkIgnoreNew Then
                    If .Path <> "" Then
                        .Selected = True
                    End If
                Else
                    .Selected = True
                End If
            Else
```

```
            .Selected = False
        End If
    End With
Next 'i
'
' Disable and rebuild the list
'
lstDocs.Enabled = False
Call BuildDocList()
End Sub
```

The Active Document Only Option

If you activate the Active Document Only option, it means that only the active document will be selected in the list. This option button is named `optActive`, and its `Click` event handler checks for the element of `arrDocs` in which the `Name` property equals the `Name` property of the `ActiveWorkbook` object, as shown in Listing 28.4.

Listing 28.4. The `Click` event handler for the Active Document Only option button.

```
Private Sub optActive_Click()
    Dim i As Integer     ' Counter
    '
    ' Set Selected property to True for active document
    '
    For i = 0 To UBound(arrDocs) - 1
        With arrDocs(i)
            If .Name = ActiveWorkbook.Name Then
                '
                ' Check to see if the "Ignore New,
                ' Unsaved Documents" check box is activated.
                '
                If chkIgnoreNew Then
                    If .Path <> "" Then
                        .Selected = True
                    End If
                Else
                    .Selected = True
                End If
            Else
                .Selected = False
            End If
        End With
    Next 'i
    '
    ' Disable and rebuild the list
    '
    lstDocs.Enabled = False
    Call BuildDocList()
End Sub
```

The Selected Open Documents Only Option

Activating the Selected Open Documents Only option button (optSelected) enables the list box so that you can select individual documents for the backup. Listing 28.5 shows the Click event handler that enables the list box.

Listing 28.5. The Click event handler for the Selected Open Documents Only option button.

```
Private Sub optSelected_Click()
    lstDocs.Enabled = True
End Sub
```

The Documents List Box

The list box that holds the names of the open documents is called lstDocs. It's a regular list box, but it uses some unusual properties:

ColumnCount: This property is set to 2. This allows the program to show the filenames in the first column and the file's "state" (Saved or Unsaved) in the second column.

ColumnWidths: This property determines the width of each column. The widths of columns 1 and 2 are set to 105 points and 15 points, respectively.

ListStyle: This property is set to fmListStyleOption, which displays a check box beside each item.

MultiSelect: This property is set to True to let the user select multiple items.

Later in this chapter I'll show you how to populate a list box that has multiple columns (see "The BuildDocList Procedure"). For now, Listing 28.6 shows the list's Change event handler. This event fires each time an item in the list is selected or deselected. The event handler runs through the elements in arrDocs and looks for the one that matches whichever list element has changed. When the match is found, the Selected property is updated to .Selected(.ListIndex), which returns the selected state of the list item in question.

Listing 28.6. The Change event handler for the list of documents.

```
Private Sub lstDocs_Change()
    Dim i As Integer     ' Counter
    '
    ' Avoid this event while we're populating
    ' the list box during the Initialize event
    '
    If initializing Then Exit Sub
    With lstDocs
        '
        ' Run through the document array
        '
        For i = 0 To UBound(arrDocs) - 1
```

```
            '
            ' Look for the array document that has the
            ' same name as the selected list item
            '
            If arrDocs(i).Name = .List(.ListIndex, 0) Then
                '
                ' Adjust its Selected property
                '
                arrDocs(i).Selected = .Selected(.ListIndex)
            End If
        Next 'i
    End With
    Call DisplaySourceData
End Sub
```

The Ignore New, Unsaved Check Box

When the Ignore New, Unsaved check box is activated, Backup automatically deselects all documents that are new and unsaved. These items remain deselected even if you activate All Open Files or Unsaved Documents Only. The `Click` event handler shown in Listing 28.7 is designed to update the selected list items, depending on the state of the check box (which is named `chkIgnoreNew`). The procedure runs through the `arrDocs` array, looking for documents in which the `Path` is the null string.

Given such a document, the easiest case is when `chkIgnoreNew` is `True`, because we simply set the `Selected` property to `False` for all the new and unsaved files.

The opposite case—when `chkIgnoreNew` is `False`—is a bit trickier, because we can't just set `Selected` to `True` for all the new and unsaved files. Instead, we have to take into account the currently selected option button. For example, if the Active Document Only option button is activated, we set a new and unsaved document's `Selected` property to `True` only if that document happens to be the active file.

Listing 28.7. The `Click` event handler for the Ignore New, Unsaved Documents check box.

```
Private Sub chkIgnoreNew_Click()
    Dim i As Integer
    If initializing Then Exit Sub
    '
    ' Run through the document array
    '
    For i = 0 To UBound(arrDocs) - 1
        '
        ' Look for array documents with no path
        '
        If arrDocs(i).Path = "" Then
            '
            ' Adjust its Selected property
            '
            If chkIgnoreNew = True Then
```

continues

28 MAKING BACKUPS AS YOU WORK

Listing 28.7. continued

```
                    '
                    ' Selected is always False here
                    '
                    arrDocs(i).Selected = False
                Else
                    '
                    ' Selected depends on current option
                    '
                    If optAll Or optUnsaved Then
                        '
                        ' Select it if option is All or Unsaved
                        '
                        arrDocs(i).Selected = True
                    ElseIf optActive And arrDocs(i).Name = ActiveWorkbook.Name Then
                        '
                        ' If option is Active, select only if doc is active
                        '
                        arrDocs(i).Selected = True
                    End If
                End If
            End If
        Next 'i
        '
        ' Redisplay the list of documents
        '
        Call BuildDocList()
End Sub
```

The Destination Tab

The Destination tab has only a few controls, and only one—the Back Up To combo box—traps any events. The next two sections tell you about the `BeforeUpdate` and `Click` events for this combo box.

Back Up To: The `BeforeUpdate` Event

The `BeforeUpdate` event fires when the user attempts to move out of the combo box. Backup uses this event to check the folder value that the user entered, as shown in Listing 28.8.

After first making sure that the folder path ends with a backslash (\), the procedure runs through the current list entries to see if the new entry matches any of them. If it does, the values in the Destination Drive Data group are updated (by calling the `DisplayDestinationData` function, which is explained later).

If no match was found, the return value of `DisplayDestinationData` is tested. If it's `True`, no problems were found with the folder's drive, so the procedure then runs `Dir` to see if the folder exists. If it does, the folder is added to the list.

Listing 28.8. The `BeforeUpdate` event handler for the Back Up To list box.

```
Private Sub cboDestination_BeforeUpdate(ByVal Cancel As MSForms.ReturnBoolean)
    Dim i As Integer     ' Counter

    With cboDestination
        '
        ' Make sure the path ends with "\"
        '
        If Right(.Value, 1) <> "\" Then .Value = .Value & "\"
        '
        ' See if the current value is already in the list
        '
        For i = 0 To .ListCount - 1
            If .Value = .List(i) Then
                '
                ' Found it, so just redisplay the drive data
                '
                Call DisplayDestinationData
                Exit Sub
            End If
        Next 'i
        '
        ' Display the drive data. DisplayDestinationData returns True
        ' only if the destination drive is available or otherwise valid.
        '
        If DisplayDestinationData = True Then
            '
            ' Check the destination folder
            '
            If Dir(.Value) <> "" Then
                '
                ' Destination folder exists, so add it to the list
                '
                .AddItem .Value
            End If
        End If
    End With
End Sub
```

Back Up To: The `Click` Event

The Back Up To control's `Click` event fires when the user drops down the list box and chooses an item. Since we already know that the list items are all legitimate paths, we only need to call `DisplayDestinationData` to redisplay the Destination Drive Data values, as shown in Listing 28.9.

Listing 28.9. The `Click` event handler for the Back Up To list box.

```
Private Sub cboDestination_Click()
    If Not initializing Then
        '
        ' Display the data for the selected destination
        '
```

continues

Listing 28.9. continued

```
        DisplayDestinationData
    End If
End Sub
```

The Mode Tab

The Mode tab determines the Backup mode the user wants to work with. To do this, the tab uses two option buttons and three text boxes, as described in the next few sections.

The Manual Option Button

The Manual option button is named `optManual`, and its `Click` event handler is shown in Listing 28.10. This procedure modifies the Backup Mode Description text (the `lblModeDesc` label) and then disables the three text boxes.

Listing 28.10. The `Click` event handler for the Manual option button.

```
Private Sub optManual_Click()
    lblModeDesc = "Manual Mode: Backs up the selected files and then unloads the
    ➥Backup dialog box."
    txtIntervalHours.Enabled = False
    txtIntervalMinutes.Enabled = False
    txtIntervalSeconds.Enabled = False
End Sub
```

The Reminder Option Button

The Reminder option button is named `optReminder`, and the event handler for its `Click` event is given in Listing 28.11. This procedure also modifies the Backup Mode Description text, and then it enables the three text boxes.

Listing 28.11. The `Click` event handler for the Reminder option button.

```
Private Sub optReminder_Click()
    lblModeDesc = "Reminder Mode: Backs up the selected files and then redisplays
    ➥the Backup dialog box at the scheduled time."
    txtIntervalHours.Enabled = True
    txtIntervalMinutes.Enabled = True
    txtIntervalSeconds.Enabled = True
End Sub
```

The Hour(s) Text Box

You'll see later that the values given by the three text boxes in the Mode tab are used to construct the argument for a `TimeValue` function. To ensure that this function receives a legal argument, Backup keeps an eye on the values in these text boxes.

The first text box is labeled Hour(s) in the Mode tab, and it's named `txtIntervalHours` in the project. In this case, our only concern is that we don't end up with either a null string or a negative value. To that end, the `BeforeUpdate` event handler shown in Listing 28.12 checks for these values and adjusts the text box to `0` in both cases.

Listing 28.12. This event handler checks the value of the Hour(s) text box.

```
Private Sub txtIntervalHours_BeforeUpdate(ByVal Cancel As MSForms.ReturnBoolean)
    With txtIntervalHours
        If .Value = "" Then
            .Value = 0
        ElseIf CInt(.Value) < 0 Then
            .Value = 0
        End If
    End With
End Sub
```


The Minutes(s) Text Box

The `BeforeUpdate` event handler for the Minutes(s) text box (named `txtIntervalMinutes`) must also watch out for null and negative values, as shown in Listing 28.13. However, we also want to make sure that this text box doesn't end up with a value that's greater than or equal to 60. If the handler encounters such a value, it does two things:

- It divides the value by 60, grabs the integer portion, and adds this value to the `txtIntervalHours` text box.
- It uses VBA's `Mod` operator to return the remainder when the value is divided by 60. This remainder is stored in the `txtIntervalMinutes` text box.

Listing 28.13. This event handler checks the value of the Minute(s) text box.

```
Private Sub txtIntervalMinutes_BeforeUpdate(ByVal Cancel As MSForms.ReturnBoolean)
    With txtIntervalMinutes
        If .Value = "" Then
            .Value = 0
        ElseIf CInt(.Value) < 0 Then
            .Value = 0
        ElseIf CInt(.Value) >= 60 Then
            txtIntervalHours = txtIntervalHours + Int(CInt(.Value) / 60)
            .Value = .Value Mod 60
        End If
    End With
End Sub
```

The Second(s) Text Box

The Second(s) text box (named `txtIntervalSeconds`) is almost identical to the Minute(s) text box discussed in the preceding section. Again, the `BeforeUpdate` event handler, shown in Listing 28.14, checks for null and negative values, as well as values that are greater than or equal to 60.

Listing 28.14. This event handler checks the value of the Second(s) text box.

```
Private Sub txtIntervalSeconds_BeforeUpdate(ByVal Cancel As MSForms.ReturnBoolean)
    With txtIntervalSeconds
        If .Value = "" Then
            .Value = 0
        ElseIf CInt(.Value) < 0 Then
            .Value = 0
        ElseIf CInt(.Value) >= 60 Then
            txtIntervalMinutes = txtIntervalMinutes + Int(CInt(.Value) / 60)
            .Value = .Value Mod 60
        End If
    End With
End Sub
```

The Command Buttons

With the three tabs now taken care of, we can turn our attention to the three command buttons that set things in motion in the Backup application: Back Up, Save Settings, and Cancel.

The Back Up Button

Clicking the Back Up button (named `cmdBackUp`) launches the backup process. The `Click` event handler for this button is shown in Listing 28.15. After first checking to make sure that, given an active Reminder option, the three text boxes aren't all 0, the procedure performs four tasks:

- It calls `BackUpSelectedFiles` to perform the backup.
- It calls `ProcessBackupMode` to perform mode-related chores (such as setting the reminder).
- It calls `SaveRegistrySettings` to store the current Backup settings in the Registry.
- It runs `Unload Me` to unload the form from memory.

The first three tasks are explained in detail later in this chapter.

Listing 28.15. The `Click` event handler for the Back Up button.

```
Private Sub cmdBackUp_Click()
    '
    ' Make sure at least one interval box has data
    '
    If optReminder And _
```

```
        txtIntervalHours = 0 And _
        txtIntervalMinutes = 0 And _
        txtIntervalSeconds = 0 Then
            MsgBox "Please enter a Reminder interval!"
            Exit Sub
    End If
    '
    ' Run the backup
    '
    Call BackUpSelectedFiles
    '
    ' Process the Backup mode
    '
    Call ProcessBackupMode
    '
    ' Save the settings and then dump the form
    '
    Call SaveRegistrySettings
    Unload Me
End Sub
```


The Save Settings Button

You click the Save Settings button (`cmdSaveSettings`) to save the current Backup settings without performing a backup. To that end, the `Click` event handler shown in Listing 28.16 calls `ProcessBackupMode`, calls `SaveRegistrySettings`, and unloads the form.

Why do we call `ProcessBackupMode`? Well, as you'll see later, one of the chores performed by this procedure is to cancel a pending reminder. So this lets you cancel a reminder without having to run a backup to do so.

Listing 28.16. The `Click` event handler for the Save Settings button.

```
Private Sub cmdSaveSettings_Click()
    '
    ' Process the Backup mode
    '
    Call ProcessBackupMode
    '
    ' Save the settings and shut down the form
    '
    Call SaveRegistrySettings
    Unload Me
End Sub
```

The Cancel Button

The Cancel button (`cmdCancel`) does nothing more than unload the form, as you can see from its `Click` event handler, shown in Listing 28.17.

Listing 28.17. The `Click` event handler for the Cancel button.

```
Private Sub cmdCancel_Click()
    '
    ' Close the form
    '
    Unload Me
End Sub
```

Backup's Support Procedures

As you've seen, Backup's event handlers leave much of the processing to various support procedures. These Sub and Function procedures do the real grunt work of the Backup application, and they're the subject of the rest of this chapter.

The `ParseSelectedFiles` Procedure

When you click Back Up or Save Settings when the Selected Open Documents Only option button (Source tab) is activated, Backup stores the filenames of the currently selected documents in the Registry (see the section "The `SaveRegistrySettings` Procedure"). This lets the program reselect those files (those that are still open) the next time the Backup form is displayed.

It's the job of the `ParseSelectedFiles` procedure, shown in Listing 28.18, to read in the string of filenames from the Registry, extract each name, find the appropriate file in the array of documents, and then set its `Selected` property to `True`.

To accomplish this, the `GetSetting` function retrieves the current string in the `SelectedDocuments` Registry key and stores it in the `filenames` variable. This string is a delimited list of filenames, where the delimiting character is a semicolon (;):

`filename1;filename2;...filenamen;`

`ParseSelectedFiles` uses a `Do While...Loop` to extract the filenames. The `InStr` function locates the next semicolon, and then the `Mid$` function is used to extract the filename.

Three variables are used: `start` holds the starting character position of each filename, `scPos` holds the character position of the next semicolon, and `filename` holds the extracted name. Here's the basic procedure:

1. Set `start` to 1 and use `InStr` to set `scPos` to the position of the first semicolon.
2. Set up a `Do While...Loop` to monitor the value of `scPos`. Exit the loop when it hits 0 (that is, when `InStr` returns 0, which means there are no more semicolons to find).
3. Use `Mid$` to extract the filename that lies from the `start` character position to the `scPos - start` character position, and store the result in `filename`.

4. Run through `arrDocs` and see if the extracted filename is still open. If it is, set its `Selected` property to `True`.
5. Set `start` to 1 more than `scPos`, and set `scPos` to the next semicolon position.
6. Repeat steps 3 through 5 until done.

The procedure finishes by calling `BuildDocList` to rebuild the list of documents (see the next section).

Listing 28.18. This procedure parses the Registry's list of selected files.

```
Private Sub ParseSelectedFiles()
    Dim filenames As String ' Temporary string buffer
    Dim filename As String  ' Temporary string buffer
    Dim start As Long       ' Parse: start position
    Dim scPos As Integer    ' Parse: semicolon position
    Dim i As Integer        ' Counter
    '
    ' Get the list of selected files from the Registry
    '
    filenames = GetSetting("VBA Unleashed", "Backup", "SelectedDocuments", "")
    '
    ' Parse the filenames from the string
    ' String structure is "filename1;filename2;..."
    '
    If filenames <> "" Then
        '
        ' Set the initial start and end points
        '
        start = 1
        scPos = InStr(filenames, ";")
        Do While scPos <> 0
            '
            ' Extract the filename
            '
            filename = Mid$(filenames, start, scPos - start)
            '
            ' Look for the filename in the document array
            '
            For i = 0 To UBound(arrDocs) - 1
                '
                ' If found, set Selected to True
                '
                If arrDocs(i).Name = filename Then
                    arrDocs(i).Selected = True
                    Exit For
                End If
            Next 'i
            '
            ' Update the start and end points
            '
            start = scPos + 1
            scPos = InStr(scPos + 1, filenames, ";")
        Loop
        Call BuildDocList()
    End If
End Sub
```

The BuildDocList Procedure

A few of the routines that we've looked at so far have made calls to the `BuildDocList` procedure, shown in Listing 28.19. The purpose of this procedure is to populate the Source tab's `lstDocs` list box. The bulk of this procedure is a `For...Next` loop that runs through the entire `arrDocs` array. For each element in the array, the procedure does the following:

- A new list item is added using the document's `Name` property. This value is placed in column 0 (the first column).
- The document's `State` (Saved or Unsaved) is placed in column 1 (the second column). This is accomplished by using the list box `List(row, column)` property, where *row* is the list row (starting at 0) and *column* is the list column (also starting at 0).
- The list item's `Selected` property is set to the document's `Selected` property.
- If the document is the active document, its name is appended to the caption of the Active Document Only option button.

Listing 28.19. This procedure uses the `arrDocs` array to build the list box items.

```
Private Sub BuildDocList()
    Dim i As Integer     ' Counter
    '
    ' Run through the list of documents
    '
    With lstDocs
        .Clear
        optActive.Caption = "Active Document Only"
        For i = 0 To UBound(arrDocs) - 1
            .AddItem arrDocs(i).Name
            .List(i, 1) = arrDocs(i).State
            .Selected(i) = arrDocs(i).Selected
            If arrDocs(i).Name = ActiveWorkbook.Name Then
                '
                ' Include active filename in Active caption
                '
                With optActive
                    .Caption = .Caption & " (" & arrDocs(i).Name & ")"
                End With
            End If
        Next 'i
    End With
    Call DisplaySourceData
End Sub
```

The DisplaySourceData Procedure

The bottom of the Backup form has two groups that display information about the current selections. The left group is labeled Source File Data. It tells you the number of files selected for backup and the size in bytes of those files.

This data is calculated and displayed by the `DisplaySourceData` procedure, shown in Listing 28.20. Two variables are used to track the totals:

`totFiles`: Holds the total number of files selected for backup.

`totBytes`: Holds the total number of bytes for the selected files.

A `For...Next` loop runs through the documents array, and, if a document's `Selected` property is `True`, the `totFiles` variable is incremented, and the `Size` property is added to `totBytes`. Once the loop is complete, the data is placed into the two label controls in the Source File Data group, `lblTotalFiles` and `lblTotalBytes`. Finally, `CheckBackupStatus` is called to see if the new data affects whether the backup can proceed (see "The `CheckBackupStatus` Procedure").

Listing 28.20. This procedure calculates the total number of files selected for backup, as well as the total number of bytes in the selected files.

```
Private Sub DisplaySourceData()
    Dim i As Integer          ' Counter
    Dim totFiles As Integer ' Holds the total files selected
    Dim totBytes As Long      ' Holds the total bytes selected
    '
    ' Add up file sizes for all documents that have
    ' Selected=True, and then display the total
    '
    totFiles = 0
    totBytes = 0
    For i = 0 To UBound(arrDocs) - 1
        If arrDocs(i).Selected Then
            totFiles = totFiles + 1
            totBytes = totBytes + arrDocs(i).Size
        End If
    Next 'i
    '
    ' Write the data
    '
    lblTotalFiles.Caption = totFiles
    lblTotalBytes.Caption = Format(totBytes, "#,##0")
    Call CheckBackupStatus
End Sub
```

The DisplayDestinationData Procedure

The Backup form's other information area—Destination Drive Data—shows the drive type and number of free bytes on whatever disk drive is the container for the folder displayed in the Back Up To combo box. More drive information is displayed in the Destination tab's Drive Status group.

All of this data is determined by the `DisplayDestinationData` procedure, shown in Listing 28.21. This procedure uses API calls and other means to glean the data, as follows:

- The procedure first stores the drive's root folder in the `nDrive` variable by running the `GetRoot` function (shown at the bottom of Listing 28.21).
- If `nDrive` equals the `currDestDrive` global variable, there's no point in repeating the entire procedure, so we exit. However, the code first checks the `lblBytesFree` label. If it's `N/A`, this means there was a problem with the drive, so we should repeat the procedure to see if the problem was fixed.
- If no value was entered into the Back Up To combo box, the `GetRoot` function returns `\`. In this case, the procedure writes `N/A` to the Destination Drive Data group's two labels (`lblDriveType` and `lblBytesFree`), sets the Drive Status group's label (`lblDriveStatus`) to `No drive specified`, and returns `False`.
- Otherwise, the `GetDriveType` API function is called to determine the type of drive that was specified. The translated result is stored in the `lblDriveType` label.
- The `GetDiskFreeSpace` API function is then called to determine the number of bytes available on the disk. If the function is successful, the result is stored in the `lblBytesFree` label, and the procedure returns `True`; otherwise, `N/A` is displayed, and the procedure returns `False`.
- With the new destination data in hand, the function calls `CheckBackupStatus` to see if the backup can proceed.

Listing 28.21. This procedure displays data for the selected destination drive.

```
Private Function DisplayDestinationData() As Boolean
    Dim lpSectorsPerCluster As Long      ' Used in GetFreeDiskSpace
    Dim lpBytesPerSector As Long         ' Used in GetFreeDiskSpace
    Dim lpNumberOfFreeClusters As Long   ' Used in GetFreeDiskSpace
    Dim lpTotalNumberOfClusters As Long  ' Used in GetFreeDiskSpace
    Dim retVal As Long                   ' Return value for API functions
    Dim nDrive As String                 ' Holds the destination drive
    '
    ' Determine the root folder
    '
    nDrive = GetRoot(cboDestination.Value)
    '
    ' Is it the same drive?
    '
    If nDrive = currDestDrive Then
        '
        ' If so, exit if there was no problem
        '
        If lblBytesFree <> "N/A" Then Exit Function
    Else
        '
        ' Otherwise, set the global variable
        '
        currDestDrive = nDrive
    End If
    '
    ' nDrive will be "\" if no folder was specified
    '
```

```
    If nDrive = "\" Then
        lblDriveType = "N/A"
        lblBytesFree = "N/A"
        fraDriveStatus.Caption = "Drive Status:"
        lblDriveStatus = "No drive specified."
        cboDestination.Value = ""
        DisplayDestinationData = False
    Else
        fraDriveStatus.Caption = "Drive Status (" & nDrive & "):"
        '
        ' Get the drive type and translate it
        '
        retVal = GetDriveType(nDrive)
        Select Case retVal
            Case 0, 1
                lblDriveType = "N/A"
            Case DRIVE_REMOVABLE
                lblDriveType = "Removable drive"
            Case DRIVE_FIXED
                lblDriveType = "Fixed drive"
            Case DRIVE_REMOTE
                lblDriveType = "Network drive"
            Case DRIVE_CDROM
                lblDriveType = "CD-ROM drive"
            Case DRIVE_RAMDISK
                lblDriveType = "RAM disk"
        End Select
        '
        ' Check the free disk space
        '
        retVal = GetDiskFreeSpace(nDrive, lpSectorsPerCluster, lpBytesPerSector,
        ➥lpNumberOfFreeClusters, lpTotalNumberOfClusters)
        If retVal <> 0 Then
            lblBytesFree = Format(lpSectorsPerCluster * lpBytesPerSector *
            ➥lpNumberOfFreeClusters, "#,##0")
            DisplayDestinationData = True
        Else
            '
            ' Couldn't get free space value
            '
            lblDriveStatus = "Drive is unavailable or invalid."
            lblBytesFree = "N/A"
            DisplayDestinationData = False
        End If
    End If
    Call CheckBackupStatus
End Function
'
' This function extracts the root folder of the specified drive
'
Private Function GetRoot(drive As String) As String
    Dim firstSlash As Integer
    Dim secondSlash As Integer
    '
    ' Are we dealing with a UNC path?
    '
    If Left(drive, 2) = "\\" Then
        firstSlash = InStr(3, drive, "\")
```

continues

Listing 28.21. continued

```
        secondSlash = InStr(firstSlash + 1, drive, "\")
        If secondSlash = 0 Then
            '
            ' Make sure the root ends with "\"
            '
            GetRoot = drive & "\"
        Else
            GetRoot = Left(drive, secondSlash)
        End If
    Else
        drive = Left(drive, 3)
        '
        ' Make sure the root ends with "\"
        '
        If Right(drive, 1) <> "\" Then
            GetRoot = drive & "\"
        Else
            GetRoot = drive
        End If
    End If
End Function
```

The CheckBackupStatus Procedure

Before the backup can proceed, certain conditions must be met. For example, at least one file must be selected for backup. The purpose of the `CheckBackupStatus` procedure, shown in Listing 28.22, is to run various checks that determine whether or not it's okay for the backup to proceed. If any of these checks fail, the Back Up button is disabled. This procedure makes four checks in all:

- Is at least one file selected for backup? Here, the procedure checks the current value of the `lblTotalFiles` label.
- Is the destination drive valid? To determine this, the procedure checks the current value of the `lblBytesFree` label.
- Does the destination folder exist? The procedure uses the `Dir` function to check the folder.
- Is there enough free space on the destination drive? To determine this, the procedure compares the values in the `lblTotalBytes` and `lblBytesFree` labels.

Listing 28.22. This procedure checks various items to see if the backup can proceed. If not, the Back Up button is disabled.

```
Private Sub CheckBackupStatus()
    '
    ' Skip this if we're initializing
    '
```

```
    If initializing Then Exit Sub
    '
    ' Can't back up if no files are selected
    '
    If CInt(lblTotalFiles) = 0 Then
        cmdBackUp.Enabled = False
        Exit Sub
    End If
    '
    ' Can't back up if the destination drive isn't valid
    '
    If lblBytesFree = "N/A" Then
        Beep
        cmdBackUp.Enabled = False
        Exit Sub
    End If
    '
    ' Can't back up if the destination folder doesn't exist
    '
    If Dir(cboDestination.Value) = "" Then
        Beep
        cmdBackUp.Enabled = False
        lblDriveStatus = "The specified folder does not exist."
        Exit Sub
    End If
    '
    ' Can't back up if there isn't enough space to hold the selected files
    '
    If CSng(lblTotalBytes) < CSng(lblBytesFree) Then
        lblDriveStatus = "Drive is OK."
    Else
        Beep
        lblDriveStatus = "There is not enough room on the drive to back up all the
        ➥selected files."
        cmdBackUp.Enabled = False
        Exit Sub
    End If
    '
    ' If we made it this far, all is well
    '
    cmdBackUp.Enabled = True
End Sub
```

The BackUpSelectedFiles Procedure

The actual backup is performed by the `BackUpSelectedFiles` procedure, shown in Listing 28.23. Here's a quick overview of how this lengthy procedure works:

- The procedure loops through the array of documents, looking for those in which the `Selected` property is `True`.
- If the file is new and unsaved, a `Do...Loop` runs `GetSaveAsFilename` to get a name for the file, which is then saved using the `SaveAs` method.

- If the file has unsaved changes, the file is saved.
- If the Overwrite Existing Destination Files check box (`chkOverwrite`) is activated, the procedure prompts the user for a new filename.
- The source path (`strSource`) and destination path (`strDest`) are stored.

The rest of the procedure uses low-level file I/O techniques (described in Chapter 26) to perform the backup. The source file is opened in Binary mode, and the file's entire contents are read into a buffer (the `buff` variable) with the following two statements:

```
buff = Space(LOF(fn))
Get #fn, , buff
```

Then the destination file is opened in Binary mode, and `Put` is used to write the buffer contents to the file:

```
Put #fn, , buff
```

Listing 28.23. This procedure performs the backup.

```
Private Sub BackUpSelectedFiles()
    Dim i As Integer            ' Counter
    Dim str As Variant          ' Temporary string (variant) buffer
    Dim strSource As String     ' The full path for each source file
    Dim strDest As String       ' The destination path for each file
    Dim fn As Long              ' File number for low-level I/O
    Dim buff As String          ' String buffer for low-level I/O
    '
    ' Turn off screen updating
    '
    Application.ScreenUpdating = False
    '
    ' Run through the documents array
    '
    For i = 0 To UBound(arrDocs) - 1
        '
        ' Only back up documents where Selected = True
        '
        If arrDocs(i).Selected Then
            With Workbooks(arrDocs(i).Name)
                '
                ' Is the file new? If so, save it.
                ' Note that you must save a new file or
                ' this loop will continue indefinitely.
                '
                If .Path = "" Then
                    Do
                        str = Application.GetSaveAsFilename(, "Excel Files
                        ➥(*.xls), *.xls")
                    Loop Until str <> False
                    .SaveAs filename:=str
                End If
                '
                ' If the file is unsaved, save it
                '
```

```
            If .unsaved Then .Save
            '
            ' Build the destination
            '
            If Not chkOverwrite Then
                strDest = InputBox(.Name & _
                    " already exists on the destination drive." & _
                    Chr(13) & _
                    "Please enter a new filename for the backup file:", _
                    "Backup", .Name)
                If strDest = "" Then Exit Sub
            Else
                strDest = .Name
            End If
            If Right(cboDestination.Value, 1) <> "\" Then
                strDest = cboDestination.Value & "\" & strDest
            Else
                strDest = cboDestination.Value & strDest
            End If
            '
            ' Store the source path
            '
            strSource = .FullName
            '
            ' Open the source file in Binary mode
            '
            fn = FreeFile
            Open strSource For Binary Access Read As #fn
            '
            ' Allocate space and then Get the entire file
            '
            buff = Space(LOF(fn))
            Get #fn, , buff
            Close #fn
            '
            ' Open the destination file in Binary mode
            '
            fn = FreeFile
            Open strDest For Binary Access Write As #fn
            Application.StatusBar = "Backing up to " & strDest
            '
            ' Write the buffer to the destination file
            '
            Put #fn, , buff
            Close #fn
        End With
        Application.StatusBar = ""
    End If
Next 'i
'
' Resume screen updating
'
Application.ScreenUpdating = True
End Sub
```

The ProcessBackupMode Procedure

If the user clicks either the Back Up button or the Save Settings button, the program needs to process the current Backup Mode selection. This is the job of the `ProcessBackupMode` procedure, shown in Listing 28.24. It has two branches:

- If the Reminder option was selected, use the values in the three Mode tab text boxes to construct the time of the next reminder. Then use the `OnTime` statement to run the `ShowBackup` procedure at the specified time.
- If the Manual option was selected, cancel the pending `OnTime` procedure if one exists. (If no `OnTime` procedure was set, the `nextReminder` variable will equal its default value of `12:00:00` AM.)

Listing 28.24. This procedure processes the selected Backup mode.

```
Private Sub ProcessBackupMode()
    '
    ' Check for Reminder mode selected
    '
    If optReminder Then
        '
        ' Determine the next backup time
        '
        nextReminder = Now + TimeValue(txtIntervalHours & ":" & txtIntervalMinutes &
        ➥":" & txtIntervalSeconds)
        '
        ' Set the timer
        '
        Application.OnTime nextReminder, "Chaptr28.Backup.ShowBackup"
    Else
        '
        ' Cancel pending OnTime, if there is one
        '
        If nextReminder <> TimeValue("12:00:00 AM") Then
            Application.OnTime nextReminder, "Chaptr28.Backup.ShowBackup", , False
        End If
    End If
End Sub
```

The SaveRegistrySettings Procedure

The final support procedure is `SaveRegistrySettings`, and it's shown in Listing 28.25. This procedure runs a series of `SaveSetting` statements that store the current Backup options in the Registry.

Listing 28.25. This procedure saves the current Backup settings to the Registry.

```
Private Sub SaveRegistrySettings()
    Dim j As Integer    ' Counter
```

```
    Dim k As Integer      ' Counter
    Dim str As String     ' Temporary string buffer
    '
    ' Save destination items to the Registry
    '
    With cboDestination
        '
        ' Add the current item first
        '
        SaveSetting "VBA Unleashed", "Backup", "MRUFolder0", .Value
        '
        ' Now add the rest of the items (maximum 10)
        '
        k = 1
        For j = 0 To .ListCount - 1
            If .List(j) <> .Value Then
                SaveSetting "VBA Unleashed", "Backup", "MRUFolder" & k, .List(j)
                k = k + 1
                If k = 10 Then Exit For
            End If
        Next 'j
    End With
    '
    ' Save other options to the Registry
    '
    If optAll Then
        SaveSetting "VBA Unleashed", "Backup", "BackupFilter", "All"
    ElseIf optUnsaved Then
        SaveSetting "VBA Unleashed", "Backup", "BackupFilter", "Unsaved"
    ElseIf optActive Then
        SaveSetting "VBA Unleashed", "Backup", "BackupFilter", "Active"
    Else
        SaveSetting "VBA Unleashed", "Backup", "BackupFilter", "Selected"
        str = ""
        For j = 0 To UBound(arrDocs) - 1
            If arrDocs(j).Selected Then
                str = str & arrDocs(j).Name & ";"
            End If
        Next 'j
        SaveSetting "VBA Unleashed", "Backup", "SelectedDocuments", str
    End If

    SaveSetting "VBA Unleashed", "Backup", "IgnoreNewAndUnsaved", chkIgnoreNew
    SaveSetting "VBA Unleashed", "Backup", "OverwriteDestFiles", chkOverwrite
    If optManual Then
        SaveSetting "VBA Unleashed", "Backup", "BackupMode", "Manual"
        SaveSetting "VBA Unleashed", "Backup", "NextReminder", "12:00:00 AM"
    Else
        SaveSetting "VBA Unleashed", "Backup", "BackupMode", "Reminder"
        SaveSetting "VBA Unleashed", "Backup", "NextReminder", nextReminder
    End If
    SaveSetting "VBA Unleashed", "Backup", "IntervalHours", txtIntervalHours
    SaveSetting "VBA Unleashed", "Backup", "IntervalMinutes", txtIntervalMinutes
    SaveSetting "VBA Unleashed", "Backup", "IntervalSeconds", txtIntervalSeconds
End Sub
```

Summary

This chapter took you through the Backup application, which, with minor modifications, can be used in any VBA-enabled application. This project used quite a few advanced VBA techniques, so here's a summary of the relevant chapters you should check for more information on these topics:

- For an extensive look at user forms and form objects, see Chapter 11, "Working with Microsoft Forms."
- To keep things uncluttered, I included no error-trapping code in the Backup procedures. I'll leave it as an exercise for you. You can find out all you need to know in Chapter 23, "Trapping Program Errors."
- I cover the Win32 API in Chapter 25, "Programming the Windows API."
- Turn to Chapter 26, "VBA Tips and Techniques," to learn more about the `GetSetting` function and the `SaveSetting` statement.
- Chapter 26 is also the place to go for information on working with the file system, including the `Dir` and `FileLen` functions, and low-level file I/O.

CHAPTER 29

Access and Outlook: E-Mail Merge

IN THIS CHAPTER

Neither snow, nor rain, nor heat, nor gloom of night stays these couriers from the swift completion of their appointed rounds.

—Herodotus

For my final VBA trick, I'll pull out of my electronic hat an application that combines Access and Outlook. You saw in Chapter 22, "E-Mail and Groupware Programming with Outlook," that you can use VBA to jack in to Outlook's Automation interface and control programmatically just about any aspect of the Outlook environment. In particular, you can log on to a MAPI session and create and send e-mail messages. That's where this project comes in. I've set up an Access application that lets you create form letters that are sent electronically to any number of recipients you choose. This chapter shows you how to operate the application and shows you how everything works.

What E-Mail Merge Does

Even if you've never used it, you've probably at least heard of Word's Mail Merge feature. The basic idea is that you set up a main document in which you combine regular text with one or more *fields,* like so:

```
Dear <<FirstName>> <<LastName>>,
```

These fields correspond to fields in a separate data source (such as an Access table). In this example, the data source would have a FirstName field and a LastName field. When you merge the main document and the data source, Word creates a new document for each data source record and fills in the document fields with the appropriate data from each record.

With all this in mind, you can think of this chapter's application as an electronic version of Mail Merge—hence the name "E-Mail Merge." In this case, the main document is the body of an e-mail message that contains one or more fields. These fields correspond to field names in a data source—an Access table that contains contact data (or whatever you like). You use the application to create "mailings" that consist of a particular message and a selection of recipients. When you send the mailing, the application creates an e-mail message for each recipient, makes the appropriate substitutions in the message body, and uses Outlook to ship all the messages.

It would also be possible to use E-Mail Merge as a simple "no post" mailing list. You'd only need to set up a data source for the list's members and associate that data source with each message you send out (I'll explain how this works in a moment).

As you can imagine, there are lots of interesting things going on behind the scenes in this application. Before we get to that, however, let's see how you use the application to create and send a mailing.

Creating a Mailing

E-Mail Merge can be found on this book's CD in the Access database file named E-MailMe.mdb. When you open this database, you'll see the Main Switchboard window, shown in Figure 29.1. You use this window to interact with the application (but you can feel free to work with the tables, queries, and forms directly).

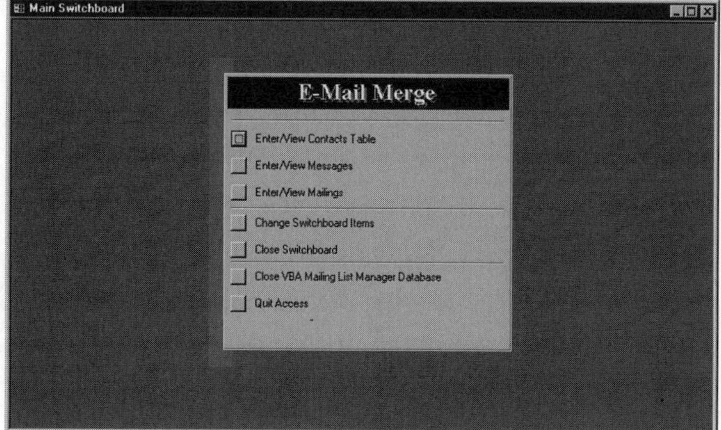

FIGURE 29.1.
The Main Switchboard window is the front-end for the E-Mail Merge application.

Step 1: Create the Data Source

Although E-Mail Merge comes with sample data, you'll need to specify your own data sources if you plan on using the application for anything useful. Happily, E-Mail Merge is extremely flexible when it comes to the data sources it can work with. In fact, there is only one requirement for a table or query to qualify as an E-Mail Merge data source: It must have a field that contains e-mail addresses. With this in mind, you have a number of options for setting up a data source:

- You can create an Access table from scratch.
- You can use the Contacts table that comes with the E-Mail Merge application.
- You can import external data (such as your Outlook address book).

Note, too, that E-Mail Merge is also perfectly happy to work with the dynasets produced by SELECT queries. This lets you create focused recipient lists by defining subsets of your data based on whatever criteria is appropriate.

The Contacts Table

If you'd like to use the Contacts list that comes with E-Mail Merge, you can display the Contacts form, shown in Figure 29.2, by clicking Enter/View Contacts Table in the Main Switchboard. (You can also open the Contacts form directly from the E-Mail Merge database window.)

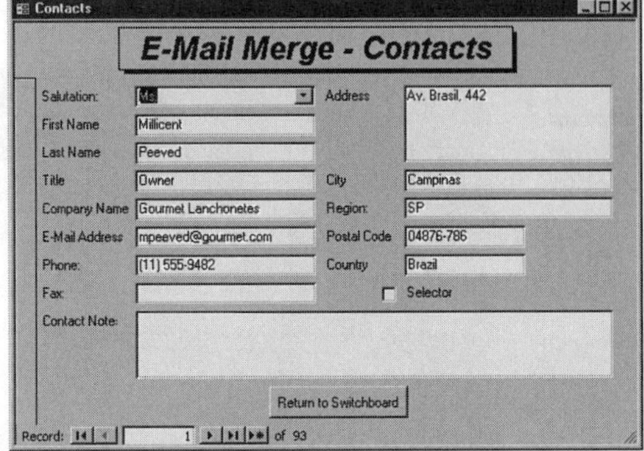

FIGURE 29.2.
Use the Contacts form to add and edit your contact data.

The only required field is E-Mail Address; the rest you can fill in as you please. Bear in mind, however, that E-Mail Merge uses the information in these fields to perform the message substitutions. So, for example, if you'll be starting your message with `Dear <<firstname>>` (I'll explain these field codes a bit later), you'll want to make sure that you fill in the FirstName field for all the contacts.

Also, the Salutation field contains the appropriate salutation (Ms., Mr., Dr., and so on) for the contact. This is a drop-down list that uses a lookup operation to get values from a separate Salutation table. If you want to use different salutations, or if you want to remove some salutations, work with the Salutations table directly.

Creating Queries

Once you've entered the data (or imported it), you have two ways to proceed to get a data source: You can work with the data as whole, or you can create select queries that knock the data down to size. For example, the Contacts table has a Contact Title field in which you enter each person's job title. You could then query this table to extract, say, only those contacts who are managers. E-Mail Merge comes with several sample queries that demonstrate this.

Working with Individual Recipients

What if the recipients you want to select aren't related in any way (or, at least, in any way that can be expressed as a `SELECT` query)? The Contacts table includes a Selector field that can help. This is a Yes/No field that you can toggle on and off either in the Contacts form or in the datasheet. The idea is that you activate this field for the individual recipients you want to work with. E-Mail Merge comes with a query called Contacts: Selected Recipients that selects only those Contacts records where the Selector field is `True`.

Note, too, that I've also included an `UPDATE` query called Contacts: Clear Selected Recipients, which sets the Selector field to `False` for all records in the Contacts table.

Step 2: Create the Message

With your data source (or sources) defined, you can now move to the next step, which involves creating the e-mail message that will be sent. The vehicle for this is the Messages form, shown in Figure 29.3. You can display this form either by selecting Enter/View Messages in the Main Switchboard or by opening the Messages form directly from the database window.

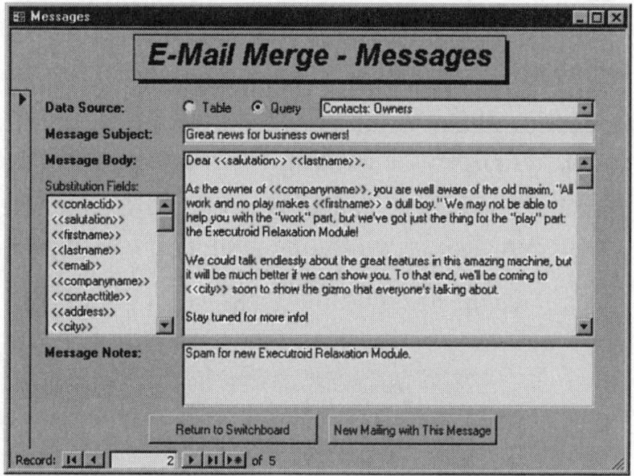

FIGURE 29.3.
Use the Messages form to construct the E-Mail Merge messages.

Here are the steps to follow to create a new message:

1. Click the New Record button, or select Insert | New Record.
2. To define the data source for the message, first activate either the Table or the Query option, and then select a table or query from the drop-down list provided.
3. If the table or query you chose doesn't contain a field named Email, you'll see the Select E-Mail Field dialog box, shown in Figure 29.4. Click the field that contains the e-mail messages and then close the dialog box.

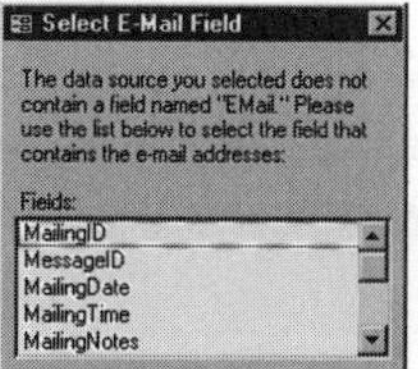

FIGURE 29.4.
This dialog box appears if E-Mail Merge isn't sure which table or query field contains the e-mail addresses.

4. Use the Message Subject text box to enter the subject line of the message.
5. Use the Message Body text box to enter the body of the message.
6. The Substitution Fields list displays the fields that are available in the selected data source. To include one of these fields in either the subject or the body, click the field, select Edit | Copy (or press Ctrl-C), position the cursor in the Message Subject or Message Body text box, and select Edit | Paste (or press Ctrl-V).
7. Use the Message Notes text box to enter a description or other information about the message.
8. Select Records | Save Record to write your changes to the Messages table.

Step 3: Create the Mailing

At this point, you've done all the hard work and you're only a couple of simple procedures away from sending the mailing. First, though, you have to create the mailing itself. You have two ways to proceed:

- To work with all the mailings, either select Enter/View Mailings from the Main Switchboard or open the Mailings form directly from the database window.
- To display a single, new mailing based on a message, select the message in the Messages form and click New Mailing with This Message.

Either way, you'll see the Mailings form, shown in Figure 29.5.

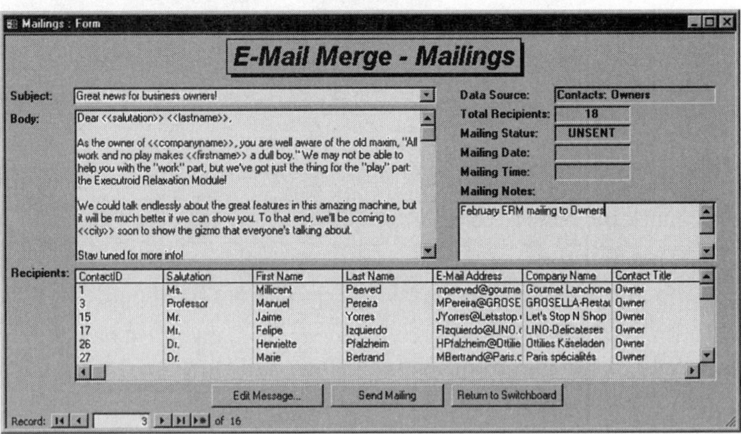

FIGURE 29.5.
Use the Mailings form to define your e-mailings.

The point of the Mailings form is to define which message you want to send, which you do by selecting a message subject from the Subject drop-down list. Once you've done that, the Mailings form then updates the following data:

Body: This is the message body associated with the selected subject line. If you'd like to make changes to the message body, edit the Body text box and then select Records | Save Record. However, if you want to add substitution fields, change the subject line, or change the data source, you need to work with the Messages form. In this case, click Edit Message to open the message in the Messages form.

Recipients: This is an uneditable list box that displays the data source associated with the selected message.

Data Source: This is the name of the data source associated with the selected message.

Total Recipients: This is the total number of records in the data source.

Mailing Status: This field displays `UNSENT` for mailings that haven't been sent. Once you send a mailing, this field changes to `SENT`.

Mailing Date: This field shows the date the mailing was sent.

Mailing Time: This field shows the time the mailing was sent.

Mailing Notes: Use this field to enter a description or other information about the mailing.

Here are the steps to follow to create a new mailing:

1. Click on the New Record button or select Insert | New Record.
2. The Mailings form will suggest a default message (whatever message was displayed before you created the new record). To select a different message, use the Subject drop-down list.
3. Edit the body text if necessary.
4. Enter a description in the Mailing Notes text box.
5. Select Records | Save Record to write your changes to the Mailings table.

Step 4: Send the Mailing

That's it—your mailing is ready to roll. All you have to do now is click the Send Mailing button, and E-Mail Merge does the rest. Keep an eye on the status bar to view the progress of the send.

When the mailing has been sent, E-Mail Merge updates the Mailing Status field to `SENT`, records the date and time the mailing was shipped out, and disables the Subject and Body fields. (The latter occurs so that you always have a record of the subject and body that were sent in the mailing.) Figure 29.6 shows the updated Mailings form.

To give you some idea of the changes E-Mail Merge makes to the messages it sends out, Figure 29.7 shows a message that was sent from the sample mailing. As you can see, E-Mail Merge has substituted the message fields with the actual field values from the data source. (Figure 29.7 also shows the hazards of form letters: I'm sure Ms. Peeved was *thrilled* to be called a "dull boy"!)

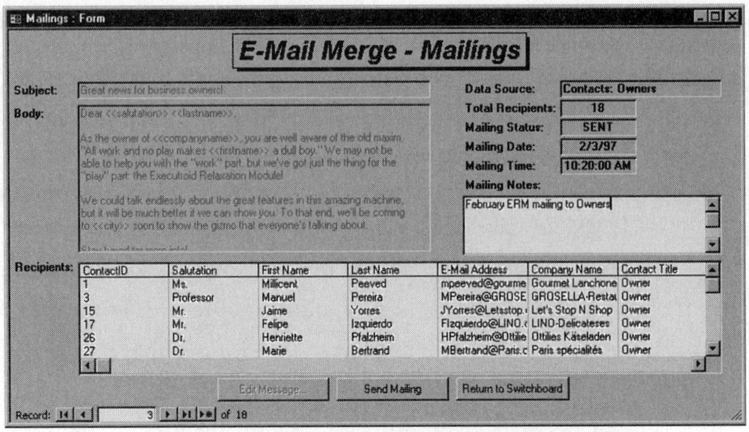

FIGURE 29.6.
Once a mailing has been sent, E-Mail Merge updates the Mailings display.

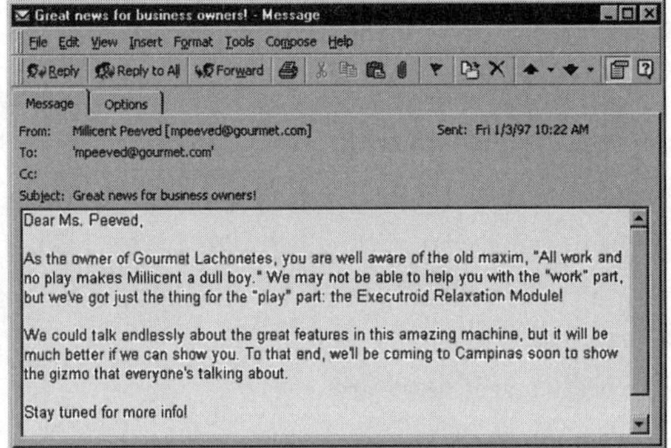

FIGURE 29.7.
A message sent by E-Mail Merge.

A Tour of the E-Mail Merge Database

Now that you know how to use E-Mail Merge, it's time to see how this application works. For starters, this section takes a look at the various components of the E-Mail Merge database.

The Tables

Tables are the heart of any Access application, and E-Mail Merge is no different. I mentioned earlier that you can import or create any data for use with E-Mail Merge, but here's a rundown of the tables that you get in the basic package.

The Contacts Table

As you've seen, the Contacts table contains contact data, including salutation, first name, last name, and e-mail address. The Salutation field is a drop-down list that gets its values from the Salutations table (described in a moment).

The Mailings Table

The Mailings table holds the data for each mailing, most of which you saw earlier in the Mailings form. Here's a summary of the fields in this table:

MailingID: This is an AutoNumber field that is the primary key for the table.

MessageID: This field is a drop-down list that specifies the message to send with the mailing. Its values are derived via a SELECT lookup on the MessageSubject field of the Messages table. Note, too, that the Messages and Mailings tables are related (one-to-many) via the MessageID field.

MailingDate: If Sent is Yes, this field holds the date the mailing was sent.

MailingTime: If Sent is Yes, this field holds the time the mailing was sent.

MailingNotes: A description of the mailing.

Sent: A Yes/No field that specifies whether or not the mailing has been sent.

SentSubject: If Sent is Yes, this field holds the subject line of the message that was sent.

SentBody: If Sent is Yes, this field holds the body of the message that was sent.

The Messages Table

The Messages table holds the data for E-Mail Merge messages:

MessageID: An AutoNumber field that is the primary key for the table.

MessageSubject: The subject line of the message.

MessageBody: The body of the message.

DataSource: The name of the data source.

DataSourceType: The type of data source. 1 represents a table, and 2 represents a query.

EMailFieldName: The name of the data source field that contains the e-mail addresses.

The Salutations Table

Salutations is a simple table that stores the various salutations used in the Contacts table. It contains just two fields: the SalutationID primary key and Salutation (Mr., Ms., Dr., and so on).

The Switchboard Items Table

This table contains data about the various commands displayed in the Main Switchboard. Instead of working with this table directly, however, you should select the Change Switchboard Items command in the E-Mail Merge Main Switchboard form. This displays the Access Switchboard Manager, which lets you add, edit, and delete switchboard items.

The Queries

As you can imagine, queries represent the real convenience of the E-Mail Merge application, because they let you create targeted mailing lists based on specific criteria. Using `SELECT` queries, you can create data sources based on job title, company name, city, state, or whatever data exists in the underlying table. E-Mail Merge ships with several `SELECT` queries that give you examples of this. For example, the Contacts: Managers query selects only those records in the Contacts table that include the word "Manager" in the ContactTitle field.

As I mentioned earlier, E-Mail Merge also comes with two queries that let you work with individual message recipients:

Contacts: Selected Recipients: This query selects records in the Contacts table where the Selector field is activated.

Contacts: Clear Selected Recipients: This is an `UPDATE` query that clears the Selector field in the Contacts table. Run this query to start from scratch whenever you need to make wholesale changes to the selected recipients.

The Forms

E-Mail Merge is really a forms-based application. Although it's certainly possible to work with the Contacts table via the datasheet, the Messages and Mailings tables only really work well if you access them via their forms. This section gives you a rundown of the various forms that ship with E-Mail Merge.

The Contacts Form

As you saw in Figure 29.2, the Contacts form is a simple collection of fields for entering and editing data in the Contacts table. The only code attached to this form is the event handler that processes the `Click` event for the command button.

The Messages Form

You saw the form view of the Messages form in Figure 29.3, but Figure 29.8 shows the design view. Most of the elements in this form are bound controls associated with the various fields in the Messages table. There are a few extras, however:

- The Table and Query option buttons are bound to the DataSourceType field. Recall that this field stores 1 for a table and 2 for a query. To allow for this, the option buttons are stored in a group, and the buttons are assigned the values 1 and 2, respectively.
- The Substitution Fields list box is unbound. The various items in this list are added via VBA code (see the section "Under the Hood: The Code").
- The two command buttons have associated `Click` event handlers that run their commands. (Again, I'll run through these procedures when I discuss the VBA code.)

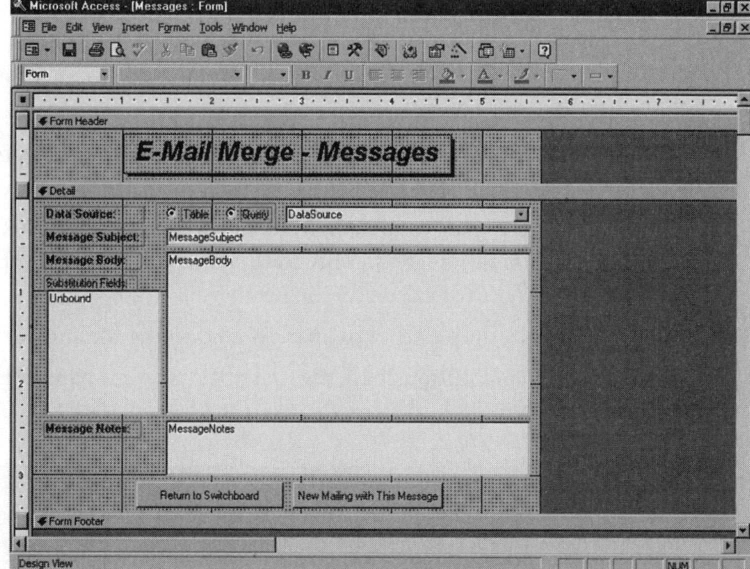

FIGURE 29.8.
The design view of the Messages form.

The Select E-Mail Field Dialog Form

Associated with the Messages form is the Select E-Mail Field Dialog form. Recall that this dialog box is displayed if the data source you choose in the Messages form doesn't have a field named Email (see Figure 29.4). To set up an Access form as a dialog box, you need to set the following form properties at design time:

- Set the `Border Style` property to `Dialog`.
- Set the `Pop Up` property to `Yes`.
- Set the `Min Max Buttons` property to `None`.
- Set the `Modal` property to `Yes`.

The Mailings Form

The form view of the Mailings form was shown in Figure 29.5. Figure 29.9 shows the design view of this well-populated form.

Here are a few notes that should help you make sense of this form:

- Two controls are used for the Subject field. If the mailing has been sent, a disabled text box that is bound to the SentSubject field is displayed. If the mailing hasn't been sent, a drop-down list bound to the MessageID field is displayed. (As you'll see later, which of these fields is visible at any one time is controlled via VBA code.)
- The Body field is also represented by two controls. If the mailing has been sent, E-Mail Merge displays a disabled text box that is bound to the SentBody field. If the

mailing hasn't been sent, the form displays the Message Body subform instead. This is a form that displays only the MessageBody field from the Messages table. The link between the two tables (which is governed by the subform's `Link Child Fields` and `Link Master Fields` properties) is the MessageID field.

- The Recipients list is an unbound list box. VBA code is used to populate this list box based on the data source of whatever message is associated with the current mailing.
- The Data Source, Total Recipients, Mailing Status, Mailing Date, and Mailing Time controls are all unbound labels. VBA code is used to adjust the `Caption` properties of these labels to reflect (or calculate) the data.
- Mailing Notes is a simple text box that's bound to the MailingNotes field.
- The three command buttons have associated `Click` event handlers that run their commands.

FIGURE 29.9.
The design view of the Mailings form.

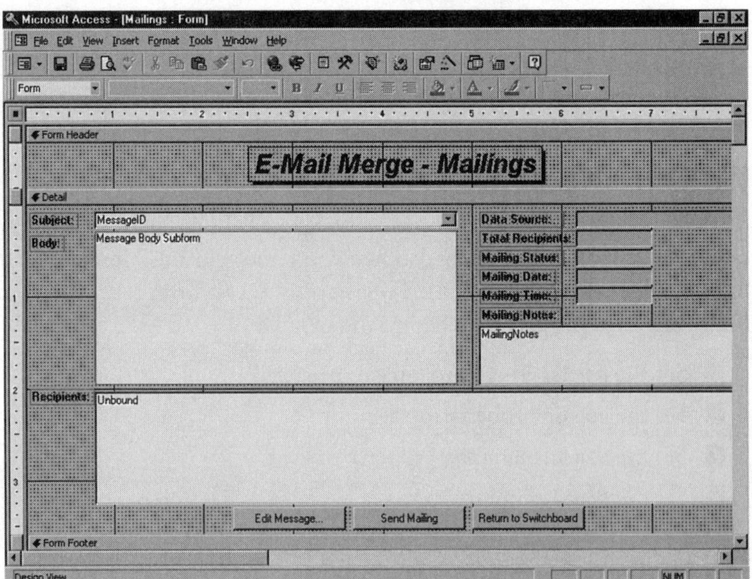

The Switchboard Form

This is the form that displays the Main Switchboard. If you'd rather not see this form every time you start E-Mail Merge, follow these steps to disable it:

1. Select Tools | Startup to display the Startup dialog box, shown in Figure 29.10.
2. Use the Display Form drop-down list either to select a different startup form or to select `(none)` to prevent any form from loading at startup.
3. Click OK to put the changes into effect.

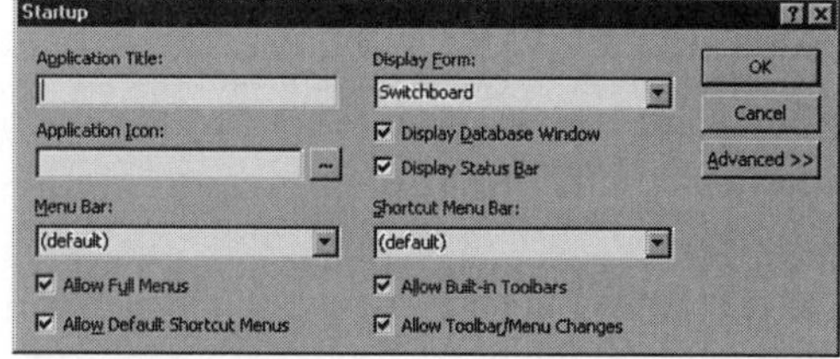

FIGURE 29.10.
Use the Startup form to control the database startup options.

Under the Hood: The Code

The final piece of the E-Mail Merge puzzle is the VBA code that underlies the Messages and Mailings forms. (The Contacts form also has some VBA code—the `Click` event handler for the Return to Switchboard command button. However, the Messages form also uses this code (as does the Mailings form), so I'll explain it when I run through the rest of the Messages code.) This code is mostly a collection of event handlers that are used to initialize the forms, adjust the data as you move from record to record, and run command buttons. The rest of this chapter explains each of these procedures.

The Code in the Messages Form

This section examines the event handlers and other procedures that are used in the Messages form.

The Load Event

The `Load` event fires when you first display a form. Listing 29.1 shows the event handler that runs each time you load the Messages form. This procedure spends most of its time setting up the data for the Data Source combo box. The various sections of this lengthy procedure are explained in depth after Listing 29.1.

Listing 29.1. This event procedure initializes the form.

```
Private Sub Form_Load()
    Dim db As Database   ' The current database
    Dim td As TableDef   ' Loop object
    Dim qd As QueryDef   ' Loop object
    Dim i As Integer     ' A counter
    '
    ' Create the list of Table objects
    '
    Set db = CurrentDb
    strTableList = ""
    For Each td In db.TableDefs
        '
        ' Avoid system objects
        '
```

continues

Listing 29.1. continued

```
        If (td.Attributes And dbSystemObject) = 0 Then
            strTableList = strTableList & td.Name & ";"
        End If
    Next 'td
    '
    ' Store the name of the first table
    '
    strFirstTable = Left(strTableList, InStr(strTableList, ";") - 1)
    '
    ' Create the list of Query objects
    '
    strQueryList = ""
    For Each qd In db.QueryDefs
        '
        ' Avoid temporary objects
        '
        If Left(qd.Name, 1) <> "~" Then
            strQueryList = strQueryList & qd.Name & ";"
        End If
    Next 'qd
    '
    ' Store the name of the first query
    '
    strFirstQuery = Left(strQueryList, InStr(strQueryList, ";") - 1)
    '
    ' Assign one of the lists to the Data Source combo box
    '
    cboDataSource.RowSourceType = "Value List"
    If fraDataSourceType.Value = TABLE Then
        cboDataSource.RowSource = strTableList
    Else
        cboDataSource.RowSource = strQueryList
    End If
    '
    ' Read the field names from the Data Source
    '
    UpdateSubstitutionList
    Set db = Nothing
End Sub
```

This procedure begins by setting a `Database` object variable named `db` equal to `CurrentDB` (which, in Access, represents the currently open database):

```
Set db = CurrentDb
```

Now the procedure creates a list of the available Table objects in the database. This will be a semicolon-delimited string suitable for displaying in the Data Source combo box. This string is named `strTableList`, and it's defined globally at the top of the module. To construct the list, the code uses a `For Each...Next` loop to run through all the `TableDef` objects, and it adds the `Name` of each one to the string, as shown in the following code. (To avoid system tables, the code uses a bitwise `And` to bypass tables in which the `Attributes` property includes the `dbSystemObject` constant.) When that's done, the name of the first table in the list is stored in the global `strFirstTable` variable.

```
strTableList = ""
For Each td In db.TableDefs
    '
    ' Avoid system objects
    '
    If (td.Attributes And dbSystemObject) = 0 Then
        strTableList = strTableList & td.Name & ";"
    End If
Next 'td
'
' Store the name of the first table
'
strFirstTable = Left(strTableList, InStr(strTableList, ";") - 1)
```

Now the procedure runs through a similar process for the Query objects in the database. As shown in the following code, a `For Each...Next` loop runs through the `QueryDef` objects (bypassing temporary queries created by Access), stores the query names in the `strQueryList` global variable, and assigns the first query to `strFirstQuery`.

```
strQueryList = ""
For i = 0 To db.QueryDefs.Count - 1
    With db.QueryDefs(i)
        '
        ' Avoid temporary objects
        '
        If Left(.Name, 1) <> "~" Then
            strQueryList = strQueryList & .Name & ";"
        End If
    End With
Next 'i
'
' Store the name of the first query
'
strFirstQuery = Left(strQueryList, InStr(strQueryList, ";") - 1)
```

With the lists in hand, the next step is to assign one of them to the Data Source combo box (named `cboDataSource`). The list's `RowSourceType` property is first set to `Value List` to let the list know that it should expect a semicolon-delimited string. Then the code examines the value of `fraDataSourceType`. This is the frame that holds the Table and Query option buttons. If Table is activated, the frame value is 1, which is represented by the `TABLE` constant. In this case, `strTableList` is assigned to the list's `RowSource` property. Otherwise, `strQueryList` is used.


```
'
' Assign one of the lists to the Data Source combo box
'
cboDataSource.RowSourceType = "Value List"
If fraDataSourceType.Value = TABLE Then
    cboDataSource.RowSource = strTableList
Else
    cboDataSource.RowSource = strQueryList
End If
```

Finally, the procedure calls the `UpdateSubstitutionList` function to populate the Substitution Fields list box. I'll explain this function later in this section.

The Current Event

In an Access form, each time you navigate from one record to another, the `Current` event fires. For our purposes, we can use this event to change the Data Source list according to the record's `DataSourceType` value, update the Substitution Fields list, and check to make sure that the record's data source still exists. Listing 29.2 shows the event handler. Here's a summary of what this procedure does:

- The procedure first checks to see if the record is a new record (as given by the form's `NewRecord` property). If it is, the data source type is set to `QUERY`, and the Data Source combo box is assigned the list of Query objects.
- Otherwise, the code then updates the data source combo box by assigning the appropriate object list.
- With the list in place, the code then checks to see if the record's DataSource value is in the list. If it's not, the procedure assigns a default object (the first value in the list) and displays a message.
- `UpdateSubstitutionList` is called again to adjust the Substitution Fields list.

Listing 29.2. The event fires each time you move to a different record.

```
Private Sub Form_Current()
    Dim i As Integer          ' Counter
    Dim sourceOK As Boolean ' True if data source exists
    '
    ' If this is a new record, set the default data source values
    '
    If Me.NewRecord Then
        fraDataSourceType = QUERY
        cboDataSource = strFirstQuery
        Exit Sub
    End If
    '
    ' Otherwise, check the data source
    '
    With cboDataSource
        '
        ' Make sure we're not just starting out
        '
        If IsNull(.ItemData(0)) Then Exit Sub
        '
        ' Assign one of the lists to the Data Source combo box
        '
        If fraDataSourceType.Value = TABLE Then
            .RowSource = strTableList
        Else
            .RowSource = strQueryList
        End If
        '
        ' Otherwise, run through the list of data sources
        '
```

```
        sourceOK = False
        For i = 0 To .ListCount - 1
            '
            ' If the data source is in the list, there's no problem
            '
            If Me!DataSource = .ItemData(i) Then sourceOK = True
        Next 'i
        '
        ' Is the source OK?
        '
        '
        If Not sourceOK Then
            '
            ' If not, just use the first item as a default
            '
            If Me!DataSourceType = TABLE Then
                .Value = strFirstTable
            Else
                .Value = strFirstQuery
            End If
            MsgBox "The data source specified for this message no longer " & _
               "exists. A default data source has been assigned, instead.", _
               vbInformation + vbOKOnly, "E-Mail Merge"
        End If
    End With
    '
    ' Read the field names from the Data Source
    '
    UpdateSubstitutionList
End Sub
```

The Data Source Procedures

The Messages form module also includes a couple of `BeforeUpdate` event handlers for the Data Source controls. The first is shown in Listing 29.3. It traps the `BeforeUpdate` event for the frame that holds the Table and Query option buttons. If the frame's value is `TABLE` (that is, 1), the `RowSource` property of the combo box is set to `strTableList`, and its `Value` property is set to the first item in this list. Otherwise, the combo box is set to the list of queries.

Listing 29.3. This event handler adjusts the Data Source list according to the currently selected option button.

```
Private Sub fraDataSourceType_BeforeUpdate(Cancel As Integer)
    If fraDataSourceType.Value = TABLE Then
        cboDataSource.RowSource = strTableList
        cboDataSource.Value = strFirstTable
    Else
        cboDataSource.RowSource = strQueryList
        cboDataSource.Value = strFirstQuery
    End If
End Sub
```

The event handler for the combo box is shown in Listing 29.4. This procedure checks the return value of the `UpdateSubstitutionList` function. If it returns `False`, the Select E-Mail Field Dialog form is displayed. Note in particular that the `OpenForm` method sends the current combo box value as the `OpenArgs` parameter. This value is then used as an argument that can be read by the Select E-Mail Field Dialog form (discussed later in this chapter).

Listing 29.4. This event handler adjusts the Substitution Fields list according to the currently selected data source.

```
Private Sub cboDataSource_BeforeUpdate(Cancel As Integer)
    If Not UpdateSubstitutionList Then
        DoCmd.OpenForm _
            FormName:="Select E-Mail Field Dialog", _
            OpenArgs:=cboDataSource.Value
    End If
End Sub
```

The `Click` Events for the Command Buttons

The Messages form has a Return to Switchboard command button (as do the Contacts and Mailings forms) that closes the form and displays the Main Switchboard. This button is named `cmdSwitchboard`, and the code for its `Click` event is shown in Listing 29.5. This procedure runs two `DoCmd` methods: `OpenForm` opens the Switchboard form, and `Close` shuts down the current form.

Listing 29.5. This procedure returns the user to the Switchboard.

```
Private Sub cmdSwitchboard_Click()
    '
    ' Open the Switchboard form
    '
    DoCmd.OpenForm "Switchboard"
    '
    ' Close this form
    '
    DoCmd.Close acForm, Me.Name
End Sub
```

The other command button is New Mailing with This Message (named `cmdNewMailing`), which is designed to create a new mailing based on the current message. The event handler for this button's `Click` event, shown in Listing 29.6, performs three tasks:

- The procedure checks to see if the Mailings form is already open and closes it if it is. To check for an open form, the code uses a `For Each...Next` loop to run through the `Forms` collection and check the `Name` property. If Mailings is found, `DoCmd.Close` shuts down the form.

- A new recordset based on the Mailings table is opened. The `AddNew` method creates a new record, its MessageID field is set to the current value of MessageID, and the MailingID of the new record is stored in the `newMailingID` variable.
- The Mailings form is opened using `DoCmd.OpenForm`. This method's `WhereCondition` argument is used to filter the form's messages. In this case, the code uses the argument to filter the form to show only the record it just created.

Listing 29.6. This event handler displays the Mailings form with a new mailing based on the current message.

```
Private Sub cmdNewMailing_Click()
    Dim frm As Form
    Dim db As Database
    Dim rsMailings As Recordset
    Dim newMailingID As Integer
    '
    ' If Mailings form is open, close it
    '
    For Each frm In Forms
        If frm.Name = "Mailings" Then
            DoCmd.Close acForm, "Mailings"
            Exit For
        End If
    Next 'frm
    '
    ' Create the new mailing
    '
    Set db = CurrentDb
    Set rsMailings = db.OpenRecordset("Mailings", dbOpenTable)
    With rsMailings
        .Edit
        .AddNew
        !MessageID = Me!MessageID
        .Update
        .MoveLast
        newMailingID = !MailingID
        .Close
    End With
    db.Close
    '
    ' Display Mailings form with the MailingID we just created
    '
    DoCmd.OpenForm _
        FormName:="Mailings", _
        WhereCondition:="MailingID=" & newMailingID
End Sub
```

The `UpdateSubstitutionList` Procedure

The final procedure associated with the Messages form is the `UpdateSubstitutionList` function, shown in Listing 29.7, which is called from several of the other procedures. This purpose of this function is to populate the Substitution Fields list box (named `lstDataSourceFields`) with the field codes associated with the current data source.

This is accomplished via a `For...Next` loop that runs through the `Fields` collection of the current data source. This loop creates a semicolon-delimited string named `strFieldList` that is used as the `RowSource` property of the list box. Each field name is added to the string, along with double angle brackets before (<<) and after (>>). The loop also checks for a field named Email. If this field doesn't exist, the function returns `False`.

Listing 29.7. This function populates the Substitution Fields list box based on the currently selected data source. It returns `False` if the data source doesn't contain a field named Email.

```
Private Function UpdateSubstitutionList() As Boolean
    Dim db As Database            ' The current database
    Dim src As Object             ' The data source object
    Dim i As Integer              ' A counter
    Dim strFieldList As String    ' The list of fields in the data source
    Dim emailField As Boolean     ' Tracks whether or not an "Email" feld exists
    '
    ' Get the current data source
    '
    Set db = CurrentDb
    If fraDataSourceType = TABLE Then
        Set src = db.TableDefs(cboDataSource.Value)
    Else
        Set src = db.QueryDefs(cboDataSource.Value)
    End If
    '
    ' Create the field string
    '
    strFieldList = ""
    For i = 0 To src.Fields.Count - 1
        strFieldList = strFieldList & "<<" & LCase$(src.Fields(i).Name) & ">>;"
        If src.Fields(i).Name = "Email" Then
            Me!emailfieldname = "Email"
            emailField = True
        End If
    Next 'i
    '
    ' Add the field names to the combo box
    '
    With lstDataSourceFields
        .RowSourceType = "Value List"
        .RowSource = strFieldList
    End With
    '
    ' Return the value
    '
    UpdateSubstitutionList = emailField
End Function
```

The Select E-Mail Field Dialog Form

Earlier you saw that the Messages form will display the Select E-Mail Field Dialog form if the selected data source doesn't contain a field named Email. The `OpenForm` method that was used passed the name of the data source as its `OpenArgs` argument.

The purpose of the Select E-Mail Field Dialog form is to display a list of the data source fields so that the user can choose which of the fields contains the e-mail addresses. The list box (it's named `lstFields`) is defined with its `RowSourceType` property set to `Field List`. This means that you only need to set the `RowSource` property to a table or query object, and the list will show the field names automatically.

To accomplish this, the form's `Load` event handler, shown in Listing 29.8, first checks to make sure that `OpenArgs` isn't `Null` (as it would be if you opened this form by hand). If it's not, the `OpenArgs` value is set to the list's `RowSource` property.

Listing 29.8. The form's `Load` event handler.

```
Private Sub Form_Load()
    If Not IsNull(Me.OpenArgs) Then
        lstFields.RowSource = Me.OpenArgs
    End If
End Sub
```

The form's `Unload` event handler, shown in Listing 29.9, is used to process the selected list value. A `For Each...Next` loop checks to make sure the Messages form is open. If it is, the list's value is checked to make sure it isn't `Null` (that is, the user must select a value). If it's not, the value is stored in the EmailFieldName field of the current Messages record.

Listing 29.9. The form's `Unload` event handler.

```
Private Sub Form_Unload(Cancel As Integer)
    Dim frm As Form
    '
    ' If Messages form is open, store the selected value
    '
    For Each frm In Forms
        If frm.Name = "Messages" Then
            If IsNull(lstFields.Value) Then
                Beep
                Cancel = True
            Else
                frm!EmailFieldName = lstFields.Value
            End If
            Exit For
        End If
    Next 'frm
End Sub
```

The Code in the Mailings Form

The Mailings form is a bit more complex than the other E-Mail Merge forms, and this complexity is reflected in the slightly more ambitious procedures that the form uses. The next few sections examine each of the event handlers and procedures utilized by the Mailings form.

The Load Event

The `Load` event handler for the Mailings form is a simple affair, as you can see from Listing 29.10. In fact, there's only one statement: a call to the `UpdateMailingData` procedure, which displays the various chunks of data associated with each mailing.

Listing 29.10. The form's `Load` event handler.

```
Private Sub Form_Load()
    UpdateMailingData
End Sub
```

The Current Event

Listing 29.11 shows the event handler for the Mailings form's `Current` event. As I mentioned earlier, a form's `Current` event fires when you navigate between the form's records. In this case, we want to trap the `Current` event so that we can update the Mailings form according to the mailing data in each record. However, note that the `Current` event also fires when you navigate to a *new* record and that the code must respond differently depending on whether it's dealing with an existing record or a new one.

The achieve this, the procedure checks the form's `NewRecord` property. If this property returns `False`, we're dealing with an existing record, and the code performs two tasks:

- The `UpdateMailingData` procedure is called. This procedure—which I'll run through in the next section—displays the mailing data for the current record.
- The current value of the MailingID field is stored in the global `currSubject` variable for later use.

If the current record is new, the procedure makes the new record "official" by setting the required `MessageID` field equal to the `currSubject` variable.

From here, the procedure checks the current value of the Sent field. If the mailing has been sent, the code displays the controls for the SentSubject and SentBody fields, hides the `MessageID` control and the Message Body subform, and disables the Edit Message button. If the mailing hasn't been sent, the opposite tasks are performed. In other words, the controls for the SentSubject and SentBody fields are hidden, the `MessageID` control and the Message Body subform are displayed, and the Edit Message button is enabled.

Listing 29.11. The form's `Current` event handler.

```
Private Sub Form_Current()
    If Not NewRecord Then
        '
        ' We're working with an existing mailing, so update the message data
        '
        UpdateMailingData
        currSubject = MessageID
    Else
        '
        ' We must be adding a new mailing.
        ' The new mailing record isn't official until
        ' we set the required MessageID field. Set it
        ' to the current Subject.
        '
        MessageID = currSubject
    End If
    '
    ' Adjust visible controls depending on Sent field value
    '
    If Sent Then
        '
        ' If mailing has been sent, make SentSubject
        ' and SentBody fields visible, hide the
        ' Subject combo box and the MessageBody field,
        ' and disable the Edit Message button.
        '
        SentSubject.Visible = True
        SentBody.Visible = True
        MessageID.Visible = False
        sfMessageBody.Visible = False
        cmdEditMessage.Enabled = False
    Else
        '
        ' Otherwise, do the opposite
        '
        SentSubject.Visible = False
        SentBody.Visible = False
        MessageID.Visible = True
        sfMessageBody.Visible = True
        cmdEditMessage.Enabled = True
    End If
End Sub
```


The `Click` Event for the Subject Combo Box

If you select a different subject from the Subject combo box, the control's `Click` event fires. As shown in Listing 29.12, the event handler simply calls the `UpdateMailingData` procedure.

Listing 29.12. The `Click` event handler for the MessageID drop-down list.

```
Private Sub MessageID_Click()
    UpdateMailingData
End Sub
```

The UpdateMailingData Procedure

In the previous three sections, you saw how the code called the `UpdateMailingData` procedure to display the data for each record in the Mailings table. Listing 29.13 shows this procedure. The following is a quick summary of the various chores performed by this code:

- The Messages table is opened, and the message associated with the current mailing is found. When this is done, the Data Source label is set to display the name of the data source, and the name is added to a SQL `SELECT` statement (the `strSQL` variable).
- Using this `SELECT` statement, the data source is opened, and the total number of recipients is calculated.
- The list of recipients is then initialized. For example, the list's `RowSource` property is set to `strSQL`.
- The other labels are filled in with mailing data.

Listing 29.13. This procedure updates the data for the current mailing.

```
Private Sub UpdateMailingData()
    Dim db As Database              ' The current database
    Dim rsMessages As Recordset     ' The Messages table
    Dim strSQL As String            ' A SQL statement
    Dim rsDataSource As Recordset   ' The message data source
    Dim i As Integer                ' A counter
    '
    ' Open the Messages table and find the
    ' message associated with this mailing.
    '
    Set db = CurrentDb
    strSQL = "SELECT DISTINCTROW * FROM ["
    Set rsMessages = db.OpenRecordset("Messages", dbOpenDynaset)
    rsMessages.FindFirst "MessageID=" & MessageID
    If Not rsMessages.NoMatch Then
        '
        ' We found it, so display the data source
        ' and add it to the SQL statement
        '
        lblDataSource.Caption = rsMessages!DataSource
        strSQL = strSQL & lblDataSource.Caption & "];"
    End If
    rsMessages.Close
    '
    ' Open the data source
    '
    Set rsDataSource = db.OpenRecordset(lblDataSource.Caption, dbOpenDynaset)
    '
    ' Get the number of recipients
    '
    rsDataSource.MoveLast
    lblTotalRecipients.Caption = rsDataSource.RecordCount
```

```
    '
    ' Set up the recipients list
    '
    With lstRecipients
        .RowSource = strSQL
        .ColumnCount = rsDataSource.Fields.Count
        .ColumnWidths = "1"""
        For i = 1 To .ColumnCount
            .ColumnWidths = .ColumnWidths & ";1"""
        Next 'i
    End With
    rsDataSource.Close
    '
    ' Display the rest of the mailing data
    '
    If Sent Then
        lblMailingStatus.Caption = "SENT"
        If Not IsNull(MailingDate) Then lblMailingDate.Caption = MailingDate
        If Not IsNull(MailingTime) Then lblMailingTime.Caption = MailingTime
    Else
        lblMailingStatus.Caption = "UNSENT"
        lblMailingDate.Caption = ""
        lblMailingTime.Caption = ""
    End If
End Sub
```

The Click Event for the Edit Message Command Button

Listing 29.14 shows the event handler for the `Click` event associated with the Edit Message command button. This procedure simply runs an `OpenForm` method to open the Messages form with a filter that restricts the Messages records to just the `MessageID` of the current mailing.

Listing 29.14. The `Click` event handler for the Edit Messages button.

```
Private Sub cmdEditMessage_Click()
    '
    ' Display the Messages form where the MessageID
    ' equals the MessageID of the current mailing
    '
    DoCmd.OpenForm _
        FormName:="Messages", _
        WhereCondition:="[MessageID]=" & Me![MessageID]
End Sub
```

The Click Event for the Send Mailing Command Button

The code that runs when you click the Send Mailing command button is shown in Listing 29.15. A detailed explanation of this code follows the listing.

Listing 29.15. The Click event handler for the Send Mailing button.

```
Private Sub cmdSendMailing_Click()
    Dim db As Database                ' The current database
    Dim strSQL As String              ' A SQL statement
    Dim strEMailField As String       ' The field containing the e-mail addresses
    Dim strSubject As String          ' The message subject
    Dim strBody As String             ' The message body
    Dim rsTemp As Recordset           ' Temporary recordset object
    Dim ol As Outlook.Application     ' Outlook Automation object
    Dim ns As NameSpace               ' Outlook NameSpace object
    Dim newMessage As MailItem        ' Stores each new mail item
    Dim i As Integer                  ' Counter
    '
    ' Make sure there is at least one recipient
    '
    If Val(lblTotalRecipients.Caption) = 0 Then
        MsgBox "There are no recipients marked! Aborting Send..."
        Exit Sub
    End If
    '
    ' Establish a connection and log on
    '
    Application.SysCmd acSysCmdSetStatus, "Creating Outlook Automation objects..."
    Set ol = CreateObject("Outlook.Application")
    Set ns = ol.GetNamespace("MAPI")
    Application.SysCmd acSysCmdSetStatus, "Logging on to MAPI session..."
    ns.Logon
    '
    ' Get the message Subject and Body if necessary
    '
    Set db = CurrentDb
    If Not Sent Then
        Set rsTemp = db.OpenRecordset("Messages", dbOpenDynaset)
        rsTemp.FindFirst "MessageID=" & MessageID
        If Not rsTemp.NoMatch Then
            strEMailField = rsTemp!EmailFieldName
            strSubject = rsTemp!MessageSubject
            strBody = rsTemp!MessageBody
        Else
            MsgBox "Could not find message data! Aborting Send..."
            rsTemp.Close
            Exit Sub
        End If
        rsTemp.Close
    End If
    '
    ' Open and loop through the source data
    '
    Set rsTemp = db.OpenRecordset(lblDataSource.Caption, dbOpenDynaset)
    i = 0
    Do While Not rsTemp.EOF
        i = i + 1
        Application.SysCmd acSysCmdSetStatus, "Sending message " & i & " of " & _
➥lblTotalRecipients.Caption
        '
        ' Create the new MailItem
        '
```

```
        Set newMessage = ol.CreateItem(olMailItem)
        '
        ' Specify the recipient, subject, and body, and then send the message
        '
        With newMessage
            .Recipients.Add rsTemp(strEMailField)
            If Not Sent Then
                .Subject = strSubject
                .Body = ReplaceFields(rsTemp, strBody)
            Else
                .Subject = SentSubject
                .Body = ReplaceFields(rsTemp, SentBody)
            End If
            .Send
        End With
        rsTemp.MoveNext
    Loop
    '
    ' Log off the session
    '
    ns.Logoff
    Set ol = Nothing
    '
    ' Update mailing data
    '
    If Not Sent Then
        MailingDate = Date
        MailingTime = Time
        SentSubject = strSubject
        SentBody = strBody
        Sent = True
        lblMailingStatus.Caption = IIf(Sent, "SENT", "UNSENT")
        lblMailingDate.Caption = MailingDate
        lblMailingTime.Caption = MailingTime
    End If
    '
    ' Format the controls for a Sent mailing
    '
    SentSubject.Visible = True
    SentBody.Visible = True
    MessageID.Visible = False
    sfMessageBody.Visible = False
    cmdEditMessage.Enabled = False
    Me.Refresh
    Application.SysCmd acSysCmdClearStatus
End Sub
```

The first thing the code does is check to make sure that there is at least one recipient. Because the form has been tracking the total number of recipients in the Total Recipients label (named `lblTotalRecipients`), we only need to check the value of the caption:

```
    If Val(lblTotalRecipients.Caption) = 0 Then
        MsgBox "There are no recipients marked! Aborting Send..."
        Exit Sub
    End If
```

If there is at least one recipient, the code continues by setting up the Automation link to Outlook and logging on:

```
Application.SysCmd acSysCmdSetStatus, "Creating Outlook Automation objects..."
Set ol = CreateObject("Outlook.Application")
Set ns = ol.GetNamespace("MAPI")
Application.SysCmd acSysCmdSetStatus, "Logging on to MAPI session..."
ns.Logon
```

In preparation for the mailing, the code next opens the Messages table, finds the message for the current mailing, and extracts the name of the e-mail field, the message subject, and the message body:

```
Set db = CurrentDb
If Not Sent Then
    Set rsTemp = db.OpenRecordset("Messages", dbOpenDynaset)
    rsTemp.FindFirst "MessageID=" & MessageID
    If Not rsTemp.NoMatch Then
        strEMailField = rsTemp!EmailFieldName
        strSubject = rsTemp!MessageSubject
        strBody = rsTemp!MessageBody
    Else
        MsgBox "Could not find message data! Aborting Send..."
        rsTemp.Close
        Exit Sub
    End If
    rsTemp.Close
End If
```

Now the procedure is ready to send the messages. As shown next, the code opens the data source and then uses a `Do While...Loop` to run through each record. For each recipient, a new mail message item is created, the recipient is added, the `Subject` and `Body` properties are set (I'll explain the `ReplaceFields` function in the next section), and the `Send` method sends the message.

```
Set rsTemp = db.OpenRecordset(lblDataSource.Caption, dbOpenDynaset)
i = 0
Do While Not rsTemp.EOF
    i = i + 1
    Application.SysCmd acSysCmdSetStatus, "Sending message " & i & " of " &
    ➥lblTotalRecipients.Caption
    '
    ' Create the new MailItem
    '
    Set newMessage = ol.CreateItem(olMailItem)
    '
    ' Specify the recipient, subject, and body, and then send the message
    '
    With newMessage
        .Recipients.Add rsTemp(strEMailField)
        If Not Sent Then
            .Subject = strSubject
            .Body = ReplaceFields(rsTemp, strBody)
        Else
            .Subject = SentSubject
            .Body = ReplaceFields(rsTemp, SentBody)
        End If
        .Send
```

```
        End With
        rsTemp.MoveNext
    Loop
```

The rest of the procedure performs various housekeeping chores: The MAPI session is logged off, the Mailings table record is updated with the date and time the message was sent and so on, and the controls are adjusted for a sent mailing:

```
    ns.Logoff
    Set ol = Nothing
    '
    ' Update mailing data
    '
    If Not Sent Then
        MailingDate = Date
        MailingTime = Time
        SentSubject = strSubject
        SentBody = strBody
        Sent = True
        lblMailingStatus.Caption = IIf(Sent, "SENT", "UNSENT")
        lblMailingDate.Caption = MailingDate
        lblMailingTime.Caption = MailingTime
    End If
    '
    ' Format the controls for a Sent mailing
    '
    SentSubject.Visible = True
    SentBody.Visible = True
    MessageID.Visible = False
    sfMessageBody.Visible = False
    cmdEditMessage.Enabled = False
    Me.Refresh
    Application.SysCmd acSysCmdClearStatus
```

The ReplaceFields Function

It's the job of the `ReplaceFields` function to take a message body and replace the field codes with the actual data from a data source record. As you can see in Listing 29.16, this function takes two arguments: `rsTemp` is the data source, and `strOriginalText` is the message body (which is subsequently stored in the local `str` variable). The bulk of the code is taken up by a `Do While...Loop` that checks the return value of `Instr(1, str, "<<")`. This value, which is stored in the `leftBracket` variable, represents the beginning of a field code. Although this value isn't 0 (in other words, there are still field codes to replace), the code extracts the name of the field from between the `"<<"` and `">>"` brackets, gets the current value of that field from the data source, and replaces the field code with the value.

TIP: USING FIELD CODES IN THE SUBJECT LINE

Although my code uses `ReplaceFields` only on the message body, there's no reason why you couldn't add field codes to the message subject and use `ReplaceFields` on the subject text.

Listing 29.16. This function takes a recordset for the data source and a string (the Message Body) and replaces the fields with the data from the current record.

```
Private Function ReplaceFields(rsTemp As Recordset, strOriginalText As String)
➥As String
    Dim str As String
    Dim leftBracket As Long
    Dim rightBracket As Long
    Dim fldName As String
    Dim rsDataSource As Recordset
    Dim fldValue As Variant
    '
    ' Get the position of the first field
    '
    str = strOriginalText
    leftBracket = InStr(1, str, "<<")
    '
    ' Run through the text
    '
    Do While leftBracket <> 0
        '
        ' Get the right field marker
        '
        rightBracket = InStr(leftBracket, str, ">>")
        '
        ' Extract the field name from between << and >>
        '
        fldName = UCase$(Mid$(str, leftBracket + 2, rightBracket - leftBracket - 2))
        '
        ' Get field value for the current data source record
        '
        fldValue = rsTemp(fldName)
        '
        ' Replace the entire field code with the value
        '
        str = Left$(str, leftBracket - 1) & fldValue & Right(str, Len(str) -
        ➥rightBracket - 1)
        '
        ' Get the position of the next field
        '
        leftBracket = InStr(1, str, "<<")
    Loop
    ReplaceFields = str
End Function
```

Summary

This chapter took you through the VBA Mailing List Manager, an Access application that uses VBA and Automation to send mass e-mailings via Outlook's Inbox. To get more information on the topics covered in this chapter, try the following chapters on for size:

- To learn more about how VBA and Access get along, head for Chapter 9, "VBA and Access."

- For the full story on how Automation works, read Chapter 15, "Controlling Applications Via OLE Automation."
- I cover DAO in depth in Chapter 18, "Programming Data Access Objects."
- The nitty-gritty of programming Outlook's Inbox module can be found in Chapter 22, "E-Mail and Groupware Programming with Outlook."

APPENDIX A

VBA Statements

Throughout this book, I've introduced you to various VBA statements. These statements appeared on an "as-needed" basis whenever I wanted to explain a particular VBA topic (such as the control structures we looked at in Chapter 5, "Controlling Your VBA Code"). Although I covered the vast majority of the VBA statements in this book, a bit of VBA's 89-statement repertoire was overlooked. However, most of the missing statements are either obscure or rarely used (such as the repugnant `GoTo` statement). (Note that, in this context, a *statement* is any VBA keyword or construct that isn't a function, object, property, or method.)

In an effort to put some finishing touches on our VBA coverage, this appendix presents a brief, but complete, look at every VBA statement. I give a short description of each statement and, where appropriate, I refer you to the relevant chapter where you can get more detailed information. For the other statements, you can get full explanations and examples from the Statements section of the VBA Help file. Also note that I've indicated which statements are new to VBA 5.0.

Table A.1. VBA statements.

Statement	*Chapter*	*Description*
`AppActivate` ***`title`***`,` *`wait`*	13	Activates the running application with the title or task ID given by ***`title`***.
`Beep`	10	Beeps the speaker.
`Call` ***`name`***`,` *`argumentlist`*	1	Calls the ***`name`*** procedure. (Because you can call a procedure just by using its name, the `Call` statement is rarely used in VBA programming.)
`ChDir` ***`path`***	26	Changes the current directory (folder) to ***`path`***.
`ChDrive` ***`drive`***	26	Changes the current drive to ***`drive`***.
`Close` *`filenumberlist`*	26	Closes one or more I/O files opened with the `Open` statement.
`Const` ***`CONSTNAME`***	2	Declares a constant variable named ***`CONSTNAME`***.
`Date =` ***`date`***		Changes the system date to ***`date`***.
`Declare` ***`name`***	25	Declares a procedure from a dynamic link library (DLL).

Statement	Chapter	Description
`DefBool` ***letterrange***	2	A module-level statement that sets the default data type to `Boolean` for all variables that begin with the letters in ***letterrange*** (for example, `DefBool A-F`).
`DefByte` ***letterrange***	2	Sets the default data type to `Byte` for all variables that begin with the letters in ***letterrange***. VBA 5.0
`DefCur` ***letterrange***	2	Sets the default data type to `Currency` for all variables that begin with the letters in ***letterrange***.
`DefDate` ***letterrange***	2	Sets the default data type to `Date` for all variables that begin with the letters in ***letterrange***.
`DefDbl` ***letterrange***	2	Sets the default data type to `Double` for all variables that begin with the letters in ***letterrange***.
`DefInt` ***letterrange***	2	Sets the default data type to `Integer` for all variables that begin with the letters in ***letterrange***.
`DefLng` ***letterrange***	2	Sets the default data type to `Long` for all variables that begin with the letters in ***letterrange***.
`DefObj` ***letterrange***	2	Sets the default data type to `Object` for all variables that begin with the letters in ***letterrange***.
`DefSng` ***letterrange***	2	Sets the default data type to `Single` for all variables that begin with the letters in ***letterrange***.
`DefStr` ***letterrange***	2	Sets the default data type to `String` for all variables that begin with the letters in ***letterrange***.
`DefVar` ***letterrange***	2	Sets the default data type to `Variant` for all variables that begin with the letters in ***letterrange***.
`Dim` ***varname***	2	Declares a variable named ***varname***.

continues

Table A.1. continued

Statement	*Chapter*	*Description*
`Do...Loop`	5	Loops through one or more statements while a logical condition is `True`.
`DoEvents`	5, 25	Yields execution to the operating system so that it can process pending events from other applications (such as keystrokes and mouse clicks).
`End` ***`keyword`***	1, 5	Ends a procedure, function, or control structure.
`Erase` ***`arraylist`***		Frees the memory allocated to a dynamic array or reinitializes a fixed-size array.
`Err =` ***`errornumber`***	23	Sets `Err` (the current error status) to ***`errornumber`***.
`Error` ***`errornumber`***	23	Simulates an error by setting `Err` to ***`errornumber`***.
`Exit` ***`keyword`***	1, 5	Exits a procedure, function, or control structure.
`FileCopy` ***`source, destination`***	26	Copies the ***`source`*** file to ***`destination`***.
`For Each...Next`	5	Loops through each member of a collection.
`For...Next`	5	Loops through one or more statements until a counter hits a specified value.
`Function`	1	Declares a user-defined function procedure.
`Get #`*`filenumber, varname`*	26	Reads an I/O file opened by the `Open` statement into a variable.
`GoSub...Return`		Branches to and returns from a subroutine within a procedure. (However, creating separate procedures makes your code more readable.)

Statement	Chapter	Description
`GoTo` ***line***		Sends the code to the line label given by ***line***.
`If...Then...Else`	5	Runs one of two sections of code based on the result of a logical test.
`Input` ***#filenumber, varlist***	26	Reads data from an I/O file into variables.
`Kill` ***pathname***	26	Deletes the file ***pathname*** from a disk.
`Let` ***varname = expression***		Sets the variable ***varname*** equal to ***expression***. `Let` is optional and is almost never used.
`Line Input` ***#filenumber, var***	26	Reads a line from an I/O file and stores it in ***var***.
`Load`	11	Loads a user form into memory without displaying it.
`Lock` ***#filenumber***, *recordrange*	26	Controls access to an I/O file.
`LSet` ***stringvar = string***		Left-aligns a string within a `String` variable.
`LSet` ***var1 = var2***		Copies a variable of one user-defined type into another variable of a different user-defined type.
`Mid`		Replaces characters in a `String` variable with characters from a different string.
`MidB`		Replaces byte data in a `String` variable with characters from a different string.
`MkDir` ***path***	26	Creates the directory (folder) named ***path***.
`Name` ***oldpathname*** `As` ***newpathname***	26	Renames a file or directory (folder).
`On Error`	23	Sets up an error-handling routine.
`On...GoSub`, `On...GoTo`		Branches to a line based on the result of an expression.
`Open` ***pathname***, etc.	26	Opens an input/output (I/O) file.

continues

Table A.1. continued

Statement	*Chapter*	*Description*
`Option Base 0¦1`	2	Determines (at the module level) the default lower bound for arrays.
`Option Compare Text¦Binary`	3	Determines (at the module level) the default mode for string comparisons.
`Option Explicit`	2	Forces you to declare all variables used in a module. Enter this statement at the module level.
`Option Private`	1	Indicates that the module is private and can't be accessed by other procedures outside the module. Enter this statement at the module level.
`Print #`***`filenumber`***	26	Writes data to an I/O file.
`Private `***`varname`***	2	Declares the ***`varname`*** variable to be a private variable that can be used only in the module in which it's declared. Enter this statement at the module level.
`Property Get`	16	Declares a property procedure.
`Property Let`	16	Assigns a value to a property in a property procedure.
`Property Set`	16	Sets a reference to an object in a property procedure.
`Public `***`varname`***	2	Makes the ***`varname`*** variable available to all procedures in a module.
`Put #`***`filenumber, varname`***	26	Writes data from the variable ***`varname`*** to an I/O file.
`Randomize `*`number`*	3	Initializes the random-number generator. Omit *`number`* to get a different random number each time.
`ReDim `***`varname`***	2	Reallocates memory in a dynamic array.

Statement	Chapter	Description
`Rem` *comment*		Tells VBA that the following text is a comment. The apostrophe (') is more widely used.
`Reset`	26	Closes all I/O files that were opened with `Open`.
`Resume`	23	After an error, resumes program execution at the line that caused the error.
`Return`		See `GoSub...Return`.
`RmDir` ***path***	26	Deletes a directory (folder).
`RSet` ***stringvar*** `=` ***string***		Right-aligns a string within a `String` variable.
`SaveSetting` ***appname***, etc.	26	Retrieves a setting from the Windows Registry.
`Seek` ***#filenumber, position***	26	Sets the current position in an I/O file.
`Select Case`	5	Executes one of several groups of statements based on the value of an expression.
`SendKeys` ***string,*** *wait*	13	Sends the keystrokes given by ***string*** to the active application.
`Set` ***objectvar*** `=` ***object***	4	Assigns an ***object*** to an `Object` variable named ***objectvar***.
`SetAttr` ***pathname, attr***	26	Assigns the attributes given by ***attr*** (for example, `vbReadOnly`) to the file given by ***pathname***.
`Static` ***varname***	2	Declares ***varname*** to be a variable that will retain its value as long as the code is running.
`Stop`	24	Places VBA in Pause mode.
`Sub`	1	Declares a procedure.
`Time =` ***time***		Sets the system time to ***time***.
`Type` ***varname***	2	Declares a user-defined data type. (Used at the module level only.)
`Unload`	11	Removes a user form from memory.

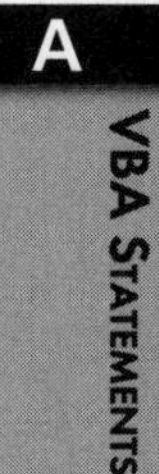

continues

Table A.1. continued

Statement	*Chapter*	*Description*
`Unlock #filenumber, recordrange`	26	Removes access controls on an I/O file.
`While...Wend`	5	Loops through a block of code while a condition is `True`.
`Width #filenumber, width`		Assigns an output line width to an I/O file.
`With...End With`	5	Executes a block of statements on a specified object.
`Write #filenumber`	26	Writes data to an I/O file.

VBA Functions

Although I discussed quite a few VBA functions in this book, I was by no means exhaustive in my coverage. VBA boasts over 160 built-in functions that cover data conversion, dates and times, math, strings, and much more. This appendix presents a categorical list of each VBA function and the arguments it uses. You can get full explanations and examples for all the functions in the Functions section of the VBA Help file. Also note that I've indicated which of the functions are new to VBA 5.0.

Table B.1. Conversion functions.

	Function	*What It Returns*
	`CBool(`***`expression`***`)`	An ***`expression`*** converted to a `Boolean` value.
VBA 5.0	`CByte(`***`expression`***`)`	An ***`expression`*** converted to a `Byte` value.
	`CCur(`***`expression`***`)`	An ***`expression`*** converted to a `Currency` value.
	`CDate(`***`expression`***`)`	An ***`expression`*** converted to a `Date` value.
	`CDbl(`***`expression`***`)`	An ***`expression`*** converted to a `Double` value.
	`CInt(`***`expression`***`)`	An ***`expression`*** converted to an `Integer` value.
	`CLng(`***`expression`***`)`	An ***`expression`*** converted to a `Long` value.
	`CSng(`***`expression`***`)`	An ***`expression`*** converted to a `Single` value.
	`CStr(`***`expression`***`)`	An ***`expression`*** converted to a `String` value.
	`CVar(`***`expression`***`)`	An ***`expression`*** converted to a `Variant` value.
	`CVDate(`***`expression`***`)`	An ***`expression`*** converted to a `Date` value. (Provided for backward compatibility. Use `CDate` instead.)
	`CVErr(`***`errornumber`***`)`	A `Variant` of subtype `Error` that contains ***`errornumber`***.

Table B.2. Date and time functions.

	Function	*What It Returns*
	`Date`	The current system date as a `Variant`.
	`Date$()`	The current system date as a `String`.
VBA 5.0	`DateAdd(`***`interval, number, date`***`)`	A `Date` value derived by adding ***`number`*** time intervals to ***`date`***.
VBA 5.0	`DateDiff(`***`interval, date1, date2,...`***`)`	The number of time intervals between ***`date1`*** and ***`date2`***.
VBA 5.0	`DatePart(`***`interval, date,...`***`)`	The ***`interval`*** (month, quarter, and so on) given by ***`date`***.

Function	*What It Returns*
`DateSerial(year, month, day)`	A `Date` value for the specified **`year`**, **`month`**, and **`day`**.
`DateValue(date)`	A `Date` value for the **`date`** string.
`Day(date)`	The day of the month given by **`date`**.
`Hour(time)`	The hour component of **`time`**.
`Minute(time)`	The minute component of **`time`**.
`Month(date)`	The month component of **`date`**.
`Now`	The current system date and time.
`Second(time)`	The second component of **`time`**.
`Time`	The current system time as a `Variant`.
`Time$`	The current system time as a `String`.
`Timer`	The number of seconds since midnight.
`TimeSerial(hour, minute, second)`	A `Date` value for the specified **`hour`**, **`minute`**, and **`second`**.
`TimeValue(time)`	A `Date` value for the **`time`** string.
`Weekday(date)`	The day of the week, as a number, given by **`date`**.
`Year(date)`	The year component of **`date`**.

Table B.3. Error functions.

Function	*What It Returns*
`Erl`	A value that specifies the line number where the most recent error occurred.
`Err`	A value that specifies the runtime error number of the most recent error.
`Error(errornumber)`	The error message, as a `Variant`, that corresponds to the *`errornumber`*.
`Error$(errornumber)`	The error message, as a `String`, that corresponds to the *`errornumber`*.

Table B.4. File and directory functions.

Function	*What It Returns*
`CurDir(`*`drive`*`)`	The current directory as a `Variant`.
`CurDir$(`*`drive`*`)`	The current directory as a `String`.
`Dir(`***`pathname`***`, `*`attributes`*`)`	The name, as a `Variant`, of the file or directory (folder) specified by ***`pathname`*** and satisfying the optional *`attributes`* (for example, `vbHidden`). Returns `Null` if the file or directory doesn't exist.
`Dir$(`***`pathname`***`, `*`attributes`*`)`	The name, as a `String`, of the file or directory (folder) specified by ***`pathname`*** and satisfying the optional *`attributes`* (for example, `vbHidden`). Returns `Null` if the file or directory doesn't exist.
`EOF(`***`filenumber`***`)`	`True` if the end of file specified by ***`filenumber`*** has been reached; `False` otherwise.
`FileAttr(`***`filenumber, returnType`***`)`	The file mode (if ***`returnType`*** is 1) or the file handle (if ***`returnType`*** is 2) of the file given by ***`filenumber`***.
`FileDateTime(`***`pathname`***`)`	The `Date` that the file given by ***`pathname`*** was created or last modified.
`FileLen(`***`pathname`***`)`	The length, in bytes, of the file given by ***`pathname`***.
`FreeFile(`*`rangenumber`*`)`	The next available file number available to the `Open` statement.
`GetAttr(`***`pathname`***`)`	An integer representing the attributes of the file given by ***`pathname`***.
`Loc(`***`filenumber`***`)`	The current read/write position in an open I/O file.
`LOF(`***`filenumber`***`)`	The size, in bytes, of an open I/O file.
`Seek(`***`filenumber`***`)`	The current read/write position, as a `Variant`, in an open I/O file.
`Shell(`***`pathname`***`, `*`windowstyle`*`)`	The task ID of the executed program given by ***`pathname`***.

Table B.5. Financial functions.

Function	*What It Returns*
`DDB(`***`cost, salvage, life, period`***`, `*`factor`*`)`	Returns the depreciation of an asset over a specified period using the double-declining balance method.
`FV(`***`rate, nper, pmt`***`, `*`pv, type`*`)`	Returns the future value of an investment or loan.
`IPmt(`***`rate, per, nper, pv`***`, `*`fv, type`*`)`	Returns the interest payment for a specified period of a loan.
`IRR(`***`values`***`, `*`guess`*`)`	Returns the internal rate of return for a series of cash flows.
`MIRR(`***`values, finance_rate, reinvest_rate`***`)`	Returns the modified internal rate of return for a series of periodic cash flows.
`NPer(`**`rate, pmt, pv`**`, `*`fv, type`*`)`	Returns the number of periods for an investment or loan.
`NPV(`***`rate, value1`***`, `*`value2...`*`)`	Returns the net present value of an investment based on a series of cash flows and a discount rate.
`Pmt(`***`rate, nper, pv`***`, `*`fv, type`*`)`	Returns the periodic payment for a loan or investment.
`PPmt(`***`rate, per, nper, pv`***`, `*`fv, type`*`)`	Returns the principal payment for a specified period of a loan.
`PV(`***`rate, nper, pmt`***`, `*`fv, type`*`)`	Returns the present value of an investment.
`Rate(`***`nper, pmt, pv`***`, `*`fv, type, guess`*`)`	Returns the periodic interest rate for a loan or investment.
`SLN(`***`cost, salvage, life`***`)`	Returns the straight-line depreciation of an asset over one period.
`SYD(`***`cost, salvage, life, period`***`)`	Returns sum-of-years digits depreciation of an asset over a specified period.

Table B.6. Math functions.

Function	*What It Returns*
`Abs(`***`number`***`)`	The absolute value of ***`number`***.
`Atn(`***`number`***`)`	The arctangent of ***`number`***.

continues

Table B.6. continued

Function	What It Returns
`Cos(`***`number`***`)`	The cosine of ***`number`***.
`Exp(`***`number`***`)`	*e* (the base of the natural logarithm) raised to the power of ***`number`***.
`Fix(`***`number`***`)`	The integer portion of ***`number`***. If ***`number`*** is negative, `Fix` returns the first negative integer greater than or equal to ***`number`***.
`Hex(`***`number`***`)`	The hexadecimal value, as a `Variant`, of ***`number`***.
`Hex$(`***`number`***`)`	The hexadecimal value, as a `String`, of ***`number`***.
`Int(`***`number`***`)`	The integer portion of ***`number`***. If ***`number`*** is negative, `Int` returns the first negative integer less than or equal to ***`number`***.
`Log(`***`number`***`)`	The natural logarithm of ***`number`***.
`Oct(`***`number`***`)`	The octal value, as a `Variant`, of ***`number`***.
`Oct$(`***`number`***`)`	The octal value, as a `String`, of ***`number`***.
`Rnd(`***`number`***`)`	A random number.
`Sgn(`***`number`***`)`	The sign of ***`number`***.
`Sin(`***`number`***`)`	The sine of ***`number`***.
`Sqr(`***`number`***`)`	The square root of ***`number`***.
`Tan(`***`number`***`)`	The tangent of ***`number`***.

Table B.7. Miscellaneous functions.

Function	What It Returns
`Array(`**`arglist`**`)`	A `Variant` array containing the values in **`arglist`**.
VBA 5.0 `Choose(`***`index`***`, `***`choice1`***`, `*`etc.`*`)`	Returns a value from a list of choices.
`CreateObject(`***`class`***`)`	An Automation object of type ***`class`***.
VBA 5.0 `Environ(`*`envstring`*`¦`*`number`*`)`	A `String` value that represents the operating system environment variable given by *`envstring`* or *`number`*.
`Format(`***`expression`***`, `*`format`*`)`	The ***`expression`***, as a `Variant`, according to the string *`format`*.
`Format$(`***`expression`***`, `*`format`*`)`	The ***`expression`***, as a `String`, according to the string *`format`*.

Function	*What It Returns*
`GetAllSettings(`***`appname, section`***`)`	Retrieves from the Registry all the settings in the specified ***`section`***. VBA5.0
`GetObject(`*`pathname, class`*`)`	The Automation object given by *`pathname`* and *`class`*.
`GetSetting(`***`appname`***`, `*`etc.`*`)`	Retrieves a setting from the Registry. VBA5.0
`IIf(`***`expr, truepart, falsepart`***`)`	Returns ***`truepart`*** if ***`expr`*** is `True`; returns ***`falsepart`*** otherwise. VBA5.0
`Input(`***`number, #filenumber`***`)`	***`number`*** characters, as a `Variant`, from the I/O file given by ***`filenumber`***.
`Input$(`***`number, #filenumber`***`)`	***`number`*** characters, as a `String`, from the I/O file given by ***`filenumber`***.
`InputB(`***`number, #filenumber`***`)`	***`number`*** bytes, as a `Variant`, from the I/O file given by ***`filenumber`***.
`InputB$(`***`number, #filenumber`***`)`	***`number`*** bytes, as a `String`, from the I/O file given by ***`filenumber`***.
`InputBox(`***`prompt`***`, `*`etc.`*`)`	Prompts the user for information.
`IsArray(`***`varname`***`)`	`True` if ***`varname`*** is an array.
`IsDate(`***`expression`***`)`	`True` if ***`expression`*** can be converted into a date.
`IsEmpty(`***`expression`***`)`	`True` if ***`expression`*** is empty.
`IsError(`***`expression`***`)`	`True` if ***`expression`*** is an error.
`IsMissing(`***`argname`***`)`	`True` if the argument specified by ***`argname`*** was not passed to the procedure.
`IsNull(`***`expression`***`)`	`True` if ***`expression`*** is the null string (`""`).
`IsNumeric(`***`expression`***`)`	`True` if ***`expression`*** is a number.
`IsObject(`***`expression`***`)`	`True` if ***`expression`*** is an object.
`LBound(`***`arrayname`***`, `*`dimension`*`)`	The lowest possible subscript for the array given by ***`arrayname`***.
`MsgBox(`***`prompt`***`, `*`etc.`*`)`	The button a user selects from the `MsgBox` dialog box.
`Partition(`***`number, start, stop,...`***`)`	Returns a `String` that indicates where ***`number`*** occurs within a series of ranges. VBA5.0
`QBColor(`***`color`***`)`	Returns the RGB color code that corresponds to ***`color`*** (a number between 1 and 15). VBA5.0

continues

Table B.7. continued

Function	What It Returns
`RGB(red, green, blue)`	The color that corresponds to the ***red***, ***green***, and ***blue*** components.
VBA5.0 `Switch(expr1, value1, etc.)`	Evaluates the expressions (***expr1*** and so on) and returns the associated value (***value1*** and so on) for the first expression that evaluates to `True`.
`Tab(n)`	Positions output for the `Print #` statement or the `Print` method.
`TypeName(varname)`	A string that indicates the data type of the ***varname*** variable.
`UBound(arrayname, dimension)`	The highest possible subscript for the array given by ***arrayname***.
`VarType(varname)`	A constant that indicates the data type of the ***varname*** variable.

Table B.8. String functions.

Function	What It Returns
`Asc(string)`	The ANSI character code of the first letter in ***string***.
VBA5.0 `AscB(string)`	The byte corresponding to the first letter in ***string***.
VBA5.0 `AscW(string)`	The Unicode character code of the first letter in ***string***.
`Chr(charcode)`	The character, as a `Variant`, that corresponds to the ANSI code given by ***charcode***.
`Chr$(charcode)`	The character, as a `String`, that corresponds to the ANSI code given by ***charcode***.
VBA5.0 `ChrB(charcode)`	The byte that corresponds to the ANSI code given by ***charcode***.
VBA5.0 `ChrW(charcode)`	The Unicode character that corresponds to the ANSI code given by ***charcode***.
`InStr(start, string1, string2)`	The character position of the first occurrence of ***string2*** in ***string1***, starting at *start*.
`InStrB(start, string1, string2)`	The byte position of the first occurrence of ***string2*** in ***string1***, starting at *start*.

Function	*What It Returns*
`LCase(`***`string`***`)`	***`string`*** converted to lowercase as a `Variant`.
`LCase$(`***`string`***`)`	***`string`*** converted to lowercase as a `String`.
`Left(`***`string, length`***`)`	The leftmost ***`length`*** characters from ***`string`*** as a `Variant`.
`Left$(`***`string, length`***`)`	The leftmost ***`length`*** characters from ***`string`*** as a `String`.
`LeftB(`***`string`***`)`	The leftmost ***`length`*** bytes from ***`string`*** as a `Variant`.
`LeftB$(`***`string`***`)`	The leftmost ***`length`*** bytes from ***`string`*** as a `String`.
`Len(`***`string`***`)`	The number of characters in ***`string`***.
`LenB(`***`string`***`)`	The number of bytes in ***`string`***.
`LTrim(`***`string`***`)`	A string, as a `Variant`, without the leading spaces in ***`string`***.
`LTrim$(`***`string`***`)`	A string, as a `String`, without the leading spaces in ***`string`***.
`Mid(`***`string, start,`***` `*`length`*`)`	*`length`* characters, as a `Variant`, from ***`string`*** beginning at ***`start`***.
`Mid$(`***`string, start,`***` `*`length`*`)`	*`length`* characters, as a `String`, from ***`string`*** beginning at ***`start`***.
`MidB(`***`string, start,`***` `*`length`*`)`	*`length`* bytes, as a `Variant`, from ***`string`*** beginning at ***`start`***.
`MidB$(`***`string, start,`***` `*`length`*`)`	*`length`* bytes, as a `String`, from ***`string`*** beginning at ***`start`***.
`Right(`***`string, length`***`)`	The rightmost ***`length`*** characters from ***`string`*** as a `Variant`.
`Right$(`***`string, length`***`)`	The rightmost ***`length`*** characters from ***`string`*** as a `String`.
`RightB(`***`string, length`***`)`	The rightmost ***`length`*** bytes from ***`string`*** as a `Variant`.
`RightB$(`***`string, length`***`)`	The rightmost ***`length`*** bytes from ***`string`*** as a `String`.
`RTrim(`***`string`***`)`	A string, as a `Variant`, without the trailing spaces in ***`string`***.

continues

Table B.8. continued

Function	*What It Returns*
`RTrim$(`***`string`***`)`	A string, as a `String`, without the trailing spaces in ***`string`***.
`Space(`***`number`***`)`	A string, as a `Variant`, with ***`number`*** spaces.
`Space$(`***`number`***`)`	A string, as a `String`, with ***`number`*** spaces.
`Str(`***`number`***`)`	The string representation, as a `Variant`, of ***`number`***.
`Str$(`***`number`***`)`	The string representation, as a `String`, of ***`number`***.
`StrComp(`***`string2, string2,`*** *`compare`*`)`	A value indicating the result of comparing ***`string1`*** and ***`string2`***.
`String(`***`number, character`***`)`	***`character`***, as a `Variant`, repeated ***`number`*** times.
`String$(`***`number, character`***`)`	***`character`***, as a `String`, repeated ***`number`*** times.
`Trim(`***`string`***`)`	A string, as a `Variant`, without the leading and trailing spaces in ***`string`***.
`Trim$(`***`string`***`)`	A string, as a `String`, without the leading and trailing spaces in ***`string`***.
`UCase(`***`string`***`)`	***`string`*** converted to uppercase as a `Variant`.
`UCase$(`***`string`***`)`	***`string`*** converted to uppercase as a `String`.
`Val(`***`string`***`)`	The number contained in ***`string`***.

The Windows ANSI Character Set

This appendix presents the Windows ANSI character set. Table C.1 lists the ANSI numbers from 32 to 255. The first 32 numbers—0 to 31—are reserved for control characters such as ANSI 13, the carriage return. There are three columns for each number:

Column	*Description*
Text	The ANSI characters that correspond to normal text fonts such as Arial (Excel's default font), Courier New, and Times New Roman.
Symbol	The ANSI characters for the Symbol font.
Wingdings	The ANSI characters for the Wingdings font.

To enter these characters into your worksheets, you can use any of the following four methods:

- For the ANSI numbers 32 through 127, you can either type the character directly using the keyboard, or hold down the Alt key and type the ANSI number using the keyboard's numeric keypad.
- For the ANSI numbers 128 through 255, hold down the Alt key and use the keyboard's numeric keypad to enter the ANSI number, including the leading 0 shown in the table. For example, to enter the registered trademark symbol (ANSI 174), you would press Alt-0174.
- Use the `CHAR(`***`number`***`)` worksheet function, where ***`number`*** is the ANSI number for the character you want to display.
- In a Visual Basic procedure, use the `Chr(`***`charcode`***`)` function, where ***`charcode`*** is the ANSI number for the character.

Table C.1. The Windows ANSI character set.

ANSI	*Text*	*Symbol*	*Wingdings*
32			
33	!	!	✏
34	"	∀	✂
35	#	#	✁
36	$	∃	👓
37	%	%	🔔
38	&	&	🕮
39	'	∍	🕯
40	(	(	☎
41	)	)	✆

ANSI	Text	Symbol	Wingdings
42	*	*	
43	+	+	
44	,	,	
45	-	−	
46	.	.	
47	/	/	
48	0	0	
49	1	1	
50	2	2	
51	3	3	
52	4	4	
53	5	5	
54	6	6	
55	7	7	
56	8	8	
57	9	9	
58	:	:	
59	;	;	
60	<	<	
61	=	=	
62	>	>	
63	?	?	
64	@	≅	
65	A	A	
66	B	B	
67	C	Χ	
68	D	Δ	
69	E	E	
70	F	Φ	
71	G	Γ	
72	H	H	
73	I	I	
74	J	ϑ	
75	K	K	
76	L	Λ	
77	M	M	
78	N	N	
79	O	O	
80	P	Π	
81	Q	Θ	

continues

Table C.1. continued

ANSI	Text	Symbol	Wingdings
82	R	Ρ	☼
83	S	Σ	💧
84	T	Τ	❄
85	U	Υ	🕆
86	V	ς	✝
87	W	Ω	🕈
88	X	Ξ	✠
89	Y	Ψ	✡
90	Z	Ζ	☪
91	[	[	☯
92	\	∴	ॐ
93	]	]	☸
94	^	⊥	♈
95	_	_	♉
96	`	‾	♊
97	a	α	♋
98	b	β	♌
99	c	χ	♍
100	d	δ	♎
101	e	ε	♏
102	f	ϕ	♐
103	g	γ	♑
104	h	η	♒
105	i	ι	♓
106	j	φ	🙰
107	k	κ	🙵
108	l	λ	●
109	m	μ	❍
110	n	ν	■
111	o	ο	□
112	p	π	🞐
113	q	θ	❑
114	r	ρ	❒
115	s	σ	⬧
116	t	τ	⧫
117	u	υ	◆
118	v	ϖ	❖
119	w	ω	⬥
120	x	ξ	⌧
121	y	ψ	⍓
122	z	ζ	⌘

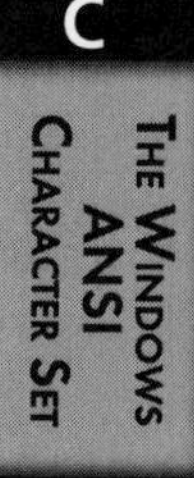

ANSI	*Text*	*Symbol*	*Wingdings*
123	{	{	✿
124	|	|	❀
125	}	}	❝
126	~	~	❞
127			▯
0128			⓪
0129			①
0130	‚		②
0131	ƒ		③
0132	„		④
0133	…		⑤
0134	†		⑥
0135	‡		⑦
0136	ˆ		⑧
0137	‰		⑨
0138	Š		⑩
0139	‹		⓿
0140	Œ		❶
0141			❷
0142			❸
0143			❹
0144			❺
0145	‘		❻
0146	’		❼
0147	“		❽
0148	”		❾
0149	•		❿
0150	–		🙖
0151	—		🙔
0152	˜		🙕
0153	™		🙗
0154	š		🙞
0155	›		🙜
0156	œ		🙝
0157			🙟
0158			·
0159	Ÿ		•
0160			
0161	¡	ϒ	○
0162	¢	′	⭕
0163	£	≤	◉
0164	¤	⁄	⊙

continues

Table C.1. continued

ANSI	*Text*	*Symbol*	*Wingdings*
0165	¥	∞	◉
0166	¦	ƒ	❍
0167	§	♣	▪
0168	¨	♦	◻
0169	©	♥	⅄
0170	ª	♠	✦
0171	«	↔	★
0172	¬	←	✶
0173	-	↑	✴
0174	®	→	✹
0175	¯	↓	✵
0176	°	°	⌖
0177	±	±	⌖
0178	²	″	✧
0179	³	≥	⌑
0180	´	×	⍰
0181	µ	∝	✪
0182	¶	∂	✰
0183	·	•	🕐
0184	¸	÷	🕑
0185	¹	≠	🕒
0186	º	≡	🕓
0187	»	≈	🕔
0188	¼	…	🕕
0189	½	⏐	🕖
0190	¾	⎯	🕗
0191	¿	↵	🕘
0192	À	ℵ	🕙
0193	Á	ℑ	🕚
0194	Â	ℜ	🕛
0195	Ã	℘	⮰
0196	Ä	⊗	⮱
0197	Å	⊕	⮲
0198	Æ	∅	⮳
0199	Ç	∩	⮴
0200	È	∪	⮵
0201	É	⊃	⮶
0202	Ê	⊇	⮷
0203	Ë	⊄	🙰
0204	Ì	⊂	🙵
0205	Í	⊆	🙐
0206	Î	∈	🙒

ANSI	Text	Symbol	Wingdings
0207	Ï	∉	🙜
0208	Ð	∠	🙞
0209	Ñ	∇	🙝
0210	Ò	®	🙟
0211	Ó	©	🙚
0212	Ô	™	🙛
0213	Õ	∏	⌫
0214	Ö	√	⌦
0215	×	⋅	⮘
0216	Ø	¬	⮚
0217	Ù	∧	⮙
0218	Ú	∨	⮛
0219	Û	⇔	⮈
0220	Ü	⇐	⮊
0221	Ý	⇑	⮉
0222	Þ	⇒	⮋
0223	ß	⇓	🡨
0224	à	◊	🡪
0225	á	〈	🡩
0226	â	®	🡫
0227	ã	©	🡬
0228	ä	™	🡭
0229	å	∑	🡯
0230	æ	⎛	🡮
0231	ç	⎜	🡸
0232	è	⎝	🡺
0233	é	⎡	🡹
0234	ê	⎢	🡻
0235	ë	⎣	🡼
0236	ì	⎧	🡽
0237	í	⎨	🡿
0238	î	⎩	🡾
0239	ï	⎪	⇦
0240	ð		⇨
0241	ñ	〉	⇧
0242	ò	∫	⇩
0243	ó	⌠	⬄
0244	ô	⎮	⇳
0245	õ	⌡	⬁
0246	ö	⎞	⬀
0247	÷	⎟	⬃
0248	ø	⎠	⬂

continues

Table C.1. continued

ANSI	*Text*	*Symbol*	*Wingdings*
0249	ù	⎤	▫
0250	ú	⎥	▫
0251	û	⎦	✖
0252	ü	⎫	✔
0253	ý	⎬	☒
0254	þ	⎭	☑
0255	ÿ		

APPENDIX D

An HTML Primer

IN THIS APPENDIX

If you've seen some World Wide Web pages in your Internet travels, you might think you need a high-end word processor or page layout application to achieve all those fancy effects. Well, although you *can* use a sophisticated software package, the truth is that any basic text editor (such as the Notepad accessory that comes with Windows) is all you need to create attractive Web pages. This appendix shows you how by giving you a primer on the basic elements that constitute HTML—HyperText Markup Language.

Understanding HTML Tags

The Web's secret is that, underneath all the bells and whistles, pages are relatively simple affairs. You just type in your text and then insert markers—called *tags*—that dictate how you want things to look. For example, if you'd like a word on your page to appear in bold text, you surround that word with the appropriate tags for boldness.

In general, tags use the following format:

```
<TAG>The text to be affected</TAG>
```

The `TAG` part is a code (usually one or two letters) that specifies the type of effect you want. For example, the tag for bolding is `<B>`. So if you wanted the phrase `ACME Coyote Supplies` to appear in bold, you'd type the following into your document:

```
<B>ACME Coyote Supplies</B>
```

The first `<B>` tells the browser to display all the text that follows in a bold font. This continues until the `</B>` is reached. The slash (`/`) defines this as an *end tag*, which tells the browser to turn off the effect. As you'll see, there are tags for lots of other effects, including italics, paragraphs, headings, page titles, lists, and much more. HTML is just the sum total of all these tags.

These days you don't need to know HTML tags in order to create Web pages. For example, you can use Word 97's menus and toolbars to construct pages. However, you need to bear in mind that all the techniques you use in Word are, in the end, creating HTML tags (albeit behind the scenes). So knowing a bit about how HTML tags work will help you understand what's going on. And, if you're having trouble getting Word or some other Office program to get your pages just right, you can always examine the HTML code and make some adjustments manually.

NOTE: HTML REFERENCE

This appendix presents only the briefest of introductions to HTML. Most of the tags I'll be talking about have a number of attributes that you can use to refine each tag's behavior. The ActiveX Control Pad that I talked about in Chapter 21, "Web Page Programming: ActiveX and VBScript," has an HTML reference that you can use to get the full story on each tag. To view this reference, start the ActiveX Control Pad and then select Help | HTML Reference.

The Basic Structure of Web Pages

Web pages range from dull to dynamic, inane to indispensable, but they all have the same underlying structure. This consistent structure—which, as you'll see, is nothing more than a small collection of HTML tags—is the reason why almost all browser programs running on almost all types of computers can successfully display almost all Web pages.

HTML files always start with the <HTML> tag. This tag doesn't do much except tell any Web browser that tries to read the file that it's dealing with a file that contains HTML codes. Similarly, the last line in your document will always be the </HTML> tag, which you can think of as the HTML equivalent of "The End."

The next items in the HTML tag catalog serve to divide the document into two sections: the *head* and the *body*.

The head section is like an introduction to the page. Web browsers use the head to glean various types of information about the page. Although a number of items can appear in the head section, the most common is the title of the page, which I'll talk about shortly. To define the head, you add a <HEAD> tag and a </HEAD> tag immediately below the <HTML> tag.

The body section is where you enter the text that will appear on the Web page and the tags that control the page's appearance. To define the body, you place a <BODY> tag and a </BODY> tag after the head section (that is, below the </HEAD> tag).

These tags define the basic structure of every Web page:

```
<HTML>
<HEAD>
Header tags go here.
</HEAD>
<BODY>
The Web page text and tags go here.
</BODY>
</HTML>
```

Adding a Title

The next item you need to add is the title of the Web page. The page's title is just about what you might think it is: the overall name of the page (not to be confused with the name of the file you're creating). If someone views the page in a graphical browser (such as Netscape or Internet Explorer), the title appears in the title bar of the browser's window.

To define a title, you surround the text with the <TITLE> and </TITLE> tags. For example, if you want the title of your page to be *My Home Sweet Home Page,* you would enter it as follows:

```
<TITLE>My Home Sweet Home Page</TITLE>
```

Note that you always place the title inside the head section. Your basic HTML document will now look like this:

```
<HTML>
<HEAD>
<TITLE>My Home Sweet Home Page</TITLE>
</HEAD>
<BODY>
</BODY>
</HTML>
```

Text and Paragraphs

With your page title firmly in place, you can now think about the text you want to appear in the body of the page. For the most part, you can simply type the text between the <BODY> and </BODY> tags.

Things get a little tricky when you want to start a new paragraph. In most text editors and word processors, starting a new paragraph is a simple matter of pressing the Enter key to move to a new line. You can try doing that in your Web page, but the browsers that read your page will ignore this "white space." Instead, you have to use the <P> tag to tell the browser that you want to move to a new paragraph:

```
<HTML>
<HEAD>
<TITLE>My Home Sweet Home Page</TITLE>
</HEAD>
<BODY>
This text appears in the body of the Web page.
<P>
This text appears in a new paragraph.
</BODY>
</HTML>
```

Adding Formatting and Headings

HTML has lots of tags that will spruce up your page text. You saw earlier how a word or phrase surrounded by the <B> and </B> tags will appear in **bold** in a browser. You can also display text in *italic* by bracketing it with the <I> and </I> tags, and you can make your words appear in `monospace` by surrounding them with the <TT> and </TT> tags.

NOTE: MORE FONT FUN

Internet Explorer also supports the <FONT> tag:

<FONT SIZE=*n* FACE=*name* COLOR=*color*>

Here, the SIZE attribute specifies the text size, FACE specifies a font name, and COLOR specifies the text color. See the HTML reference for details on these attributes.

Like the chapters of a book, many Web pages have their contents divided into several sections. To help separate these sections and make life easier for the reader, you can use *headings*. Ideally, these headings act as mini-titles that convey some idea of what each section is all about. To make these titles stand out, HTML has a series of heading tags that display text in a larger, bold font. There are six heading tags in all, ranging from `<H1>`, which uses the largest font, down to `<H6>`, which uses the smallest font.

To illustrate these text formatting and heading tags, Figure D.1 shows how Internet Explorer displays the following text (see Formats.htm on the CD):

```
<HTML>
<HEAD>
<TITLE>My Home Sweet Home Page</TITLE>
</HEAD>
<BODY>
This text appears in the body of the Web page.
<P>
This text appears in a new paragraph.
<P>
You can create various text formatting effects,
including <B>bold text</B>, <I>italic text</I>,
and <TT>monospaced text</TT>.
<H1>An H1 Heading</H1>
<H2>An H2 Heading</H2>
<H3>An H3 Heading</H3>
<H4>An H4 Heading</H4>
<H5>An H5 Heading</H5>
<H6>An H6 Heading</H6>
</BODY>
</HTML>
```


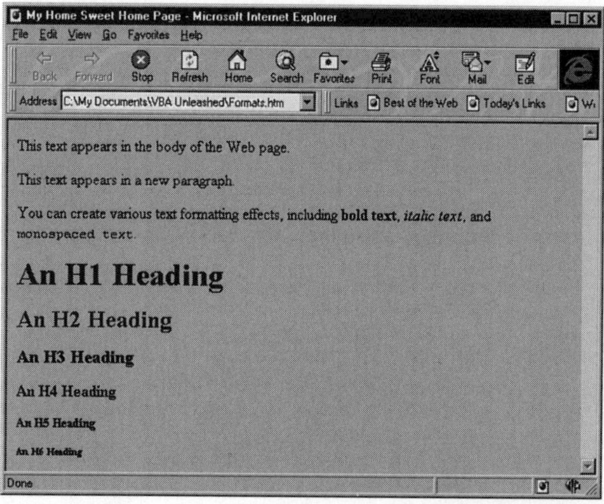

FIGURE D.1.
Examples of text formatting and heading tags.

Setting Up Lists

HTML offers three different list styles: numbered lists, bulleted lists, and definition lists. This section takes you through the basics of each list type.

If you want to include a numbered list of items—a Top Ten list, bowling league standings, or any kind of ranking—you don't need to add the numbers yourself. Instead, you can use HTML *ordered lists* to make the Web browser generate the numbers for you.

Ordered lists use two types of tags:

- The entire list is surrounded by the `<OL>` and `</OL>` tags.
- Each item in the list is preceded by the `<LI>` (list item) tag.

The general setup looks like this:

```
<OL>
<LI>First item.
<LI>Second item.
<LI>Third item.
<LI>You get the idea.
</OL>
```

Of course, numbered lists aren't the only kinds of lists. If you want to list just a few points, a *bulleted list* might be more your style. They're called "bulleted" lists because a Web browser displays a small dot or square (depending on the browser) called a *bullet* to the left of each item.

The HTML tags for a bulleted list are pretty close to the ones you saw for a numbered list. As before, you precede each list item with the `<LI>` tag, but you enclose the entire list in the `<UL>` and `</UL>` tags. Why `<UL>`? Well, what the rest of the world calls a bulleted list, the HTML powers-that-be call an *unordered list.* Here's how they work:

```
<UL>
<LI>First bullet point.
<LI>Second bullet point.
<LI>Third bullet point.
<LI>And so on
</UL>
```

The final type of list is called a *definition list.* It was originally used for dictionary-like lists in which each entry had two parts: a term and a definition. However, definition lists are useful for more than just definitions.

To define the two different parts of each entry in these lists, you need two different tags. The term is preceded by the `<DT>` tag, and the definition is preceded by the `<DD>` tag:

```
<DT>Term<DD>Definition
```

You then surround all your entries with the `<DL>` and `</DL>` tags to complete your definition list. Here's how the whole thing looks:

```
<DL>
<DT>A Term<DD>Its Definition
<DT>Another Term<DD>Another Definition
<DT>Yet Another Term<DD>Yet Another Definition
<DT>Etc.<DD>Abbreviation of a Latin phrase that means "and so forth."
</DL>
```

Figure D.2 shows how the various types of lists appear in Internet Explorer (see Lists.htm on the CD).

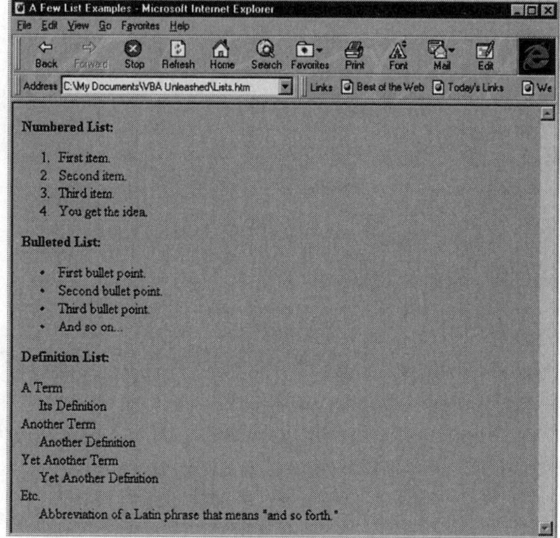

FIGURE D.2.
How HTML lists appear in a browser.

Working with Hyperlinks

The "H" in HTML stands for *hypertext,* which is dynamic text that defines a *link* to another document. The user clicks the hypertext, and the browser takes him to the linked document.

The HTML tags that set up links are `<A>` and `</A>`. The `<A>` tag is a little different from the other tags you've seen. Specifically, you don't use it by itself; instead, you add the address of the document to which you want to link. Here's how it works:

```
<A HREF="address">
```

Here, `HREF` stands for *hypertext reference.* Just replace *`address`* with the actual address of the Web page you want to use for the link (and, yes, you have to enclose the address in quotation marks). Here's an example:

```
<A HREF="http://www.mcp.com/sams/">
```

You're not done yet, though. Next, you have to give the reader some descriptive link text to click on. All you do is insert the text between the `<A>` and `</A>` tags, like so:

```
<A HREF="address">Link text goes here</A>
```

Here's an example:

```
Why not head to the <A HREF="http://www.mcp.com/sams">Sams home page</A>?
```

Figure D.3 shows how this looks in a Web browser (see Link.htm on the CD). Notice how the browser highlights and underlines the link text. When you point the mouse cursor at the link, the address you specified appears in the status bar.

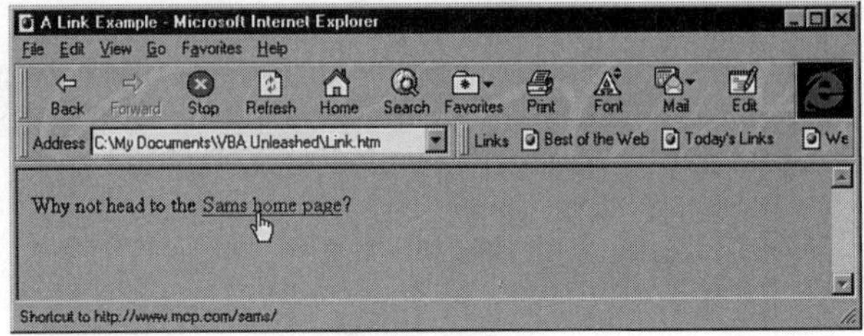

FIGURE D.3.
How Internet Explorer displays the hypertext link.

Inserting Images

If you're looking to make your Web site really stand out from the crowd, you need to go graphical with a few well-chosen images. How do you insert images if HTML files are text-only? As you'll see a bit later, all you'll really be doing (for each image you want to use) is adding a tag to the document that says, in effect, "Insert image here." This tag specifies the name of the graphics file, so the browser opens the file and displays the image.

Some computer wag once said that the nice thing about standards is that there are so many of them! Graphics files are no exception. It seems that every geek who ever gawked at a graphic has invented his own format for storing them on disk. There are images in GIF, JPEG, BMP, PCX, TIFF, DIB, EPS, and TGA formats, and those are just the ones I can think of off the top of my head. How's a budding Web page architect supposed to make sense of all this?

The good news is that the vast majority of browsers can handle only two formats: GIF and JPEG. (And some older browsers can't even handle JPEG.) Internet Explorer, however, can also work with Windows' native BMP and DIB formats.

As I mentioned a moment ago, there's an HTML code that tells a browser to display an image: the <IMG> tag. Here's how it works:

```
<IMG SRC="filename">
```

Here, SRC is short for *source,* and *filename* is the name and path of the graphics file you want to display. For example, suppose you have an image named logo.gif and it's located in the Graphics folder. To add it to your page, you'd use the following line:

```
<IMG SRC="/Graphics/logo.gif">
```

NOTE: HANDLING NONGRAPHICAL BROWSERS

Some browsers can't handle images, and some surfers speed up their downloads by turning graphics off in their browser. In these situations, you should include a text description of the image by including the ALT attribute in the <IMG> tag:

```
<IMG SRC="filename" ALT="Alternative text">
```

Setting Up Tables

An HTML table is a rectangular grid of rows and columns in a Web page. You can enter all kinds of information into a table, including text, numbers, links, and even images. Your tables will always begin with the following basic container:

```
<TABLE>
</TABLE>
```

All the other table tags fit between these two tags. There are two things you need to know about the <TABLE> tag:

- If you want your table to show a border, use the <TABLE BORDER> tag.
- If you don't want a border, just use <TABLE>.

Once that's done, most of your remaining table chores will involve the following four-step process:

1. Add a row.
2. Divide the row into the number of columns you want.
3. Insert data into each cell.
4. Repeat steps 1 through 3 until done.

To add a row, you toss a <TR> (table row) tag and a </TR> tag (its corresponding end tag) between <TABLE> and </TABLE>:

```
<TABLE BORDER>
<TR>
</TR>
</TABLE>
```

Now you divide that row into columns by placing the <TD> (table data) and </TD> tags between <TR> and </TR>. Each <TD>/</TD> combination represents one column (or, more specifically, an individual cell in the row). Therefore, if you want a three-column table, you'd do this:

```
<TABLE BORDER>
<TR>
<TD></TD>
<TD></TD>
<TD></TD>
</TR>
</TABLE>
```

Now you enter the row's cell data by typing text between each <TD> tag and its </TD> end tag:

```
<TABLE BORDER>
<TR>
<TD>Row 1, Column1</TD>
<TD>Row 1, Column2</TD>
<TD>Row 1, Column3</TD>
</TR>
</TABLE>
```

Remember that you can put any of the following within the <TD> and </TD> tags:

- Text
- HTML text-formatting tags (such as <B> and <I>)
- Links
- Lists
- Images

Once you've got your first row firmly in place, you simply repeat the procedure for the other rows in the table. For our sample table, here's the HTML that includes the data for all the rows (see Table.htm on the CD):

```
<TABLE BORDER>
<TR>
<TD>Row 1,  Column1</TD>
<TD>Row 1, Column2</TD>
<TD>Row 1, Column3</TD>
</TR>
<TR>
<TD>Row 2,  Column1</TD>
<TD>Row 2, Column2</TD>
<TD>Row 2, Column3</TD>
</TR>
<TR>
<TD>Row 3,  Column1</TD>
<TD>Row 3, Column2</TD>
<TD>Row 3, Column3</TD>
</TR>
</TABLE>
```

Figure D.4 shows the result in Internet Explorer.

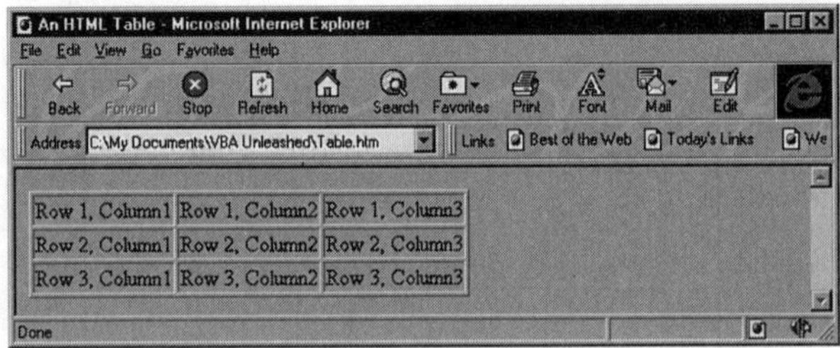

FIGURE D.4.
An HTML table in Internet Explorer.

NOTE: TABLE HEADINGS

If you want to include headings at the top of each column, use <TH> (table heading) tags in the first row. Most browsers display text within a <TH>/</TH> combination in bold type. (Note, too, that you can just as easily use <TH> tags in the first column to create headers for each row.)

Working with HTML Forms

The Web pages we've talked about so far have been more or less static—just a collection of text and images that provide no user interaction. It's possible to provide a very basic level of interaction by including hyperlinks in your pages, as described earlier. Beyond this, however, there lies a whole genre of interactive Web pages called *forms.* The rest of this appendix introduces you to HTML forms.

To understand forms, think of the humble dialog box. Most modern applications display a dialog box whenever they need to extract information from you. For example, selecting a program's Print command will most likely result in some kind of Print dialog box showing up. The purpose of this dialog box is to pester you for information such as the number of copies you want, which pages you want to print, and so on.

A form is simply the Web page equivalent of a dialog box. It's a page that's populated with dialog box-like controls—such as text boxes, drop-down lists, and command buttons—that are used to obtain information from the reader. For example, Figure D.5 shows a form from my Web site. This is a "guest book" that people "sign" when they visit my Web abode. (At this point it's worth mentioning that although most new browsers can handle forms, some older browsers might choke on them.)

As you can imagine, guest books are only the beginning of what you can do with forms. If you publish a newsletter or magazine, you can use forms to gather information from subscribers. If your Web site includes pages with restricted access, you can use a form to get a person's user name and password for verification. If you have information in a database, you can use a form to construct a query.

It's one thing to build a form, but it's quite another to actually make it do something useful. In other words, having a form on your Web site doesn't do you much good unless you have some way to process whatever data the user enters into the form. There are a number of ways to go about this, but the most common is to create a "script" that runs on the Web server. This script reads the form data, performs some sort of operation on the data (such as adding it to a database), and then returns some kind of "results" page (which might only be a simple "Thanks!" message). These scripts must conform to the Common Gateway Interface (CGI) standard, which defines how the browser sends the form data to the server.

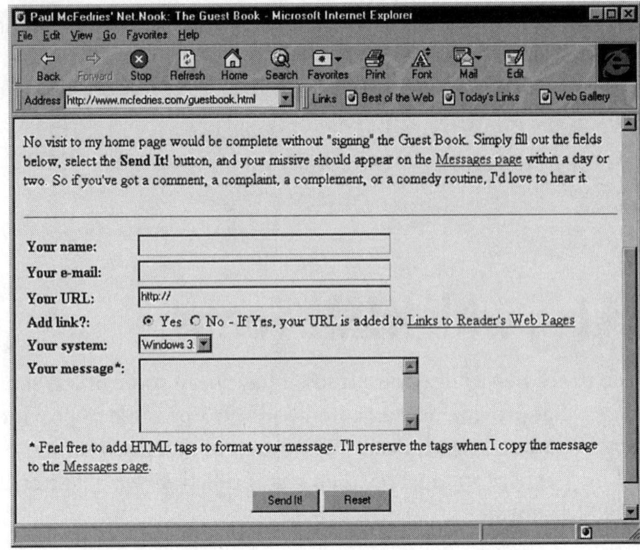

FIGURE D.5.
A form used as a guest book.

CGI is a complex topic that is beyond the scope of this book. If you'd like to learn more about it, I recommend the book *HTML & CGI Unleashed* (Sams Publishing, 1995). However, if you'll be using the form to work with an Access database on Microsoft's Internet Information Server (IIS), you can also use Internet Database Connector (IDC) files and Active Server Pages to construct dynamic pages.

Defining the Form

In HTML, you define a form by entering the `<FORM>` and `</FORM>` tags within the body of the page. The `<FORM>` tag always includes a couple of extra attributes that tell the Web server how to process the form. Here's the general format:

```
<FORM ACTION="URL" METHOD=METHOD>
</FORM>
```

Here, the `ACTION` attribute tells the browser where to send the form's data. This will almost always be the script that you've set up to process the data. The *`URL`* part is the program's address.

The `METHOD` attribute tells the browser how to send the form's data to the URL specified by `ACTION`. You have two choices for `METHOD`:

`GET`: The browser appends a question mark (`?`) and the data to the end of the `ACTION` attribute's URL and then requests this URL/data combination from the server.

`POST`: The browser sends the data to the server in a separate message.

When deciding which method to use, bear in mind that each control on your form sends two things to the server: the name of the control and the data the user entered into the control.

This means that a form could end up sending quite a bit of data to the server (especially if the form contains many controls or text boxes that could potentially hold long strings). However, some systems restrict the size of a URL sent to a Web server. This means that the GET method's URL/data combination might end up truncated. The POST method doesn't suffer from this problem, so you should always use it when large amounts of form data are involved. If you're not sure, use POST.

Let's look at an example. If you don't have a script for processing the form, you can still test the form by using one of the NCSA's public scripts. There's one for the POST method and one for the GET method. Here's how to use the POST method version:

```
<FORM ACTION="http://hoohoo.ncsa.uiuc.edu/htbin-post/post-query" METHOD=POST>
```

For the GET method, use the following:

```
<FORM ACTION="http://hoohoo.ncsa.uiuc.edu/htbin/query" METHOD=GET>
```

You can try this after you build a working form.

The Submit Button

Most dialog boxes, as I'm sure you know by now, have an OK button. Clicking this button says, in effect, "All right, I've made my choices. Now go put everything into effect." Forms also have command buttons that come in two flavors: submit and reset.

A submit button is the form equivalent of an OK dialog box button. When the reader clicks the submit button, the form data is shipped out to the program specified by the <FORM> tag's ACTION attribute. Here's the simplest format for the submit button:

```
<INPUT TYPE=SUBMIT>
```

As you'll see, most form elements use some variation of the <INPUT> tag. In this case, the TYPE=SUBMIT attribute tells the browser to display a command button labeled Submit (or, on some browsers, Submit Query or Send). Note that each form can have just one submit button.

If the standard Submit label is too prosaic for your needs, you can make up your own label, as follows:

```
<INPUT TYPE=SUBMIT VALUE="Label">
```

Here, *Label* is the label that will appear on the button.

Using a Submit Image

A variation on the submit button theme is the *submit image*. This is similar to a submit button, but the user clicks a picture instead. Here's the general tag syntax:

```
<INPUT TYPE=IMAGE SRC="Path">
```

Here, *Path* is the path and filename of the image file.

Starting Over: The Reset Button

If you plan on creating fairly large forms, you can do your readers a big favor by including a reset button somewhere on the form. A reset button clears all the data from the form's fields and reenters any default values that you specified in the fields. (I'll explain how to set up default values for each type of field as we go along.) Here's the tag to use to include a reset button:

```
<INPUT TYPE=RESET>
```

You can create a custom label by tossing the VALUE attribute into the <INPUT> tag, as in the following example:

```
<INPUT TYPE=RESET VALUE="Start From Scratch">
```

Using Text Boxes for Single-Line Text

For simple text entries, such as a person's name or address, use text boxes. Here's the basic format for a text box tag:

```
<INPUT TYPE=TEXT NAME="FieldName">
```

In this case, *FieldName* is a name you assign to the field that's unique among the other fields in the form. For example, to create a text box named FirstName, you'd enter the following:

```
<INPUT TYPE=TEXT NAME="FirstName">
```

Here's some HTML code that utilizes a few text boxes to gather some information from the user (see TextBox.htm on the CD):

```
<HTML>
<HEAD>
<TITLE>Text Box Example</TITLE>
</HEAD>
<BODY>
<H3>Please tell me about yourself:</H3>
<FORM ACTION="http://hoohoo.ncsa.uiuc.edu/htbin-post/post-query" METHOD=POST>
First Name: <INPUT TYPE=TEXT NAME="First">
<P>
Last Name: <INPUT TYPE=TEXT NAME="Last">
<P>
Nickname: <INPUT TYPE=TEXT NAME="Nick">
<P>
Stage Name: <INPUT TYPE=TEXT NAME="Stage">
<P>
<INPUT TYPE=SUBMIT VALUE="Just Do It!">
<INPUT TYPE=RESET VALUE="Just Reset It!">
</FORM>
</BODY>
</HTML>
```

Figure D.6 shows how this code looks in Internet Explorer, and Figure D.7 shows the page that's returned by the NCSA server if you click the Just Do It! button. Notice how the page shows the names of the fields followed by the value the user entered.

FIGURE D.6.
A form with a few text boxes.

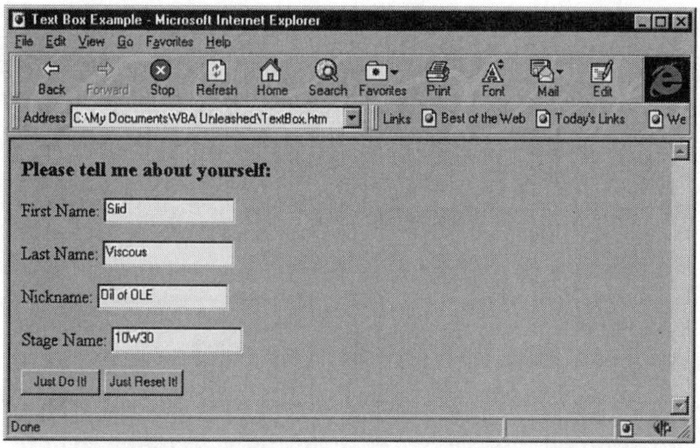

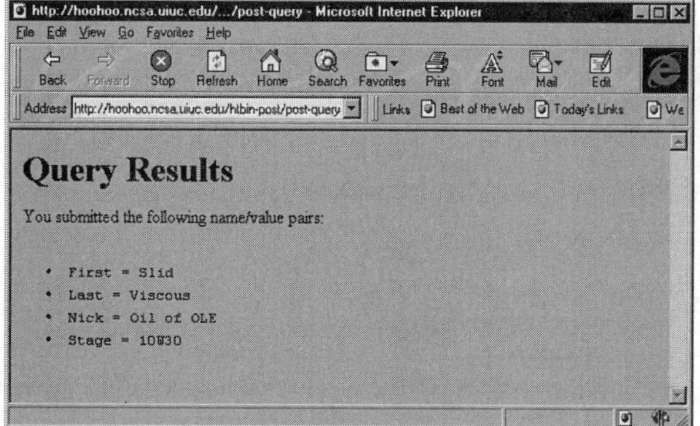

FIGURE D.7.
An example of the page that's returned when you send the form data to the NCSA public server.

Text boxes also come with the following bells and whistles:

Setting the default value: If you'd like some text to appear in the field by default, include the `VALUE` attribute in the `<INPUT>` tag. For example, suppose you want to know the URL of the reader's home page. To include `http://` in the field, you'd use the following tag:

```
<INPUT TYPE=TEXT NAME="URL" VALUE="http://">
```

Setting the size of the box: To determine the length of the text box, use the `SIZE` attribute. (Note that this attribute affects only the size of the box, not the length of the entry; for the latter, use the `MAXLENGTH` attribute.) For example, the following tag displays a text box that is 40 characters long:

```
<INPUT TYPE=TEXT NAME="Address" SIZE=40>
```

Limiting the length of the text: In a standard text box, the reader can type away until his fingers are numb. If you'd prefer to restrict the length of the entry, use the `MAXLENGTH` attribute. For example, the following text box is used to enter a person's age; it restricts the length of the entry to three characters:

```
<INPUT TYPE=TEXT NAME="Age" MAXLENGTH=3>
```

NOTE: PASSWORD TEXT BOXES

A slight variation on the text box theme is the password box:

```
<INPUT TYPE=PASSWORD NAME="FieldName">
```

This is a text box that displays only asterisks as the user types.

Using Text Areas for Multiline Text

If you want to give your readers extra room to type their text, or if you need multiline entries (such as an address), you're better off using a *text area* than a text box. A text area is also a rectangle that accepts text input, but text areas can display two or more lines at once. Here's how they work:

```
<TEXTAREA NAME="FieldName" VALUE="Text" ROWS=TotalRows COLS=TotalCols WRAP>
</TEXTAREA>
```

Here, *FieldName* is a unique name for the field, *Text* is the initial text that appears in the field, *TotalRows* specifies the total number of lines displayed, and *TotalCols* specifies the total number of columns displayed. The WRAP attribute tells the browser to wrap the text onto the next line whenever the user's typing hits the right edge of the text area. (The WRAP attribute is supported by most browsers, but not all of them.) Note, too, that the <TEXTAREA> tag requires the </TEXTAREA> end tag. (If you want to include default values in the text area, just enter them—on separate lines, if necessary—between <TEXTAREA> and </TEXTAREA>.)

The following HTML tags show a text area in action, and Figure D.8 shows how it looks in a browser (see TextArea.htm on the CD).

```
<HTML>
<HEAD>
<TITLE>Text Area Example</TITLE>
</HEAD>
<BODY>
<H3>Today's Burning Question</H3>
<HR>
<FORM ACTION="http://hoohoo.ncsa.uiuc.edu/htbin-post/post-query" METHOD=POST>
First Name: <INPUT TYPE=TEXT NAME="FirstName">
<P>
Last Name: <INPUT TYPE=TEXT NAME="LastName">
<P>
Today's <I>Burning Question</I>: <B>Why is Jerry Lewis so popular in France?</B>
<P>
Please enter your answer in the text area below:
<BR>
<TEXTAREA NAME="Answer" ROWS=10 COLS=60 WRAP>
</TEXTAREA>
<P>
<INPUT TYPE=SUBMIT VALUE="I Know!">
<INPUT TYPE=RESET>
</FORM>
</BODY>
</HTML>
```

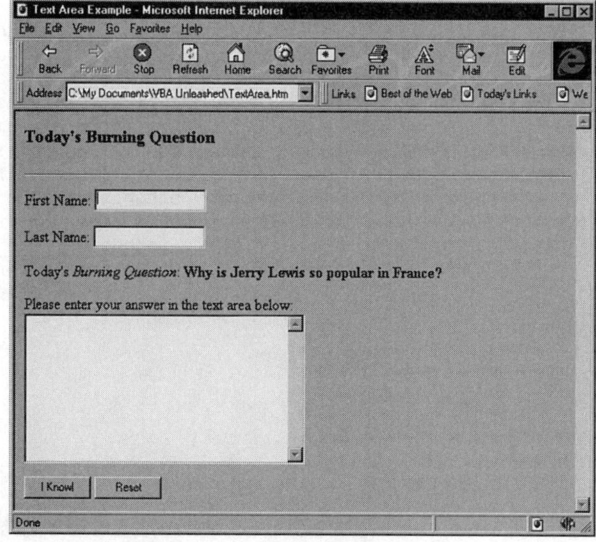

FIGURE D.8.
An example of a text area.

Toggling an Option On and Off with Check Boxes

If you want to elicit yes/no or true/false information from your readers, check boxes are a lot easier than having the user type in the required data. Here's the general format for an HTML check box:

```
<INPUT TYPE=CHECKBOX NAME="FieldName">
```

As usual, *FieldName* is a unique name for the field. You can also add the attribute CHECKED to the <INPUT> tag, which tells the browser to display the check box "pre-checked." Here's an example:

```
<INPUT TYPE=CHECKBOX NAME="Species" CHECKED>Human
```

Notice in this example that I placed some text beside the <INPUT> tag. This text is used as a label that tells the reader what the check box represents. Here's a longer example that uses a few check boxes (see CheckBox.htm on the CD). Figure D.9 shows how it looks.

```
<HTML>
<HEAD>
<TITLE>Check Box Example</TITLE>
</HEAD>
<BODY>
<H3>Welcome to Hooked On Phobics!</H3>
<HR>
<FORM ACTION="http://hoohoo.ncsa.uiuc.edu/htbin-post/post-query" METHOD=POST>
What's <I>your</I> phobia? (Please check all that apply):
```

```
<P>
<INPUT TYPE=CHECKBOX NAME="Ants">Myrmecophobia (Fear of ants)<BR>
<INPUT TYPE=CHECKBOX NAME="Bald">Peladophobia (Fear of becoming bald)<BR>
<INPUT TYPE=CHECKBOX NAME="Beards">Pogonophobia (Fear of beards)<BR>
<INPUT TYPE=CHECKBOX NAME="Bed">Clinophobia (Fear of going to bed)<BR>
<INPUT TYPE=CHECKBOX NAME="Chins">Geniophobia (Fear of chins)<BR>
<INPUT TYPE=CHECKBOX NAME="Flowers">Anthophobia (Fear of flowers)<BR>
<INPUT TYPE=CHECKBOX NAME="Flying">Aviatophobia (Fear of flying)<BR>
<INPUT TYPE=CHECKBOX NAME="Purple">Porphyrophobia (Fear of the color purple)<BR>
<INPUT TYPE=CHECKBOX NAME="Teeth">Odontophobia (Fear of teeth)<BR>
<INPUT TYPE=CHECKBOX NAME="Thinking">Phronemophobia (Fear of thinking)<BR>
<INPUT TYPE=CHECKBOX NAME="Vegetables">Lachanophobia (Fear of vegetables)<BR>
<INPUT TYPE=CHECKBOX NAME="Fear">Phobophobia (Fear of fear)<BR>
<INPUT TYPE=CHECKBOX NAME="Everything">Pantophobia (Fear of everything)<BR>
<P>
<INPUT TYPE=SUBMIT VALUE="Submit">
<INPUT TYPE=RESET>
</FORM>
</BODY>
</HTML>
```

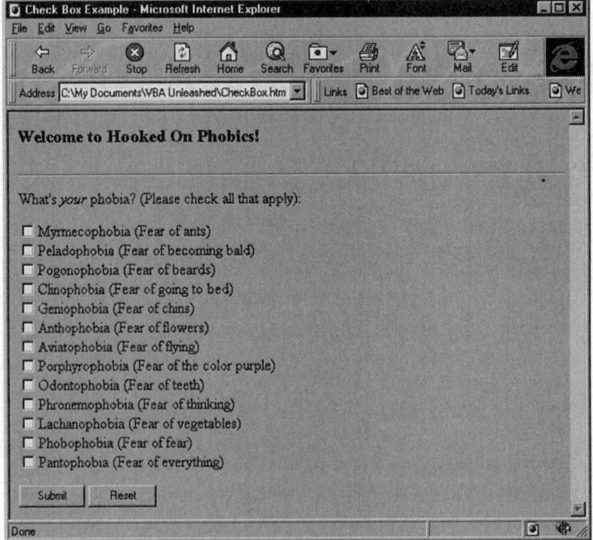

FIGURE D.9.
Some check box examples.

Multiple Choice: Option Buttons

Instead of yes/no choices, you might want your readers to have a choice of three of four options. In this case, option buttons are your best bet. With option buttons, the user gets two or more choices, but he can choose only one. Here's the general format:

```
<INPUT TYPE=RADIO NAME="FieldName" VALUE="Value">
```

`FieldName` is the usual field name, but in this case you supply the same name to *all* the option buttons. That way, the browser knows which buttons are grouped. `Value` is a unique text string that specifies the value of the option when it's selected. In addition, you can also add CHECKED to one of the buttons to have the browser activate the option by default.

The following HTML document (see RadioBtn.htm on the CD) puts a few option buttons through their paces, as shown in Figure D.10.

```
<HTML>
<HEAD>
<TITLE>Radio Button Example</TITLE>
</HEAD>
<BODY>
<H3>Survey</H3>
<HR>
<FORM ACTION="http://hoohoo.ncsa.uiuc.edu/htbin-post/post-query" METHOD=POST>
Which of the following best describes your current salary level:
<UL>
<INPUT TYPE=RADIO NAME="Salary" VALUE="Salary1" CHECKED>Below the poverty line<BR>
<INPUT TYPE=RADIO NAME="Salary" VALUE="Salary2">Living wage<BR>
<INPUT TYPE=RADIO NAME="Salary" VALUE="Salary3">Comfy<BR>
<INPUT TYPE=RADIO NAME="Salary" VALUE="Salary4">DINK (Double Income, No Kids)<BR>
<INPUT TYPE=RADIO NAME="Salary" VALUE="Salary5">Rockefellerish<BR>
</UL>
Which of the following best describes your political leanings:
<UL>
<INPUT TYPE=RADIO NAME="Politics" VALUE="Politics1" CHECKED>So far left,
➥I'm right<BR>
<INPUT TYPE=RADIO NAME="Politics" VALUE="Politics2">Yellow Dog Democrat<BR>
<INPUT TYPE=RADIO NAME="Politics" VALUE="Politics3">Right down the middle<BR>
<INPUT TYPE=RADIO NAME="Politics" VALUE="Politics4">Country Club Republican<BR>
<INPUT TYPE=RADIO NAME="Politics" VALUE="Politics5">So far right, I'm left<BR>
</UL>
<P>
<INPUT TYPE=SUBMIT VALUE="Submit">
<INPUT TYPE=RESET>
</FORM>
</BODY>
</HTML>
```

Selecting from Lists

Option buttons are a great way to give your readers multiple choices, but they get unwieldy if you have more than about five or six options. For longer sets of options, you're better off using lists. Setting up a list requires a bit more work than the other form tags. Here's the general format:

```
<SELECT NAME="FieldName" SIZE=Items>
<OPTION>First item text</OPTION>
<OPTION>Second item text</OPTION>
<OPTION>And so on...</OPTION>
</SELECT>
```

For the SIZE attribute, *Items* is the number of items you want the browser to display. If you omit SIZE, the list becomes a drop-down list. If SIZE is 2 or more, the list becomes a rectangle with scrollbars for navigating the choices. Also, you can insert the MULTIPLE attribute into the <SELECT> tag. This tells the browser to allow the user to select multiple items from the list.

FIGURE D.10.
A form that uses radio buttons for multiple-choice input.

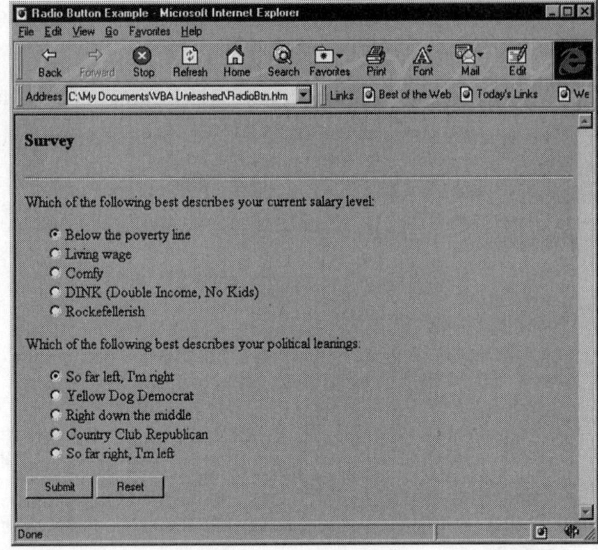

Between the `<SELECT>` and `</SELECT>` tags are the `<OPTION>` and `</OPTION>` tags; these define the list items. If you add the `SELECTED` attribute to one of the items, the browser selects that item by default.

To show you some examples, the following document defines no less than three selection lists (see Lists2.htm on the CD). Figure D.11 shows what the Internet Explorer browser does with them.

```
<HTML>
<HEAD>
<TITLE>Selection List Example</TITLE>
</HEAD>
<BODY>
<H3>Putting On Hairs: Reader Survey</H3>
<HR>
<FORM ACTION="http://hoohoo.ncsa.uiuc.edu/htbin-post/post-query" METHOD=POST>
Select your hair color:<BR>
<SELECT NAME="Color">
<OPTION>Black</OPTION>
<OPTION>Blonde</OPTION>
<OPTION SELECTED>Brunette</OPTION>
<OPTION>Red</OPTION>
<OPTION>Something neon</OPTION>
<OPTION>None</OPTION>
</SELECT>
<P>
Select your hair style:<BR>
<SELECT NAME="Style" SIZE=7>
<OPTION>Bouffant</OPTION>
<OPTION>Mohawk</OPTION>
<OPTION>Page Boy</OPTION>
<OPTION>Permed</OPTION>
<OPTION>Shag</OPTION>
```

```
<OPTION SELECTED>Straight</OPTION>
<OPTION>Style? What style?</OPTION>
</SELECT>
<P>
Hair products used in the last year:<BR>
<SELECT NAME="Products" SIZE=5 MULTIPLE>
<OPTION>Gel</OPTION>
<OPTION>Grecian Formula</OPTION>
<OPTION>Mousse</OPTION>
<OPTION>Peroxide</OPTION>
<OPTION>Shoe black</OPTION>
</SELECT>
<P>
<INPUT TYPE=SUBMIT VALUE="Hair Mail It!">
<INPUT TYPE=RESET>
</FORM>
</BODY>
</HTML>
```

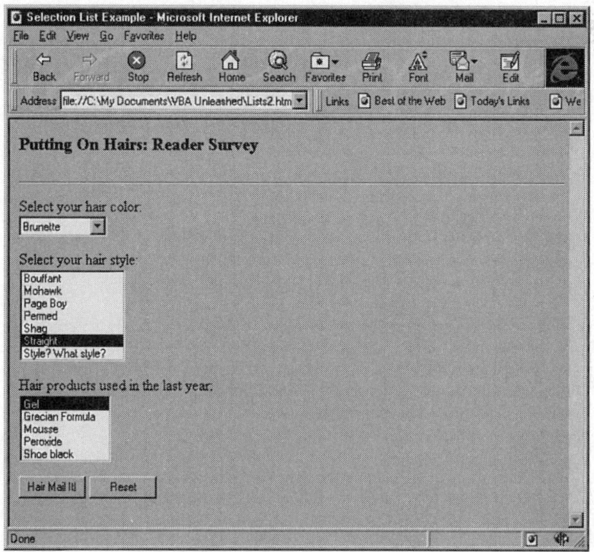

FIGURE D.11.
A form with a few selection list examples.

Hidden Controls

If you put together a lot of forms, you might find that some of them use similar layouts and controls. For forms that are only slightly dissimilar, it might not make sense to write separate scripts to handle the data. It would be nice if you could use a single script and have it branch depending on which form was being used.

An easy way to accomplish this is to include a “hidden” control in each form:

```
<INPUT TYPE=HIDDEN NAME="FieldName" VALUE="Value">
```

As the HIDDEN type implies, these controls aren't visible to the user. However, their NAME and VALUE attributes get sent to the script along with the rest of the form data. Consider the following example:

```
<INPUT TYPE=HIDDEN NAME="FormName" VALUE="Form A">
```

A script could test the FormName variable. If its value were Form A, it could process one set of instructions. If it were Form B, it could process a different set of instructions.

I

INDEX

Symbols

A

G

H

L

M

O

P

T

U

V

X-Y-Z

Technical Support:

If you need assistance with the information in this book or with a CD/Disk accompanying the book, please access the Knowledge Base on our Web site at **http://www.superlibrary.com/general/support**. Our most Frequently Asked Questions are answered there. If you do not find the answer to your questions on our Web site, you may contact Macmillan Technical Support **(317) 581-3833** or e-mail us at **support@mcp.com**.

Teach Yourself Visual Basic 5 in 21 Days, Fourth Edition

Nathan Gurewich and Ori Gurewich

Using a logical, easy-to-follow approach, this international bestseller teaches readers the fundamentals of developing programs. It starts with the basics of writing a program and then moves on to adding voice, music, sound, and graphics. This books uses shaded syntax boxes, techniques, and Q&A, Do/Don't, and workshop sections to highlight key points and reinforce learning.

Price: $29.99 USA/$42.95 CDN
ISBN 0-672-30978-5 *1,000 pages*
New - Casual *Programming*

Teach Yourself Microsoft Office 97 in 24 Hours

Greg Perry

An estimated 22 million people use Microsoft Office, and with the new features of Office 97, much of that market will want the upgrade. To address that market, Sams has published a mass-market version of its best-selling *Teach Yourself* series. This book shows readers how to use the most widely requested features of Office. This entry-level book includes many figures and a step-by-step plan for learning Office 97. It teaches you how to use each Office product and shows you how to create documents in Word that include hypertext links to files created with one of the other Office products.

Price: $19.99 USA/$28.95 CDN
ISBN 0-672-31009-0 *450 pages*
New - Casual - Accomplished *Integrated Software/Suites*

Microsoft Office 97 Unleashed

Paul McFedries and Sue Charlesworth

Microsoft has brought the Web to its Office suite of products. Hyperlinking, Office Assistants, and Active Document Support let users publish documents to the Web or an intranet site. The Web also completely integrates with Microsoft FrontPage, making it possible to point-and-click a Web page into existence. This book details each of the Office products—Excel, Access, PowerPoint, Word, and Outlook—and shows you how to create presentations and Web documents. You'll see how to extend Office to work on a network, and you'll learn how to use the various Office Solution Kits.

Price: $39.99 USA/$56.95 CDN
ISBN 0-672-31010-4 *1,316 pages*
Accomplished - Expert *Integrated Software/Suites*

ActiveX Programming Unleashed

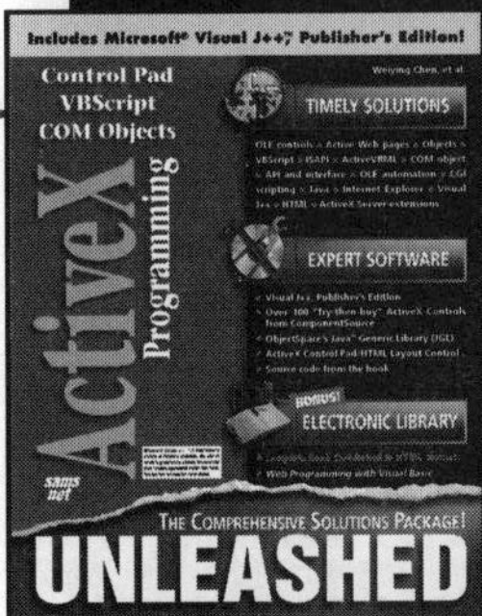

Weiying Chen, et al

ActiveX is Microsoft's core Internet communication technology. This book describes and details that technology, giving programmers the knowledge they need to create powerful ActiveX programs for the Web and beyond. It covers ActiveX controls—the full-featured components of the Internet. It also teaches you how to use ActiveX documents, server framework, ISAPI, and security.

Price: $39.99 USA/$56.95 CDN
ISBN 1-57521-154-8 *700 pages*
Accomplished - Expert *Internet/Programming*

Laura Lemay's Web Workshop: ActiveX and VBScript

Paul Lomax and Rogers Cadenhead

ActiveX is an umbrella term for a series of Microsoft products and technologies that add activity to Web pages. VBScript is an essential element of the ActiveX family. With it, you can add animation, multimedia, sound, graphics, and interactivity to a Web site. This book is a compilation of individual workshops that show the reader how to use VBScript and other ActiveX technologies within a Web site. The CD-ROM contains the entire book in HTML format, as well as a selection of the best ActiveX development tools, scripts, templates, backgrounds, borders, and graphics.

Price: $39.99 USA/$56.95 CDN
ISBN 1-57521-207-2 *450 pages*
Casual - Accomplished *Internet/Programming*

Access 97 Unleashed, Second Edition

Dwayne Gifford, et al

Access, one of Microsoft's database managers for Windows, has become one of the most accepted standards of database management for PCs. The *Unleashed* format allows current and new users to quickly and easily find the information they need on the new features. It also serves as a complete reference for database programmers new to Access. You'll learn advanced techniques for working with tables, queries, forms, and data. You'll also see how to program Access and how to integrate it with the Internet. The CD-ROM includes Access utilities and applications and an electronic Access reference library.

Price: $49.99 USA/$70.95 CDN
ISBN 0-672-30983-1 *1,100 pages*
Accomplished - Expert *Databases*

Develop programs that exploit Access 97's speed and efficiency
ALISON BALTER'S
MASTERING
ACCESS 97
DEVELOPMENT
SECOND EDITION

Alison Balter's Mastering Access 97 Development, Second Premier Edition

Alison Balter

One of the premier corporate database applications, Access is a powerful application that can be programmed and customized. This book shows users how to develop simple and complex applications for Access 97. You'll see how to create tables, forms, queries, reports, and objects. You'll also learn how to program Access applications for a client/server environment. The CD-ROM includes source code, reusable functions, forms, and reports.

Price: $49.99 USA/$70.95 CDN
ISBN 0-672-30999-8 *1,100 pages*
Accomplished - Expert *Databases*

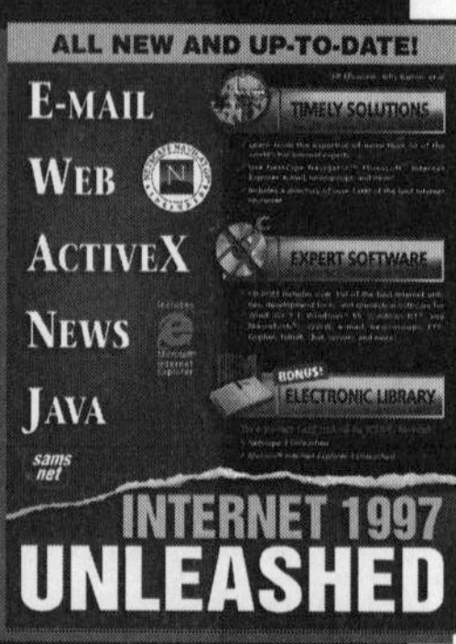

The Internet 1997 Unleashed

Jill Ellsworth, et al

This book is the definitive bible for Internet users. This comprehensive guide stakes out new ground as it details the hottest Internet tools and upcoming technologies. Written by the world's top experts in Internet fields, this book provides improved coverage of common tools and looks at the Internet of tomorrow. This book includes an easy-to-use, well-organized listing of the top 1,000 resources on the Internet. This book also covers WWW browsers, Internet commerce, and Internet Virtual Reality. The CD-ROM contains all the software you need to get connected to the Internet, regardless of your platform—Windows 3.1, Windows 95, Macintosh, or UNIX.

Price: $49.99 USA/$70.95 CDN
ISBN 1-57521-185-8 *1,328 pages*
Intermediate - Advanced *Internet/General/WWW Applications*

Book ISBN 0-672-31046-5

What's on the CD-ROM

The CD-ROM that comes with this book contains all of the VBA examples that I used throughout the book, plus an assortment of third-party tools and product demos. The CD-ROM is designed to be explored using a CD-ROM Menu program. Using the Menu program, you can view information concerning products and companies and install programs with a single click of the mouse. To run the Menu program, follow the next steps.

Windows 95/NT Installation Instructions

1. Insert the CD-ROM into your CD-ROM drive.
2. If Windows 95/NT is installed on your computer and the AutoPlay feature is enabled, a Program Group for this book is automatically created whenever you insert the CD-ROM into your CD-ROM drive.

   If AutoPlay isn't enabled, using Windows Explorer, choose Setup from the CD drive to create the Program Group for this book.
3. Double-click the CD-ROM Product Browser icon in the newly created Program Group to access the installation programs of the software or source code included on the CD-ROM.

   To review the latest information about the CD-ROM, double-click the About this CD-ROM icon.

NOTE

For best results, set your monitor to display between 256 and 64,000 colors. A screen resolution of 640×480 pixels is also recommended. If necessary, adjust your monitor settings before using the CD-ROM.